T0235454

Lecture Notes in Computer Science 9097

Commenced Publication in 1973
Founding and Former Series Editors:
Gerhard Goos, Juris Hartmanis, and Jan van Leeuwen

More information about this series at http://www.springer.com/series/7409

Jelena Zdravkovic · Marite Kirikova
Paul Johannesson (Eds.)

Advanced Information Systems Engineering

27th International Conference, CAiSE 2015
Stockholm, Sweden, June 8–12, 2015
Proceedings

 Springer

Editors
Jelena Zdravkovic
Stockholm University
Stockholm
Sweden

Paul Johannesson
Stockholm University
Stockholm
Sweden

Marite Kirikova
Riga Technical University
Riga
Latvia

ISSN 0302-9743   ISSN 1611-3349   (electronic)
Lecture Notes in Computer Science
ISBN 978-3-319-19068-6   ISBN 978-3-319-19069-3   (eBook)
DOI 10.1007/978-3-319-19069-3

Library of Congress Control Number: 2015938745

LNCS Sublibrary: SL3 – Information Systems and Applications, incl. Internet/Web and HCI

Springer Cham Heidelberg New York Dordrecht London

Printed on acid-free paper

Springer International Publishing AG Switzerland is part of Springer Science+Business Media
(www.springer.com)

Preface

This volume of the LNCS series includes the papers accepted for the presentation at the 27th International Conference on Advanced Information Systems Engineering (CAiSE 2015), held in Stockholm, during June 08–12, 2015. Stockholm is the cultural, media, political, and economic center of Sweden. The city is home to some of Europe's top ranking universities, and it hosts the annual Nobel Prize ceremonies at the City Hall – the place where the reception ceremony of CAiSE 2015 was held.

After 15 years CAiSE has returned again to Stockholm where it was founded in 1989 as a Nordic conference on IS Engineering, and hosted again in 1990 and in 2000. Over the time CAiSE has established itself as a leading venue of information systems engineering. It is a forum of exchange for researchers, industrials, and students, as well as a place to learn, identify future trends, and start new collaborations.

The theme for this year's edition of the conference was *Creativity, Ability and Integrity in Information Systems Engineering* (CAISE). As systems are moving beyond traditional information management and need to organically blend into the environment, appealing to large and diverse user bases – creativity, ability, and integrity are some important components to address. Creativity is becoming ever more important as Information Systems are designed in novel and unexpected ways making use of information from different sources that need to be merged and molded to become meaningful and valuable. Ability enables systems to be capable of delivering business in excellent, competitive, and agile way. The task of integrity is to ensure quality in ethical codes – modifications by authorized parties, or only in authorized ways.

CAiSE 2015 received 236 full-paper submissions from all over the world: Europe (25 countries), Algeria, Brazil, Australia, Canada, China, Columbia, Egypt, India, Iran, Israel, Japan, New Zealand, Pakistan, Saudi Arabia, Singapore, Tunisia, United Arab Emirates, USA, and Vietnam. The papers reflected different topics – models, methods, techniques, architectures, platforms, as well as domain-specific, multi aspect, and new-generation solutions in the information systems engineering discipline. Each submitted paper was evaluated by at least three independent members of the Program Committee (PC), further the papers were discussed online under the supervision of a member of the Program Board (PB), and again at the PB meeting held in Stockholm during February 5–6, 2015.

The proceedings of CAiSE 2015 reflect the high quality of included contributions. Together with the 31 accepted papers, they contain the abstracts of three keynote speeches and five tutorials presented at the conference. The papers were classified into the sessions organized by themes: social and collaborative computing, business process modeling and languages, high volume and complex information management, requirements elicitation and management, enterprise data management, model conceptualization and evolution, process mining, monitoring, and predicting, intra- and interorganizational process engineering, process compliance and alignment, enterprise IT integration and management, and service science and computing. The three keynote speeches were "Attaining a Systems Perspective" by Harold W. "Bud" Lawson – a pioneer in hardware and software technologies of the 20th century, "The Age of Data & the New Era of Computing" by Aleksandra Mojsilovic – an IBM Fellow specialized in Data Science, and "From Opinions to Facts – Building Products Customers Actually Use" by Jan Bosch – a professor in Software Engineering at Chalmers University. The tutorials reflected various topics, such as business-IT alignment, matching of IS models, know-how to organize, map, and manage knowledge by IT means, IT change management, as well as design science for IS/IT.

As a tradition at CAiSE, the conference program was preceded by 10 workshops and 2 associated working conferences: EMMSAD and BPMDS. Separate proceedings were published for all these events. The main conference included research paper sessions, tutorials, panels, doctoral Symposium, forum for short visionary papers, case studies, and tools' applications, as well as a whole-day industry track dedicated to the subject of Big Data and Business Analytics.

In our role as the editors of this volume, we owe special thanks to the authors submitting their novel research results to the conference; members of the Program Committee and Program Board for promoting the conference, their support in attracting submissions, as well as for providing valuable reviews for the submitted papers. We also thank the external reviewers. Special thanks go to Richard van de Stadt who timely and efficiently helped us with the CyberChairPRO conference management system. Finally, we warmly thank the Department of Computer and Systems Sciences (DSV) of Stockholm University and its local organization team, publicity chairs, workshop organization chairs, forum chairs, tutorial and panel chairs, doctoral symposium chairs, and industry track chairs.

April 2015

Jelena Zdravkovic
Marite Kirikova
Paul Johannesson

Organization

Steering Committee

Barbara Pernici	Politecnico di Milano, Italy
Óscar Pastor	Universitat Politècnica de València, Spain
John Krogstie	Norwegian University of Science and Technology, Norway

Advisory Committee

Janis Bubenko Jr	Royal Institute of Technology, Sweden
Arne Sølvberg	Norwegian University of Science and Technology, Norway
Colette Rolland	Université Paris 1 Panthéon Sorbonne, France

General Chair

Paul Johannesson	Stockholm University, Sweden

Program Chairs

Jelena Zdravkovic	Stockholm University, Sweden
Marite Kirikova	Riga Technical University, Latvia

Organization Chairs

Åsa Smedberg	Stockholm University, Sweden
Eric-Oluf Svee	Stockholm University, Sweden
Birger Andersson	Stockholm University, Sweden

Workshop Chairs

Janis Stirna	Stockholm University, Sweden
Anne Persson	University of Skövde, Sweden

Forum Chairs

Janis Grabis	Riga Technical University, Latvia
Kurt Sandkuhl	University of Rostock, Germany

Doctoral Consortium Chairs

Peri Loucopoulos   University of Manchester, UK
Selmin Nurcan   Université Paris 1 Panthéon Sorbonne, France
Hans Weigand   Tilburg University, The Netherlands

Tutorial and Panel Chairs

Ilia Bider   Stockholm University, Sweden
Pnina Soffer   University of Haifa, Israel

Publicity Chairs

Dimitris Karagiannis   University of Vienna, Austria
Jolita Ralyté   University of Geneva, Switzerland
Erik Perjons   Stockholm University, Sweden

Industry Chairs

Gustaf Juell-Skielse   Stockholm University, Sweden
John Krogstie   Norwegian University of Science and Technology,
                          Norway
Vandana Kabilan   Accenture, Sweden

Technical Chair

Iyad Zikra   Stockholm University, Sweden

Program Committee Board

Eric Dubois, Luxembourg   Óscar Pastor, Spain
Johann Eder, Austria   Barbara Pernici, Italy
Xavier Franch, Spain   Anne Persson, Sweden
Remigijus Gustas, Sweden   Michaël Petit, Belgium
John Krogstie, Norway   Klaus Pohl, Germany
Michel Léonard, Switzerland   Collete Rolland, France
Peri Loucopoulos, UK   Pnina Soffer, Israel
Haralambos Mouratidis, UK   Janis Stirna, Sweden
Selmin Nurcan, France   Hans Weigand, The Netherlands
Andreas L. Opdahl, Norway   Mathias Weske, Germany

Program Committee

Wil van der Aalst, The Netherlands
João Paulo Almeida, Brazil
Yuan An, USA
Paris Avgeriou, The Netherlands
Marko Bajec, Slovenia
Luciano Baresi, Italy
Carlo Batini, Italy
Boualem Benatallah, Australia
Giuseppe Berio, France
Nacer Boudjlida, France
Sjaak Brinkkemper, The Netherlands
Jordi Cabot, France
Albertas Caplinskas, Lithuania
Silvana Castano, Italy
Jaelson Castro, Brazil
Corine Cauvet, France
Julio Cesar Leite, Brazil
Lawrence Chung, USA
Isabelle Comyn-Wattiau, France
Panos Constantopoulos, Greece
Fabiano Dalpiaz, The Netherlands
Valeria De Antonellis, Italy
Rébeccca Deneckère, France
Michael Derntl, Germany
Marlon Dumas, Estonia
Neil Ernst, USA
Sergio Espana, Spain
Ulrich Frank, Germany
Avigdor Gal, Israel
Paolo Giorgini, Italy
Aniruddha Gokhale, USA
Michael Grossniklaus, Germany
Francesco Guerra, Italy
Renata Guizzardi, Brazil
Giancarlo Guizzardi, Brazil
Irit Hadar, Israel
Anne Hakånsson, Sweden
Brian Henderson-Sellers, Sydney
Jennifer Horkoff, UK
Marta Indulska, Australia
Matthias Jarke, Germany
Manfred Jeusfeld, Sweden
Ivan Jureta, Belgium
Haruhiko Kaiya, Japan

Dimitri Karagiannis, Austria
Evangelia Kavakli, Greece
David Kensche, Germany
Larry Kerschberg, USA
Christian Kop, Austria
Lea Kutvonen, Finland
Regine Laleau, France
Alexei Lapouchnian, Canada
Sotirios Liaskos, Canada
Rimantas Butleris, Lithuania
Lech Madeyski, Poland
Alexander Mädche, Germany
Raimundas Matulevicius, Estonia
Heinrich Mayr, Austria
Jan Mendling, Austria
Miguel Mira da Silva, Portugal
Isabelle Mirbel, France
Ana Moreira, Portugal
John Mylopoulos, Italy
Michael Pantazoglou, Greece
Anna Perini, Italy
Gilles Perrouin, Belgium
Mario Piattini, Spain
Geert Poels, Belgium
Jaroslav Pokorny, Czech Republic
Erik Proper, Luxembourg
Christoph Quix, Germany
Jolita Ralyté, Switzerland
Francisco Valverde Girome, Spain
Manfred Reichert, Germany
Iris Reinhartz-Berger, Israel
Dominique Rieu, France
Stefanie Rinderle-Ma, Austria
Thomas Rose, Germany
Michael Rosemann, Australia
Gustavo Rossi, Argentina
Matti Rossi, Finland
Antonio Ruiz Cortés, Spain
Irina Rychkova, France
Motoshi Saeki, Japan
Camille Salinesi, France
Michael Schrefl, Austria
Samira Si-Said Cherfi, France
Vítor Silva Souza, Brazil

Guttorm Sindre, Norway
Monique Snoeck, Belgium
Arnon Sturm, Israel
Angelo Susi, Italy
David Taniar, Australia
Ernest Teniente, Spain
Juan-Carlos Trujillo Mondéjar, Spain
Aphrodite Tsalgatidou, Greece
Irene Vanderfeesten, The Netherlands

Olegas Vasilecas, Lithuania
Panos Vassiliadis, Greece
Gianluigi Viscusi, Switzerland
Barbara Weber, Austria
Alain Wegmann, Switzerland
Roel Wieringa, The Netherlands
Eric Yu, Canada
Yijun Yu, UK

Additional Referees

Kiki Adhinugraha
Moussa Amrani
Kevin Andrews
George Athanasopoulos
Fatma Basak Aydemir
Seyed-Mehdi-Reza Beheshti
Pierre Berlioux
Floris Bex
Devis Bianchini
Neli Blagus
Alexander Bock
Dominik Bork
Quentin Boucher
Isabel Sofia Brito
Kristof Böhmer
Javier Canovas
Evellin Cardoso
Michele Catasta
Marco Comerio
Fabiano Dalpiaz
Cristiano De Faveri
Sophie Dupuy-Chessa
Hella Faller
Walid Fdhila
Christophe Feltus
Pablo Fernandez
Alfio Ferrara
Marília Ferreira
Hans-Georg Fill
Jose Maria Garcia
Lorenzo Genta
Frederic Gervais
Sepideh Ghanavati

David Gil
Fáber D. Giraldo
Christophe Gnaho
Evangelos Gongolidis
Bertrand Grégoire
Saulius Gudas
Jens Gulden
Phillip Haake
Tom Haegemans
Tobias Hildebrandt
Markus Hipp
Amin Jalali
Slinger Jansen
Florian Johannsen
Monika Kaczmarek
Georg Kaes
Diana Kalibatiene
Christos Kalloniatis
Kęstutis Kapočius
István Koren
Eleni Koutrouli
Milos Kravcik
Harald Kuehn
Philippe Lalanda
Andreas Lanz
Jens Lauterbach
Maria Leitner
Feng-Lin Li
Tong Li
Rima Linaburgyte
Matthias Lohrmann
Garm Lucassen
Amel Mammar

Diana Marosin
Irini Marouskou
Alejandro Maté
Andrea Maurino
Michele Melchiori
Gytenis Mikulenas
Stefano Montanelli
Stefan Morana
Christoph Moser
Bernd Neumayr
Kestutis Normantas
Karolyne Oliveira
Sietse Overbeek
Elda Paja
Matteo Palmonari
Otto Parra
João Pimentel
Rüdiger Pryss
Philippe Ramadour
Itzel Morales Ramirez
Eric Rocha de Souza
Marcela Ruiz
Mattia Salnitri

Titas Savickas
Carola Schauer
Marc Schickler
Johannes Schobel
Christoph Schütz
Sergio Segura
Farida Semmak
Arik Senderovich
Vladimir Shekhovtsov
Elias Silva
Tomas Skersys
Marco Spruit
Lovro Subelj
Michalis Titsias
Justas Trikunas
Christina Tsagkani
Wilfrid Utz
Maria José Villanueva
Gianluigi Viscusi
Jan Martijn van der Werf
Marinka Zitnik
Slavko Zitnik

Keynotes

Attaining a Systems Perspective

Harold W. "Bud" Lawson

bud@lawson.com

Abstract. Obtaining and utilizing a systems perspective that enables the capability to "think" and "act" in terms of systems is vital for Information Systems Engineers that develop and deploy products and services that are integrated into wider systems in various environments. To be able to use concepts, principles and paradigms as common mental models as well as to share a vocabulary of terminology all are essential for achieving understanding and communication. This applies to individuals as well as for all forms of organized group activities in treating the life cycle aspects of an information system. In this keynote address, a proven approach to attaining a broad common systems perspective is presented and related to information systems.

About the Speaker

Harold W. "Bud" Lawson has been active in the computing and systems arena since 1958 and has broad international experience in private and public organizations as well as academic environments. Experienced in many facets of computing and computer-based systems, including systems and software engineering, computer architecture, real-time, programming languages and compilers, operating systems, life-cycle process standards, various application domains as well as computer and systems related education and training. He contributed to several pioneering efforts in hardware and software technologies at Univac, IBM, Standard Computer Corporation, and Datasaab. In 2000, he received the prestigious IEEE Computer Pioneer Charles Babbage medal award for his 1964 invention of the pointer variable concept for programming languages.

Harold Lawson has held permanent and visiting professorial appointments at several universities including Polytechnic Institute of Brooklyn, University of California, Irvine, Universidad Politecnica de Barcelona, Linköpings University, Royal Technical University, University of Malaya and Keio University. He is a Fellow of the Association for Computing Machinery, Fellow and Life Member of the IEEE and Fellow of the International Council on Systems Engineering.

The Age of Data and the New Era of Computing

Aleksandra Mojsilovic

Thomas J. Watson Research Center
aleksand@ibm.us

Abstract. The emergence of social networking, sensors, mobile devices, business data warehouses, scientific and government records creates an abundance of information. We like to call it "Big Data." Big Data comes in all forms: sound, video, images, symbols, measurements and natural language. It is changing the way we live and work, the way businesses operate and the way governments are run. And it is fundamentally changing the Information Technology landscape, giving rise to a new generation of cognitive systems that sense, predict, infer, recommend, hypothesize, and in some ways, reason. The combination of people and computers will be able to think in a way that neither people nor computers have ever done before; it will amplify human abilities and lead to new breakthroughs, assist us in making better choices, look out for us, and help us navigate our world in powerful new ways.

About the Speaker

Aleksandra "Saška" Mojsilović manages Data Science Group at the IBM T. J. Watson Research Center in Yorktown Heights, New York. Aleksandra is one of the pioneers of business analytics at IBM; throughout her career she championed innovative uses of analytics for business decision support: from the early identification of client risk via predictive modeling, to the estimation of outsourcing benefits via signal analysis in support of IBM marketing campaigns. Over the last decade, as a lead scientist, Aleksandra drove the development of a portfolio of Smarter Workforce solutions and led their deployment within IBM for the enterprise-wide transformation. Working with key IBM clients in healthcare she led the development of differentiating analytics capabilities for healthcare payers. For her technical contributions and the business impact of her work, Aleksandra was appointed an IBM Fellow, the company's highest technical honor. Saška's research interests include multidimensional signal processing, pattern recognition, machine learning and predictive modeling, with applications to business analytics, healthcare, finance, multimedia, social and biomedical systems. She is the author of over 100 publications and holds 14 patents. Saška received a number of awards for her work, including the IEEE Young Author Best Paper Award, INFORMS Wagner Prize, IEEE International Conference on Service Operations and Logistics and Informatics Best Paper Award, European Conference on Computer Vision Best Paper Award, IBM Gerstner Award, IBM Market Intelligence Award and several IBM Outstanding Technical Achievement Awards.

From Opinions to Facts – Building Products Customers Actually Use

Jan Bosch

Chalmers University of Technology
janbosch@chalmers.se

Abstract. Research shows that for a typical system, more than half of all the features are never used. This is a colossal waste of R&D effort and is caused by companies asking customers and users what they want. Users don't know what they want and it's the engineer's job to find this out. Answering this question requires a systematic approach to exploring a broad set of hypotheses about functionality that might add value for users at different stages of development. The talk introduces the notion of Innovation Experiment Systems as a systematic method for optimising the user experience of existing features, developing new features as well as developing new products. The method uses different techniques dependent on the stage of development, including pre-development, development and commercial deployment. In each stage, frequent customer involvement, both active and passive, is used to constantly establish and improve the user experience. The method is based on data from eight industrial cases and stresses the importance of speed and rapid iterations in development. The talk uses numerous examples from industry are used to illustrate the concepts.

About the Speaker

Jan Bosch is professor of software engineering and director of the Software Center at Chalmers University Technology in Gothenburg, Sweden. Earlier, he worked as Vice President Engineering Process at Intuit Inc where he also lead Intuit's Open Innovation efforts and headed the central mobile technologies team. Before Intuit, he was head of the Software and Application Technologies Laboratory at Nokia Research Center, Finland. Prior to joining Nokia, he headed the software engineering research group at the University of Groningen, The Netherlands, where he holds a professorship in software engineering. His research activities include open innovation, innovation experiment systems, compositional software engineering, software ecosystems, software architecture, software product families and software variability management. He is the author of a book "Design and Use of Software Architectures: Adopting and Evolving a Product Line Approach" Jan also runs a consulting firm, Boschonian AB, that offers its clients support around R&D and innovation management. More information about his background can be found at his website: www.janbosch.com.

Contents

Social and Collaborative Computing

Game Aspect: An Approach to Separation of Concerns in Crowdsourced
Data Management   3
   Shun Fukusumi, Atsuyuki Morishima, and Hiroyuki Kitagawa

Editing Anxiety in Corporate Wikis: From Private Drafting to Public Edits . . .   20
   Cristóbal Arellano, Oscar Díaz, and Maider Azanza

Run-Time and Task-Based Performance of Event Detection Techniques
for Twitter   35
   Andreas Weiler, Michael Grossniklaus, and Marc H. Scholl

Business Process Modeling and Languages

RALph: A Graphical Notation for Resource Assignments in Business
Processes   53
   Cristina Cabanillas, David Knuplesch, Manuel Resinas,
   Manfred Reichert, Jan Mendling, and Antonio Ruiz-Cortés

Revising the Vocabulary of Business Process Element Labels   69
   Agnes Koschmider, Meike Ullrich, Antje Heine, and Andreas Oberweis

Declarative Process Modeling in BPMN   84
   Giuseppe De Giacomo, Marlon Dumas, Fabrizio Maria Maggi,
   and Marco Montali

High Volume and Complex Information Management

The Requirements and Needs of Global Data Usage in Product Lifecycle
Management   103
   Anni Siren, Kari Smolander, and Mikko Jokela

Probabilistic Keys for Data Quality Management   118
   Pieta Brown and Sebastian Link

A Clustering Approach for Protecting GIS Vector Data   133
   Ahmed Abubahia and Mihaela Cocea

Requirements Elicitation and Management

Need-to-Share and Non-diffusion Requirements Verification
in Exchange Policies   151
   Rémi Delmas and Thomas Polacsek

Virtual Business Role-Play: Leveraging Familiar Environments to Prime
Stakeholder Memory During Process Elicitation   166
   Joel Harman, Ross Brown, Daniel Johnson, Stefanie Rinderle-Ma,
   and Udo Kannengiesser

Handling Regulatory Goal Model Families as Software Product Lines   181
   Anthony Palmieri, Philippe Collet, and Daniel Amyot

Enterprise Data Management

Managing Data Warehouse Traceability: A Life-Cycle Driven Approach . . .   199
   Selma Khouri, Kamel Semassel, and Ladjel Bellatreche

Specification and Incremental Maintenance of Linked Data Mashup Views . . .   214
   Vânia M.P. Vidal, Marco A. Casanova, Narciso Arruda,
   Mariano Roberval, Luiz Paes Leme, Giseli Rabello Lopes,
   and Chiara Renso

A Model-Driven Approach to Enterprise Data Migration   230
   Raghavendra Reddy Yeddula, Prasenjit Das, and Sreedhar Reddy

Model Conceptualisation and Evolution

Interactive Recovery of Requirements Traceability Links Using
User Feedback and Configuration Management Logs   247
   Ryosuke Tsuchiya, Hironori Washizaki, Yoshiaki Fukazawa,
   Keishi Oshima, and Ryota Mibe

Detecting Complex Changes During Metamodel Evolution   263
   Djamel Eddine Khelladi, Regina Hebig, Reda Bendraou,
   Jacques Robin, and Marie-Pierre Gervais

"We Need to Discuss the *Relationship*": Revisiting Relationships
as Modeling Constructs   279
   Nicola Guarino and Giancarlo Guizzardi

Process Mining, Monitoring and Predicting

PM^2: A Process Mining Project Methodology   297
   Maikel L. van Eck, Xixi Lu, Sander J.J. Leemans,
   and Wil M.P. van der Aalst

Completing Workflow Traces Using Action Languages 314
  Chiara Di Francescomarino, Chiara Ghidini, Sergio Tessaris,
  and Itzel Vázquez Sandoval

A Novel Top-Down Approach for Clustering Traces 331
  Yaguang Sun and Bernhard Bauer

Intra- and Inter-Organizational Process Engineering

Extracting Decision Logic from Process Models 349
  Kimon Batoulis, Andreas Meyer, Ekaterina Bazhenova, Gero Decker,
  and Mathias Weske

Equivalence Transformations for the Design of Interorganizational
Data-Flow 367
  Julius Köpke and Johann Eder

Automatic Generation of Optimized Process Models from Declarative
Specifications 382
  Richard Mrasek, Jutta Mülle, and Klemens Böhm

Process Compliance and Alignment

Towards the Automated Annotation of Process Models 401
  Henrik Leopold, Christian Meilicke, Michael Fellmann,
  Fabian Pittke, Heiner Stuckenschmidt, and Jan Mendling

Discovery and Validation of Queueing Networks in Scheduled Processes . . . 417
  Arik Senderovich, Matthias Weidlich, Avigdor Gal, Avishai Mandelbaum,
  Sarah Kadish, and Craig A. Bunnell

Verification and Validation of UML Artifact-Centric Business
Process Models 434
  Montserrat Estañol, Maria-Ribera Sancho, and Ernest Teniente

Enterprise IT Integration and Management

Empirical Challenges in the Implementation of IT Portfolio Management:
A Survey in Three Companies 453
  Lucy Ellen Lwakatare, Pasi Kuvaja, Harri Haapasalo, and Arto Tolonen

Integration Adapter Modeling 468
  Daniel Ritter and Manuel Holzleitner

Service Science and Computing

Modelling Service Level Agreements for Business Process
Outsourcing Services.   485
   Adela del–Río–Ortega, Antonio Manuel Gutiérrez,
   Amador Durán, Manuel Resinas, and Antonio Ruiz–Cortés

Deriving Artefact-Centric Interfaces for Overloaded Web Services.   501
   Fuguo Wei, Alistair Barros, and Chun Ouyang

Tutorials

CAiSE 2015 Tutorials.   519
   Ilia Bider and Pnina Soffer

Work System Theory: A Bridge Between Business and IT Views
of Systems.   520
   Steven Alter

Fundamental Systems Thinking Concepts for IS Engineering:
Balancing between Change and Non-change   522
   Gil Regev

Know-how Mapping with ME-map.   523
   Eric Yu and Arnon Sturm

Model Matching - Processes and Beyond   525
   Avigdor Gal and Matthias Weidlich

FEDS2: A Practical Tutorial on the Framework for Evaluation in Design
Science Research (v. 2).   527
   John R. Venable

Author Index   529

Social and Collaborative Computing

Game Aspect: An Approach to Separation of Concerns in Crowdsourced Data Management

Shun Fukusumi, Atsuyuki Morishima$^{(\boxtimes)}$, and Hiroyuki Kitagawa

University of Tsukuba, Tsukuba, Japan
shun.fukusumi.2011b@mlab.info, mori@slis.tsukuba.ac.jp,
kitagawa@cs.tsukuba.ac.jp

Abstract. In data-centric crowdsourcing, it is well known that the incentive structure connected to workers' behavior greatly affects output data. This paper proposes to use a declarative language to deal with both of data computation and the incentive structure explicitly. In the language, computation is modeled as a set of Datalog-like rules, and the incentive structures for the crowd are modeled as games in which the actions taken by players (workers) affect how much payoff they will obtain. The language is unique in that it introduces the game aspect that separates the code for the incentive structure from the other logic encoded in the program. This paper shows that the game aspect not only makes it easier to analyze and maintain the incentive structures, it gives a principled model of the fusion of human and machine computations. In addition, it reports the results of experiments with a real set of data.

Keywords: Crowdsourcing · Declarative languages · Databases · Separation of concerns

1 Introduction

Much crowdsourcing is *data-centric*, i.e., we ask workers to perform microtasks to enter data or to help collect, process, and manage data [5] [20]. In data-centric crowdsourcing, it is well known that the incentive structure connected to workers' behavior greatly affects output data [10]. However, for many existing data-centric declarative frameworks [6] [19] [22], the design space for the incentive structure is relatively limited. For example, each worker receives a fixed amount of payment for each task, and the payment for each task is the only parameter for the incentive space. The reason for this is that complex incentive structures are often strongly connected to the logic of applications. In addition, such incentive structures are difficult to analyze and maintain.

This paper proposes to use a declarative language to deal with both of data computation and the incentive structure explicitly. In the language, computation is modeled as a set of Datalog-like (or Prolog-like) rules, and the incentive structures for the crowd are modeled as *games* in which the actions taken by players (workers) affect how much payoff they will obtain. The language can be used to implement both microtask-based and game-style crowdsourcing applications.

© Springer International Publishing Switzerland 2015
J. Zdravkovic et al. (Eds.): CAiSE 2015, LNCS 9097, pp. 3–19, 2015.
DOI: 10.1007/978-3-319-19069-3_1

The language is unique in that it adopts *separation of concerns*, which is an important principle in software development. The language introduces the *game aspect* that separates the code for the incentive structures from the other logic encoded in the program. With the game aspect, the code for the incentive structure is localized and described in terms taken from game theory[1]. Game theory is known to be useful when discussing not just real "games" but any system that involves incentive structure, and the game aspect makes analyzing and maintaining the incentive structure easier. In contrast, in traditional programming abstractions, it is difficult to find what kind of game is implemented in the code.

Interestingly, a logic-based language with the game aspect provides us with a natural and principled model of integration of human and machine intelligence. In the model, the incentive structure affects workers' behavior to determine two things that cannot be determined by the machine. Workers determine: (1) which rule to execute first when we have multiple rules but the evaluation order cannot be determined by logic, and (2) what value will be entered when the values cannot be derived by logic and the stored data. We will show that given an appropriate incentive, human intelligence can be used to find an effective ordering for evaluating rules to find good results without exploring the whole search space.

As a running example, we discuss four variations of a game-style crowd-sourcing application for extracting structured data from tweets. To show the potential of the language, some variations are complex: the players (workers) are asked to not only enter the extraction results, but also to enter *extraction rules to be processed by the machine*. Therefore, we obtain the extraction rules as the result of crowdsourcing. In addition, the obtained rules are used during the same crowdsourcing process so that the main contributor of the extraction is gradually changed from humans to the machine. Although there are many approaches to apply machine learning techniques to find rules [16], there are many cases wherein we cannot apply machine learning techniques, such as a case in which the rules are very complex or we need to find rules with a small set of training data. In such cases, crowdsourcing is a promising approach.

Related Work. There have been many attempts to develop languages for data-centric crowdsourcing. Most of them are SQL-like languages [6] [19] [21]. Other approaches to help develop crowdsourcing applications include toolkits (e.g., TurKit [15]) and abstractions for crowdsourcing [13][17]. Existing languages have no explicit component to describe the incentive structure, and how workers behave is out of their scope.

There are several crowdsourcing systems that introduce the notion of games. Verbosity [4] is a Game-With-A-Purpose system (GWAP) [2] that collects common-sense knowledge during gameplay. The ESP Game [1] collects tags for

---

[1] Strictly speaking, the game aspect localizes the code required to define the unit of games and compute feedback to workers, regardless whether the feedback serves as a meaningful incentive or not. However, the game aspect helps us analyze and maintain the incentive structure. Detail is given in Section 4.

images, wherein each player is shown an image and guesses the tag another player would enter for the image. Our paper shows that declarative languages with the game aspect description offer a simple and powerful approach to help analyze the behavior of the code.

Recently, integration of human and machine computations is a hot issue [9] [14]. This paper shows that we can use a logic-based formalization to bridge the gap between human-only and machine-only computations in a unique way.

There have been many attempts to investigate connections between game theory and logic [12]. Our language is unique in that games are defined in the code, and that the games are used to not only define the semantics of the code, but leverage human intelligence to solve problems efficiently. The literature on algorithmic game theory has addressed various aspects involving both algorithms and games, such as complexities of computing equilibrium of games [23]. We hope that results from the area are helpful in discussing computational complexity of programs involving human activities.

This paper proposes an implementation language for crowdsourcing. Applying the research results on higher-level issues [7][8] to our language is an interesting challenge. Aspect oriented programming were first introduced in [11]. Applying various results on AOP to our context, such as finding aspects (in our case, games) in the early stages of software development [25], is also our interesting future work.

Summary of Contributions. First, we introduce a declarative framework that supports the game aspect. The game aspect not only makes it easier to analyze and maintain the incentive structures, it gives a principled model of the fusion of human and machine computations. Second, with a running example, we show that the game aspect allows us to easily apply game theory to prove some properties of complex crowdsourcing applications. We believe that this is an important first step to discuss the semantics of the code involving human behavior, although the assumption that workers are rational is not always true. We also conducted experiments with a real set of data. The results show that appropriately designed complex crowdsourcing applications obtain good results, especially in terms of the quality of data extraction rules. The results are consistent with the results of theoretical analysis using the game aspect.

2   Running Example: TweetPecker

As a running example, we explain TweetPecker [18], a game-style Web application to crowdsource extracting structured data from a set of tweets to populate a relation.

Figure 1 shows the dataflow in TweetPecker. It takes as inputs (1) a set of tweets and (2) the relation (table) schema $St(\mathtt{tw}, a_1, a_2, \ldots, a_N)$ to store extracted values (Figure 1(1)) where $\mathtt{tw}$ is a mandatory attribute to store tweets, and a_is are attributes to store values extracted from the tweet $\mathtt{tw}$. Then, Tweet-Pecker shows workers each tweet one by one and asks them to enter values for attributes a_is for the tweet. Each result is represented as a tuple (row)

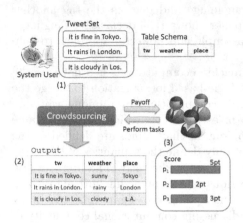

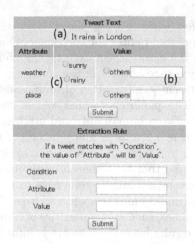

Fig. 1. Overview of TweetPecker

Fig. 2. Interface for entering values (top) entering extraction rules (bottom)

and inserted into the `Output` relation (Figure 1(2)). Workers receive feedbacks (Figure 1(3)) according to their inputs.

We can design variations of TweetPecker by changing what workers do and how they receive feedback. The following are four variations of TweetPecker: VE, VE/I, VRE, and VRE/I.

(1) Value-Entry (VE) crowdsources workers directly extracting values from tweets. Figure 2 (top) is the interface for workers. In VE (and VE/I we explain next), the radio buttons in Figure 2 (c) do not appear. In VE, the player (worker) is given a tweet "It rains in London" (Figure 2 (a)) and is asked to enter values for `weather` and `place` attributes into the text form (Figure 2 (b)). If she enters the values, the next tweet shows up. Each attribute value of an `Output` tuple is determined when two distinct workers give the same value. Each worker receives a fixed score (e.g., 1) whenever she performs a task regardless of the entered value.

(2) Value-Entry with Incentive (VE/I) is the same as VE except that workers receive positive scores only if their entered values match with each other (Section 4 for details).

(3) Value-Rule-Entry (VRE) allows workers to not only directly extract values from tweets but give extraction rules to be used by the machine with the interface in Figure 2 (bottom) (Section 5.1).

(4) Value-Rule-Entry with Incentives (VRE/I) is the same as VRE except that workers receive scores according to their behaviors (Section 5.2).

3   CyLog

CyLog [18] is an executable abstraction for crowdsourcing. It is a rule-based language whose syntax is similar to Datalog. CyLog is adopted by Crowd4U [27],

```
rules: Pre1: TweetOriginal(tw:"It rains in London", loc:"London");
Pre2: ValidCity(cname:"London"); Pre3: Tweet(tw) <-
TweetOriginal(tw, loc), ValidCity(cname:loc); Pre4: Worker(pid:1,
name:"Shun"); Pre5: Worker(pid:2, name:"Ken");

VE1: Input(tw, attr:"weather", value, p)/open[p] <- Tweet(tw), Worker(p);
VE2: Output(tw, weather:value) <- Input(tw, attr:"weather", value, p:p1),
                        Input(tw, attr:"weather", value, p:p2), p1!=p2;
```

Fig. 3. Fragment of a CyLog program

an open crowdsourcing platform being developed and operated by universities. Crowd4U is similar to Amazon Mechanical Turk but workers (most of them are students and faculty members of universities) perform tasks voluntarily. This section first summarizes the basics of CyLog. Then, it explains the code for VE, the simplest variation of TweetPecker.

Overview. The basic data structure in CyLog is a *relation*, which is a table to deal with a set of *tuples* that conform to the *schema* of the relation. A program written in CyLog consists of four sections. The **schema** section describes the schema of relations. The **rules** section has a set of rules each of which *fires* (is executed) if its condition is satisfied. The **views** section describes the interface with workers in HTML (e.g., the ones in Figure 2). The **games** section describes the game aspect of the program (Section 4). In the following discussions, we explain only the **rules** section and the **games** section. The **schema** and **views** sections are straightforward and we assume that they are appropriately given.

Facts and Rules. The main component of a CyLog program is the set of *statements* written in the **rules** section. Figure 3 shows a set of statements, each of which is preceded by a label for explanation purposes. A statement is either a *fact* or a *rule*. In the figure, Pre1, Pre2, Pre4, and Pre5 are facts, and Pre3, VE1, VE2 are rules. A rule has the form of *head ← body*. Each *fact* or *head* is given in the form of an *atom*, while each atom consists of a predicate name (e.g., Tweet) followed by a set of *attributes* (e.g., loc). Optionally, each attribute can be followed by a colon with a value (e.g., :"London") or an alias name (e.g., :p1). Each *body* consists of a sequence of atoms.

A fact describes that the specified tuple is inserted into a relation. For example, Pre1 is a fact that inserts a tuple whose values for attributes tw and loc are ''It rains in London'' and ''London'' into relation TweetOriginal[2].

A rule specifies that, for each combination of tuples satisfying the condition specified in the *body*, the tuple described in *head* is inserted to a relation. Atoms in the body are evaluated from left to right and variables are bound to values that are stored in the relation specified by each atom. For example, Pre3 is a rule that inserts a tuple having a tweet tw into relation Tweet if tw is in the TweetOriginal and its location is a valid city contained in ValidCity. In other words, for each combination of a tuple in TweetOriginal and a tuple in

---

[2] CyLog adopts the *named perspective* [3] which means that variables and values in each atom are associated to attributes by explicit *attribute names*, not by their positions in the attribute sequence.

`ValidCity` whose `loc` attributes match to each other, it inserts a tuple having `tw` value into relation `Tweet`.

Open Predicates. CyLog allows predicates to be *open*, which means that the decision as to whether a tuple exists in the relation or not is performed by humans when the data cannot be derived from the data in the database. For example, the head of VE1 is followed by `/open` and is an open predicate. If a head is an open predicate, CyLog asks humans to give values to the variables that are not bound to any values in the body (e.g., `value` in VE1)[3]. Optionally, each `/open` can be followed by `[..]` (e.g., `[p]`) to specify the worker CyLog asks for the values through the interface. Therefore, VE1 means that for each combination of a tweet `tw` and a worker `p`, the code asks the worker `p` to enter a value for the `value` attribute.

Evaluation Order. Each rule fires when its condition is satisfied. If more than one rule are ready to fire *at the same time* because all of their body conditions are satisfied, logic cannot determine in which order the rules should be executed. As with many languages, CyLog evaluates all such rules with a default ordering if the rules have no open predicates: a rule that appears earlier in the code with tuples appearing at earlier rows in relations is given higher priority. However, evaluation of any rule with an open predicate is suspended until a worker enters values for the open predicate, even if its body condition is satisfied. This allows workers to determine which rule to or not to fire, under the control by the incentive mechanism we explain in Section 4.

Block Style Rules. Each rule $P \leftarrow P_1, P_2, \ldots, P_n$ can be written in the *block style* $P_1\{P_2\{\ldots\{P_n\{P;\}\ldots\}\}$. For example, Pre3 in Figure 3 can be written as:

```
TweetOriginal(tw, loc) {
    ValidCity(cname:loc) {
        Tweet(tw);
    }
}
```

where `Tweet(tw)` is the head of the rule. The block style provides a concise expression when we have many rules that have the same body atoms, because we can write more than one atom inside each bracket (e.g., $P_1\{P_2; P_3;\}$ for $P_2 \leftarrow P_1; P_3 \leftarrow P_1;$).

Value-Entry: A Variation of TweetPecker. The code in Figure 3 implements VE. we assume that the relation generated by TweetPecker is `Output(tw, weather)`[4]. Pre1 to Pre3 construct a set of tweets. Pre4 and Pre5 define two workers. VE1 and VE2 implement the essential part of VE. VE1 asks the two workers to extract values for attribute `weather` from tweets (there is only one tweet in the code) and generates tuples for relation `Input`, an intermediate relation to store the workers' inputs. The omitted code in the view section shows

---

[3] If all variables in the head are bounded to values in the rule body, CyLog asks workers whether the tuple should exist in the relation.

[4] For simplicity, we deal with only one attribute for extracted values. It is straightforward to deal with more than one attribute.

Player A/Player B	Fine	Rainy
Fine	(1,1)	(0,0)
Rainy	(0,0)	(1,1)

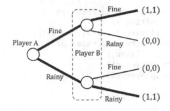

Fig. 4. Payoff matrix for a game and its extensive form

workers the tweet (Figure 2(a)) and the text input form (Figure 2(b)). VE2 states that if two different workers enter the same value for `weather` attribute of the same tweet, the agreed value is stored in the `Output`.

4   Game Aspect

Semantics of Open Predicates. Open predicates make it difficult to define the semantics of the code. First, we have no clue on what value each worker gives for open predicates. Second, the order in which we evaluate rules with open predicates is undefined. CyLog introduces a mechanism to support for describing the incentive structure at the language level to give the code a clear semantics using game theory.

The idea is to model the incentive structure as "games" in which the behaviors of players (workers) determine payoffs to them. We use VE/I (Section 2) to explain this concept. VE/I can be seen as having a collection of games, each of which is associated to one tweet: In each game, a tweet is shown to players, and each player is required to predict a term to represent the weather written in the tweet, which others would give for the same tweet. If two players give the same term, the players are rewarded, and the matched term will be stored into `Output` as the value of the `weather` attribute of the tuple for the tweet.

In game theory, a game is often written as a *payoff matrix*; Figure 4 (left) shows a part of the payoff matrix of the game (only two terms are shown in the matrix). The Y and X axis show the possible *actions* of Player A and B, respectively. The matrix shows that each player can enter `fine` or `rainy` for a given tweet. It also describes how payoffs are given to players. In each cell, (v_1, v_2) means that Players A and B receive v_1 and v_2 as their payoffs when they choose the actions on the X and Y axes. In the game, if they give the same term, they receive the payoffs. Such an incentive structure is known as a coordination game [24] in game theory.

Figure 4 (right) illustrates the same game in a tree style called the *extensive form* [24]. Each *path* from the root to a terminal node corresponds to each cell in the payoff matrix and represents a possible play of the game. The leaf nodes are associated with payoffs to the players. The dotted circle means that the player B does not know the choice Player A took for her action. Then, we can define the semantics of open values as actions in the *solutions* of the game, which are the paths taken by rational workers. For example, the solution of the game in Figure

```
games:
      VEI(tw,attr){    // Skolem function
      /* Path definition */
VEI1:   Path(action:["value",value],player:p)
               <- Inputs(tw,attr,value,p);
      /* Payoff definition */
VEI2:   Path(action,player:p1),
        Path(action,player:p2),
        p1!=p2 {
VEI2.1:      Payoff[p1+=1,p2+=1]
        }
      }
```

Order	Date	Player	Action
1	10:10am	Kate	["value", "fine"]
2	10:11am	Pam	["value", "rainy"]
3	10:12am	Ann	["value", "fine"]

Fig. 5. Game aspect of VE/I   **Fig. 6.** Path table

4 (right) is the paths in which the players provide the same term (bold lines), because the best strategy for them is to choose the same one that the other player would choose. To compute the payoff values for them, it is important to maintain the information on the path in each game play.

Separation of Concerns by the Game Aspect. If we write code to maintain paths of the game and to compute payoffs to players in existing programming languages, the code fragments related to the games are implicitly encoded in many different places in the code. Therefore, analyzing and changing the incentive structure will be a cumbersome task. As our example will show, the incentive structure is often complicated, which makes it almost impossible to analyze and maintain the incentive structure.

An important principle in software development is the *separation of concerns.* We propose the *game aspect,* which separates the code for the incentive structures from the other logic encoded in the program, by allowing the code to be localized and described in terms taken from game theory. Therefore, the game aspect makes analyzing and maintaining the incentive structure easy.

Figure 5 shows the game aspect of VE/I. The whole code for VE/I is the combination of the **rules** section (Figure 3) and the game aspect. Therefore, the code clearly shows that VE/I is the same as VE except its incentive structure.

A game aspect consists of three parts: a Skolem function, the path definition, and the payoff definition.

1. Skolem Function. The first line has a function named a Skolem function to create a game for each specified parameters. Intuitively, it defines the unit of games. For example, **VEI(tw,attr)** creates a **VEI** game for each combination of a tweet and one of its attributes (e.g., **weather**). We call each game a *game instance.*

For each game instance, a special table called a *path table* is automatically constructed (Figure 6). The path table maintains the *path* (i.e., a line from the root to a leaf in Figure 4 (right)) of the play of the game instance to show how the game reached the last state. Its schema is **Path(<u>Order</u>,Date,Player,Action)**, where each tuple records when and who took what action on the executed path. Figure 6 shows an example of the path table. Here, **["value",***value***]** is a list

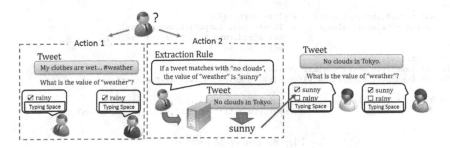

Fig. 7. VRE and VRE/I

containing two strings, which means that the action is to enter *value* for the
"`value`" attribute.

2. Path Definition. The rule whose head is `Path` (i.e., VEI1) supplies tuples
inserted to the path table of a game instance created for the parameters of the
Skolem function (i.e., a combination of `tw` and `attr`). VEI1 states that the inputs
to the `value` attribute of the relation `Inputs` are inserted into the table to be
recorded as actions of players.

3. Payoff Definition. The rule whose head is `Payoff` (i.e., VEI2 to VEI2.1. Note
that VEI2.1 is the head in the block style rule) computes the payoffs to players. `Payoff` is a relation that maintains payoff values to players. The head
`Payoff[p1+=1, p2+=1]` is a syntactic sugar of a rule to update the values of
payoffs for players (we can write rules without the syntactic sugar by writing a
more complicated rule). The rule implements the same game as that in Figure 4
except that it extends the payoff matrix with an infinite number of players and
terms (values).

Value-Entry with Incentive (VE/I). To summarize, the combination of the
codes in Figures 3 and 5 implements VE/I. Each `VRI` game is instantiated for
each combination of a tweet and an attribute. If people behave rationally, it is
expected that values are computed by the solution of the coordination game.
Assume that we have the path table shown in Figure 6 for a game instance,
which was constructed by the game aspect in Figure 5. Then, the payoff values
for `Kate`, `Pam`, and `Ann`, are 1, 0, and 1, respectively, because `Kate` and `Ann` agreed
on the value. The players can see their accumulated payoff values as the scores
shown in the screen (the code is omitted) (Figure 1(3)).

5 Complex Crowdsourcing

5.1 Value-Rule-Entry (VRE)

In contrast to VE and VE/I, VRE allows each worker to take two types of actions
in arbitrary order (Figure 7):

```
rules:
VRE1: Rules(cond,attr,value,p)/open[p] <- Workers(p);
VRE2: Extracts(tw,attr,value,rid) <- Tweets(tw), Output(tw,weather:null),
                                      Rules(rid,cond,attr:"weather",value),
                                      matches(cond, tw);
VRE3: Tweets(tw), Workers(p){
  VRE3.1: Inputs(tw,attr:"weather",value, p)/open[p];
  VRE3.2: Inputs(tw,attr,value,p)/open[p] <- Extracts(tw,attr:"weather",value);
      }
VRE4: Output(tw, weather:value) <- Inputs(tw,attr:"weather",value,p:p1),
                                   Inputs(tw,attr:"weather",value,p:p2), p1!=p2;
```

Fig. 8. The code for VRE

Action 1: directly enter values extracted from tweets as in VE and VE/I. The default interface of VRE is the same as that for VE (Figure 2 (top)) in which the worker takes Action 1, except that it shows workers the candidate values extracted by the machine (Figure 2(c)).

Action 2: give extraction rules to be used by the machine. If the worker chooses to take Action 2, the interface is changed to the one shown in Figure 2 (bottom), in which she enters extraction rules. We allow regular expressions in the *condition* part.

The entered rules are used by the machine to extract values from the tweets whose values have not been determined yet. The values extracted from a tweet by the machine using the extraction rules are shown to other workers who are taking Action 1, as possible candidates for attribute values of the tweet (Figure 2(c)). This allows the workers to choose a shown value, instead of directly extracting and typing values in the text input form in Figure 2 (b).

Note that workers take Actions 1 and 2 in *arbitrarily order*. As we will explain in Section 5.1, the two actions are implemented by two independent CyLog rules with open predicates. And as explained in Section 3, the rules with open predicates are suspended until workers enter values, even if the both rules are ready to fire (i.e., logically, they have the same priority in the evaluation order). Therefore, the order of user's taking actions determines the order of evaluating such rules. Here, we want to utilize the intelligence of workers, because we expect that workers are able to determine whether they should directly extract values or enter extraction rules for future tweets, for efficient extraction of values. We will be back to this issue in Section 5.2.

Extraction Rules. In VRE, workers enter extraction rules in an HTML form (Figure 2 (bottom)). Logically, each extraction rule is a triple (*condition, attribute, value*). It means that if a tweet matches with the *condition*, the value of *attribute* will be *value*. For example, extraction rule ("clear", "weather", "sunny") means that if a tweet contains "clear", the value of weather will be "sunny".

CyLog Description. Figure 8 is the CyLog code for VRE. We assume that we already have valid tweets and workers. Compared to the code of VE (Figure 3), Figure 8 has two additional rules for relations Rules (VRE1) and Extracts

(VRE2). However, VRE3 and VRE4 are similar to VE1 and VE2, respectively. Details are shown below.

VRE1. The rule asks workers to enter extraction rules. The `Rules` relation maintains the extraction rules entered by workers. Its schema is `Rules(`<u>`rid`</u>`, cond, attr, value, p)`. Here, we have two additional attributes for management purposes: `rid` is an auto-increment key and `p` is the worker who entered the rule.

VRE2. The rule extracts a value if `Output` records no value for the `weather` attribute of a tweet `tw` and there is an extraction rule that matches with the tweet. Relation `Extracts(`<u>`tw, attr, value`</u>`, rid)` records the values extracted by the machine. Each tuple records the fact that an extraction rule with id `rid` extracted `value` as the value for attribute `attr` of tweet `tw`. In the omitted schema section, we define the key of the `Extracts` as a combination of `tw`, `attr`, `value` attributes. Hence the machine can extract `value` for an attribute `attr` of a tweet `tw` only once.

VRE3. The rule from VRE3 to VRE3.1 is the same as VE1 except that it is written in the block style. The rule from VRE3 to VRE3.2 deals with the case wherein the machine extracted a value and shows it in the interface in Figure 2 (c): if `Extracts` has a tuple that records `value` for "weather" attribute of `tw`, we ask the worker if the `value` is correct or not.

VRE4. This is the same as VE2.

5.2 Value-Rule-Entry with Incentives (VRE/I)

In VRE, there was no theoretical guarantee that the workers use their intelligence to take actions so that the results are generated efficiently and effectively, and we left the results up to fate. VRE/I is a solution to the problem. It is the same as VRE but implements the `VREI` game that defines the incentive for workers that affects workers' decision on how to interleave and take Action 1 (encoded as VRE3) and Action 2 (encoded as VRE1).

Incentive Structure of VRE/I. The incentive structure for VRE/I is as follows:

Payoffs related to Action 1: As with VE/I, the worker receives w_1 if she entered a value for a tweet in the interface in Figure 2 (top) and the value matched with the value entered by another worker. Note that if the machine used extraction rules to extract values for the tweet, candidate values show up as in Figure 2 (c). Regardless which interface the worker uses ((b) or (c)), she receives payoffs if another worker gives the same value. We call this *payoff 1*.

Payoffs related to Action 2: The worker receives w_2 if all of the following conditions hold: (1) she enters an extraction rule in the form of Figure 2 (bottom), (2) the machine uses the extraction rule to extract a value for a tweet, and (3) the value is adopted as an agreed value by two other workers with the interface in Figure 2 (top). We call this *payoff 2a*. If there are more than one worker that satisfy the conditions above, the worker who entered the extraction rule *earliest* receives w_2. However, she loses w_3 if the value extracted by her extraction rule is *not* adopted as an agreed value. We call this *payoff 2b*.

In VE/I, we defined one game for each combination of a tweet and an attribute. However, the incentive structure of VRE/I involves all tweets and extraction rules in the process. Therefore, we cannot divide VRE/I into many small independent game instances. Instead, we define only one game for VRE/I as explained below.

CyLog Description. Figure 9 shows the game section of VRE/I (the rule section is the same as that of VRE in Figure 8). Note that since VREI has no parameter, there is only one VREI game instance in VRE/I.

As the incentive structure of VRE/I contains that of VE/I, the game aspect VREI naturally contains that of VEI. In the path definition, VREI1 is the same as VEI1 except that each action records tw and attr, which are used to differentiate the action from the ones for other tweets. We need to do so because VREI has only one game instance for all tweets and attributes. In the payoff definition, the rule from VREI3 to VREI 3.1 is the same as the rule from VEI2 to VEI2.1, and computes *payoff 1*.

Other lines deal with the case where extraction rules are involved. In the path definition, VREI2 means that the path table records an action if a worker enters an extraction rule. In the payoff definition, the rules VREI3 and VREI3.2 implement *payoff 2a*: if a worker entered an extraction rule to extract a value and other two workers agreed on the value, she receives w_2. Similarly, the rules VREI3 and VREI3.3 implement *payoff 2b*.

Note that in VREI3.2, the key of Extract relation is a combination of tw, attr and value. As explained in Section 3, the evaluation priority of CyLog rules guarantees that the extraction rule entered earliest will be used for extracting the value. Therefore, payoff is given to the worker who entered the first extraction rule that extracted value for attr of tw.

6   Theoretical Analysis

Since the game aspect directly describes the incentive structure embedded in the program using the terms of game theory, it is easy to analyze the game aspect of the code. Moreover, it is easy to change the incentive structure because the game aspect is separated from other logic. In this section, we prove two theorems on properties of VRE/I, which we cannot guarantee to hold without an appropriate incentive structure. We can prove the theorems easily by looking at the code in the game aspect. Due to the space limitation, the complete proofs are given in [26].

Theorem 1. (Data Quality) *Let p_1 be a worker of VRE/I who enters an extraction rule. Let p_2 and p_3 be workers who enter values for an attribute of a tweet*

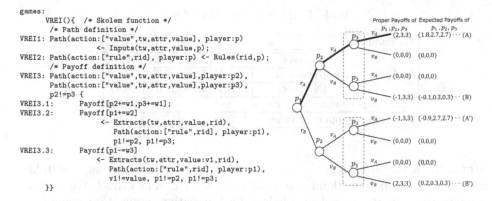

```
games:
      VREI(){   /* Skolem function */
            /* Path definition */
VREI1: Path(action:["value",tw,attr,value], player:p)
                  <- Inputs(tw,attr,value,p);
VREI2: Path(action:["rule",rid], player:p) <- Rules(rid,p);
            /* Payoff definition */
VREI3: Path(action:["value",tw,attr,value],player:p2),
       Path(action:["value",tw,attr,value],player:p3),
       p2!=p3 {
VREI3.1:      Payoff[p2+=w1,p3+=w1];
VREI3.2:      Payoff[p1+=w2]
                  <- Extracts(tw,attr,value,rid),
                     Path(action:["rule",rid], player:p1),
                     p1!=p2, p1!=p3;
VREI3.3:      Payoff[p1-=w3]
                  <- Extracts(tw,attr,value:v1,rid),
                     Path(action:["rule",rid], player:p1),
                     v1!=value, p1!=p2, p1!=p3;
      }}
```

Fig. 9. Game aspect of VRE/I   **Fig. 10.** Game tree of VRE/I

for which the extraction rule extracted an value. Then, if the workers behave rationally, all of them enter correct extraction rules or values.

Proof Outline. From the game aspect of VRE/I, we can easily develop the game tree for VREI (A fragment of the game tree is shown in Figure 10 with expected payoffs for workers). A simple game-theoretic analysis proves the theorem holds.   □

Theorem 2. (Termination) *VRE/I terminates if the number of tweets is finite.*

Proof outline. In VREI3.2 of the game aspect, payment is given to only the worker who entered the first extraction rule that extracted `value` for `attr` of `tw`, because the key attributes of `Extract` are `tw`, `attr` and `value`. Thus, the number of extraction rules that yield payoffs is finite and rational workers eventually stop entering rules.   □

7   Experiment

We conducted an experiment to compare the four variations of TweetPecker. Workers in our experiment were basically diligent and their extracted values were generally good in the quality even with variations without incentives for good data quality (i.e., VE and VRE). This is not surprising, because the theorem 1 does not guarantee that workers without incentives generate bad-quality data. However, an interesting finding is that *even for such diligent workers*, the incentive structure heavily affected the quality of extraction rules and workers' behavior, as supported by theorems 1 and 2. The result suggests that giving workers an appropriate incentive structure improves data quality. The comparision of this approach and other approaches such as training workers is an interesting issue but is out of the scope of this paper.

Due to the space limitation, we cannot show all results of our experiments and detailed analysis. The complete set of results is given in [26].

Table 1. Quality of acquired data

Technique		VE	VE/I	VRE	VRE/I
A: Agreed values	Correct	73.5%	72.2%	71.2%	72.0%
	Incorrect	6.7%	7.9%	7.2%	7.6%
	Neither	19.8%	19.9%	21.6%	20.4%
B: Average confidence of rules		-	-	60.9%	77.0%
C: Average support of rules		-	-	2.71%	6.32%

Method. In the first phase, we recruited four sets of five workers, and told each set of workers to work for one of VE, VE/I, VRE, and VRE/I. We used a common set of tweets as explained below. Each variation terminates when all of attribute values for all tweets are determined.

In the second phase, we asked an independent set of three persons to evaluate the quality of the extracted (agreed) attribute values. This phase was performed off-line. They discussed the quality of each value to classify it to one of "correct", "incorrect", and "neither" groups (Row A of Table 1).

Data. We collected tweets tweeted for a successive 16 days in 2013 with the tag "#tenki" (Japanese word to denote the weather). The number of tweets was 463. The relation schema was defined as Output(tw, weather, place).

Quality of Generated Attribute Values and Extraction Rules. As Row A of Table 1 shows, the quality of data generated by the four variations are almost the same and the difference is not significant in statistics. The reason is that the workers are university students, and they are relatively reliable even without the incentive for improving the quality of their work.

However, an interesting fact was that even if they are reliable workers who work diligently without an incentive that is connected to the quality of their work, the quality of extraction rules became much better with an appropriate incentive structure. Given an extraction rule r_i, we compute the confidence ($conf_i$) and support (sup_i) for r_i and compared them to each other. Here, $conf_i$ and sup_i are defined as follows:

$$conf_i = \frac{\#\text{agreed values}}{\#\text{values extracted by } r_i} \qquad sup_i = \frac{\#\text{tweets matched with } r_i}{\#\text{all tweets}}$$

Rows B and C of Table 1 shows that the average confidence and support for VRE/I are clearly higher than those for VRE. In fact, our statistical analysis shows that the differences are significant at the 0.01 significance level, assuming that population variances of VRE and VRE/I are the same in computing $conf_i$ and sup_i.

Workers' Behavior. For the detailed analysis, we examined the log of actions to compare the workers' behavior in both VRE/I and VRE. Figure 11 has two graphs each of which visualizes the behavior of workers for VRE or VRE/I. In each graph, the X axis is the completion rate of extracting attribute values from

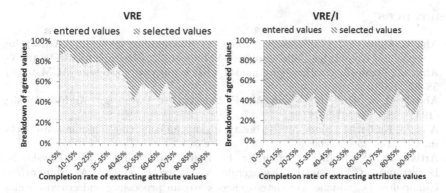

Fig. 11. Breakdown of agreed values into entered and selected values

all the tweets. The Y axis shows the breakdown of agreed values: whether each agreement was on entered values or on selected values. If we compare the two graphs, we can see that the percentage of agreement on selected values (i.e., the percentage of the values extracted by the machine, out of all adopted values) is clearly higher in the early stages in VRE/I.

We examined the log of actions in more detail [26]. Then, we found that workers in VRE/I took the strategy that they enter high-quality extraction rules in earlier stages to try (1) to maximize the number of values extracted by the rules and agreed by workers and (2) to obtain more payoff by taking Action 1 in later stages, instead of entering extraction rules that they cannot expect to give them much payoff. The strategy is consistent with Theorems 1 and 2, and in fact, generated high-quality extraction rules.

8 Conclusion

This paper introduced a declarative language that supports the game aspect for data-centric crowdsourcing. With a running example, we showed that the game aspect not only makes it easier to maintain and analyze the code using game theory, but gives a principled model of the fusion of human and machine computations. In addition, we showed experimental results with a real data set. The results are consistent with the results of the theoretical analysis, and showed that appropriately designed complex crowdsourcing applications obtain good results.

Acknowledgments. The authors are grateful to the contributors to Crowd4U, whose names are partially listed at http://crowd4u.org. They are also grateful to Prof. Yasuhiro Hayase for giving valuable comments on AOP for CyLog. This research was partially supported by PRESTO from the Japan Science and Technology Agency, and by the Grant-in-Aid for Scientific Research (#25240012) from MEXT, Japan.

References

1. Ahn, L., Dabbish, L.: ESP: labeling images with a computer game. In: AAAI Spring Symposium: Knowledge Collection from Volunteer Contributors, pp. 91–98 (2005)
2. Ahn, L., Dabbish, L.: Designing games with a purpose. Commun. ACM **51**(8), 58–67 (2008)
3. Abiteboul, S., Hull, R., Vianu, V.: Foundations of Databases. Addison-Wesley (1995), ISBN 0-201-53771-0
4. Ahn, L., Kedia, M., Blum, M.: Verbosity: a game for collecting common-sense facts. In: CHI, pp. 75–78 (2006)
5. Artikis, A., Weidlich, M., Schnitzler, F., Boutsis, I., Liebig, T., Piatkowski, N., Bockermann, C., Morik, K., Kalogeraki, V., Marecek, J., Gal, A., Mannor, S., Gunopulos, D., Kinane, D.: Heterogeneous stream processing and crowdsourcing for urban traffic management. In: EDBT, pp. 712–723 (2014)
6. Franklin, M.J., Kossmann, D., Kraska, T., Ramesh, S., Xin, R.: CrowdDB: answering queries with crowdsourcing. In: SIGMOD Conference, pp. 61–72 (2011)
7. Gustas, R., Gustiene, P.: Conceptual Modeling Method for Separation of Concerns and Integration of Structure and Behavior. IJISMD **3**(1), 48–77 (2012)
8. Geiger, D., Rosemann, M., Fielt, E., Schader, M.: Crowdsourcing information systems - definition, typology, and design. In: ICIS (2012)
9. Goldberg, S.L., Wang, D.Z., Kraska, T.: CASTLE: Crowd-assisted system for text labeling and extraction. In: HCOMP (2013)
10. Jain, S., Parkes, D.C.: The role of game theory in human computation systems. In: HCOMP 2009, pp. 58–61 (2009)
11. Kiczales, G., Lamping, J., Mendhekar, A., Maeda, C., Lopes, C., Loingtier, J.-M., Irwin, J.: Aspect-oriented programming. In: Akşit, M., Matsuoka, S. (eds.) ECOOP 1997. LNCS, vol. 1241. Springer, Heidelberg (1997)
12. Hodges, W.: Logic and Games. The Stanford Encyclopedia of Philosophy (Spring 2013 Edition), Zalta, E.N., (ed.). http://plato.stanford.edu/archives/spr2013/entries/logic-games
13. Kittur, A., Smus, B., Kraut, R.: CrowdForge: crowdsourcing complex work. In: CHI Extended Abstracts, pp. 1801–1806 (2011)
14. Kondreddi, S.K., Triantafillou, P., Weikum, G.: Combining information extraction and human computing for crowdsourced knowledge acquisition. In: ICDE, pp. 988–999 (2014)
15. Little, G., Chilton, L.B., Goldman, M., Miller, R.C.: TurKit: human computation algorithms on mechanical turk. In: UIST, pp. 57–66 (2010)
16. Langley, P., Simon, H.A.: Applications of Machine Learning and Rule Induction. Commun. ACM **38**(11), 54–64 (1995)
17. Minder, P., Bernstein, A.: CrowdLang: a programming language for the systematic exploration of human computation systems. In: Aberer, K., Flache, A., Jager, W., Liu, L., Tang, J., Guéret, C. (eds.) Social Informatics. LNCS, vol. 7710, pp. 124–137. Springer, Heidelberg (2012)
18. Morishima, A., Shinagawa, N., Mitsuishi, T., Aoki, H., Fukusumi, S.: CyLog/Crowd4U: a declarative platform for complex data-centric crowdsourcing. VLDB **5**(12), 1918–1921 (2012)
19. Marcus, A., Wu, E., Karger, D., Madden, S., Miller, R.: Human-powered Sorts and Joins. PVLDB **5**(1), 13–24 (2011)
20. Nebeling, M., Speicher, M., Grossniklaus, M., Norrie, M.C.: Crowdsourced web site evaluation with crowdstudy. In: Brambilla, M., Tokuda, T., Tolksdorf, R. (eds.) ICWE 2012. LNCS, vol. 7387, pp. 494–497. Springer, Heidelberg (2012)

21. Parameswaran, A.G., Park, H., Garcia-Molina, H., Polyzotis, N., Widom, J.: Deco: declarative crowdsourcing. In: CIKM, pp. 1203–1212 (2012)
22. Park, H., Pang, R., Parameswaran, A.G., Garcia-Molina, H., Polyzotis, N., Widom, J.: An overview of the deco system: data model and query language; query processing and optimization. SIGMOD Record 41(4), 22–27 (2012)
23. Roughgarden, T.: Algorithmic game theory. Commun. ACM 53(7), 78–86 (2010)
24. Vega-Redondo, F.: Economics and Theory of Games. Cambridge University Press (2003)
25. Yu, Y., Cesar, J., Leite, S.P., Mylopoulos, J.: From goals to aspects: discovering aspects from requirements goal models. In: RE, pp. 38–47 (2004)
26. Fukusumi, S., Morishima, A., Kitagawa, H.: Game Aspect: An Approach to Separation of Concerns in Crowdsourced Data Management, Technical Report. http://mlab.info/t-reports/game_aspect-full.pdf
27. Crowd4U. http://crowd4u.org

Editing Anxiety in Corporate Wikis: From Private Drafting to Public Edits

Cristóbal Arellano[1,2]($\boxtimes$), Oscar Díaz[1], and Maider Azanza[1]

[1] Onekin Research Group, University of the Basque Country (UPV/EHU),
San Sebastián, Spain
{cristobal.arellano,oscar.diaz,oscar.diaz,maider.azanza}@ehu.es
[2] IK4-IKERLAN Research Centre, Mondragón, Spain
CArellano@ikerlan.es

Abstract. Wikis promote work to be reviewed *after* publication, not before. This vision might not always fit organizations where a common employee concern is that sharing work-in-progress may negatively affect the assessments they receive. This might lead users to edit in distress, thus affecting task performance, and may minimize their participation in wikis. On this premise, this work advocates for complementing wiki editing with in-line drafting. By "drafting" is meant the personal process of collecting references or gradually forging a new structure of ideas, till the result is good-enough to be published. By "in-line", we highlight that drafts will end up being article edits, and as such, their elaboration should take place *within* the wiki rather than being offloaded to third-party tools. This vision is realized by *Wikinote*, an extension for *Google Chrome* that leverages *MediaWiki's Visual Editor* with drafting facilities. First evidence indicates that *Wikinote* reduces contribution judgement anxiety, and to a lesser extent, editing anxiety.

Keywords: Wikis · Note-taking · Editing anxiety

1 Introduction

Wikis have recently erupted on to the Knowledge Management scene. However, their organizational and social impact is not yet fully understood. Wikis enjoy a great popularity partially due to the success of *Wikipedia*. Key to this success is a crucial innovation in the publishing model: review work *after* publication, not before [18]. This approach has been extremely successful for open communities. Spurred by this success, organizations have rushed to tap into this facility for knowledge sharing and co-creation [14–16,21]. Specifically, wikis have been suggested as "a place for *ideation* to occur by providing an open and democratic environment for individuals and teams to share ideas. Wikis' open and organic nature can allow the capture of ideas quickly and promotes the growth of ideas as they develop" [20]. However, the basis on which *Wikipedia's* success is based might not apply to other organizations. *Wikipedia* culture is characterized by volunteer, hobbyist, potentially anonymous, peer-based, no-deadline,

© Springer International Publishing Switzerland 2015
J. Zdravkovic et al. (Eds.): CAiSE 2015, LNCS 9097, pp. 20–34, 2015.
DOI: 10.1007/978-3-319-19069-3_2

factual contributions. If these contextual factors change, then results might vary [9,11]. Moving from open communities to closed organizations might change these contextual factors (e.g. named contributions, existence of power relationships, possible compulsory editing). This begs the questions as to whether wikis are still "a place for ideation to occur".

Today's wikis support collaborative writing. However, ideation (a.k.a. idea generation) precedes writing. Flower states that "a writer in the act of discovery is hard at work searching memory, forming concepts, and forging a new structure of ideas, while at the same time trying to juggle all the constraints imposed by his or her purpose, audience, and language itself ...This act of creating ideas, not finding them, is at the heart of significant writing" [8]. Open wikis suggest that these activities (i.e. searching memory, forming concepts, forging a structure of ideas) are collaboratively fleshed out. However, when wiki content goes beyond facts to enter the fuzzy realms of ideas, this model is challenged. For enterprises, Lykourentzou et al. report that a common employee concern is that sharing work-in-progress may negatively affect the assessments they receive [15]. This might be due to corporate users "often feel strong personal ownership of content they add (and are organizationally accountable for it) and a corresponding unwillingness to edit content *owned* by others". This leads some authors to state that enterprises often use wikis as a technology but let the wiki philosophy of openness leave behind [18].

These insights undercut the usage of wikis for idea generation in organizations. Yet, wikis are being used for other Knowledge Management activities [14], and hence, wikis might well be the place were ideas arise. Studies recommend anchoring ideas at the place where they emerge for easy remembering and contextualization [1]. This raises this paper's research question: *how to reconcile the convenience of elaborating ideas within the Corporate wiki while, at the same time, overcoming the reluctance to publish work-in-progress.*

To this end, we advocate for complementing the *review-after-publication* wiki model with *in-line drafting*. "In-line" indicates that drafting should occur within the wiki. "Drafting" suggests that idea generation is not off-the-cuff. Rather, ideas are the result of a crafting process where contribution opportunities are first spotted; next, raw material is collected and elaborated upon, till it eventually ends up as a draft ready to be published. This paper delves into *in-line drafting* as follows:

- providing a model for in-line wiki drafting (Section 2),
- realizing this model through *Wikinote*, a browser extension on top of *MediaWiki's Visual Editor* (Section 3), and
- validating this extension through the *Wiki Anxiety Inventory-Editing* questionnaire [3] (Section 4).

The latter supports the hypothesis that *Wikinote* reduces user anxiety when contributing to a Corporate wiki. We hypothesize that the fact that *Wikinote* allows users to share ideas once in a mature state is the major anxiety reducer, hence increasing positive affect towards wiki editing and reducing contribution judgement anxiety.

2   Theoretical Framework

This section looks into what compels people to edit in a wiki. According to one hypothesis [4], people contribute to solve cognitive incongruities between the current state of a wiki article and their own knowledge. Cress et al. hypothesize that the likelihood for this to happen is a function of two features: the size of the incongruity between the individual's knowledge and the wiki's information on the one hand, and the valence which the topic has for people on the other hand[1]. Cross et al. conclude that "only a medium-level incongruity causes a cognitive conflict which motivates people to engage" in wiki editing [4]. According to this model, the flow between the social system (i.e. the wiki) and the cognitive systems (i.e. the individual) is regulated along two processes:

- *Externalization.* For contributing to the development of a wiki, people first have to externalize their knowledge. For that purpose, a person's own knowledge has to be conveyed into a wiki article in a form that maps the person's knowledge. The mental effort necessary for the externalization can extend people's individual knowledge, because externalization requires deeper processing and clarification.
- *Internalization.* Inter-individual knowledge transfer and collaborative knowledge building take place when people have the opportunity to work with a wiki and to internalize the information available in the wiki. This individual knowledge is enriched in two ways: (1) absorbing facts already existing in the wiki and (2), developing new knowledge as a result of the existing personal knowledge being somehow challenged by the wiki facts (a.k.a. emergent knowledge). The latter is described through Piaget's model of equilibration where the learning trigger is the cognitive conflict between individual knowledge and external knowledge (e.g. the one in the wiki).

Externalization and internalization intermingle to output collaborative knowledge building, and emergent knowledge creation. This model might well explain people's impulse to edit on open wikis. However, Corporate wikis bring into play other considerations. For a *Justin Bieber* fan who spots a mistake on *Bieber's Wikipedia* article about his birthday date, the high valence of the topic, the easily-identifiable incongruity, and the lightweight effort required, will most likely lead to restore coherence (i.e. editing Bieber's article, and correct the date). But, what if the incongruity emerges when reading a workmate's edit in the Corporate wiki? Unlike the *Bieber* example, this alters both the subject matter and the context:

- *Subject matter: facts* vs. *ideas.* Encyclopaedia entries tend to be about facts. For instance, *Wikipedia* articles *must* not contain original research. That is, there is no room in *Wikipedia* to refer to "material for which no reliable,

---

[1] Valence, as used in psychology, especially in discussing emotions, means the intrinsic attractiveness (positive valence) or aversiveness (negative valence) of an event, object, or situation (*Wikipedia*).

published sources exist. This includes any analysis or synthesis of published material that serves to reach or imply a conclusion not stated by the sources"[2]. We depart from this setting to move to idea generation, i.e. the process whereby ideas are created. Unlike facts, idea elaboration goes beyond writing. Ideas need first to be articulated, structured and worked out in a way that others can understand it. Here, externalization is more costly and time consuming, and on top of that, the employee's prestige might be at stake.

– *Context: open* vs. *close.* Prestige and power relationships might act as stressors, making people reluctant to expose edits prematurely. People perhaps are afraid of making incorrect statements, or they feel that they have not reflected upon their contributions long enough to write them down. This results in *editability anxiety* and *contribution judgment anxiety* [3].

This new setting might prevent "the incongruity impulse" from surmounting the larger externalization effort and the anxiety brought by peer pressure. Notice however that the impulse is still there. The issue is how to channel this impulse into a medium-run effort that increases the chances of ending up in an edit. Our premise is that personal drafting might be such a channel, and that *publishing more elaborated edits might reduce both editability anxiety and contribution judgment anxiety, hence, leading to a more participatory wiki.* This begs the question of what is meant by "elaborated edits", i.e. how much elaboration is needed before being ready to publication.

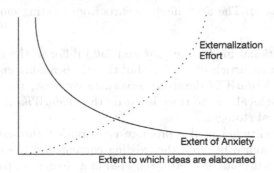

Fig. 1. Finding a balance between the externalization effort and the anxiety growth w.r.t. the degree of elaboration of edits

Figure 1 sketches the likely tension between the externalization effort and the anxiety growth w.r.t. the degree of edit elaboration. If edits are published prematurely, then it might have a negative impact on the user prestige, hence, increasing user anxiety and eventually, putting users off. However, if users wait for edits to be fully elaborated, then the externalization effort increases, and so

---

[2] http://en.wikipedia.org/wiki/Wikipedia:No_original_research

do the chances of conflicts with other wiki users, both aspects also discouraging editing. Our hypothesis is that a compromise can be found for **"paragraph edits"** (approx. less than 300 characters) where the upfront investment of externalization pays off in terms of a reduction in anxiety.

Previous considerations guide our design of a wiki-specific drafting facility, namely:

- Internalization (specifically, emergent knowledge) results from being exposed to the wiki where "the cognitive conflict" emerges. This sustains *in-line* drafting.
- Externalization does not require the interaction with other people in a narrow sense. People can externalize their knowledge (and thereby extend their own knowledge) without necessarily addressing other people in the first place. This sustains *personal* drafting.
- Externalization might imply an important upfront investment that can later be challenged by the community. This sustains *paragraph* drafting (as opposed to document drafting) as a "breakeven point".

The next section addresses how these insights guide *Wikinote* design.

3   Facilitating Externalization: The *Draft* Mode

This section advocates a third wiki mode: the *draft* mode. Today's wiki engines support two main modes: the *edit* mode (for article editing) and the *talk* mode (for article discussion). The *draft* mode departs from existing modes in the following aspects:

- Storage. Traditional modes (i.e. *edit* and *talk*) differ in the subject matter (article content *vs.* article discussion) but the text is readily made public (i.e. moved to the *MediaWiki* database server). In contrast, when on the *draft* mode, edits are local, i.e. no trace is left on the *MediaWiki* database but on the browser local storage.
- Rendering. Traditional modes promote contribution through WYSIWYG editors: no difference between the existing content and the new additions. By contrast, draft edits are better reflected in a change-control manner.
- Lifecycle. In traditional modes, edits are readily followed by publication. In contrast, drafts go through a maturity process before being published.

Figure 2 depicts the *idea maturity model* along the following landmarks: *spark, gather, elaborate* and *consolidate*. Each landmark has a GUI counterpart. *Wikinote* extends *MediaWiki's Visual Editor*[3] with the *draft* mode, i.e. a set of Graphical-User Interactions (GUIs) that realize each of the abovementioned actions. *Wikinote* has been tested with *Google's Chrome* version 39, *MediaWiki's* version 1.25 and *Visual Editor's* version 0.1.0. It is available at the *Chrome Web Store*: https://chrome.google.com/webstore/detail/lohjainijkgonhljngepoaphjpljeiii. Next, we

---

[3] http://en.wikipedia.org/wiki/VisualEditor

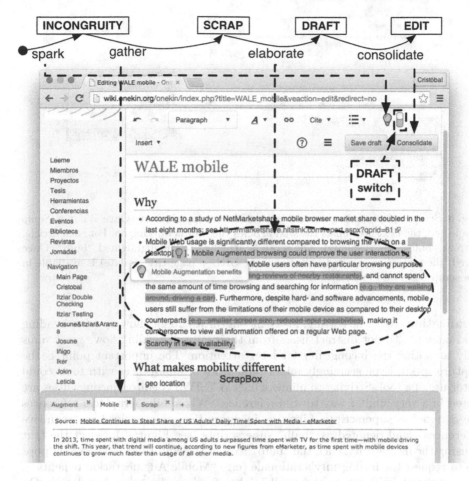

Fig. 2. The Idea Maturity Model: from "light-bulb" moments to public edits

describe each action's purpose and its support in *Wikinote*. These actions become available as soon as the user puts the *draft switch* on. Worth noticing the *draft* mode only makes sense for contributions of a certain calibre and size. Typo corrections and minor rewritings are not worth the effort.

3.1 Spark

Purpose. Firstly, we consider the process of translating a thought into a physical or digital format. The "light-bulb moment" can come at any time. It might well happen when the user is engaged in other activities with no time to further elaborate the idea. Frequently, users resort to digital/physical artefacts (e.g. *Post-it* notes) to record the idea. This calls for capturing ideas at the place where they arise. In addition, it contextualizes the idea by the setting where it emerges, hence, facilitating recovering [1].

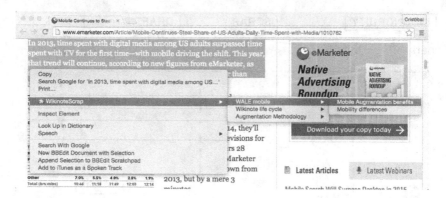

Fig. 3. Scrap capture through nested right-click contextual menus. Once *WikinoteScrap* is selected, the next menu lists the wiki articles the user is working on. For each article, current "bulbs" are displayed. The scrap is attached to the highlighted "bulb". Once saved, the scrap (i.e. selected text + current URL + page title + date) is available in the scrap box (see Figure 2).

Realization. In a wiki setting, ideas/incongruities might show up when reading wiki content. To not distract users from their current reading flow, *spark* aims only at noting the incongruity for later attention. The important point is the capture speed. Even seemingly minor difficulties or annoyances with tools could deter use of a tool. Striving to mimic wiki's WYSIWYG editor, incongruities are noted in a very similar way to wiki references. Wikis' bibliographical references are denoted as superscripts. Likewise, incongruities are conceived as "cognitive references", and denoted as "bulb" superscripts (see Figure 2). Select the text causing the incongruity, click the "bulb" icon in the editor bar, and a menu pops up to request the incongruity's rationale (e.g. "Mobile Augmentation benefits"). This rationale will act as the "bulb" label for later indexing (see later). On acceptance, the "bulb" superscript appears by the wiki sentence.

3.2   Gather

Purpose. Externalization is not a one-shot process but time is needed for the idea to mature. This might imply collecting evidence, thoughts and references that can be sought on purpose or stumbled upon. This is realized in terms of **scraps**. While bulbs act as reminders, scraps refer to generally small, disconnected sentences that develop some of the twist brought about by the incongruity. Hence, scraps do not exist in a vacuum but qualify an incongruity.

Realization. Again lightweight mechanisms become a must for both scrap gathering and posterior recovering. Coming across an interesting scrap might well occur when users are performing some other attentionally engaging primary tasks. For this reason, lowering both the actual and perceived cost of cognitive and physical effort may improve gathering.

Scraps can be originated in different settings: when reading the wiki, when browsing the web, when reading an article at the desktop, when traveling, etc. So far, *Wikinote* supports two settings. In both cases, gathering is a click away:

- When browsing the Web, the right-click contextual menu has been extended with the *WikinoteScrap* menu (see Figure 3). Select the content to be gathered from the current page, right click, and a menu pops up for the user to indicate the bulb label to which this clipboard-generated scrap is going to be attached to.
- When reading the wiki, manually-typed scraps can be created. Select first a "bulb", and next, click on the "+" icon to create a scrap associated with this bulb.

No matter how they are obtained, scraps are collected into **the scrap box** (see Figure 2). *Wikinote* only shows those scraps attached to the currently-selected "bulb". Move to a different "bulb", and so will do the scrap box. If no "bulb" is selected, the scrap box hides behind the namesake tab, so that it does not interfere with the reading.

3.3   Elaborate

Purpose. So far, the article's content has been left untouched. Except for the "bulb" annotation, we have not yet addressed changes on the content of the article. This has been so for presentation sake. Actually, users might change article content at wish. Nevertheless, directly changing article content makes sense for minor edits (e.g. typos, spelling mistakes, etc.) but this is not the scenario under consideration. Rather, we target changes that require some previous elaboration before being substantiated as article paragraphs. "Bulbs" and scraps help to stage this development that will eventually produce a **draft**, i.e. a set of changes on the article content that stands for a meaningful unit to tackle a given "bulb".

Realization. This action does not imply a change on the WYSIGYG way in which users are accustomed to modifying the article's content. However, and unlike *Visual Editor*, modifications are reflected in a change-control manner. This is recommended when working on top of somewhere else's content. Besides acting directly upon the wiki content, users might also drag&drop scraps. This permits first working on the scrap box (e.g. rephrasing/tinging content obtained from the Web, merging scraps which convey a similar argument, etc.) till a scrap is elaborated enough to be moved to the content canvas. The scrap then becomes part of the draft.

Two aspects are worth noticing. First, the scrap's references are automatically attached to the so-generated draft's paragraph. In this way, *Wikinote* automatically supports provenance, i.e. keeping track of the sources. Second, draft changes are local, i.e. they have any no impact on the content of the underlying article. Except the author, no one can yet see the draft. Basically, actions *gather* and *elaborate* intertwine to gradually produce the draft. During this process, the underlying article can be changed by other wiki users. Those changes are visible for the draft author. On the upside, this implies that draft authors are always aware of the most recent version of the article. On the downside, article upgrades might unsettle draft edits. Indeed, drafts are implemented as *layers* on top of the article content, i.e. draft edits are "anchored" to the article content. Different mechanisms are implemented to make drafts resilient to changes on the underlying article content [5]. Nevertheless, it can happen that the article text that underpins a draft annotation is eventually removed[4]. In this case, the annotation becomes dangling, and it is up to the author to re-anchor it again. Eventually, the draft is ready for consolidation.

3.4   Consolidate

Purpose. *Consolidate* is the process whereby drafts become published, i.e. all the article's drafts are publicly exposed as if they were a single *MediaWiki* edit.

Realization. The "*Consolidate*" button achieves this transition. From an external reader, no differences should exist between edits achieved via *Visual Editor* or those obtained through *Wikinote*. Only the *edit summary*[5] reflects the origin of the edit. An edit summary is a brief explanation of an edit to a wiki page. For *Wikinote* edits, this summary is automatically generated indicating the fact that this is a *Wikinote* edit. The summary also includes the incongruity rationale that triggered the edit in the first place.

4   Evaluation

Wikinote aims at reducing anxiety users might feel when editing a Corporate wiki, thus fostering contributions. This section evaluates whether *Wikinote* fulfils such a goal while intending to quantify its effect. The driving hypothesis follows:

> *Wikinote reduces user anxiety when contributing to a Corporate wiki.*

In a Corporate setting, users edit a wiki on a normal basis. Hence, we opted for evaluating *Wikinote* in their normal environment instead of bringing participants to a laboratory, where the anxiety motivated by the setting itself could interfere with our measures. The following section delves into the details of the experimental design.

4.1   Experimental Design

We state the **goal of the experiment** using the Goal/Question/Metric (GQM) method: *analyse* the wiki anxiety of users working with *Wikinote*, *for the purpose of* comparing it with a baseline alternative (*MediaWiki* alone), *with respect to*

---

[4] Text re-allocation is not a big issue since annotations move along their anchoring text.

[5] http://en.wikipedia.org/wiki/Help:Edit_summary

user anxiety, *from the point of view of* a researcher trying to assess *Wikinote*, *in the context of* user's usual wiki editing activities.

Wikinote, or the lack thereof, will be the *independent variable*. The anxiety users feel when editing the wiki will be the *dependent variable*. These variables lead to a unifactorial design [19]. As we want to evaluate the difference *Wikinote* introduces, we designed an experiment with repeated measures, where the same participants edited with and without *Wikinote*. In order to counteract the impact of the order in which participants edited, we counterbalanced it, i.e. half of the participants first edited without *Wikinote* and then tried it whereas the other half performed the edits in the opposite order.

Wiki anxiety was measured using the *Wiki Anxiety Inventory-Editing (WAI-E)*, a questionnaire that has shown high validity and reliability ($=0.93$) [3]. This instrument presents significant and strong correlation with state anxiety measured directly after wiki editing [$r(48) =0.73$, P$_i$0.001] as well as with fear of negative evaluation [$r(48)= 0.42,P=0.002$]. It, however, has not shown significant correlation with trait anxiety [$r(48) =0.27,P=0.06$], suggesting that the anxiety it measures is more based on the context of a wiki edit than on the traits of the users performing it. A component analysis of WAI-E revealed three factors that explain 62% of the variance. They were termed *positive affect, editability anxiety*, and *contribution judgement anxiety* that allow understanding different aspects of user anxiety in wiki editing [3].

Participants were recruited at the Computer Science Faculty of the University of the Basque Country using volunteer sampling. Three faculty members and five Ph.D. students, who all use a wiki on a daily basis in the context of a research group, answered the call. In particular Ph.D. students use the wiki as the main means to summarize their work and discuss it with their advisor. The experiment took place over a week and a half. The aim was to compare Wikinote (i.e. in-line drafting) with the baseline case (i.e. traditional review-after-publication as supported by MediaWiki). Since *editability anxiety* very much depends on what is being written and who reads it, we did not devise specific tasks but instructed participants to keep writing their reports in the wiki as usual. To counterbalance the effect of tool order (i.e., with and without Wikinote), participants were randomly assigned to two groups. The first group was asked to fill out the WAI-E questionnaire shortly after it had performed a substantial edit to the wiki (i.e., one that involved at least two paragraphs). They were given Monday and Tuesday for this task. Wikinote was then presented to both groups in a 45' session on Wednesday. Next, both groups were requested to complete the WAI-E questionnaire after a substantial edit they made using Wikinote during Thursday or Friday. Lastly, participants in the second group were asked to uninstall Wikinote and to answer the WAI-E questionnaire after a substantial edit during the following Monday or Tuesday, this time without Wikinote. In all cases, participants were requested to start the questionnaire (see less Table 1) than five minutes after the edit, so that the state anxiety generated by the wiki editing could be measured.

Table 1. Descriptive Statistics for WAI-E items

	Baseline		Wikinote	
	Mean	SD	Mean	SD
I felt confident when contributing to the wiki	3.25	1.04	4.25	0.46
I felt excited when editing the wiki	2.25	0.89	3.75	0.71
I felt comfortable about editing the wiki	2.75	0.89	4.63	0.52
I was happy to contribute content to the wiki	3.13	1.13	4.25	0.71
I felt secure when editing the wiki	2.63	0.74	4.63	0.52
I felt relaxed whilst editing the wiki	2.38	1.19	4.38	0.52
I felt at ease editing the wiki	2.38	0.52	3.88	0.64
I was confident that the information I was contributing was correct	3.13	0.83	3.75	1.04
I felt intimidated while editing the wiki	2.88	1.13	1.75	0.71
The fact that the content could be changed made me uneasy	2.63	1.19	1.88	0.64
I was worried about making a mistake that I could not correct when editing the wiki	3.13	1.25	1.63	0.52
It scared me to think that I could accidentally destroy somebody else's content	3.38	1.30	1.88	0.64
I was nervous about changing existing content on the wiki	3.38	1.30	1.75	0.46
I was afraid that I might do something wrong when editing the wiki	3.38	0.92	1.50	0.53
I was certain I could overcome any difficulties I encountered in editing the wiki	2.88	0.99	3.50	0.93
I was concerned that people would know it was me that was contributing to the wiki	3.13	1.13	2.63	1.31
I was afraid that people would find faults with any edits I made	3.50	1.31	2.25	0.71
Thoughts about being judged by other users made me feel tense	3.62	1.19	2.75	1.04
I was nervous of what other users might think of my edits	3.38	1.30	2.00	0.93
I felt apprehensive when editing the wiki	3.13	1.13	2.13	0.64
When editing the wiki I felt anxious about making a mistake	3.50	1.31	1.88	1.13
I found it hard to concentrate when editing the wiki	2.88	0.83	2.38	0.92

4.2 Analysis

The data collected did not fulfil the assumptions of parametric tests. Specifically, Shapiro-Wilk tests showed a significant deviance from normality (as we had less than 50 subjects). Hence, we resorted to non-parametric Wilcoxon signed-rank tests for this analysis. Eight subjects participated in the experiment (3 lecturers and 5 Ph.D. students), of whom 50% were male and 50% female. Regarding age, the average was 32.5 years with a standard deviation of 8.14. All of them use a wiki on a normal basis as part of their work: they all add content to a wiki from one to five times a week. Table 1 shows the descriptive statistics for the WAI-E items. All items correspond to a five point Likert scale (1-Strongly Disagree, 5-Strongly Agree).

Table 2. Test Results

	Baseline		Wikinote				
	Mean	SD	Mean	SD	T	p	r
WAI-E	71.13	17.41	43.38	8.39	-2.37	0.018	-0.592
Positive Affect	21.88	5.19	33.50	3.38	2.53	0.011	0.633
Editability Anxiety	19.00	5.86	11.13	1.36	-2.25	0.025	-0.563
Contribution Judgement Anxiety	17.13	6.06	11.00	3.85	-2.83	0.017	-0.706

The test outcome is summarized in Table 2. First the mean and standard deviation values of participants' responses to the WAI-E scale and its subscales are presented: *Baseline* stands for editing with MediaWiki built-in facilities whereas *Wikinote* refers to editing with the namesake extension. T and p columns represent the T value of the Wilcoxon signed-rank test and the significance, respectively. In metrics where statistically significant differences were found (i.e., $p < 0.05$), the effect size was calculated using r. A value of this parameter above 0.5 in absolute values denotes a large effect size as a result of the independent variable (i.e., the use of *Wikinote*). The r values are presented in the last column of the table.

These preliminary results show that there is a statistically significant difference when *Wikinote* is introduced as measured by WAI-E, and also, in each of its subscales (i.e., positive affect, editability anxiety and contribution judgement anxiety). *Wikinote* introduces the largest effect in increasing participants' positive affect towards wiki editing (r=0.633) and decreasing their contribution judgement anxiety (r=-0.706).

All in all, these preliminary results support our hypothesis that *Wikinote* reduces user anxiety when contributing to a Corporate wiki. We hypothesize that the fact that *Wikinote* allows users to share ideas once they are in a mature state is the major anxiety reducer, hence increasing positive affect towards wiki editing and reducing contribution judgement anxiety.

Threats to Validity. A main concern for internal validity is the appropriateness of the sample. The first issue relates to sample size. Even though our results show statistically significant differences and large effect sizes, larger groups are needed to corroborate these findings. A second issue involves the participants' background. Participants are technically savvy, which may have had an impact in their attitude towards wiki editing. Moreover, the wiki they work with, is relatively small and only 15 people have access to it. The last issue concerns the external validity. We used an opportunistic sample of faculty and Ph.D. students. We hypothesize that contribution anxiety in a corporate setting might be larger than in academia. While this hypothesis might likely result in *Wikinote* performing better, the different environments might lead to different results. Specifically, *Wikinote* might delay idea sharing, specifically for people too perfectionist or image conscious, hindering the chances of integrating someone else's viewpoints in the early stage of idea conception.

5   Related Work

Wikinote combines features of an editor (i.e. it acts upon article content), an annotator (i.e. it introduces "bulb" annotations) and a note-taking facility (i.e. the scrap box). This unique blend and its wiki-oriented purpose differentiate *Wikinote* from related tools. The next paragraphs provide a review.

Wiki Editors. *Wikinote* can be aligned with efforts of promoting wiki contribution. Recent research shows that the number of active contributors in *Wikipedia* has been declining steadily for years. The blame is put on the restrictiveness of the encyclopaedia's primary quality control mechanisms, and the algorithmic tools used to reject contributions [10]. As a result, "both newcomers and experienced editors are moving increasingly toward less formal spaces" [10]. *Wikinote* can be regarded as providing one possible realization of this "less formal" space. In the same vein (i.e. promoting contributions among newcomers), other works give support for validating content (e.g. *ConstrainedWiki* [6]), enhancing content (e.g. *VisualWikiCurator* [13]) or socially elaborating content (e.g. *Teahouse* [17]). *Wikinote* provides a different support by providing a secluded setting for drafting once the article is in full swing.

Note Taking. Note-taking is the practice of recording information captured from another source. In the commercial front, *Evernote* is one of the best-known examples. In academia, *MADCOW* [2] and *SPREADCRUMBS* [12] present similitudes with *Wikinote*: the use of contextual menus for note-taking. Differences stem from the architecture. Both *MADCOW* and *SPREADCRUMBS* resort to a server for note storage. In contrast, we purposefully design *Wikinote* to be uniquely browser-based. No need to open an account in someone else's server (like in *Evernote*). All *wikinotes* are locally kept. This feature might be specially attractive for organizations that could be reluctant to offload sensitive information into third-party servers. *Wikinote* can afford to limit itself to local storage since it is not thought of for long-term storage (like *Evernote*) but transient memory till the draft gets ready for wiki consolidation.

Annotation Systems. There is a wide range of annotation tools for Web pages (e.g. *Diigo*; see [7] for an overview). An annotation is an added note that explains something in a text. Hence, annotations are not the text as such but meta-data about the text. Most tools are generic. This is at the same time their strength and their weakness. The advantage is that they annotate no matter the website. The downside is that such decoupling forces users to cope with two different Web experiences: the one of the annotation tool (e.g. *Diigo*) and the one of the annotated website (e.g. *Wikipedia*). By contrast, *Wikinote* explores a different approach: wiki-specific annotation. This accounts for a seamless integration of editing and annotation commands (e.g. the "bulb" icon), hence promoting prompt in-line annotation, and eventually, editing. The bottom line is that if annotation is the prelude of editing, then facilitating annotation becomes a main wiki concern, not to be left to third-party generic software.

6   Conclusions

This study addresses idea generation in Corporate wikis on two main premises. First, incongruities raised during wiki reading may spur contributions. This momentum should be readily captured and sustained as smoothly as possible, and ideally, supported within the wiki realm. Second, lowering the bar for drafting might result in more elaborated edits being published. This, in turn, might decrease both editing anxiety and contribution judgement anxiety. To test this out, a personal in-line drafting browser extension is developed: *Wikinote*. *Wikinote* extends *MediaWiki's Visual Editor* with the *draft* mode. First validations suggest that *Wikinote* is effective in reducing editing anxiety. Additional validations are needed to assess not only effectiveness but also usability. In this respect, we are currently addressing scrap portability, i.e. notes captured by no matter the tool to be easily contextualized/rendered within wiki articles. Specifically, we are planning to capitalize on *Evernote* and *Mendeley* note-taking facilities to be seamlessly accessible through *Wikinote's* scrap box.

Acknowledgments. This work is co-supported by the Spanish Ministry of Education, and the European Social Fund under contract TIN2011-23839 *(Scriptongue)*.

References

1. Bernstein, M., Van Kleek, M., Karger, D., Schraefel, M.C.: Information Scraps: How and Why Information Eludes Our Personal Information Management Tools. ACM Transactions on Information Systems **26**(4) (2008)
2. Bottoni, P., Levialdi, S., Labella, A., Panizzi, E., Trinchese, R., Gigli, L.: MAD-COW: a visual interface for annotating web pages. In: Working Conference on Advanced Visual Interfaces (AVI 2006), Venezia, Italy (2006)
3. Cowan, B.R., Jack, M.A.: Measuring Anxiety Towards Wiki Editing: Investigating the Dimensionality of the Wiki Anxiety Inventory-Editing. Interacting with Computers **26**(6) (2014)
4. Cress, U., Kimmerle, J.: A Systemic and Cognitive View on Collaborative Knowledge Building with Wikis. International Journal of Computer-Supported Collaborative Learning **3**(2) (2008)

5. Csillag, K.: Fuzzy anchoring, April 2013. http://hypothes.is/blog/ fuzzy-anchoring/, November 2014
6. Di Lorio, A., Draicchio, F., Vitali, F., Zacchiroli, S.: Constrained Wiki: The Wikiway to Validating Content. Advances in Human-Computer Intelligence **2012** (2012)
7. Fance, C.: Top Web Annotation And Markup Tools, April 2010. http://www. hongkiat.com/blog/top-web-annotation-and-markup-tools/, November 2014
8. Flower, L., Hayes, J.R.: The Cognition of Discovery: Defining a Rhetorical Problem. College Composition and Communication **31**(1), February 1980
9. Giordano, R.: An investigation of the use of a wiki to support knowledge exchange in public health. In: International ACM SIGGROUP Conference on Supporting Group Work (GROUP 2007), Sanibel Island, Florida, USA (2007)
10. Halfaker, A., Geiger, R.S., Morgan, J., Riedl, J.: The Rise and Decline of an Open Collaboration System: How Wikipedia's reaction to sudden popularity is causing its decline. American Behavioral Scientist **57**(5), May 2013
11. Holtzblatt, L.J., Damianos, L.E., Weiss, D.: Factors impeding wiki use in the enterprise: a case study. In: Extended Abstracts on Human Factors in Computing Systems (CHI 2010), Atlanta, Georgia, USA (2010)
12. Kawase, R., Herder, E., Papadakis, G., Nejdl, W.: In-context annotations for refinding and sharing. In: Filipe, J., Cordeiro, J. (eds.) WEBIST 2010. LNBIP, vol. 75, pp. 85–100. Springer, Heidelberg (2011)
13. Kong, N., Hanrahan, B.V., Weksteen, T., Convertino, G., Chi, E.H.: VisualWikiCurator: human and machine intelligence for organizing wiki content. In: 16th International Conference on Intelligent User Interfaces (IUI 2011), Palo Alto, CA, USA (2011)
14. Kussmaul, C., Jack, R.: Wikis for knowledge management: business cases, best practices, promises, & pitfalls. In: Lytras, M.D., Damiani, E., Ordóñez de Pablos, P. (eds.) Web 2.0. Springer, US (2009)
15. Lykourentzou, I., Djaghloul, Y., Papadaki, K., Dagka, F., Latour, T.: Planning for a Successful Corporate Wiki. In: Ariwa, E., El-Qawasmeh, E. (eds.) DEIS 2011. CCIS, vol. 194, pp. 425–439. Springer, Heidelberg (2011)
16. Majchrzak, A., Wagner, C., Yates, D.: Corporate wiki users: results of a survey. In: International Symposium on Wikis (WikiSym 2006), Odense, Denmark (2006)
17. Morgan, J.T., Bouterse, S., Walls, H., Stierch, S.: Tea and sympathy: crafting positive new user experiences on wikipedia. In: 16th ACM Conference on Computer Supported Cooperative Work (CSCW 2013), San Antonio, Texas, USA (2013)
18. Priedhorsky, R., Terveen, L.G.: Wiki grows up: arbitrary data models, access control, and beyond. In: 7th International Symposium on Wikis and Open Collaboration (WikiSym 2011), Mountain View, CA, USA, 3–5 October 2011 (2011)
19. Shadish, W., Cook, T., Campbell, D.: Experimental and Quasi-experimental Designs for Generalized Causal Inference. Cengage Learning (2002)
20. Standing, C., Kiniti, S.: How Can Organizations Use Wikis for Innovation? Technovation **31**(7) (2011)
21. Swisher, K.: 'Wiki' May Alter How Employees Work Together. The Wall Street Journal, July 2004. http://online.wsj.com/news/articles/SB109105974578777189

Run-Time and Task-Based Performance of Event Detection Techniques for Twitter

Andreas Weiler[✉], Michael Grossniklaus, and Marc H. Scholl

Department of Computer and Information Science,
University of Konstanz, P.O. Box 188, 78457 Konstanz, Germany
{andreas.weiler,michael.grossniklaus,marc.scholl}@uni-konstanz.de

Abstract. Twitter's increasing popularity as a source of up to date news and information about current events has spawned a body of research on event detection techniques for social media data streams. Although all proposed approaches provide some evidence as to the quality of the detected events, none relate this task-based performance to their run-time performance in terms of processing speed or data throughput. In particular, neither a quantitative nor a comparative evaluation of these aspects has been performed to date. In this paper, we study the run-time and task-based performance of several state-of-the-art event detection techniques for Twitter. In order to reproducibly compare run-time performance, our approach is based on a general-purpose data stream management system, whereas task-based performance is automatically assessed based on a series of novel measures.

Keywords: Event detection · Performance evaluation · Twitter streams

1 Introduction

With 271 million monthly active users[1] that produce over 500 million tweets per day[2], Twitter is the most popular and fastest-growing microblogging service. Microblogging is a form of social media that enables users to broadcast short messages, links, and audiovisual content. In the case of Twitter, these so-called *tweets* can contain 140 characters and are posted to a network of *followers* as well as to a user's public timeline. The brevity of tweets make them an ideal mobile communication medium and Twitter is therefore increasingly used as an information source for current events as they unfold. For example, Twitter data has been used to detect earthquakes [17], to track epidemics [10], or to monitor elections [21].

In this context, an *event* is defined as a real-world occurrence that takes place in a certain geographical location and over a certain time period [3]. For traditional media such as newspaper archives and news websites, the problem of event

---

[1] http://www.statista.com/study/9920/twityter-statista-dossier/
[2] http://www.sec.gov/Archives/edgar/data/1418091/000119312513390321/
d564001ds1.htm

© Springer International Publishing Switzerland 2015
J. Zdravkovic et al. (Eds.): CAiSE 2015, LNCS 9097, pp. 35–49, 2015.
DOI: 10.1007/978-3-319-19069-3_3

detection has been addressed by research from the area of Topic Detection and Tracking (TDT). However, topic detection in Twitter data streams introduces new challenges. First, Twitter "documents" are much shorter than traditional news articles and therefore harder to classify. Second, tweets are not redacted and thus contain a substantial amount of spam, typos, slang, etc. Finally, the rate at which tweets are produced is very bursty and continually increases as more people adopt Twitter every day.

Several techniques for event detection in Twitter have been proposed. However, most of these approaches suffer from two major shortcomings. First, they tend to focus exclusively on the information extraction aspect and often ignore the streaming nature of the input. As a consequence, they make unrealistic assumptions, which limit their practical value. Examples of such assumptions include buffering entire months of Twitter data before processing it or fixing a complex set of parameters at design-time using sample data. Second, very few authors have evaluated their technique quantitatively or comparatively. While most provide some qualitative evidence demonstrating their task-based performance, very few consider run-time performance. Therefore, little or no research to date has measured the computing cost of the same result quality for different approaches. We argue that understanding this trade-off is particularly important in a streaming setting, where processing needs to happen in real-time.

In this paper, we present a method to study the task-based and the run-time performance of current and future event detection techniques. In order to measure comparable run-time performance numbers, we propose to "standardize" event detection techniques by implementing them based on a single data stream management system. Additionally, we developed several scalable measures to assess the task-based performance of event detection techniques automatically, i.e., without painstakingly crafting a gold standard manually. The specific contributions of this paper are as follows.

1. Streaming implementations of state-of-the-art event detection techniques for Twitter that are consistent with respect to each other.
2. Detailed study of the task-based and run-time performance of well-known event detection techniques.
3. Platform-based approach that will enable further systematic performance studies for novel event detection techniques in the future.

The remainder of this paper is structured as follows. Section 2 provides the background of this work by summarizing the state of the art in event detection for Twitter data streams. In Sect. 3, we give a brief overview of Niagarino, the data stream management system that we used as an implementation platform. Section 4 describes the selected event detection techniques and their streaming implementations using Niagarino. Section 5 presents the results of the evaluation that we performed in order to study the selected task-based and run-time performance of these event detection techniques. Finally, concluding remarks are given in Sect. 6.

2   Background

Our work is situated in the research field of analysis and knowledge discovery for social media data. Bontcheva *et al.* [8] provides a good general overview of sense making of social media data by surveying state-of-the-art approaches for mining semantics from social media streams. Due to the fast propagation speed of information in social media networks, a large number of works focus on event or topic detection and tracking for various domains. In this setting, Farzindar and Khreich [11] surveyed techniques for event detection in Twitter. The work presented in this paper targets approaches that support the detection of general (unknown) events [3] and we will therefore focus the following discussion on approaches that share this goal.

Petrović *et al.* [16] propose to use an online clustering approach that is based on locality sensitive hashing. The approach uses the number of tweets and hashtags, but also introduces a novel measure of entropy for the analysis. The method was evaluated using six months of data containing 163.5 million tweets and an average precision score was calculated against a manually labeled result set. Becker *et al.* [6] present an approach for "real-world event detection on Twitter" that uses an online clustering method in combination with a support vector machine classifier. They focus on hashtags with special capitalization and check for retweets, replies, and mentions. The method is evaluated against a manually labeled result set for a one-month data set with 2.6 million tweets. Long *et al.* [14] use divisive clustering, whereas Weng and Lee [21] use discrete wavelet analysis and graph partitioning. Both of these approaches use word frequencies of individual words for event detection. The latter approach was evaluated by using a self-built ground truth, which is prepared by using a latent dirichlet allocation (LDA) method [7]. Cordeiro [9] proposes the use of continuous wavelet analysis to detect event peaks in the signal of hashtags and summarizes the detected events by using LDA. For evaluation purposes, they used a visual illustration of their results obtained from an eight-day data set with 13.6 million tweets. Zimmermann *et al.* [22] present a text stream clustering method that detects, tracks, and updates large and small bursts in a two-level (global and local) topic hierarchy by using collected news articles. The technique proposed by enBloque [4] to detect emergent events relies on statistics about tags and pairs of tags. These statistics are computed using a time-sliding window and monitored for shifts in order to capture unpredictable and thus interesting developments. It has been evaluated on a two-week Twitter data set by conducting experiments to measure run-time performance and a user study to assess task-based performance.

In summarizing the state of the art in event detection techniques for Twitter, it is important to note that all existing approaches are realized as custom ad-hoc implementations, which limits the reproducibility and comparative evaluation of their results. As a consequence, little to no comparative evaluations of different event detection methods exist. In particular, none of these approaches have been evaluated to relate their task-based (result quality) and run-time performance (tweets per second). Therefore, there is a comprehensive lack of evaluation methods for event detection techniques for social media data.

3   Niagarino Overview

In order to realize streaming implementations of state-of-the-art event detection techniques for Twitter, we use Niagarino[3], a data stream management system that is developed and maintained by our research group. The main purpose of Niagarino is to serve as an easy-to-use and extensible research platform for streaming applications such as the one presented in the paper. The concepts embodied by Niagarino can be traced back to a series of pioneering data stream management systems, such as Aurora [2], Borealis [1], and STREAM/CQL [5]. In particular, Niagarino is an offshoot of NiagaraST [13], with which it shares the most common ground. In this section, we briefly summarize the parts of Niagarino that are relevant for this paper.

In Niagarino, a query is represented as a directed acyclic graph $Q = (O, S)$, where O is the set of operators used in the query and S is the set of streams used to connect the operators. The Niagarino data model is based on relational tuples that follow the first normal form, i.e., have no nesting. Two types of tuples can be distinguished, data and metadata tuples. Data tuples are strongly typed and have a schema that defines the domains of all attributes. All data tuples in a stream share the same schema, which corresponds to the output schema of the operator that generates the tuples and must comply with the input schema of the operator that consumes the tuples. In contrast, metadata tuples, so-called messages, are untyped and typically self-describing. Therefore, different messages can travel in the same stream. Messages are primarily used to transmit data and operator statistics in order to coordinate the operators in a query. Each stream is bidirectional consisting of a forward and a backward direction. While data tuples can only travel forward, messages can travel in both directions.

Based on its relational data model, Niagarino implements a series of operators. The selection (σ) and projection (π) operator work exactly the same as their counterparts in relational databases. Other tuple-based operators include the derive (f) and the unnest (μ) operator. The derive operator applies a function to a single tuple and appends the result value to the tuple. The unnest operator splits a "nested" attribute value and emits a tuple for each new value. A typical use case for the unnest operator is to split a string and to produce a tuple for each term it contains. Apart from these general operators, Niagarino provides a number of stream-specific operators that can be used to segment the unbounded stream for processing. Apart from the well-known time and tuple-based window operators (ω) that can be tumbling or sliding [12], Niagarino also implements data-driven windows, so-called frames [15]. Stream segments form the input for join ($\bowtie$) and aggregation (Σ) operators. As with derive operators, Niagarino also supports user-defined aggregation functions. Niagarino operators can be partitioned into three groups. The operators described above are general operators, whereas source operators read input streams and sink operators output results. Each query can have multiple source and sink operators.

---

[3] http://www.informatik.uni-konstanz.de/grossniklaus/software/niagarino/

This classification is similar to the notion of spouts and bolts used in Twitter's data stream management system Storm [19].

Niagarino is implemented in Java 8 and relies heavily on its new language features. In particular, anonymous functions (λ-expressions) are used in several operators in order to support lightweight extensibility with user-defined functionality. The current implementation runs every operator in its own thread. Operator threads are scheduled implicitly using fixed-size input/output buffers and explicitly through backwards messages.

4 Event Detection Techniques

We focus on techniques with the specific task of first story detection, i.e., the detection of general (unknown) events, which is defined as a subtask of TDT [3]. In this section, we briefly describe the five state-of-the-art techniques that we selected for our study in terms of their functionality and the parameters used. Figure 1 illustrates these techniques by means of Niagarino query plans that use the operators described in the previous section. As can be seen in the figure, all of these techniques use the same pre-processing steps before the streaming tuples enter the actual event detection phase. The pre-processing selects all tweets that are non-retweets and in English. Additionally, each tuple is enriched with the derived distinct terms of the tweet that are not contained in a standard English stop-word list or can be considered noise (e.g., less than three characters, unknown characters, repetition of the same pattern, or terms without vowels).

The *TopN* algorithm assigns each individual term a single value based on the inverse document frequency (IDF) [18] over an entire time window. All values are then sorted and the top n terms are reported as events together with their top m most frequently co-occurring terms, which are also obtained by using the IDF measure.

The *Latent Dirichlet Allocation (LDA)* [7] is a hierarchical Bayesian model that explains the variation in a set of documents in terms of a set of n latent "topics", i.e., distributions over the vocabulary. Since LDA is normally used for topic modeling, we equate a topic to an event. For each time window, LDA extracts n events that are described by m terms. The parameter i defines the number of iterations performed in the modeling phase, where a higher value typically increases the quality of the detected events. To perform the LDA, we use *Mallet*[4], an existing Java library.

Our own *Shifty* [20] technique calculates a measure that is based on the shift of IDF values of single terms in pairs of successive sliding windows of a pre-defined size. First, the IDF value of each term in a single window (with size s_{input}) is continuously computed and compared to the average IDF value of all terms within that window. Terms with an IDF value above the average are filtered out. The next step builds a window with size s_1 that slides with range r_1 in order to calculate the shift from one window to the next. In this step,

---

[4] http://mallet.cs.umass.edu

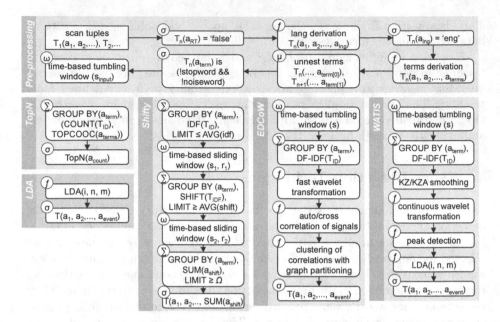

Fig. 1. Niagarino query plans of the five selected event detection techniques

the shift value is again checked against the average shift of all terms and only terms with a shift above the average are retained. In the last step, a new sliding window with size s_2 that slides with range r_2 is created. The total shift value is computed as the sum of all shift values of the sub-windows of this window. If this total shift value is greater than the pre-defined threshold Ω, the term is detected as event and reported together with its top 4 co-occurring terms.

The first step of the *Event Detection with Clustering of Wavelet-based Signals (EDCoW)* [21] algorithm is to partition the stream into intervals of s seconds and to build DF-IDF signals for each distinct term in the interval. These signals are further analyzed using discrete wavelet analysis that builds a second signal for the individual terms. Each data point of this second signal summarizes a sequence of values from the first signal with length Δ. The next step then filters out trivial terms by checking the corresponding signal auto-correlations against a threshold γ. The remaining terms are then clustered to form events with a modularity-based graph partitioning technique. Insignificant events are filtered out using a threshold parameter ϵ. Since this approach detects events with a minimum of two terms, we introduced an additional enrichment step that adds the top co-occurring terms to obtain events with at least five terms.

The *Wavelet Analysis Topic Inference Summarization (WATIS)* [9] algorithm also partitions the stream into intervals of s seconds and builds DF-IDF signals for each distinct term. Due to the noisy nature of the Twitter data stream, signals are then processed by applying the adaptive Kolmogorov-Zurbenko filter (KZA), a low-pass filter that smoothens the signal by calculating a moving average with

i_{kz} iterations over n intervals. It then uses continuous wavelet transformation to construct a time/frequency representation of the signal and two wavelet analyses, the tree map of the continuous wavelet extrema and the local maxima detection, to detect abrupt increases in the frequency of a term. To enrich events with more information, the previously mentioned LDA algorithm (with i_{lda} iterations) is used to finally report events that consist of five terms each.

5   Evaluation

The evaluation of event detection techniques is itself a challenging task. Determining an F_1 score in terms of precision and recall would require a ground truth (gold standard) to which the detected events can be compared. Due to the lack of such a ground truth for the Twitter data stream, some existing approaches have been evaluated using a manually created ground truth or based on user studies, if at all. Since both of these methods are very time-consuming and do not scale, we have experimented with a number of measures that can be applied automatically. In this section, we discuss the motivation behind these measures and present detailed results that were obtained by using them.

5.1   Measures

In order to evaluate different techniques automatically, we defined five main measures (some with sub-measures), which are used for the individual ratings. The measures are described in the following.

Precision (Search Engine). This measure describes the percentage of events that can be verified with the use of a search engine (www.google.com). For each detected event, the search engine is queried using the five event terms and a specific date range. A rating between 1 and 10 (*GoogleN*) is computed by checking how many of the first ten result hits point to a news website. News websites are identified based on a whitelist of domain names containing sites such as CNN, CBS, Reuters, NYTimes, and the Guardian. Based on this measure, detected events can be rated with respect to their newsworthiness on or at least one day after the detection date.

Precision (DBPedia). This measure is calculated using the DBPedia[5] data set, which contains the abstracts (long versions) from all Wikipedia articles. In order to query the roughly four million English abstract, the native XML database BaseX[6] is used. For each detected event, the number of matching abstracts in DBPedia is computed using XQuery Full Text. We have defined three sub-measures. *DBPedia5* is the precision using all five event terms, *DBPedia4S* only uses the top four event terms, and *DBPedia4A* queries DBPedia with all subsets of cardinality four. For the first two measures, an abstract is considered a match to an event if it contains *all* terms that were used in the query. For the third measure, an abstract matches if it contains all terms of *one* of the combinations.

---

[5] http://dbpedia.org/
[6] http://basex.org

Recall. In order to compute the recall, *Bloomberg*[7] was crawled as their archive maintains a list of the most important news articles for each day. Crawling individual days leads to an average of about 200 events per day. Each crawled news item is then tokenized and cleaned by the same processes as the tweets. As a consequence, the short description of each news item by a series of terms can be very similar to the one obtained from the tweets. In order to calculate the similarity between detected events and a news item, **eventSim**(e_1, e_2) is used, which is based on the Levenshtein distance.

$$\textbf{levSim}(t_1, t_2) = 1.0 - \text{lev}(t_1, t_2) \; / \; \max(\{|t_1|, |t_2|\}) \tag{1}$$

$$\textbf{termSim}(t_1, t_2) = \begin{cases} 0 & \text{levSim}(t_1, t_2) < minTermSim \\ 1 & \text{otherwise} \end{cases} \tag{2}$$

$$\textbf{eventSim}(e_1, e_2) = \frac{1}{N} \sum_{i=0, j=0}^{N} \text{termSim}(e_1[t_i], e_2[t_j]) \tag{3}$$

The motivation behind **eventSim**(e_1, e_2) is to compensate for misspellings or alternate spellings of terms as well as for different term sets describing similar events. An event is represented as an alphabetically sorted list of terms $e = [t_0, \ldots, t_n]$. Each term $t_1 \in e_1$ is compared to each term $t_2 \in e_2$ using the **levSim**(t_1, t_2), which is the Levenshtein distance normalized to the range $[0 \ldots 1]$. If the similarity of a term of e_1 to a term of e_2 is above the threshold *minTermSim*, this combination is marked as hit and the algorithm continues with the next term of e_1. Finally, **eventSim**(e_1, e_2) aggregates the number of hits and normalizes it with the number of terms.

In an effort to obtain a reasonable amount of hits, the parameters of this formula are set rather low. The parameter *minTermSim* is set to 0.7 and the overall limit for **eventSim** is set to 0.2. Two sub-measures are defined for the recall. *Bloom1D* calculates the recall just for the given date, whereas *Bloom2D* also includes the following day.

Duplicate Event Detection Rate (DEDR). This measure is also based on the event similarity defined above in order to calculate the similarity of the events for one single technique and data set. Two sub-measures have been defined. For *ADEDR* (almost duplicate event detection rate) the parameter *minTermSim* is set to 0.8 and the limit for *eventSim* is set to 0.5, whereas for *FDEDR* (full duplicate event detection rate) the *minTermSim* is the same but the limit for *eventSim* is set to 0.9.

Run-time Performance. Run-time performance is measured as the number of tweets per second that a technique is able to process.

---

[7] http://www.bloomberg.com/archive/news/

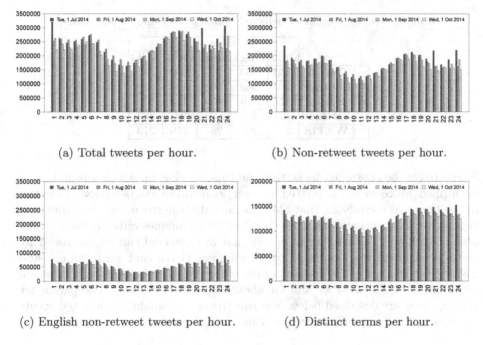

(a) Total tweets per hour.

(b) Non-retweet tweets per hour.

(c) English non-retweet tweets per hour.

(d) Distinct terms per hour.

Fig. 2. Statistics of the Twitter data set

5.2 Data Sets

The data sets used in the study presented in this paper consist of 10% of the public live stream of Twitter for four days. Using the Twitter Streaming API[8] with the so-called "Gardenhose" access level, which is a randomly sampled substream, we collected data for the first day of June, August, September, and October. Figure 2 provides statistics of the initial data set as well as for the processing steps that are common to all techniques (cf. Fig. 1). Figure 2a presents the total number of tweets for the chosen days grouped by the hour (given in GMT+1). As can be seen, the rate of tweets follows a regular daily pattern. On average, the incoming stream contains 2.3 million tweets/hour and 35,000 tweets/minute. Figure 2b shows the hourly tweet volumes after filtering out retweets at an average of 1.6 million tweets/hour. After the next step, shown in Fig. 2c, the data sets are further reduced to an average of 500,000 tweets/hour by filtering out tweets that are not in English. Finally, Fig. 2d shows an average of 120,000 distinct terms/hour that have been derived from all English tweets.

5.3 Experimental Setup

In order to be able to compare the results of the five chosen techniques in a fair way, they have to be aligned in terms of the rate and number of events detected.

---

[8] https://dev.twitter.com

Table 1. Average number of detected events per techniques and dataset

<table>
<tr><td rowspan="2"></td><td rowspan="2"></td><td colspan="5">dataset</td></tr>
<tr><td>Jul1</td><td>Aug1</td><td>Sep1</td><td>Oct1</td><td>AVG</td></tr>
<tr><td rowspan="5">technique</td><td>Top15</td><td>360</td><td>360</td><td>360</td><td>360</td><td>360</td></tr>
<tr><td>LDA500</td><td>360</td><td>360</td><td>360</td><td>360</td><td>360</td></tr>
<tr><td>Shifty</td><td>327</td><td>316</td><td>354</td><td>402</td><td>350</td></tr>
<tr><td>EDCoW</td><td>353</td><td>375</td><td>396</td><td>409</td><td>383</td></tr>
<tr><td>WATIS</td><td>270</td><td>261</td><td>287</td><td>276</td><td>273</td></tr>
</table>

The rate can be controlled by setting the time window on which a technique is performed. Since we are interested in (near) real-time event detection, a window of one hour was used. Note, that *Shifty* is the only true streaming algorithm that reports results continuously, whereas all other techniques only produce results after each hour. The number of events that are detected can be controlled by setting the specific parameters of each technique. Given that our recall measure assumes an average of 200 events per day and compensating for events that are detected multiple times, we aim for about 350 events per day. The parameter settings used are described below, whereas the actual number of detected events per day and technique are shown in Tab. 1.

TopN. Per hour, the top $n = 15$ events are reported together with $m = 5$ co-occurring terms to obtain a total of 360 events per day

LDA. LDA is set to perform $i = 500$ iterations and to report 15 events, described by $m = 5$ terms each, per hour, yielding again a total of 360 events per day.

Shifty. The IDF value is calculated over 1-minute intervals. The size of the window used to compute the IDF shift is $s_1 = 2$ minutes. The size of the window that aggregates and filters the IDF shift is $s_2 = 4$ minutes. Both windows slide by range $r_1 = r_2 = 1$ minute. By setting the threshold $\Omega = 0.35$, we obtain all terms with a minute by minute IDF value that increases more than 35% over four minutes.

EDCoW. The size of the initial intervals is set to $s = 10$ seconds and the number of intervals that are combined by the wavelet analysis to $\Delta = 32$, yielding a total window size per value of 320 seconds. The other parameters are set to the same values as in the original paper ($\gamma = 1$ and $\epsilon = 0.2$). As the original paper fails to mention the wavelet type that was used, we experimented with several types. The results reported in this paper are based on the *Discrete Meyer* wavelet, which showed the best performance.

WATIS. The length of initial intervals is set to $s = 85$ seconds. For the KZ/KZA analysis, $n = 5$ intervals and $i_{kz} = 5$ iterations are used, yielding a total window size of 425 seconds. LDA is set to perform $i_{lda} = 500$ iterations and report a description with five terms per detected event.

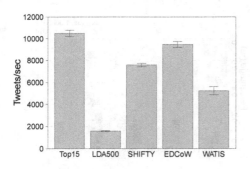

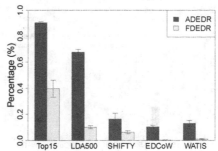

Fig. 3. Average run-time performance

Fig. 4. Average duplicate rate

5.4   Results

In the following, we present the results of our evaluation of event detection techniques in terms of run-time and task-based performance. Rather than discussing all results that we have obtained, we focus on the most significant measures and outcomes. While we do not claim that our measures are absolute, it should be noted that these results support relative conclusions.

Run-Time Performance. Run-time performance was measured using Oracle Java 1.8.0_25 (64 bit) on server-grade hardware with 2 Intel Xeon E5345s processors at 2.33 GHz with 4 cores each and 24 GB of main memory. The corresponding results for all techniques in terms of throughput (tweets/second) are given in Fig. 3. We note that the performance of all techniques is very stable across the four days for which experiments were run. Taking into account the average rate of 35,000 tweets/minute (583 tweets/second), we can derive that all techniques are able to process the 10% stream in real-time on the tested hardware. However, taking a 100% stream ($\sim 5,830$ tweets/second) into account, both *LDA500* and *WATIS* would be too slow to process the stream in real-time on the tested hardware. In both techniques, the number of LDA iterations could be reduced, i.e., trading off result quality for performance. Finally, we point out that our experimental setup is stacked against our own technique, *Shifty*. In contrast to the other approaches that can only process tweets at the end of each one-hour window, *Shifty* processes tweets continuously and can therefore amortize its processing cost over the one-hour window.

Task-Based Performance. The first measure of task-based performance that we will examine is the duplicate event detection rate. Results obtained using both the *ADEDR* and *FDEDR* sub-measures are given in Fig. 4. In comparison to the other three techniques, both *Top15* and *LDA500* detect a large number of duplicates. This result is explained by the fact that these techniques identify events based on the absolute frequency of terms, i.e., without considering changes

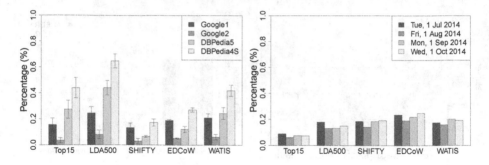

Fig. 5. Average precision   **Fig. 6.** Recall using *Bloom1D*

in the relative frequency. The *ADEDR* of the remaining three techniques is relatively low in the range of 15–18%. *Shifty*'s *FDEDR* stayed consistently below 10% in all our experiments, whereas *EDCoW* and *WATIS* do hardly detect any duplicates at all. Finally, the results also show that there is little deviation in the detected number of duplicates over the four days in our data set.

Apart from the duplicate event detection rate, we have also studied the task-based performance of the selected techniques in terms of precision and recall. Figure 5 summarizes the precision results of all techniques obtained with the *Google1*, *Google2*, *DBPedia5*, and *DBPedia4S* measures. We omit results from the *DBPedia4A* as our experiments showed that they are not discriminating. Even though the measures we defined yield a wide range of precision values, their relative ratio is always the same. Since our goal is to comparatively evaluate event detection techniques, we conclude that our measures are sound with respect to this criterion. Again, *Top15* and *LDA500* stand out with higher precision values than the other three techniques. The reason for this result is that our precision measures are slightly biased towards approaches that report duplicates.

Figure 6 shows the recall results for the *Bloom1D* measure. *Bloom2D* is omitted as the results are almost exactly the same. First of all, it can be seen from the figure that the recall of all techniques is relatively low at 10–20%. Note that our recall measure is based on the Bloomberg news website, which lists an average of 200 topics per day. Even though techniques were configured to report about $1.5\times$ as many events, our recall measure is nevertheless ambitious. For example, it is difficult to imagine that enough people will tweet about a topic such as Heathrow's cargo statistics in order to detect it as an event. However, since we are only interested in relative measures, these low recall figures are not a problem. Rather, we can observe that *Top15* and *LDA500* generally have a lower recall than the other three techniques. As this outcome is to be expected due to the high duplicate event detection rate of these techniques, we can again conclude that our measure for recall is sound.

In order to summarize the most discriminating measures presented in this paper, we define three scoring functions that can be used to compare the run-time and task-based performance of event detection techniques. The three scoring functions are defined as follows.

$$\text{FScore} = 2 \times \frac{\text{precision} \times \text{recall}}{\text{precision} + \text{recall}} \tag{4}$$

$$\text{PFScore} = (\text{FScore} \times \text{performance}) \tag{5}$$

$$\text{DPFScore} = \text{PFScore} \times (1 - DEDR) \tag{6}$$

The first score, *FScore*, denotes the F_1 score that is calculated by using the value of the *Google1* and *Bloom1D* measures for precision and recall, respectively. Alternatively, using *DBPedia5* leads to very similar results. The second score, *PFScore*, also factors in the performance rate of the technique. Performance values are normalized to the range $[0 \ldots 1]$ by setting the maximum processing rate that we measured to 1. Finally, the last measure, *DPFScore*, also includes the duplicate event detection rate of the technique. In the following, we have used the value of the *FDEDR* measure to calculate *DPFScore*.

Based on these definitions, Fig. 7 shows the scores that were assigned to each of the five techniques as averages over the four days in the evaluation data set. Even though *Top15* scores relatively high in terms of precision, its *FScore* is low due to a poor recall because of duplicates. As *Top15* is consistently the fastest technique in our experiments, its *PFScore* is equal to its *FScore*. The high *DEDR* of *Top15* has a noticeable negative effect

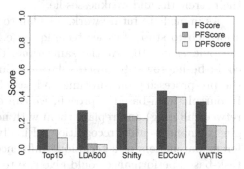

Fig. 7. Average rating scores

on its *DPFScore*. *LDA500*'s *FScore* is relatively high, but comes at a high performance penalty, which negatively affects both its *PFScore* and *DPFScore*. Based on these results, we can conclude that neither *Top15* nor *LDA500* are suitable event detection techniques. This result is not surprising as both of these techniques have originally not been developed for this task.

In contrast, the scores of *Shifty*, *EDCoW*, and *WATIS* are much better. In particular, none of these techniques suffer significantly from duplicate event detection. *Shifty* and *WATIS* have a similar *FScore*, but are both negatively affected by their performance score. However, since *Shifty*'s streaming algorithm was forced to an hourly reporting scheme for the sake of comparability, this score is still a good result for our technique. *EDCoW* scores impressive results for all scoring functions, which confirms that its status as the most cited event detection technique is well-deserved. This work however is the first to provide comparative and quantitative evidence for *EDCoW*'s quality.

Finally, we note that duplicate events are not always undesired, e.g., when tracking re-occurring events or changes in event descriptions. The need to study event detection techniques in both settings, motivates our separate definitions of *FScore*, *PFScore*, and *DPFScore*. Both *LDA500* and *Top15* could be extended to explicitly avoid the detection of duplicate events. However, since the other techniques do allow for duplicates, we have chosen not to do so in this study.

6   Conclusion

In this paper, we addressed the problem of comparatively and quantitatively studying the task-based and run-time performance of state-of-the-art event detection techniques for Twitter. In order to do so, we have presented a two-pronged approach. First, we ensure comparable run-time performance results by providing streaming implementations of all techniques based on a data stream management system. Second, we propose several new measures that can assess the relative task-based performance of event detection techniques. The detailed study described in this paper has shown that these measures are sound and which of them are most discriminating. Finally, we defined scoring functions based on selected measures that revealed how the different techniques relate to each other as well as where their strengths and weaknesses lie.

As immediate future work, we plan to take advantage of our platform-based approach to study further techniques, e.g., enBloque [4] and the approach of Petrović et al. [16]. At the same time, the currently implemented techniques could be improved to process data continuously. Furthermore, the influence of the pre-processing on run-time and task-based performance should be studied. In our platform-based approach, we can easily remove existing operators (e.g., retweet filtering) and replace them with new operators (e.g., part-of-speech tagging or named-entity recognition). Finally, a deeper evaluation of how the different parameters of a technique influence the trade-off between run-time and task-based performance could give rise to adaptive event detection techniques.

Acknowledgments. We would like to thank our students Christina Papavasileiou and Harry Schilling for their contributions to the implementation of *WATIS* and *EDCoW*.

References

1. Abadi, D.J., Ahmad, Y., Balazinska, M., Çetintemel, U., Cherniack, M., Hwang, J., Lindner, W., Maskey, A., Rasin, A., Ryvkina, E., Tatbul, N., Xing, Y., Zdonik, S.B.: The design of the borealis stream processing engine. In: Proc. Intl. Conf. on Innovative Data Systems Research (CIDR), pp. 277–289 (2005)
2. Abadi, D.J., Carney, D., Çetintemel, U., Cherniack, M., Convey, C., Lee, S., Stonebraker, M., Tatbul, N., Zdonik, S.: Aurora: A New Model and Architecture for Data Stream Management. The VLDB Journal **12**(2), 120–139 (2003)
3. Allan, J.: Topic Detection and Tracking: Event-based Information Organization. Kluwer Academic Publishers (2002)
4. Alvanaki, F., Michel, S., Ramamritham, K., Weikum, G.: See what's enBlogue: real-time emergent topic identification in social media. In: Proc. Intl. Conf. on Extending Database Technology (EDBT), pp. 336–347 (2012)
5. Arasu, A., Babu, S., Widom, J.: The CQL Continuous Query Language: Semantic Foundations and Query Execution. The VLDB Journal **15**(2), 121–142 (2006)

6. Becker, H., Naaman, M., Gravano, L.: Beyond trending topics: real-world event identification on twitter. In: Proc. Intl. Conf on Weblogs and Social Media (ICWSM), pp. 438–441 (2011)
7. Blei, D.M., Ng, A.Y., Jordan, M.I.: Latent Dirichlet Allocation. J. Mach. Learn. Res. **3**, 993–1022 (2003)
8. Bontcheva, K., Rout, D.: Making Sense of Social Media Streams through Semantics: a Survey. Semantic Web **5**(5), 373–403 (2014)
9. Cordeiro, M.: Twitter event detection: combining wavelet analysis and topic inference summarization. In: Proc. Doctoral Symposium on Informatics Engineering (DSIE) (2012)
10. Culotta, A.: Towards detecting influenza epidemics by analyzing twitter messages. In: Proc. Workshop on Social Media Analytics (SOMA), pp. 115–122 (2010)
11. Farzindar, A., Khreich, W.: A Survey of Techniques for Event Detection in Twitter. Computational Intelligence (2013). http://dx.doi.org/10.1111/coin.12017
12. Li, J., Maier, D., Tufte, K., Papadimos, V., Tucker, P.A.: No Pane, No Gain: Efficient Evaluation of Sliding-Window Aggregates over Data Streams. SIGMOD Record **34**(1), 39–44 (2005)
13. Li, J., Tufte, K., Shkapenyuk, V., Papadimos, V., Johnson, T., Maier, D.: Out-of-Order Processing: A New Architecture for High-Performance Stream Systems. PVLDB **1**(1), 274–288 (2008)
14. Long, R., Wang, H., Chen, Y., Jin, O., Yu, Y.: Towards effective event detection, tracking and summarization on microblog data. In: Wang, H., Li, S., Oyama, S., Hu, X., Qian, T. (eds.) WAIM 2011. LNCS, vol. 6897, pp. 652–663. Springer, Heidelberg (2011)
15. Maier, D., Grossniklaus, M., Moorthy, S., Tufte, K.: Capturing episodes: may the frame be with you. In: Proc. Intl. Conf. on Distributed Event-Based Systems (DEBS), pp. 1–11 (2012)
16. Petrović, S., Osborne, M., Lavrenko, V.: Streaming first story detection with application to twitter. In: Proc. Conf. of the North American Chapter of the Association for Computational Linguistics (HLT), pp. 181–189 (2010)
17. Sakaki, T., Okazaki, M., Matsuo, Y.: Earthquake shakes twitter users: real-time event detection by social sensors. In: Proc. Intl. Conf. on World Wide Web (WWW), pp. 851–860 (2010)
18. Sparck Jones, K.: A Statistical Interpretation of Term Specificity and Its Application in Retrieval, pp. 132–142. Taylor Graham Publishing (1988)
19. Toshniwal, A., Taneja, S., Shukla, A., Ramasamy, K., Patel, J.M., Kulkarni, S., Jackson, J., Gade, K., Fu, M., Donham, J., Bhagat, N., Mittal, S., Ryaboy, D.V.: Storm @Twitter. In: Proc. Intl. Conf. on Management of Data (SIGMOD), pp. 147–156 (2014)
20. Weiler, A., Grossniklaus, M., Scholl, M.H.: Event identification and tracking in social media streaming data. In: Proc. EDBT Workshop on Multimodal Social Data Management (MSDM), pp. 282–287 (2014)
21. Weng, J., Lee, B.S.: Event detection in twitter. In: Proc. Intl. Conf on Weblogs and Social Media (ICWSM), pp. 401–408 (2011)
22. Zimmermann, M., Ntoutsi, I., Siddiqui, Z.F., Spiliopoulou, M., Kriegel, H.P.: Discovering global and local bursts in a stream of news. In: Proc. Symp. on Applied Computing (SAC), pp. 807–812 (2012)

Business Process Modeling
and Languages

RALph: A Graphical Notation for Resource Assignments in Business Processes

Cristina Cabanillas[1](✉), David Knuplesch[2], Manuel Resinas[3],
Manfred Reichert[2], Jan Mendling[1], and Antonio Ruiz-Cortés[3]

[1] Vienna University of Economics and Business, Vienna, Austria
{cristina.cabanillas,jan.mendling}@wu.ac.at
[2] Ulm University, Ulm, Germany
{david.knuplesch,manfred.reichert}@uni-ulm.de
[3] University of Seville, Seville, Spain
{resinas,aruiz}@us.es

Abstract. The business process (BP) resource perspective deals with the management of human as well as non-human resources throughout the process lifecycle. Although it has received increasing attention recently, there exists no graphical notation for it up until now that is both expressive enough to cover well-known resource selection conditions and independent of any BP modelling language. In this paper, we introduce RALph, a graphical notation for the assignment of human resources to BP activities. We define its semantics by mapping this notation to a language that has been formally defined in description logics, which enables its automated analysis. Although we show how RALph can be seamlessly integrated with BPMN, it is noteworthy that the notation is independent of the BP modelling language. Altogether, RALph will foster the visual modelling of the resource perspective in BPs.

Keywords: BPM · Graphical notation · RALph · Resource assignment

1 Introduction

The Business Process (BP) resource perspective deals with the management of human as well as non-human resources throughout the process lifecycle [1]. The management of resources in this context involves the definition of assignments at design time, i.e. by querying those actors that are supposed to work on tasks, the allocation of resources at runtime, and the analysis of resource utilisation after execution for process improvement. While it is widely accepted that models and visual notations can be beneficial for system development [2], it is striking to note that a notation for modelling these aspects in an integrated way is still missing.

This work was funded by the Austrian Research Funding Association (FFG) and Science Fund (FWF), the German Research Foundation (DFG), the European Commission (FEDER), the Spanish and the Andalusian R&D&I programmes (grants 845638 (SHAPE), I743, RE 1402/2-1 (C3Pro), TIN2012-32273 (TAPAS), P12-TIC-1867 (COPAS), TIC-5906 (THEOS)).

© Springer International Publishing Switzerland 2015
J. Zdravkovic et al. (Eds.): CAiSE 2015, LNCS 9097, pp. 53–68, 2015.
DOI: 10.1007/978-3-319-19069-3_4

The support of resource management in current process modelling approaches can be roughly categorised as follows. On the one hand, languages like Business Process Model and Notation (BPMN) [3] emphasise modelling of the control flow and data in its graphical notation. Resource assignments can be expressed in a rather basic fashion visually, with partial extensions in structured but non-visual attributes. On the other hand, implementations like the YAWL system [4] provide a rich support for the resource perspective, but not as part of the visual notation. A few works have contributed towards a better integration of a visual notation for defining resource assignments with extensive semantics recently [5,6]. Still, they expose gaps towards a full visual support.

In this paper, we want to bridge this gap by introducing RALph, a graphical notation for defining the assignments of human resources to BP activities. RALph has the following characteristics: (i) It is expressive. In particular, it allows defining all the resource selection conditions covered by the workflow resource patterns [7] as well as those we discovered in a real scenario from the healthcare domain. (ii) Resource assignments specified with RALph can be automatically analysed. In turn, this enables automatic answers to questions such as "Is the BP consistent regarding the use of resources?" or "Which activities may Mr. B perform in the context of BP X?". This is achieved by defining the semantics of RALph through its semantic mapping to Resource Assignment Language (RAL) [5], a textual language for resource assignment whose formal semantics was defined in description logics. (iii) It is independent of any BP modelling language. For that, it can be seamlessly integrated with existing notations (e.g., BPMN), as demonstrated with a proof-of-concept prototype we developed.

The remainder of the paper is structured as follows: Section 2 describes a real scenario that serves as use case throughout the paper, and evidences the need of a graphical notation for resource specification in Business Process Management (BPM) by studying related work. Section 3 introduces RALph's graphical notation and its formal syntax. Section 4 describes RALph's formal semantics. Section 5 discusses expressiveness issues and presents RALph's integration capabilities with existing tools. Finally, Section 6 concludes this work and gives an outlook of future work.

2   Background

In this section, we discuss the background of our research. Section 2.1 presents the running example that we use in this paper. Section 2.2 discusses prior work related to resource specification. Section 2.3 summarises requirements for a graphical notation for resource assignment.

2.1   Running Example

Throughout this paper, we will use the process of patient examination as running example. Figure 1 shows this process modelled in BPMN according to the

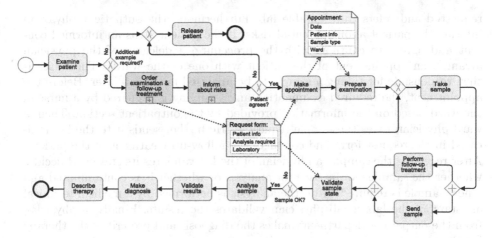

Fig. 1. Process of patient examination

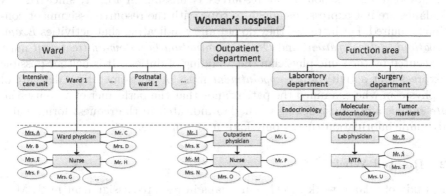

Fig. 2. Organisational model

description provided by the Women's Hospital of Ulm. Furthermore, we refer to the organisational model of this hospital that is shown in Figure 2 [8,9]. In it, the rectangles with rounded corners represent organisational units that are structured hierarchically; rectangles with straight corners are hierarchies of organisational positions within the units; and ellipses represent people[1] that occupy the positions defined.

The examination process can be summarised as follows. The process starts when the female patient is examined by an outpatient physician, who decides whether she is healthy or needs to undertake an additional examination. In the former case, the physician fills out the examination form and the patient can leave. In the latter case, an examination and follow-up treatment order is placed by the physician who additionally fills out a request form. Beyond information about the patient, the request form includes details about the examination

---

[1] Please, note that due to privacy issues the names have been anonymised.

requested and refers to a suitable lab. Furthermore, the outpatient physician informs the patient about potential risks. If the patient signs an informed consent and agrees to continue with the procedure, a delegate of the physician arranges an appointment of the patient with one of the wards. The latter is then responsible for taking a sample to be analysed in the lab later. Before the appointment, the required examination and sampling is prepared by a nurse of the ward based on the information provided by the outpatient section. Then, a ward physician takes the sample requested. He further sends it to the lab indicated in the request form and conducts the follow-up treatment of the patient. After receiving the sample, a physician of the lab validates its state and decides whether the sample can be used for analysis or whether it is contaminated and a new sample is required. After the analysis is performed by a medical technical assistant of the lab, a lab physician validates the results. Finally, a physician from the outpatient department makes the diagnosis and prescribes the therapy for the patient.

Note that information about resources is missing in Fig. 1, since BPMN swimlanes are not expressive enough to cope with the resource assignment conditions required. For instance, they do not allow indicating that activities *Examine patient*, *Release patient* and *Order examination & follow-up treatment* must be executed by the same physician (i.e., binding of duties). It is neither possible to express that activity *Make appointment* must be performed by a delegate of the physician who examined the patient, nor that the performer of activity *Validate sample state* must belong to the lab indicated in the request form, which is dynamic information that is only known at run time.

2.2 Related Work

The study of related work reveals some gaps in resource assignment in BPM.

Several metamodels [10,11] and expressive resource assignment languages [5, 12] have been developed, but they do not provide any graphical representation of the concepts they handle and the resource selection conditions they allow for. Some of them provide display notations in the form of user interfaces that help non-technical users to define the conditions [4,13], but these are not visualised together with the elements of the BP model.

The main drawback of the graphical notations proposed so far is that they lack formal semantics, which makes them inappropriate for automated resource analysis in BP models. This is the case of the swimlanes offered by the de-facto standard BPMN [3]. Event-driven Process Chains(EPCs) [14] also allow for the graphical assignment of organisational entities to process activities, but semantics are not defined.

Some approaches have been developed to overcome this drawback. However, they either present a lack of expressive power regarding the conditions for resource selection they allow defining, or have been developed for specific BP modelling notations, or both. The workflow resource patterns [7] (see also Section 5.1) are used to assess the former criterion. Business Activities [6] is a Role-based access control (RBAC) [15] extension of Unified Modeling Language (UML) activity diagrams to define separation of duties and binding of duties between the activities of a process. Some ad-hoc analysis mechanisms have been developed for them as well. However, their scope does not cover resource selection conditions based on other organisational entities, people's skills or runtime information. Several approaches extended the BPMN metamodel to graphically define specific types of conditions along with the swimlanes or with process activities. For instance, Wolter and Schaad introduced access-control constraints in BPMN models through an extension based on authorisation constraints [16]. Awad et al. [17] and Stroppi et al. [18], in turn, developed extensions that cover all the assignment patterns defined by the workflow resource patterns. In all these approaches, however, the definition of the resource selection conditions is mainly done textually, though graphically associated to BPMN elements, e.g. by making use of BPMN text annotations or group artifacts.

2.3 Requirements for a Graphical Resource Assignment Notation

We have studied the related work according to well-defined criteria in order to discover the gaps that should be bridged. Table 1 depicts the result of the evaluation, where ✓ indicates full support for a criterion, ∼ indicates partial support, and − indicates no support. Specifically, the criteria included in the comparison framework are the following:

Extent of language specification. The syntactic, semantic and pragmatic perspectives of the language for resource assignment are evaluated. In particular, we have checked whether it has formal syntax and semantics, and whether there is a graphical notation to model the resource selection conditions together with the other elements of a BP model.

Table 1. Study of resource assignment approaches

Approach	Language Specification			Domain Concepts					Reuse
	Syntax	Semantics	Graph.	Entity	AC	Capability	Deferred	History	
HRMM [10]	−	✓	−	∼	−	−	−	−	✓
Team [11]	−	✓	−	∼	✓	✓	−	−	✓
RAL[5]	✓	✓	−	✓	✓	✓	✓	✓	✓
CSL[12]	✓	✓	−	∼	✓	−	−	−	✓
YAWL[4]	✓	✓	∼	✓	✓	✓	✓	✓	−
XACML N.[13]	✓	✓	∼	∼	−	✓	−	−	✓
BPMN[3]	✓	−	✓	✓	−	−	−	−	−
EPCs[14]	✓	−	✓	✓	−	−	−	−	−
Business A.[6]	✓	✓	✓	∼	✓	−	−	−	−
BPMN E.[16]	✓	✓	∼	∼	✓	−	−	✓	−
BPMN E.[17]	✓	✓	∼	∼	✓	✓	−	✓	−
BPMN E.[18]	✓	✓	∼	✓	✓	✓	✓	✓	−

Extent of domain concepts. The expressiveness of the graphical notation is assessed according to the workflow resource patterns [7], which have been used as evaluation framework to assess the expressiveness of a number of proposals on resource assignment in BPM [6,11,17,19,20]. Specifically, we use the creation patterns, as they are related to resource selection. These patterns include:

- *Direct Allocation* is the ability to specify at design time the identity of the resource that will execute a task.
- *Role-Based Allocation* is the ability to specify at design time that a task can only be executed by resources that correspond to a given role.
- *Organisational Allocation* is the ability to offer or allocate activity instances to resources based their organisational position and their relationship with other resources.
- *Separation of duties* is the ability to specify that two tasks must be allocated to different resources in a given BP instance.
- *Case Handling* is the ability to allocate the activity instances within a given process instance to the same resource.
- *Retain Familiar* is the ability to allocate an activity instance within a given BP instance to the same resource that performed a preceding activity instance, when several resources are available to perform it. This pattern is also known as binding of duties.
- *Capability-Based Allocation* is the ability to offer or allocate instances of an activity to resources based on their specific capabilities.
- *Deferred Allocation* is the ability to defer specifying the identity of the resource that will execute a task until run time.
- *History-Based Allocation* is the ability to offer or allocate activity instances to resources based on their execution history.

For the sake of brevity, in Table 1 the first three patterns have been grouped as entity-based assignments, and the three subsequent patterns have beed grouped as access-control assignments.

Note that creation patterns *Authorisation* and *Automatic Execution* are not on the list. The former is excluded since it is not related to the definition of conditions for resource selection, and the latter since it is not related to the assignment language and is inherently supported by all Business Process Management System (BPMS).

Extent of reusability. We have also checked whether the current graphical notations for resource assignment are independent of any BP modelling language. Independent notations are likely to be applicable in different domains along with different existing notations.

3   RALph: Resource Assignment Language Graph

This section presents the RAL graph (RALph) visual notation for specifying resource assignments in BP models. RALph represents resources as different kinds of entities instead of using pools and lanes like in BPMN [3]. In turn, resource assignments are expressed by connectors, which either link resources to activities or link activities among each other in order to express access-control constraints (i.e., separation and binding of duties).

The semantic concepts underlying the elements (i.e., entities and connectors) of RALph have been identified based on the experience we gained in the context of (textual) resource assignment languages [5] and case studies we applied in the healthcare domain [8,9,21]. In turn, we iteratively elaborated their visual representation (cf. Fig. 3) in eleven steps and during discussions with domain experts.

3.1 Graphical Notation

The RALph graphical notation provides various visual elements (i.e., entities and connectors) that enable the visual modelling of resource selection conditions in process models (cf. Fig. 3). For this purpose, activities may either be connected with *resource entities* using the *resource assignment connector* as well as *hierarchy connectors* or with other activities using *history connectors*.

The *resource assignment connector* enables the explicit specification of responsibilities by connecting resource or capability entities to activities. RALph provides four *resource entities* that cover *persons*, *roles*, *positions*, and *organizational units*. In order to refer to a particular resource, its name must be specified as a label on them. In turn, unlabeled resource entities are wildcards to be further restricted through *data-driven connectors*, which use fields of data objects to specify the name of the resource. In addition, *roles* can be linked with *organizational units* using the *resource assignment connector* in order to select only those actors that play a specific role within a specific unit of an organisation. Finally, *capability entities* refer to persons having a particular capability or skill.

RALph assumes that the organisation is structured hierarchically based on positions, similarly to other approaches [5,7,20]. Hence, the *hierarchy connectors* apply hierarchical relationships and assign an activity to the super- or subordinated persons of a specific position, which is specified using the *position resource entity*. One may want to refer to direct reporting, i.e. to the positions immediately superior in the hierarchy, or to transitive reporting, i.e. scaling up in the hierarchy by transitivity. In order to distinguish between them, hierarchy connectors may either use single arrow heads (direct) or doubled ones (transitive).

Finally, RALph provides four different kinds of *history connectors*. They assign an activity to those actors that have been responsible for the execution of another activity, which is connected by a connector that ends up with an empty circle. The activity referenced represents an activity instance (i) in the context of the same process instance (solid line), (ii) the same or any previous process instance (solid line and log symbol), (iii) any previous process instance (dashed line and log symbol), or (iv) any process instance that was executed in a specified period of time (dashed line and calendar symbol).

RALph applies an AND-semantics, i.e., all the resource selection conditions defined for an activity must be considered in the assignment. Nonetheless,

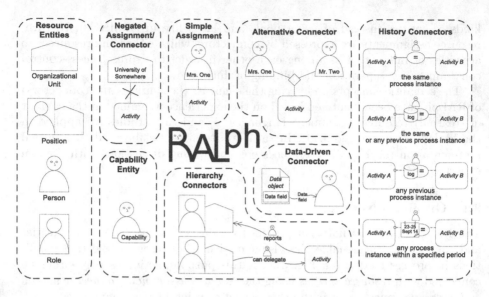

Fig. 3. The RALph language

diamonds may be used to express that only one of the conditions defined needs to be satisfied in order to assign resources to the activity. In order to specify negations, connectors can be crossed-out (cf. *negated assignment/connector in Fig. 3*).

Fig. 4 applies the RALph language to the patient examination process of our running example (cf. Sect. 2.1 and Fig. 1). For example, Fig. 4 *assigns* position *outpatient physician* of unit *outpatient department* (cf. Fig. 2) to task *examine patient*. Furthermore, a *history connector* expresses that the same person is also assigned to task *release patient*. In turn, a *hierarchy connector* is applied in order to specify that a delegate of the *outpatient physician* (i.e., someone to whom the physician can delegate work) is responsible for task *make appointment*. Finally, an example of a *data-driven connector* refers to field *ward* of data object *appointment* in order to specify the organizational unit, which is responsible for taking the sample. In particular, a *nurse* and a *ward physician* of the respective ward are assigned to the tasks *prepare examination* and *take sample* and subsequent steps.

3.2   Formal Specification

In order to provide a clear syntax as well as to enable the specification of a formal semantics for RALph, this section introduces a set-based definition of RALph. Since RALph extends process models, first of all, Definition 1 provides a fundamental definition of the latter. Note that Definition 1 abstracts from those details of process models that are not relevant for the formal specification of RALph. For example, types of activities are not specified. Furthermore, all gateways and events, respectively, are combined in one set.

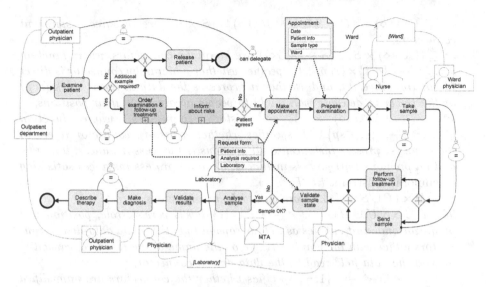

Fig. 4. Process of patient examination with RAL graph

Definition 1 (Process Model). *A process model PM is a tuple PM =* $(A, G, E, D, .\text{-}, \text{-})$ *where*

- *A is a set of activities,*
- *G is a set of gateways,*
- *E is a set of events,*
- *D is a set of data objects,*
- *.* $\text{-} \subseteq (A \cup G \cup E) \times (A \cup G \cup E)$ *is a sequence flow relation, and*
- *-* $\subseteq (A \times D) \cup (D \times A)$ *is an information flow relation.*

Based on Definition 1, we formally specify RALph in Definition 2. Specifically, Definition 2 includes four sets of resource entities and one set for capability entities. In addition, it comprises six sets specifying the different kinds of connectors and, finally, four functions labeling and annotating entities and connectors.

Definition 2 (RAL Graph (RALph)). *Let PM = $(A, G, E, D, .\text{-}, \text{-})$ be a process model (cf. Definition 1). Further, let $\mathcal{L}$ be a set of labels and ϵ be the empty string. Then: A RAL graph (RALph) for PM is a tuple $\Psi = (P, S, U, R, C,$ per, $\diamond$, $\diagup$, $\diagup$, $\diagup$, $\diagup\!\!\!\bullet$, lbl, hr, hs, σ) with PM is a tuple $\Psi = (P, S, U, R, C, \diamond, \diagup,$ $\diagup$, $\diagup$, $\diagup\!\!\!\bullet$, lbl, hr, hs, σ) where*

- *P is a set of person entities,*
- *S is a set of position entities,*
- *U is a set of organizational unit entities,*
- *R is a set of role entities,*
- *C is a set of capability entities,*
- *$\diamond$ is a set of alternative connectors,*

- $\diagup \subseteq (A \cup \diamond) \times (P \cup S \cup U \cup R \cup \diamond) \cup (S \times U)$ *are resource assignment connectors,*
- $\diagup \subseteq ((A \cup \diamond) \times S) \cup (S \times (A \cup \diamond))$ *are hierarchy connectors, where function* $hr : \diagup \longrightarrow \{d, t\} \times \{rep, del\}$ *specifies whether a hierarchy connector is direct (d) or transitive (t), and whether it expresses the duty to report work (rep) or the power to delegate work (del) to people according to their positions,*
- $\diagup\bullet \subseteq (A \cup \diamond) \times A$ *are history connectors, where function* $hs : \diagup\bullet \longrightarrow \{s, p, sp\} \cup T$ *specifies whether a history connector refers to the same (s) process instance, to all previous (p) process instances, the same and all previous (sp) process instances, or to all process instances satisfying a temporal constraint* $t \in T$,
- $\diagup \subseteq D \times (P \cup S \cup U \cup R)$ *are data-driven connectors,*
- $lbl : P \cup S \cup U \cup R \cup C \cup \diagup \longrightarrow \mathcal{L} \cup \{\epsilon\}$ *labels person, role, position and organizational unit entities as well as capability entities and data-driven connectors either with the empty string ϵ or the name of the resource, capability or with the data field read by the data-driven connector,*
- $\sigma : \diagup \cup \diagup \cup \diagup\bullet \longrightarrow \{1, \neg\}$ *specifies whether the connectors are unmodified (1) or negated ($\neg$) - i.e., crossed out in the graphical notation.*

Note that Definition 2 specifies how the elements of a RALph specification can be connected with each other and with elements of the corresponding process model. However, Definition 2 still allows for ambiguities and conflicts (e.g., two or more data-driven connectors may be connected to the same resource entity or cycles of history connectors may occur). In order to enable the specification of correctness criteria dealing with these issues, Definition 3 introduces different sets of nodes and edges as well as a special subgraph of a RALph model.

Definition 3 (Nodes, Edges and Subgraphs of a RAL Graph). *Let* $PM = (A, G, E, D, \diagup, \diagup)$ *be a process model (cf. Definition 1) and let* $\Psi = (P, S, U, R, C, \diamond, \diagup, \diagup, \diagup, \diagup\bullet, lbl, hr, hs, \sigma)$ *be a RAL graph for PM. Then:*

- $N_\Psi := A \cup O \cup P \cup S \cup U \cup R \cup C \cup \diamond$ *is the set containing all nodes of RAL graph Ψ, including the activities and data objects of the related process model,*
- $\diagup^+ := \diagup \cup \diagup \cup \diagup\bullet$ *are the extended resource assignment connectors of RAL graph Ψ that also include hierarchy and history connectors,*
- $\diagup_T := \{(n_1, n_2) \in \diagup | n_2 \in T\} \subseteq \diagup$ *are the resource connectors, which are connected to resources of entity type $T \in \{P, S, U, R, C\}$ (e.g., all elements of $\diagup_P$ are connected to person entities),*
- $G^i_\Psi := (A \cup \diamond, \{(n1, n2) \in \diagup^+ | n_1, n_2 \in A \cup \diamond\})$ *is the inner subgraph of Ψ, which is derived from Ψ after removing all resource entities and connected edges. Note that G^i_Ψ only includes resource and history connectors.*

Based on Definition 3, we can specify correctness criteria for RALph. In particular, we specify whether or not a RAL graph is well-formed as follows.

Definition 4 (Well-formed RAL Graph). *Let* $PM = (A, G, E, D, .\neg, \nearrow)$ *be a process model (cf. Definition 1) and let* $\Psi = (P, S, U, R, C, \diamond, \nearrow, \nearrow, \circ\nearrow, \circ\bullet, lbl, hr, hs, \sigma)$ *be a RAL graph for* PM *(cf. Definition 2). Then,* Ψ *is* well-formed, *iff each of the following constraints holds:*

C1: Resource entities must be either labeled or be target of a data-driven connector; i.e., $\forall n \in P \cup S \cup U \cup R \cup C$ *exactly one of the following conditions must be* true:
- $lbl(n) \neq \epsilon$,
- $\exists(f, n) \in \circ\nearrow$.

C2: Data-driven connectors must be always labeled; i.e., $\forall d \in \circ\nearrow : lbl(d) \neq \epsilon$,

C3: Resource entities must not be target of more than one data-driven connector; i.e., $\forall n \in P \cup S \cup U \cup R : |\{e \in \circ\nearrow | e = (f, n)\}| \leq 1$

C4: There exists no cycle of history connectors; i.e., G_Ψ^i *is acyclic.*

Note that Definition 4 does only ensure that a RAL Graph itself is well-formed. However, the interplay of sequence flow, information flow and resource assignments might cause other errors. Further, note that the italic labels in square brackets on the organizational units *ward* and *laboratory* in Fig. 4 constitute comments that are only used to ease understanding. Therefore, they are not part of the RAL graph; i.e., for both, labeling function *lbl* returns the empty string ϵ (cf. C1 in Definition 4).

4   RALph Semantics

We provide RALph with a well-defined semantics to enable its automated analysis and verification. In particular, we establish a semantic mapping to an existing textual resource assignment language called RAL [5]. RAL presents the following advantages: (i) It is expressive regarding the types of resource selection conditions that can be defined; (ii) It is independent of any BP modelling language; and (iii) Its semantics are well-defined, which enables automated analyses of RAL expressions [5]. In addition, RAL's syntax is close to natural language to improve its readability. In the following, we textually describe the resource assignments for some activities[2] of the running example (cf. Fig. 4) together with the expressions that define them in RAL.

Release patient. The patient is released by the physician who examined her.

    IS ANY PERSON responsible for ACTIVITY Examine patient

Make appointment. An appointment is made by checking availability with a delegate of the ward physician.

    CAN HAVE WORK DELEGATED BY POSITION Ward physician

Prepare examination. The required examination is prepared by a nurse of the ward indicated in the request form.

---

[2] Due to space limitations, we have selected a representative subset of assignments.

```
(HAS POSITION NURSE) AND (HAS UNIT IN DATA FIELD Appointment.Ward)
```

In the following, we define the mapping of RALph to RAL as a mapping function $\mu : A \longrightarrow RALExpr$ that maps the resource assignment specified by RALph to any activity $a \in A$ to a RAL expression. However, we first must introduce three auxiliary mappings, namely: η, ρ and ρ_n

The label mapping function $\eta : P \cup S \cup U \cup R \longrightarrow \mathcal{L} \cup \mathcal{L}_D$ maps each resource entity to either its label or the data field that specify its name. $\mathcal{L}_D$ is the set obtained as the result of prefixing IN DATA FIELD to all $l \in \mathcal{L}$. Specifically, for all $x \in P \cup S \cup U \cup R$:

- $lbl(x) \neq \epsilon \Rightarrow \eta(x) = lbl(x)$
- $\exists(o, x) \in \sigma^{\nearrow} \Rightarrow \eta(x) = $ IS PERSON IN DATA FIELD $lbl(o, x)$

The resource selection condition mapping function $\rho : \nearrow^+ \longrightarrow RALExpr$ maps resource selection conditions specified by RALph connectors to RAL expressions. Specifically:

- $\forall(o, p) \in \nearrow_P \Rightarrow \rho(o, p) = $ IS $\eta(p)$
- $\forall(o, s) \in \nearrow_S \Rightarrow \rho(o, s) = $ HAS POSITION $\eta(s)$
- $\forall(o, r) \in \nearrow_R$:
    - $\exists(r, u) \in \nearrow, u \in U \Rightarrow \rho(o, r) = $ HAS ROLE $\eta(r)$ IN UNIT $\eta(u)$
    - Otherwise, $\rho(o, r) = $ HAS ROLE $\eta(r)$
- $\forall(o, u) \in \nearrow_U, o \notin R \Rightarrow \rho(o, u) = $ HAS UNIT $\eta(u)$
- $\forall(o, c) \in \nearrow_C \Rightarrow \rho(o, c) = $ HAS CAPABILITY $lbl(s)$
- $\forall(o, s) \in \nearrow$, then:
    - $hr(o, s) = (d, rep) \Rightarrow \rho(o, s) = $ DIRECTLY REPORTS TO POSITION s
    - $hr(o, s) = (t, rep) \Rightarrow \rho(o, s) = $ REPORTS TO POSITION s
    - $hr(o, s) = (t, del) \Rightarrow \rho(o, s) = $ CAN DELEGATE WORK TO POSITION s
- $\forall(o, a) \in \sigma^{\bullet}$, then:
    - $hr(o, a) = s \Rightarrow \rho(o, a) = $ IS ANY PERSON responsible for ACTIVITY a
    - $hr(o, a) = p \Rightarrow \rho(o, a) = $ IS ANY PERSON responsible for ACTIVITY a IN ANOTHER INSTANCE
    - $hr(o, a) = sp \Rightarrow \rho(o, a) = $ IS ANY PERSON responsible for ACTIVITY a IN ANY INSTANCE
    - $hr(o, a) = \{t_1, t_2\}, \{t_1, t_2\} \in \mathcal{T} \Rightarrow \rho(o, a) = $ IS ANY PERSON responsible for ACTIVITY a FROM t_1 TO t_2
- $\forall(o, \diamond) \in \nearrow \Rightarrow \rho(o, \diamond) = (\rho_n(\diamond, x_1))$ OR ... OR $(\rho_n(\diamond, x_n))$, for all $(\diamond, x_i) \in \nearrow^+$ with $1 \leq i \leq n$.

The negation mapping function $\rho_n : \nearrow^+ \longrightarrow RALExpr$ extends mapping function ρ by taking negations into account. Specifically, $\forall(o, x) \in \nearrow^+$:

- $\sigma(o, x) = \neg \Rightarrow \rho_n(o, x) = $ NOT $(\rho(o, x))$
- $\sigma(o, x) = 1 \Rightarrow \rho_n(o, x) = \rho(o, x)$

Finally, since RALph applies an AND-semantics for all resource selection conditions defined for an activity, the mapping of RALph to RAL $\mu : A \longrightarrow RALExpr$ can be defined as follows: $\mu(a) = (\rho_n(a, x_1))$ AND ... AND $(\rho_n(a, x_n))$, for all $(a, x_i) \in \nearrow^+$ with $1 \leq i \leq n$.

5   Evaluation

The evaluation of RALph described below is two-fold. On the one hand, we assess its expressive power using the workflow resource patterns as evaluation framework. On the other hand, its usage with existing BP modelling notations has been tested by integrating it into a platform that uses BPMN for process modelling. Its applicability was already shown in Fig. 4 by modelling the resource assignments defined in the real scenario from Section 2.1.

5.1   Support for the Workflow Resource Patterns

In the following, we describe how RALph covers all the creation patterns, which were used for the evaluation of existing approaches in Section 2.3:

- *Direct Allocation.* Connection of resource entity Person to an activity.
- *Role-Based Allocation.* Connection of resource entity Role to an activity.
- *Deferred Allocation.* Connection of a data object to any resource entity with a data-driven connector: e.g., for activities *Prepare examination*, *Take sample* and *Analyse sample* (cf. Fig. 4), the organisational unit is indicated in a data field. In particular, the value of the data field selected is only known at run time.
- *Separation of duties.* Connection of two activities with a history connector, which indicates that the activity instances belong to the same BP instance, and crossing it out to indicate it is a negated assignment. For example, it is expressed like the assignments for activities *Release patient, Inform about risks* and *Send sample* (cf. Fig. 4) but using a negated connector instead of the simple one.
- *Case Handling.* To implement this pattern with RALph, we should specify a separation of duties for all the activities of a process.

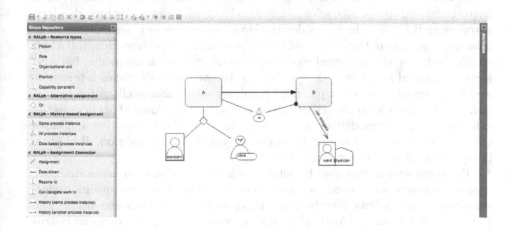

Fig. 5. RALph web–based editor

- *Retain Familiar.* Connection of two activities with a history connector that indicates that the activity instances belong to the same BP instance: e.g., activities *Release patient* and *Inform about risks* (cf. Fig. 4) have a binding of duties with activity *Examine patient.*
- *Capability-Based Allocation.* Connection of a capability entity to an activity.
- *History-Based Allocation.* Connection of two activities with a history connector that indicates that the referenced activity belongs to (i) the same or any previous BP instance, (ii) a previous BP instance, or (iii) any BP instance executed within a specific period of time.
- *Organisational Allocation.* Connection of resource entity Position to an activity, e.g. in activities *Examine patient* and *Make diagnosis* of Fig. 4.

5.2   Implementation

We provide a graphical editor for RALph diagrams at http://www.isa.us.es/cristal. This editor is based on Oryx [22], which is an open–source platform to build web–based diagram editors. Oryx provides native support for several graphical notations such as BPMN, and allows for the definition of new graphical notations by means of the so–called *stencil sets*. Consequently, RALph has been implemented as an Oryx stencil set that extends the Oryx–native BPMN stencil set with the symbols described in this paper. Figure 5 depicts a screenshot of RALph web–based editor.

6   Conclusions and Future Work

In this paper we have introduced RALph, a graphical notation for defining resource assignments in BP models. RALph is more expressive than existing approaches. Specifically, it deals with real selection conditions as discovered, e.g., in the healthcare domain. Furthermore, it provides support for all the creation patterns related to resource selection. It also has formal semantics provided by a mapping to RAL [5], which uses description logics as semantic formalism and as a means to automate the analysis of the BP resource perspective. Hence, RALph enables not only the graphical representation of resource assignments, but also their automated analysis at design time to discover inconsistencies a-priori, as well as at run time to detect potential problems with resource allocation (e.g., a lack of performers for some activity given previous allocations). This bridges the existing gap in BP modelling notations for the resource perspective and eases the way resources are handled by non-technical users. In addition, RALph is independent of any BP modelling notation.

There are several directions for future work. First, we want to assess RALph's expressive power with more use cases. Second, we want to evaluate its understandability and learnability by conducting experiments with end users. The Physics of Notations by Moody [23] with the corresponding measurement instrument by Figl et al. [24] provide the basis for that work. Finally, we want to extend the notation to be able to consider several degrees of responsibilities for a process activity beyond the resource responsible for its execution (i.e., the performer of the work). For instance, there may be a resource in charge of approving the work performed, or there may be resources that must be informed when the activity has been completed (cf. the Generic Human Roles defined in BPEL4People [19] and RACI matrices [25]). For these involvements, it should also be possible to specify resource selection conditions.

References

1. Dumas, M., Rosa, M.L., Mendling, J., Reijers, H.A.: Fundamentals of Business Process Management. Springer (2013)
2. Whittle, J., Hutchinson, J., Rouncefield, M.: The State of Practice in Model-Driven Engineering. IEEE Software **31**(3), 79–85 (2014)
3. OMG, BPMN 2.0. Recommendation, OMG (2011)
4. van der Aalst, W.M.P., ter Hofstede, A.H.M.: YAWL: Yet Another Workflow Language. Inf. Syst. **30**(4), 245–275 (2005)
5. Cabanillas, C., Resinas, M., Cortés, A.R.: Specification and Automated Design-Time Analysis of the Business Process Human Resource Perspective. Inf. Syst. (in press, 2015)
6. Strembeck, M., Mendling, J.: Modeling process-related RBAC models with extended UML activity models. Inf. Softw. Technol. **53**, 456–483 (2011)
7. Russell, N., ter Hofstede, A., Edmond, D., van der Aalst, W.M.P.: Workflow resource patterns. In: Tech. Rep., BETA, WP 127. Eindhoven Univ. of Tech (2004)
8. Konyen, I., Reichert, M., Schultheiss, B.: Prozessentwurf eines ablaufs im labor. In: Tech. Rep. Ulm University (1996)
9. Semmelrodt, F.: Modellierung klinischer Prozesse und Compliance Regeln mittels BPMN 2.0 und eCRG. Master's thesis, University of Ulm (2013)
10. Koschmider, A., Yingbo, L., Schuster, T.: Role assignment in business process models. In: Daniel, F., Barkaoui, K., Dustdar, S. (eds.) BPM Workshops 2011, Part I. LNBIP, vol. 99, pp. 37–49. Springer, Heidelberg (2012)
11. van der Aalst, W.M.P., Kumar, A.: A Reference Model for Team-enabled Workflow Management Systems. Data Knowl. Eng. **38**(3), 335–363 (2001)
12. Bertino, E., Ferrari, E., Atluri, V.: The specification and enforcement of authorization constraints in workflow management systems. ACM Trans. Inf. Syst. Secur. **2**, 65–104 (1999)
13. Stepien, B., Felty, A., Matwin, S.: A non-technical user-oriented display notation for XACML conditions. In: Babin, G., Kropf, P., Weiss, M. (eds.) E-Technologies: Innovation in an Open World. LNBIP, vol. 26, pp. 53–64. Springer, Heidelberg (2009)
14. van der Aalst, W.: Formalization and verification of event-driven process chains. Information and Software Technology **41**(10), 639–650 (1999)
15. Ferraiolo, D.F., et al.: Proposed NIST standard for role-based access control. ACM Trans. Inf. Syst. Secur. **4**, 224–274 (2001)
16. Wolter, C., Schaad, A.: Modeling of task-based authorization constraints in BPMN. In: Alonso, G., Dadam, P., Rosemann, M. (eds.) BPM 2007. LNCS, vol. 4714, pp. 64–79. Springer, Heidelberg (2007)
17. Awad, A., Grosskopf, A., Meyer, A., Weske, M.: Enabling resource assignment constraints in BPMN. In: Tech. Rep., BPT (2009)

18. Stroppi, L.J.R., Chiotti, O., Villarreal, P.D.: A BPMN 2.0 extension to define the resource perspective of business process models. In: CIbS 2011 (2011)
19. WS-BPEL Extension for People (BPEL4People). In: Tech. Rep., OASIS (2009)
20. Adams, M.: YAWL v2.3-User Manual (2012)
21. Semmelrodt, F., Knuplesch, D., Reichert, M.: Modeling the resource perspective of business process compliance rules with the extended compliance rule graph. In: Bider, I., Gaaloul, K., Krogstie, J., Nurcan, S., Proper, H.A., Schmidt, R., Soffer, P. (eds.) BPMDS 2014 and EMMSAD 2014. LNBIP, vol. 175, pp. 48–63. Springer, Heidelberg (2014)
22. Decker, G., Overdick, H., Weske, M.: Oryx – an open modeling platform for the BPM community. In: Dumas, M., Reichert, M., Shan, M.-C. (eds.) BPM 2008. LNCS, vol. 5240, pp. 382–385. Springer, Heidelberg (2008)
23. Moody, D.L.: The Physics of Notations: Toward a Scientific Basis for Constructing Visual Notations in Software Engineering. IEEE Trans. Software Eng. **35**(6), 756–779 (2009)
24. Figl, K., Recker, J., Mendling, J.: A study on the effects of routing symbol design on process model comprehension. Decision Support Systems **54**(2), 1104–1118 (2013)
25. Smith, M., Erwin, J., Diaferio, S.: Role and responsibility charting (RACI). In: Project Management Forum (PMForum) (2005)

Revising the Vocabulary of Business Process Element Labels

Agnes Koschmider[1(✉)], Meike Ullrich[1], Antje Heine[2], and Andreas Oberweis[1]

[1] Institute AIFB, Karlsruhe Institute of Technology, Karlsruhe, Germany
{agnes.koschmider,meike.ullrich,andreas.oberweis}@kit.edu
[2] Institut für Deutsche Philologie, Ernst-Moritz-Arndt-Universität,
Greifswald, Germany
antje.heine@uni-greifswald.de

Abstract. A variety of methods devoted to the behavior analysis of business process models has been suggested, which diminish the task of inspecting the correctness of the model by the process modeler. Although a correct behavior has been attested, the process model might still not be feasible because the modeler or intended user is hampered in her comprehension (and thus hesitates e.g., to reuse the process model). This paper addresses the improvement of comprehension of process element labels by revising their vocabulary. Process element labels are critical for an appropriate association between the symbol instance and the real world. If users do not (fully) understand the process element labels, an improper notion of the real process might arise. To improve the comprehension of element labels algorithms are presented, which base on common hints how to effectively recognize written words. Results from an empirical study indicate a preference for such revised process element labels.

1 Introduction

The labeling of business process model elements is still a mainly manual task and requires a great deal of experience of the process modeler. Highly skilled process modelers tend to find easier (and better) labels for process model elements than modeling beginners, who also might omit activities or might have problems to find an appropriate abstraction level for activities [1]. Process element labels are critical for an appropriate association between the symbol instance and the real world [2]. If users do not (fully) understand the process element labels, an improper notion of the real process might arise. Assigning unambiguous label names to process elements is a challenging task, particularly because process modelers are usually not experts in linguistics.

This paper presents algorithms that revise the vocabulary of process model element labels, which should increase the comprehension of the business process model. The algorithms are founded on effects from word recognition, which we applied to business process models, and also empirical results studying vocabulary preferences of process element labels. Figure 1 gives an overview of our approach. Exemplarily, the vocabulary revision algorithms should be applied on the business process model "handle exam results" (see the **input** business process

© Springer International Publishing Switzerland 2015
J. Zdravkovic et al. (Eds.): CAiSE 2015, LNCS 9097, pp. 69–83, 2015.
DOI: 10.1007/978-3-319-19069-3_5

model). Initially, the labels are extracted and segmented according to their part-of-speech (e.g., noun, verb) using a tagger. Additionally, structural information of the process element label[1] is stored (i.e., the position, the predecessor(s) and successor(s) of the label)[2]. The tagger also derives morphosyntactic information of labels (i.e., case, genus). After tagging, the labels are checked with respect to their linguistic fitness based upon a dictionary and/or on a domain ontology. The results of this analysis are linguistically revised process activity labels. Also no cleansing of the vocabulary might be required (if no indication for improvement is given) and the original label remains unchanged. The algorithms presented in

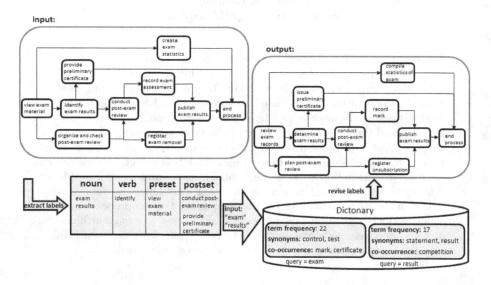

Fig. 1. Process of revising the vocabulary of process element labels

this paper are based on the following methodological foundation. To understand how the vocabulary of labels might be improved, we checked effects from word recognition, which give hints how to efficiently recognize written words. These effects are explained in Section 2. Linguists are well-versed in applying these effects and therefore, we asked linguistics students to revise labels for exemplary business process models, which was part of a first empirical study. To benchmark the linguistic suggestions and to see whether users prefer the linguistically revised vocabulary, we performed a second empirical study with business process modelers. Both studies are summarized in Section 3. The algorithms for vocabulary revision are described in Section 4. The implementation of our approach is given in Section 5. Implications and limitations are discussed in Section 6. The

---

[1] The revision algorithms works on a process activity graph of business process models. The output of activities (e.g., places, events) are not considered since they use the same vocabulary but with a different grammatical conjugation.

[2] Note that the information of one activity label is stored within one row in order to keep the linguistic information.

add-on of our contribution is compared with related approaches in Section 7. Finally, the paper ends with a summary and an outlook.

2 Effects in Word Recognition

Process element labels are a concatenation of words. Frequently, a verb-noun style (e.g., initiate registration) is used to label process model elements. Common labeling styles are also a deverbalized-noun + "of" + noun (e.g., evaluation of flights), a noun + deverbalized-noun (flight evaluation) or a gerund + noun (e.g., evaluating flights). Additionally, descriptives (e.g., by officer) or further part of speech (e.g., adjectives) can be used to label the process element[3]. Several effects have been identified in word recognition, which impact the access to words:

- *word frequency effect*: more often used (common) words are recognized more quickly in a text than less common words [3].
- *neighborhood frequency effect*: words are processed more slowly (errors can occur) when the neighboring words are orthographically similar to the stimulus word [4]. A further impact on this effect was found, which confirms that the existence of higher frequency neighbors facilitates processing of the stimulus word [5].
- *neighborhood size effect*: large neighborhood facilitates access for low-frequency words [5].

The word frequency effect is applied to process activity labels through assessing the *relative word frequency* of lexemes[4] of the original noun in a text corpus, a glossary or a domain ontology. The word frequency effect is also considered by determining an appropriate *collocation* of verbs and nouns[5]. Neighborhood frequency and size effects are addressed by the revision of the neighborhood of process activity labels. Each process activity has a direct dir_N and indirect ind_N neighborhood. Process activities, which directly precede (preset) or directly succeed (postset) a process activity are part of the direct neighborhood. Indirect neighbors are all remaining process elements of the business process model. The corresponding linguistic concepts that inspect the neighborhood are *co-occurrence* and *lexical field*. We consider co-occurrence as cohesion quality that is determined by mathematical and statistical computation and the results are to be interpreted. Lexical field is useful for the inspection of distinct activities of direct neighbors of a process activity label. Figure 2 applies exemplarily for the label "identify exam results" the four linguistic concepts. The term "exam

---

[3] The algorithms presented in Section 4 are implemented and tested for labels in German language. Terms discussed in this paper were translated to English by ourselves. The respective implications are discussed in Section 6.

[4] Particularly, we consider lexemes, which are in a synonym or hierarchical relationship (i.e., hypernyms, hyponyms), and lexemes, which belong to the same part of speech and have at least one common feature and thus belong to the same lexical field.

[5] Collocations are combinations of words that are preferred over other combinations that otherwise appear to be semantically equivalent [6].

result" is a compound, which however does not occur as one single term in the text corpus. Therefore, it is segmented into two terms, which are recognized as nouns by the tagger. Lexemes of the noun "exam" are "examination" (with rel. frequency of 12.5), "control" (with rel. frequency of 19) and "exam" (with rel. frequency of 22). Lexemes of the noun "result" are "report" (with rel. frequency of 11), "statement" (with rel. frequency of 9) and "result" (with rel. frequency of 17). Assume that terms with the highest word frequency are further considered. This means that "exam result" does not require any revision and remains "exam result" (both terms have the highest rel. word frequency among their lexemes). Verbs that occur near the term "exam results"[6] and are of the same lexical field than the verb "identify" are "calculate" (with rel. frequency of 7), measure (with rel. frequency of 10) and "determine" (with rel. frequency of 11). The collocator with the highest word frequency is "determine", which means that the original verb "identify" is replaced by "determine". For instance, a verb, which is not considered as collocator, is "initiate" because the verb does not belong to the same lexical field (i.e., is not a synonym of the input verb). Frequently the terms "certificate" and "class" cooccur with the term "exam", which means, it is checked whether exactly these terms are used in the business process model. If their synonyms were found then a replacement is performed (replacement of synonyms by the proper terms from the co-occurrence analysis). In the context

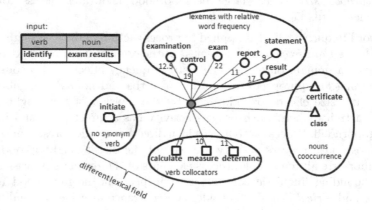

Fig. 2. Concepts used for revision of vocabulary

of an empirical study we asked students of German linguistics to revise process activity labels bearing in mind the four linguistic concepts. The intention of the study was to inspect the validity of the linguistic concepts. Subsequently, process modelers bench-marked the revised process activity labels. The results of the studies are presented in the next section.

---

[6] In case of compounds appropriate collocators are searched first for the second noun since the second noun is the primary word that refines the first noun.

3   Results from a Two-Stage Study

In the first stage of the study (run in December 2013), Bachelor students of German linguistics at the University of Greifswald had to revise the process activity labels of two business process models. The background qualifying the students to take part in the study is their attendance of a seminar of corpus linguistics. The first process model to revise was "handle and review exams", which should have been familiar to the students since all of them already should have passed through an exam. The second process model was the ITIL process "Incident Management", which should have been unfamiliar to the students. The process models were not designed with a particular modeling language. The students received an introduction to business process models and both process models were explained. Participants were free to answer the questions. The motivation to answer the questionnaire was a learning effect for the exam. To measure the understandability of the original process activity labels we used the perceived ease of use (PEOU) measure [7]. Prior to revision, the students were asked to complete on a Likert 5 point scale to each business process model the statement "It was easy for me to understand the meaning of the business process model".

Finally, we received 44 questionnaires, collected the suggestions in a spreadsheet file and applied a sorting for the suggestions. The revision suggestions were sorted according to identical names and identical labeling style. We observed that the participants mainly followed a verb-noun style (e.g., mark exam), which was also the predominant labeling style of the original process models. Also a deverbalized-noun+"of"+noun style (e.g., registration of students) was used. We observed that the deverbalized-noun+"of"+noun labeling style was used if the verb of the original activity label was unusual and instead a synonym noun was found to be more common (e.g., prevent problem → analysis of problems)[7]. Due to numerous domain-specific expressions in the ITIL process model, the students had difficulties (compared to the improvement of the "handle and review exams" process) to revise the labels. The suggestions for labels of the ITIL process model were less effective (i.e., we received a lower number of revision suggestions than for the other more understandable process model). The difficulty of revising the process activity labels of the ITIL process model is also indicated in the degree of the understandability measure. The cumulative frequency for PEOU of the original "handle and review exams" process model (judged by the students) is 38.46% for strong agree and agree, 38.46% for neutral and 23.1% for disagree and strong disagree. The cumulative frequency for PEOU of the original ITIL process model is 14.28% for strong agree and agree, 42.85% for neutral and 42.86% for disagree and strong disagree. These values indicate that more participants found the original "handle and review exams" process model easier to understand. For the ITIL process model it was vice versa.

In the second phase of the empirical study (run in February till April 2014) 49 process modeling beginners (graduates) and experts from different European

---

[7] An analysis in a German text corpus also indicates a higher relative frequency for the noun "analysis" ("Analyse") vs. "prevent" ("vorbeugen").

universities and research-driven institutes bench-marked the label suggestions in a paper-based questionnaire. The questionnaire was splitted up in group A and group B[8] and the participants had to indicate for each process model variant (original and revised labels) "It was easy for me to understand the meaning of the process elements" and to give a preference for a process model variant. The split into two groups should avoid crossover effects. The PEOU measures for the revised "handle and review exams" process model for group A are 87.2% and for group B 100.0% for strong agree and agree. The PEOU measures for the revised ITIL process model for group A is 77.9% and for group B 91.7% for strong agree and agree. These results mean that the revised process models were highly understandable for the respondents. To determine the degree of agreement (consensus) among interviewees of group A (beginners and experts) we used the Cohens Kappa coefficient. The coefficient has the value of 0.71, which indicates a good agreement among the interviewees. Thus, the understandability of process activity labels does not depend on modeling experiences. After reviewing the original process model versus the revised process model, the participants judged the usefulness of the process models against each other. Group A received first the original process model followed by the revised process model. Group B received the process models in a reversed order. Table 1 shows the statistical results for group A (left hand side) and Group B (right hand side). The process modelers preferred the revised "handle and review exams" process model over the original process model while the original ITIL process model was preferred over the revised ITIL process model by both groups. The conclusion from the

Table 1. Statistical test results for the process modeler preferences

Usefulness	$Mean_A$	St.Dev.	t-value	p	$Mean_B$	St.Dev.	t-value	p
$exam_o$ vs. $exam_r$	43.46	27.27	9.9526	< 0.0001	44.54	20.88	7.9815	< 0.0001
$exam_r$ vs. $exam_o$	69.23	26.32	16.4263	< 0.0001	67.27	24.52	10.2651	< 0.0001
$ITIL_o$ vs. $ITIL_r$	80.0	16.32	30.6127	< 0.0001	71.0	26.69	9.9535	< 0.0001
$ITIL_r$ vs. $ITIL_o$	38.18	17.99	13.2537	< 0.0001	50.96	25.0	7.627	< 0.0001

two-stage study is that the application of effects from word recognition impacts the understandability and users also prefer linguistically superior labels. This assumption was observed for process models where no domain specific vocabulary was used. Therefore, when a common vocabulary is used it might be sufficient to access standard language dictionaries in order to revise the vocabulary. For domain dependent labels a domain ontology or a glossary is recommended in order to provide better suggestions for the revision of the vocabulary.

4   Revision Algorithm for the Vocabulary of Labels

Based on these findings from the study revision algorithms were designed.

---

[8] 37 persons (19 beginners, 18 advanced) answered the group A questionnaire. 12 persons (12 advanced) answered the group B questionnaire.

4.1   Preliminary Steps

Before the revision can be initiated, three preliminary steps are necessary. Firstly, a part-of-speech tagging (POS tagging) must be applied in order to assign parts of speech (e.g., noun, verb) to each term in the label [8]. The tagger should work on a data and tag set, which consider peculiarities of the language in use[9]. The part-of-speech assignment allows to categorize labels to a labeling style (i.e., verb-noun style, deverbalized-noun +"of"+ noun, noun + deverbalized-noun, gerund + noun). Secondly, process activities with labels using one or more composition operators (i.e. here: *and*, *or*) are decomposed into several atomic activities. The decomposition for the composition operator *and* is illustrated in Figure 3. The same holds for the decomposition of a process activity whose

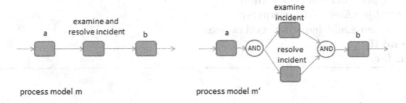

Fig. 3. Excerpt of a process model *m* before (left) and after preprocessing transformation into model *m'* (right)

label contains the composition *or*. Such labels are decomposed into two (or more) process activities with the routing element XOR or possibly AND (this is case dependent). Thirdly, it is required to determine the subject area of the business process model. This step prevents that synonyms of higher relative word frequency but different subject area (e.g., a synonym of the term "exam" with higher word frequency is "monastery", which however does not fit in the context of exam) are considered as appropriate candidates. The algorithm determining the subject area is as follows (see Algorithm 1). All nouns of the business process model are extracted and the hypernyms for each noun are determined. The subject area corresponds to the most frequently found hypernym(s). Finally, all lexemes of the most frequently given hypernym(s) are extracted (this step is required for Algorithm 2).

4.2   Revision Algorithms

Based upon these preliminary steps, revision algorithms depending on the labeling style are executed (see Algorithm 2). The process of each algorithm is to analyze the noun(s) of the label (Step 1), subsequently the verbs undergo an analysis (Step 2). Finally, the vocabulary of the neighborhood of process activities is inspected, which might result in a further revision of the vocabulary of the label (Step 3).

---

[9] For instance, compounds are in the German language composite terms, which must be segmented to single terms by the tagger.

Algorithm 1. Algorithm to determine the subject area

```
1: input: ProcessModel model;
2: output: List subjectArea, List lexemes;
3: List elements = model.extractElements(); CountList hypernyms;
4: for all element: elements do
5:     for all noun: element.getNouns() do
6:         for all hypernym: noun.getHypernyms() do
7:             hypernyms.add(hypernym);
8:         end for
9:     end for
10: end for
11: List subjectArea; List lexemes;
12: for all hypernym: hypernym do
13:     if hypernym.count() > 1 then
14:         subjectArea.add(hypernym);
15:         lexemes.add(hypernym.getLexemes());
16:     end if
17: end for
```

Step 1 of the vocabulary revision is identical for the four labeling styles, which is to determine the lexemes of each noun[10] with its relative word frequency. The algorithm extracts lexemes, which belong to same part of speech and have at least one common feature (e.g., synonyms or hierarchical relationship). A combination frequency is checked for compounds using co-occurrence (i.e., which lexemes of a compound are often combined with each other). Next, intersections between the extracted lexemes of each noun and the lexemes of the subject area (hypernym(s)) are determined. Lexemes of intersection with high relative word frequency are considered as potential candidates. Lexemes, which do not intersect the subject area and are part of compounds, are selected based upon the relative word frequency. All candidates are collected within a list.

Step 2 of the revision algorithm depends on the labeling style. Given a verb-noun style (see Algorithm 2), verb collocators are determined. It is searched for verbs, which are often combined with the candidate noun(s) and which are in the lexical field (e.g., synonyms) of the original verb as well. The collocator with the highest relative word frequency is considered as candidate. As subsequent step the algorithm checks if the verb candidates perform a distinct action to its neighborhood process activities. Particularly, the direct neighborhood dir_N is considered (see Section 2). When revising the vocabulary of process activities, it should be taken into account that process activities in the preset and postset should perform distinct actions. The lexical field theory [9] is applied for this purpose. For each process activity it is inspected if nouns of process activities in the direct neighborhood are synonyms or belong to identical lexical field. If so, then the verb collocator must be of different lexical field. Note that the structural

---

[10] All nouns of the element labels and compounds were already extracted and segmented into single terms (see preliminary steps).

transformation shown in Figure 3 does not affect the vocabulary analysis in terms of dir_N as $b_m\bullet = a$ and $b_{m'}\bullet = A$ and $\bullet c_m = a$ and $\bullet c_{m'} = A$ where $A = \{a_1, ..., a_n\}$[11]. An indirect neighborhood ind_N of a process activity includes all process activities that precede and succeed a process activity without its direct neighborhood. ind_N is used to revise the process activity label with respect to the linguistic concept of co-occurrence. For each original noun a co-occurrence analysis is performed based upon a matching of terms of occurrence.

Algorithm 2. Algorithm to revise the vocabulary of verb-noun style labels

---

1: input: ProcessElement element;
2: output: ProcessElement elementRevised;
3: List dir_{Ns} = element.getDir$_{Ns}$();
4: List collocators = element.getVerb().getCollocators();
5: Collocator candidate = collocators.selectBestCandidate();
6: **for all** $dir_N : dir_{Ns}$ **do**
7:    **if**
      (isSynonym(dir_N.getVerb(),element.getVerb()) OR
      identicalLexicalField(dir_N.getVerb(),element.getVerb()) AND
      differentLexicalField(dir_N.getVerb(),candidate) **then**
8:       elementRevised = candidate;
9:    **else**
10:       elementRevised = element;
11:    **end if**
12: **end for**

The algorithm to revise the vocabulary of a deverbalized-noun+of+noun style works as described in the following[12]. Here, the collocator is a deverbalized noun instead of a verb. After extracting the lexemes of the noun, lexemes of the deverbalized noun are determined. Subsequently, the combination of deverbalized noun + revised noun is compared versus revised noun + verb collocators of the same lexical field as the deverbalized noun (based upon rel. word frequency). The combination with the highest relative word frequency is selected. This algorithm is also applied for a noun+deverbalized-noun and a gerund+noun labeling style. The next section applies the algorithms for the input business process model in Figure 1.

4.3   Application of the Algorithms

Consider the input business process model in Figure 1. Initially, a part-of-speech tagging is applied and the labeling style "verb-noun" has been identified 10 or 11

---

[11] $\bullet x$ is called *preset*, which is the set of all preceding activities. $x\bullet$ is called *postset*, which is the set of all succeeding activities.

[12] Due to space restrictions we do not include pseudo code for this algorithm in this paper. However we plan to publish both source code and used data set online in the near future, in order to support the repeatability of our scientific work.

times respectively. The process activity "organize and check post-exam review" is decomposed into the process activities "organize post-exam review" and "check post-exam review" (after decomposition the verb-noun labeling style is used 11 times). The parts of speech are stored within rows of a table additionally with the labels of dir_N. Nouns of the considered business process model are "exam material", "exam review", "exam result", "certificate", "exam statistics", "exam assessment", "exam removal" and "process". The subject area is determined by the most frequently used noun in this list, which is "exam". Subsequently, hypernyms of the term "exam" are determined. Next, lexemes (hypernyms, hyponyms and synonyms) of the four hypernyms of "exam" are extracted. The results are shown in Table 2. Hypernyms and lexemes of the subject area are used when

Table 2. Hypernyms and lexemes of the subject area term

most frequently used noun (subject area)	hypernyms	lexemes
exam	control, performance test, test, examination	control, performance test, test, examination, written test, exam, examination, exercise, inquiry, evaluation, study, assessment, activity, process.

intersections between the lexemes of each original noun and the lexemes of the subject area (hypernym(s)) are determined. Prior to this step it is required to extract the lexemes of each original noun with its relative word frequency. Table 3 shows this process for an excerpt of nouns. In case of compounds it is checked

Table 3. Suggestions for input nouns of process model in Figure 1

$noun_{orig}$	lexemes	comparison	$l_{intersec}$	$noun_{new}$
(exam) material	material (7.2), records (9.0), documentation (11.1), evidence (4.5), proof (3.5), paper (9.7)	exam - material (7.2), exam - records (11.2), exam - documentation (10.7)	-	(exam) record
certificate	certificate (10.0), testimonial (5.5), letter of reference (4.3), credentials (2.7), attestation (9.3), report (10.2)	-	-	report

whether and which lexemes frequently co-occur. For instance, the terms "exam" and "record" are more frequently combined than "exam" and "material". The new noun of a label is the term, which is most frequently used and is in the range of the subject area. Lexemes of the terms "material" and "certificate" do not intersect with lexemes of the subject area. Therefore, a selection is done based upon the relative word frequency.

Subsequently, verb collocators are determined. Exemplarily, verb collocators for the term "certificate" (the label is "provide preliminary certificate"), which are in the lexical field of the verb "provide" are "issue" (with rel. word frequency of 14.2), "acquire" (with rel. word frequency of 6.2), "prepare" (with rel. word frequency of 10.1) and "provide" (with rel. word frequency of 2.1). Since "issue" has the highest relative word frequency, it is considered as a better verb collocator than "provide". After improving the collocators for all labels, the verbs of dir_N of a label are inspected. Label of dir_N of the label "issue preliminary certificate" are "determine exam results" and "end process". Since the nouns "certificate", "exam results" and "process" are not synonyms of each other, no further consideration is required. Finally, a co-occurrence analysis is performed. Figure 4 shows individual co-occurrence graphs for the terms "exam" and "result" to visualize terms of occurrence.

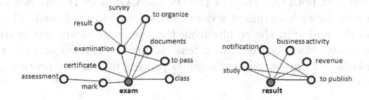

Fig. 4. co-occurrence graphs

Nouns frequently used with the term "exam" are "certificate", "class", "document", "examination" and "mark". The revision algorithms suggested to replace the term "certificate" by "report" (due to the higher rel. word frequency). Since the term "certificate" is more frequently used with the term "exam", the term "certificate" is overwritten and is the candidate term.

5   Implementation and Analysis

The revision of the vocabulary of process activity labels has been implemented for the German language and a verb-noun labeling style. However, we do not expect that significant extensions are required to make the algorithms suitable for the English language. In contrast, the high frequency of morphological compounding in the German language makes finding of unknown words more difficult than for the English language [10].

To tag the labels the Stanford POS-Tagger is used. This tagger has been selected due to its high accuracy and its validation on the English and German language [11]. The tagger uses the negra corpus[13] and the STTS tag set[14]. Additionally, a list of German prefix and particle verbs has been created and

---

[13] http://www.coli.uni-saarland.de/projects/sfb378/negra-corpus/negra-corpus.html
[14] http://www.ims.uni-stuttgart.de/forschung/ressourcen/lexika/TagSets/stts-table.html

is applied. Two German corpora are used to revise the vocabulary, which are DWDS[15] and COSMAS II[16]. The subject area of a business process model is derived from the component *OpenThesaurus* of DWDS. This thesaurus suggests synonyms, hypernyms and hyponyms of a query term. Verb collocators are derived through the *word field analysis* component of DWDS. The co-occurrence analysis is performed with COSMAS II. In the current implementation the revision based upon the co-occurrence analysis is done manually by the user. The tool suggests a list of nouns, which might be more appropriate than the revision. Thus, the revision of labels according to the co-occurrence concept depends on the decision of users. In future we plan to integrate machine learning techniques in order to make automatic suggestions based upon user's preferences.

The implementation has been validated on several business process models. We observed that the results clearly depend on the domain specificity of the vocabulary. We manually created a glossary for a set of ITIL process models and observed that both text corpora DWDS and COSMAS II were not suitable in this context. In such a context a domain ontology must be used. The initial analysis results underpin the results from the two-stage study where students of the linguistics acted according to a text corpus like DWDS and the revised process models were preferred over original process models for process models with common terms.

6   Discussion

Implications. From our point of view the revision approach has implications on all approaches that deal with process element labels. For instance, our approach concerns approaches detecting the similarity between process models. Algorithm 1, which determines the subject area of business process models can be used to uncover the semantic field between terms (similarity algorithms searches for semantic fields). Additionally, the revision algorithm might serve as a data cleaning approach before applying any approach for similarity calculation. It searches for similar terms in a context where lexemes of terms were identified and already revised. It is expected that similarity searches are performed more effectively and efficiently. Since linguistically revised process element labels strikes agreement, such a feature should also be integral part of a process modeling tool. This would relieve the process modeler from this manual task.

Limitations. The participants of the first study were linguistic students, which, from our point of view, qualified them revising process activity labels due to their background knowledge in corpus linguistics. However, the involvement of students always raises discussions about the external validity of the results. Although the students were not highly familiar with the process model paradigm (they received an introduction to business process modeling) the number of the highly qualitative suggestions for new process activity labels must be pointed

---

[15] http://www.dwds.de/
[16] www.ids-mannheim.de/cosmas2/

out. The quality was attested by an expert of the linguistics. Thus negative consequences due to the education level of the participants were not observed.

The techniques presented in this paper have been developed for the German language. The high morphological occurrence of terms in the German language makes the application of the revision approach even more difficult than for the English language. For instance, the English language has only few prefixes, which are a common feature in the German language[17]. The frequent usage of compounds in the German language also makes the revision approach more difficult than for the less morphological occurrence of compounds in the English language.

Lastly, the implementation of the revision algorithms is limited by ongoing research in corpus linguistics (e.g., the algorithms to detect homonyms are still not satisfying), which however, point to open research directions that must be tackled in order to improve the quality of business process models. Thus, the topic addressed in this paper also paves the way for additional research.

7   Related Work

Revising the vocabulary of process activity labels impacts the quality of the process element labels and finally of the complete business process model. Related approaches which also address the improvement of process element label quality perform this task by (1) improving the labeling style, or (2) assisting in the labeling of process elements.

Process model elements can be labeled according to several styles, which impact the understandability of the user in a different way. An empirical study of [12] found out that a verb-noun style is the preferable labeling style. Transformation algorithms exist, which convert an improper labeling style to this preferable style [13]. Although the preference for a verb-noun style over, e.g., a deverbalized-noun+"of"+noun style is comprehensible, no vocabulary revision has been performed for the process models used in this study. Our observation in the empirical study summarized in Section 3 was, that the preference for a labeling style highly depends on the familiarity of terms and thus a general recommendation for a verb-noun style might not be maintained. This observation calls for a further empirical study investigating preferences for labeling styles after vocabulary revision.

The second stream of related approaches automates the labeling of process model elements and thus relieves the manual and error-prone task, which is called to decrease label quality. Process model elements might be automatically generated based upon a glossary [14] or the linguistic analysis of process model elements [15]. Process element names are generated in the approach of [14] by a label suggestion component that also incorporates a label checker. The suggestion component works on a glossary being aware of control flow aspects of process models (this also allows to detect control-flow errors during labeling).

---

[17] http://www.bu.edu/isle/files/2012/01/-Stefan-Diemer-Corpus-Linguistics-with-Google.pdf

The glossary is created from a given collection of process models without improving the vocabulary. The approach of [15] makes suggestions for labels based upon the inspection of labels that were gathered from a collection of business process models. Particularly, suggestions for element labels are based on the analysis of holonyms (a word representing the whole of a part-of relation) and hypernyms (a more general word) relationships. The authors propagate their approach for finding element labels for process model abstraction. This is also reasonable due to the limitation of analyzing holonyms and hypernyms. The label repository gathered by [15] might be suitable as foundation for revision techniques suggested in this paper. For instance, relative word frequency count and verb collocation might be used to determine the label with the highest linguistics among all similar labels. Thus, synergies can be found here. A further approach related to the assistance of element labeling is suggested by [16]. This approach detects naming conflicts already during the modeling process using a repository of domain specific vocabulary. The approach of [16] might be complementary when a business process model is described by a domain specific vocabulary. For instance, a glossary or domain ontology might be created from the domain specific repository. A domain ontology supports the revision of domain specific process models.

To sum up, our approach can be considered as a preprocessing step for most of these related approaches that could profit from an adjusted and improved vocabulary since these approaches rely on the labeling of process model elements.

8   Conclusion and Outlook

The revision of the vocabulary of process activity labels is connected with the quality of business process models. Several approaches addressed the quality improvement of process element labels by, for instance, postulating a labeling style, which improves comprehension. This paper suggested the revision of the vocabulary of process element labels as a research step to improve the quality of business process models. Four linguistic concepts were applied to business process elements. These concepts were derived from word recognition effects that give hints how to better recognize written words. Results from an empirical study indicate the validity of these concepts. In the future we plan to incorporate the analysis of all common labeling styles and to perform the analysis for the English language. To finally find determinants of the understandability of process element labels we are also conducting several empirical studies investigating the visual design of element labels (e.g., their textual segmentation).

References

1. Wilmont, I., Brinkkemper, S., van de Weerd, I., Hoppenbrouwers, S.: Exploring intuitive modelling behaviour. In: Bider, I., Halpin, T., Krogstie, J., Nurcan, S., Proper, E., Schmidt, R., Ukor, R. (eds.) BPMDS 2010 and EMMSAD 2010. LNBIP, vol. 50, pp. 301–313. Springer, Heidelberg (2010)

2. Moody, D.: The 'physics' of notations: Toward a scientific basis for constructing visual notations in software engineering. IEEE Trans. Softw. Eng. **35**, 756–779 (2009)
3. Balota, D.A., Spieler, D.H.: Word frequency, repetition, and lexicality effects in word recognition tasks: Beyond measures of central tendency. Journal of Experimental Psychology: General **128**, 32–55 (1998)
4. Grainger, J., ORegan, J.K., Jacobs, A.M., Segui, J.: On the role of competing word units in visual word recognition: the neighborhood frequency effect. Percept Psychophys **45**, 189–195 (1989)
5. Sears, C.R., Hino, Y., Lupker, S.J.: Neighborhood size and neighborhood frequency effects in word recognition. Journal of Experimental Psychology: Human Perception and Performance **21**, 876–900 (1995)
6. Croft, W., Cruse, D.A. (eds.): Cognitive Linguistics. Cambridge University Press (2004)
7. Maes, A., Poels, G.: Evaluating quality of conceptual modelling scripts based on user perceptions. Data Knowl. Eng. **63**, 701–724 (2007)
8. Ratnaparkhi, A.: A maximum entropy model for part-of-speech tagging. In: Brill, E., Church, K. (eds.): Proceedings of the Empirical Methods in Natural Language Processing, pp. 133–142 (1996)
9. Coseriu, E., Geckeler, H.: Trends in Structural Semantics. Tübinger Beiträge zur Linguistik, Narr (1981)
10. Tseng, H., Jurafsky, D., Manning, C.: Morphological features help pos tagging of unknown words across language varieties. In: Proceedings of the Fourth SIGHAN Workshop on Chinese Language Processing, pp. 32–39 (2005)
11. Toutanova, K., Manning, C.D.: Enriching the knowledge sources used in a maximum entropy part-of-speech tagger. In: Proceedings of the 2000 Joint SIGDAT Conference on Empirical Methods in Natural Language Processing and Very Large Corpora, EMNLP 2000. Association for Computational Linguistics, pp. 63–70 (2000)
12. Mendling, J., Reijers, H.A., Recker, J.: Activity labeling in process modeling: Empirical insights and recommendations. Inf. Syst. **35**, 467–482 (2010)
13. Leopold, H., Smirnov, S., Mendling, J.: On the refactoring of activity labels in business process models. Information Systems **37**, 443–459 (2012)
14. Peters, N., Weidlich, M.: Using glossaries to enhance the label quality in business process models. In: Proceedings of the 8th GI-Workshop Geschäftsprozessmanagement mit Ereignisgesteuerten Prozessketten (EPK), CEUR-WS.org, pp. 75–90 (2009)
15. Leopold, H., Mendling, J., Reijers, H.A., Rosa, M.L.: Simplifying process model abstraction: Techniques for generating model names. Information Systems **39**, 134–151 (2014)
16. Delfmann, P., Herwig, S., Lis, L., Stein, A.: Supporting distributed conceptual modelling through naming conventions - a tool-based linguistic approach. Enterprise Modelling and Information Systems Architectures **4**, 3–19 (2009)

Declarative Process Modeling in BPMN

Giuseppe De Giacomo[1], Marlon Dumas[2], Fabrizio Maria Maggi[2(✉)],
and Marco Montali[3]

[1] Sapienza Università di Roma, Rome, Italy
degiacomo@dis.uniroma1.it
[2] University of Tartu, Tartu, Estonia
{marlon.dumas,f.m.maggi}@ut.ee
[3] Free University of Bozen-Bolzano, Bolzano, Italy
montali@inf.unibz.it

Abstract. Traditional business process modeling notations, including
the standard Business Process Model and Notation (BPMN), rely on
an imperative paradigm wherein the process model captures all allowed
activity flows. In other words, every flow that is not specified is implicitly disallowed. In the past decade, several researchers have exposed the
limitations of this paradigm in the context of business processes with
high variability. As an alternative, declarative process modeling notations have been proposed (e.g., Declare). These notations allow modelers to capture constraints on the allowed activity flows, meaning that
all flows are allowed provided that they do not violate the specified constraints. Recently, it has been recognized that the boundary between
imperative and declarative process modeling is not crisp. Instead, mixtures of declarative and imperative process modeling styles are sometimes
preferable, leading to proposals for hybrid process modeling notations.
These developments raise the question of whether completely new notations are needed to support hybrid process modeling. This paper answers
this question negatively. The paper presents a conservative extension of
BPMN for declarative process modeling, namely BPMN-D, and shows
that Declare models can be transformed into readable BPMN-D models.

Keywords: BPMN · Declarative process modeling · Declare

1 Introduction

The standard Business Process Model and Notation (BPMN) [13] and related
approaches rely on an imperative paradigm wherein the process model captures all allowed activity flows. Underpinning these notations is a "closed world"
assumption, meaning that the process model captures all possible activity flows
and hence any unspecified activity flow is disallowed. This paradigm has proved
suitable in the context of regular and predictable processes, where there is
in essence one primary way of performing a process, with relatively few and
well-scoped variations.

© Springer International Publishing Switzerland 2015
J. Zdravkovic et al. (Eds.): CAiSE 2015, LNCS 9097, pp. 84–100, 2015.
DOI: 10.1007/978-3-319-19069-3_6

In the past decade, several researchers have exposed the limitations of this imperative paradigm in the context of business processes with high variability, such as customer lead management processes, product design processes, patient treatment and related healthcare processes [17,19]. As an alternative, declarative process modeling notations have been proposed, e.g., Declare [1,14], Guard-Stage-Milestones (GSM) [9] and the Case Management Model and Notation (CMMN) [11]. Unlike their imperative counterparts, a declarative model captures a process under an "open world" assumption, such that everything is allowed unless it is explicitly forbidden by a rule. In this context, a rule may take the form of a binary relation between pairs of tasks that must be satisfied in every execution of a process, like for example "task B can only be performed if task A has been previously performed in the same case".

More recently, it has been recognized that the boundary between imperative and declarative process modeling is not crisp. Instead, mixtures of declarative and imperative modeling styles are sometimes preferable, leading to proposals for hybrid process modeling notations [6,21]. These developments raise the question of whether completely new notations are needed to support hybrid process modeling.

Given this question, this paper analyzes the possibility of seamlessly extending BPMN with declarative constructs. The main contribution of the paper is an extension of BPMN, namely BPMN-D. BPMN-D is a conservative extension in the sense that it only adds constructs, such that any BPMN model is a BPMN-D model. Furthermore, BPMN-D is a macro-extension, i.e., it is designed so that any BPMN-D model can be translated into a (larger and potentially less readable) BPMN model. The paper also shows that any Declare model can be translated into a readable BPMN-D model via constraint automata. More generally, any declarative process modeling language defined in terms of Linear Temporal Logic over finite traces (LTL_f) can be translated into BPMN-D using the proposed translation method.

The paper is structured as follows. Section 2 provides an overview of declarative process modeling – specifically the Declare notation – and discusses previous research on linking declarative and imperative process modeling approaches. Section 3 introduces the BPMN-D notation and shows how the extended constructs of BPMN-D can be re-written into standard BPMN. Next, Section 4 outlines the translation from Declare to BPMN-D. Finally, Section 5 draws conclusions and outlines future work.

2 Background and Related Work

Declare [1,14] is a declarative process modeling language wherein a process is specified via a set of constraints between activities, which must be satisfied by every execution of the process. Declare constraints are captured based on templates. Templates are patterns that define parameterized classes of properties, while constraints are their concrete instantiations. Herein, we write template

Table 1. Semantics for some Declare templates

Template	LTL$_f$ semantics	Activation
responded existence	$\Diamond A \rightarrow \Diamond B$	A ●—| B
response	$\Box(A \rightarrow \Diamond B)$	A ●—▶ B
alternate response	$\Box(A \rightarrow \bigcirc(\neg A \sqcup B))$	A ⬅═ B
chain response	$\Box(A \rightarrow \bigcirc B)$	A ══▶ B
precedence	$(\neg B \sqcup A) \vee \Box(\neg B)$	A |—▶● B
alternate precedence	$(\neg B \sqcup A) \vee \Box(\neg B) \wedge$ $\Box(B \rightarrow \bigcirc((\neg B \sqcup A) \vee \Box(\neg B)))$	A ═—▶● B
chain precedence	$\Box(\bigcirc B \rightarrow A)$	A ══▶● B

parameters in upper-case and concrete activities in their instantiations in lower-case. Constraints have a graphical representation. The semantics of templates can be formalized using different logics [12], for example LTL$_f$.

Table 1 summarizes some Declare templates and their corresponding formalization in LTL$_f$. (The reader can refer to [1] for a full description of the language.) The $\Diamond$, $\bigcirc$, $\Box$, and $\sqcup$ LTL$_f$ operators have the following intuitive meaning: formula $\Diamond\phi_1$ means that ϕ_1 holds sometime in the future, $\bigcirc\phi_1$ means that ϕ_1 holds in the next position, $\Box\phi_1$ says that ϕ_1 holds forever, and, lastly, $\phi_1 \sqcup \phi_2$ means that sometime in the future ϕ_2 will hold and until that moment ϕ_1 holds (with ϕ_1 and ϕ_2 LTL$_f$ formulas).

Consider, for example, the *response* constraint $\Box(a \rightarrow \Diamond b)$. This constraint indicates that if a *occurs*, b must eventually *follow*. Therefore, this constraint is satisfied for traces such as $\mathbf{t}_1 = \langle a, a, b, c \rangle$, $\mathbf{t}_2 = \langle b, b, c, d \rangle$, and $\mathbf{t}_3 = \langle a, b, c, b \rangle$, but not for $\mathbf{t}_4 = \langle a, b, a, c \rangle$ because, in this case, the second occurrence of a is not followed by an occurrence of b. A constraint can define more than one activity for each parameter specified in its template. In this case, we say that the parameters *branch out* and, in the graphical representation, they are replaced by multiple arcs to all branched activities. In the LTL$_f$ semantics, the parameters are replaced by a disjunction of branching activities. For example, the LTL$_f$ semantics of the response template with two branches on the target parameter is $\Box(A \rightarrow \Diamond(B \vee C))$.

Example 1. Consider the Declare model that represents a fragment of a purchase order process, as shown in Figure 1. The process is as follows:
- a payment cannot be done until the order is closed (*precedence* constraint);
- whenever a payment is done, then a receipt or an invoice must be produced (*branching response* constraint).

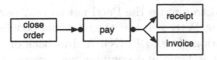

Fig. 1. Example of a Declare model

Like any declarative model, this model should be interpreted according to an "open-world" semantics: It is possible to send a receipt or an invoice without paying beforehand and, also, to close an order without eventually paying. In addition, an activity in the model can be executed several times. Closing an order several times has no effect on the process execution, whereas it is possible to pay several times (this is the case, for example, of installments) and, also, to send invoices and receipts several times.

Besides Declare, other declarative process modeling notations include Condition Response Graphs (DCR) graphs [8] and GSM [9]. DCR graphs rely on binary relations between tasks (as in Declare) but employ a smaller set of five core relations and support decomposition (nesting). GSM differs from Declare and DCR in that it does not rely on binary relations. Instead it relies on three core concepts: guard, stage and milestone. A stage is a phase in the execution of a process where a certain number of tasks (or other stages) may occur in any order and any number of times (similar to *ad hoc* activities in BPMN). The opening of a stage is subject to one of its guards (event-condition rules) becoming true. The stage is closed when one of its milestones is achieved (i.e., becomes true). A milestone is also defined by means of an event-condition rule. The guards of a stage may refer to data associated to the process and/or to the status of other stages or milestones (e.g., whether a given stage is currently "open" or "closed"). Tasks are modeled as atomic stages and may have their own guards and milestone(s). Several concepts proposed in the GSM notation have made their way into the CMMN standard [11].

Initially, declarative process modeling notations were proposed as alternatives to imperative ones. Recent research though has put into evidence synergies between these two approaches [15,18]. Accordingly, hybrid process modeling notations have been proposed. In particular, [21] proposes to extend Colored Petri nets with the possibility of linking transitions to Declare constraints (in the same model). The notion of *transition enablement* is extended to handle declarative links between transitions. Meanwhile, [6,10] combine imperative and declarative styles in the context of automated discovery of process models from event logs. Specifically, the approach in [10] discovers hierarchical models with sub-processes that can be either imperative (Petri nets) or declarative (Declare constraints). Meanwhile, the method in [6] discovers a process model with two types of arcs: imperative (sequence flows) and declarative (Declare constraints).

Another contribution that bridges declarative and imperative process modeling styles is [16], which proposes a translation from Declare to Petri nets. The idea is to first produce a Finite State Machine (FSM) from a Declare model using standard techniques for mapping regular expressions to automata. The FSM is then mapped into a sequential Petri net and methods related to "theory of regions" [3] are used to rewrite the Petri net so that parallelism is explicitly captured. The resulting Petri net can then be mapped into other imperative process modeling notations (e.g., BPMN). A drawback of this approach is that the resulting Petri net is large and complex relative to the initial declarative model. This drawback is illustrated in [16] where a Declare model with 4 tasks and 7 constraints leads to an FSM with 10 states and 24 arcs. This FSM in turn leads to a Petri net with 25 transitions, 13 places and over 40 arcs. The issue at stake is that a given constraint may be satisfied by a large number of distinct possible execution paths. Capturing these paths in an imperative style leads to significant amounts of task duplication (e.g., transitions with duplicate labels in the case of Petri nets).

3   BPMN-D

This section introduces the BPMN-D notation and gives it a semantics by means of a translation from BPMN-D to plain BPMN, for which different formal semantics have been specified in previous work [7].

3.1   Overview

BPMN-D is an extension of BPMN partly inspired by BPMN-Q [2] – a language previously proposed to capture queries over collections of BPMN models. Like BPMN-Q, BPMN-D is a conservative (additive) extension of BPMN, implying that any BPMN model is also a BPMN-D model. Fig. 2 shows an example of a BPMN-D model. In particular, a BPMN-D model may have *start* and *end event nodes*, with the same semantics as in standard BPMN. For instance, in Fig. 2, there is one start event and two end events. Similarly, *behavioral XOR split/join* represents (exclusive) alternative behaviors that are allowed during the process execution, following the standard BPMN semantics of *deferred choice* (i.e., choice freely taken by the resources responsible for the process execution). As shown in Fig. 2, the graphical representation for a XOR gateway is the same as in BPMN. In this paper, we only discuss XOR gateways as they are sufficient to demonstrate the extensions proposed in BPMN-D and the translation from Declare to BPMN-D. In the remainder of the paper, we denote by Σ the set of all tasks that can be performed in a given business context.

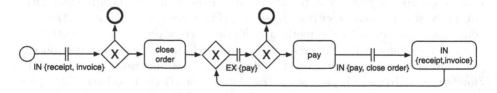

Fig. 2. Example of a BPMN-D model

Table 2. Overview of BPMN-D activity nodes

Notation	Name	Semantics
t	Atomic task	As in BPMN: perform t
IN {t1,...,tn}	Inclusive task	Perform a task among $t_1, \ldots, t_n$
EX {t1,...,tn}	Exclusive task	Perform a task different from $t_1, \ldots, t_n$
ANY	Any task	Perform any task from those available in the business context

BPMN-D extends only two constructs in BPMN, namely activity nodes and sequence flows connectors. An *activity node* represents a task in the process, and is represented as a labeled, rounded rectangle. As in standard BPMN, this in turn corresponds to an execution step inside the process. Differently from BPMN, though, a BPMN-D activity node can be labeled not only with a single task name $t \in \Sigma$, but with a set T of multiple tasks, such that T is nonempty and does not coincide with Σ. When the label denotes a single task t, the semantics coincides with that of BPMN: the activity node is executed whenever t is performed. When the label is instead a set T of tasks, the activity node is considered to be executed whenever a task t is executed, such that either $t \in T$ (*inclusive task*), or $t \notin T$ (*exclusive task*). To distinguish between these two cases, a set-labeled BPMN-D task is also annotated with a property IN or EX, so as to indicate whether the task is inclusive or exclusive. For example, in Fig. 2, the *pay*-labeled activity node indicates that a payment must be done, whereas the set-labeled activity node IN({*receipt, invoice*}) indicates that one task between *receipt* or *invoice* must be performed. In addition to these three types of activity nodes, we consider also the case in which the process expects participants to do "something", that is, to engage in an execution step by freely choosing a task from the global set Σ. In this case, we assume that the activity node is just labeled with label ANY. The different BPMN-D activity nodes are summarized in Table 2.

A *flow connector* is a binary, directed relation between nodes in the process. It indicates an ordering relationship between the connected nodes, and implicitly also the state of the process when the process has traversed the source node but has still to traverse the destination node. Differently from BPMN, in BPMN-D sequence-flow connectors do not only represent a direct ordering relationship (stating that the destination node comes next to the source one), but also a "loose" ordering relationship, which indicates that the destination node will be traversed *after* the source one, but that other BPMN-D tasks can be performed in between. First of all, BPMN-D supports the ordinary BPMN sequence flow, adopting its semantics and notation (a solid arrow from the source to the destination node). Loose flow connectors are instead visually depicted as an interrupted solid arrow, and their specific semantics is defined by labeling and annotating

Table 3. Overview of BPMN-D flow connectors

Notation	Name	Semantics
A ⟶ B	Sequence flow	As in BPMN: node B is traversed next to A
A ⟶ B IN {t₁,...,tₙ}	Inclusive flow	B is traversed after A, with 0 or more repetitions of tasks from $t_1, \ldots, t_n$ in between
A ⟶ B EX {t₁,...,tₙ}	Exclusive flow	B is traversed after A, with 0 or more repetitions of tasks different from $t_1, \ldots, t_n$ in between
A ⟶ B ANY	Any flow	B is traversed after A, with 0 or more repetitions of tasks in between

the connector with additional information, similarly to the case of BPMN-D activity nodes. As summarized in Table 3, three loose connectors are supported. The first two, namely *inclusive flow* and *exclusive flow*, label the flow connectors with a set of T of tasks, and indicate that while moving from the source to the destination node along the flow connector, 0 or more repetitions of tasks respectively from or not in T can be executed. To distinguish between the two cases, the set T is also annotated with a property IN or EX, so as to indicate whether the flow connector is inclusive or exclusive. For example, in Fig. 2, the first flow connector indicates that when the process starts, 0 or more repetitions of tasks *receipt* and *invoice* may occur while moving to the first decision point. In addition, we consider also the case in which while moving from a node to another node, 0 or more repetitions of any task may occur. In this case, we assume that the flow connector is just labeled with label ANY, and we consequently call it *any flow*.

3.2   BPMN-D Models

We now turn to the formal definition of BPMN-D model, substantiating the overview of the previous section. Given a set Σ of tasks, a BPMN-D model $\mathcal{M}$ is a tuple $\langle N, type_N, \ell_N, F, type_F, \ell_F \rangle$, where:

- N is a finite set of nodes, partitioned into activity nodes, event nodes, and gateways.
- $type_N$ is a total function from N to a finite set of *node types*; the following types are considered in this paper:
  - ATOMIC-TASK, IN-TASK, EX-TASK, and ANY-TASK for activity nodes (cf. Table 2);
  - START and END for event nodes;
  - XOR-SPLIT and XOR-JOIN for gateways.
  We consequently define:
  - the set A of *activity nodes* as
    $\{n \mid n \in N \text{ and } type_N(n) \in \{\text{ATOMIC-TASK}, \text{IN-TASK}, \text{EX-TASK},$ ANY-TASK$\}\}$;

- the set E of *event nodes* as $\{n \mid n \in N \text{ and } type_N(n) \in \{\text{START}, \text{END}\}\}$;
- the set G of *gateways* as $\{n \mid n \in N \text{ and } type_N(n) \in \{\text{XOR-SPLIT}, \text{XOR-JOIN}\}\}$;

  Notice that $N = A \uplus E \uplus G$.
- $\ell_N : A \longrightarrow 2^\Sigma$ is a function that assigns task names to activity nodes in N. To guarantee that each activity node is mapped to a set of tasks consistently with its specific type, ℓ_N must satisfy the following conditions:
  - for every $a \in A$ such that $type_N(a) = \text{ATOMIC-TASK}$, $|\ell_N(a)| = 1$;
  - for every $a \in A$ such that $type_N(a) \in \{\text{IN-TASK}, \text{EX-TASK}\}$, $\emptyset \subset \ell_N(a) \subset \Sigma$;
  - for every $a \in A$ such that $type_N(a) = \text{ANY-TASK}$, $\ell_N(a) = \emptyset$.
- $F \subseteq N \times N$ is a set of flow connectors that obeys to the following restrictions: *(i)* every start event node has no incoming sequence flow, and a single outgoing sequence flow; *(ii)* every end event node has a single incoming sequence flow, and no outgoing sequence flow; *(iii)* every activity node has a single incoming and a single outgoing sequence flow; *(iv)* every XOR split gateway has a single incoming and at least two outgoing sequence flows; *(v)* every XOR join gateway has a single outgoing and at least two incoming sequence flows.[1]
- $type_F$ is a total function from F to the finite set of *flow connector types* $\{\text{SEQ-FLOW}, \text{IN-FLOW}, \text{EX-FLOW}, \text{ANY-FLOW}\}$ (cf. Table 3).
- $\ell_F : F \longrightarrow 2^\Sigma$ is a function that assigns task names to flow connectors in F. To guarantee that each flow connector is mapped to a set of tasks consistently with its specific type, ℓ_F must satisfy the following conditions:
  - for every $f \in F$ such that $type_F(f) \in \{\text{SEQ-FLOW}, \text{ANY-TASK}\}$, $\ell_F(f) = \emptyset$;
  - for every $f \in F$ such that $type_F(f) \in \{\text{IN-TASK}, \text{EX-TASK}\}$, $\emptyset \subset \ell_F(f) \subset \Sigma$.

3.3   Translating BPMN-D to Standard BPMN

Any BPMN-D diagram can be faithfully represented as a (trace-equivalent) corresponding standard BPMN diagram, at the price of conciseness. In this section, we discuss this translation, which has a twofold purpose: (i) it shows that, in principle, a BPMN-D process can be enacted on top of a standard BPMN engine; (ii) it provides an implicit execution semantics for BPMN-D in terms of standard BPMN.

For the translation, we assume that the overall set of tasks Σ is fixed. In this respect, it is sufficient to discuss how elements annotated with IN or ANY have to be translated: each label of the kind $\text{EX}(T)$ can be in fact equivalently re-expressed as $\text{IN}(\Sigma \setminus T)$. As shown in Table 4 (top row), an inclusive task with label $\{t_1, \ldots, t_n\}$ is translated into a deferred choice where one of the tasks $t_1, \ldots, t_n$ is selected. An ANY-labeled task is translated in the same way, considering all tasks in Σ as possible alternatives. The translation of an inclusive path sequence flow with label $\{t_1, \ldots, t_n\}$ is also depicted in Table 4 (bottom

---

[1] Graphically, we sometimes collapse a XOR join, connected to a XOR split via a standard BPMN sequence flow, into a single XOR gateway acting simultaneously as split/join.

Table 4. Translation of the key BPMN-D elements into standard BPMN

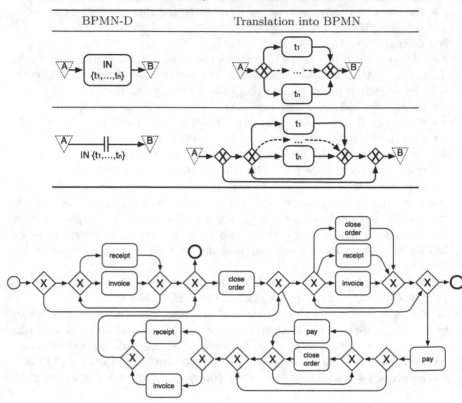

Fig. 3. Standard BPMN representation of the BPMN-D diagram of Figure 2

row). In this case, two alternative behaviors are obtained: either the inclusive path sequence flow behaves as a normal sequence flow (thereby directly connecting node A to node B), or it allows the executors to repeatedly execute tasks $t_1, \ldots, t_n$ in between. As for tasks, also the case of a ANY-labeled sequence flow is handled in the same way, just considering all tasks in Σ as possible alternatives. Figure 3 shows the result obtained by applying this translation procedure to the BPMN-D model shown in Figure 2.

4   From Declare to BPMN-D

We now propose a translation mechanism that, given a declarative, constraint-based process model, produces a corresponding readable BPMN-D diagram that faithfully represents the original intended behaviors. As source language, we consider Linear Temporal Logic on finite traces (LTL$_f$), which is the logic underpinning the Declare notation. However, it is worth noting that our approach can be directly applied to the more expressive logic LDL$_f$ [5], which has been recently adopted to formalize and monitor Declare constraints and meta-constraints [4].

The algorithm proceeds in two phases. In the first phase, the given Declare (or LTL$_f$/LDL$_f$) specification is translated into a corresponding finite-state automaton that employs a form of declarative labels, and can therefore represent the given specification more compactly than for standard finite-state automata. In the second phase, this so-called "constraint automaton" is translated into a corresponding BPMN-D model. Both steps are such that the produced model accepts exactly the same traces as the input model, in turn guaranteeing that the BPMN-D model is a faithful, equivalent representation of the input Declare model.

In the remainder of this section, we provide a detailed account of these two phases.

4.1   From Declare to Constraint Automata

It is well-known that a Declare model can be transformed into a corresponding finite-state automaton that accepts exactly those traces that satisfy all the constraints present in the model [4,16,20]. A *finite-state automaton* (FSA) is a tuple $\langle \Sigma, S, I, F, \delta \rangle$, where: *(i)* Σ is the *alphabet* of symbols; *(ii)* S is a finite set of *states*; *(iii)* $I \subseteq S$ is the set of *initial states*; *(iv)* $F \subseteq S$ is the set of *final states*; *(v)* $\delta : S \times \Sigma \to 2^S$ is the *state transition function*, which maps each state and symbol to a set of successor states. Hereby, we assume that symbols represent atomic tasks, and consequently that the symbol alphabet is constituted by all atomic tasks that can be executed in the targeted domain. The *language* of an FSA A, written $\mathcal{L}(A)$, is the set of *finite traces* (i.e., words) over Σ that are accepted by A. The notions of deterministic finite-state automaton (DFA) and of minimal automaton are as usual.

Once the Declare model is translated into its corresponding FSA, the FSA can be determinized and minimized using standard techniques. This minimal DFA can be used to enact the Declare model [14]: at any time, the DFA states whether the process can be terminated or not, and indicates which tasks that can/must be executed next.

A drawback of this automata-based representation is that every transition of the automaton is labeled with a single, atomic task. This means that the same pair of states can be connected through several transitions, each associated to a different task. All such transitions connect the same source state to the same destination state, and hence express different ways to achieve the same "effect" on the process. This closely resembles the notion of inclusive task in BPMN-D. To fully exploit this analogy, and make the automaton closer to BPMN-D, we introduce a variant of finite-state automata, called *constraint automata*. Differently from FSAs, constraint automata are finite-state automata whose transitions are associated to "declarative" labels, each of which acts as a *constraint* on the possible atomic tasks that can navigate the transition. In particular, a constraint automaton moves from one state to a successor state if the next symbol s to be analyzed *satisfies* the constraint C attached to the corresponding transition.

Given a task alphabet Σ, we consider the following *task constraints*, which are directly inspired from BPMN-D and consequently provide the basis for a natural translation of constraint automata to BPMN-D:

- t, with $t \in \Sigma$; an atomic task $t' \in \Sigma$ satisfies t iff $t = t'$.
- $\mathrm{IN}(T)$, with $\emptyset \subset T \subset \Sigma$; an atomic task $t \in \Sigma$ satisfies $\mathrm{IN}(T)$ iff $t \in T$.
- $\mathrm{EX}(T)$, with $\emptyset \subset T \subset \Sigma$; an atomic task $t \in \Sigma$ satisfies $\mathrm{EX}(T)$ iff $t \notin T$.
- ANY; every atomic task $t \in \Sigma$ satisfies ANY.

Intuitively, t represents the execution of an atomic task, $\mathrm{IN}(T)$ the execution of a task belonging to the set T of alternatives, $\mathrm{EX}(T)$ the execution of a task that does not fall inside the set T of forbidden tasks, and ANY the execution of some task. Like for BPMN-D, the following correspondences hold, consistently with the notion of satisfaction as defined above: *(i)* $t = \mathrm{IN}(\{t\})$; *(ii)* $\mathrm{IN}(T) = \mathrm{EX}(\Sigma \setminus T)$.

In the following, we denote by $\mathcal{C}_\Sigma$ the set of all possible constraints that can be expressed over Σ. Technically, a *finite-state constraint automaton* (FCA) A_c is a tuple $\langle \Sigma, S_c, I_c, F_c, \delta_c, \ell_c \rangle$, where: *(i)* Σ is the (task) alphabet; *(ii)* S_c is a finite set of states; *(iii)* $I_c \subseteq S_c$ is the set of initial states; *(iv)* $F_c \subseteq S_c$ is the set of final states; *(v)* $\delta_c \subseteq S_c \times S_c$ is a transition relation between states; *(vi)* $\ell_c : \delta_c \to \mathcal{C}_\Sigma$ is a labeling function that, given a transition in δ_c, returns a task constraint over Σ.

Given a finite trace $\pi = \langle t_1, \ldots, t_n \rangle$ over Σ, we say that π is *accepted* by A_c if there exists a sequence of states $\langle s_1, \ldots, s_{n+1} \rangle$ over S_c such that: *(i)* $s_1 \in I_c$; *(ii)* $s_n \in F_c$; *(iii)* $\langle s_i, s_{i+1} \rangle \in \delta_c$ for $i \in \{1, n\}$; *(iv)* t_i satisfies constraint $\ell_c(\langle s_i, s_{i+1} \rangle)$ for $i \in \{1, n\}$. As usual, the *language* of a constraint automaton A_c, written $\mathcal{L}(A_c)$, is the set of *finite traces* over Σ that are accepted by A_c. We say that A_c is a *deterministic constraint automaton* (DCA) if $|I_c| = 1$ and, for every state $s \in S_c$ and every task $t \in \Sigma$, there exists *at most one* state $s' \in S_c$ such that $\langle s, s' \rangle \in \delta_c$ and t satisfies $\ell(\langle s, s' \rangle)$. If this is not the case, then A_c is a *nondeterministic constraint automaton* (NCA).

It is important to notice that in a constraint automaton, at most one transition can exist between a given pair of states. In fact, multiple simple transitions connecting the same pair of states can be compacted into a unique transition labeled with a constraint obtained from the combination of the original labels. We make this intuition systematic by introducing a translation mechanism that, given a standard finite-state automaton on Σ, produces a corresponding constraint automaton that employs the "most compact" constraints on arcs. In this context, "most compact" means that the constraint explicitly refers to the minimum number of tasks in Σ. For example, if $\Sigma = \{a, b, c\}$, we prefer $\mathrm{EX}(\{a\})$ over the equivalent constraint $\mathrm{IN}(\{b, c\})$.

The translation mechanism is defined in Algorithm 1, and it is straightforward to prove that it enjoys the following key properties:

Lemma 1. *For every* FSA *A: (i)* FSA2CA *is correct, i.e.,* $\mathcal{L}(A) = \mathcal{L}(\mathrm{FSA2CA}(A))$; *(ii)* FSA2CA *preserves determinism, i.e., if A is a* DFA, *then* FSA2CA(A) *is a* DCA.

The mechanism of transition compaction shown in Algorithm 1 can be either applied on-the-fly, during the construction of the automaton starting from the

---

Algorithm 1. Translation of a standard FSA to an equivalent FCA

1: **procedure** FSA2CA
2: **input** FSA $\langle \Sigma, S, I, F, \delta \rangle$
3: **output** FCA $\langle \Sigma, S_c, I_c, F_c, \delta_c, \ell_c \rangle$
4:    $S_c := S, I_c := I, F_c := F, \delta_c := \emptyset$
5:    **for all** $s_1, s_2 \in S$ **do**
6:        $T := \emptyset$
7:        **for all** $t \in \Sigma$ **do**
8:            **if** $s_2 \in \delta(s_1, t)$ **then** $T := T \cup \{t\}$
9:        **if** $T = \Sigma$ **then** $\delta_c := \delta_c \cup \langle s_1, s_2 \rangle, \ell_c(\langle s_1, s_2 \rangle) = $ ANY
10:       **else if** $|T| \leq |\Sigma \setminus T|$ **then** $\delta_c := \delta_c \cup \langle s_1, s_2 \rangle, \ell_c(\langle s_1, s_2 \rangle) = $ IN(T)
11:       **else if** $T \neq \emptyset$ **then** $\delta_c := \delta_c \cup \langle s_1, s_2 \rangle, \ell_c(\langle s_1, s_2 \rangle) = $ EX$(\Sigma \setminus T)$

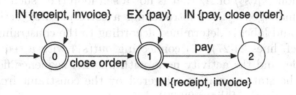

Fig. 4. Minimal DCA for the Declare model shown in Figure 1

Declare model, or as a final post-processing step (using FSA2CA itself). Both strategies do not affect the computational complexity of the automaton construction, and do not interfere with determinization (cf. Lemma 1). Furthermore, the correctness of FSA2CA guarantees that, after this first phase, the input Declare model is transformed into a constraint automaton that accepts exactly the same behaviors.

Figure 4 represents the minimal DCA that corresponds to the Declare model shown in Figure 1, assuming $\Sigma = \{close\ order, pay, receipt, invoice\}$ as task alphabet.

4.2   From Constraint Automata to BPMN-D

The algorithm for translating a constraint automaton A_c into a corresponding BPMN-D specification $\mathcal{M}$ is described in this section. We assume that the input constraint automaton is deterministic, and thus the unique initial state of A_c corresponds to a single start event node in $\mathcal{M}$. Consistently with the fact that automata are centered around states, while BPMN (and hence also BPMN-D) is centered around tasks, the translation maps states of A_c into flow connectors of $\mathcal{M}$, and transitions of A_c into activity nodes of $\mathcal{M}$.

The full translation mechanism is provided in Algorithm 2. It is immediate to see that the translation is linear in the size of the input automaton (measured by considering the number of its states and transitions). Each state s of A_c is handled according to the following rules: (1) State s is mapped to a flow connector f_s that connects a dedicated xor-join $in(s)$ to a dedicated xor-split

$out(s)$ (cf. lines 7-9 of Algorithm 2); $in(s)$ accounts for the incoming transitions in s, while $out(s)$ accounts for the outgoing transitions from s. (2) If s has a self-loop t, then the type and label of f_s are set according to the constraint c attached to t (cf. lines 10-13); this accounts for the fact that as long as tasks satisfying c are executed, the process continues to stay in state s, which in turn means that it is still flowing through f_s. If instead s has no self-loop, f_s is a simple sequence flow connector (cf. line 14). (3) If s is an input state, then the start event node of $\mathcal{M}$ is connected with a sequence flow to $in(s)$ (cf. lines 15-16); this models that when the process starts, it immediately flows through f_s. (4) If s is an output state, then $out(s)$ is connected with a sequence flow to an end event node in $\mathcal{M}$ (cf. lines 17-20); this models the fact that, while the process is flowing through f_s, the process executors can decide to terminate it.

Each transition $\langle s_1, s_2 \rangle$ of A_c that is not a self-loop (i.e., such that $s_1 \neq s_2$), is then simply managed by: (1) introducing a corresponding activity node in $\mathcal{M}$, whose type and label is determined according to the constraint attached to the transition (cf. lines 24-27); (2) connecting $out(s_1)$ with a sequence flow to the activity node, and the activity node with another sequence flow to $in(s_2)$, reconstructing the state transition triggered by the constraint from which the activity node is derived (cf. lines 28-30).

Obviously, the technique so presented may lead to introduce several "inconsistent" x-or split and join gateways with only one input and one output attached sequence flow. To compensate for this issue, $\mathcal{M}$ is finally post-processed by removing all such unnecessary gateways (cf. the REMOVE-UNNECESSARY-XOR procedure on line 31 of Algorithm 2). This is quite straightforward, hence its actual code is omitted.

By considering the language of a DCA, and by modularly applying the translation procedure from BPMN-D to BPMN of Section 3.3 to the BPMN-D fragments produced by the different components of Algorithm 2, we have that:

Lemma 2. *The* FCA2BPMND *procedure is correct: for every* DCA, FCA2BPMND (DCA) *produces a proper BPMN-D model (according to the definition of Sec. 3.2), which accepts all and only the traces in* $\mathcal{L}$(DCA).

We close this section by illustrating, in Figure 5, the result of the FCA2BPMND procedure the FCA of Figure 4.

4.3   The Whole Translation Procedure

By combining the contributions of Sections 4.1 and 4.2, we can finally set up the whole translation procedure DECLARE2BPMND, which transforms a Declare model into BPMN-D, as shown in Algorithm 3. The following key result witnesses the correctness of this transformation:

Theorem 1. DECLARE2BPMND *is correct: for every Declare model* $\mathcal{D}$, *the BPMN-D model produced by* DECLARE2BPMND *accepts all and only the traces accepted by* $\mathcal{D}$.

Algorithm 2. Translation of an FCA to BPMN-D

1: **procedure** FCA2BPMND
2: **input** FCA $\langle \Sigma, S_c, I_c, F_c, \delta_c, \ell_c \rangle$
3: **output** BPMN-D model $\mathcal{M} = \langle N, type_N, \ell_N, F, type_F, \ell_F \rangle$
4: **pick** fresh node se
5: $F := \emptyset$ $N := \{se\}$, $type_N(se) :=$ START
6: **for all** $s \in S_c$ **do**
7:    **pick** fresh nodes $in(s)$ and $out(s)$
8:    $f_s := \langle in(s), out(s) \rangle$, $N := N \cup \{in(s), out(s)\}$, $F := F \cup \{f_s\}$
9:    $type_N(in(s)) :=$ XOR-JOIN, $type_N(out(s)) :=$ XOR-SPLIT
10:    **if** $\langle s, s \rangle \in \delta_c$ and $\ell_c(\langle s, s \rangle) = t$ **then** $type_F(f_s) :=$ IN-FLOW, $\ell_F(f_s) := \{t\}$
11:    **else if** $\langle s, s \rangle \in \delta_c$ and $\ell_c(\langle s, s \rangle) =$ IN(T) **then** $type_F(f_s) :=$ IN-FLOW, $\ell_F(f_s) := T$
12:    **else if** $\langle s, s \rangle \in \delta_c$ and $\ell_c(\langle s, s \rangle) =$ EX(T) **then** $type_F(f_s) :=$ EX-FLOW, $\ell_F(f_s) := T$
13:    **else if** $\langle s, s \rangle \in \delta_c$ and $\ell_c(\langle s, s \rangle) =$ ANY **then** $type_F(f_s) :=$ ANY-FLOW, $\ell_F(f_s) := \emptyset$
14:    **else** $type_F(f_s) :=$ SEQ-FLOW, $\ell_F(f_s) := \emptyset$ ▷ $\langle s, s \rangle \notin \delta_c$
15:    **if** $s \in I_c$ **then**
16:      $F := F \cup \{\langle se, in(s) \rangle\}$, $type_F(\langle se, in(s) \rangle) :=$ SEQ-FLOW, $\ell_F(\langle se, in(s) \rangle) := \emptyset$
17:    **if** $s \in F_c$ **then**
18:      **pick** fresh node ee_s
19:      $N := N \cup \{ee_s\}$, $type_N(ee_s) :=$ END, $F := F \cup \{\langle out(s), ee_s \rangle\}$
20:      $type_F(\langle out(s), ee_s \rangle) :=$ SEQ-FLOW, $\ell_F(\langle out(s), ee_s \rangle) := \emptyset$
21:    **for all** $\langle s_1, s_2 \rangle \in \delta_c$ such that $s_1 \neq s_2$ **do**
22:    **pick** fresh node a
23:    $N := N \cup \{a\}$
24:    **if** $\ell_c(\langle s_1, s_2 \rangle) = t$ **then** $type_N(a) :=$ ATOMIC-TASK, $\ell_N(a) := \{t\}$
25:    **else if** $\ell_c(\langle s_1, s_2 \rangle) =$ IN(T) **then** $type_N(a) :=$ IN-TASK, $\ell_N(a) := T$
26:    **else if** $\ell_c(\langle s_1, s_2 \rangle) =$ EX(T) **then** $type_N(a) :=$ EX-TASK, $\ell_N(a) := T$
27:    **else** $type_N(a) :=$ ANY-TASK, $\ell_N(a) := \emptyset$ ▷ $\ell_c(\langle s_1, s_2 \rangle) =$ ANY
28:    $F := F \cup \{\langle out(s_1), a \rangle, \langle a, in(s_2) \rangle\}$
29:    $type_F(\langle out(s_1), a \rangle) :=$ SEQ-FLOW, $\ell_F(\langle out(s_1), a \rangle) := \emptyset$
30:    $type_F(\langle a, in(s_2) \rangle) :=$ SEQ-FLOW, $\ell_F(\langle a, in(s_2) \rangle) := \emptyset$
31:    REMOVE-UNNECESSARY-XOR$(\mathcal{M})$

Proof. First of all, by Lemma 1, since FSA2CA is applied on A after the determinization, also the produced constraint automaton is actually an FCA, and hence it can be correctly fed into FCA2BPMND. The correctness of line 5 is obtained from [4], and that of line 7 is obtained by applying Lemma 1 and 2.

5 Conclusion

We have provided elements to support a negative answer to the original question: "Are completely new notations needed to support hybrid process modeling?". The definition of BPMN-D as a conservative extension to BPMN shows that

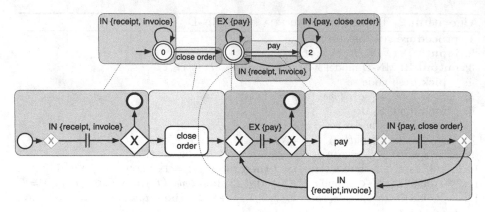

Fig. 5. Application of FCA2BPMND procedure to the FCA of Fig. 4; the small, light xor gateways are removed (cf. last line of the algorithm) leading to the diagram in Fig. 2

Algorithm 3. Translation of a Declare model to BPMN-D

1: **procedure** DECLARE2BPMND
2: **input** Declare model $\mathcal{D}$
3: **output** BPMN-D model $\mathcal{M}$
4:     $\Phi := \bigwedge_{c \text{ constraint of } \mathcal{D}} \text{LTL}_f(c)$ ▷ Obtained from the LTL$_f$ formalization of Declare
5:     $A := \text{LDL}_f 2\text{NFA}(\Phi)$ ▷ A is an NFA produced using the technique in [4]
6:     $A := \text{MINIMIZE}(\text{DETERMINIZE}(A))$ ▷ Standard automata operations
7:     $\mathcal{M} := \text{FCA2BPMND}(\text{FSA2CA}(A))$

"open-world" modeling constructs can be embedded into existing imperative process modeling notations without fundamentally extending their semantics. Indeed, the proposed BPMN-D notation is a macro-extension of BPMN. Moreover, we have shown that this notation can capture the range of constraints present in the Declare notation in an intuitive manner.

In its present form, the translation from Declare to BPMN-D generates process models with exclusive (XOR) gateways only, thus without parallelism. A direction for future work is to extend this translation with the ability to generate BPMN-D models with inclusive and parallel gateways. A possible approach is to adapt existing techniques from theory of regions [3], which extract parallelism in the context of Petri nets. A direct application of this approach can lead to unreadable process models as put into evidence in [16]. However, if we take constraint automata as a basis – as in our translation approach – it may be possible to adapt techniques from theory of regions to produce simpler constraint-annotated Petri nets that explicitly capture parallelism, and from there we could generate a BPMN-D process model.

Acknowledgments. This research is partly by ERDF via the Estonian Centre of Excellence in Computer Science and by the Estonian Research Council.

References

1. van der Aalst, W., Pesic, M., Schonenberg, H.: Declarative workflows: Balancing between flexibility and support. Computer Science - Research and Development **23** (2009)
2. Awad, A., Sakr, S.: On efficient processing of BPMN-Q queries. Computers in Industry **63**(9) (2012)
3. Carmona, J.: Projection approaches to process mining using region-based techniques. Data Min. Knowl. Discov. **24**(1) (2012)
4. De Giacomo, G., De Masellis, R., Grasso, M., Maggi, F., Montali, M.: Monitoring business metaconstraints based on LTL and LDL for finite traces. In: Sadiq, S., Soffer, P., Völzer, H. (eds.) Business Process Management. LNCS, vol. 8659, pp. 1–17. Springer, Heidelberg (2014)
5. De Giacomo, G., Vardi, M.Y.: Linear temporal logic and linear dynamic logic on finite traces. In: 23rd Int. Joint Conf. on Artificial Intelligence (IJCAI). AAAI (2013)
6. De Smedt, J., De Weerdt, J., Vanthienen, J.: Multi-paradigm process mining: retrieving better models by combining rules and sequences. In: Meersman, R., Panetto, H., Dillon, T., Missikoff, M., Liu, L., Pastor, O., Cuzzocrea, A., Sellis, T. (eds.) OTM 2014. LNCS, vol. 8841, pp. 446–453. Springer, Heidelberg (2014)
7. Dijkman, R.M., Dumas, M., Ouyang, C.: Semantics and analysis of business process models in BPMN. Information & Software Technology **50**(12), 1281–1294 (2008)
8. Hildebrandt, T., Mukkamala, R.R., Slaats, T.: Nested dynamic condition response graphs. In: Arbab, F., Sirjani, M. (eds.) FSEN 2011. LNCS, vol. 7141, pp. 343–350. Springer, Heidelberg (2012)
9. Hull, R., Damaggio, E., Masellis, R.D., Fournier, F., Gupta, M., Heath, F., Hobson, S., Linehan, M., Maradugu, S., Nigam, A., Noi Sukaviriya, P., Vaculín, R.: Business artifacts with guard-stage-milestone lifecycles: managing artifact interactions with conditions and events. In: 5th ACM Int. Conf. on Distributed Event-Based Systems (DEBS). ACM (2011)
10. Maggi, F.M., Slaats, T., Reijers, H.A.: The automated discovery of hybrid processes. In: Sadiq, S., Soffer, P., Völzer, H. (eds.) BPM 2014. LNCS, vol. 8659, pp. 392–399. Springer, Heidelberg (2014)
11. Marin, M., Hull, R., Vaculín, R.: Data centric BPM and the emerging case management standard: a short survey. In: La Rosa, M., Soffer, P. (eds.) BPM Workshops 2012. LNBIP, vol. 132, pp. 24–30. Springer, Heidelberg (2013)
12. Montali, M., Pesic, M., van der Aalst, W.M.P., Chesani, F., Mello, P., Storari, S.: Declarative Specification and Verification of Service Choreographies. ACM Transactions on Information Systems (2010)
13. Object Management Group: Business Process Modeling Notation Version 2.0. Tech. rep., Object Management Group Final Adopted Specification (2011)
14. Pesic, M., Schonenberg, H., van der Aalst, W.M.P.: Declare: Full support for loosely-structured processes. In: EDOC 2007 (2007)
15. Pichler, P., Weber, B., Zugal, S., Pinggera, J., Mendling, J., Reijers, H.A.: Imperative versus declarative process modeling languages: an empirical investigation. In: Daniel, F., Barkaoui, K., Dustdar, S. (eds.) BPM Workshops 2011, Part I. LNBIP, vol. 99, pp. 383–394. Springer, Heidelberg (2012)
16. Prescher, J., Di Ciccio, C., Mendling, J.: From declarative processes to imperative models. In: 4th Int. Symp. on Data-Driven Process Discovery and Analysis (SIMPDA). CEUR-WS.org (2014)

17. Reichert, M., Weber, B.: Enabling Flexibility in Process-Aware Information Systems - Challenges, Methods, Technologies. Springer (2012)
18. Reijers, H.A., Slaats, T., Stahl, C.: Declarative modeling–an academic dream or the future for BPM? In: Daniel, F., Wang, J., Weber, B. (eds.) BPM 2013. LNCS, vol. 8094, pp. 307–322. Springer, Heidelberg (2013)
19. Schonenberg, H., Mans, R., Russell, N., Mulyar, N., van der Aalst, W.: Towards a taxonomy of process flexibility. In: Forum at the CAiSE 2008 Conf., vol. 344. CEUR-WS.org (2008)
20. Westergaard, M.: Better algorithms for analyzing and enacting declarative workflow languages using LTL. In: Rinderle-Ma, S., Toumani, F., Wolf, K. (eds.) BPM 2011. LNCS, vol. 6896, pp. 83–98. Springer, Heidelberg (2011)
21. Westergaard, M., Slaats, T.: Mixing paradigms for more comprehensible models. In: Daniel, F., Wang, J., Weber, B. (eds.) BPM 2013. LNCS, vol. 8094, pp. 283–290. Springer, Heidelberg (2013)

High Volume and Complex
Information Management

The Requirements and Needs of Global Data Usage in Product Lifecycle Management

Anni Siren[1(✉)], Kari Smolander[1], and Mikko Jokela[2]

[1] Lappeenranta University of Technology, Lappeenranta, Finland
anni.siren@gmail.com, kari.smolander@lut.fi
[2] ABB Ltd., Espoo, Finland
mikko.jokela@fi.abb.com

Abstract. This study examines global data movement in large businesses from a product data management (PDM) and enterprise resource planning (ERP) point-of-view. The purpose of this study was to understand and map out how a large global business handles its data in a multiple site structure and how it can be applied in practice. This was done by doing an empirical interview study on five different global businesses with design locations in multiple countries. Their master data management (MDM) solutions were inspected and analyzed to understand which solution would best benefit a large global architecture with many design locations. One working solution is a transactional hub which negates the effects of multisite transfers and reduces lead times.

Keywords: ERP · PLM · MDM · Data management · Global data · Multisite

1   Introduction

In the last twenty years, large businesses have become more international with design, manufacturing, and production located around the globe. This means that each of these sites needs to be connected for smooth data transactions. To achieve this, a reliable software system is needed.

The objective of this study is to understand global design in an enterprise resource planning (ERP) and product data management (PDM) environment. An ERP system provides an all-in-one solution for seamless integration of information flows across an organization [1]; while a PDM system is used for product data management and publication while facilitating the splitting of resources such as designers and product manufacturing between various global sites [2].

The goal of this study is to determine how data flows between different global sites. The main focus of this study is how current PDM and ERP data transfer systems work in practice and how data is transferred between sites. This study is limited to five global machine manufacturing companies with design teams located in Finland. This study is also limited to a PDM and ERP environment. The main target is observing the boundary between PDM and ERP systems in a multinational organization where data is moved between sites on a daily basis.

© Springer International Publishing Switzerland 2015
J. Zdravkovic et al. (Eds.): CAiSE 2015, LNCS 9097, pp. 103–117, 2015.
DOI: 10.1007/978-3-319-19069-3_7

The structure of this paper is split into five main chapters. The second chapter will discuss the background of product lifecycle management (PLM) and how PDM and ERP systems are connected. Chapter 3 will discuss master data management and chapter 4 will consist of a case study in which five companies are interviewed about their global PDM systems. Chapter 5 concludes this study.

2   Understanding PDM and ERP Systems in a Global Environment

Product lifecycle management (PLM) is essentially a business strategy for creating a project-centric environment [3] [4]. The purpose of PLM is to chart the whole lifecycle of a product from concept to retirement and is deeply associated with computer aided design (CAD) and product data management (PDM) systems.

PLM is used to spread the influence of PDM systems beyond design and manufacturing and towards areas such as marketing and sales, in this case through an enterprise resource planning (ERP) system. The main purpose for linking PDM and ERP systems in a CAD design environment is to ensure the efficient movement of designs through the CAD environment into the PDM system which feeds it to the ERP system and subsequently to manufacturing.

To understand product data management it is important to understand PDM systems. According to [5], [2] and [6], PDM is a software framework which enables manufacturers to manage engineering information such as the data needed for new product designs and engineering processes. It allows the control of product information throughout the entire product lifecycle (PLC) and thus takes a more team-oriented approach to product development. The PDM system helps control how manufacturing data is created, reviewed, modified, approved and archived. One of the main functions of a PDM system is to ensure that data modifications happen in an organized manner. It controls data access with a check-in/-out function and controls authorized users [7]. It is also common to use a PDM system to determine the state of an object. A state indicates if an object has been approved to enter the next stage of development [8].

A PDM system needs an authoring tool, such as a CAD program, which supplies data to the PDM system [9]. CAD tools are used to design and modify content such as 3D MCAD and ECAD documents. However, a PDM system is not used to handle physical parts and this is where an enterprise resource planning (ERP) system is needed. An ERP system controls the physical ordering and distribution of parts after the design process. By adding an ERP system with a PDM system, they can be made to work in tandem to control the flow of information from conception to shipping a finished product. It is difficult to get a smoothly working integrated PDM/ERP system because they are fundamentally different ways of looking at data management [2].

[9], introduce a framework for PDM/ERP interoperability in which the user has one interface where they can use both systems and [10] introduces a method for digital manufacturing that eases the way data flows between PDM and ERP systems.

3 MDM in Large Business

Master data management (MDM) is a general term which refers to the "disciplines, technologies, and solutions that are used to create and maintain consistent and accurate master data from all stakeholders across and beyond the enterprise" [11]. MDM is a tool which provides a way to incrementally reduce the amount of superfluous information in an enterprise.

With an excellent MDM system, a company will have correct and authoritative master data. Master data itself is a central prerequisite for companies to perform acceptably [12]. A company's master data is used throughout the whole organization and thus it is imperative that the data is organized accordingly. According to [13], master data includes data models, attributes and definitions. An important part of master data is information systems (IS), which includes the applications and technology used to integrate and share data.

When considering master data implementation it is important to remember that not only is quality and consistency of the data important, but the usage of the data should be available throughout the enterprise. Another advantage of MDM is cost reduction and avoidance, since it can lead to the reduction of data storage costs and remove redundant data copies in consolidation and transactional hub styles of MDM [11]. This is due to MDM enabling the reuse of key processes.

There are three types of MDM implementation styles: (i) consolidation implementation, (ii) coexistence style implementation, and (iii) transactional hub implementation [11]. The consolidation implementation has an analytical focus, while the other two are more operationally oriented [14].

A consolidation implementation brings master data from multiple existing systems and places them into a single MDM hub where a golden record of the data exists. A golden record serves as a trusted source to downstream systems for reporting and analytics or as a system of reference to other operational applications. In a coexistence style implementation master data can be authored and stored in multiple locations. It has a golden record constructed similarly to the one in the consolidation method, typically through batch imports, and can be both queried and updated within the MDM system. A transactional hub implementation is the goal of every MDM system. It is a centralized, complete set of master data for one or more domains. It is a system of record while the other two are systems of reference. Master data in an ideal MDM implementation can be considered a system of record while a system of reference is a replica of the master data which is known to be synchronized with the system of record [11].

4 Case Study

To better understand how a multisite works in practice, five companies were interviewed. These companies are all machine manufacturing companies with design teams located in Finland. The interviewed persons were PDM experts. For the purpose of this study all company data is kept anonymous.

4.1   Company A

Company A is a medium sized company with 100+ employees with one main site in Finland and sub-sites located internationally. The main PDM database is located at the main site and all data from sub-sites is replicated there daily. This keeps the master copy of the data at the main site up-to-date. This indicates that they are using a consolidation style MDM implementation.

There has been no need to handle data ownership as most sites have their own design projects and products which are site based. This causes little conflict between sites. Technically there is only one database which is at the main-site and when a new part is created the meta-data is created in the main database. The documentation is then synchronized nightly. Most product design and product maintenance is located at the main site. However, sometimes assemblies will have the same subassemblies. This causes some data management issues, because there is no data locking mechanisms. This is not seen as a large problem since most of the design work is order engineering.

Approval processes are relaxed since many drawings are created and used only once so if problems do arise the drawings can be redone easily. However, purchased components have their own approval processes which are mostly related to internal system specific details e.g. naming and grouping. When the approval is complete the data is sent to the main site PDM and ERP systems. There is no process to check for the quality of the data or if the synchronization of data was successful.

All purchases are done through the ERP system. Long-term components are purchased at an early date in the design cycle, then the main quantity of parts and finally any other parts that are needed. It is not enough to approve an item in the PDM system and move it to the ERP system for purchases to be made; they need to be activated separately from the assembly's purchase order located in the ERP system.

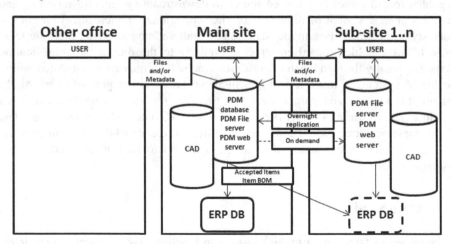

Fig. 1. Company A: PDM Architecture

Design tasks are monitored poorly. Designers inform project managers on how a task is progressing, but no clear system exists for monitoring tasks. Design hours are calculated and fixed accordingly. These hours are used as a loose baseline on how complete a design project is. This is a very difficult process since the design progress also constitutes the timeline for part purchases.

Figure 1 shows the PDM architecture for company A. Each site has its own PDM file server and PDM web server which are used as a physical client for the PDM software. The main site has the main PDM database which sends information to the global ERP database. Sub-sites send data to the main site in an overnight replication process. There are also other offices which need to use the PDM information so the needed files and metadata is sent accordingly.

All sites, including daughter companies, are connected through the ERP and PDM systems so no other data movement is necessary. Designers use a local file database to access information and non-designer users are connected to their own systems where they can locate the necessary information. Company A has one data storage location which collects all information into a central location. The design data moves only in one direction and sub-sites are not able to access data from other sub-sites without additional synchronization. Synchronization to the central site works well. Moving data toward sub-sites, however, is more complicated and designers have to wait for the data to arrive. Sometimes after a manual data sync, parts of the assembly data will be missing which causes further problems. Usually, sites handle their own projects, but some capacity sharing is done when needed. Designers will then get additional CAD data while assembly data is available through the ERP system.

Design approval transparency is very poor. The only way to see if something goes wrong with design approval is when it cannot be found in the ERP system. Technically the ERP has a monitoring element, but it is so sensitive it suffers from major inflation of messages. Another problem with PDM-ERP transfers is the way certain parameters are handled e.g. groups, types, and units. They need to be manually transferred across to the ERP if any changes are done after the initial transfer. Another large issue with transfers is how parts are moved straight to project structures. Even though the structure should not change after creation, most errors occur when two BOM lines are placed under the same number or something changes on the PDM side which has not transferred correctly.

PDM-ERP transfers for individual items work really well. Product structures are created automatically for each item and when product specifications e.g. group, unit, are kept in check in the ERP system there are little problems with it. The night replication also works well.

4.2 Company B

Company B is a large multinational company with 16,000+ employees. Their headquarters are located in Helsinki, Finland with sub-sites abroad. There are two PDM systems, an internal EDM (Teamcenter) and a global PDM (Aton) which makes things more complex. The higher level PDM system sends data to the global ERP.

Currently, CAD systems are loosely integrated into the PDM system. Items are approved as prototypes or final products. Final products are sent to the ERP system. When objects are approved in Teamcenter they are sent to Aton. Aton is used for final approvals and items are then sent to the global ERP system. The reason Teamcenter is not used for final approvals is because electrical and hydraulics designs are not available in the design process. Thus, the full assembly is not available until Aton. Only marginal changes are possible in Aton as almost everything is done in Teamcenter e.g. Aton cannot create new revisions, instead certain assembly attributes are filled in and final approval processes happen here The ERP system is used for some designer monitoring, but the main methods are email and meetings.

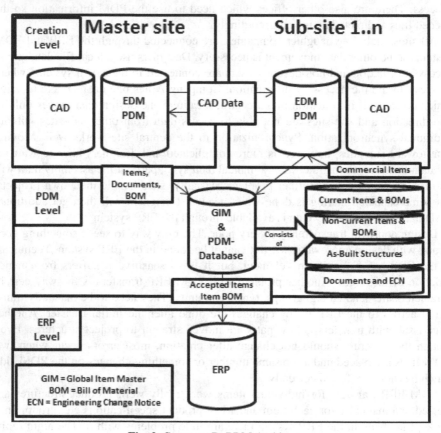

Fig. 2. Company B: PDM Architecture

All data is moved from the PDM system to the ERP system. ERP has no backward compatibility, except with commercial items which need to be modified in the PDM system before they can be readmitted to the ERP system. Basic data movement between PDM and ERP systems is satisfactory. The multisite only works on-demand. There is little need for moving data between sites as most assemblies are completed at one site. Sometimes, different product modules are designed at other sites. This does add the need for multisite data transfers. Replication is only done on-demand. Users can access it from the PDM client interface and administration can access it through the server scripts. Items that have been replicated before can be transferred by users, but other items must be handled by the administration. The PDM client interface will inform the user that the data has been sent, but it will not report if the transfer was successful. Ownership can only be transferred by an admin.

Figure 2 shows the PDM architecture for company B. There is one master site and multiple sub-sites, but they are technically on the same creation level as both can submit information to the main PDM database, Aton. CAD data is moved between the creation level PDM sites, but other PDM information is approved on the PDM level. Aton can then be used to send the PDM information into the global ERP system. This indicates that Company B currently has a consolidation method system, but they are moving toward a transactional hub with a single PDM and ERP system.

There is no need for improvements, even though all processes could be moved to Teamcenter. There is also no backward data movement from ERP to PDM where some information such as order information, average prices, warehouse inventory could be very useful.

This was an affordable PDM solution; stable and relatively high quality. The fact that there are two PDM systems interlinked is unnecessary from a user's perspective. The simplest solution would be to move to use just the Teamcenter PDM, but many other business units only use Aton.

4.3   Company C

Company C is a large multinational company with 18,000+ employees and headquarters in Helsinki, Finland. They have 2 main sites; one located in Europe and one in Asia. With a large company, such as company C, the amount of business divisions creates a need for a complex PDM solution which will cater to all divisions with equal efficiency. Currently, there are multiple PDM systems which are being replaced by Teamcenter. The current global PDM system reflects the coexistence implementation style.

Company C, like so many others, is trying to move toward a transactional hub, but current data latency issues for data movement across the world this is a hard goal to achieve. There are two main sites with a single central database which will result in faster data queries. An additional future feature will be a cloud portal which lessens the need for multisite transfers and creates a faster connection to the central database.

Figure 3 shows the PDM architecture for company C. The main site and sub-sites are all on the same creation level and feed to a global PDM system. This data can then be moved to the global ERP system. From a PDM-ERP connection perspective there is only one ERP system at Company C. This makes data transfers to ERP simple. There is one PDM to ERP connection located in the EU and another in Asia.

There is very strict access management built into the PDM system, which increases data protection as a user is allowed to only create, modify, or view materials in their own user group. Data is owned by one site with replicas at other sites, but the strict data access management keeps anyone outside the correct user group from tampering. There is also an enterprise content management (ECM) in production which allows all items to be covered by a change item. This allows drawings to be watermarked and sent to joint ventures and partners before its approval is finalized. When the final approval is performed the watermark is removed.

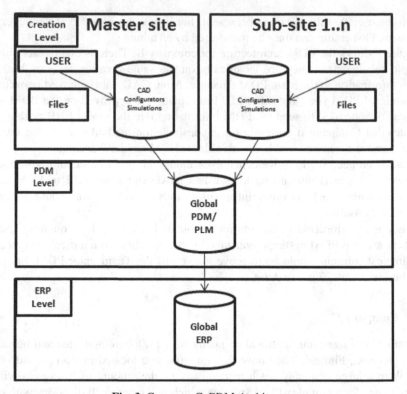

Fig. 3. Company C: PDM Architecture

Data is moved in the PDM system and then released to the global ERP. Design approvals are monitored by multiple stakeholders, which makes workflows very complex. This allows for quality insurance and change management of designs. Items can have two flags: approval and sent to ERP flags. This is useful since long time components are sent to the ERP before they are approved in the PDM system and are essentially placeholders for purchasing.

Currently no assembly structure skeletons are available. Assembly data is handled through a material master since configurators are not connected to the PDM system at this time. This causes materials to be released to the ERP system before they are approved in the PDM system. Approvals are not moved between sites; instead they are moved between the PDM and ERP systems. One product approval has a dedicated workflow to send data to the ERP and another is embedded into change management. Many things are done during the approval process including the creation of CAD PDFs and PDXs files. Thus new checkpoints need to be established to keep track of what has been delivered to the ERP system. This causes workflows to become a bottleneck when there is an internal failure or when data does not meet the checkpoints of a workflow.

One challenge is the growing user base. Currently, the number of users is around 1000, but through a PDM merger project the number should double. Most multisite issues are reduced by merging sites which eliminates the need for replicas. Not all problems are solved with a global ERP and by merging sites and transfer speeds suffer from latency between sites with site consolidations e.g. Norway to Finland.

4.4   Company D

Company D is a multinational company with headquarters in Finland and they have more than 10,000 employees. The main design sites are located in Europe, Asia and the USA. Company D has design teams in 15-20 countries and it is an inherent feature that each sales representative has a technical specialist or designer for support. This adds many more countries where small change design work is done. This company is going through a large PDM project moving from a cluster of systems to one centralized PDM-ERP system. This means that Company D is moving from a coexistence implementation style to a transactional hub. This new centralized system is the first platform which enables a global PDM-ERP environment.

Data ownership is handled poorly. Items can be viewed and edited by different user groups, but with such a large company there are many divisions and outside sources that need to manage the data. Data is not locked unless it is being modified by CAD tools.

Figure 4 shows the PDM architecture of company D. Data is created at main and sub-sites and moved to a regional cache database which is located in e.g. Europe or Asia. It is then replicated to the global PDM database located in Finland. Only the metadata is available instantly in the global PDM system as it takes time for the information to transfer. However, this shows designers what information will be available almost instantaneously. The data can then be moved to the global ERP system.

Design data is approved in stages and they do not move directly into the ERP system. There are different workflows for approving items and other workflows which combine the approval and transfer processes. A designer who does research and development has a stricter approval process while order engineering designers can approve their own work to a certain status which allows production. The different status can be used to see if an item is meant for further production or if it is just a one-time assembly.

Data is moved between sites through a store and forward cache system. Data is moved into a central database with the metadata sent straight to the destination system. The central database then moves the data to the destination site at its own pace. Currently, this is an on-demand type of cache system. This means that when design data is saved in the PDM system it is sent to a country cache after which it is moved to the central database. The metadata is moved first which will show up quickly while the actual CAD data will appear when the full transfer is done.

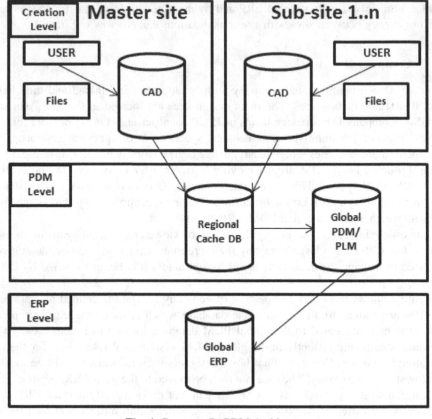

Fig. 4. Company D: PDM Architecture

Currently, most data moves from PDM-ERP, but some aspects are starting to flow from ERP-PDM e.g. sales orders. The most crucial improvement would be to performance; large data amounts are difficult to move in a short period of time.

4.5   Company E

Company E is a large multinational company with headquarters in Zurich, Switzerland. It employs 150,000+ employees with 16,000 employees in the business unit this PDM system serves. The main PDM sites are located in Europe and Asia. There is currently a large PDM project underway in which many new PDM sites are added into the global PDM collective. Company E has a coexistence implementation style and each site has its own PDM and ERP systems which communicate through a multisite collaboration system.

Assemblies are approved through the PDM system and they are sent to the ERP system during the approval process. Product structures are first sent to ERP as an assembly structure skeleton which is used as a base for the final assembly. Approved items will be flagged, but there is no indicator that it has been sent to ERP. This has caused some problems when drawings or structure data is missing.

Items are locked when they are in use. This means that nothing can use the item at that time, i.e. another designer or approval process. This ensures quality of data at that time. However, this also causes problems when a process or designer has locked an item which needs to be used somewhere else.

Designers are located in multiple locations and can work on the same assemblies or subassemblies. This makes it very important for multisite transfers to work efficiently. Data is sent to other sites on-demand and after the object is located somewhere it is kept up-to-date with a nightly data synchronization. Not all sites are connected to each other as most sites are paired up with one or two other sites.

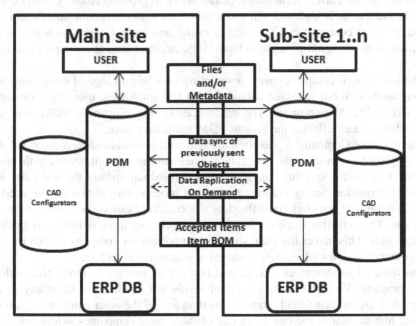

Fig. 5. Company E: PDM Architecture

Figure 5 shows the PDM architecture of company E. Each main site and sub-site is used to create their own data. This data is then replicated on-demand between sites. Each site also has their own ERP system, thus they need to move the PDM data to each ERP separately as needed.

The design process is poorly monitored through Excel spreadsheets and internal communication. Purchases are handled by the ERP system where assembly structure skeletons are run to ensure that long term components are delivered on time.

There have been some issues with multisite transfers. Large assemblies take a long time to transfer and might contain errors. The amount of errors has lessened, but there are still connection difficulties to Asia. The daily synchronizations work relatively well and the number of error messages are manageable.

4.6   Data Analysis

Since computer systems have become common place in the last two decades, PDM systems projects have become more vital for organizations. Each of the interviewed companies was in the middle of an extensive PDM project to improve their product data management. The method that everyone strives for is the transactional hub, because it consists of one large database which encompasses the whole organization. This would make data sharing between sites obsolete and in theory all data would be available for every designer at any time. In practice this is close to impossible to accomplish with the current technology. Data latency to growing industry centers, such as India and China, is high and will cause problems with connection speeds and synchronizing to a central hub. Even with a cache and store system, such as the one Company D has, it is not possible to have 100% accurate data at a central point at all times.

The interviewed companies were a sampling of a broad range of companies with various needs with one midsized company with 100 employees, four large companies with 10,000-18,000 employees. The differences in the companies' PDM structures were extensive and reflected the various PDM needs they have.

The midsized Company A was the only one with a consolidation method solution with no plans to convert in the near future. Their data movement needs are the smallest, but they have a working data transfer system which updates the main site with updated information during a nightly replication process. This eliminates the need for extensive multisite transfers since the data's normal replication need was only to the main site. The sub-sites work on their own projects and there is little collaboration between sites. This makes the main site more important for company A than they are in the other companies where data is moved at a more rigorous pace.

The three large companies – B, C, and D – are all moving toward a transactional hub. Company B's and C's data creation levels are similar, but Company D and Company E create significantly more items than any of the other companies. A transactional hub solution is the one every one of these three companies strides for. It has its advantages, but also comes with its own risks as data ownership becomes a serious issue.

Companies B and C are close in the number of items created in a year. They also have low data movement needs and when a working transactional hub is in place that need will disappear altogether. The methods of data transfer are very different however. Company B is crippled with having to essentially use two PDM software solutions at once, while company C is moving toward a one PDM system solution.

Company D is the only one with a working transactional hub solution currently in use with a store and cache system. It negates the need for multisite transfers and it seems to be working efficiently. However, their data ownership processes are poorly handled, unlike in companies B, C and E where data ownership is done efficiently.

Company E has the largest need for data transfers, but they also have the weakest multisite system. Company E is using a coexistence method which works with a large number of main sites. Many assembly designs are split between sites, which causes a high need to move data through a multisite solution. This data is moved manually and after the data exists at another site it is replicated automatically when changes are made. This lessens the burden of having to move updated information manually. However, this does not lessen the strain on the system and causes problems with ERP since new data needs to be manually sent to the ERP system.

Even with such different types of companies they also have their similarities. Four out of the five interviewed companies used Teamcenter as their main user oriented PDM system and SAP as their main ERP system. This can be due to the fact that each company has their main PDM teams in Finland.

Table 1. Company summaries

	A	B	C	D	E
PDM/ERP software	Aton, LEAN, AB+, SAP	Aton, Team-center, SAP, other ERP systems	Transition to: Teamcenter, SAP	Transition to: Teamcenter, SAP	Teamcenter, SAP
MDM type	Consolidation method	Consolidation method -> Transactional hub	Coexistence method -> Transactional hub	Consolidation method -> Transactional hub	Coexistence method
Number of sites	1 main site	1 main site, 3 major sub-sites	2 main sites	7 main sites	7 main sites, 3 major sub-sites
Company size	100+ em-ployees	16,000+ em-ployees	18,000+ employees	10,000+ employees	16,000+ employees
Product lifecycle	30+ years	10-40+ years	30-40+ years	15-30+ years	20-30+ years
Estimated item crea-tion per year	15,000	20,000	16,000-40,000	120,000	50,000-100,000 per site
Data movement needs	Low, All sites are connected to PDM-ERP. No other data movement necessary	Low, some modules are designed at different sites	Low, Only one ERP	Low, Only one ERP and global PDM	High, many multiple site design projects
Data movement between sites	Automatic from sub-site to main site, multisite transfer from main site to sub-sites.	Only on-demand, users can only move replicated material, others by admins	Data approv-als not moved between sites but between PDM and ERP	Store and cache system. Data is moved from central database	Multisite transfer, replicated data synched each night
Data movement between PDM and ERP	During ap-proval	During ap-proval, no backwards compatibility	Its own ap-proval process, sends a sent to ERP flag	Its own ap-proval process	Each site sends to their own ERP during ap-proval process
Data own-ership	No handling	Only admins can change ownership	Very strict access man-agement	Poorly	Items are owned by site, locked when in use

4.7   Case Summary

A store and cache mechanism, like the one used by company D, is a good method to move data between sites as it negates the need for manual data transfers with one central database. It moves the metadata instantly to all sites, which allows designers to see what data is available, even if the actual CAD data has not been moved yet.

Company C has a very strict access management system which monitors data ownership and authoring. This is a very useful as each designer only sees what data they need. This allows for less accidental data tampering. Company C also has different approval flags; sent to ERP, basic and final approval flags. This is useful, as a designer can instantly see what status an item has. As they have a single PDM and ERP systems data approvals do not need to move between sites, but are moved inside the PDM and ERP systems themselves.

Companies A, B and D have stable working environments where the multisite works well and efficiently according to their data movement needs. Company C is currently undergoing a large PDM project to move away from a multiple PDM system solution to a single PDM system solution. Company E has the most problems with their multisite system, but this is due to the large quantities of data that need to be moved compared to the other companies.

There were some clear similarities between the five companies, such as each of the large companies had chosen to use Teamcenter as their main PDM software and SAP for their main ERP software. This could be due to the fact that all were large machine manufacturing companies where the main PDM site was located in Finland and so the study is quite limited to their point-of-view.

5   Conclusion

Data management is an important part of a company's business structure as it controls everything from design to manufacturing. This study looks at how global design effects data management in a multinational company through the use of product data management and enterprise resource planning systems. In this environment, design data moves between the PDM and ERP systems within one site and between sites through a multisite connection.

Five different companies were interviewed to see how different companies handle their multisite connections through different master data management solutions. The best method to gain a working solution was to nullify the need for a multisite system and instead focus on rendering a working transactional hub. This makes sharing designs simpler and more efficient. The downside of this system is the long distance and current infrastructure in places such as China and India which causes bad data latency issues.

There were some clear similarities between the five interviewed companies, such as each large company had chosen to use Teamcenter as their main PDM software and SAP for their main ERP software. This could be due to the fact that all were large machine manufacturing companies where the main PDM site was located in Finland. This could have skewed the results to favor a similar view.

Global design is a very important research subject which will only expand as more companies turn to multinational solutions. As technology advances some issues such as data latency can be rectified. This will cause global PDM and ERP solutions to become more popular.

Acknowledgements. This study was partly funded by Academy of Finland grant #259454.

References

1. Davenport, T.H.: Putting the enterprise into the enterprise system. Harvard Business Review, vol. 76 (1998)
2. Peltonen, H., Martio, A., Sulonen, R.: PDM Tuotetiedon hallinta. Edita Prima Oy, Helsinki (2002)
3. Ameri, F., Dutta, D.: Product Lifecycle Management: Closing the Knowledge Loops. Computer-Aided Design and Applications **2**, 577–590 (2005)
4. Saaksvuori, A., Immonen, A.: Product Lifecycle Management. Springer-Verlag, Berlin (2008)
5. Gascoigne, B.: PDM: the essential technology for concurrent engineering. World Class Design to Manufacture **2**, 38–42 (1995)
6. Crnkovic, I., Asklund, U., Dahlqvist Persson, A.: Implementing and Integrating Product Data Management and Software Configuration Management. Artech House, p. 19. Norwood (2003)
7. Kääriäinen, J., Savolainen, P., Taramaa, J., Leppälä, K.: Product Data Management (PDM) Design, exchange and integration viewpoints. Technical Research Center of Finland (VTT), Espoo (2000)
8. Peltonen, H.: Concepts and an Implementation for Product Data Management. The Finnish Academies of Technology, Espoo (2000)
9. Paviot, T., Cheutet, V., Lamouri, S.: A PLCS framework for PDM/ERP interoperability. International Journal of Product Lifecycle Management **5**, 295–313 (2011)
10. Lee, C., Leem, C.S., Hwang, I.: PDM and ERP integration methodology using digital manufacturing to support global manufacturing. The International Journal of Advanced Manufacturing Technology **53**, 399–409 (2011)
11. Dreibelbis, A., Hechler, E., Milman, I., Oberhofer, M., van Run, P., Wolfson, D.: Enterprise Master Data Management: An SOA Approach to Managing Core Information. Pearson Education, Boston (2008)
12. Otto, B., Huner, K.M.: Functional Reference Architecture for Corporate Master Data Management. Institute of Information Management, University of St. Gallan, St. Gallan (2009)
13. Silvola, R., Jaaskelainen, O., Kropsu-Vehkapera, H., Haapasalo, H.: Managing one master data - challenges and preconditions. Industrial Management and Data Systems **111**, 146–162 (2011)
14. Radcliffe, J., White, A., Newman, D.: How to choose the right architectural style for master data management. Gartner Research (2006)

Probabilistic Keys for Data Quality Management

Pieta Brown and Sebastian Link[(✉)]

Department of Computer Science, University of Auckland, Auckland, New Zealand
{pieta.brown,s.link}@auckland.ac.nz

Abstract. Probabilistic databases address well the requirements of an increasing number of modern applications that produce large volumes of uncertain data from a variety of sources. We propose probabilistic keys as a principled tool helping organizations balance the consistency and completeness targets for their data quality. For this purpose, algorithms are established for an agile schema- and data-driven acquisition of the marginal probability by which keys should hold in a given application domain, and for reasoning about these keys. The efficiency of our acquisition framework is demonstrated theoretically and experimentally.

Keywords: Acquisition · Key · Probability · Quality · Visualization

1 Introduction

Background. The notion of a key is fundamental for understanding the structure and semantics of data. For relational databases, keys were already introduced in Codd's seminal paper [6]. Here, a key is a set of attributes that holds on a relation if there are no two different tuples in the relation that have matching values on all the attributes of the key. Keys uniquely identify tuples of data, and are applied in data cleaning, integration, modeling, processing, and retrieval.

Motivation. Relational databases target applications with certain data, such as accounting, inventory and payroll. Modern applications, such as data integration, information extraction, and financial risk assessment produce large volumes of uncertain data from a variety of sources. For instance, RFID (radio frequency identification) is used to track movements of endangered species of animals, such as wolverines. Here it is sensible to apply probabilistic databases. Table 1 shows a probabilistic relation (p-relation), which is a probability distribution over a finite set of possible worlds, each being a relation.

Keys address the consistency dimension of data quality in traditional databases. Due to the veracity inherent to probabilistic databases as well as the variety of sources the data originates from, the traditional concept of a key requires revision in this context. In our example, for instance, there is no non-trivial key that is satisfied by all possible worlds: the key $k1 = k\{time, zone\}$ holds in the worlds W_1 and W_2, $k2 = k\{rfid, time\}$ holds in W_2 and W_3, and $k3 = k\{rfid, zone\}$ holds in W_3 and W_4. One may argue to remove possible worlds that violate a key but this would neither address the completeness dimension of

© Springer International Publishing Switzerland 2015
J. Zdravkovic et al. (Eds.): CAiSE 2015, LNCS 9097, pp. 118–132, 2015.
DOI: 10.1007/978-3-319-19069-3_8

Table 1. Probabilistic relation

W_1 $(p_1 = 0.2)$			W_2 $(p_2 = 0.45)$			W_3 $(p_3 = 0.3)$			W_4 $(p_4 = .05)$		
rfid	time	zone	rfid	time	zone	rfid	time	zone	rfid	time	zone
w1	2pm	z1	w1	2pm	z1	w1	2pm	z1	w1	3pm	z1
w1	3pm	z1	w1	3pm	z1	w1	3pm	z2	w1	3pm	z2
w1	3pm	z2	w2	3pm	z2	w2	3pm	z2	w2	3pm	z2

data quality nor would it make sensible use of probabilistic databases. Instead, we propose the new concept of a *probabilistic key*, or p-key for short, which stipulates a lower bound on the marginal probability by which a traditional key holds in a probabilistic database. In our example, $k1$, $k2$, and $k3$ have marginal probability 0.65, 0.75, and 0.35, respectively, which is the sum of the probabilities of those possible worlds which satisfy the key. Indeed, the marginal probability of a key provides a control mechanism to balance consistency and completeness targets for the quality of data. Larger marginal probabilities represent stricter consistency and more liberal completeness targets, while smaller marginal probabilities represent more liberal consistency and stricter completeness targets. Having fixed these targets in the form of a marginal probability, p-keys can be utilized to control these data quality dimensions during updates. When new data arrives, p-keys can help detect anomalous patterns of data in the form of p-key violations. That is, alerts can be automatically sent out when a data set would not meet a desired lower bound on the marginal probability of a key. In a different showcase, p-keys can also be used to infer probabilities that query answers are unique. In our example, we may wonder about the chance that different wolverines are in the same zone at the same time, indicating potential mating behavior. We may ask

SELECT DISTINCT *rfid* FROM TRACKING WHERE *zone*='z2' AND *time*='2pm'

and using our p-keys enables us to derive a minimum probability of 0.65 that a unique answer is returned, that is, different wolverines are in zone z2 at 2pm at most with probability 0.35. These bounds can be inferred without accessing any portion of a potentially big data source at all, only requiring that the key $k1$ has at least marginal probability 0.65 on the given data set.

Contributions. The examples motivate us to stipulate lower bounds on the marginal probability of keys. The main inhibitor for the uptake of p-keys is the identification of the right lower bounds on their marginal probabilities. While it is already challenging to identify traditional keys which are semantically meaningful in a given application domain, identifying the right probabilities is an even harder problem. Lower bounds appear to be a realistic compromise here. Our contributions can be summarized as follows. **Modeling.** We propose p-keys $kX_{\geq p}$ as a natural class of semantic integrity constraints over uncertain data. Their main target is to help organizations balance consistency and completeness targets for the quality of their data. P-keys can distinguish semantically meaningful from meaningless patterns in large volumes of uncertain data from

	CD table				P table	
rfid	time	zone	W		W	P
w1	2:00pm	z1	1, 2, 3		1	.2
w1	3:00pm	z1	1, 2, 4		2	.45
w1	3:00pm	z2	1, 3, 4		3	.3
w2	3:00pm	z2	2, 3, 4		4	.05

rfid, time, zone
1

rfid, time   rfid, zone   time, zone
0.75   0.35   0.65

rfid   time   zone
0   0   0

∅
0

Fig. 1. Armstrong PC-table for $\{k1_{\geq 0.65}, k2_{\geq 0.75}, k3_{\geq 0.35}\}$ and its profile of p-keys

a variety of sources, and help quantify the probability for unique query answers. **Reasoning.** We characterize the implication problem of p-keys by a simple finite set of Horn rules, as well as a linear time decision algorithm. This enables organizations to reduce the overhead of data quality management by p-keys to a minimal level necessary. For example, enforcing $k\{rfid\}_{\geq 0.3}$, $k\{rfid,time\}_{\geq 0.25}$, and $k\{rfid,zone\}_{\geq 0.35}$, would be redundant as the enforcement of $k\{rfid,time\}_{\geq 0.25}$ is already implicitly done by enforcing $k\{rfid\}_{\geq 0.3}$. **Visualization.** For the schema-driven acquisition of the right marginal probabilities by which keys should hold, we show how to visualize concisely any given system of p-keys in the form of an Armstrong PC-table. An Armstrong PC-table is a perfect semantic summary of all p-keys currently perceived meaningful by the analysts. That is, the Armstrong PC-table satisfies every key with the exact marginal probability that is perceived to best represent the application domain. Any problems with such perceptions are explicitly pointed out by the PC-table. For example, the left of Figure 1 shows an Armstrong PC-table for $\{k1_{\geq 0.65}, k2_{\geq 0.75}, k3_{\geq 0.35}\}$. In the CD table, the W column of a tuple shows the identifiers of possible worlds to which the tuple belongs. The P-table shows the probability distribution on the possible worlds. Any p-key that is not implied by this set is violated, in particular the keys $k\{rfid\}$, $k\{time\}$ and $k\{zone\}$ all have marginal probability zero in the p-relation from Table 1, which is represented by this PC-table. **Profiling.** For the data-driven acquisition of p-keys we compute the marginal probability of every key from a given PC-table. This is also known as data profiling, and our paper is the first to propose probabilistic data profiling techniques. For example, if we want to know the marginal probabilities by which an attribute set forms a key in the PC-table from Figure 1, then our algorithm would return the profile $k\emptyset_{\geq 0}$, $k\{rfid\}_{\geq 0}$, $k\{time\}_{\geq 0}$, $k\{zone\}_{\geq 0}$, $k\{rfid,time\}_{\geq 0.75}$, $k\{rfid,zone\}_{\geq 0.35}$, $k\{time,zone\}_{\geq 0.65}$, and $k\{rfid,time,zone\}_{\geq 1}$, as visualized on the right of Figure 1. **Experiments.** Our experiments demonstrate that our visualization and profiling techniques work efficiently in the context of our acquisition framework.

Organization. We discuss related work in Section 2. P-keys are introduced in Section 3, and axiomatic and linear-time algorithmic characterizations of their implication problem are established in Section 4. These lay the foundation for the schema- and data-driven discovery algorithms of p-keys in Section 5. Experiments with these algorithms are presented in Section 6. We conclude and sketch future work in Section 7.

2   Related Work

Poor data quality is arguably the biggest inhibitor to deriving value from big data [31]. P-keys provide a principled tool to balance the consistency and completeness requirements of an organization on the quality of their data [23,30]. Primary impact areas of p-keys include data integration [5] where keys cannot be expected to hold with probability one; data modeling [27] where p-keys may represent target constraints that avoid data redundancy with certain degrees of probability; data processing [18] where p-keys facilitate updates and query answer exploration of targeted degrees of quality; compliance validation of business rules [25] where data is uncertain; in duplicate detection [3] where anomalous patterns of uncertain data are found; and in data cleaning and linkage [2]. The concept of probabilistic keys is new but naturally derived from previous research.

Our contributions extend results on keys from traditional relations, covered by our framework as the special case where the p-relation consists of one possible world only. Extensions include work on the classical implication problem [1,7, 11,13–15], Armstrong relations [4,9,12,13,21,29] and the discovery of keys from relations [16,22,29]. In fact, our axiomatic and algorithmic characterizations of the implication problem as well as the schema- and data-driven discovery of the right probabilities of keys is novel. Specifically, Armstrong databases and data profiling have not been studied yet for probabilistic data. For certain relations there is empirical evidence that Armstrong databases help with the acquisition of meaningful business rules [4,20,21,29]. Our techniques will make it possible to conduct such empirical studies for p-keys in the future.

There is a large body of work on the discovery of "approximate" business rules, such as keys, functional and inclusion dependencies [10,17,24]. Approximate means here that not all tuples satisfy the given rule, but some exceptions are tolerable. Our constraints are not approximate since they are either satisfied or violated by the given p-relation or the PC-table that represents it. Again, it is future work to investigate approximate versions of probabilistic keys.

Closest to our approach is the work on possibilistic keys [19], where tuples are attributed some degree of possibility and keys some degree of certainty saying to which tuples they apply. In general, possibility theory is a qualitative approach, while probability theory is a quantitative approach to uncertainty. This research thereby complements the qualitative approach to keys in [19] by a quantitative approach.

Keys have also been included in description logic research [26,33], but we are unaware of any work concerning keys on probabilistic data.

3   Probabilistic Keys

We introduce some preliminary concepts from probabilistic databases and the central notion of a probabilistic key.

A *relation schema* is a finite set R of attributes A. Each attribute A is associated with a domain $dom(A)$ of values. A tuple t over R is a function that assigns to each attribute A of R an element $t(A)$ from the domain $dom(A)$. A *relation* over R is a finite set of tuples over R. Relations over R are also called *possible worlds* of R here. An expression kX over R with $X \subseteq R$ is called a *key*. A key kX is said to hold in a possible world W of R, denoted by $W \models kX$, if and only if there no two tuples $t_1, t_2 \in W$ such that $t_1 \neq t_2$ and $t_1(X) = t_2(X)$. A *probabilistic relation* (p-relation) over R is a pair $r = (\mathcal{W}, P)$ of a finite non-empty set $\mathcal{W}$ of possible worlds over R and a probability distribution $P : \mathcal{W} \rightarrow (0, 1]$ such that $\sum_{W \in \mathcal{W}} P(W) = 1$ holds. Table 1 shows a probabilistic relation over relation schema WOLVERINE$=\{rfid, time, zone\}$. World W_2, for example, satisfies the keys $k\{rfid, time\}$ and $k\{zone, time\}$, but violates the key $k\{rfid, zone\}$. The *marginal probability* of a key kX in the p-relation $r = (\mathcal{W}, P)$ over relation schema R is the sum of the probabilities of those possible worlds in r which satisfy the key. We will now introduce the central notion of a probabilistic key.

Definition 1. *A probabilistic key, or p-key for short, over relation schema R is an expression $kX_{\geq p}$ where $X \subseteq R$ and $p \in [0, 1]$. The p-key $kX_{\geq p}$ over R is satisfied by, or said to hold in, the p-relation r over R if and only if the marginal probability of kX in r is not smaller than p.*

In our running example over relation schema WOLVERINE, the p-relation from Table 1 satisfies the p-keys $k\{rfid, time\}_{\geq 0.75}$ and $k\{rfid, zone\}_{\geq 0.35}$, but violates the p-keys $k\{rfid, time\}_{\geq 0.9}$ and $k\{rfid, zone\}_{\geq 0.351}$.

4   Reasoning Tools

When using sets of p-keys to manage the consistency and completeness targets on the quality of an organization's data, it is important that their overhead is reduced to a minimal level necessary. In practice, this requires us to reason about p-keys efficiently. It is the goal of this section to establish basic tools to reason about the interaction of p-keys. This will help us identify efficiently the largest probability by which a given key is implied from a given set of p-keys, and to optimize the efficiency of updates and query answers, for example. The results will also help us develop our acquisition framework later.

Let $\Sigma \cup \{\varphi\}$ denote a set of constraints over relation schema R. We say Σ *implies* φ, denoted by $\Sigma \models \varphi$, if every p-relation r over R that satisfies Σ, also satisfies φ. We use $\Sigma^* = \{\varphi : \Sigma \models \varphi\}$ to denote the *semantic closure* of Σ. For a class $\mathcal{C}$ of constraints, the $\mathcal{C}$-implication problem is to decide for a given relation schema R and a given set $\Sigma \cup \{\varphi\}$ of constraints in $\mathcal{C}$ over R, whether Σ implies φ. We will now characterize the $\mathcal{C}$-implication problem for the class of p-keys axiomatically by a simple finite set of Horn rules, and algorithmically by a linear time algorithm.

Axioms. We determine the semantic closure by applying *inference rules* of the form $\dfrac{\text{premise}}{\text{conclusion}}$. For a set $\mathfrak{R}$ of inference rules let $\Sigma \vdash_{\mathfrak{R}} \varphi$ denote the

Table 2. Axiomatization $\mathfrak{P} = \{\mathcal{T}, \mathcal{Z}, \mathcal{S}, \mathcal{W}\}$

$\overline{kR_{\geq 1}}$ (Trivial, $\mathcal{T}$)	$\overline{kX_{\geq 0}}$ (Zero, $\mathcal{Z}$)	$\dfrac{kX_{\geq p}}{kXY_{\geq p}}$ (Superkey, $\mathcal{S}$)	$\dfrac{kX_{\geq p+q}}{kX_{\geq p}}$ (Weakening, $\mathcal{W}$)

inference of φ from Σ by $\mathfrak{R}$. That is, there is some sequence $\sigma_1, \ldots, \sigma_n$ such that $\sigma_n = \varphi$ and every σ_i is an element of Σ or is the conclusion that results from an application of an inference rule in $\mathfrak{R}$ to some premises in $\{\sigma_1, \ldots, \sigma_{i-1}\}$. Let $\Sigma_{\mathfrak{R}}^+ = \{\varphi : \Sigma \vdash_{\mathfrak{R}} \varphi\}$ be the *syntactic closure* of Σ under inferences by $\mathfrak{R}$. $\mathfrak{R}$ is *sound* (*complete*) if for every set Σ over every R we have $\Sigma_{\mathfrak{R}}^+ \subseteq \Sigma^*$ ($\Sigma^* \subseteq \Sigma_{\mathfrak{R}}^+$). The (finite) set $\mathfrak{R}$ is a (finite) *axiomatization* if $\mathfrak{R}$ is both sound and complete. The set $\mathfrak{P}$ of inference rules from Table 2 forms a finite axiomatization for the implication of p-keys. Here, R denotes the underlying relation schema, X and Y form attribute subsets of R, and p, q as well as $p + q$ are probabilities.

Theorem 1. $\mathfrak{P}$ *forms a finite axiomatization for p-keys.* □

For example, the set $\Sigma = \{k\{time\}_{\geq 0.2}, k\{rfid\}_{\geq 0.3}\}$ imply the p-key $\varphi = k\{rfid, time\}_{\geq 0.25}$, but not the p-key $\varphi' = k\{rfid, time\}_{\geq 0.35}$. Indeed, φ can be inferred from Σ by applying $\mathcal{S}$ to $k\{rfid\}_{\geq 0.3}$ to infer $k\{rfid, time\}_{\geq 0.3}$, and applying $\mathcal{W}$ to $k\{rfid, time\}_{\geq 0.3}$ to infer φ. If a data set is valid for the set Σ of p-keys, it is also valid for every p-key φ implied by Σ. The larger the data set, the more time we save by avoiding redundant validation checks.

Algorithms. In practice, the semantic closure Σ^* of a finite set Σ is infinite and even though it can always be represented finitely, it is often unnecessary to determine all implied p-keys. In fact, the implication problem for p-keys has as input $\Sigma \cup \{\varphi\}$ and the question is whether Σ implies φ. Computing Σ^* and checking whether $\varphi \in \Sigma^*$ is not feasible. In fact, we will now establish a linear-time algorithm for computing the maximum probability p, such that $kX_{\geq p}$ is implied by Σ. The following theorem allows us to reduce the implication problem for p-keys to a single scan of the input.

Theorem 2. *Let $\Sigma \cup \{kX_{\geq p}\}$ denote a set of p-keys over relation schema R. Then Σ implies $kX_{\geq p}$ if and only if $X = R$ or $p = 0$ or there is some $kZ_{\geq q} \in \Sigma$ such that $Z \subseteq X$ and $q \geq p$.* □

Theorem 2 enables us to design Algorithm 1, which returns the maximum probability p by which a given key kX is implied by a given set Σ of p-keys over R. If $X = R$, then we return probability 1. Otherwise, starting with $p = 0$ the algorithm scans all input keys $kZ_{\geq q}$ and sets p to q whenever q is larger than the current p and X contains Z. We use $|\Sigma|$ and R to denote the total number of attributes that occur in Σ and R, respectively.

Theorem 3. *On input (R, Σ, kX), Algorithm 1 returns in $\mathcal{O}(|\Sigma| + |R|)$ time the maximum probability p with which $kX_{\geq p}$ is implied by Σ.* □

Algorithm 1. Inference

Require: R, Σ, kX
Ensure: $\max\{p : \Sigma \models kX_{\geq p}\}$
 1: **if** $X = R$ **then**
 2:     $p \leftarrow 1;$
 3: **else**
 4:     $p \leftarrow 0;$
 5:     **for all** $kZ_{\geq q} \in \Sigma$ **do**
 6:         **if** $Z \subseteq X$ and $q > p$ **then**
 7:             $p \leftarrow q;$
 8: **return** $p;$

Given $R, \Sigma, kX_{\geq p}$ as an input to the implication problem we can use Algorithm 1 to compute $p' := \max\{q : \Sigma \models kX_{\geq q}\}$ and return an affirmative answer if and only if $p' \geq p$.

Corollary 1. *The implication problem of p-keys is decidable in linear time.* □

Given the p-key set $\Sigma = \{k\{time\}_{\geq 0.2}, k\{rfid\}_{\geq 0.3}\}$ and the key $k\{rfid, time\}$, Algorithm 1 returns $p = 0.3$. Consequently, the p-key $k\{rfid, time\}_{\geq 0.25}$ is implied by Σ, but $k\{rfid, time\}_{\geq 0.35}$ is not implied by Σ.

5   Tools for Acquiring Probabilistic Keys

Applications will benefit from the ability of analysts to acquire a good lower bound for the marginal probability by which keys hold in the domain of the application. For that purpose, analysts should communicate with domain experts. We establish two major tools that help analysts to communicate effectively with domain experts. We follow the framework in Figure 2. Here, analysts use our algorithm to visualize abstract sets Σ of p-keys in the form of some Armstrong PC-table, which is then inspected jointly with domain experts. In particular, the PC-table represents simultaneously for every key kX the marginal probability that quality data sets in the target domain should exhibit. Domain experts may change the PC-table or supply new PC-tables to the analysts. For that case we establish an algorithm that profiles p-keys.

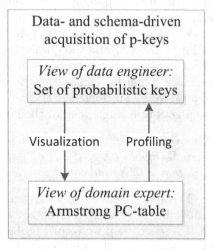

Fig. 2. Acquisition framework

That is, the algorithm computes the marginal probability of each key in the given PC-table. Such profiles are also useful for query optimization, for example.

5.1 Visualizing Abstract Sets of p-keys as Armstrong PC-tables

Our results will show that every abstract set of p-keys can be visualized in the form of a single PC-table that represents a p-relation that satisfies all given p-keys and violates all those p-keys not implied by the given set. This notion is known as an *Armstrong database*, which we formally recall here [8]. Let Σ denote a set of p-keys over a given relation schema R. A p-relation $r = (\mathcal{W}, P)$ over R is *Armstrong* for Σ if and only if for all p-keys φ it holds that r satisfies φ if and only if Σ implies φ. The following theorem shows that every distribution of probabilities to keys, that follows the inference rules from Table 2, can be represented by a single p-relation which exhibits this distribution in the form of marginal probabilities.

Theorem 4. *Let $l : R \to [0,1]$ be a function such that $l(R) = 1$ and for all $X, Y \subseteq R$, $l(XY) \geq l(X)$ holds. Then there is some p-relation r over R such that r satisfies $kX_{\geq l(X)}$, and for all $X \subseteq R$ and for all $p \in [0,1]$ such that $p > l(X)$, r violates $kX_{\geq p}$.*

Proof. Let $\{l_1, \ldots, l_n\} = \{l(X) : X \subseteq R\}$ such that $l_1 < l_2 < \ldots < l_n$, and let $l_0 = 0$. Define a probabilistic relation $r = (\{W_1, \ldots, W_n\}, P)$ as follows. For all $i = 1, \ldots, n$, the world W_i is an Armstrong relation for the key set $\Sigma_i = \{kY : l(Y) \geq l_i\}$, and $P(W_i) = l_i - l_{i-1}$. For all $X \subseteq R$, let $l(X) = l_j$ for $j \in \{1, \ldots, n\}$. Then, kX holds on W_i if and only if $i \leq j$. Consequently, kX has marginal probability $l(X)$ with respect to r, and $kX_{\geq l(X)}$ is satisfied. However, r violates $kX_{\geq p}$ for every $p > l(X)$. $\qquad\square$

Let Σ be a set of p-keys. For all $X \subseteq R$, let $p_X := \sup\{p : \exists Y \subseteq X(kY_{\geq p} \in \Sigma \cup \{kR_{\geq 1}\})\}$. Then for all $Z \subseteq R$, Σ implies $kZ_{\geq p}$ if and only if $p \leq p_Z$. Now, let $l(X) := p_X$. Then $l(R) = p_R = 1$ and $l(XY) = p_{XY} \geq p_X = l(X)$. By Theorem 4 it follows that there is some Armstrong p-relation r, since for all $Z \subseteq R$ and all $p \in [0,1]$, Σ implies $kZ_{\geq p}$ if and only if r satisfies $kZ_{\geq p}$.

Instead of computing Armstrong p-relations we compute PC-tables that are concise representations of Armstrong p-relations. We call these *Armstrong PC-tables*. Recall the following standard definition from probabilistic databases [32]. A *conditional table* or *c-table*, is a tuple $CD = \langle r, W \rangle$, where r is a relation, and W assigns to each tuple t in r a finite set W_t of positive integers. The set of *world identifiers* of CD is the union of the sets W_t for all tuples t of r. Given a world identifier i of CD, the possible world associated with i is $W_i = \{t | t \in r \text{ and } i \in W_t\}$. The semantics of a c-table $CD = \langle r, W \rangle$, called *representation*, is the set $\mathcal{W}$ of possible worlds W_i where i denotes some world identifier of CD. A *probabilistic conditional database* or *PC-table*, is a pair $\langle CD, P \rangle$ where CD is a c-table, and P is a probability distribution over the set of world identifiers of CD. The set of possible worlds of a PC-table $\langle CD, P \rangle$ is the representation of CD, and the probability of each possible world W_i is defined as the probability of its world identifier. For example, Figure 1 shows a PC-table $\langle CD, P \rangle$ that is Armstrong for the p-relation in Table 1.

We will now describe an algorithm that computes an Armstrong PC-table for every given set Σ of p-keys. In our construction, the number of possible worlds

---

Algorithm 2. Armstrong PC-table

Require: R, Σ
Ensure: Armstrong PC-table $\langle CD, P \rangle$ for Σ
1: Let $p_1, \ldots, p_n$ denote the i-th smallest probabilities p_i occurring in Σ; ▷ If $p_n < 1$, $n \leftarrow n + 1$ and $p_n \leftarrow 1$
2: $p_0 \leftarrow 0$;
3: $P \leftarrow \emptyset$;
4: **for** $i = 1, \ldots, n$ **do**
5:    $P \leftarrow P \cup \{(i, p_i - p_{i-1})\}$;   ▷ World i has probability $p_i - p_{i-1}$
6:    $A_i^{-1} \leftarrow$ Set of anti-keys for Σ_{p_i};   ▷ Anti-keys to be realized in world i
7: $A^{-1} \leftarrow \emptyset$;
8: **for all** $X \in A_1^{-1} \cup \cdots \cup A_n^{-1}$ **do**
9:    $A^{-1} \leftarrow A^{-1} \cup \{(X, \{i : X \in A_i^{-1}\})\}$;   ▷ Worlds in which X is an anti-key
10: **for all** $A \in R$ **do**
11:    $t_0(A) \leftarrow c_{A,0}$;
12: $CD \leftarrow \{(t_0, \{1, \ldots, n\})\}$;   ▷ Tuple t_0 is part of every world
13: $j \leftarrow 0$;
14: **for all** $(X, W) \in A^{-1}$ **do** ▷ For each X that is an anti-key in every world in W...
15:    $j \leftarrow j + 1$;
16:    **for all** $A \in R$ **do**▷ Add some t_j that realizes agree set X in every world in W
17:    $t_j(A) \leftarrow \begin{cases} c_{A,0}, & \text{if } A \in X \\ c_{A,j}, & \text{otherwise} \end{cases}$;
18:    $CD \leftarrow CD \cup \{(t_j, W)\}$;
19: **return** $\langle CD, P \rangle$;

---

is determined by the number of distinct probabilities that occur in Σ. For that purpose, for every given set Σ of p-keys over R and every probability $p \in [0, 1]$, let $\Sigma_p = \{kX : \exists kX_{\geq q} \in \Sigma \wedge q \geq p\}$ denote the p-cut of Σ, i.e., the set of keys over R which have at least marginal probability p. It is possible that Σ does not contain any p-key $kX_{\geq p}$ where $p = 1$. In this case, Algorithm 2 computes an Armstrong PC-table for Σ that contains one more possible world than the number of distinct probabilities occurring in Σ. Processing the probabilities Σ from smallest p_1 to largest p_n, the algorithm computes as possible world with probability $p_i - p_{i-1}$ (line 5) a traditional Armstrong relation for the p_i-cut Σ_{p_i}. For this purpose, the anti-keys are computed for each p_i-cut (line 6), and the set W of those worlds i is recorded for which X is an anti-key with respect to Σ_{p_i} (line 9). The CD-table contains one tuple t_0 which occurs in all possible worlds (line 12), and for each anti-key X another tuple t_j that occurs in all worlds for which X is an anti-key and that has matching values with t_0 in exactly the columns of X (lines 14-18).

Theorem 5. *For every set Σ of p-keys over relation schema R, Algorithm 2 computes an Armstrong PC-table for Σ in which the number of possible worlds coincides with the number of distinct probabilities that occur in $\Sigma \cup \{kR_{\geq 1}\}$.* □

In our running example, Σ contains $k\{rfid, time\}_{\geq 0.75}$, $k\{time, zone\}_{\geq 0.65}$, and $k\{rfid, zone\}_{\geq 0.35}$. Applying Algorithm 2 to WOLVERINE and Σ may result in the Armstrong PC-table of Figure 3. Finally, we derive some bounds on the time complexity of finding Armstrong PC-tables. Additional insight is given by our experiments in Section 6.

Theorem 6. *The time complexity to find an Armstrong PC-table for a given set Σ of p-keys over relation schema R is precisely exponential in $|\Sigma|$.*

Fig. 3. An Armstrong PC-table

CD table

rfid	time	zone	W
w1	2pm	z1	$1, 2, 3, 4$
w1	3pm	z2	1
w2	4pm	z1	1
w3	2pm	z3	$1, 2$
w1	5pm	z1	$2, 3, 4$
w4	2pm	z1	$3, 4$
w1	2pm	z4	4

P table

W	$\mathcal{P}$
1	.35
2	.3
3	.1
4	.25

Proof. Given R and Σ as input, Algorithm 2 computes an Armstrong PC-table for Σ in time at most exponential in $|\Sigma|$. Indeed, an Armstrong relation for Σ_{p_i} can be computed in time at most exponential in $|\Sigma_{p_i}| \leq |\Sigma|$, and we require no more than $|\Sigma|$ computations of such relations.

There are cases where the number of tuples in any Armstrong PC-table for Σ over R is exponential in $|\Sigma|$. Such a case is given by $R_n = \{A_1, \ldots, A_{2n}\}$ and $\Sigma_n = \{\{A_1, A_2\}_{\geq 1}, \ldots, \{A_{2n-1}, A_{2n}\}_{\geq 1}\}$ with $|\Sigma_n| = 2 \cdot n$. Every Armstrong PC-table requires $2^n + 1$ tuples, and there is only one possible world. $\square$

There are also cases where the number of tuples in some Armstrong PC-table for Σ over R is logarithmic in $|\Sigma|$. Such a case is given by $R_n = \{A_1, \ldots, A_{2n}\}$ and $\Sigma_n = \{(X_1 \cdots X_n)_{\geq 1} : X_i \in \{A_{2i-1}, A_{2i}\} \text{ for } i = 1, \ldots, n\}$ with $|\Sigma_n| = n \cdot 2^n$. One Armstrong PC-table for Σ represents a single possible world which has $n + 1$ tuples that realize the n agree sets $R - \{A_{2i-1}, A_{2i}\}$, the sets of attributes on which some pair of distinct tuples have matching values.

5.2   Profiling of p-keys from PC-tables

The profiling problem of p-keys from a given PC-table $\langle CD, P \rangle$ over a relation schema R is to determine for all $X \subset R$, the marginal probability p_X of kX in the p-relation $r = (W, P)$ that $\langle CD, P \rangle$ represents. The problem can be solved as follows: for each $X \subset R$, initialize $p_X \leftarrow 0$ and for all worlds $W \in \mathcal{W}$, add the probability p_W of W to p_X, if X contains some minimal key of W, see Algorithm 3. The set of minimal keys of a world W is given by the set of minimal transversals over the disagree sets of W (the complements of agree sets) [28]. Applying Algorithm 3 to the PC-table from Figure 1 returns the p-keys $k\{time, zone\}_{\geq 0.65}$, $k\{rfid, time\}_{\geq 0.75}$, $k\{rfid, zone\}_{\geq 0.35}$ and $kX_{\geq 0}$ for all remaining $X \subset R$, as illustrated on the right of Figure 1.

Algorithm 3. Profiling

Require: PC-table $\langle CD, P \rangle$ over relation schema R
Ensure: For all $X \subset R$, the maximum p_X such that $kX_{\geq p_X}$ holds on p-relation
  $r = (\mathcal{W}, P)$ that $\langle CD, P \rangle$ represents
1: **for all** $X \subset R$ **do**
2:     $p_X \leftarrow 0$;
3: **for all** $W \in \mathcal{W}$ **do**
4:     $\mathcal{M}(W) \leftarrow$ Set of minimal keys on W;   ▷ by known algorithm, e.g., [28]
5:     **for all** $X \subset R$ **do**
6:         **if** X contains some $M \in \mathcal{M}(W)$ **then**
7:             $p_X \leftarrow p_X + P(W)$;
8: **return** $\{(X, p_X) : X \subseteq R\}$;

---

6 Experiments

In this section we report on some experiments regarding the computational complexity of our algorithms for the visualization and discovery of probabilistic keys.

6.1 Visualization

The Armstrong construction takes as input a set Σ of randomly generated p-keys, and outputs an Armstrong PC-table for Σ. The random generation of Σ was achieved by firstly sampling n probabilities p_n from $[0, 1]$ and for each attribute set $X \subset R$, we assign a probability randomly sampled from the set $\{0\} \cup \{p_1, p_2, \ldots, p_n\}$. For our experiments, n was at most 15.

The left of Figure 4 shows the number of tuples in the Armstrong PC-table as a function of applying Algorithm 2 to the exponential case from the proof of Theorem 6 (black line), the logarithmic case described after Theorem 6 (blue line), and the random generation (red line). The figure illustrates that the average size of an Armstrong PC-table grows linearly in the input key size. The worst-case exponential growth occurs rarely on average. This demonstrates that Armstrong PC-tables exhibit small sizes on average, which makes them a practical tool to acquire meaningful p-keys in a joint effort with domain experts.

The right of Figure 4 shows the time for computing Armstrong PC-tables from the given sets of randomly created p-keys. It shows that Armstrong PC-tables can be computed efficiently for the input sizes considered. In fact, their computation hardly ever exceeded 1 second. The left of Figure 6 shows the graphical user interface of our visualization tool, developed in R. The input interface is shown on the left, and the output PC-table on the right.

6.2 Profiling

Figure 6 shows the time for profiling p-keys from the given Armstrong PC-tables we randomly created previously. It illustrates that the profiling problem can be solved efficiently for input sizes typical for our acquisition framework, see Figure 2. Large input sizes will require more sophisticated techniques.

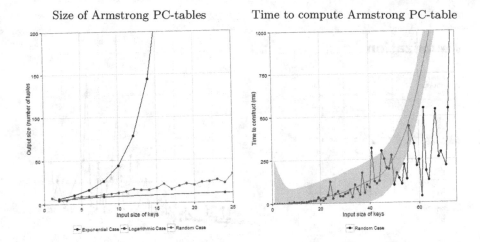

Fig. 4. Results of experiments with visualization

7 Conclusion and Future Work

We have introduced probabilistic keys that stipulate lower bounds on the marginal probability by which keys shall hold on large volumes of uncertain data. The marginal probability of keys provides a principled mechanism to control the consistency and completeness targets for the quality of an organization's data, as illustrated in Figure 5.

We have established axiomatic and algorithmic tools to reason about probabilistic keys. This can minimize the overhead in using them for data quality management and query processing. These applications are effectively unlocked by developing support for identifying the right marginal probabilities by which keys should hold in a given application domain. For this challenging problem, we have developed schema- and data-driven algorithms that can be used by analysts to communicate more effectively with domain experts. The schema-driven algorithm converts any input in the form of an abstract set of probabilistic keys into an Armstrong PC-table that satisfies the input and violates all probabilistic keys not implied by the input. Analysts and domain experts can jointly inspect the Armstrong PC-table which points out any flaws in the current perception of marginal probabilities. The data-driven algorithm computes a profile of the probabilistic keys that a given PC-table satisfies.

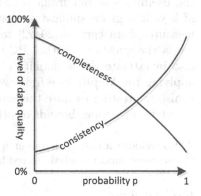

Fig. 5. Control mechanism p

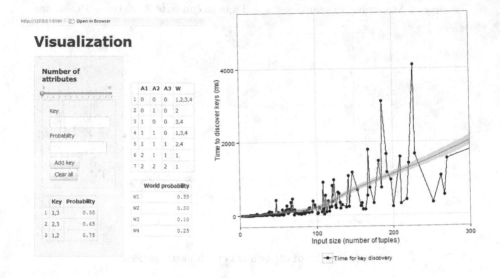

Fig. 6. GUI for visualization and times for profiling p-keys

Such PC-tables may represent some exemplary data sets or result from changes to a given Armstrong PC-table in response to identifying some flaws during their inspection. Experiments confirm that the computation of Armstrong PC-tables is typically efficient, their size is small, and profiles of probabilistic keys can be efficiently computed from PC-tables of reasonable size.

In future research we will apply our algorithms to investigate empirically the usefulness of our framework for acquiring the right marginal probabilities of keys in a given application domain. This will require us to extend empirical measures from certain [20–22] to probabilistic data sets. Particularly intriguing is the question whether PC-tables or p-relations are more useful. We will also investigate the scalability of the profiling problem to large data sets, by applying the MapReduce framework to recent data profiling techniques [16]. It is also interesting to raise the expressivity of probabilistic keys by allowing the stipulation of upper bounds or other features.

Acknowledgments. This research is supported by the Marsden fund council from Government funding, administered by the Royal Society of New Zealand.

References

1. Armstrong, W.W.: Dependency structures of data base relationships. In: IFIP Congress. pp. 580–583 (1974)
2. Atencia, M., David, J., Scharffe, F.: Keys and pseudo-keys detection for web datasets cleansing and interlinking. In: ten Teije, A., Völker, J., Handschuh, S., Stuckenschmidt, H., d'Acquin, M., Nikolov, A., Aussenac-Gilles, N., Hernandez, N. (eds.) EKAW 2012. LNCS, vol. 7603, pp. 144–153. Springer, Heidelberg (2012)

3. de Bakker, M., Frasincar, F., Vandic, D.: A hybrid model words-driven approach for web product duplicate detection. In: Salinesi, C., Norrie, M.C., Pastor, Ó. (eds.) CAiSE 2013. LNCS, vol. 7908, pp. 149–161. Springer, Heidelberg (2013)
4. Beeri, C., Dowd, M., Fagin, R., Statman, R.: On the structure of Armstrong relations for functional dependencies. J. ACM **31**(1), 30–46 (1984)
5. Blanco, L., Crescenzi, V., Merialdo, P., Papotti, P.: Probabilistic models to reconcile complex data from inaccurate data sources. In: Pernici, B. (ed.) CAiSE 2010. LNCS, vol. 6051, pp. 83–97. Springer, Heidelberg (2010)
6. Codd, E.F.: A relational model of data for large shared data banks. Commun. ACM **13**(6), 377–387 (1970)
7. Diederich, J., Milton, J.: New methods and fast algorithms for database normalization. ACM Trans. Database Syst. **13**(3), 339–365 (1988)
8. Fagin, R.: Horn clauses and database dependencies. J. ACM **29**(4), 952–985 (1982)
9. Geiger, D., Pearl, J.: Logical and algorithmic properties of conditional independence and graphical models. The Annals of Statistics **21**(4), 2001–2021 (1993)
10. Giannella, C., Robertson, E.L.: On approximation measures for functional dependencies. Inf. Syst. **29**(6), 483–507 (2004)
11. Hannula, M., Kontinen, J., Link, S.: On independence atoms and keys. In: Li, J., Wang, X.S., Garofalakis, M.N., Soboroff, I., Suel, T., Wang, M. (eds.) Proceedings of the 23rd ACM International Conference on Conference on Information and Knowledge Management, CIKM 2014, Shanghai, China, November 3–7, 2014, pp. 1229–1238 (2014)
12. Hartmann, S., Kirchberg, M., Link, S.: Design by example for SQL table definitions with functional dependencies. VLDB J. **21**(1), 121–144 (2012)
13. Hartmann, S., Leck, U., Link, S.: On Codd families of keys over incomplete relations. Comput. J. **54**(7), 1166–1180 (2011)
14. Hartmann, S., Link, S.: Efficient reasoning about a robust XML key fragment. ACM Trans. Database Syst. **34**(2) (2009)
15. Hartmann, S., Link, S.: The implication problem of data dependencies over SQL table definitions. ACM Trans. Database Syst. **37**(2), 13 (2012)
16. Heise, A., Jorge-Arnulfo, Q.-R., Abedjan, Z., Jentzsch, A., Naumann, F.: Scalable discovery of unique column combinations. PVLDB **7**(4), 301–312 (2013)
17. Huhtala, Y., Kärkkäinen, J., Porkka, P., Toivonen, H.: TANE: an efficient algorithm for discovering functional and approximate dependencies. Comput. J. **42**(2), 100–111 (1999)
18. Jha, A.K., Rastogi, V., Suciu, D.: Query evaluation with soft-key constraints. In: PODS. pp. 119–128 (2008)
19. Koehler, H., Leck, U., Link, S., Prade, H.: Logical foundations of possibilistic keys. In: Fermé, E., Leite, J. (eds.) JELIA 2014. LNCS, vol. 8761, pp. 181–195. Springer, Heidelberg (2014)
20. Langeveldt, W., Link, S.: Empirical evidence for the usefulness of armstrong relations in the acquisition of meaningful functional dependencies. Inf. Syst. **35**(3), 352–374 (2010)
21. Le, V.B.T., Link, S., Ferrarotti, F.: Effective recognition and visualization of semantic requirements by perfect SQL samples. In: Ng, W., Storey, V.C., Trujillo, J.C. (eds.) ER 2013. LNCS, vol. 8217, pp. 227–240. Springer, Heidelberg (2013)
22. Le, V.B.T., Link, S., Memari, M.: Schema- and data-driven discovery of SQL keys. JCSE **6**(3), 193–206 (2012)
23. Link, S.: Consistency enforcement in databases. In: Bertossi, L.E., Katona, G.O.H., Schewe, K., Thalheim, B. (eds.) Semantics in Databases. LNCS 2582, vol. 2582, pp. 139–159. Springer, Heidelberg (2003)

24. Liu, J., Li, J., Liu, C., Chen, Y.: Discover dependencies from data - A review. IEEE Trans. Knowl. Data Eng. **24**(2), 251–264 (2012)
25. López, M.T.G., Gasca, R.M., Pérez-Álvarez, J.M.: Compliance validation and diagnosis of business data constraints in business processes at runtime. Inf. Syst. **48**, 26–43 (2015)
26. Lutz, C., Areces, C., Horrocks, I., Sattler, U.: Keys, nominals, and concrete domains. J. Artif. Intell. Res. (JAIR) **23**, 667–726 (2005)
27. Malhotra, K., Medhekar, S., Navathe, S.B., Laborde, M.D.D.: Towards a form based dynamic database schema creation and modification system. In: Jarke, M., Mylopoulos, J., Quix, C., Rolland, C., Manolopoulos, Y., Mouratidis, H., Horkoff, J. (eds.) CAiSE 2014. LNCS, vol. 8484, pp. 595–609. Springer, Heidelberg (2014)
28. Mannila, H., Räihä, K.J.: Algorithms for inferring functional dependencies from relations. Data Knowl. Eng. **12**(1), 83–99 (1994)
29. Ramdoyal, R., Hainaut, J.-L.: Interactively eliciting database constraints and dependencies. In: Mouratidis, H., Rolland, C. (eds.) CAiSE 2011. LNCS, vol. 6741, pp. 184–198. Springer, Heidelberg (2011)
30. Sadiq, S.: Handbook of Data Quality. Springer (2013)
31. Saha, B., Srivastava, D.: Data quality: The other face of big data. In: ICDE. pp. 1294–1297 (2014)
32. Suciu, D., Olteanu, D., Ré, C., Koch, C.: Probabilistic Databases. Synthesis Lectures on Data Management, Morgan & Claypool Publishers (2011)
33. Toman, D., Weddell, G.E.: On keys and functional dependencies as first-class citizens in description logics. J. Autom. Reasoning **40**(2–3), 117–132 (2008)

A Clustering Approach for Protecting GIS Vector Data

Ahmed Abubahia(✉) and Mihaela Cocea

School of Computing, University of Portsmouth, Portsmouth PO1 3HE, UK
{ahmed.abubahia,mihaela.cocea}@port.ac.uk

Abstract. The availability of Geographic Information System (GIS) data has increased in recent years, as well as the need to prevent its unauthorized use. One way of protecting this type of data is by embedding within it a digital watermark. In this paper, we build on our previous work on watermarking vector map data, to improve the robustness to (unwanted) modifications to the maps that may prevent the identification of the rightful owner of the data. More specifically, we address the simplification (removing some vertices from GIS vector data) and interpolation (adding new vertices to GIS data) modifications by exploiting a particular property of vector data called a bounding box. In addition, we experiment with bigger maps to establish the feasibility of the approach for larger maps.

Keywords: Geographic Information System · Vector map data · Cluster analysis · Data protection · Security · Digital copyright

1 Introduction

Research in the area of Geographic Information Systems (GIS) has been growing in recent years, and digital GIS data is now widely available on numerous Internet websites. Consequently, this valuable GIS data is liable to be illegally copied, modified or distributed due to its digital nature. This stands for a compelling need of copyright protection to combat illegal use of GIS data. A popular solution for the protection of GIS data is using digital watermarking systems that enable the identification of unauthorized use of GIS data.

GIS data can be divided into two main models[1]: raster data model and vector data model. The raster model (image) stores the geographic information into a form of grid cells, and each cell represents the natural corresponding value on the ground (e.g. color scale). On the other hand, the vector data model stores the geographic information into geometrical entities which have properties such as length, a starting point and an ending point [15]. GIS vector data is defined by a sequence of coordinates, and includes shapes such as points, polylines and polygons [1]. This paper focuses on the vector format of GIS data.

---

[1] http://www.ordnancesurvey.co.uk/support/understanding-gis/raster-vector.html

© Springer International Publishing Switzerland 2015
J. Zdravkovic et al. (Eds.): CAiSE 2015, LNCS 9097, pp. 133–147, 2015.
DOI: 10.1007/978-3-319-19069-3_9

Data mining in general and clustering in particular, have been recently used for analysing GIS data for a variety of applications such as government and public services; business and service planning; logistics and transportation; and environmental studies [5], [6], [19]. There are, however, only a limited number of approaches using clustering methods in the watermarking field [2].

In addition, although many watermarking methods have been proposed for digital multimedia data (e.g. images, audio, texts and videos) copyright protection, e.g. [20], [23], [25], digital vector data received less attention, as pointed out in several recent review papers [1], [4], [28].

Our previous work is based on the use of k-medoids clustering for watermarking ESRI (Environmental Systems Research Institute) shapefiles of polygon type [2]; which is discussed in more detail in Section 2.

In this paper, we propose an improvement to our previous work [2], by using the bounding box property of vector map data, to achieve: (a) robustness to simplification (i.e. deletion of some vertices) [14] and interpolation (i.e. adding new vertices) [26] attacks, and (b) preservation of the balance between the map fidelity (the imperceptibility of the inserted watermark) and capacity (distribution of the watermark bits within the data) for GIS vector map copyright protection. These terms are discussed in more detail in Section 2.

The rest of this paper is organized as in the following. In Section 2, the GIS map watermarking process is briefly explained and a detailed overview of relevant previous work is presented. Section 3 describes the GIS vector data format and the platform used for the experimental evaluation of the proposed approach. Section 4 presents in detail our approach, while Section 5 discusses the experimental results. Section 6 concludes the paper.

2   Research Background

A digital GIS watermarking system consists of three main stages: embedding, attack/modification and extraction (Fig. 1). The embedding stage aims to insert a watermark (e.g. digital binary sequence) into the GIS vector map points, by using a specific computing approach; the embedding space is normally the Cartesian coordinates [14], [22]. The attack or modification stage is the process of distorting the digital map content. The extraction stage refers to obtaining the watermark from the host GIS data in order to retrieve the original map. There are three key requirements for reliable GIS watermarking system: fidelity, capacity and robustness [1], [4].

The fidelity requirement refers to the quality of the watermarked GIS data, in the sense that the watermark embedding process should not affect the quality of the host data and that the watermark should not be noticeable to the human eye [21]. The fidelity also indicates the similarity between the original data and the watermarked data. In the case of GIS raster data (image), which offers an extended range (color-scale) for a pixel, this can be solved easily by maintaining the pixel value within a specific range. In contrast, the fidelity requirement stands as a crucial issue in GIS vector data context due to their Cartesian coordinates

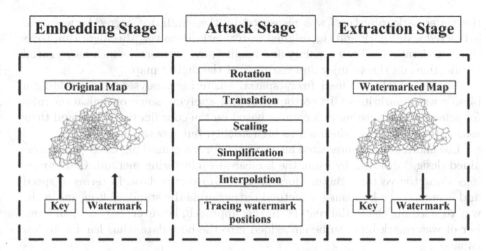

Fig. 1. Digital GIS Map Watermarking System

values sensitivity, which if changed will affect the map shape, and, consequently, will have a negative impact on the usability of GIS map.

The capacity requirement refers to the number of watermark bits that can be embedded in the host map data. The more watermark bits are embedded, the more secure the watermark becomes. Moreover, it is important not only to have high capacity, but also to have the watermark distributed across the entire map [2]. This could also leads to a loss of fidelity: the more watermark bits are embedded, the more the host vector map is changed, thus, leading to a loss of map quality. Consequently, the fidelity and capacity requirements need to be balanced to achieve both map quality and watermark quality, in order to ensure the effectiveness of the watermarking method. We refer to this relation between fidelity and capacity as a trade-off, given that an increase in one leads to a decrease in the other, and vice versa.

The robustness requirement refers to the ability of the watermarked data to withstand malicious modifications to the host GIS map, called attacks. There are many types of attacks [31], of which geometric modifications are particularly important for GIS vector data; such modification processes are rotation, translation and scaling. Rotation means turning the vector map around its center by a specific angle [16]. Translation means moving the whole map by a specific distance towards a specific direction [29]. Scaling refers to altering the size of the map, in both axes by a specific value [16]. Other relevant types of attacks are interpolation [26] and simplification [14] attacks. Simplification attacks refer to the process of removing vertices from the map [14], while interpolation attacks refer to the process of adding new vertices in the map [26].

In the following, research using clustering approaches for watermarking GIS vector data are reviewed in relation to the trade-off between fidelity and capacity.

Haowen [11] developed an algorithm for embedding a binary image watermark into GIS vector data of point geometry type. The evaluation of the watermark robustness was measured by the similarity degree between the extracted watermark and the original watermark. However, this algorithm lacks the consideration of both capacity and fidelity measurements, which have crucial implications on the security and usability of the digital map.

Jianguo et al. [14] used fuzzy spatial clustering analysis for embedding a binary watermark into GIS vector data, and applying some optimization rules for selecting the watermark locations based on the coordinates' values and their associated attributes, which led to high fidelity, but low capacity.

Lee and Kwon [17] presented an approach for watermarking CAD (computer-aided design) drawing by using the k-means++ clustering method. CAD drawings share the vector structure format with GIS vector data. In terms of speed and accuracy, the k-means++ method outperforms the standard k-means in the way of selecting the initial centers. In this approach, however, only a small number of watermark bits can be embedded into the host data, thus leading to low capacity.

Huo et al. [12] used a k-means partitioning clustering method for inserting a watermark into GIS vector data, based on ESRI shapefile format, according to the polygons' mean centers. Although their fidelity achievement is considerably high, the capacity of the watermark was relatively low for the size of the map they used. Therefore, their approach, like the previous ones, does not achieve a good trade-off between fidelity and capacity.

All previously mentioned approaches have three limitations: (a) low capacity, which leads to vulnerability to simplification and interpolation attacks; (b) lack of balance between the fidelity and capacity requirements, which has an impact on the map usability and security, and (c) experimentation with small maps, i.e. with small number of polygons, which questions the ability of the proposed approaches to deal with the higher computational complexity brought by bigger maps; as data nowadays is increasing in size, there is a need to demonstrate that the proposed approaches can deal with bigger maps.

To address the trade-off issue, our previous work [2] introduced the use of k-medoids-based partition clustering for embedding watermark bits into three digital GIS vector maps of 27, 53 and 132 polygons, and using mean polygons' centers for locating the optimum position to embed watermark bits into the digital map; the aim was mainly to improve the approach of Huo et al. [12]. Although our approach achieved a considerable improvement in terms of the balance between capacity and fidelity, like the other approaches, it is still vulnerable to simplification and interpolation attacks, and has not been shown to work on larger maps.

In this paper, we build on our previous work to address the vulnerability to simplification and interpolation attacks and to show that the proposed approach is feasible for larger maps. Thus, we argue that using a particular property of vector data called a bounding box in combination with our k-medoids approach, addresses the vulnerability to the two mentioned attacks, while also preserving a good trade-off between fidelity and capacity.

3   GIS Vector Data

This section describes the GIS vector data that has been used for testing the proposed approach. As shown in Fig. (2a), (2b) and (2c), the used GIS maps are polygon-based maps that represent administrative boundaries of 3 countries in Africa: Benin, Angola and Burkina Faso. These GIS vector maps are freely available, in ESRI shapefile format, from the Natural Earth website.[2]

ESRI Shapefiles (.shp) are produced by ESRI [3], and considered as a popular format for geographic information system applications [18]. It has several prominent features: small storage space, easy reading and writing, fast shape editing, storing both spatial and attribute information, and supporting point, polyline and polygon geometry types [7].

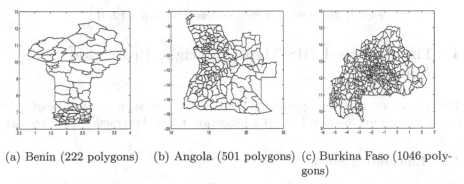

(a) Benin (222 polygons)   (b) Angola (501 polygons) (c) Burkina Faso (1046 polygons)

Fig. 2. The GIS maps used in the experiments

Despite the use of ESRI shapefiles in GIS vector data watermarking research [24], [12], the advantage of the shape bounding box feature in the shapefile header has not yet been exploited in this context. As shown in Fig. 3, the bounding box properties we are interested in are the minimum and maximum coordinates' values in both horizontal and vertical axes.

For the watermark embedding and extraction processes, we implemented our approach in MATLAB version R2013b (8.2.0.701). For more information regarding MATLAB, see the Mathworks website[4].

The following section presents our approach based on k-medoids clustering and using the bounding box information in the ESRI shapefile. We compare the results of this approach with our previous work [2], which used k-medoids clustering with mean polygon centers, to establish the role of the bounding box property in addressing the vulnerability to simplification and interpolation attacks, and to investigate if the trade-off between fidelity and capacity is preserved.

---

[2] http://www.mapmakerdata.co.uk.s3-website-eu-west-1.amazonaws.com/library/stacks/Africa/index.htm

[3] http://www.esri.com/

[4] http://www.mathworks.co.uk/

Position	Field	Value	Type
Byte 0	File Code	9994	Integer
Byte 4	Unused	0	Integer
Byte 8	Unused	0	Integer
Byte 12	Unused	0	Integer
Byte 16	Unused	0	Integer
Byte 20	Unused	0	Integer
Byte 24	File Length	File Length	Integer
Byte 28	Version	1000	Integer
Byte 32	Shape Type	Shape Type	Integer
Byte 36	Bounding Box	Xmin	Double
Byte 44	Bounding Box	Ymin	Double
Byte 52	Bounding Box	Xmax	Double
Byte 60	Bounding Box	Ymax	Double
Byte 68*	Bounding Box	Zmin	Double
Byte 76*	Bounding Box	Zmax	Double
Byte 84*	Bounding Box	Mmin	Double
Byte 92*	Bounding Box	Mmax	Double

Fig. 3. The Header of Polygon-based Shapefile, ESRI [7]

4   The Proposed GIS-Map Copyright Protection Approach

This section presents our approach following the three stages outlined earlier in Fig. 1: embedding (Section 4.1), attack (Section 4.2) and extraction (Section 4.3).

4.1   Embedding Stage

The embedding approach, as illustrated in Fig. 4, consists of several steps. First, the locations for inserting the watermark are identified by computing the polygon's centers using the bounding box information for each polygon, and then

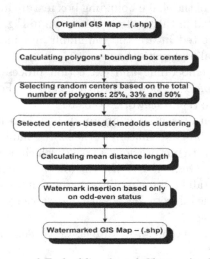

Fig. 4. The Proposed Embedding-based Cluster Analysis Framework

applying k-medoids to cluster the computed centers. The number of clusters establishes in how many polygons the watermark will be inserted. We experimented with three different proportions of numbers of polygons in the vector map, i.e. 25%, 33% and 50%. After identifying the locations for watermark insertion, the mean distance length is calculated for the selected polygons and the watermark is inserted into the means distance length by utilizing an odd-even indexing rule.

Embedding Location Identification

The approaches given by our previous work [2] and Huo et al. [12] calculate polygons' centers by summing up all vertices coordinates, in both axes, for each polygon and dividing the sum by the number of vertices minus one; the minus one is due to the the last vertex coordinates being the same as for the first vertex, according to the polygon shapefile format [7].

In this approach we exploit polygons' bounding boxes property for calculating polygons' centers. Bounding boxes refer to the stored values that represent the extent of the geometry shape in the shape file [7]. Polygons' bounding box centers are calculated in both axes, as shown in Equation(1) and Equation(2), respectively.

$$x_c = \frac{x_{min} + x_{max}}{2} \tag{1}$$

$$y_c = \frac{y_{min} + y_{max}}{2} \tag{2}$$

where: x_c and y_c are the coordinates of polygon's center in both x and y axes respectively; x_{min} is the minimum vertex coordinate in x-axis; x_{max} is the maximum vertex coordinate in x-axis; y_{min} is the minimum vertex coordinate in y-axis; y_{max} is the maximum vertex coordinate in y-axis. x_{min}, x_{max}, y_{min} and y_{max} are each of 8-byte length [7].

The key characteristics of the k-medoids partitioning clustering method are robustness to outliers and the fact that the medoids (representative objects) of clusters are represented by actual points in the dataset [9], [10], unlike other methods, such as k-means, where the representative objects of clusters are artificial points which are not present in the dateset [12]. Therefore, the k-medoids approach can efficiently manage most forms of GIS Vector data.

We use a k-medoids based clustering method called PAM (Partitioning Around Medoids), as shown in Algorithm 1, to cluster the bounding box centers in order to determine the best positions for embedding the watermark. The PAM method assigns seeds, i.e initial representative objects, for the given polygons' centers. These seeds are replaced by other representative objects, called medoids, through a number of iterations until the resulting medoids can not be improved or changed. Polygons' centers are clustered into k-clusters and the resulting medoids are kept as a secret key ($key1$). The polygons corresponding to the medoids resulted from clustering are then used for watermark insertion.

Algorithm 1. k-medoids method for GIS vector data clustering

Input:
k: the number of clusters,
D_c^n: a data set containing number of polygons' centers.
Output: k clusters.
Method:

- select k polygons' centers in D_c^n as the initial representative polygons' centers; arbitrarily
- repeat
- each remaining polygon's center is assigned to the cluster with the nearest representative polygon's center, measured by Euclidean distance;
- choose, randomly, a non-representative polygon's center, C_p^{random};
- calculate the total cost, T, of swapped representative polygon's center, C_p^j, with C_p^{random};
- if $T < 0$ then swap C_p^j with C_p^{random} to form the new set of k representative polygons' centers;
- continue until no change;

Watermark Insertion

The concept of zero watermarking [27] is utilized in our proposed watermark embedding process. Zero watermarking aims to exploit some of the host GIS data characteristics in order to generate a more robust watermark. In this case, the topological characteristic of the host GIS data that is used, is the mean-distance length of polygons. This is calculated for the polygons identified through the clustering process.

The watermark is constructed by adding or subtracting a bit value of 1 from the mean-distance length of polygons. The mean-distance length of each polygon is defined by the average value of distance lengths from that polygon's vertices to its center [12], [29], where the center is calculated as described in Equation(1) and Equation(2). This is illustrated in Fig. 5, while Equation(3) demonstrates the way of calculating the mean-distance length of selected polygons.

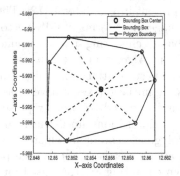

Fig. 5. Distances from bounding box center to the vertices of polygon

$$L_c = \frac{1}{n-1} \sum_{v=1}^{n-1} \sqrt{(x_c - x_v)^2 + (y_c - y_v)^2} \qquad (3)$$

where: L_c is the mean distance length; n is the number of vertices in a polygon; x_c and y_c are the center coordinates in x and y axes, respectively; x_v and y_v are the vertex coordinates in x and y axes, respectively.

The values of mean-distance lengths are stored as a secret key ($key2$) and they represent the selective positions for embedding the watermark. These are based on the polygons whose bounding box centers were selected as final medoids by the k-medoids clustering method. The watermark is embedded by applying odd-even indexing [12], [3], as outlined in Equation (4).

$$W_i = \begin{cases} T - 1, & \text{if } OES(I) = odd \\ T + 1, & \text{if } OES(I) = even \end{cases} \qquad (4)$$

where: W_i is the ith bit value of the watermark; OES stands for Odd-Even Status; I is the order index of the mean-distance length value in the matrix; T is the value of the 4th digit of the mean-distance length value, after the decimal point [12].

The index of each mean-distance value is used in this approach, instead of using an additional random sequence proposed by [12], to get more consistent positions for embedding the watermark. This consistency sums up both: (a) the indexing as a vital role in the clustering process, and (b) maintaining the security of the watermark position by storing the index values as a key instead of utilizing a random sequence that is not relevant to the used data. This also offers the ability to control the watermark capacity in order to preserve the map fidelity, whereas the use of a random sequence [12] will limit that choice of control.

As shown in Equation (4), the watermark is embedded by comparing the OES (Odd-Even Status) of the I and T variables. The conditions are set based on two scenarios as in the following:

– If the OES of I is odd, 1 will be subtracted from the value of T
– In contrast, if the OES of I is even, 1 will be added to the value of T.

After applying the OES to change the values of L_c, the new values of mean-distance length will be represented by L_c^*. The indexes of new mean-distance length values are stored as another secret key ($key3$), to secure the positions in which the watermark is embedded. The change rate α_c is calculated as depicted in Equation (5):

$$\alpha_c = \frac{L_c^*}{L_c} \qquad (5)$$

The change rate α_c is used to change all vertices of polygons identified through clustering on the basis of the embedding condition, as given in equations 6 and 7:

$$v_x^* = \alpha_c v_x + x_c(1 - \alpha_c) \qquad (6)$$

$$v_y^* = \alpha_c v_y + y_c(1 - \alpha_c) \tag{7}$$

where: v_x^* and v_y^* are the new vertices' coordinates after embedding the watermark according to the aforementioned condition in Equation (4).

4.2 Attack Stage

Robustness reflects the watermark's resistance to a set of attacks or modifications. This paper addresses geometric attacks such as rotation, translation and scaling due to their relevance to the geometrical properties of polygons in the GIS vector maps context. Also other relevant attacks such as simplification, interpolation and tracing the positions of watermark bits are taken into account.

1. Rotation Attack: rotation means turning the vector map around its center by a specific angle [16]. Rotation is of crucial importance because it changes spatial locations of the vector map points. In our approach this problem is tackled by using the mean distance length which is known for its resilience to the rotation process [2], [12].
2. Translation Attack: translation means moving the whole map by a specific distance towards a specific direction [29]. Translation also has the property of changing the positions of vector map points, but has no effect on the mean distance length because the distances between the vector map points will remain unchanged [2], [12].
3. Scaling Attack: the scaling attack refers to altering the size of the map, in both axes by a specific value [16]. Although the scaling attack could change the distances between the vector map points, the scaling factor could be computed by dividing the mean-distance values of the scaled map by the mean-distance values of the original map [2], [12]. Consequently, the scaled map can be easily retrieved to its original form after it undergoes the scaling attack.
4. Simplification Attack: the simplification attack refers to the process of removing vertices from the map [14]. If the polygons' centers are calculated as the average of the vertices, removing some vertices, will change that average. The bounding box centers, however, are not affected by the number of vertices in a polygon; consequently, our approach has more robustness to the simplification attack.
5. Interpolation Attack: the interpolation attack refers to the process of adding new vertices to map's borders [26]. Similary to the simplification attack, when the centers of polygons are calculated by averaging the vertices, adding more vertices will change that average. As the bounding box is independent of the number of vertices in a polygon, out approach will lead to more robustness to interpolation attacks.
6. Tracing watermark bits positions: the positions of the embedded watermark are secured by using a set of three different keys, which are kept secret from the attackers, and stored for the use in the extraction stage. These keys are: (a) the values of computed clusters' centers, (b) the values of mean-distance lengths and (c) the indexes of the new mean-distance values.

4.3   Extraction Stage

In the literature, the extraction stage is classified into three categories: blind, semi-blind and non-blind approaches [1]. In the blind approach the original map is not needed in the watermark extraction stage. Semi-blind extraction refers to the case in which the original watermark is used instead of the original map in the watermark extraction stage. Non-blind extraction means that the original map is needed in the watermark extraction stage.

Our proposed approach is blind extraction and characterized by flexibility, which means that both the watermark embedding and the watermark extraction processes are quite similar. The keys stored in the embedding process are used in the process of extraction. Firstly, the bounding box center of each polygon is recalculated, and then the polygons' centers are divided into k-clusters by using the k-medoids method, in order to compare with the stored $key1$ (Section 4.1). The assumption here is that the attacker will not change the bounding box information, which identifies the boundaries of the whole map, as well as each polygon in the map, because such a change will destroy the map's quality and usability. In the next step, the mean-distance length for the watermarked map is calculated in the same way as in the embedding process. By comparing the computed mean-distance to the stored $key2$ and $key3$ (Section 4.1), it becomes easy to extract the watermark bits (1 or -1), and restore the original map even when the watermarked GIS vector map has undergone the attacks mentioned in Section 4.2.

5   Experimental Results and Discussion

A set of experiments was implemented to assess the balance between fidelity and capacity achieved by our proposed approach. These experiments are carried out on GIS vector maps of 222, 501 and 1046 polygons, as shown in Fig. (2a), (2b) and (2c). The capacity and fidelity results are displayed in Table 1.

The fidelity metric aims to measure the imperceptibility of the watermark and reflects its degree of invisibility. This metric is significant because it has two crucial effects in the context of GIS vector data: one on the map shape, and another, consequently, on the usability of the GIS vector map. Fidelity is measured by using PSNR (Peak Signal to Noise Ratio), in decibels [12]; there is no specific range for PSNR values but a higher PSNR would normally indicate that the data is of higher quality [13]. Typical values are considered to be between 30 and 50 dB, in the context of digital images [8]. In order to use this metric, we stored the watermarked GIS vector maps in JPEG image format (jpg) for the measurement purpose.

Capacity refers to the number of vertices that carry the watermark bits. The importance of the watermark capacity is specified by its vital implication on increasing the watermark robustness to cropping attacks. Cropping is the process of cutting some parts of the watermarked GIS vector map [30]. Consequently, it is important not only to have high capacity, but also to have the watermark distributed across the entire map [2], to avoid having areas of the map with no

Table 1. The results of bounding box approach versus mean polygon centers using k-medoids

Map (proportion of data used)	k-medoids with bounding box centers		k-medoids with mean polygon centers [2]	
	Capacity (No. of vertices)	Fidelity (PSNR)	Capacity (No. of vertices)	Fidelity (PSNR)
Benin Map (25%)	1428	42.3485	1321	41.1902
Benin Map (33%)	2187	41.9815	1730	40.8308
Benin Map (50%)	3226	39.2617	2661	38.6129
Angola Map (25%)	4334	46.5627	4118	44.6826
Angola Map (33%)	6379	44.2873	5823	43.3034
Angola Map (50%)	10062	43.6553	9936	41.9183
Burkina Faso Map (25%)	15630	41.1364	15350	40.6581
Burkina Faso Map (33%)	21572	41.6359	19044	40.5387
Burkina Faso Map (50%)	31680	36.8983	31277	36.4201

watermark, which can be then cut off and used without being able to identify ownership. In our approach, the distribution across the map is achieved through the clustering process.

Table 1 compares the results of our approach described in this paper, using the bounding box centers, with the results of our previous work [2], using polygons' mean centers, to investigate how the performance of the two approaches compare in terms of the trade-off between fidelity and capacity.

There are two considerable differences between our approach and the previous one [2]. The first difference is in the way of calculating the polygons' centers, i.e. using the bounding box as explained in Section 4.1 versus using the mean of vertices coordinates in our previous approach [2]. Consequently, the given results can be attributed to the use of the bounding box properties. The second difference is the use of GIS vector maps that contain large numbers of polygons in contrary to [2], which was tested only on small number of polygons (27, 53 and 132 polygons). This should indicate if the approach is suitable for maps with large number of polygons.

As shown in Table 1, the trade-off between fidelity and capacity is balanced by increasing the watermark capacity (number of vertices) while keeping higher watermark invisibility (PSNR). Three different proportions of map size, i.e. 25%, 33% and 50%, were used to observe the effect of increased capacity and its effect on fidelity. These proportions represent approximately a quarter, a third and (exactly) half of the number of polygons in the used maps.

The relation between the map size proportions and the number of clusters is illustrated in the following for each of the three maps used in the experiments. Thus, for the map of Benin, 25%, 33% and 50% corresponds to 56, 74 and 111 clusters, respectively; for the map of Angola, 25%, 33% and 50% corresponds to 126, 167 and 251 clusters, respectively; and for the map of South Africa, 25%, 33% and 50% corresponds to 262, 349 and 523 clusters, respectively. This shows that our approach is valid for GIS maps that contain large numbers of polygons.

When looking at the results for the 25% sizes of the three maps in Table 1, we notice that the capacity values for the approach proposed in this paper (bounding box-based k-medoids), i.e. 1428, 4334 and 15630, are higher than those from our previous approach [2], i.e. 1321, 4118 and 15350. At the same time, it is noticeable that the fidelity values are also higher than the approach of [2], despite the increase in capacity. The same can be observed for the 33% and 50% sizes on all three maps.

As pointed out in the previous section, one key characteristic of using the bounding box centers is that it does not depend on the number of vertices in a polygon, which has an advantages of more robustness to the interpolation and simplification attacks. Therefore, the approach proposed in this paper improves our previous approach [2] by achieving robustness to simplification and inter-polation attacks, while also increasing the fidelity and capacity metrics, and, at the same time, preserving the balance between the two metrics.

6 Conclusions

The influence of using the bounding box properties for protecting the copyright of GIS vector data was investigated in this paper. We introduced the use of bounding box centers in the context of watermarking research, and compared our approach with previous work [2].

To assess the effectiveness of our approach, we looked at two important aspects: fidelity and capacity. The experimental results show that the use of the bounding box centers has a significant implication on the trade-off between the fidelity and the capacity metrics, and resulted in higher fidelity as capacity increased.

In addition to the improvement of the trade-off between fidelity and capacity, the use of bounding box centers adds more robustness to the simplification and interpolation attacks due to their independence from the number of vertices in a polygon. By using vector maps with large numbers of polygons, the approach has been shown to be feasible for large maps.

For measuring fidelity, PSNR was used to be consistent with the previous work in this area, including our previous work [2], which is an improved work of the approach by Huo et al. [12]. This metric, however, is used in image water-marking and is not necessarily the best metric for GIS vector data [22], as it does not exploit the properties of vector data. As there is no current alternative for measuring fidelity, in future work, we will investigate different metrics that would be more suitable for vector map data.

Further research and experiments will be carried out on computing a fixed set of initial representatives for our k-medoids-based watermarking approach to achieve more predictability and efficiency, to eliminate the randomness involved in the initial selection of the centers involved in the typical PAM-based k-medoids method [2]. Also, we will experiment with other clustering approaches proposed in the literature, such as grid-based and density-based approaches, to explore the capability of different cluster analysis tools in the research context of GIS vector map data copyright protection.

References

1. Abbas, T., Jawad, M.: Digital Vector Map Watermarking: Applications, Techniques and Attacks. J. Oriental J. Computer Science & Technology **6**(3), 333–339 (2013)
2. Abubahia, A., Cocea, M.: Partition clustering for GIS map data protection. In: 26th IEEE International Conference on Tools with Artificial Intelligence, pp. 830–837 (2014)
3. Baiyan, W., Wei, W., Dandan, M.: 2D vector map watermarking based on spatial relations. In: International Conference on Earth Observation Data Processing and Analysis, pp. 532–537 (2008)
4. Bhanuchandar, P., Prasad, M., Srinivas, K.: A Survey on Various Watermarking Methods for GIS Vector Data. Int. J. Computer and Electronics Research **2**, 5–7 (2013)
5. Choi, J., Lee, D., Jung, H.: Knowledge discovery and integration: a case study of housing planning support system. In: Park, J.J.J.H., Adeli, H., Park, N., Woungang, I. (eds.) Mobile, Ubiquitous, and Intelligent Computing. LNEE, vol. 274, pp. 287–291. Springer, Heidelberg (2014)
6. Croitoru, A., Crooks, A., Radzikowski, J., Stefanidis, A.: Geosocial Gauge: A System Prototype for Knowledge Discovery from Social Media. Int. J. Geographical Information Science **27**(12), 2483–2508 (2013)
7. ESRI.: ESRI Shapefile Technical Description. Technical Report, Environmental Systems Research Institute, Inc., 380 New York Street, Redlands, CA 92373–8100 USA, July 1998. http://www.esri.com/library/whitepapers/pdfs/shapefile.pdf
8. Hamzaoui, R., Saupe, D.: Fractal image compression. In: Barni, M. (eds.) Document and Image Compression, pp. 145–177. CRC (2006)
9. Han, J., Kamber, M., Pei, J.: Data Mining: Concept and Techniques. Morgan Kaufmann, Waltham (2012)
10. Han, J., Lee, J.G., Kamber, M.: An Overview of Clustering Methods in Geographic Data Analysis. Taylor & Francis Group, LLC (2009)
11. Haowen, Y.: Watermarking algorithm for vector point clusters. In: 7th International Conference on Wireless Communications, Networking and Mobile Computing, pp. 1–4 (2011)
12. Huo, X.J., Moon, K.S., Lee, S.H., Seung, T.Y., Kwon, S.G.: Protecting GIS vector map using the k-means clustering algorithm and odd-even coding. In: 17th Korea-Japan Joint Workshop on Frontiers of Computer Vision, pp. 1–5. IEEE, February 2011
13. Huynh, Q., Ghanbari, M.: Scope of Validity of PSNR in Image/Video Quality Assessment. IEEE Electronic Letters **44**(13), 800–801 (2008)
14. Jianguo, S., Liang, K., Songzhu, X.: Research of Lossless Digital Watermarking Technology. J. Applied Mechanics and Materials **333**, 1219–1223 (2013)
15. Kennedy, M.: Introducing Geographic Information Systems with ArcGIS. John Wiley and Sons (2013)
16. Lee, S.H., Kwon, K.R.: Vector Watermarking Scheme for GIS Vector Map Management. J. Multimedia Tools and Applications **63**, 757–790 (2013)
17. Lee, S.H., Kwon, K.R.: CAD Drawing Watermarking Scheme. J. Digital Signal Processing **20**(5), 1379–1399 (2010)
18. Longley, P., Goodchild, M., Maguire, D., Rhind, D.: Geographic Information Systems and Science. John Wiley and Sons (2011)
19. Miller, H.J., Han, J.: Geographic Data Mining and Knowledge Discovery. CRC Press (2009)

20. Mohammed, G., Yasin, A., Zeki, A.: Robust image watermarking based on dual intermediate significant bit. In: 6th International Conference on Computer Science and Information Technology, pp. 18–22 (2014)

21. Nin, J., Ricciardi, S.: Digital watermarking techniques and security issues in the information and communication society. In: 27th International Conference on Advanced Information Networking and Applications Workshops, pp. 1553–1558 (2013)

22. Niu, X.M., Shao, C.Y., Wang, X.T.: A Survey of Digital Vector Map Watermarking. Int. J. Innovative Computing Information and Control 2(6), 1301–1316 (2006)

23. Peng, F., Liu, Y., Long, M.: Reversible Watermarking for 2D CAD Engineering Graphics Based on Improved Histogram Shifting. J. Computer-Aided Design 49, 42–50 (2014)

24. Sha-Sha, L., Wei, Z., An-Bo, L.: Image Watermark Similarity Calculation of GIS Vector Data. Procedia Engineering 29, 1331–1337 (2012)

25. Urvoy, M., Goudia, D., Autrusseau, F.: Perceptual DFT Watermarking with Improved Detection and Robustness to Geometrical Distortions. IEEE Trans. on Information Forensics and Security 9(7), 1108–1119 (2014)

26. Wang, N., Men, C.: Reversible fragile watermarking for locating tampered blocks in 2D vector maps. J. Multimedia Tools and Applications 67, 709–739 (2013). Springer

27. Wang, X., Huang, D., Zhang, Z.: A Robust Zero-Watermarking Algorithm for vector digital maps based on statistical characteristics. J. Software 7(10), 2349–2356 (2012)

28. Wu, J., Yang, F., Wu, C.: Review of digital watermarking for 2D-vector map. In: IEEE International Conference on Green Computing and Communications and IEEE Internet of Things and IEEE Cyber, Physical and Social Computing, pp. 2098–2101 (2013)

29. Xun, W., Ding-jun, H., Zhi-yong, Z.: A robust zero-watermarking algorithm for 2D vector digital maps. In: He, X., Hua, E., Lin, Y., Liu, X. (eds.) Computer, Informatics, Cybernetics and Applications. LNEE, vol. 107, pp. 533–541. Springer, Netherlands (2012)

30. Zhao, Q., Sui, L., Wang, C., Yin, X.: Publicly verify the integrity of the geographical data using public watermarking scheme. In: Bian, F., Xie, Y., Cui, X., Zeng, Y. (eds.) GRMSE 2013, Part I. CCIS, vol. 398, pp. 646–652. Springer, Heidelberg (2013)

31. Zope-Chaudhari, S., Venkatachalam, P.: Evaluation of spatial relations in watermarked geospatial data. In: 3rd ACM SIGSPATIAL International Workshop on GeoStreaming, pp. 78–83 (2012)

Requirements Elicitation
and Management

Need-to-Share and Non-diffusion Requirements Verification in Exchange Policies

Rémi Delmas[✉] and Thomas Polacsek

ONERA, 2 Avenue Édouard Belin, F31055 Toulouse, France
remi.delmas@onera.fr

Abstract. Whether be it for Earth observation, risk management or even companies relations, more and more interconnected organizations form decentralized systems in which the exchange, in terms of diffusion or non-diffusion of information between agents, can have critical consequences. In this paper, we present a formal framework to specify information exchange policies for such kinds of systems and two specific requirements, the need-to-share and the non-diffusion requirements, as well as properties strongly related to them. Wiser from these formal definitions, we see how to reconcile these sometimes antagonist requirements in a same policy specification with information filtering operations. We also explain how we use state of the art theorem provers to perform automatic analysis of these policies.

Keywords: Requirements engineering · Information exchange policies · Formal specification · Formal verification

1 Introduction

Today, individuals, companies, organizations and national agencies are increasingly interconnected, forming complex and decentralized information systems. In some of these systems, the very fact of exchanging information can constitute a safety critical concern. Take for instance Space Situation Awareness applications (SSA), in which space observation capabilities belonging to different nations are mutualized in order to build a complex information gathering, analysis and alert diffusion system. The mission of the system is to warn when situations of potential collision between orbiting objects are detected. The system must, in case of potential collision, send relevant alerts and associated information to the right agents so as to allow them to avoid the collision, while guaranteeing that sensitive information about the orbiting objects, such as their exact nature, their trajectories, manœuvre capabilities, *etc.* will not be leaked. Another example is Global Earth Observation and Surveillance Systems (GEOSS). Observation information is exchanged by cooperating agencies or states, and it must be ensured that information about natural disasters will always reach the relevant authorities so that population protection measures can be taken in due time, while not revealing sensitive information about the earth observation means of the members taking part in the surveillance effort.

J. Zdravkovic et al. (Eds.): CAiSE 2015, LNCS 9097, pp. 151–165, 2015.
DOI: 10.1007/978-3-319-19069-3_10

In systems like SSA or GEOSS, qualified authorities *must absolutely be warned* as soon as evidence showing imminent natural disaster is acquired. We call such requirements: *need-to-share* requirement. In fact, the true requirement is the authorities need to know the information and from that we derive the need-to-share requirement. In a paradoxical way, because agents from different organizations share information, any risk of leakage of private or sensitive information about the cooperating parties must be prevented. So, the challenge is to reconcile these two antagonist requirements: firstly, ensuring that actors will always receive the information they need to perform their designated mission; secondly, ensuring that no sensitive information will be released in an uncontrolled manner.

To do so, need-to-share and *non-diffusion* requirements should be expressed in a specification language which allows to formally specify the conditions under which agents have either the obligation, the permission or the interdiction to communicate information to other agents in the system. We call such specifications *information exchange policies*. Besides the formalization of requirements, our goal is also to provide means of automatic formal verification of a number of generic properties of policies. To obtain the high degree of automation needed by system designers while retaining a high performance of analysis, we provide PEPS-analyzer, an automatic semantic analyzer for policies, which works by translating property verification problems for policies to *satisfiability modulo theory* problems, which are resolved using a state-of-the-art SMT solver, Microsoft Z3 in our case.

In this paper, we give in section 2 a brief overview of an existing framework to specify information exchange policies and explain how we use satisfiability checkers to perform automatic analyses on them. After that, in section 3 we detail the running example of this paper. In sections 4 and 5, we give formal definitions of two classes of generic properties, related to the need-to-share requirement on the one hand, and to the non-diffusion of information requirement on the other hand. Then, in section 6, we proceed to identify cases in which these properties become logically incompatible and detail how the need of information filtering operations arises naturally. Last, section 7 concludes the paper and outlines perspectives to this work.

2   Exchange Policy Specification

In [5], we provided a formal framework named PEPS[1], for the specification and verification of information diffusion policies. In this section, we show how we extend PEPS to take into account both diffusion and non-diffusion requirements explicitly.

The benefit of using unified frameworks has previously been studied in the context of information access. In [11] for instance, the authors propose a modelling language, in fact a meta-model, which allows to express security and privacy requirements; In [1] and [12] the authors propose similar approaches for security requirements.

---

[1] PEPS is a recursive acronym for *Peps for Exchange Policy Specification*.

2.1   The peps Formal Language

The formal system underlying PEPS is many sorted first-order logic with equality [7] (MSFOL). So, PEPS allows the use of sorts $(\mathcal{A}, \mathcal{B}, \dots)$, free constants $(A, B, \dots)$, functions and predicates (first letter in uppercase), polymorphic equality $(=)$, usual logical connectors $(\neg, \wedge, \vee, \implies)$ as well as sorted variables $x : \mathcal{S}$ (first letter in lowercase), together with universal $(\forall)$ and existential $(\exists)$ quantifiers. Full details about the PEPS syntax and semantics can be found in [5].

The PEPS language is extensible, *ie* users can declare their own sorts, functions and predicates. However, PEPS comes equipped with a minimalist set of core concepts, in the form of predefined sorts, functions and predicates: Sorts $\mathcal{A}, \mathcal{I}, \mathcal{T}$ represent respectively agents, information items and information topics. In addition, we have the following *domain-predicates*, or *D-predicates* for short: $K(A, I)$ is used to express that an agent A knows an information item I; the predicate $Topic(I, T)$ is used to express that information item I is relevant of topic T (a single information item can be relevant of many different topics).

Unlike standard deontic logic [3], we do not have a generic obligation operator, because we focus on the concept of *obligation to send information item i from agent a to agent b*. So, dedicated *normative-predicates*, called *N-predicates*, are provided: $O_{Send}(A, B, I)$, $P_{Send}(A, B, I)$ and $F_{Send}(A, B, I)$, which respectively encode the obligation, permission and interdiction for an agent A to send an information I to another agent B.

Note that, to express obligation and related concepts, we could have used deontic logic. However tools dedicated to modal logic are less efficient than standard logic solver tools [13] such as SAT solvers or SMT-solvers. By not representing obligation with a modal operator we lose expressiveness, but we gain the use of efficient logic solvers to perform fully automatic analyses.

In standard deontic logic, obligation and permission operators are linked by axiom (D) which expresses that if a proposition P is obligatory then P is also permitted. In PEPS, we translate this axiom to a first-order property we also call (D): if communication of an information item is mandatory between two agents, then it is also permitted.

Definition 1 (D).

$$D \equiv \forall a, \forall b, \forall i, O_{Send}(a, b, i) \implies P_{Send}(a, b, i)$$

In PEPS, an *exchange rule* expresses conditions under which agents have the obligation, permission or interdiction to send a piece of information to another agent. An *exchange policy* (*EP*) is a collection of exchange rule formulas.

Definition 2 (Exchange Rule). *An exchange rule is a closed* PEPS *formula of one of the following syntactical forms:*

$$\forall x_1, \dots, \forall x_n, (\phi \implies O_{Send}(t_1, t_2, t_3))$$
$$\forall x_1, \dots, \forall x_n, (\phi \implies P_{Send}(t_1, t_2, t_3))$$
$$\forall x_1, \dots, \forall x_n, (\phi \implies F_{Send}(t_1, t_2, t_3))$$

where:

- $x_1, \ldots, x_n$ are all variables identifiers occurring in ϕ, t_1, t_2 and t_3;
- ϕ is a quantifier-free and N-predicate-free formula;
- t_1, t_2 are quantifier-free terms of sort $\mathcal{A}$;
- t_3 is a quantifier-free term of sort $\mathcal{I}$.

Also part of a PEPS specification is a formal description of Σ, the domain in which the policy is meant to apply. The declaration of additional sorts and domain predicates needed to build a domain model suitable for a particular application is left to the user. These new predicates and sorts can be used in the left member ϕ of the implication forming a rule, but not in the right member (PEPS is extensible only with new sorts, functions and D-predicates, and not with new N-predicates).

The combination of an exchange policy EP and set of domain constraints Σ is called an *exchange policy specification* and is noted $EPS = \langle \Sigma, EP \rangle$.

In the following sections, we will often have to assert that a policy specification EPS is in effect under the domain constraints and the D property. We hence introduce the following notation for what we call the *policy formula*.

Definition 3 (Policy Formula).

$$\mathcal{EPS} \equiv \Sigma \wedge (\bigwedge_{r \in EP} r) \wedge D$$

Last, we will use the notation $P \models Q$ to state that Q is a logical consequence of P, *ie* that any model of P is also a model of Q.

2.2   Formal Policy Verification

In this section we first provide details on satisfiability checking algorithms used in the PEPS-analyzer tool, and then provide details on the generic properties that can be checked using the tool.

The Peps-Analyzer Tool. We provide a tool which can be used both to find bugs in policies and to check that properties hold on policies. A semantic verification tool such as PEPS-analyzer is a valuable help. Even with as few as a dozen of rules, complex interactions between rules make it hard to identify and understand incoherences, incompleteness or redundancy using solely a mental model of the policy, or using test cases, or to be absolutely sure the policy indeed works as intended. With PEPS-analyzer we address verification problems which can be expressed as (one or more) satisfiability checks. In order to verify that $P \models Q$, meaning Q *is a logical consequence of* P, where P and Q are both MSFOL formulas, the unsatisfiability of $P \wedge \neg Q$ is checked using an MSFOL satisfiability solver.

Earlier versions of PEPS-analyzer were based on a pure SAT encoding of MSFOL satisfiability problems, where sorts were interpreted over finite domains, and by using a bounded model checking approach: domain cardinalities were increased iteratively up to user-specified bounds, and quantifiers grounded on these finite domains. This approach was fully automatic, but the validity of the analyses was only up to a finite and relatively small number of information items, agents, topics, etc.

The latest version of PEPS-analyzer still works by reducing property verification to satisfiability, however MSFOL formulas generated by PEPS-analyzer (always involving quantifiers) are now directly given to an MSFOL-capable satisfiabilit solver which natively supports quantifiers, and handles quantifier instantiation internally using advanced algorithms. Quantifier handling in SMT solvers has come a long way since the early days, and Microsoft Z3 [10], the back-end solver used by PEPS-analyzer, is able to handle the quantified formulas arising from policy verification without user interaction or manual tuning. The huge advantage is that proofs obtained this way hold for sort interpretation domains of infinite cardinality. Models returned by Z3 for satisfiable formulas are presented to the user when they represent counter example to policy properties.

Generic Policy Properties. PEPS-analyzer allows to either prove or disprove four generic properties: *consistency, applicability minimality,* and *completeness*.

The *consistency* property holds if and only if there is no situation allowed by the domain model such that an agent is both obliged (or permitted) and prohibited to send an information to another agent. The *applicability* property holds if for each rule, there exists at least one situation allowed by the domain model in which the rule applies. The *minimality* property holds if no rule can be deduced from a combination of the other rules, under the domain constraints.

For the *completeness* property, the following definition is used: the completeness property holds if and only if, in any situation allowed by the domain model, for any information topic, any agent who knows an information item is either obliged, permitted or prohibited to send it to any other agent. Completeness checking aims at detecting situations in which the policy does not tell the agent what to do with a piece of information.

This definition of completeness is fairly standard and similar to the definition given by [2] [6] in the context of access control policies. It can also be found in numerous works with few variations, as in the case of access control in a multi-level security context [4] or in the problem of merging two policies [8].

However, this strict and global definition of completeness does not allow to deal efficiently with the following practical situations: first, the design of a policy is most of the time decomposed in phases, and in each phase the designer(s) might want to focus on a subset of the possible information topics covered by the policy. Second, policies might be designed collaboratively by distinct parties, each one paying attention only to a certain subset of all possible topics. In the context of Earth observation for instance, military operators may want to ensure that the policy is complete for any military-relevant topic, without much care for other topics.

In situations like these, the completeness check will fail as long as the policy is in an intermediary state and missing rules. It could be interesting to define a restricted form of completeness, which would be checkable as the design of the policy progresses, without waiting for the policy to be in its final state.

So, we propose to adapt the completeness notion by making it relative to a given information topic T. We call this restricted form of completeness T-completeness.

Definition 4 (T-Completeness of a Policy Specification). *Let* $EPS = \langle \Sigma, EP \rangle$ *be an exchange policy specification, and* T *a constant of sort* $\mathcal{T}$. *We say that* EPS *is* complete *relative to* T, *or* T-complete *if and only if the following holds:*

$$\mathcal{EPS} \models \forall a, \forall b, \forall i, (K(a, i) \wedge Topic(i, T)$$
$$\implies (P_{Send}(a, b, i) \vee O_{Send}(a, b, i) \vee F_{Send}(a, b, i)))$$

So, a policy is T-complete if and only if for any agent who knows a piece of information relevant of a topic T, the policy specifies whether the agent is obliged, permitted or prohibited to send it to any other agent.

3   Example

We now introduce a simple running example which will help us illustrate the rest of the paper. In this example, agents represent anything from individuals to organizations in possession of earth observation means. We distinguish a specific group of agents: the *Geohazard Management Group*, noted *GMG*, whose mission is to prevent false geohazard warnings and to organize disaster management plans. The policy for this system is very simple and consists of four rules:

r1 "Any agent not part of the GMG has the obligation to communicate any geohazard-related information to at least one member of the GMG."

r1b "Any agent not part of the GMG has the permission to communicate any geohazard-related information to any agent part of the GMG."

r2 "Any agent which is not part of the GMG is forbidden to communicate geohazard-related information to any agent not part of the GMG."

r3 "Agents of the GMG have the permission to communicate geohazard-related information to any agent."

The rule ($r1$) shows that we are indeed dealing with the need-to-share requirement, the necessity for other agents to communicate geohazard-relevant information to a member of the GMG is essential for the GMG to accomplish its mission.

The rule ($r1b$) handles the cases ignored by ($r1$), any agent external to GMG knows what to do with respect to any agent of the GMG besides the one for which communication is mandatory. The rule ($r2$) prevents the risk of mass-panic movements which could result from a brutal dissemination of geohazard information to the general public. The rule ($r3$) illustrates the benefits of the permission modality: details of the criteria used by the GMG, which could involve human appreciation, to eventually issue a public alert or not are abstracted away by the optional nature of the permission. *The permission operator hence allows to model policies at a high abstraction level*, which is desirable for an early use of this formalism in the design process.

In order to model these rules in PEPS, we first declare a new constant Geo of sort $\mathcal{T}$ representing the *geohazard* information topic and a new domain predicate GMG ranging over the agent sort $\mathcal{A}$.

In fact, because PEPS is extensible language, we can add predicates whenever we need it. In this example, and for the rest of this paper, we choose to model groups in a simple and abstract way. For that, we introduce a predicate over the agent sort for each group. These predicates can be viewed as membership predicates, characterizing groups of agents. Each predicate acts as a characteristic function for the group it represents, *i.e.* the predicate evaluates to $\top$ for agents which are part of the group, and to $\bot$ for agent which are not part of the group. Note that, of course other ways to model groups are possible in PEPS, for instance by introducing a sort $\mathcal{G}$ to represent the groups, and by using a predicate $mb(g : \mathcal{G}, a : \mathcal{A})$ for membership testing, as found in OrBAC [9] models.

In our example, $GMG(a)$ is true whenever a is part of the GMG group and false when it is not.

The four rules of the exchange policy of our example are then expressed in PEPS as follows:

$$r1 : \forall a, \forall i, \exists b, K(a, i) \wedge Topic(i, Geo) \wedge \neg GMG(a) \wedge \quad GMG(b) \implies O_{Send}(a, b, i)$$
$$r1b : \forall a, \forall i, \forall b, K(a, i) \wedge Topic(i, Geo) \wedge \neg GMG(a) \wedge \quad GMG(b) \implies P_{Send}(a, b, i)$$
$$r2 : \forall a, \forall i, \forall b, K(a, i) \wedge Topic(i, Geo) \wedge \neg GMG(a) \wedge \neg GMG(b) \implies F_{Send}(a, b, i)$$
$$r3 : \forall a, \forall i, \forall b, K(a, i) \wedge Topic(i, Geo) \wedge \quad GMG(a) \quad\quad\quad \implies P_{Send}(a, b, i)$$

In addition, we assert that there is no information without topic in the system, by adding the domain constraint d: *"Any information is relevant of at least one topic."* to the policy, which is written in PEPS as follows: $d : \forall i, \exists t, Topic(i, t)$.

Using the tool PEPS-analyzer, we can check that the policy specification $\langle \{d\}, \{r1, r1b, r2, r3\} \rangle$ is Geo-complete, consistent, applicable and minimal.

4 Need-to-Share Requirement: The Awareness Property

In systems like GEOSS or SSA, it is frequent that some designated group of agents has missions requiring it being aware of any piece of information relevant of some topic T. In our example, the group GMG needs to know any piece of information related to the topic Geo. It can hence be desirable to check that the rules of a policy guarantee that the said group never misses such T-related information. We call this notion T-awareness, and define it formally as follows:

Definition 5 (T-Awareness of a Group G). *Let $EPS = \langle \Sigma, EP \rangle$ be an exchange policy specification, T be a constant of sort $\mathcal{T}$ and G be a predicate* *ranging over the sort* $\mathcal{A}$, *characterizing a group of agents*[2]. *We say that G is T-aware according to EPS if and only if:*

$$\mathcal{EPS} \models (\forall a, \forall i, \exists b, K(a, i) \wedge Topic(i, T) \wedge \neg G(a) \wedge G(b) \implies O_{Send}(a, b, i))$$

So, the group G is T-aware according to EPS if and only if any agent outside of G knowing a T-relevant information item has the obligation to send it to at least one agent belonging to the group G.

If the group contains only one agent A, then $G(a)$ is equivalent to the test $(a = A)$, and after simplification we get the following definition of agent-awareness.

Definition 6 (T-Awareness of an Agent A). *Let $EPS = \langle \Sigma, EP \rangle$ be an exchange policy specification, T be a constant of sort $\mathcal{T}$ and A be a constant of sort $\mathcal{A}$. We say that A is T-aware according to EPS if and only if:*

$$\mathcal{EPS} \models \forall b, \forall i, K(b, i) \wedge Topic(i, T) \wedge \neg(b = A) \implies O_{Send}(b, A, i)$$

So, the agent A is T-aware according to EPS if and only if any other agent knowing a T-relevant information item has the obligation to send it to A.

On a side note, if an agent is T-aware for all possible topics it is called *omniscient*, but this case somehow lies at the border of our scope of study. Indeed, an omniscient agent is an agent which has a total knowledge of the system, meaning information is centralized by one agent, which does not correspond to systems we are studying here.

Using PEPS-analyzer, we check that the example policy $\langle \{d\}, \{r1, r1b, r2, r3\} \rangle$ satisfies the *Geo*-awareness property for group GMG (indeed, rule $(r1)$ is a direct instantiation of the property).

5   Non-diffusion Requirement: The Restriction Properties

If the T-awareness property allows to verify that T-related information is sent to the right group of agents in a system, it can be interesting to verify a dual property, namely that information about some topic (presumably a sensitive one) cannot reach a group of agents, a single agent or can simply not be disseminated at all. Given a group of agents, one can be interested in regulating the diffusion of information in the following cases: purely outside of the group, from outside to inside or from inside to outside the group. The case of diffusion within the group is not relevant here since we are interested in characterizing the diffusion of information with respect to the boundary defined by the group.

Definition 7 (T-Restriction to a Group G). *Let T be a constant of sort $\mathcal{T}$, G be a predicate ranging over the sort $\mathcal{A}$, characterizing a group of agents, and let EPS be a policy specification.*

---

[2] Groups are modelled with a domain predicate G ranging over the agent sort $\mathcal{A}$. $G(a)$ is true whenever the agent a is part of the group and false otherwise (see Section 3).

Topic T is said to be:

(a) T-out-out-restricted according to EPS if and only if:

$$\mathcal{EPS} \models (\forall a, \forall b, \forall i, K(a,i) \wedge Topic(i,T) \wedge \neg G(a) \wedge \neg G(b) \implies F_{Send}(a,b,i))$$

(b) T-out-in-restricted according to EPS if and only if:

$$\mathcal{EPS} \models (\forall a, \forall b, \forall i, K(a,i) \wedge Topic(i,T) \wedge \neg G(a) \wedge G(b) \implies F_{Send}(a,b,i))$$

(c) T-int-out-restricted according to EPS if and only if:

$$\mathcal{EPS} \models (\forall a, \forall b, \forall i, K(a,i) \wedge Topic(i,T) \wedge G(a) \wedge \neg G(b) \implies F_{Send}(a,b,i))$$

A system satisfying (a) (b) and (c) is completely sealed, which means diffusion of T-relevant information is only allowed within the group.

One can also be interested by the strict non-diffusion of T-relevant information in a system, expressed as: communication of T-relevant information is forbidden between any pair of agents.

Definition 8 (Strict T-Restriction). *Let T be a constant of sort $\mathcal{T}$ and let EPS be a policy specification. The topic T is said to be strictly restricted according to EPS if and only if:*

$$\mathcal{EPS} \models (\forall a, \forall b, \forall i, K(a,i) \wedge Topic(i,T) \implies F_{Send}(a,b,i))$$

Note that this definition is just a particular case of Definition 7 with an empty G group, modelled as $\forall a, G(a) \equiv \bot$.

We check automatically with PEPS-analyzer that the policy $\langle \{d\}, \{r1, r1b, r2, r3\} \rangle$ satisfies the *Geo*-out-out-restriction for the group *GMG*. Indeed, *Geo*-relevant information cannot be sent between agents outside of *GMG*, however agents of *GMG* can receive information from external agents, and also have the permission to communicate with other agents outside of the group.

6 Need-to-Share Versus Non-diffusion Requirements

6.1 Incompatibility between Awareness and Restriction Properties

Let us further assume that the example system will also have to deal with sensitive information, and that we would like to ensure strict non-diffusion of this new kind of information. We add the following rule ($r4$) to the exchange policy:

$r4$ *"It is forbidden to exchange any piece of sensitive information."*

To model this new rule in PEPS, we simply introduce a new constant *Sens* of sort $\mathcal{T}$ to model the new topic, and add the following rule:

$$r4 : \forall a, \forall b, \forall i, K(a,i) \wedge Topic(i, Sens) \implies F_{Send}(a,b,i)$$

The consequences of adding $(r4)$ are rather important, since the example policy $\langle \{d\}, \{r1, r1b, r2, r3, r4\} \rangle$ is now inconsistent.

The phenomenon is the following: if an agent knows a piece of information which is relevant of both *Geo* and *Sens* topics (imagine for instance a single satellite picture taken by a military satellite, showing a risk of natural disaster next to both a city and a secret research facility), then rules $(r1)$ and $(r4)$ apply, entailing the interdiction for the agent to send this piece of info to any agent of the group *GMG* (according to $(r4)$), as well as the obligation to send it to at least one agent of *GMG* (according to $(r1)$). These two requirements are obviously contradictory, and violate the consistency property defined for PEPS policies (see section 2.2). Note that rules $(r3)$ and $(r4)$ also entail the inconsistency of the policy by permitting and forbidding the communication of an information item relevant of both *Geo* and *Sens* topics.

In fact, the problem is not specifically tied to this example, it is more general. If we consider the T_1-awareness property for a group G_1 and one of the T_2-restriction properties for a group G_2 in a strictly logical way, depending on the domain constraints and on how G_1 and G_2 behave under them, it can be possible to build models satisfying both properties and where it is both mandatory and forbidden to send an information from an agent to another agent[3]. These models all have the same structure: at least one piece of information relevant of both topics T_1 and T_2 exists, and the group predicates G_1 and G_2 are such that some agents exist inside and/or outside G_1 and G_2 while satisfying the premises of the properties.

6.2   An Ad-Hoc Solution

In order to fix the problem of possible conflict between the necessity of diffusion and the obligation of non-diffusion, we propose to introduce an abstract operator in the framework, noted P, and to give it properties allowing to obtain both *Geo*-awareness for *GMG* and strict non-diffusion for the topic *Sens*. Information being a multidimensional entity, a piece of information can be relevant or more than one topic, we might be able to resolve the conflict by having this new operator selectively *forget* or *erase* the problematic topic from a multi-topic information item.

In the case of our example policy, we introduce the new operator as a function taking an information item and returning an information item, with the signature $P(i : \mathcal{I}) : \mathcal{I}$. We want this operator to forget about the sensitive part of an otherwise geohazard-related piece of information, so we have two domain constraints: $(p1)$ an information produced by P is never relevant of the *Sens* topic and $(p2)$ an information remains *Geo*-relevant when P is applied on it.

$$p1 : \forall i, \neg Topic(P(i), Sens)$$
$$p2 : \forall i, Topic(i, Geo) \implies Topic(P(i), Geo)$$

---

[3] The PEPS theory contains no axioms to prevent such situations, they are just identified and labelled as inconsistent by the consistency checking algorithm of the PEPS-analyzer [5].

We might also want to adapt the original policy by specifying the cases in which the operator needs to be used and the ones where it does not. Firstly, we split rule $(r1)$ in two new rules, $(r11)$ and $(r12)$, to express that if an information item is related to Geo and not to $Sens$, agents have the obligation to send it to a member of the GMG, but if the item is also $Sens$-relevant, the agents need to apply the abstract operation P before sending it.

$$r11 : \forall a, \forall i, \exists b, \; K(a,i) \wedge Topic(i, Geo) \wedge Topic(i, Sens)$$
$$\wedge \neg GMG(a) \wedge GMG(b) \implies O_{Send}(a, b, P(i))$$
$$r12 : \forall a, \forall i, \exists b, \; K(a,i) \wedge Topic(i, Geo) \wedge \neg Topic(i, Sens)$$
$$\wedge \neg GMG(a) \wedge GMG(b) \implies O_{Send}(a, b, i)$$

Secondly, in the same way as above, we decompose the rule $(r1b)$ in two new rules $(r1b1)$ and $(r1b2)$ to take the new $Sens$ topic into account.

$$r1b1 : \forall a, \forall i, \forall b, \; K(a,i) \wedge Topic(i, Geo) \wedge Topic(i, Sens)$$
$$\implies \wedge \neg GMG(a) \wedge GMG(b) P_{Send}(a, b, P(i))$$
$$r1b2 : \forall a, \forall i, \forall b, \; K(a,i) \wedge Topic(i, Geo) \wedge \neg Topic(i, Sens)$$
$$\wedge \neg GMG(a) \wedge GMG(b) \implies P_{Send}(a, b, i)$$

Thirdly, we need to modify the rule $(r3)$ in $(r3')$ which expresses that any member of the GMG is allowed to communicate a piece of information related to geohazards to any other agent if the piece of information is not sensitive.

$$r3' : \forall a, \forall b, \forall i, K(a,i) \wedge Topic(i, Geo) \wedge \neg Topic(i, Sens) \wedge GMG(a)$$
$$\implies P_{Send}(a, b, i)$$

With this modification, using PEPS-analyzer, we check that the new policy $\langle \{d, p1, p2\}, \{r11, r12, r1b1, r1b2, r2, r3', r4\} \rangle$ is Geo-complete, $Sens$-complete, consistent, applicable, minimal and satisfies the strict restriction property for topic $Sens$.

However, this new policy does not satisfy the property of Geo-awareness anymore, for the following reason: in some situations the rules specify to send the result of applying the P operation to a Geo-relevant information item instead of the information item itself, whereas the awareness property requires this information to be sent.

A first important point in the mission of GMG is that its agents need to be sent all possible information items related to the Geo topic, be it the raw items or the items after a modification such as P, as long as the Geo-relevant part is preserved. So, the Geo-awareness property for the GMG group needs to be reformulated to reflect this nuance. We will now consider that the GMG group is Geo-aware if and only if any agent outside of the GMG and knowing a Geo-relevant information has the obligation to send it to a GMG member, or the obligation to send it to a GMG member after applying P, as long as P preserves the Geo-relevant part of the information.

$$\forall a, \forall i, K(a,i) \wedge Topic(i, Geo) \wedge \neg GMG(a) \implies$$
$$(\exists b, GMG(b) \wedge (O_{Send}(a, b, i) \vee (Topic(P(i), Geo) \wedge O_{Send}(a, b, P(i)))))$$

Another important point to remark here is that the conditions specifying when to use or not to use P are not given in this property, for the following reason: we want this property to be generic and more abstract than the policies against which it will be checked, and we want it to be only expressed in terms of the *Geo* topic, and not the *Sens* topic.

In fact, the operator P operates as a topic-filtering operator, and corresponds to an operation already routinely performed by any organization managing sensitive data, prior to releasing it to a tier. Depending on the field and exact purpose, this practice is called *declassification, sanitization, anonimization, etc.*

In the next sections, we will propose more elegant and general definitions of the filtering operation and awareness property.

6.3   A Generic Information Filtering Operator

In order to model operations such as declassification and its variants in PEPS, we introduce a new generic *filtering operator*, parameterized by a *filtering mode*. Each mode specifies which topics are *preserved* by the filtering and which topics are *removed* from the information item by the filtering.

In PEPS this is modelled by introducing a sort $\mathcal{M}$ representing the filtering modes, the filtering operator as a function with signature $Filter(m : \mathcal{M}, i : \mathcal{I}) : \mathcal{I}$ and two predicates $Preserves(m : \mathcal{M}, t : \mathcal{T})$ and $Removes(m : \mathcal{M}, t : \mathcal{T})$ specifying if a given topic is preserved or respectively removed by a mode.

The following axioms formalize the behaviour of the filtering operator with respect to the mode properties.

Definition 9 (F Axioms).

$$\begin{aligned} \forall t, \forall m, & & Preserves(m, t) &\implies \neg Removes(m, t) \\ \forall i, \forall t, \forall m, \; Topic(i, t) \wedge Preserves(m, t) &\implies Topic(Filter(m, i), t) \\ \forall i, \forall t, \forall m, \; Topic(i, t) \wedge \; Removes(m, t) &\implies \neg Topic(Filter(m, i), t) \end{aligned}$$

The first axiom enforces coherence between preservation and removal predicates, it states that if a mode preserves a topic, then it does not remove it. The second (respectively, third) axiom states that if an information item is relevant of a topic preserved (respectively, removed) by a mode, then it is still relevant (respectively, not anymore relevant) of this topic after filtering using this mode.

The ad-hoc P operator, defined in the last section for the running example, can now be replaced by the generic *Filter* operator. First, we declare a constant *FilterSens* of sort $\mathcal{M}$, representing the mode which filters the sensitive contents out of an information item. Second, we add the following domain constraint stating that the mode *FilterSens* preserves the topic *Geo* and removes the topic *Sens*:

$$f : \quad Preserves(FilterSens, Geo) \wedge Removes(FilterSens, Sens)$$

Last, all occurrences of $P(i)$ in the rules of the policy are replaced with $Filter(FilterSens, i)$, to obtain a specification expressed in terms of the generic *Filter* operator, and satisfying the same properties.

This characterization of the filtering modes using the *Preserves* and *Removes* predicates is only partial, since other conditions must be taken into account when using the operator, such as the agent capacity to actually perform the filtering, the fact that filtering could be applicable only on information items satisfying specific conditions, *etc.* All extra conditions characterizing filtering modes can be grouped to form what we call a *filtering policy*. Similar notions already exist in the real world, for instance *declassification policies*, *sanitization policies*, *etc.* The extensibility of PEPS and the expressive power of the underlying logic certainly allows to model such details, but we deliberately do not develop further this topic in the present paper.

6.4   Generic Awareness and Restriction Properties

Wiser from the filtering operator definition we can redefine the awareness property, originally given in Definition 5, into a version not entering in conflict with the restriction properties of Definition 7. Now, a group of agents is T-aware if and only if any agent outside the group knowing a T-relevant information item I has the obligation to send I directly, or to send $Filter(M, I)$ using a filtering mode M preserving the topic T, to at least one agent belonging to the group.

Definition 10 (T-awareness for a Group G). *The group G is said T-aware in the presence of filtering if and only if the following property holds:*

$$\mathcal{EPS}, F \models (\forall a, \forall i, K(a, i) \wedge Topic(i, T) \wedge G(a) \implies$$
$$(\exists b, G(b) \wedge (O_{Send}(a, b, i) \vee \exists m, Preserves(m, T) \wedge O_{Send}(a, b, Filter(m, i)))))$$

Unlike the awareness property, the restriction properties do not need reformulation. The non-diffusion of a piece of information related to a restricted topic is achieved by using the filtering operation in the exchange policy. This motivates the use of the *Removes* predicate to specify which topics are removed by each filtering mode.

It can now be checked automatically using the PEPS-analyzer that the policy $\langle \{d, f\}, \{r11, r12, r1b1, r1b2, r2, r3', r4\} \rangle$, rewritten in terms of the *Filter* operator, satisfies both the new *Geo*-awareness and the *Geo*-out-out restriction for the group GMG and the strict restriction for *Sens* topic, in addition to *Geo*-completeness, *Sens*-completeness, consistency, applicability and minimality.

7   Conclusion

In this paper, after giving a brief reminder about PEPS, a formal information exchange policy specification language, and about PEPS-analyzer, an SMT-based property checker for PEPS, we introduced and formalized two new antagonist classes of properties: the awareness and the restriction properties. We showed that in some cases satisfying both properties can be logically impossible, which in turn motivated the definition of an *information filtering* operator. Thanks to this new operator, we obtain a framework in which both exchange policies and filtering policies can be specified, and *awareness* and *diffusion restriction* properties can be formally verified.

Ongoing work aims at extending the core PEPS modelling language with notions of *organization* and agent *roles*, taking inspiration from existing work on organization-based and role-based access control policies (OrBAC [9]). This will allow PEPS users to specify more generic and high-level diffusion rules in terms of roles and organizations, and let them assign specific agents to roles and organizations in a second step, for a particular application context of the policy.

Another important topic on our road-map is that of automatically deriving information filtering requirements, based on counter-examples to non-diffusion requirements: for rules involved in the violation of a non-diffusion requirement, PEPS-analyzer will identify where to insert relevant information filtering operation to prevent non-diffusion violation, while preserving diffusion properties, and present suggestions of modifications of rules to the user.

References

1. Abramov, J., Anson, O., Dahan, M., Shoval, P., Sturm, A.: A methodology for integrating access control policies within database development. Computers & Security **31**(3), 299–314 (2012)
2. Akl, S.G., Denning, D.E.: Checking classification constraints for consistency and completeness. In: IEEE Symposium on Security and Privacy, pp. 196–201. IEEE Computer Society (1987)
3. Castanēda, H.N.: Thinking and doing. D. Reidel, Dordrecht (1975)
4. Cuppens, F., Demolombe, R.: A modal logical framework for security policies. In: Raś, Z.W., Skowron, A. (eds.) ISMIS 1997. LNCS, vol. 1325, pp. 579–589. Springer, Heidelberg (1997)
5. Delmas, R., Polacsek, T.: Formal methods for exchange policy specification. In: Salinesi, C., Norrie, M.C., Pastor, Ó. (eds.) CAiSE 2013. LNCS, vol. 7908, pp. 288–303. Springer, Heidelberg (2013)
6. Denning, D.E., Akl, S.G., Heckman, M., Lunt, T.F., Morgenstern, M., Neumann, P.G., Schell, R.R.: Views for multilevel database security. IEEE Trans. Software Eng. **13**(2), 129–140 (1987)
7. Gallier, J.H.: Logic for Computer Science: Foundations of Automatic Theorem Proving, chapter 10, pp. 448–476. Wiley (1987)
8. Halpern, J.Y., Weissman, V.: Using first-order logic to reason about policies. ACM Transactions on Information and System Security (TISSEC) **11**(4) (2008)
9. Kalam, A.A.E., Benferhat, S., Miège, A., Baida, R.E., Cuppens, F., Saurel, C., Balbiani, P., Deswarte, Y., Trouessin, G.: Organization based access contro. In: POLICY, p. 120. IEEE Computer Society (2003)
10. de Moura, L., Bjørner, N.S.: Z3: an efficient SMT solver. In: Ramakrishnan, C.R., Rehof, J. (eds.) TACAS 2008. LNCS, vol. 4963, pp. 337–340. Springer, Heidelberg (2008)

11. Mouratidis, H., Kalloniatis, C., Islam, S., Huget, M.P., Gritzalis, S.: Aligning security and privacy to support the development of secure information systems. J. UCS **18**(12), 1608–1627 (2012)

12. Paja, E., Dalpiaz, F., Poggianella, M., Roberti, P., Giorgini, P.: Modelling security requirements in socio-technical systems with sts-tool. In: Kirikova, M., Stirna, J. (eds.) CEUR Workshop Proceedings of the CAiSE Forum, vol. 855, pp. 155–162. CEUR-WS.org (2012)

13. Sebastiani, R., Vescovi, M.: Automated reasoning in modal and description logics via sat encoding: the case study of k(m)/alc-satisfiability. J. Artif. Intell. Res. (JAIR) **35**, 343–389 (2009)

Virtual Business Role-Play: Leveraging Familiar Environments to Prime Stakeholder Memory During Process Elicitation

Joel Harman[1][✉], Ross Brown[1], Daniel Johnson[1],
Stefanie Rinderle-Ma[2], and Udo Kannengiesser[3]

[1] Science and Technology Faculty,
Queensland University of Technology, Brisbane, Australia
joel.harman@hdr.qut.edu.au, {r.brown,dm.johnson}@qut.edu.au
[2] Faculty of Computer Science, University of Vienna, Vienna, Austria
stefanie.rinderle-ma@univie.ac.at
[3] Metasonic GmbH, Münchner Strasse 29 - Hettenshausen,
Pfaffenhofen 85276, Germany
udo.kannengiesser@metasonic.de

Abstract. Business process models have traditionally been an effective way of examining business practices to identify areas for improvement. While common information gathering approaches are generally efficacious, they can be quite time consuming and have the risk of developing inaccuracies when information is forgotten or incorrectly interpreted by analysts. In this study, the potential of a role-playing approach for process elicitation and specification has been examined. This method allows stakeholders to enter a virtual world and role-play actions as they would in reality. As actions are completed, a model is automatically developed, removing the need for stakeholders to learn and understand a modelling grammar. Empirical data obtained in this study suggests that this approach may not only improve both the number of individual process task steps remembered and the correctness of task ordering, but also provide a reduction in the time required for stakeholders to model a process view.

Keywords: Business process management · Process elicitation · Subject-oriented business process management · 3D virtual worlds · Human-computer interaction

1 Introduction

Expert knowledge elicitation has traditionally been a problem of much significance within a wide range of fields [7]. Tasks ranging from software requirements elicitation to graphic design all require an accurate flow of information between developers and end users. The inaccurate communication of this information has the potential to manifest in a variety of ways[27], including extended development times, higher construction costs or irrelevant products.

© Springer International Publishing Switzerland 2015
J. Zdravkovic et al. (Eds.): CAiSE 2015, LNCS 9097, pp. 166–180, 2015.
DOI: 10.1007/978-3-319-19069-3_11

While each of these fields does not necessarily use the same exact approaches to elicit this information, the same general concepts and methodologies are implemented. This commonly involves having users try and articulate their requirements either verbally or technically, or using an observational approach to have analysts better understand the client perspective and the exact requirements for the task in question [7].

These elicitation approaches, however, do not always provide accurate and succinct information. While the end users may be able to visualise their exact requirements, it is common that they are not able to fully express them correctly [2]. This may be caused by assumptions that end users believe are universally understood, despite them not being explicitly stated [6]. This issue is compounded by the fact that the people who access this elicited information often adhere strictly to what has been outlined in an attempt to ensure that the end product closely matches what they believe is expected [20]. It is suggested that this is done because those who use this knowledge do not necessarily have the requisite background to evaluate the correctness and completeness of the information.

Business Process Management (BPM) is an approach which is commonly used to better formalise, analyse and optimise core business practices [25]. To achieve this, formal models are constructed outlining each of the potential tasks involved in various processes along with their respective execution structure. The goal in doing this is to analyse running processes over time to identify any metrics which may require attention [13]. Common examples include the time required to build goods, perform services or respond to clients. After issues are detected with existing processes, the business can then examine these process models to identify areas for improvement, either refining the models or reworking them entirely [25]. Despite these benefits, issues which arise in process modelling have the potential to result in a variety of concerns for businesses. In 2013, 46% of companies adopting BPM principles were spending upwards of half a million dollars annually on the methodology [15]. As accurate models are critical for business analysis and refinement [29], incorrect models can result in large amounts of wasted spending within a business.

The benefit of evaluating this role-playing elicitation approach with regards to BPM is that the accurate specification of task information is critical to the overall methodology [13]. Without accurate base models to capture task information, effective model analysis and refinement cannot easily be performed [11]. Furthermore, many of these processes are spatially distributed, involving tasks which closely map to real world items [33]. This suggests that priming users with the 3D virtual world will result in the recollection of task steps which may otherwise be forgotten [12].

1.1 Aim

In this study, an alternate method for eliciting process information from stakeholders will be examined. Rather than having these stakeholders try and verbally explain all of the various steps involved in a large task, they will instead specify this information with a role-playing approach. To facilitate this, a 3D virtual world has been developed which closely mirrors the process execution environment of the stakeholder. The user is then able to traverse this world and role-play each step they would normally complete in the process. As this is done, the tool captures the tasks performed as well as their sequence and other flow structures (such as conditions) to build a formal specification. Figure 1 provides an example of the virtual world developed for this study.

Fig. 1. Screen captures of virtual world airport scene

The goal of this approach is to place experts into a more familiar environment during task specification. In doing this, there is also the potential to prime user memory and adjust cognitive thought processes to assist with memory recollection [3].

1.2 Approach

To evaluate this role-play elicitation methodology, a tool using this role-playing approach has been constructed which utilizes the subject-oriented business process management (S-BPM) modelling grammar [10]. The efficacy of this new virtual world approach has been evaluated using the build-evaluate design science methodology [1]. This evaluation has been done in the form of an A/B comparative experiment, comparing the virtual world with a custom S-BPM process modeller also developed in this work. The experiment goal was to evaluate the ability of participants to accurately recall and order a series of process tasks while also exploring the way in which users interact with the world to construct process models. This has been compared with a 2D modelling approach in order to identify any major differences in both the modelling approach and the final model outputs.

Section 2 of this paper will examine the S-BPM language, particularly the individual subject views, as the virtual world currently generates outputs using this grammar. Section 3 outlines the features of the developed virtual world, with a focus on how users interact with the environment to complete tasks. Section 4 provides an overview of the experiment design, including hypotheses and approach. Section 5 provides results and section 6 analyses the significance of these results and whether they match original predictions. Section 7 considers the limitations of these findings in addition to any potential threats to validity. Section 8 considers similar research which has previously been conducted in this area. Finally, section 9 will conclude by summarising areas of interest and identifying the logical next steps to further evaluate this approach.

2   The S-BPM Language

The S-BPM modelling language follows a view-based modelling approach. Unlike traditional languages, complete S-BPM models are constructed by merging several individual subject views [10]. Each subject view describes the actions of a single entity. The language has been designed to follow closely with standard *subject-predicate-object* constructs, allowing stakeholders to both understand and construct their own process views [19]. These views are constructed by linking three possible states: *internal action, send* and *receive*. Internal actions represent actions completed by the subject, while send and receive states represent communication between subjects. An example S-BPM subject view can be seen in figure 4. This language has been chosen as it provides concise mapping between first-person virtual world actions and S-BPM model components without requiring participants to model the process from multiple viewpoints. Figure 2 shows an example of virtual world actions mapping to S-BPM components.

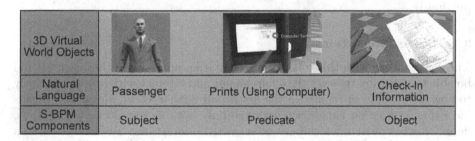

Fig. 2. Sample mapping of S-BPM natural language constructs to 3D Virtual World Objects

It should be noted that while the S-BPM language is believed to be the best fit for this particular elicitation approach, it does not mean that other modelling languages could not also map to virtual world actions. Work has been done investigating the possibility of producing a BPMN model from subjective viewpoints [28]. There is even potential for this world to output models of varying languages, as object interactions can be mapped in a largely language independent manner.

3   Virtual World Implementation

Virtual worlds are synthetic environments which provide users with an avatar through which they can interact with other users, or interact with the world itself to perform various tasks [9]. Virtual world research is extremely broad, examining potential in a number of fields including education, training and simulation [16]. A major issue in virtual world research, however, is that many of these worlds can be difficult to use without extensive training [30]. With this in mind, the features of the virtual world were carefully considered, with a user design experiment previously being conducted to evaluate tool usability [14].

The virtual world used in this work has been constructed using the Unity3D[1] game engine with the environments containing a mix of both modelled and prebuilt assets. The user is given an avatar through which they can traverse the world to interact with objects, as this is a core component for a role-playing based approach to process elicitation. The world used in this study has been constructed with a high degree of fidelity, including both high quality assets as well as well as objects which do not necessarily have core importance to process execution, despite previous work indicating that they do not meaningfully affect user priming in these environments [12]. The reasoning behind this choice is that while the walls of a building and other objects may be superfluous for priming memory, they are still critical for role-playing a process naturally. Furthermore, easy assess to recent 3D asset banks such as *Unity Asset Store*[2] or *3D Sketchup Warehouse*[3] has allowed the environments used in this study to be constructed in only a few hours, rather than the days or weeks which would have been needed previously.

3.1   Scene Interactions

The core concept with this role-playing elicitation approach is that users should be able to naturally traverse the environment and interact with objects similarly to how they would in reality. In the developed virtual world, almost all objects have this interaction capability, with the only notable exceptions being walls, floors or other objects which have no standard interactions. To interact with an object, users simply click on the object they wish to use. This will produce a list of common generic actions or allow the user to create an entirely new one if necessary. By providing a list of structured generic options, user commands are tagged, thereby providing additional structure to their responses and allowing for better categorisation and merging of different process views. This is particularly beneficial when working with view-based models as views are often merged by searching for matching strings [5]. After the user has selected their chosen generic action, they will be prompted to enter a more comprehensive explanation of the specific task being performed. Figure 3 shows each of these steps in detail, with a corresponding task output.

---

[1] Unity3D: www.unity3d.com, accessed: November, 2014.

[2] Unity Asset Store: www.assetstore.unity3d.com, accessed: November, 2014.

[3] 3D Sketchup Warehouse: 3dwarehouse.sketchup.com, accessed: November, 2014.

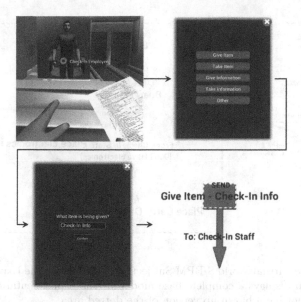

Fig. 3. Virtual world commands required to specify the handing of check-in information to airline staff

After the user has finished performing an interaction, the system will construct an S-BPM model which matches the actions which have been completed to that point[4]. This information is extracted from the virtual world using the *subject-predicate-object* approach described in S-BPM. This highlights a major benefit in using this modelling language with virtual world integration, as this task information can easily be extracted from the world data and encoded into the model quite easily. The virtual world model output for the experiment task is shown in Figure 4 below.

4   Experiment Outline

The experiment conducted in this study aimed to to identify differences in process model outputs and modelling methods between participants who use the virtual world to construct models, and participants who use a standard grammar-based modelling approach. The custom S-BPM modelling tool shown in Figure 4 was used for the comparison case in this experiment, as it allowed both tools to output the same model types and enforced a similar interface as they were designed to be used together. Participants for this study were randomly sourced from the Queensland University of Technology, Brisbane, Australia. This group was chosen as it provided sufficient statistical power to perform the proposed analyses while still having a group which could adequately play the given role for

---

[4] An example video showing in detail how these states, splits and joins are created can be found at https://www.youtube.com/watch?v=zezPX7do-xY

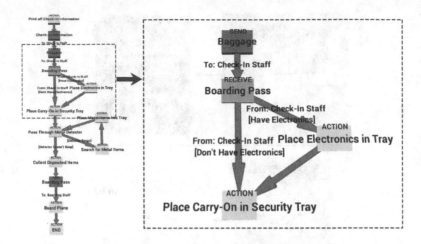

Fig. 4. Complete Virtual World S-BPM Subject-View Model for the Experiment Task. The left diagram displays a complete base model for the experimental case, with the right diagram showing a blown-up version of the dotted area.

the described process (i.e. university students are proposed as adequate proxies for people boarding a plane). Each participant was randomly assigned to one of the two test cases. In this experiment, there were three main hypotheses which were examined:

- Hypothesis 1: Users will correctly specify a larger number of task steps in the virtual world than in the S-BPM modelling tool.
- Hypothesis 2: Users will create fewer erroneous task sequences in the virtual world than in the S-BPM modelling tool.
- Hypothesis 3: Users in the virtual world will use a more consistent set of words to describe tasks than those in the S-BPM modelling tool.

There is significant theory to support the first hypothesis. While this priming effect has been shown to have positive responses in memory recall [23], the potential for eliciting procedural knowledge within a virtual world has not yet been tested. This positive effect may be attributed to situated cognition theory, which suggests that our memories are not wholly autonomous and are instead tied to the situations in which they were created [4]. As the virtual world is able to partially simulate this situation, it may trigger better memory responses then in a standard interview setting. Furthermore, lack of stakeholder engagement has been identified as a major problem during standard process construction [10]. Virtual worlds, however, have been shown to improve engagement [31], which may result in the these participants simply being more motivated to construct a correct model.

Much of the theory for the second hypothesis aligns closely with the first. If participants in the virtual world are primed to remember more information about the process, they are also likely to remember the sequence in which steps are executed. In addition to this, research has shown that training participants with images and videos resulted in better task ordering then text based descriptions [32]. This suggests that being able to view aspects of the environment clearly is critical. A virtual world provides the next logical step for this, allowing participants to achieve much greater levels of presence through interaction with the environment [8]. Furthermore, having the participants role-play the process within the world also provides much greater spatial awareness. If a participant was to enter an airport, pass the security checkpoint and then have to backtrack to the front desk to pick up their boarding pass, they are much more likely to notice their mistake then a participant who did not visually see this issue.

The third hypothesis once again draws heavily on memory recall stated earlier [23]. As the participants are given a short description of the task beforehand (as a series of annotated images), it is primarily testing their ability to remember the keywords used and apply them in their descriptions. Furthermore, this also tests the participants ability to apply these words consistently. The goal is that by have participants associate keywords with objects in the environment, they will continue to use those same words throughout the task. Additionally, it is expected that participants in the virtual world will better remember the original images when primed by similar environments within the world. This may allow them to more accurately recall the original keywords used in the description.

4.1 Modelling Scenario

For this experiment, participants used their assigned tool to describe all of the actions which may be necessary in boarding an airplane for a short domestic flight. To limit the scope of potential responses, participants were asked to only consider tasks occurring after they had already arrived at the airport and before they boarded the plane. To assist in normalising knowledge of the process, participants were given a series of real world images showing each of the core steps involved in the process alongside text based descriptions of the corresponding actions. This task priming technique has been used successfully in other studies which examine the ability of a stakeholder to model a task [24]. Examples of described tasks include:

- Collecting a Boarding Pass
- Handing Baggage to Airport Check-In Staff
- Placing Carry-On Luggage into Security Trays

In addition to the core process tasks, participants were also encouraged to include any *additional* tasks (without removing or reordering existing steps) that they would normally perform when boarding an airplane. This was done to better identify whether participants were primed by past experience in the process, or simply by the task that had been explained.

4.2   Participant Training

Despite the development of both elicitation tools targeting process stakeholders, it is unrealistic to expect that they can be easily operated without any training, background knowledge or outside assistance. To counter this issue, participants were provided with basic training on their assigned tool in the form of an annotated video. As both tools require different forms of training, however, this factor needed to be controlled. This was done by ensuring both videos had the exact same play length (four minutes) and covered identical topics. Furthermore, a 7-point Likert-scale item was included in the questionnaire which asked participants to rate how well they believed they had been trained for the task to further control for any differences which may have existed in the training videos.

5   Results

Participants were randomly assigned to one of the two conditions, with each condition having 32 participants. There were two dropouts in the S-BPM treatment which needed to be replaced. The average age of this cohort was 21.2 (SD $= 2.9$), with a gender distribution of 45 males and 19 females. The level of prior process modelling knowledge was quite low, with an average response of 1.9 on a seven-point Likert scale (SD $= 1.27$). Perceived understanding of the airport boarding process was quite high, with an average response of 5.2 (SD $= 1.4$). Of the 64 respondents, 38 reported that they had boarded an airplane sometime during the year. Finally, participants in the virtual world reported moderate virtual world exposure, with an average response of 4.3 (SD $= 2.4$). As multiple tests of significance are performed below, a Bonferonni correction has been applied to keep the family-wise error rate to 0.05. In total, 8 individual univariate tests were performed with a revised significance level of 0.00625.

5.1   Hypothesis 1: Tasks Remembered

The first hypothesis aimed to evaluate whether participants in the virtual world would remember a larger number of task steps than those given an S-BPM modelling tool. In the evaluation off this hypothesis, three main measures were considered: the number of base explanation steps recalled, the number of additional steps added and the total number of overall steps. Results from these tests showed that participants in the virtual world remembered a larger number of base tasks (M $= 11.22$, SE $= 0.26$) than the S-BPM tool (M $= 9.03$, SE $= 0.31$), $t(62) = 5.37$, $p < 0.0001$, r $= 0.56$. Participants in the virtual world also produced models with a larger number of additional task steps (M $= 2.19$, SE $= 0.32$) than the S-BPM tool (M $= 0.84$, SE $= 0.21$), $t(62) = 3.54$, $p = 0.0008$, r $= 0.41$. Finally, the overall number of task steps was also higher in the virtual world (M $= 13.41$, SE $= 0.50$) than the S-BPM tool (M $= 9.88$, SE $= 0.38$), $t(62) = 5.58$, $p < 0.0001$, r $= 0.58$.

5.2   Hypothesis 2: Task Ordering

The second hypothesis in this experiment stated that the virtual world participants would be less likely to place tasks in an incorrect order than their S-BPM counterparts. To evaluate this hypothesis, the average number of incorrectly ordered tasks was considered. Results from this test showed that participants in the virtual world placed fewer tasks in an incorrect order (M = 0.19, SE = 0.07) than participants in the S-BPM modelling tool (M = 0.72, SE = 0.16), $t(62) = 3.09$, $p = 0.0003$, r = 0.37.

5.3   Hypothesis 3: Consistent Naming

The third hypothesis in this experiment stated that participants in the virtual world would be more consistent with their naming conventions. To evaluate this, the total number of distinct words used by participants has been examined, both as an absolute value and as a ratio of unique words to total words used - also known as *lexical density* [21]. Texts with lower lexical densities are considered to be easier to understand. Furthermore, if the overall wording pool from participants contains fewer unique words, this may suggest that participants are referring to actions and objects more consistently with their naming. Results from these tests show that participants in the virtual world used a smaller set of unique words to explain the process (M = 38.15, SE = 4.25) than those using the S-BPM tool (M = 67.92, SE = 5.11), $t(62) = 4.48$, $p < 0.0001$, r = 0.49. Comparing lexical density shows a similar affect, with participants in the virtual world having much lower lexical density scores (M = 0.24, SE = 0.01) than those in the S-BPM tool (M = 0.41, SE = 0.02), $t(62) = 7.38$, $p < 0.0001$, r = 0.68.

The results from this test indicate a noteworthy effect, with participants in the virtual world constraining their grammar more heavily than participants in the S-BPM modelling tool. To verify that this result did impact on their task labeling, an analysis of frequent words has also been performed. The below table shows how the virtual world resulted a larger count of consistent word usage for each item than the 2D S-BPM modeller, eg. Boarding Pass (49 VW vs 28 2D S-BPM).

Table 1. Most Frequent Word Choices by Treatment Case

Expected Name	Virtual World Tool	2D Modelling Tool
Boarding Pass	Boarding Pass (49), Ticket (4)	Boarding Pass (28), Ticket (16)
Metal Items	Metal Items (11), Metal Objects (9)	Metal Items (4), Metallics (2)
Carry-On	Carry-On (19), Bag (8)	Bag (9), Carry-On (7)
Metal Detector	Metal Detector (30), Scanner (1)	Metal Detector (8), Scanner (6)

This analysis shows that when referring to a specific object, participants in the virtual world more commonly use the same naming style, while participants in the S-BPM modelling tool had a much more evenly distributed spread of responses. Note that this effect occured even for the *Boarding Pass* and *Carry-On* items, despite the names of these objects never appearing within the world.

5.4   Model Construction Time

In addition to the hypotheses stated above, the time taken to construct these models was also a value of interest in this study. Results from this test measuring the total seconds required to fully construct a model showed that participants in the virtual world constructed their models faster (M = 377, SE = 30.80) than those in the S-BPM modelling tool (M = 668, SE = 57.41), $t(62) = 4.47$, $p <$ 0.0001, r = 0.49.

5.5   Model Alterations

The final factor which was considered in this experiment examined the method behind how users arrived at their final process model. From the beginning of the modelling session, participants may perform actions which they later consider to be incorrect. This could result in wording changes, task reordering or task deletions. For this analysis, the combined total of each of these values has been considered. The results of this test showed that participants in the S-BPM tool made more modifications to their model (M = 0.81, SE = 0.23) than those in the virtual world (M = 3.38, SE = 0.45), $t(62) = 5.10$, $p < 0.0001$, r = 0.54.

6   Discussion

The result of the first and second hypotheses in this experiment closely match the expected results. It does appear that the virtual world did prime user memory and enables participants to remember the overall process structure more clearly. This closely matches with theoretical literature which suggests that providing a user with an environment encourages them to think about tasks specific to that environment [26]. The result from the third hypothesis is quite interesting. Despite participants in the virtual world using more overall words to explain their models, their choice of words was more concise, having a lexical density approximately half that of the S-BPM participants. Concise and consistent naming is of great importance when either analysing a group of models for similarities, or trying to merge multiple views into a single process [5]. If descriptions are not consistent, analysts may not recognise that these varying action descriptions correspond to the same task.

The analysis investigating the time taken to construct the final output models is also of great interest. A major concern noted in earlier experiments was that it may become too time consuming for participants to model complex processes using the virtual world [14]. In particular, the time required for users to move about the world and interact with objects was considered to be a risk with this approach, as stakeholders are often unwilling to spend copious amounts of time constructing their models [10]. This experiment, however, suggests that the virtual world users were able to construct their models much faster than those in a 2D S-BPM modelling tool. The larger number of model changes made by the S-BPM treatment may be a factor in this result, but further analysis is needed to determine exactly where this time was spent.

7   Limitations and Threats to Validity

As this was primarily an exploratory study which aimed to generate some preliminary data on the use of virtual worlds in the scope of task elicitation, the results presented come with certain limitations. All virtual worlds are not equal, the level of detail in the environment, user controls and the level of interaction within the world have the potential to greatly affect the observed outcome. To develop rigorous claims about the efficacy of virtual worlds for elicitation, these results need to be replicated within other environments. Furthermore, this work evaluated the two interfaces against a single business process. The results obtained may have varied greatly if participants were exposed to a different process, particularly one which was not as spatial as the airport scenario. There are also limitations in this study with regards to the modelling language chosen. In this work, the S-BPM modelling language was chosen as the comparative case, but the grammar exposed to participants in the 2D modeller treatment may impact on the number of tasks participants are able to specify. As this experiment involved the use of two distinct tools, there was the potential for usability differences to impact on the results discovered. To try and control for this, a software usability questionnaire [18] consisting of several seven-point Likert scale questions was provided to participants with analysis revealing no significant differences between the overall usability scores in the virtual world (M = 5.65, SE = 0.12) and the 2D S-BPM modelling tool (M = 5.56, SE = 0.10), $t(62) = 0.62$, $p < 0.53$. This does not mean that no differences in usability were present, but does suggest that the observed differences were more likely caused by the modelling approach to which they were exposed. Finally, as the training videos given to the two user groups also had differences, it is possible that one group was trained better than the other. In an attempt to control for this, participants were asked to rate how well they believed they were trained for the given task, with similar responses being observed in both the virtual world (M = 6.09, SE = 0.18) and S-BPM modeller (M = 6.25, SE = 0.13), $t(62) = 0.71$, $p = 0.48$. Despite this, there is still the potential that differences in the training videos may have impacted on the results obtained.

In addition to these limitations, there are certain threats to the ecological validity of these findings. The participants were generally quite young, with many coming from a technology background and reporting previous virtual world usage. This suggests that while the virtual world cohort in this experiment may have found the tool easy to use, the target audience of expert process stakeholders may not have this same background. Additionally, participant knowledge of the process was normalised by providing them with a summary of the tasks before they began. While this approach has been used previously when looking to prime novice modellers [24], it does result in the outcome potentially being influenced by the participant's ability to recall short-term information, rather than commonly repeated actions. This issue was partially controlled by asking participants to provide additional information not included in the task description, but it nevertheless did prime participants with knowledge they may not otherwise have recalled.

8   Related Work

Process elicitation is tremendously important and difficult at the same time. Process elicitation methods comprise workshops, interviews, and process modeling by domain experts (top-down) as well as process discovery based on mining techniques (bottom-up). Several novel top-down approaches have been recently proposed. Some of these methods aim to extend current techniques by providing stakeholders with tangible modelling interfaces to assist in visualisation [11], with further work integrating these interfaces directly into existing modelling tools [19]. In [17], an alternate approach to process elicitation (BPME) based on to-do lists and combining content analysis and process mining is described. In particular, based on the to-do lists, the individual views of the process participants are derived in terms of process models. These individual process models are then to be integrated into the process model that reflects the overall business process. This method is extended to the BPMEVW method by using a complementary virtual world approach [5]. Specifically, the meta data that is necessary to integrate the individual process models can be enriched by the virtual world context, e.g., exploiting information on shared resources. Other virtual world applications in this scope have also been examined, with an aim to improve remote collaborative modelling by allowing modellers to use natural gestures (such as pointing or waving), which would not be possible in a standard tool [22].

9   Conclusion and Future Work

The results from this study have highlighted several key areas of interest. In particular, they suggest that virtual worlds do provide an effective platform for stakeholder knowledge elicitation. In addition to requiring little outside assistance, the results also suggest that users were able to remember a larger amount of process tasks and place tasks in correct order more often than in the 2D S-BPM modeller. This result holds much significance as accurate knowledge elicitation and model generation is critical for quality analysis to be performed. Additionally, results also suggest that stakeholders are able to fully construct these models much faster in the virtual world than they could using a standard modelling approach. This study also indicates that the large virtual world time construction barriers have been reduced significantly with the introduction of freely available development tools and pre-built assets. Full 3D virtual environments can easily be constructed in a matter of hours, with participants being able to operate and efficiently complete tasks with little formal training and no outside assistance.

As this is the first empirical evaluation which has been performed with regards to virtual world potential in process elicitation, there is a significant amount of work which still needs to be done. While the results from this study indicated that a virtual world tool is effective at priming user memory, further research needs to be conducted to determine the ecological validity of these results. In particular, evaluating the effectiveness of this world when used by expert stakeholders would be the logical next step in the evaluation of this approach.

Acknowledgments. We acknowledge the financial support of this project by Metasonic via an Honours degree scholarship.

References

1. von Alan, R.H., March, S.T., Park, J., Ram, S.: Design science in information systems research. MIS Quarterly **28**(1), 75–105 (2004)
2. Balota, D.A., Marsh, E.J.: Cognitive psychology: Key readings. Psychology Press (2004)
3. Barsalou, L.W., Niedenthal, P.M., Barbey, A.K., Ruppert, J.A.: Social embodiment. Psychology of Learning and Motivation **43**, 43–92 (2003)
4. Brown, J.S., Collins, A., Duguid, P.: Situated cognition and the culture of learning. Educational Researcher **18**(1), 32–42 (1989)
5. Brown, R., Rinderle-Ma, S., Kriglstein, S., Kabicher-Fuchs, S.: Augmenting and assisting model elicitation tasks with 3D virtual world context metadata. In: Meersman, R., Panetto, H., Dillon, T., Missikoff, M., Liu, L., Pastor, O., Cuzzocrea, A., Sellis, T. (eds.) OTM 2014. LNCS, vol. 8841, pp. 39–56. Springer, Heidelberg (2014)
6. Coughlan, J., Lycett, M., Macredie, R.D.: Communication issues in requirements elicitation: a content analysis of stakeholder experiences. Information and Software Technology **45**(8), 525–537 (2003)
7. Davis, A., Dieste, O., Hickey, A., Juristo, N., Moreno, A.: Effectiveness of requirements elicitation techniques: empirical results derived from a systematic review. In: 14th IEEE International Conference Requirements Engineering, pp. 179–188 (2006)
8. Dinh, H.Q., Walker, N., Hodges, L.F., Song, C., Kobayashi, A.: Evaluating the importance of multi-sensory input on memory and the sense of presence in virtual environments. In: Proceedings of the IEEE Virtual Reality, 1999, pp. 222–228. IEEE (1999)
9. Duncan, I., Miller, A., Jiang, S.: A taxonomy of virtual worlds usage in education. British Journal of Educational Technology **43**(6), 949–964 (2012)
10. Fleischmann, A., Ra, S., Singer, R.: S-BPM Illustrated. Springer (2013)
11. Grosskopf, A., Edelman, J., Weske, M.: Tangible business process modeling – methodology and experiment design. In: Rinderle-Ma, S., Sadiq, S., Leymann, F. (eds.) BPM 2009. LNBIP, vol. 43, pp. 489–500. Springer, Heidelberg (2010)
12. Guo, H., Brown, R., Rasmussen, R.: A theoretical basis for using virtual worlds as a personalised process visualisation approach. In: Franch, X., Soffer, P. (eds.) CAiSE Workshops 2013. LNBIP, vol. 148, pp. 229–240. Springer, Heidelberg (2013)
13. Hammer, M.: What is business process management? In: Rosemann, M., vom Brocke, J. (eds.) Handbook on Business Process Management, pp. 3–16. Springer (2010)

14. Harman, J., Brown, R., Kannengiesser, U., Meyer, N., Rothschädl, T.: Model as you do: engaging an S-BPM vendor on process modelling in 3D virtual worlds. In: Fleischmann, A., Schmidt, W., Stary, C. (eds.) S-BPM In the Wild - A Field Study Book. Springer (2015)
15. Harmon, P., Wolf, C.: The state of business process management 2014, BPTrends Technical Report (2014)
16. Hew, K.F., Cheung, W.S.: Use of three-dimensional (3-D) immersive virtual worlds in k-12 and higher education settings: A review of the research. British Journal of Educational Technology 41(1), 33–55 (2010)
17. Kabicher, S., Rinderle-Ma, S.: Human-centered process engineering based on content analysis and process view aggregation. In: Mouratidis, H., Rolland, C. (eds.) CAiSE 2011. LNCS, vol. 6741, pp. 467–481. Springer, Heidelberg (2011)
18. Lewis, J.R.: IBM computer usability satisfaction questionnaires: psychometric evaluation and instructions for use. International Journal of Human-Computer Interaction 7(1), 57–78 (1995)
19. Oppl, S., Rothschädl, T.: Separation of concerns in model elicitation – role-based actor-driven business process modeling. In: Zehbold, C. (ed.) S-BPM ONE 2014. CCIS, vol. 422, pp. 3–20. Springer, Heidelberg (2014)
20. Parsaye, K., Chignell, M.: Expert systems for experts. Wiley (1988)
21. Perfetti, C.A.: Lexical density and phrase structure depth as variables in sentence retention. Journal of Verbal Learning and Verbal Behavior 8(6), 719–724 (1969)
22. Poppe, E., Brown, R., Recker, J., Johnson, D.: Improving remote collaborative process modelling using embodiment in 3D virtual environments. In: Proceedings of the Ninth Asia-Pacific Conference on Conceptual Modelling, vol. 143, pp. 51–60. APCCM 2013. Australian Computer Society Inc, Darlinghurst, Australia (2013)
23. Qu, C., Brinkman, W., Wiggers, P., Heynderickx, I.: The effect of priming pictures and videos on a question-answer dialog scenario in a virtual environment. Presence 22(2), 91–109 (2013)
24. Recker, J., Safrudin, N., Rosemann, M.: How novices model business processes. In: Hull, R., Mendling, J., Tai, S. (eds.) BPM 2010. LNCS, vol. 6336, pp. 29–44. Springer, Heidelberg (2010)
25. Rosemann, M., vom Brocke, J.: The six core elements of business process management. In: Brocke, J., Rosemann, M. (eds.) Handbook on Business Process Management 1. IHIS, pp. 107–122. Springer, Berlin Heidelberg (2010)
26. Schacter, D.L., Buckner, R.L.: Priming and the brain. Neuron 20(2), 185–195 (1998)
27. Smith, E.A.: The role of tacit and explicit knowledge in the workplace. Journal of Knowledge Management 5(4), 311–321 (2001)
28. Sneed, S.: Mapping possibilities of S-BPM and BPMN 2.0. In: Oppl, S., Fleischmann, A. (eds.) S-BPM ONE 2012. CCIS, vol. 284, pp. 91–105. Springer, Heidelberg (2012)
29. Verner, L.: Bpm: The promise and the challenge. Queue 2(1), 82–91 (2004)
30. Virvou, M., Katsionis, G.: On the usability and likeability of virtual reality games for education: The case of VR-Engage. Computers & Education 50(1), 154–178 (2008)
31. Wiecha, J., Heyden, R., Sternthal, E., Merialdi, M.: Learning in a virtual world: experience with using second life for medical education. Journal of medical Internet research 12(1), e1 (2010)
32. Zacks, J.M., Tversky, B.: Structuring information interfaces for procedural learning. Journal of Experimental Psychology: Applied 9(2), 88 (2003)
33. Zhu, X., Recker, J., Zhu, G., Maria Santoro, F.: Exploring location-dependency in process modeling. Business Process Management Journal 20(6), 794–815 (2014)

Handling Regulatory Goal Model Families as Software Product Lines

Anthony Palmieri[1], Philippe Collet[1(✉)], and Daniel Amyot[2]

[1] Université Nice – Sophia Antipolis CNRS, I3S, UMR 7271,
06900 Sophia Antipolis, France
palmieri.anthony@etu.unice.fr, philippe.collet@unice.fr
[2] School of EECS, University of Ottawa, Ottawa, Canada
damyot@eecs.uottawa.ca

Abstract. Goal models can capture the essence of legal and regulation statements and many of their relationships, enabling compliance analysis. However, current goal modeling approaches do not scale well when handling large regulations with many variable parts that depend on different aspects of regulated organizations. In this paper, we propose a tool-supported approach that integrates the Goal-oriented Requirement Language and feature modeling to handle regulatory goal model families. We show how they can be organized as a Software Product Line (SPL), ensuring the consistency of the SPL as a whole, and providing an adapted derivation process associated to a feature model configuration. The proposed approach is also evaluated on large generated SPLs with results suggesting its capability to address scalability concerns.

Keywords: Goal modeling · Goal-oriented requirement language · Legal compliance · Variability · Software product line

1 Introduction

Goal-oriented modeling has been successfully applied to capture and reason about many forms of requirements, being functional, non-functional or even legal [1,2]. In the regulatory domain, many requirements have been modeled and used by regulators for compliance and performance monitoring across regulated organizations. Such models are crucial to improve the suitability, fairness and correctness of evolving regulations and laws. In many contexts, goal-oriented regulation models may be very large, with models containing more than one thousand elements [3,4]. Moreover, it is often the case that regulations are distinguished according to organization types (e.g., reflecting their location, their size, etc.), or simply to different interpretations or analyses [5].

In [5], an approach is proposed to capture a generic goal model with ITU-T's *Goal-oriented Requirement Language* (GRL) [6,7] as a family, enabling one to extract individual members of the family (e.g., a goal model targeting a specific type of organization) for compliance analysis. However, this approach only

© Springer International Publishing Switzerland 2015
J. Zdravkovic et al. (Eds.): CAiSE 2015, LNCS 9097, pp. 181–196, 2015.
DOI: 10.1007/978-3-319-19069-3_12

supports one dimension of variability, e.g., the type of organization, at a time. In large regulatory requirements, the different family members are characterised by complex configurations that expose a high degree of variability. This situation is representative of what is tackled by the *Software Product Line* (SPL) paradigm [8].

In this paper, we propose a tool-supported approach, based on GRL and SPL techniques with feature modeling, to handle regulatory goal model families on a large scale, with many variability dimensions. We show how regulatory GRL model families can be organized as a consistent SPL, providing an adapted derivation process. This enables regulators to obtain a valid and tailored regulatory model that fits their context and expectations.

In the following, background and motivation on goal modeling for regulations and the SPL paradigm are described in section 2. In section 3, we give an overview of our proposed SPL for regulatory goal model families. Consistency of the SPL and of its associated derivation process are described respectively in sections 4 and 5. We report on the evaluation of our current prototype in section 6. Related work is discussed in section 7, while section 8 presents our conclusions.

2   Background and Motivation

2.1   Regulatory Goal Model Families

Regulatory contexts are numerous and most existing goal-oriented languages have already been used for legal compliance modeling and assessment [1]. Regulatory goal models are becoming crucial as regulators use them to be more efficient and have standardized viewpoints on the assessed compliance. This is especially the case when evolving from a prescriptive regulation approach, which imposes specific compliance means, to an intention-centric one, which focuses on regulation goals and performance indicators rather than on implementation means [3].

In this work, we use the graphical language GRL [6] to represent goals for several reasons. First GRL provides ways to model and reason about goals and non-functional requirements in a social context. Its standardization within the User Requirements Notation [7], its support for Key Performance Indicators (KPIs), its support of standard annotations (metadata) for domain profiling, its integration of evaluation strategies, and the availability of a mature modeling and analysis tool (jUCMNav [9]) are relevant advantages over many other goal notations. GRL has also been already used with success to measure compliance of business processes with regulations [1], to analyze organizational security requirements [2] and to reason about large outcome-based regulatory requirements [3]. Tool support for importing regulations and handling large legal models is also available [4]. Finally, GRL is also the basis for the first definition of goal model families [5].

Goal model families have been proposed to handle large and complex regulation models that have to be applied to multiple types of organizations. As separate models would hinder evolution, increase maintenance costs and the risk of errors, a form of generic model must be maintained. In [5], the authors take the hypothesis that a goal language, such as GRL, can be tailored sufficiently to support the concept of a model family. Applying it to a realistic aerodrome security regulations use case, they manage to annotate/tag goal model elements with the type of aerodrome to form a kind of generic model. Being configured, one can obtain a valid GRL model conform to expectations for a specific type of aerodrome. Tailored tool-supported analysis algorithms recompute contributions levels between intentional elements when elements are removed and ensure the consistency of the obtained goal model. The main problem of this approach is that it only handles one set of tags, i.e. aerodrome types in [5], at a time. If several sets of tags have to be managed to describe the variability of a larger and more complex legal context, there is no way to ensure the consistency of either the constraints between these tags or the resulting goal model family. The approach also suffers from usability issues in that situation. We analyse this as a variability management problem as, now classically, handled by the SPL paradigm [8]. Despite different approaches that couple the SPL paradigm to goal modeling (see section 7), to the best of our knowledge, none of them tackles the problem of handling a highly variable goal model family. Most approaches actually use a goal model to guide selection of a particular SPL configuration, e.g., by taking into consideration quality aspects and potential trade-offs [10,11].

2.2   Software Product Lines and Feature Modeling

Promoting systematic reuse of sofware artifacts, SPL engineering aims to manage and generate software variants tailored to the needs of particular customers [8]. This paradigm is now gaining increasing attention in different application domains to efficiently handle software families. It mainly exploits what variants have in common and manages what varies among them. *Feature models* (FMs) are a widely used formalism to model this variability in terms of mandatory, optional and exclusive features organized in a rooted hierarchy, together with propositional *cross-tree* constraints over the features [12]. A example of FM is depicted on the right part of Fig. 1, with *snow_risk* being an optional feature, *type1* to *type3* being mutually exclusive, and some constraints expressing feature implication.

The semantics of a FM [12] characterizes the valid combinations of its features as a configuration. Automated reasoning operations can also be applied on the FM [13], notably as an FM can be encoded as a propositional formula defined over a set of Boolean variables, where each variable corresponds to a feature [14]. A configuration defines one product of the SPL on a conceptual level. It can be used as input to a variability realization mechanism, which processes all relevant realization assets to derive, i.e. create, a concrete software system as variant of the SPL. Annotative mechanisms define a so-called *150% model* that encompasses all possible variations of assets for the entire SPL [15,16]. During derivation, parts of the 150% model that are not relevant to a particular variant are removed, and mechanisms must be provided in the SPL to ensure consistency. On the other hand, compositional variability realization mechanisms assemble variants by combining elements of assets with a common core to obtain a product [17].

3   A SPL of Regulatory GRL Models

In order to handle regulatory goal model families on a large scale, we propose to organize them following the SPL paradigm. In this section, we discuss and illustrate the proposed SPL organization.

3.1   Rationale and Overview

In order to better manage the different domain elements that can influence the form of a regulatory goal model within a family, we first choose to use a separate feature model (FM) to represent the variability. For the realization mechanism, we propose to follow the approach of Czarnecki et al. [15]. The family contains all regulation possibilities in a so-called 150% model that is represented directly in GRL. We then rely on a *negative* variability principle so that the selection of a feature (within a configuration) will remove from this 150% model elements irrelevant to the configuration, so to obtain a completely tailored product (GRL model) at the end. Consequently, the FM will allow one to configure the 150% model. Together, they make up a regulatory GRL model family.

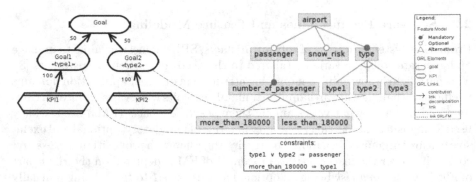

Fig. 1. Architecture of the regulatory goal model SPL

Figure 1 shows how a goal SPL is architected. The 150% GRL model is standard GRL. It contains intentional elements, like goals (e.g., Goal and Goal1), contribution links ($\rightarrow$) connecting two intentional elements with quantitative weights ([-100, 100]), AND/OR decomposition links (+) connecting elements with sub-elements, and finally KPIs, which convert values from the real world (e.g., KPI1) to a GRL satisfaction level according to a defined conversion method (involving target, threshold, and worst-case values)[1]. Intentional elements can optionally be allocated to actors, not shown here.

---

[1] In GRL, KPIs can be linked with intentional elements only if they are the source of a contribution or decomposition link.

To relate the FM and the 150% GRL model so that model elements irrelevant in a specific context can be pruned, we use annotations on GRL elements. Since regulatory models are mainly made of goals and KPIs and since KPIs are not meaningful by themselves, we choose to only annotate goals in the following examples (without loss of generality). Goal annotations are made of feature names within the associated FM. To be more expressive in annotations, we consider that they form a propositional logic formula in which terms are feature names, e.g., the goal *Goal1* is annotated with the feature *type1*. During the derivation process, a goal element containing a formula will be in the final product if and only if its associated formula is evaluated to true. Otherwise it will be removed.

Building different goal model SPLs with our approach, we realized that the complexity of annotations should not be too important so to ease their creation and maintenance. A general rule is to use simple formula in the annotations (e.g., and/or relationships between two features) and to move to the feature model more complex constraints. This simplifies annotations, but also enables one to check the consistency of constraints with feature modeling analysis operations [13].

3.2 Consistency Issues

At derivation time, annotations can be valuated with a given valid and final configuration. The resulting formula is evaluated by considering that all selected features are replaced with true, whereas all deselected features are replaced with false. When goals have been removed, the consistency of the GRL model must be preserved so that, to exist in the final product, an intentional element must be linked to the root or have at least an ancestor linked to it.

With such expressiveness in the annotation language, some annotations may be inconsistent. For example an annotation formula could always be true, so that it has not impact on the 150% GRL model. Conversely, a formula which is always false is inconsistent because the associated element can never be in the derived product. More complex issues may arise when the annotation formula, combined with the FM formula, leads to an always-true or always-false result.

Moreover, an annotation has an evaluation context, because an element can be present if its parent (through GRL links) is present as well, i.e., if the parent element is annotated, its formula should be evaluated to true. Consequently we must verify that for each ancestor, all annotations are always consistent.

Finally, another problem is related to the pruning of the 150% model. Removing elements has obviously an impact on the consistency of the GRL model, especially for contribution links. In the considered regulation models, for a given element, the sum of all incoming quantitative contributions should be less or equal to 100. If one removes a linked element contributing to a goal satisfaction, the semantics will be affected as this goal will not be as satisfiable as before.

3.3   Illustrative Example

In this paper, we use as a representative example the security regulations of Canadian airports[2] which was also used in previous work on regulatory goal modeling [3,5]. An extract of the considered GRL model is depicted in Fig. 2, with a more complete one used in section 5. This model illustrates the main elements structuring a regulatory GRL model: goals as intentional elements (e.g., Perimeter Security), contribution links ($\rightarrow$) (e.g., the goals Rules regarding signs and Perimeter Security are linked by a quantitative contribution with a weight of 10), and decomposition links (e.g., Perimeter Security and others *AND*-decomposing Airport Compliance). In addition, KPIs are, for example, used for the number of fences that do not comply with *Fence rule2*.

In our example, the airport compliance to regulation rules depends at least on two high-level requirements: the security perimeter and the firefighting equipment/personal. Each such requirement is decomposed into operational and control rules (e.g., rules regarding fences). Furthermore, each rule receives contributions from KPIs measuring the rule compliance level.

However, some requirements directly depend on airport characteristics. For instance airports can be divided into three types (*type1*, *type2* or *type3*) and some requirements must be hidden or shown according to this characteristic. Following our approach, this notion of variability is organised with others (snow risk, influx of passengers) into a feature model, which is actually the FM shown in Fig. 1 for our airport example. If different versions of the goal model were created for different combinations of types of organizations, their maintenance would be cumbersome and error-prone.

In our approach, several goals are thus going to be annotated. For example, the goal *fence rule2* is annotated with the feature "*type2*", hence this requirement will be hidden if the airport is not of type *type2*. As shown on Fig. 2, each requirement that depends on specific characteristics is then annotated. On the "*Rules regarding access control systems*" goal, one can observe another kind of annotation with a combination of features. There is then a dependency between this goal and "*Access control system rule2*" that could result in inconsistencies between annotations. To ensure safe SPL management, all annotations must be well-formed and there should not exist any conflict between them (see section 4).

Moreover, at configuration time, when features are selected (e.g., *type1*) the FM supporting tool enforces the feature model semantics so that features *type2* and *type3* are automatically deselected. After this selection, if we focus for example on "*Rules regarding fences*", elements will be pruned and this rule will only receive a contribution from "*Fence rule3*". Consequently, if we directly apply the GRL algorithm to compute satisfaction, even if all the fences are compliant, the highest reachable satisfaction level would be 33 instead of 99. The associated SPL derivation process should also ensure consistency of contributions in each derived GRL model (see section 5).

---

[2] http://bit.ly/1w7jwvo

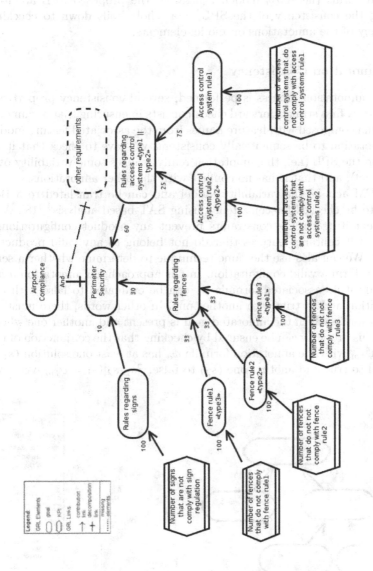

Fig. 2. Extract of the airport regulatory model with annotations

4   Consistency of the SPL as a Whole

As we follow an annotative approach, information is added to a GRL model
so that it forms the 150% model, central to the proposed SPL architecture.
Checking the consistency of the SPL as a whole boils down to checking the
consistency of the annotations on model elements.

4.1   Annotation Consistency

Once the annotation process is performed, several consistency properties must
be verified. A first straightforward check consists in ensuring that all annotations
are formula composed with feature names from the associated feature model. For
each annotation to be semantically consistent, we have to check that it has an
impact on the SPL (i.e., the annotation really realizes some variability over the
GRL model), and that it has no conflict with the other annotations.

The FM acts as the variability model and can be translated to a Boolean
formula to be checked for consistency using SAT-based analysis[3] [18]. A FM is
inconsistent if its feature constraints prevent any product configurations; it is
incorrect if it contains features that do not belong to any valid product (*dead
features*). We can also use the same technique to determine whether a selection
of features form a valid configuration. In our approach, an annotation a is valid
if and only if its associated formula ϕ_a can be evaluated to false with a given
configuration and to true with another one. In other words, there must exist a
configuration in which the annotated goal is present and another one where it is
absent. This property can be ensured by checking that the conjunction of the FM
formula ψ_{fm} with the annotation formula ϕ_a has at least one solution (s_1) to be
evaluated to true and another one (s_2) to false: $\exists s_1, s_2 | (s_1 = \psi_{fm} \wedge \phi_a) \wedge (s_2 = \neg(\psi_{fm} \wedge \phi_a))$

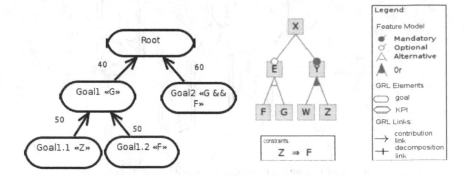

Fig. 3. Multiple inconsistent annotations

---

[3] Boolean satisfiability is a decision problem about determining whether a Boolean
formula evaluates to true for any assignment to its variables.

This verification must be complemented to ensure that two annotations are not in conflict. To do so, we must take into consideration the context of the annotation, i.e., all annotated elements that are ancestors of the element being checked. For example, in Fig. 3, checking consistency of *Goal1.2* is equivalent to checking that after the selection of G, selecting F keeps the configuration valid. Hence, we must check all annotated paths from the root to the leaves. Similarly to single annotation checking, we can check the conjunction of all annotations on a path with the FM formula. But we can also SAT-based check the same property by adding all annotations context as constraints in the feature model. This is equivalent to the previous checking technique, because if one wants that a given path exists in the derived model, one must ensure that, at the end of this path, all annotations are evaluated. The check will then simply be done on the conjunction of the augmented FM formula and the goal annotation formula.

4.2   Illustration

In Fig. 3, several inconsistencies with the feature model and between annotations are illustrated. Note that *Goal1.1* and *Goal1.2*, annotated with "Z" and "F" respectively, are the children of goal element *Goal1*, itself annotated with "G". *Goal2* contains the formula "G and F". First, the annotation "G and F" is inconsistent because in a configuration, one cannot select G and F due to the affiliation of G and F to the same XOR group in the feature model FM. The conjunction of FM and the formula "G and F" will be unsatisfiable.

Second, considering the path composed by elements {*Root, Goal1, Goal1.1*}, the annotation "Z" on *Goal1.1* is not consistent. If we search for a configuration validating all the paths, the context annotation will impose that "G" be selected by the goal "*Goal1*" and that "Z" be selected on the element "*Goal1.1*". But this selection is impossible because if Z is selected, F must be selected too (by the constraint "Z implies F" while F and G belong to an XOR group and cannot be selected together). Finally the path {*Root, Goal1.1, Goal1.2*} is also inconsistent as there exists no configuration where F and G can be selected.

4.3   Algorithm

Applying the rules determined above, we check the consistency of a regulation GRL model as follows: for all paths from the root, we perform a depth-first search (DFS). During this DFS, we build the conjunction of all encountered formula on each traversed path (cf. *getAllFormula* in Algorithm 1). For each different formula obtained, consistency is then checked. Checking the conjunction of each formula on each path is a sufficient condition as it checks that a configuration exists such that the corresponding path can exist and not exist for different solutions. It thus ensures that all elements can be present or removed in the derived GRL model.

Applying this algorithm to Fig. 3, the DFS is performed on the GRL model and creates formulas according to annotations found. ¿From the different paths,

Algorithm 1. SPL consistency checking

```
1.  Global variable: grlModel, featureModel
2.  function GETALLFORMULA(element, formula, set)
3.      if element is a leaf then
4.          add formula to set                                          ▷ no duplicate
5.      else
6.          for each children w of element do
7.              if w is annotated then
8.                  set ← GETALLFORMULA(w, formula ∧ w.formula, set)
9.              else
10.                 set ← GETALLFORMULA(w, formula, set)
11.             end if
12.         end for
13.     end if
14.     return set
15. end function
16. function MAIN
17.     GETALLFORMULA(grlModel.getRoot, new formula(), set ← new set())
18.     for each formula in set do
19.         CHECKFORMULACONSISTENCY(formula ∧ FeatureModel.formula)
20.     end for
21. end function
```

different formulas will be obtained and checked: $G \wedge Z$ is obtained from {Root, Goal1, Goal1.1} and $G \wedge F$ both from {Root, Goal1, Goal1.2} and {Root, Goal2}.

5   Consistent Derivation Process

5.1   Derivation Procedure

Assuming that all annotations are consistent within the SPL, the next step is to ensure that the derivation always gets to a valid product, namely a valid GRL model. Following the negative variability principle, this process (Algorithm 2) will prune goal elements according to a given feature model configuration. We assume that the arguments to call the following algorithm are the root element of GRL model and the *true* logic value to specify that the root element is present.

Algorithm 2. Derivation

```
1.  function DERIVE(element, evaluation)
2.      if element is annotated then
3.          evaluation ← EVALUATEFORMULA(element.formula)∧ evaluation   ▷ this function evaluates
    the formula on element according to the selection in the FM.
4.      end if
5.      if evaluation is true then
6.          add runtime annotation to keep element   ▷ handles element's shared descendants, if any
7.      end if
8.      if last visit of element then
9.          for children w of element do
10.             DERIVE(w, evaluation)
11.         end for
12.         if ∄ runtime annotations on element then
13.             remove element
14.         end if
15.     end if
16. end function
```

To apply the derivation algorithm, we first consider that a valid and complete configuration has been made on the feature model, as this can be directly ensured by relying on SAT-based analysis [18]. In Fig. 4, we illustrate the potential issues to be handled with a configuration of the airport feature model. We have selected features *type1*, *passenger*, and *more_than_180000*, and unselected *snow_risk*, *type2*, *type3*, and *less_than_180000*.

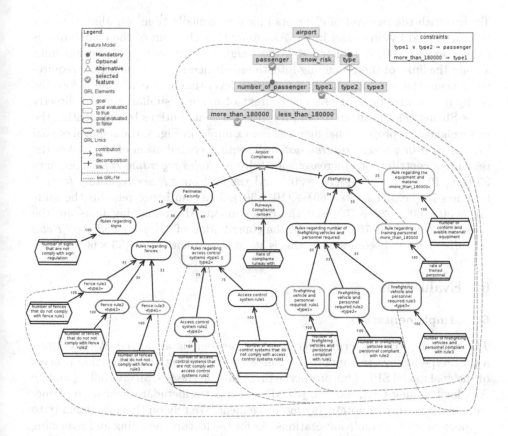

Fig. 4. Airport regulation SPL under configuration (red elements and descendants are pruned, and remaining contributions need to be balanced)

The impact on links must also be studied. Two kinds of links are present in GRL regulations models: decomposition and contribution. For decomposition links, the semantics does not change since the computation of the satisfaction of OR and IOR decompositions is the maximum of the children's values. Similarly, for the AND decomposition, the satisfaction value of the parent will be the minimum value of its children, so if at least one link exists, we can still compute the minimum value. As a result removing an element from the 150% model linked with a decomposition does not impact the semantics of the derived GRL model.

However, there are issues with contribution links. In our derivation example, after pruning, the goal element *"Rules regarding fences"* satisfaction cannot be higher than 33 even if all fences conform to the regulation. The derivation process has thus to be extended to rebalance contributions.

5.2 Maintaining Consistency in Contributions

To deal with the removal of elements linked to contributions, an algorithm has been proposed by Shamsaei in [5]. Assuming that the sum of the contributions cannot exceed 100, it redistributes the weights of removed contribution links among the links of the remaining intentional elements. Consequently, a requirement keeps the same maximum satisfaction level that was reachable before the configuration and pruning. As our context of usage is similar, we can directly reuse Shamsaei's algorithm to obtain consistent contributions by reallocating the lost weights in a proportional manner. For example, in Fig. 4, the removal of goal *"Rules regarding access control systems"*, with a contribution of 60, makes the remaining contributions increase: the 10 from *"Rules regarding signs"* becomes 25 (i.e., $10 + (10 \times 60) \div (10 + 30)$) and the 30 from *"Rules regarding fences"* becomes 75 (i.e., $30 + (30 \times 60) \div (10 + 30)$). The sum hence remains the same $(10 + 30 + 60 = 25 + 75)$, and the ratios among the remaining links are the same $(10 \div 30 = 25 \div 75)$. Similarly, the contribution of *"Fence rule3"* to *"Rules regarding fences"* becomes 99 as this is the only one left $((33 + (33 \times 66) \div (33))$.

6   Evaluation

6.1   Implementation

The whole approach described in this paper has been implemented. We developed a prototype in Java to support the consistency checking and derivation process of the goal model SPL. Our prototype first relies on the jUCMNav tool [9] and its API for handling GRL models. jUCMNav supports metadata, which are name-value pairs used to annotate any model element. We rely on this functionality to support our SPL formula annotations. As for the feature modeling and reasoning part, our prototype directly uses the FAMILIAR language and Java API [19] to manage feature models and call necessary SAT-based analysis.

The prototype is complemented by a test suite and our airport regulation SPL served as an end-to-end validation of the described algorithms. As our approach aims to manage large and highly variable goal models, we conducted an experiment to observe the behaviour of the consistency checking algorithm on large regulatory SPLs. Our SPL architecture exploits the structure of regulatory GRL models and uses SAT-solving in a way similar to feature modeling [18]. We thus expect good capabilities in handling large regulatory goal families.

6.2 Experimentation

Our experiment consists in measuring the computation time of our consistency checking algorithm on generated goal SPLs. To generate these SPLs, we first use the SPLOT software [20] to create random feature models, and vary both size (i.e., number of features) and cross-tree constraints ratio (CTCR)[4].

On the GRL side, there does not exist any model generator, so we relied on domain expert observations to design and implement a generator of random regulatory models. Due to the complexity and the important number of parameters that should be considered in GRL models, we had to make several design choices. We thus decided that the depth of a regulatory GRL model was not relevant to our study, as the complexity in annotations is due to the number of different sets of formula conjunctions that result from the paths getting from leaves to the root. From previously existing GRL regulation models, we observed that the largest one was composed of 3000 intentional elements, and that the proportion of annotated elements generally does not exceed 20%. In these annotations, 50% of formulas are identical and a formula contains around 2 features on average. We thus randomly generated GRL models with 500 to 5000 elements, with 10% to 30% of annotated elements, and with annotations being 50% to 85% different.

As for the FM characteristics, annotations were made with two kinds of feature models: the first one contains 50 features while the other one has 150 features, which was our upper bound for the largest annotated GRL model. As the CTCR is strongly influencing the complexity of the SAT solving, we varied the ratio of constraints from 10% to 30%, this latter value being a maximum observed on real feature models [18]. Finally, we took randomized feature models of the two kinds (50 and 150 features) that were related to more than 1200 GRL models that have been annotated in several ways.

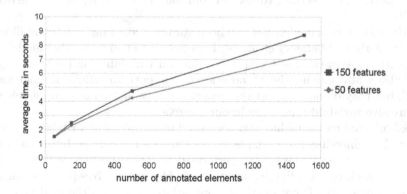

Fig. 5. Consistency checking times (averaged)

---

[4] The CTCR measures the degree of involvement of features in the constraints, by computing the ratio of the number of features in the cross-tree constraints to the total number of features.

The experiments were run on a dual-core virtual machine with 4GB RAM, representing a laptop on which the creation and the derivation of the goal models SPL could be done in practice. The average times to check consistency of the resulting SPL are shown in Fig. 5. On large SPLs, the average checking time taken is between 4 and 8 seconds. In the worst case, the consistency checking has taken 30 seconds on a GRL model with 5000 elements, including 1500 elements annotated with 85% of different annotations. We were also able to observe that the size of the feature model had little impact on the checking time (around 1 second difference for the more complex GRL models in Fig. 5). Resulting times can be seen as reasonable, as the machine used is not very powerful and the checking is only performed when new annotations or goals are modified.

In addition, we ran similar experiments on the derivation process. Results show that this operation runs in polynomial time as a function of the number of GRL model elements. This is consistent with the derivation algorithm (Algorithm 2), as it is essentially a graph traversal with formula computations.

7   Related Work

The work of Shamsaei et al. on GRL goal families [5] provides a first solution to manage variability of regulatory GRL models. As already said in section 2.1, the proposed solution directly tailors the GRL models with a single set of annotations and cannot deal with complex variability settings. In contrast, our solution makes explicit the captured variability in a feature model, provides consistency mechanisms while reusing their contribution balancing algorithm. As for the architecture of our solution, similar results would have been achieved using the Orthogonal Variability Model (OVM) approach [21]. The FM would have been related to an OVM model representing variants of the goal models, leading to a more explicit but also heavier architecture. We see our solution as more lightweight while being scalable.

Variability on goal models has also been studied according to different dimensions. Similarly to Shamsaei et al. [5], Lapouchnian et al. [10] label model elements with boolean tags, so to represent domain variability and extract a goal model. They also extend the i^* notation to support variations in goal models [22], but they do not support the quantitative evaluation of goal models nor an expressive variability model as in our approach.

Goal-oriented modeling has also been used to complement variability modeling in SPL engineering. For example, feature models are derived from goal models [23, 24], consistency checking is performed between the two models [25, 26], feature models are preconfigured using stakeholder's objectives [11] or quantitative constraints [27]. However, these approaches do not see the goal model as the product being managed within an evolving family.

8   Conclusion

Current goal modeling approaches do not scale well when handling large and highly variable regulations. We have proposed a tool-supported approach that integrates the Goal-oriented Requirement Language and feature modeling to handle regulatory goal model families. We have shown how they can be organized as an SPL by annotating a goal model with propositional formula related to features in a feature model. We have provided techniques and algorithms to check consistency of the SPL as a whole and ensure the derivation of valid tailored goal models. Our approach has been evaluated on large generated SPLs, and results suggest its capability to address scalability concerns in a practical time.

Threats to validity concern the simulated models. For the feature modeling part, the simulation parameters have been chosen to generate a wide variety of FMs, with some very high ratios of constraints, so that we are confident that this covers a majority of real FMs. For the GRL part, they are randomly but conservatively generated following patterns of already some developed regulatory GRL models [5]. If applicability is not demonstrated, the structure of the GRL models is quite regular and we expect larger and highly variable regulatory requirements to be captured and exploited with the provided approach. We plan to apply it on real regulatory settings to get new insights. We also want to extend the approach to manage variability against all elements within a GRL model, and explore less structured goal models outside the regulation domain.

References

1. Ghanavati, S., Amyot, D., Peyton, L.: A systematic review of goal-oriented require-ments management frameworks for business process compliance. In: Requirements Engineering and Law (RELAW) 2011, pp. 25–34. IEEE CS (2011)
2. Shamsaei, A., Amyot, D., Pourshahid, A.: A systematic review of compliance mea-surement based on goals and indicators. In: Salinesi, C., Pastor, O. (eds.) CAiSE Workshops 2011. LNBIP, vol. 83, pp. 228–237. Springer, Heidelberg (2011)
3. Tawhid, R., Braun, E., Cartwright, N., Alhaj, M., Mussbacher, G., Shamsaei, A., Amyot, D., Behnam, S.A., Richards, G.: Towards outcome-based regulatory com-pliance in aviation security. In: 20th IEEE International Requirements Engineering Conference (RE), pp. 267–272. IEEE CS (2012)
4. Rashidi-Tabrizi, R., Mussbacher, G., Amyot, D.: Transforming regulations into performance models in the context of reasoning for outcome-based compliance. In: Sixth International RELAW Workshop, pp. 34–43. IEEE CS (2013)
5. Shamsaei, A., Amyot, D., Pourshahid, A., Braun, E., Yu, E., Mussbacher, G., Tawhid, R., Cartwright, N.: An approach to specify and analyze goal model fam-ilies. In: Haugen, Ø., Reed, R., Gotzhein, R. (eds.) SAM 2012. LNCS, vol. 7744, pp. 34–52. Springer, Heidelberg (2013)
6. Amyot, D., Mussbacher, G.: User Requirements Notation: The first ten years, the next ten years. Journal of Software 6(5), 747–768 (2011)
7. ITU-T: Recommendation, Z.151 (11/08) - User Requirements Notation (URN)-language definition, Geneva, Switzerland (2008)
8. Pohl, K., Böckle, G., van der Linden, F.J.: Software Product Line Engineering: Foundations, Principles and Techniques. Springer-Verlag (2005)
9. Mussbacher, G., Amyot, D.: Goal and scenario modeling, analysis, and transfor-mation with jucmnav. In: ICSE-Companion 2009, pp. 431–432. IEEE CS (2009)

10. Lapouchnian, A., Mylopoulos, J.: Modeling domain variability in requirements engineering with contexts. In: Laender, A.H.F., Castano, S., Dayal, U., Casati, F., de Oliveira, J.P.M. (eds.) ER 2009. LNCS, vol. 5829, pp. 115–130. Springer, Heidelberg (2009)
11. Asadi, M., Bagheri, E., Gašević, D., Hatala, M., Mohabbati, B.: Goal-driven software product line engineering. In: Proceedings of SAC 2011, pp. 691–698. ACM (2011)
12. Schobbens, P.Y., Heymans, P., Trigaux, J.C., Bontemps, Y.: Generic semantics of feature diagrams. Computer Networks 51(2), 456–479 (2007)
13. Benavides, D., Segura, S., Cortés, A.R.: Automated analysis of feature models 20 years later: A literature review. Inf. Syst. 35(6), 615–636 (2010)
14. Czarnecki, K., Wąsowski, A.: Feature diagrams and logics: there and back again. In: Proc. of SPLC 2007, pp. 23–34. IEEE CS (2007)
15. Czarnecki, K., Antkiewicz, M.: Mapping features to models: a template approach based on superimposed variants. In: Glück, R., Lowry, M. (eds.) GPCE 2005. LNCS, vol. 3676, pp. 422–437. Springer, Heidelberg (2005)
16. Kästner, C., Apel, S., Kuhlemann, M.: Granularity in software product lines. In: ICSE 2008, pp. 311–320. ACM, New York (2008)
17. Batory, D., Sarvela, J.N., Rauschmayer, A.: Scaling step-wise refinement. IEEE Trans. Softw. Eng. 30(6), 355–371 (2004)
18. Mendonca, M., Wąsowski, A., Czarnecki, K.: SAT-based analysis of feature models is easy. In: SPLC 2009, pp. 231–240. Carnegie Mellon University, USA (2009)
19. Acher, M., Collet, P., Lahire, P., France, R.B.: Familiar: A domain-specific language for large scale management of feature models. SCP 78(6), 657–681 (2013)
20. Mendonca, M., Branco, M., Cowan, D.: SPLOT: software product lines online tools. In: OOPSLA 2009 companion, pp. 761–762. ACM (2009)
21. Metzger, A., Pohl, K., Heymans, P., Schobbens, P.Y., Saval, G.: Disambiguating the documentation of variability in software product lines: a separation of concerns, formalization and automated analysis. In: RE 2007, pp. 243–253 (2007)
22. Lapouchnian, A., Mylopoulos, J.: Capturing contextual variability in i^* models. In: 5th International i^* Workshop, vol. 766, pp. 96–101. CEUR-WS.org (2011)
23. Yu, Y., do Prado Leite, J.C.S., Lapouchnian, A., Mylopoulos, J.: Configuring features with stakeholder goals. In: SAC 2008, pp. 645–649. ACM (2008)
24. Silva, C.T., Borba, C., Castro, J.: A goal oriented approach to identify and configure feature models for software product lines. In: WER 2011 Worskop (2011)
25. Mussbacher, G., Araújo, J., Moreira, A., Amyot, D.: AoURN-based modeling and analysis of software product lines. Software Quality Journal 20(3–4), 645–687 (2012)
26. Liu, Y., Su, Y., Yin, X., Mussbacher, G.: Combined propagation-based reasoning with goal and feature models. In: MoDRE 2014 workshop, pp. 27–36. IEEE (2014)
27. Than Tun, T., Boucher, Q., Classen, A., Hubaux, A., Heymans, P.: Relating requirements and feature configurations: a systematic approach. In: SPLC 2013, pp. 201–210 (2009)

Enterprise Data Management

Managing Data Warehouse Traceability:
A Life-Cycle Driven Approach

Selma Khouri[1,2(✉)], Kamel Semassel[2], and Ladjel Bellatreche[1]

[1] LIAS/ISAE-ENSMA – Poitiers University, Poitiers, France
{selma.khouri,bellatreche}@ensma.fr
[2] National High School for Computer Science (ESI), Algiers, Algeria
k_semassel@esi.dz

Abstract. Traceability has been used as a quality attribute for softwares for some decades now. Traceability can be defined as the ability to follow the life of software artifacts. Unfortunately, making a DW traceable did not have the same spring as for software systems. Nowadays, DW systems are evolving in a dynamic environment, where DW design become a complex task involving many resources and artifacts. In order to facilitate this task, a design life-cycle has been defined including five main phases. Due to the special idiosyncrasy of DW development, a tailored traceability approach is required. Our proposal in this paper is a novel DW traceability approach, driven by its design life-cycle. This approach covers the *whole* cycle and considers its inter-relationships. This study required (i) the formalization of each life-cycle phase and (ii) the identification of the interactions between and inside these phases. The traceability approach is conducted by two main activities: the *identification* of trace artifacts and links materialized in a traceability model and the *recording* of the model. The approach is illustrated using TPC-H and ETL benchmarks. It is implemented using Postgres DBMS.

Keywords: Data warehouse · Traceability · Design life-cycle · Trace links

1 Introduction

Data warehouses (DWs) are the core components of decision support systems. DW design is a difficult task which involves many actors, tools and artifacts. In order to facilitate this task, DW design follows a design life-cycle including five main phases: requirements definition, conceptual design, logical design, Extract-Transform-Load (ETL) phase and physical design [6]. This cycle has been defined through a long process including three main evolutions [9]: (1) the *vertical* evolution which defined the five design phases. The DW design cycle first considered the logical, ETL and physical phases. This cycle vertically evolved by the addition of the requirements definition phase [10] and then the conceptual design phase [7]. (2) The *internal* evolution defined the steps of each design phase. For example, the requirements definition phase includes four steps: elicitation of

© Springer International Publishing Switzerland 2015
J. Zdravkovic et al. (Eds.): CAiSE 2015, LNCS 9097, pp. 199–213, 2015.
DOI: 10.1007/978-3-319-19069-3_13

requirements, design, specification and validation. Each design phase provides an output schema which is *transformed* to another one using some given rules or algorithms. (3) The cycle evolved horizontally due to continuous innovations in data management systems pushed by new requirements. The *horizontal* evolution diversified each design phase by adding new storage schemes (according to given data models like relational, Nosql or even newSQL schemas), database architectures (conventional DB, NoSQL BD, Semantic DB, etc.) and deployment platforms (ex. Centralized, Cloud).

These evolutions let the DW system evolve in a dynamic environment, where new functional or non-functional requirements (like the consideration of new storage schemas) must be incorporated in the system. As instance, the horizontal evolution makes the DW schema evolve very differently from the initial conceptual schema. If we consider the DW conceptual schema presented in Figure 1, this schema can be stored as illustrated in the figure using different layouts (relational, object or Nosql storage layouts). The initial schema goes through successive modifications and the resulting schema may not match with the initial one, structurally and semantically. These transformations are included: *internally* between design elements of each design phase, *vertically* between design elements of the different design phases and *horizontally* between design elements translated using diverse design schemas.

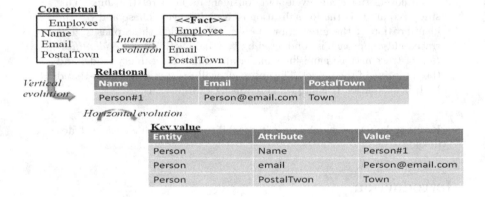

Fig. 1. Evolution links illustrated during DW design cycle

During this complex design process, the relationships between design elements are not recorded and lost, since there is no explicit traceability included. *Tracing* design elements by name matching is also not possible. Consequently, managing traceability become an important challenge for DW design, at the heart of different issues around: the validation of requirements, management of source evolution (at the instance or at the schema level), management of requirements evolution, support of change propagation and limitation of changes impact, decision support about alternative implementations, and more generally quality management of the DW system [14,18]. Actually, many quality standards such as IEEE Std. 1219, ISO 9000ff, ISO 15504 (SPICE), and SEI CMM/CMMI, recommend traceability as an attribute of software quality [18].

Traceability can be defined as the ability to follow the life of software artifacts [18]. Traceability has been studied first in requirements engineering field for software development [18]. Unfortunately, managing traceability in DW systems did not have the same spring as for software even though it can be seen as a software product. Due to the special idiosyncrasy of DW development, a traceability approach specifically tailored to face several challenges is required [13,14]. Some attempts have been made in order to manage traceability issue in DW design. However, in existing approaches, traceability is studied for some design phases and not for the whole design cycle. This is explained by the lack of a global vision of the design life-cycle, and the different relationships between the design elements. This drawback can be due to the *recent* establishment and consensus on the DW design life-cycle. As instance, most approaches study the traceability only from the sources perspective [4,5], or from the requirements perspective [13]. Our main contribution in this paper, is the proposition of *design life-cycle* driven approach for managing traceability in DW systems. Storing these traces allows an easy forward and backward navigation between design elements. As defined by the ANSI/IEEE Std 830-1993 [2], backward traceability refers to the ability to follow the traceability links from a specific artifact back to its sources from which has been derived. Forward traceability stands for following the traceability links to the artifacts that have been derived from the artifact under consideration. This proposition is motivated by some recent studies which demonstrate the importance of expliciting hidden links between design phases, like [17] which illustrates the usefulness of the implicit links between the ETL model and the DW collected requirements. Managing traceability become possible by:

Identifying the relationships between design elements: each design phase produces in output *schema*, and the navigation between phases is achieved using a design process (usually a set of rule translating an input element into an output element). The identification of design elements and their relationships required a deep study and formalization of the DW design life-cycle. The way in which we propose to achieve traceability is making use of a specific trace component in which information related to the design phase (the design schema) and the translation process between the phases is explicitly stored. Figure 4 illustrates the design artifacts and the traces that should be identified and stored.

Preserving these relationships between all design elements: in a usual design process, only the physical design schema storage is achieved inside the DBMS. Since the DBMS system is the "natural" component for storing the design schema and its meta-data, we propose to extend its meta-model by the other design elements (requirements, conceptual, logical and ETL). In order to keep trace of the design process, the reconciling items between phases (eg. The translation rules) are also stored.

The main contributions of this paper are: **(1)** the formalization of DW design-life cycle, which allowed the identification of design elements that should be considered. **(2)** An approach for managing traceability in DW systems. The approach is conducted by the DW design life-cycle and considers its three evolution dimensions. **(3)** Implementation of the traceability approach using an ETL benchmark based on the TPC-H benchmark. The trace components are stored in Postgres DBMS implementing the DW, and then retrieved. This implementation shows the feasibility of the traceability approach.

The rest of the paper is organized as follows: section 2 presents a motivating example that will also be used in the implementation section. Section 3 presents the main concepts related to traceability in software product in general, then in DW context. Section 4 presents the design cycle formalization framework. Section 5 illustrates the traceability approach we propose, which includes a traceability model and a set of traceability activities. Section 6 presents the implementation of the approach. Section 6 concludes the paper.

2   Motivating Example

In order to illustrate our proposal, let us define the following example, that uses the ETL benchmark proposed in [15]. This benchmark completes TPC-H[1] with ETL workflows. TPC-H is a decision support benchmark that describes a sales system. The conceptual schema of the benchmark can be defined by a reverse engineering process (as illustrated in[2]). The set of requirements are provided in TPC-H benchmark and defined as business questions. The set of sources and the target DW logical schemas are presented in the following table.

Simitsis et al. provided in [15] a set of ETL workflows that allows to populate the target DW schema with sources data. Each ETL workflow defines an ordered sequence of ETL expressions that are applied to some input elements. Figure 2 presents an example that populate Supplier and Partsupp tables.

In this example, the workflow uses *Partsupp* and *Supplier* source tables as inputs. It includes the following ETL operations: (1) concerning the Partsupp source, surrogate key values are generated for the "part-key" and "suppkey" fields. (2) Then, the "totalcost" field is calculated and added to each tuple. (3) Then, the transformed records are saved and loaded in the table *DW.Partsupp*. (4) Concerning the Supplier source, a surrogate key is generated for the "suppkey" field, (5) and a second activity transforms the "phone" field. (6) Then, the transformed records are saved and loaded in the table *DW.Supplier*.

A traceability approach should, as instance, define the information given by the following TPC-H requirement: *"the requirements identifies customers who might be having problems with the parts that are shipped to them. The requirement lists the customer's name, address, phone number, account balance, comment information and revenue lost. The customers are listed in descending order of lost revenue. Revenue lost is defined as sum(L_extendedprice*(1-L_discount)) for all lineitems."* This requirement has identified the following concepts in the conceptual schema: *Customer* and all its attributes, *LineItem*

---

[1] www.tpc.org/tpch/

[2] http://www.essi.upc.edu/$\sim$petar/demo.html

and its attributes (l_extendedprice and l_discount). The concept *LineItem* is identified as a fact and *Customer* as a dimension. These concepts are transformed into relations then into tables in the physical level (using corresponding translation rules). The workflows 2 and 5 (named Wishbone and Fork in the benchamrk) are used to populate these tables. The source elements that populated these tables are *Customer* and *LineItem* in source 2. The backward path can also be identified. As instance, the DW *Customer* table has been populated using only *Customer* Table of source1. The requirements that are related to the *Customer* Concept are Requirements 3, 5 and 10 (in the benchmark).

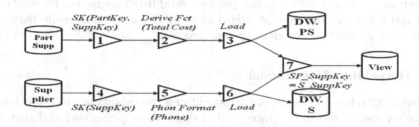

Fig. 2. ETL workflow example

DATA WAREHOUSE:
PART (rkey s_partkey, name, mfgr, brand, type, size, container, comment)
SUPPLIER (s_suppkey, name, address, nationkey, phone, acctbal, comment, totalcost)
PARTSUPP (s_partkey, s_suppkey, availqty, supplycost, comment)
CUSTOMER (s_custkey, name, address, nationkey, phone, acctball, mktsegment, comment)
ORDER (s_orderkey, custkey, orderstatus, totalprice, orderdate, orderpriority, clerk, ship-priority, comment)
LINEITEM (s_orderkey, partkey, suppkey, linenumber, quantity, extendedprice, discount, tax, returnflag, linestatus, shipdate, commitdate, receiptdate, shipinstruct, ship-mode, comment, profit)

STORAGE HOUSE SOURCE:
PART (partkey, name, mfgr, brand, type, size, container, comment)
SUPPLIER (suppkey, name, address, nationkey, phone, acctbal, comment)
PARTSUPP (partkey, suppkey, availqty, supplycost, comment)

SALES POINT SOURCE:
CUSTOMER (custkey, name, address, nationkey, phone, acctball, mktsegment, comment)
ORDER (orderkey, custkey, orderstatus, totalprice, orderdate, orderpriority, clerk, shippriority, comment)
LINEITEM (orderkey, partkey, suppkey, linenumber, quantity, extendedprice, discount, tax, returnflag, linestatus, shipdate, commitdate, receiptdate, shipinstruct, shipmode, comment)

3   Related Work

Traceability has been used as a quality attribute for software development. Traceability has started as an area of requirements engineering. It has then been used
in model-driven development area. Nowadays, traceability concept is used in
its general term, and is seen an instrument to generally follow the whole software development process [18]. Traceability is defined in the IEEE Standard
Glossary of Software Engineering Terminology [1] as: (1) the degree to which a
relationship can be established between two or more products of the development process. (2) The degree to which each element (like documents, models,
or code) in a software development product establishes its reason for existing.
A trace is defined in the same standard glossary [90] as a relationship between
two or more products of the development process.

3.1   Traceability Meta-Model

A traceability scheme is the basic component of a traceability approach. It helps
in this process of recording traces and making them persistent. Different ad
hoc traceability meta-models have been proposed in the literature [18]. These
models share the same core conception. Currently there is no single standardized
traceability meta-model. We thus use the traceability model proposed in [18],
which presents the common features of the meta-models found in literature. The
model is presented in figure 3.

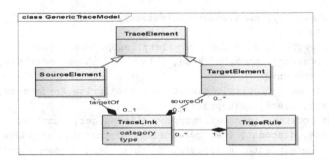

Fig. 3. Generic Traceability Model [18]

The model defines a context used to define which metamodels are used and
the values of the transformation parameters (if an automatic transformation was
used to create the traces). The trace link can contain metadata defining which
rule or operation created the trace. The most important feature of a trace is
the links to the model elements or artifacts, which are connected via the trace
(source and target elements). Spanoudakis and al. [16] defined eight *categories* of
trace links derived from an analysis of related literature: dependency links, refinement, evolution, satisfiability, overlap, conflict, rationalization and contribution.

Two *types* of traceability links are identified [14]: horizontal traceability that links elements belonging to the same project phase or level of abstraction, and vertical traceability links elements belonging to different ones.

3.2   Traceability in DW Design Context

Since DWs development can be conducted as for software products, traceability has been applied for them. In this context, existing studies that manage traceability issue focus on some aspects of DW design, and do not cover the whole design life-cycle.

Among these studies, *Chui et al.* [4] (detailed in [5]) provide an algorithm for tracing the lineage of tuples in set-based aggregate-select-project-join (ASPJ) views in relational DWs. The authors also discuss further optimizations of the tracing procedure in special-case scenarios. This study aim to trace instances of data by means of queries. However it studies traceability from source perspective, it does not support modeling and ignore the impact of user's requirements and the translations between the design phases. *Marotta et al.* [12] propose a DW design approach using a schema transformation approach. The approach identifies the trace as the links (or the path) providing the information about the sequences of primitives that were applied to each DW element starting from a source element. The approach focuses on the traces between the target DW schema and the sources schemas, and the process providing the traces is not detailed. *Trujillo et al.* [13,14] proposed a trace meta model and an approach used for expliciting the traces between the conceptual DW schema obtained from the mapping between sources and requirements. Traceability of the ETL, logical and physical phases are ignored in this study. The traceability links are defined using Query/View/Transformation (QVT) rules and ATLAS Transformation Language. As explained in [18], such frameworks allows technically to record traces as a by-product of the transformation process, but they present issues, like setting up tools and configuring transformations for traceability which is not well supported and is thus also difficult and error-prone. Additionally, these framework focus more on traceability of model elements through consecutive transformation steps, which is not the case of all DW design steps. As instance, the ETL phase does not transform the physical schema but just populates it. Few DW development tools provide some traceability capabilities,but they are usually limited to the ETL and physical phases. We believe that the recent consensus established around the cited design life-cycle including the five phases, allows us to define a global traceability approach covering this cycle. This proposition is furthermore motivated by the necessity of each design phase proved in DW literature, and by the different recent studies that exploit correlations between design phases. As instance, [17] illustrates the usefulness of the implicit links between the ETL model and the DW collected requirements. The availability of design traces become thus mandatory for the achievement of such studies. Our traceability approach is first based on a traceability model, instantiating the meta model (presented previously) for DW design context. This study requires the formalization of the outputs of each design phase and the links between them, which is presented in what follows.

4   Design Life-Cycle Formalization

The thorough analysis of $\mathcal{DW}$ design literature [8] allows us to propose a formalization of $\mathcal{DW}$ cycle as follows: $< \mathcal{RM}, \mathcal{CM}, \mathcal{LM}, \mathcal{ETL}, \mathcal{PM} >$. Note that the framework formalization must contain the model-based and the process-based facets. We start by the presentation of the model-based aspect :

Requirements Model ($\mathcal{RM}$) : $< Req, Rel, Formalism >$, such as:

- *Req*: is the set of requirements collected from users and validated.
- *Rel*: defines different types of relationships between requirements, such as *conflict, equivalent, require*, etc.
- *Formalism(RM)*: is the formalism used for analyzing the set of requirements (like goal or process oriented formalisms, etc.)

Conceptual Model ($\mathcal{CM}$) : different conceptual models have been used in DW conceptual design, among them E/R, UML class diagram, ontology models and Description logic (DL) formalism. Different studies defined DL as a high level formalism that is able to capture the most popular data *class-based modeling* formalisms presently used in *databases* [3]. We assume that the reader is familiar with the basic concepts of DL formalism. $\mathcal{CM}$ is thus formally defined as follows: $< C, R, Ref, Multidim, Formalism >$

- *C*: denotes *Concepts* of the model (atomic concepts and concept descriptions).
- *R*: denotes *Roles* of the model. Roles can be relationships relating concepts to other concepts, or relationships relating concepts to data-values.
- *Ref* : $C \cup R \rightarrow (Operator, Exp(C, R))$: Ref is a function representing the various correlations between concepts. Operators can be inclusion ($\sqsubseteq$) or equality ($\equiv$). $Exp(C, R)$ is an expression over concepts and roles of $\mathcal{CM}$ using constructors such as union, intersection, restriction, etc.
- *Multidim* : $C \cup R \rightarrow$ multidim: defines the multidimensional role (fact, dimension, measure, etc) of each concept or role
- *Formalism(CM)*: is the *formalism* followed by the global ontology model like *ER, UML, OWL*, etc.

Logical Model ($\mathcal{LM}$) : $< Construt_{LM}, Formalism(LM) >$

- $Construt_{LM}$: the constructs of the logical data schema. For the relational model, it would be the relations and their attributes.
- *Formalism(LM)*: the used formalism in logical phase (E.g. Relational, Object, etc)

Physical Model ($\mathcal{PM}$) : $< Construt_{PM}, I, Pop, OPS, Formalism(PM) >$

- $Construt_{PM}$: the constructs of the physical data schema. For the relational model, it would be tables and their columns.
- I: the set of instances
- Pop: $Construt_{PM} \rightarrow 2^I$: relates some PM constructs to their instances from the set I.
- OPS: defined optimization structures
- $Formalism(PM)$: the used formalism in the physical design phase (E.g. Relational)

The $\mathcal{ETL}$ Model : a conventional ETL process is achieved between the target physical DW schema and physical schemas of sources using some defined mappings relating their elements. The ETL model is thus formally defined by the triplet $< G, S, M >$ [11], such as:

- G: the global schema (the target physical schema as defined in this section).
- S: Each local source S_i is a data repository. We retain in the source:
  - $Construt_{PMS}$: The physical elements of the source.
  - I: the set of instances
  - Pop: $Construt_{PMS} \rightarrow 2^I$: relates some PM constructs to their instances from the set I.
- M: Mappings assertions relate a mappable element of schema $\mathcal{G}$ to a mappable element of schema $\mathcal{S}$, using an *ETL Expression*.

The process-based formalization concerns the different algorithms used during the design process, like the translation algorithms (from one design phase to another) and the ETL algorithm. These algorithms are dependent of the design context. The trace information that need to be identified and stored are related to the way in which specific design elements in each phase are translated into elements of adjacent phases. In DW design, the conceptual schema is defined either from: the sources schemas, or from the requirements schema or after confronting the source and requirements schemas. This confrontation allows identifying the set of relevant concepts that should be stored in the DW. The multidimensional role (fact, dimension, measure, dimension attribute or hierarchy level) of each concept of the conceptual schema is afterward identified. The logical schema (usually relation or multidimensional) is derived from the conceptual schema using some defined rules. The physical schema is derived from the logical schema using some defined rules. The ETL process uses the set of mappings M in order to populate the physical DW schema with data from sources. Consequently, the process-based trace information include:

- The mapping link between the source element and/or the defined requirement and the conceptual element.
- The multidimensional role of each conceptual element.
- The set of rules deriving the logical schema from the conceptual one, and the physical schema from the logical one.

- The specific rule applied for each element.
- The ETL expression used to populate the physical design elements with the identified data (related to source elements).

These trace links are vertical links since they are defined between elements of different phases. Figure 4 illustrates these trace links. Horizontal trace links are also defined. These links are observed in the requirements and conceptual phases: between conceptual elements (Ref function), between the set of requirements (Rel function). Particularly, the links between (source, requirement and conceptual elements) are tagged by their category type, eg. "satisfiable", "conflict", etc. The ETL, logical and physical schemas do not store such internal links. Figure 5 illustrates the DW trace model that we propose, based on the design cycle formalization.

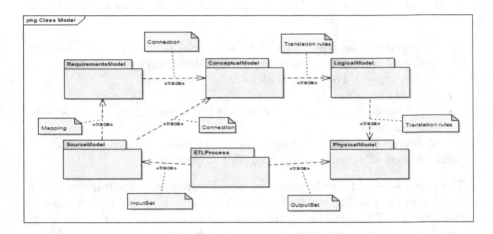

Fig. 4. Vertical Trace links

5   Proposal

This section presents the traceability approach we propose. It includes: the traceability model proposed in the previous section (defining the trace models and links) and the defined activities for recording and using the traces. Basically, there are four activities when working with traces [18]: planning for traceability, recording traces, using them, and maintaining them. These activities are performed as part of the software development process. Unfortunately, there is only little to no guidance for practitioners for applying these approaches into standard procedures [18]. We thus have to propose traceability activities dedicated for DW systems.

5.1   Planing

The outcome of this activity is a traceability model, which is described in the previous section.

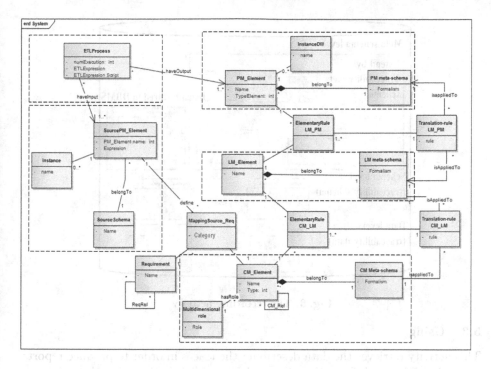

Fig. 5. DW Traceability Model

5.2   Recording

This activity leaves traces on the artifacts and make them persistent. This can be done during the design process or after the actual design process has been finished. It is recommended that traces are recorded immediately to avoid recording imprecise traces. The approach is independent of the formalisms used for each design phase (UML, ER, relational, etc). One just needs to identify the design artifacts and the translation rules used. During the DW design process, the DBMS system is used during the physical design phase, in order to record information about data and meta-data. Two components are recorded: (1) the physical model, which contains the data schema and its instances and (2) the meta-base which contains the physical meta-schema. Since the DBMS is the "natural" component used for recording DW information, we propose to use it in order to record the traceability model. The traceability model we proposed is composed of the different schemas defined in each design phase: the requirements schema, the conceptual, logical, ETL and physical schemas. Since the meta-base is the meta-data repository, it can easily be extended by additional information retracing the origin of the physical model during the whole design cycle. This recording activity is illustrated in figure 6. The instantiation of each model will record the design elements used in each design phase, and their data. This process is illustrated in the next section

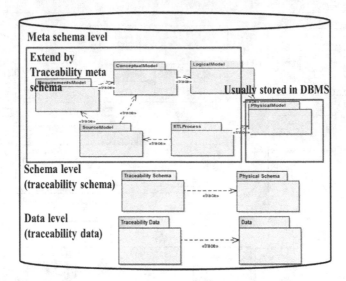

Fig. 6. The recording activity

5.3 Using

This activity retrieves the data describing the traces in order to produce reports or to find relevant information. Since the recording activity is achieved using the DBMS system, the access to data is done using the dedicated query language. Some examples are presented in the next section, where the recording activity is accomplished using Postgres DBMS. Sql query language is thus used to retrieve traceability information. Defined queries and stored procedures have been defined on each design trace in order to easily retrieve trace links.

5.4 Maintaining

The traces must be maintained in case of a structural change of the design process, or if errors in the trace data has been detected. This activity is out of the scope of the current study.

6 Implementation

The objective of this section is to show the feasibility and the advantages of our proposal. We illustrate the approach for the case of ETL traceability. The traceability approach is preceded by the implantation of the ETL workflows of the benchmark. For each ETL operation we execute what is needed in terms of traceability management. This implementation requires three steps: (1) extend the DBMS to allow the manipulation of ETL operations more easily. (2) For each ETL operation, trigger the execution of a series of instructions capturing traceability data and storing them *automatically* in the database. (3) Define queries in order to facilitate the use of the traceability meta-base.

Implementation with PostgreSQL: the implementation of our proposal can be performed on any DBMS. We decided to carry out this task using the free RDBMS PostgreSQL which offers various variability and extensibility features. It also provides the ability to program packages with internal procedures in its own language PL/pgSQL, which turned out to be completely effective.

Extending PostgreSQL to manage the ETL process: the traceability meta-model defined previously is created as an extension of the physical meta-schema of the DBMS. New meta-tables (eg. ETLProcess meta-table) are thus created related to existing "Table" and "Column" of the DBMS.

Managing and storing of traceability data: in order to provide the DBMS new commands that can be used in the ETL process, we need to create new functions for each ETL operation composing the ETL workflow. These operations are implemented using PostgreSQL functions (query language functions witch is written in SQL and procedural language functions written in PL/pgSQL). As instance, in our example, the first ETL operation in the ETL process is the generation of surrogate keys values from the source table Surrogate key SK(Partkey,Suppkey) :

```
CREATE FUNCTION SK(IN source character, IN table1 character, OUT RES boolean)
RETURNS boolean AS
$BODY$
BEGIN
ALTER TABLE source.table1 ADD COLUMN table1Id SERIAL UNIQUE;
END;
$BODY$
LANGUAGE plpgsql VOLATILE
```

Once the function created, its use generates the execution of the defined script. With the same method, we create all the functions of the ETL process such DeriveFct(Total Cost), LoadInstances (PS), etc. Each script is stored in

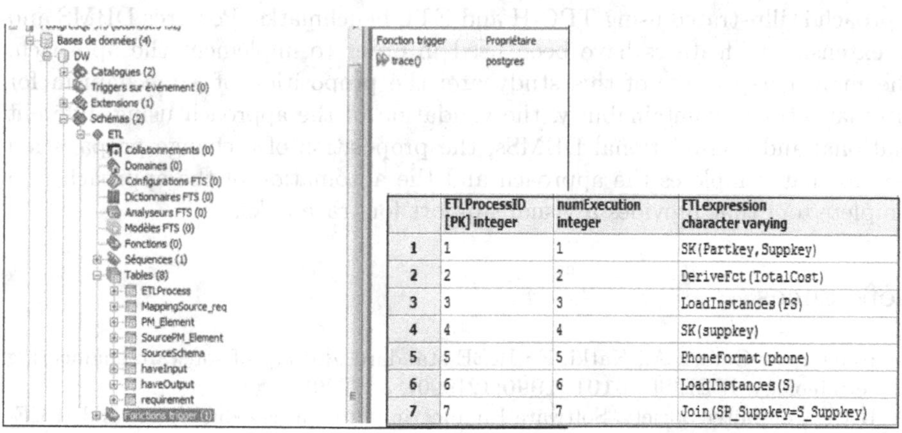

Fig. 7. Managing traceability in Postgres

the ETLProcess table (ETLScript attribute). The numExecution order or the operation in the workflow is also stored. Each ETL operation triggers instructions for managing and storing traceability data in the specific tables which instantiate the meta-tables (eg. ETLProcess table). The trigger is associated with the table 'ETLProcess' and executes the function Trace (figure 7) when a new element is inserted. The trace is created with the code:

```
CREATE TRIGGER TRIG_TRACE  AFTER INSERT ON ETL PROCESS FOR EACH ROW
EXECUTE PROCEDURE TRACE();
```

Note that in a conventional design, these traces are usually lost once the DW implemented. this implementation allows their automatic (or semi-automatic) storage during the design process. Now that the database contains traceability information, they can be easily retrieved using SQL queries. For example, if we want to know how the instances of the Partsupp table have been loaded, we can run the query selecting instances of PM_Element ID = 1 (which match to Partsupp) such as:

```
SELECT * FROM ETLProcess, haveOutput
WHERE ETLProcess.ETLProcessID = haveOutput.ETLProcessID
AND haveOutput.PM_ElementID= 1
```

7   Conclusion

We have presented in this paper a DW traceability approach in order to record explicitly the relationships between design elements during DW design life-cycle. The different evolutions of the life-cycle, which make the DW evolve in a very dynamic environment, motivated this study. The approach is based on the cycle formalization that identified the design elements and the interactions between them. The approach includes three activities: (1) planning: which identified the DW traceability model, (2) recording: the DBMS implementing the DW has been used for persisting the traces,(3) using the traces and retrieving them. The approach is illustrated using TPC-H and ETL benchmarks. Postgres DBMS and its extensibility features have been used in order to implement the approach. The main perspectives of this study are: the proposition of a mechanism for automatic trace maintainability, the validation of the approach using different relational and non-relational DBMSs, the proposition of a change propagation process that completes the approach and the automation of the approach in a complete tool that provides a visual support for trace links.

References

1. Radatz, J., Geraci, A., Katki, F.: IEEE standard glossary of software engineering terminology. IEEE Std **610121990**(121990), 3 (1990)
2. IEEE Computer Society. Software Engineering Standards Committee, and IEEE-SA Standards Board. "IEEE Recommended Practice for Software Requirements Specifications." Institute of Electrical and Electronics Engineers (1998)

3. Calvanese, D., Lenzerini, M., Nardi, D.: Description logics for conceptual data modeling. In: Logics for Databases and Information Systems, pp. 229–263. Springer, US (1998)
4. Cui, Y., Widom, J.: Practical lineage tracing in data warehouses. In: Proceedings. 16th International Conference on Data Engineering, 2000, pp. 367–378. IEEE (2000)
5. Cui, Y., Widom, J.: Lineage tracing for general data warehouse transformations. The VLDB JournalThe International Journal on Very Large Data Bases 12(1), 41–58 (2003)
6. Golfarelli, M.: From user requirements to conceptual design in data warehouse design a survey. In: Data Warehousing Design and Advanced Engineering Applications Methods for Complex Construction, pp. 1–6 (2010)
7. Golfarelli, M., Maio, D., Rizzi, S.: The dimensional fact model: a conceptual model for data warehouses. International Journal of Cooperative Information Systems 7(02n03), 215–247 (1998)
8. Khouri, S.: Cycle de vie smantique de conception de systmes de stockage et de manipulation de donnees. PhD thesis, ENSMA & ESI, October 2013
9. Khouri, S., Bellatreche, L.: Towards a configurable database design: a case of semantic data warehouses. In: Meersman, R., Panetto, H., Dillon, T., Missikoff, M., Liu, L., Pastor, O., Cuzzocrea, A., Sellis, T. (eds.) OTM 2014. LNCS, vol. 8841, pp. 760–767. Springer, Heidelberg (2014)
10. Kimball, R.: The data warehouse toolkit: practical techniques for building dimensional data warehouses. John Wiley & Sons Inc., New York (1996)
11. Lenzerini, M.: Data integration: a theoretical perspective. In: :Proceedings of the Twenty-First ACM SIGMOD-SIGACT-SIGART Symposium on Principles of Database Systems, pp. 233–246. ACM (2002)
12. Marotta, A., Ruggia, R.: Data warehouse design: a schema-transformation approach. In : Computer Science Society, SCCC 2002, Proceedings of the 22nd International Conference of the Chilean, pp. 153–161. IEEE (2002)
13. Mat, A., Trujillo, J.: A trace metamodel proposal based on the model driven architecture framework for the traceability of user requirements in data warehouses. Information Systems 37(8), 753–766 (2012)
14. Mat, A., Trujillo, J.: Tracing conceptual models' evolution in data warehouses by using the model driven architecture. Computer Standards & Interfaces 36(5), 831–843 (2014)
15. Simitsis, A., Vassiliadis, P., Dayal, U., Karagiannis, A., Tziovara, V.: Benchmarking ETL workflows. In: Nambiar, R., Poess, M. (eds.) TPCTC 2009. LNCS, vol. 5895, pp. 199–220. Springer, Heidelberg (2009)
16. Spanoudakis, G., Zisman, A.: Software traceability: a roadmap. Handbook of Software Engineering and Knowledge Engineering 3, 395–428 (2005)
17. Theodorou, V., Abelló, A., Thiele, M., Lehner, W.: A framework for user-centered declarative etl. In: Proceedings of the 17th International Workshop on Data Warehousing and OLAP, pp. 67–70. ACM (2014)
18. Winkler, S., Pilgrim, J.V.: A survey of traceability in requirements engineering and model-driven development. Software & Systems Modeling 9(4), 529–565 (2010)

Specification and Incremental Maintenance of Linked Data Mashup Views

Vânia M.P. Vidal[1], Marco A. Casanova[2(✉)], Narciso Arruda[1], Mariano Roberval[1], Luiz Paes Leme[3], Giseli Rabello Lopes[4], and Chiara Renso[5]

[1] Department of Computing, Federal University of Ceará, Fortaleza, CE, Brazil
{vvidal,narciso,mariano}@lia.ufc.br
[2] Department of Informatics,
Pontifical Catholic University of Rio de Janeiro, Rio de Janeiro, RJ, Brazil
casanova@inf.puc-rio.br
[3] Fluminense Federal University, Niteroi, RJ, Brazil
lapaesleme@ic.uff.br
[4] Computer Science Department,
Federal University of Rio de Janeiro, Rio de Janeiro, RJ, Brazil
giseli@dcc.ufrj.br
[5] ISTI Institute of National Research Council, Pisa, Italy
chiara.renso@isti.cnr.it

Abstract. The Linked Data initiative promotes the publication of previously isolated databases as interlinked RDF datasets, thereby creating a global scale data space, known as the Web of Data. Linked Data Mashup applications, which consume data from the multiple Linked Data sources in the Web of Data, are confronted with the challenge of obtaining a homogenized view of this global data space, called a Linked Data Mashup view. This paper proposes an ontology-based framework for formally specifying Linked Data Mashup views, and a strategy for the incremental maintenance of such views, based on their specifications.

Keywords: Data mashup application · RDF dataset interlinking · Linked data · View maintenance

1 Introduction

The Linked Data initiative [2] brought new opportunities for building the next generation of Semantic Mashup applications [8]. By exposing previously isolated datasets as data graphs, which can be interlinked and integrated with other datasets, Linked Data allows creating a global-scale interlinked data space, known as the Web of Data. The success of the Linked Data initiative is mainly due to the adoption of known Web standards, such as Web infrastructure standards (URIs and HTTP), Semantic Web standards (RDF and RDFS) and vocabularies, which facilitate the deployment of Linked Data sources.

© Springer International Publishing Switzerland 2015
J. Zdravkovic et al. (Eds.): CAiSE 2015, LNCS 9097, pp. 214–229, 2015.
DOI: 10.1007/978-3-319-19069-3_14

A *linked data mashup* is an (Web) application that offers new functionality by combining, aggregating, and transforming data available on the *Web of Data* [11], [19]. Thanks to the new technologies that have been developed by the Semantic Web community, a great amount of linked data mashups were recently produced [11], in several domains. A simple example of Linked Data Mashup is *BBC Music* [13] which integrates data from two Linked Data sources, *DBpedia* [3] and *MusicBrainz* [20].

Linked Data Mashup (LDM) applications are confronted with the challenge of obtaining a homogenized view of this global data space, which we call a *Linked Data Mashup view* (*LDM view*). The creation of a LDM view is a complex task which involves four major challenges: (1) selection of the Linked Data sources that are relevant for the application; (2) extraction and translation of data from different, possibly heterogeneous Linked Data sources to a common vocabulary; (3) identification of links between resources in different Linked Data sources; (4) combination and fusion of multiple representations of the same real-world object into a single representation and resolution of data inconsistencies to improve the quality of the data.

To be useful, a LDM view must be continuously maintained to reflect dynamic data sources updates. Basically, there are two strategies for materialized view maintenance. *Re-materialization* re-computes view data at pre-established times, whereas *incremental maintenance* periodically modifies part of the view data to reflect updates to the database. It has been shown that incremental maintenance generally outperforms full view recomputation [1,7,9,15].

In this paper, we investigate the problem of incremental maintenance of LDM views. First, we propose an ontology-based framework for formally specifying LDM views. In our framework, an LDM view is specified with the help of exported views, sameAs linkset views, data fusion rules and a normalization function. The LDM view specification is used to automatically materialize the mashup view. Then, we propose a strategy that uses the LDM view specification for incrementally maintain the mashup view materialization.

The incremental maintenance strategy of LDM views is the major contribution of this paper. The strategy addresses the problem of dealing with the combination and fusion of multiple representations of the same real-world object when the Linked Data sources are updated. As discussed in the related work section, this problem received little attention and yet poses new challenges due to very nature of mashup data.

The paper is organized as follows. Section 2 presents the framework to create LDM views. Section 3 discusses how to maintain LDM Views. Section 4 reviews related work. Finally, Section 5 contains the conclusions.

2   Ontology-Based Framework for LDM View Specification

2.1   Overview

In this section, we discuss a three level ontology-based framework, as summarized in Figure 1, to formally specify LDM views. In the Mashup View Layer, the mashup view ontology O_D specifies the concepts of the mashup application (i.e., the *conceptual model*), which is the common vocabulary for integrating data exported by the Linked Data sources.

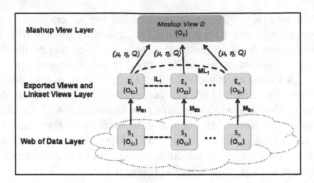

Fig. 1. Three Level Ontology-Based Framework

In the Web of Data Layer, each data source S_i is described by a *source ontology* O_{Si}, published on the Web according to the Linked Data principles. These source ontologies are depicted in the Web of Data layer in Figure 1.

Each Linked Data source S_i exports one or more views. Each such view E_i has an ontology O_{Ei} and a set of rules M_{Ei} that map concepts of O_{Si} to concepts of O_D. The vocabulary of O_{Ei} is the subset of the vocabulary of O_D whose terms occur in the head of the rules in M_{Ei}. The exported ontologies are depicted in the Exported Views and Linkset Views Layer in Figure 1.

We consider two types of sameAs links: *exported sameAs links*, which are exported by a Linked Data source, and *mashup sameAs links*, which are automatically created based on a sameAs linkset view specification [5] specifically defined for the mashup application.

As detailed in the following subsections, a *LDM view specification* is an n-tuple $\lambda = (D, O_D, E_1, ..., E_n, EL_1,..., EL_p, ML_1,...,ML_q, \mu, \eta, Q)$, where:

- D is the *name* of the mashup view
- O_D is the *mashup view ontology*
- $E_1, ..., E_n$ are *exported view specifications* with ontologies $O_{E1},...,O_{En}$, whose vocabularies are subsets of the vocabulary of O_D
- $EL_1,..., EL_p$ are *exported sameAs linkset view specifications* between $E_1, ..., E_n$
- $ML_1, ..., ML_q$ are *mashup sameAs linkset view specifications* between $E_1, ..., E_n$
- μ is a set of *fusion rules* from $O_{E1},...,O_{En}$ to O_D
- η is a *normalization function symbol* whose interpretation defines how to remap IRIs of the exported views to IRIs of the LDM view
- Q is a set of *quality assessment metrics*, which are used to quantify the quality of the Linked Data sources. This information is required by fusion rules. The specification of quality assessment metric [16] is out of the scope of this work.

The process for generating the LDM view specification λ consists of 5 steps: (1) Modeling of the mashup ontology View; (2) Generation of the exported views specifications; (3) Generation of the exported sameAs linkset view specifications; (4) Generation of the mashup sameAs linkset view specifications; (5) Definition of the normalization function, fusion rules and quality assessment metrics. Steps 2 to 5 are detailed in the following subsections.

In our framework, the materialization of a *LDM view specification* λ is automatically processed based on its specification and consists of four steps:

1. **Materialization of the exported views**. This step translates source data to the exported view vocabulary as specified by the mapping rules in the exported view specification.

2. **Materialization of the exported sameAs linksets views**. Given an exported linkset view *EL* over a Linked Data source *S*, this step exports sameAs links from *S* to the LDM view materialization.

3. **Materialization of the mashup sameAs linksets.** Given a mashup linkset view *ML*, this step computes sameAs links based on the specification of *ML*.

4. **Materialization of the mashup view**. This step materializes the mashup view by applying the normalization function and the fusion rules to the materialized exported views and the materialized sameAs Linkset views. It includes the combination and fusion of multiple representations of the same real-world object into a single representation and the resolution of data inconsistencies.

2.2   Running Example

Throughout the paper, we will adopt a simple example of a mashup application about music, called *DBB_Music*, which integrates data from two Linked Data sources: *DBpedia* [3] and *MusicBrainz* [20]. Figure 2 depicts, in UML notation, the application ontology *Music_OWL* for the *DBB_Music* mashup, which reuses terms from three well-known vocabularies: *FOAF* (Friend of a Friend), *MO* (Music Ontology) and *DC* (Dublin Core). We use the prefix *"moa:"* for the new terms defined in the *Music_OWL* ontology. *DBpedia* uses the *DBpedia Ontology [21]* which we call *DBpedia_OWL*, and we use the prefix *"dbpedia-owl:"* to refer to it. *MusicBrainz* uses the *Music Ontology* [17] and we use the prefix *"mo:"* to refer to it.

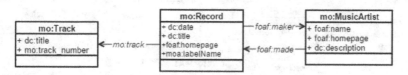

Fig. 2. Music_OWL

2.3   Specification and Materialization of Exported Views

An *exported view specification* is a quintuple (E, S, O_S, O_E, M_E), where:

- *E* is the *name* of the view
- *S* is a Linked Data source
- O_S is the ontology of *S*
- O_E is the *exported view ontology* such that the terms of its vocabulary occur in the heads of the mapping rules in *M*
- M_E is a set of mapping rules from O_S to O_E

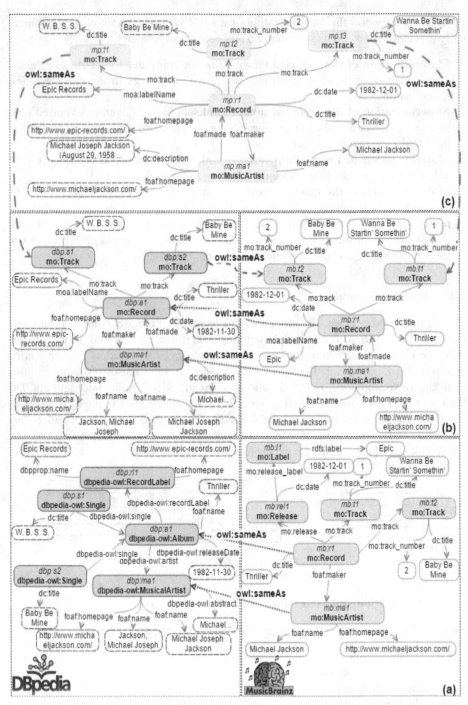

Fig. 3. (a) Data sources state; (b) Materialized Exported views and linkset views; (c) LDM view

In our framework, each linked data source exports a view whose specification is automatically generated considering the source ontology, the application ontology and the mappings between the source ontology and the application ontology. Note that, when an exported view E is part of a LDM view specification, the vocabulary of the ontology O_E must be a subset of the vocabulary of the mashup view ontology, as required in Section 2.1. The problem of generating exported views specifications is addressed in our previous work [18] and it is out of the scope of this work.

Consider the mashup application *DBB_Music* introduced in Section 2.1. An exported view specification, *DBpedia_EV*, which uses the data source *DBpedia* can be defined based on the mappings rules between *Music_OWL* and *DBpedia_OWL*. Due to space limitation, the mappings rules are omitted here. The vocabulary of the exported view ontology of *DBpedia_EV* then is:{*mo:Record*, *mo:MusicArtist*, *mo:Track*, *foaf:homepage*, *moa:labelName*, *dc:title*, *dc:date*, *foaf:name*, *dc:description*, *mo:track*, *foaf:maker*, *foaf:made*}

An exported view specification, *MusicBrainz_EV*, which uses the data source *MusicBrainz* can be likewise defined. The vocabulary of the exported view ontology of *MusicBrainz_EV* is:{*mo:Record*, *mo:MusicArtist*, *mo:Track*, *moa:labelName*, *dc:title*, *dc:date*, *foaf:name*, *foaf:homepage*, *mo:track_number*, *mo:track*, *foaf:maker*, *foaf:made*}

A materialization of an exported view requires translating source data into the exported view vocabulary as specified by the mapping rules. Referring to our case study, Figure 3(b) shows materializations of the exported views *MusicBrainz_EV* and *DBpedia_EV* obtained by applying the mappings rules.

2.4   Specification and Materialization of Exported sameAs Linkset Views

In our framework, the existing sameAs links between resources of different exported views should also be exported to the mashup view. To create exported links, the user should first specify an exported sameAs linkset view and then materialize the links.

Let $(T, S_T, O_{ST}, O_T, \mu_T)$ and $(U, S_U, O_{SU}, O_U, \mu_U)$ be two exported views. An *exported sameAs linkset view specification* is a tuple $(EL, T, U, C, C_{ST}, C_{SU})$, where:

- EL is the *name* of the view;
- $(T, S_T, O_{ST}, O_T, M_T)$ and $(U, S_U, O_{SU}, O_U, M_U)$ are exported view specifications;
- C is a class in both the vocabularies of the exported view ontologies O_T and O_U;
- C_{ST} is a class in the vocabulary of the data source ontology O_{ST} of S_T such that there is a rule in M_T, indicating that instances of C_{ST} are mapped to instances of C;
- C_{SU} is a class in the vocabulary of the data source ontology O_{SU} of S_U such that there is a rule in M_U, indicating that instances of C_{SU} are mapped to instances of C;

Let s_T and s_U be states respectively of S_T and S_U. The materialization of EL in s_T and s_U is the set $EL[s_T, s_U]$ defined as:

$(t, owl:sameAs, u) \in EL[s_T, s_U]$ iff
$(t, owl:sameAs, u) \in s_T \land (t, rdf:type, C_{ST}) \in I[s_T](C_{ST}) \land$
$(u, rdf:type, C_{SU}) \in I[s_U](C_{SU})$.

That is, *EL[s_T,s_U]* imports sameAs links from s_T whose subject is in the interpretation in s_T of the class C_{ST} and whose object is in the interpretation in s_U of the class C_{SU}.

Consider, for example, the exported views *MusicBrainz_EV* and *DBpedia_EV* introduced in Section 2.3. As shown in Figure 3(a), the data source *MusicBrainz* contains sameAs links matching instances of class *mo:Record* with instances of class *dbpedia_owl:Albums*. It also contains sameAs links matching instances of *mo:MusicArtist* with *dbpedia_owl:MusicalArtist*. In order to materialize the sameAs links for the instances of the exported views *MusicBrainz_EV* and *DBpedia_EV*, two exported linkset views should be specified:

- *(EL_1, MusicBrainz_EV, DBpedia_EV, mo:Record, mo:Record, dbpedia-owl:Album)*
- *(EL_2, MusicBrainz_EV, DBpedia_EV, mo:MusicArtist, mo:MusicArtist, dbpedia-owl:MusicalArtist)*

Referring to Figure 3(a) of our case study, the sameAs link from *mb:ma1* to *dbp:ma1* is materialized by EL_2, and the sameAs link from *mb:r1* to *dbp:a1* is materialized by EL_1.

2.5   Specification and Materialization of Mashup sameAs Linkset Views

In our framework, mashup sameAs links are inferred by matching property values of resources defined in the exported views. To create mashup links, the user should first specify the mashup sameAs linkset view and then materialize the links. More precisely, a *mashup sameAs linkset view specification* is a tuple *(ML, T, U, C, p_1,..., p_n, μ)*, where:

- *ML* is the *name* of the view
- *(T, S_T, O_{ST}, O_T, μ_T)* and *(U, S_U, O_{SU}, O_U, μ_U)* are exported view specifications
- *C* is a class in both the vocabularies of the exported view ontologies O_T and O_U;
- p_1, ..., p_n are properties of class *C* in both the vocabularies of the exported view ontologies O_T and O_U
- *μ* is a 2n-relation, called the *match predicate*

Let e_T and e_U be states respectively of *T* and *U*. The materialization of *ML* in e_T and e_U is the set *ML[e_T,e_U]* defined as:

$(t, owl:sameAs, u) \in ML[e_T,e_U]$ iff there are triples
$(t, rdf:type, C), (t, P_1, v_1),...,(t, P_n, v_n) \in e_T$ and
$(u, rdf:type, C), (u, P_1, w_1),...,(u, P_n, w_n) \in e_U$
such that $(v_1,..., v_n, w_1,..., w_n) \in μ$

Consider the exported views *MusicBrainz_EV* and *DBpedia_EV* introduced in Section 3.3. Then, sameAs linkset views could be specified for matching instances of the class *mo:Track*. As an example, consider the mashup sameAs view specification for *mo:Track*: *(ML_1, MusicBrainz_EV, DBPedia_EV, mo:Track, dc:title, p)*, where the match predicate *p* is defined as $(v_1, w_1) \in p$ iff $\sigma(v_k, w_k) \geq \alpha$, for each *k=1*, where σ

is the 3-gram distance [14] and $\alpha = 0.5$. Referring to our case study, Figure 3(b) shows the sameAs links automatically created using ML_1.

2.6   Specification of the Normalization Function and Fusion Assertions

In this section, we first introduce the concepts of normalization function and fusion assertions, then we describe how the data fusion rules are induced from the fusion assertion.

Normalization Function. The LDM view specification includes a *normalization function*, denoted η, that remaps all IRIs in the exported views that are declared to denote the same object, via sameAs links, to one canonical target IRI. The normalization function must satisfy the following axiom (using an infix notation for sameAs):

(N_1) $\forall x_1 \forall x_2 (x_1 \text{ sameAs } x_2 \Leftrightarrow \eta(x_1) = \eta(x_2))$

which says that the normalization function must remap to the same IRI two IRIs x_1 and x_2 iff they are declared to be equivalent via a sameAs statement of the form "x_1 sameAs x_2".

The normalization function partitions the IRIs of the exported views resources into a set of equivalence classes. In the materialization of the LDM view, all IRIs in the same equivalence class are homogenized by grouping all properties of those IRIs into one canonical target IRI. The canonical IRI also have owl:sameAs links pointing to the original IRIs, which makes it possible for applications to refer back to the original data sources on the Web.

Referring to our case study, the equivalence classes induced by the sameAs links in Figure 3(b) are: $\varepsilon_1 = \{dbp:ma1, mb:ma1\}$, $\varepsilon_2 = \{dbp:a1, mb:r1\}$, $\varepsilon_3 = \{dbp:s2, mb:t2\}$, $\varepsilon_4 = \{dbp:s1\}$, $\varepsilon_5 = \{ mb:t1 \}$.

Data Fusion Assertions and Data Fusion Rules. In the rest of this section, let D be a LDM view, $O_D = (V_D, \Sigma_D)$ be the ontology of D, and η be the normalization function. Let C be a class in V_D. We define

$Props(C, V_D) = \{P \mid P \text{ is a property in } V_D \text{ and } C \text{ is a subclass of the domain of } P\}$

In our approach, the user is free to define how to resolve the problem of contradictory attribute values when combining multiple representations of the same real-world object into a single representation (canonical IRI). This is specified with the help of *data fusion property assertions*.

A *data fusion property assertion (FPA)* for a property P in the context of a class C is an expression of form "$\Psi: P[C] \equiv f/Q$", where Ψ is the name of the *FPA*, C is a class in V_D, P and Q are properties in $Props(C, V_D)$, and f is a *data fusion function symbol*, which denotes a function whose domain is a set of sets of individuals and whose range is a set of individuals.

Data fusion assertions should be regarded as a shorthand notation for a class of data fusion rules. A set A of data fusion assertions defined over the vocabulary V_D of D, induces a set of fusion rules for D as follows:

- Let C be a class in V_D and P be a property in $Props(C, V_D)$. Assume that the assertion "$\Psi: P[C] \equiv f/Q$" is in A and that $S_1, ..., S_n$ are all the exported views of D

whose vocabulary contains class C and property Q. Then, the *fusion rule for P in the context C induced by A* is

$P(x,u) \leftarrow u = f(v/B[x,v])$ where:

$B[x,v] = ((C(x_1),Q(x_1,v))_{S1}, x = \eta(x_1)); ...;((C(x_n),Q(x_n,v))_{Sn}, x = \eta(x_n))$

The subscript S_i indicates the exported view against which $(C(x_i), Q(x_i,v))$ will be evaluated. Intuitively, $\{v/B[x,v]\}$ denotes the set of individuals v that satisfy $B[x,v]$. Then, $f(v/B[x,v])$ denotes the individual to which f maps the set $\{v/B[x,v]\}$.

- Let C be a class in V_D and P be a property in $Props(C, V_D)$. Assume that there is no assertion in A for property P in the context of C and that $S_1,...,S_n$ are all the exported views of D whose vocabulary contains C and P. Then, the *fusion rule for P in the context C induced by A* is

  $P(x,v) \leftarrow ((C(x_1),P(x_1,v))_{S1}, x = \eta(x_1)); ...;((C(x_n),P(x_n,v))_{Sn}, x = \eta(x_n))$

- Let C be a class in V_D. Assume that $S_1,...,S_n$ are all the exported views of D whose vocabulary contains C. Then, the *fusion rule for class C induced by A* is

  $C(x) \leftarrow ((C(x_1))_{S1}, x = \eta(x_1)); ...;((C(x_n))_{Sn}, x = \eta(x_n))$

For example, let the *FPA* for the *moa:labelName* property in the context of class *mo:Record* be

$\Psi:moa:labelName[mo:Record] \equiv KeepSingleValueByReputation/moa:labelName$

Then, this FPA *induces* the following fusion rule:

$moa:labelName(x,u) \leftarrow u = KeepSingleValueByReputation(v/$
$(mo:Record(y),moa:labelName(y,v))_{DBpedia\_EV}, x = \eta(y);$
$(mo:Record(z),(moa:labelName(z,v))_{MusicBrainz\_EV}, x = \eta(z))).$

The fusion rule creates a triple of the form "$(x, moa:labelName, u)$" in a materialization of the LDM view by taking u as the most reputable name for x found in the materialization of the two exported views, *MusicBrainz_EV* and *DBpedia_EV*.

If no *FPA* was specified for the *moa:labelName* property in the context of class *mo:Record*, then the following default fusion rule would be induced:

$moa:labelName(x,v) \leftarrow (mo:Record(y),moa:labelName(y,v))_{DBpedia\_EV}, x = \eta(y));$
$(mo:Record(z),(moa:labelName(z,v))_{MusicBrainz\_EV}, x = \eta(z))).$

This fusion rule creates a triple for each values of *moa:labelName* coming from an exported view.

2.7   Materialization of the LD Mashup View

In this section we describe how to materialize a LDM view by applying the normalization function and data fusion rules to the materialized exported views and the materialized sameAs Linkset views. The materialization process includes the combination and fusion of multiple representations of the same real-world object into a single representation and the resolution of data inconsistencies [4].

We begin by introducing the notation that will be used in this section:

- $\lambda = (D, O_D, E_1,..., E_n, EL_1,..., EL_p, ML_1,..., ML_q, \mu, \eta, Q)$ is a LDM view specification.
- V_D is the vocabulary of O_D
- $\mathbf{C} = \{ C / C$ is a class in $V_D\}$
- $\mathbf{P} = \{ P / P$ is a property in $V_D\}$
- $e_1,..., e_n$ are states of $E_1,..., E_n$ and $l_1,..., l_m$ are states of $EL_1,..., EL_p, ML_1,..., ML_q$, with $m=p+q$
- $s = (e_1,..., e_n, l_1,..., l_m)$
- $IRIs(s) = \{ x / x$ is the subject of a triple in a tripleset in $s \}$
- $\varepsilon_1,...,\varepsilon_w$ are the equivalence classes induced by $l_1,..., l_m$
- $[\varepsilon_i]$ denotes the IRI that represents ε_i
- η^s denotes the interpretation of η for the $\varepsilon_1,...,\varepsilon_w$

Definition 1: $I[s](T)$ denotes the set of triples that state s assigns to a class or property T, i.e., the interpretation of T in s, defined as follows:
- Let C be a class in V_D. Assume that μ has a fusion rule whose head uses C and that the rule is of the form
  $$C(x) \leftarrow (C(x_1)_{S1}, x=\eta(x_1)); ... ;(C(x_p)_{Sq}, x=\eta(x_n))$$
  Then, the interpretation of C *induced by* μ *in* s, also denoted $I[s](C)$, is defined as:
  $$(x, rdf{:}type, C) \in I[s](C) \text{ iff } (x, rdf{:}type, C) \in I[e_1](C), x=\eta^s(x_1)) \vee ... \vee$$
  $$(x, rdf{:}type, C) \in I[e_n](C), x=\eta^s(x_n)).$$
- Let P be a property in V_D. Assume that μ has a fusion rule whose head uses P and that the rule is of the form
  $$P(x,v) \leftarrow (C(x_1),P(x_1, v))_{S1}, x=\eta(x_1)); ...;((C(x_n), P(x_n, v))_{Sn}, x=\eta(x_n)).$$
  Then, the interpretation of P *induced by* μ *in* s, also denoted $I[s](P)$, is defined as:
  $$(x, P, v) \in I[s](P) \text{ iff } ((x, rdf{:}type, C) \in I[e_1](C), (x,P,v) \in I[e_1](P), x=\eta^s(x_1)) \vee$$
  $$... \vee ((x, rdf{:}type, C) \in I[e_n](C), (x,P,v) \in I[e_n](P), x=\eta^s(x_n))$$
- Let P be a property in V_D. Assume that μ has a fusion rule whose head uses P and that the rule is of the form
  $$P(x, u) \leftarrow u = f(v/B[x,v]) \text{ where:}$$
  $$B[x,v] = ((C(x_1),Q(x_1,v))_{S1}, x=\eta(x_1)); ...;((C(x_n),Q(x_n,v))_{Sn}, x=\eta(x_n))$$
  Then, the interpretation of P *induced by* μ *in* s, also denoted $I[s](P)$, is defined as:
  $$(x, P, u) \in I[s](P) \text{ iff } u = I[s](f)(\{v / I[s](B[x,v])=true\})$$
- If there is more than one fusion rule in μ whose head uses P, then $I[s](P)$ is the union of all sets of triples as defined on the right-hand sides of the double implications above.

Definition 2: Recall that $\mathbf{C}$ is the set of all classes in V_D and $\mathbf{P}$ is the set of all properties in V_D and ε_i is an equivalence class induced by $l_1,..., l_m$. We define the *DataFusion* function as follows:

$$DataFusion(\varepsilon_i, s) = \cup_{C \in \mathbf{C}} \{ (x, rdf{:}type, C) \in I[s](C) / x = [\varepsilon_i] \} \cup$$
$$\cup_{P \in \mathbf{P}} \{ (x, P, y) \in I[s](P) / x = [\varepsilon_i] \} \cup$$
$$\cup \{ ([\varepsilon_i], owl{:}sameAs, y) / y \in \varepsilon_i \wedge y \neq [\varepsilon_i] \}.$$

Definition 3: We define the *state d* or the *materialization* of D *induced by s* as (recall that $\varepsilon_1,...,\varepsilon_w$ are the equivalence classes induced by $l_1,..., l_m$):

$$d = \cup_{i=1,...,w} DataFusion(\varepsilon_i, s).$$

Referring to our case study, Figure 3(c) shows the state of the mashup view computed from the states of the exported views and sameAs linkset views in Figure 3 (b). The mashup view has 5 resources which are computed by applying the *DataFusion* function to equivalence classes $\varepsilon_1,...,\varepsilon_5$ defined in Section 2.6.

3   Incremental Maintenance of LDM Views

We now turn to the problem of maintaining a LDM view, when update operations are applied to the Linked Data sources. In this section, let:

- $\lambda = (D, O_D, E_1,..., E_n, EL_1,..., EL_p, ML_1,...,ML_q, \mu, \eta, Q)$ be an LDM view specification
- $e_1,..., e_n$ be states of $E_1,..., E_n$ and $l_1,..., l_m$ be states of $EL_1,..., EL_p, ML_1,..., ML_q$, with $m=p+q$
- $s = (e_1,..., e_n, l_1,..., l_m)$
- d be the state of D induced by s

The incremental view maintenance problem is schematically described by the diagram in Figure 4. The user specifies an update u against a base data source, which results in new states $e'_1,...,e'_n$ of the exported views and new states $l'_1,..., l'_m$ of the *sameAs* views. Let d' be the state of D induced by $(e'_1,...,e'_n, l'_1,...,l'_m)$. We say that a set of updates U_D over the state d correctly maintains D iff $U_D(d) = d'$.

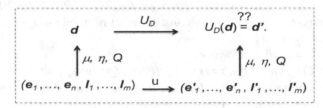

Fig. 4. Incremental View Maintenance Problem

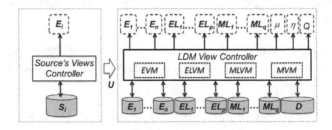

Fig. 5. Suggested Platform for LDM View Maintenance

Figure 5 shows the main components of the architecture we suggest to incrementally maintain the LDM view D. For each data source S_i that exports a view E_i to D, there is a *Source View Controller*, with the following functionality:

1. Identify updates on S_i that are relevant to D, that is, relevant to exported views or materialized linkset views used to construct D. This is computed from the specification of the exported views and linkset views.
2. For each relevant update u, create the set: $R = \{ r \mid r$ is the IRI of a resource affected by $u \}$.
3. Send R to the LDM View Controller.

Note that R can be automatically computed based on the exported and linkset views specifications. Hence, no access to the mashup view is required. The problem of computing R is out of the scope of this paper. A similar problem was addressed in a previous work [22].

The *LDM View Controller* receives R and then performs the incremental maintenance of the exported and linkset views followed by the incremental maintenance of mashup view D. The *LDM View Controller* has 4 main components (see Figure 5):

- **EVM Module**: Maintains the exported views $E_1, ..., E_n$.
- **ELVM Module:** Maintains the exported linkset views $EL_1, ..., EL_p$.
- **MLVM Module:** Maintains the mashup linkset views $ML_1, ..., ML_q$.
- **MVM Module:** Maintains the mashup view D.

The incremental maintenance of linkset views has already been addressed in our previous work [5], and the problem of incremental maintenance of exported views is very similar to the problem addressed in [22]. Therefore, we do not address those problems in this paper.

In order to accomplish incremental maintenance of mashup view D, the **MVM** module executes the procedure *Effect(R)* considering $t = (e'_1, ..., e'_n, l'_1, ..., l'_m)$, the new states of the exported views and sameAs views. The definition of *Effect* depends on the following definitions:

Definition 4: Let r be a resource in R, $DA(r) = A_{OLD}(r) \cup A_{NEW}(r)$ where:
$A_{OLD}(r) = \{ x \in IRIs(t) / (\exists y \in IRIs(d))((y, owl{:}sameAs, r) \in d @ (y, owl{:}sameAs, x) \in d) \}$
$A_{NEW}(r) = \{ x \in IRIs(t) / \eta[t](x) = \eta[t](r)$.

Definition 5: $DA(R) = \cup_{r \in R} DA(r)$.

Definition 6: $DA^*(R) = \cup_{r \in R} DA^*(r)$ where
$\quad DA^*(r) = \{ x \in IRIs(d) / (\exists y \in DA(r)) ((x, owl{:}sameAs, y) \in d) \}$.

Definition 7: $IA^*(R) = (\cup_{r \in R} IA^*(r)) - DA^*(R)$ where,
$\quad IA^*(r) = \{ x \in IRIs(d) / x \notin DA^*(r) \wedge (\exists y \in DA^*(r))((x, P, y) \in d) \}$.

The procedure *Effect* in Table 1, computes the mashup view maintenance updates in 2 steps:

<u>Step 1</u>: Computes the new state of the mashup resources in $DA^*(R)$, i.e. directly affected by the resources in R.
<u>Step 2</u>: Updates the state of the mashup resources in $IA^*(R)$, i.e. indirectly affected by the updates in step 1.

Table 1. Procedure *Effect(R)*

Parameters (as defined above):
  λ, the LDM view specification
  $t = (e'_1,..., e'_n, l'_1,..., l'_m)$
  d, the state of mashup view *D* induce by *s*
 	
Input: R, the set of IRIs of resources affected by an update
 	
Step 1. Compute the new state of the mashup resources in $DA^*(R)$.
1.1 Compute $DA(R)$ and $DA^*(R)$; /* See Definitions 4-6
1.2. Retrieve Δ_{OLD} the old states of the mashup resources in $DA^*(R)$;
    $\Delta_{OLD} := \cup_{x \in DA^*(R)} I[d](x)$, where $I[d](x)$ denotes the state of the resource x in state d,
          i.e., the set of triples in *d* where the subject of those triple is x.
1.3. Compute Δ_{NEW} the new states of the mashup resources for the resources in $DA(R)$;
    $\Delta_{NEW} := \cup_{[\varepsilon] \in s} DataFusion(\varepsilon, t)$ where $S = \{ \eta[t](x) / x \in DA(R)\}$,
          i.e., the set of equivalence classes for the resources in $DA(R)$.
1.4. $d := (d - \Delta_{OLD}) \cup \Delta_{NEW}$;
 	
Step 2. Update the state of the mashup resources in $IA^*(R)$.
 2.1 Compute $IA^*(R)$; /* see Definition 7.
 2.2 For each *m* in $IA^*(R)$ do {
    2.2.1 $AP(m) = \{ P / (\exists y \in DA^*(R)) \wedge (m, P, y) \in d)\}$;
    /*$AP(m)$ denotes the set of properties relating *m* with mashup resources in $DA^*(R)$.
    2.2.2. Computes the new states for the properties in $AP(m)$;
      For each *P* in $AP(m)$ do {
      $\Delta_{OLD} := \{(m, P, y) /(\exists y \in d) \wedge (m, P, y) \in d\}$;
      $\Delta_{NEW} := I[t](P)$; /* see Definition 1.
      $d := (d - \Delta_{OLD}) \cup \Delta_{NEW}$;

To illustrate this strategy, let *u* be the following update on *DBpedia:*

```
1.   WITH <http://dbpedia.org>
2.   DELETE { ?x dc:title "W. B. S. S." }
3.   INSERT { ?x dc:title "Wanna Be Startin' Somethin'" }
4.   WHERE{?x rdfs:type dbpedia-owl:Single.?x dc:title "W.B.S.S"}
```

Phase 1: (Executed by the *DBpedia* View Controller)
Considering the state of DBpedia in Figure 3(a), the update *u* changes the title of the instance *dbp:s1* to "Wanna Be Startin' Somethin'". Therefore, the *DBpedia* View Controller sends R={*dbp:s1*} to the *LDM View Controller*.

Phase 2: (Executed by the LDM View Controller)
The *LDM View Controller* receives *R* and then performs the incremental maintenance of the exported views and linkset views. Based on ML_1 specification, the resources *dbp:s1* and *mb:t1* are computed as equivalent. Therefore a new sameAs link (*dbp:s1, owl:sameAs, mb:t1*) is added to ML_1.

Then, the procedure *Effect*({*dbp:s1*}) computes the mashup view maintenance updates in 2 steps:

Step 1: Compute the new state of the mashup resources for the resources in
$DA*(\{dbp:s1\})$

Step 1.1: Considering the state t and d in Figures 3(b) and 3(c) we have that:

$DA(\{dbp:s1\})=\{dbp:s1, mb:t1\}$

$DA*(\{dbp:s1\})=\{mp:t1, mp:t3\}$

Step 1.2: $\Delta_{OLD} = I[d](mp:t1) \cup I[d](mp:t3)$

Step 1.3: $\Delta_{NEW} = DataFusion(\varepsilon, t)$ where $\varepsilon = \{dbp:s1, mb:t1\}$

Step 1.4: $d = (d - \Delta_{OLD}) \cup \Delta_{NEW}$

Step 2. Update the state of the mashup resources in $IA^*(\{dbp:s1\})$

Step 2.1. $IA^*(\{dbp:s1\})=\{mp:r1\}$

Step 2.2. Computes the new states for the properties in $AP(mp:r1)$

Step 2.2.1 $AP(mp:r1) = \{mo:track\}$

Step 2.2.2 $\Delta_{OLD}=\{(mp:r1, mo:track, mp:t1), (mp:r1, mo:track, mp:t3)\}$

$\Delta_{NEW} = \{(mp:r1, mo:track, mp:t4)\}$

$d := d - \Delta_{OLD} \cup \Delta_{NEW}$

4   Related Work

The problem of incremental view maintenance has been extensively studied in the
literature. However, for the most part, views are defined over a single data source,
e.g., for relational views [6], for object-oriented views [15], for semi-structured views
[1], for XLM Views [7], [23], and for RDF views [22]. None of the proposed techniques can be directly applied to data integration views.

The incremental maintenance of data integration views is address in [9], [10],
which focus on the relational views. In [10], an algorithm for the incremental maintenance of outerjoin and match views was developed. In [9], algebraic change propagation algorithms were developed for the maintenance of the outerjoin view. Despite
of their important contributions, none of those techniques can be applied to LDM
views, since the nature of linked data sources poses new challenges for dealing with
the data fusion problem, specially the treatment of sameAs.

Recently, two frameworks were proposed for creating LDM views. The ODCleanS-
tore framework [12] offers Linked Data fusion, dealing with inconsistencies. LDIF -
Linked Data Integration Framework [19] implements a mapping language, deals with
URIs remapping and uses named graphs for registering data provenance.

To the best of our knowledge, incremental maintenance of LDM views has not yet
been addressed in any framework.

5   Conclusions

In this paper, we first proposed an ontology-based framework for specifying Linked
Data Mashup views. In the framework, a Linked Data mashup view is formally

specified with the help of exported views, linkset views, data fusion function and normalization function. The LDM view specification is used to automatically materialize the mashup view. Then, we outlined a strategy that uses the mashup view specification for incrementally maintain the mashup view.

Our strategy addressed the problem of dealing with changes in the set of sameAs links between IRIs from different data sources and with the very question of recomputing mashup property values, in the presence of updates on the data sources.

Acknowledgments. This work was partly funded by CNPq, under grants 248987/2013-5, 442338/2014-7 and 303332/2013-1, by FAPERJ, under grant E-26/201.337/2014, and by CAPES, under grants PROCAD/NF 789/2010, 1410827.

References

1. Abiteboul, S., McHugh, J., Rys, M., Vassalos, V., Wiener, J.L.: Incremental Maintenance for Materialized Views over Semistructured Data. VLDB 1998, 38–49 (1998)
2. Berners-Lee, T.: Linked Data (2006). http://www.w3.org/DesignIssues/LinkedData.html
3. Bizer, C., Lehmann, J., Kobilarov, G., Auer, S., Becker, C., Cyganiak, R., Hellmann, S.: DBpedia - A crystallization point for the Web of Data. J. Web Semant. 7(3), 154–165 (2009)
4. Bleiholder, J., Naumann, F.: Data fusion. ACM Comput. Surv. 41(1), 1:1–1:41 (2009)
5. Casanova, M.A., Vidal, V.M., Lopes, G.R., Leme, L.A.P., Ruback, L.: On materialized sameAs linksets. In: Decker, H., Lhotská, L., Link, S., Spies, M., Wagner, R.R. (eds.) DEXA 2014, Part I. LNCS, vol. 8644, pp. 377–384. Springer, Heidelberg (2014)
6. Ceri, S., Widom, J.: Deriving productions rules for incremental view maintenance. VLDB 1991, 577–589 (1991)
7. Dimitrova, K., El-Sayed, M., Rundensteiner, E.A.: Order-sensitive View Maintenance of Materialized XQuery Views. ER 2003, 144–157 (2003)
8. Endres, B.N.: Semantic Mashups. Springer, Heidelberg (2013)
9. Griffin, T., Libkin, L.: Algebraic change propagation for semijoin and outerjoin queries. SIGMOD Record 27(3) (1998)
10. Gupta, A., Mumick, I.S.: Materialized Views. MIT Press (2000)
11. Hanh, H.H., Tai, N.C., Duy, K.T., Dosam, H., Jason, J.J.: Semantic Information Integration with Linked Data Mashups Approaches. Int. J. Distrib. Sens. N. (2014)
12. Knap, T., Michelfeit, J., Daniel, J., Jerman, P., Rychnovsky, D., Soukup, T., Necasky, M.: ODCleanStore: A Framework for Managing and Providing Integrated Linked Data on the Web. In: Sean Wang, X., Cruz, I., Delis, A., Hua, G. (eds.) Web Information Systems Engineering - WISE 2012. LNCS, vol. 7651, pp. 815–816. Springer, Heidelberg (2012)
13. Kobilarov, G., Scott, T., Raimond, Y., Oliver, S., Sizemore, C., Smethurst, M., Bizer, C., Lee, R.: Media Meets Semantic Web – How the BBC Uses DBpedia and Linked Data to Make Connections. In: Aroyo, L., Traverso, P., Ciravegna, F., Cimiano, P., Heath, T., Hyvönen, E., Mizoguchi, R., Oren, E., Sabou, M., Simperl, E. (eds.) ESWC 2009. LNCS, vol. 5554, pp. 723–737. Springer, Heidelberg (2009)
14. Kondrak, G.: N-Gram similarity and distance. In: Consens, M.P., Navarro, G. (eds.) SPIRE 2005. LNCS, vol. 3772, pp. 115–126. Springer, Heidelberg (2005)

15. Kuno, H.A., Rundensteiner, E.A.: Incremental Maintenance of Materialized Object-Oriented Views in MultiView: Strategies and Performance Evaluation. IEEE TDKE 10(5), 768–792 (1998)
16. Mendes, M., Mühleisen, H., Bizer, C.: Sieve: Linked Data Quality Assessment and Fusion. Invited paper at the LWDM 2012 (2012)
17. Raimond, Y., Abdallah, S., Sandler, M., Giasson, F.: The Music Ontology. In: International Conference on Music Information Retrieval, pp. 417–422 (2007)
18. Sacramento, E.R., Vidal, V.M.P., Macedo, J.A.F., Lóscio, B.F., Lopes, F.L.R., Casanova, M.A.: Towards Automatic Generation of Application Ontologies. JIDM 1(3), 535–550 (2010)
19. Schultz, A., Matteini, A., Isele, R., Mendes, P., Bizer, C., Becker, C.: LDIF - A Framework for Large-Scale Linked Data Integration. In: WWW2012, Developers Track (2012)
20. Swartz, A.: MusicBrainz: A Semantic Web Service. IEEE Intelligent Systems 17(1), 76–77 (2002)
21. The DBpedia Ontology (2014). http://wiki.dbpedia.org/Ontology2014
22. Vidal, V.M.P., Casanova, M.A., Cardoso, D.S.: Incremental Maintenance of RDF Views of Relational Data. In: Meersman, R., Panetto, H., Dillon, T., Eder, J., Bellahsene, Z., Ritter, N., De Leenheer, P., Dou, D. (eds.) ODBASE 2013. LNCS, vol. 8185, pp. 572–587. Springer, Heidelberg (2013)
23. Vidal, V.M.P., Lemos, F.C.L., Araújo, V., Casanova, M.A.: A Mapping-Driven Approach for SQL/XML View Maintenance. ICEIS 2008, 65–73 (2008)

A Model-Driven Approach to Enterprise Data Migration

Raghavendra Reddy Yeddula[(✉)], Prasenjit Das, and Sreedhar Reddy

Tata Consultancy Services, Pune 411 013, India
{raghavendrareddy.y,prasenjit.d,sreedhar.reddy}@tcs.com

Abstract. In a typical data migration project, analysts identify the mappings between source and target data models at a conceptual level using informal textual descriptions. An implementation team translates these mappings into programs that migrate the data. While doing so, the programmers have to understand how the conceptual models and business rules map to physical databases. We propose a modeling mechanism where we can specify conceptual models, physical models and mappings between them in a formal manner. We can also specify rules on conceptual models. From these models and mappings, we can automatically generate a program to migrate data from source to target. We can also generate a program to migrate data access queries from source to target. The overall approach results in a significant improvement in productivity and also a significant reduction in migration errors.

Keywords: Data migration · Conceptual models · Data model mapping · Query translation

1   Introduction

Data migration is the process of transferring an enterprise's data from one database to another. A typical data migration project starts with business analysts identifying the mappings between source and target data models. An implementation team then manually translates these mappings into programs that migrate the data. Business analysts specify the mappings in terms of conceptual data models that reflect the business domain semantics. Programmers have to write their programs in terms of physical database schemas. While doing this, programmers not only have to understand the source-to-target mappings correctly, but also how the conceptual models and the rules there of map to the physical databases, as shown in Fig. 1. This is an error prone process which is further compounded by the fact that these mappings are generally only documented informally, using sketchy textual descriptions.

In this paper we describe a model driven approach to automate this process using a model mappings based infrastructure. Using this infrastructure we can create conceptual models, physical models and specify mappings between them, formally, using a mappings language. This infrastructure also provides a set of primitive processing blocks such as mapping composer, query translator, etc. Mapping composer can compose a set of mappings to create a new mapping. Query translator can process a mapping to translate a query on a model at one end of the mapping to an equivalent

© Springer International Publishing Switzerland 2015
J. Zdravkovic et al. (Eds.): CAiSE 2015, LNCS 9097, pp. 230–243, 2015.
DOI: 10.1007/978-3-319-19069-3_15

query on the model at the other end. These blocks process not only the mappings but also the rules captured in the conceptual model.

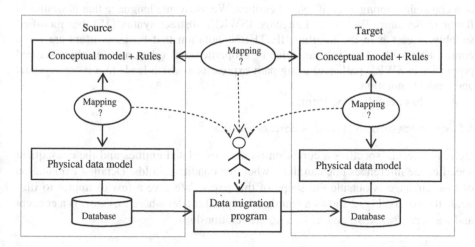

Fig. 1. Data Migration – typical scenario

In a data migration scenario, we create models and mappings as shown in Fig. 1, i.e. a mapping between source and target conceptual models, a mapping between source conceptual and physical models, and a mapping between target conceptual and physical models. Some of these models and mappings can be reverse engineered from existing systems. For instance, source-side models and mappings can be reverse engineered from an existing source system implementation, and likewise on the target side. We compose these models and mappings to automatically derive a mapping between source and target databases. From this mapping, we generate a program to migrate data from source to target. We also generate a program to migrate queries expressed on the source database into equivalent queries on the target database. The latter is important because, typically, in a data migration project, it is not only the data that has to be migrated, but also the data access programs. The overall approach results in a significant improvement in productivity. It also results in a significant reduction in migration errors.

The rest of the paper is organized as follows. Section 2 discusses the modeling infrastructure, section 3 discusses the data migration architecture and section 4 presents some results. Section 5 discusses related work. We conclude by summarizing and discussing future work.

2   Modeling Infrastructure

2.1   Conceptual Models

We use an extended version of UML object model [17] as our conceptual modeling language. Object model is extended to add rules to classes and relations. The extension to UML meta model is implemented using our in-house meta modeling tool [9].

2.2   Rules

We can specify rules on conceptual models. A rule specifies a derivative relationship or a constraint among a set of related entities. We use a rule language that is similar in flavor to Semantic Web Rule Language (SWRL) abstract syntax [18], but modified suitably to cast it in the familiar 'IF..THEN' notation that business users are more comfortable with. Also we can refer to properties and relations (i.e. object-valued properties in SWRL parlance) using path expressions which leads to a more compact and readable notation.

A rule has the following form:

```
if <antecedent> then <consequent>
```

Here, antecedent specifies a condition on a set of related entities and the consequent specifies the inferences one can draw when the condition holds. Detailed explanation of this language is outside the scope of this paper. We give a few examples to illustrate the syntax. Fig. 2 shows a simple conceptual model where Person is a concept and parent, spouse and sibling are relationships.

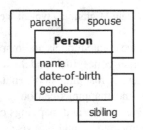

Fig. 2. A simple conceptual model

The following are some of the rules and constraints that one can express on this model:

Rule 1: Persons who have a common parent are siblings.

```
If
   Person(p1) and Person(p2) and p1.parent = p2.parent
Then
   p1.sibling = p2
```

Constraint 1: Two different parents (e.g. mother and father) of a person cannot have the same gender.

```
If
   Person(p1) and Person(p2) and Person(p3)and
   p1.parent = p2 and p1.parent = p3 and p2 <> p3
then
   p2.gender <> p3.gender
```

2.3   Physical Models

We use relational model for physical data modeling. A simplified version of the relational meta model is shown in Fig. 3. Using this model we can specify relational tables and primary-key and foreign-key relations among them.

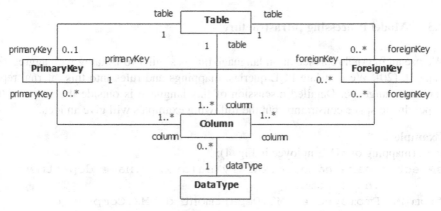

Fig. 3. Relational meta-model

2.4   Model Mappings

We map two models by defining a class or a table of one model as a view over one or more classes or tables of the other model. Views are defined declaratively using a language that is a restricted version of Object Query Language (OQL) [19]. We call this language PQL (for path expression query language). This is essentially OQL

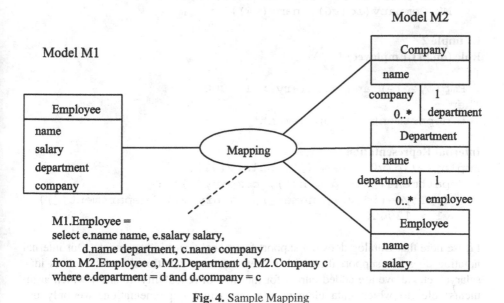

Fig. 4. Sample Mapping

without some of the procedural extensions such as method invocations on objects. We support user-defined functions but they are required to be side-effect-free, i.e. they just take inputs and return an output without leaving any side-effect in the state.

Fig. 4 shows an example mapping where a class in model M1 is mapped as a view over a set of classes in model M2.

2.5   Model Processing Infrastructure

We use an internal representation language that is similar to Datalog with aggregation [1], [3], [20]. We translate PQL queries, mappings and rules into this internal representation language. Detailed discussion of this language is outside the scope of this paper due to space constraints, but the following examples will give an idea.

Example 1
PQL (mapping of M1.Employee in Fig. 4):

```
select e.name name, e.salary salary, d.name department,
        c.name company
from M2.Employee e, M2.Department d, M2.Company c
where e.department = d and d.company = c;
```

Internal Representation

```
M1.Employee(name(v1), salary(v2), department(v3),
   company(v4)) :-
    M2.Employee(id(v0), name(v1), salary(v2)),
    M2.employee_department(id1(v0), id2(v5)),
    M2.Department(id(v5), name(v3)),
    M2.department_company(id1(v5), id2(v6)),
    M2.Company(id(v6), name(v4)).
```

Example 2
Rule (on M1.Employee)

```
If
   Employee(e) and e.salary > 120000
Then
   e.department = 'Management'
```

Internal Representation

```
Employee(id(v0), name(_), salary(v1),
   department('Management'), company(_)) :-
    Employee(id(v0), name(_), salary(v1), department(_)),
    v1 > 120000.
```

Please note that Datalog does not support functional terms in arguments. Our internal notation does not support them either. References to functional terms such as id(), salary(), etc. above are added purely for the sake of readability, to show which arguments refer to which data elements. In the actual implementation, we only use variable arguments, where the position of an argument uniquely identifies the data element it represents.

Also note the usage of object IDs (id() terms), and the codification of a relationship as a term with two ID arguments. For example, the relationship between Employee and Department is represented by the term employee_department(id1(), id2()).

With respect to a given model M, we classify the internal representation rules of mappings into two classes, the so-called global-as-view (GAV) [2], [5] and local-as-view (LAV) rules [4]. Rules of a mapping where a class of M is defined as a view over classes of other models are classified as GAV rules; whereas rules of a mapping in the other direction, i.e. a class of the other model being defined as a view over classes of M, are treated as LAV rules.

The uniform representation of rules and mappings allows us to process them together. For instance, referring to the rule above, if we have a query asking for employees of 'management' department, we can return all employees whose salary is greater than 120000.

2.6   Query Translator

We use a query translation algorithm to translate queries written on a model at one end of a mapping into an equivalent query on the other end of the mapping, as shown in Fig. 5. The algorithm is based on the well-known GAV [2] and LAV [4] query rewriting techniques. A detailed discussion of the query translation algorithm is outside the scope of this paper. A detailed discussion on the individual techniques can be found in the cited references. We combine these techniques in a layered manner, where each layer does a partial translation.

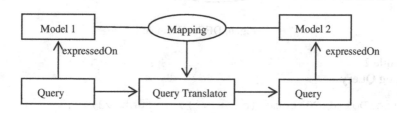

Fig. 5. Query Translation

2.7   Data Flow Graph Generator

A Data Flow Graph or DFG represents the flow of data from one system to another system and the transformations it undergoes along the way. A DFG contains nodes and directed edges. Nodes represent operators. An edge represents flow of data from one node to the other. There are various types of operators in a DFG, such as *join, union, filter, aggregation,* etc. each performing a specific operation. For example, *join* operator joins the data tuples coming in on its input edges and sends out the joined tuples on its output edge. A data flow graph is a procedural artifact. We can either execute it directly or translate it into procedural code in a standard high-level language such as java, stored procedures, etc.

We can translate a PQL query into an equivalent data flow graph. We first translate the query into our internal Datalog representation, and then generate the DFG from this internal representation. We illustrate this with a few examples:

Example 1
Datalog Query

```
Customer(name(v1))  :- CorporateCustomer(name(v1), ..).
Customer(name(v1))  :- IndividualCustomer(name(v1), ..).
```

The query is used to fetch names of customers from two sources -- corporate customers and individual customers by executing the corresponding sub queries `CorporateCustomer()` and `IndividualCustomer()`.

Fig. 6 shows the equivalent DFG. The boxes `CorporateCustomer` and `IndividualCustomer` represent the sources. The Selection operators select name of `CorporateCustomer` and `IndividualCustomer` from respective sources.

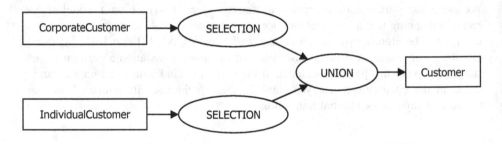

Fig. 6. DFG – Example 1

Example 2
Datalog Query

```
MillionDollarCustomer(name(v1), amount(v2))  :-
  SQ(v1, v2), v2 > 1000000.
SQ(v1, SUM(v3))  :-
  Customer(id(v0), name(v1), ..),
  Customer_Contract(customer(v0), contract(v2)),
  Contract(id(v2), amount(v3)).
```

This query is used to fetch names and total contract amount of customers whose total contract amount exceeds a million.

Fig. 7 shows the equivalent DFG.

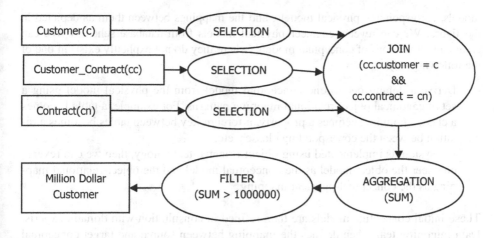

Fig. 7. DFG – Example 2

2.8   Mapping Composer

We can derive a mapping between two unmapped models by composing other known mappings. Referring to Fig. 8 below, suppose we have three models M1, M2 and M3. Suppose we know the mappings between M1 and M2, and between M2 and M3, namely MAP1 and MAP2. We can compose MAP1 and MAP2 to derive a new mapping MAP3 between M1 and M3.

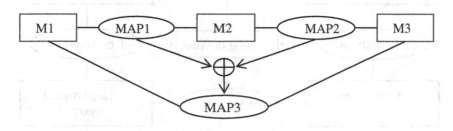

Fig. 8. Mapping composition

Composition is done by a series of query translation steps. Suppose MAP1 specifies a class C1 in M1 as a view V1 over a set of classes in M2, and MAP2 in turn specifies classes in M2 as views over classes in M3. Then a translation of the view query V1 from model M2 to model M3 gives the mapping of class C1 in terms of classes in M3.

3   Data Migration Solution

Fig. 9 below depicts the data migration solution implemented using the modeling infrastructure discussed in the previous section. We define source and target conceptual models, corresponding physical models, and the mappings between them as depicted in the figure. We can reverse engineer physical models from database schemas. We can create initial versions of conceptual models (where they do not explicitly exist) in one of the following ways:

- Derive a default one-to-one conceptual model from the physical model using a set of canonical object-relational mapping patterns. For example, a table becomes a class, a column becomes a property, a foreign-key between tables becomes a relation between the corresponding classes, etc.
- If a system is implemented using object-oriented technology, then we can reverse engineer the object model as the conceptual model and the object-relational mapping as the conceptual-physical mapping.

These initial conceptual models are then refined in consultation with domain experts. Data migration team then defines the mapping between source and target conceptual models. We can use a schema matching algorithm [15, 16] to discover initial correspondences. These are then refined into mappings in consultation with domain experts. From these mappings, we automatically derive a mapping between source and target physical models using mapping composer. Referring to Fig. 9, we derive the mapping PP_MAPPING by composing S_CP_MAPPING, CC_MAPPING and T_CP_MAPPING.

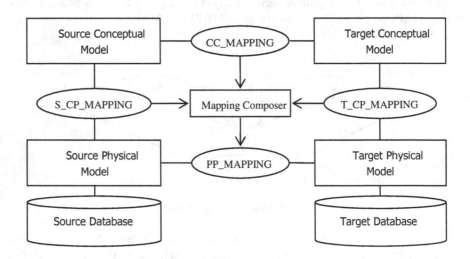

Fig. 9. Data Migration – modeling schema

A point to note here is that there is no inherent limitation on the number of source databases that can be mapped to the source conceptual model. We can have more than one source database, and so more than one source physical model and corresponding physical-conceptual mappings. This is typically the scenario when data is being migrated from a number of related databases.

3.1   Generating Data Migration Program

Conceptually the data we need in a target database table T is the data that should satisfy
the query 'select * from T'.   So for each target table T we start with this query. Then
we translate this query into an equivalent query on the source data models. From the
translated query we generate a data flow graph. This process is depicted in Fig. 10.

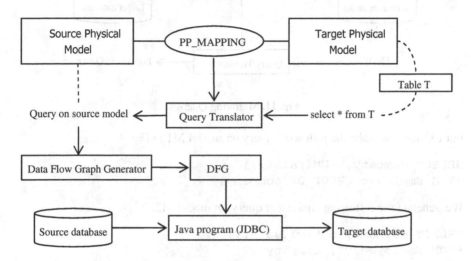

Fig. 10. Generating data migration program

We can execute the generated DFGs directly to transfer source data to the target
tables, or we can translate them into platform specific ETL [8] processes. We can also
translate the DFG to a platform specific executable program. For example, we can
translate the DFG to a program in Java and JDBC.

We also generate a master program that invokes the individual programs in an order that honors referential integrity constraints in the target database. For instance, in
a parent-child relationship, the DFG of the parent table is invoked before the DFG of
the child table.

3.2   Migrating Queries

In a data migration project, typically, it is not only the data that has to be migrated,
but also the data access programs. Query migration is at the heart of data access program migration. We can use the derived mapping PP_MAPPING to translate queries
on the source side into equivalent queries on the target side, as shown in Fig. 11.

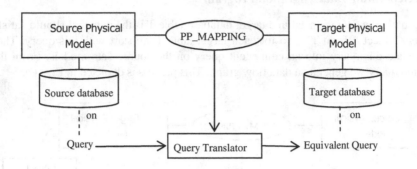

Fig. 11. Migrating Queries

For example, we take the following query on model M1 in Fig. 4.

```
SELECT company, SUM(salary)
FROM Employee GROUP BY company;
```

We generate the following equivalent query on model M2.

```
SELECT v2.name, SUM(v1.salary)
FROM Employee v1, Company v2
WHERE v1.department.company = v2 GROUP BY v2.name;
```

We generate a program that internally uses the query translator and the composed mapping to migrate source queries to the target.

4   Results

We tested our data migration approach in a product migration scenario in the financial services business domain. Our company has developed a financial services product. Deploying this product in a customer organization involves migrating a customer's existing systems to our product. Data migration is one of the first steps in the overall migration process. Customers' data is typically present in customer specific data formats and our financial services product stores its data in its own data model.

We took the case of one of our customers whose data was migrated to this financial services product. The migration was done by writing a set of custom PL/SQL programs. The customer's data was spread across two databases, with each database having more than 170 master tables. The record count in the tables ranges from a few hundred to a few millions.

Using the data migration tool, we reverse engineered the physical data models from the database schemas of customer's databases and our product database respectively. We also created corresponding conceptual models. Mappings were then identified between source and target models. Mapping specifications were of different complexities, varying from simple one-to-one mappings to complex mappings involving join conditions and sub-queries.

We then generated the data migration program to migrate data from customer's databases to our product database. Using the data migration approach discussed earlier DFGs were generated for target tables. Data migration program was then generated from these DFGs. This program had more than 400 Java Classes. This program was executed and results were compared with the data obtained from the previous hand-coded approach.

Preliminary assessment suggests that approximately 1 person year has been spent on this tool based migration approach. The corresponding effort in the old approach of creating custom PL/SQL programs was more than 5 person years. This is around 80% improvement in productivity. Based on the analysis of available defect logs from the traditional approach, our initial estimate of error reduction is around 30%. These improvements are primarily due to automated code generation from model mappings, thereby improving productivity and eliminating error-prone manual coding. Model mappings are also much easier to verify, leading to early detection of errors.

5 Related Work

Commercial data migration tools [12, 13, 14] provide a graphical environment where developers create an ETL [8] process. These tools provide a library of operators along with an execution engine. ETL processes are essentially platform specific variants of data-flow graphs discussed in this paper. ETL based approaches suffer from the same issues discussed in this paper, viz., mappings are identified at a conceptual level, and a programmer has to understand how the conceptual models and their rules map to physical models and then translate this understanding into data-flow graphs, which is an error-prone and effort-intensive process [10].

In [6] Simitsis et al propose an approach that uses semantic web technologies for designing ETL processes. They annotate data elements of data sources and warehouse using a common vocabulary, and from these annotations infer data transformations required to populate the warehouse from data sources. While this is an interesting approach, our experience suggests that it does not scale up for complex industrial scale problems. We need full-fledged conceptual models with rules and full-fledged mappings to capture the semantics. Annotations are useful but not sufficient. They also talk about generating an ontology from such annotations. This again is a useful feature to have when there is no explicitly defined ontology. Indeed we ourselves use a similar approach when we derive a conceptual model from a physical model as explained in section 3. Again, in our experience, this can only give an initial simplistic version, which has to be refined subsequently in consultation with domain experts.

In [7] Lilia et al propose a Model Driven Architecture (MDA) based framework for development of ETL processes. They talk about specifying ETL processes at two levels -- a platform independent model (PIM) (they call it a conceptual model) and a platform specific model (PSM). They use UML activity diagrams to specify ETL processes at the PIM level and use Query/View/Transformations (QVT) specifications to transform them into platform specific ETL models. While this gives a measure of independence from platform level variations, it does not significantly raise the level of abstraction. Activity diagrams are still procedural artifacts. They are not easy to reason with to support operations such as query translation.

In [11] Dessloch et al discuss Orchid, an approach for integrating declarative mappings with ETL processes. Their approach is the closest to our approach in spirit. They also talk about declarative mappings between models and generating ETL specifications from these mappings. However, they propose an operator model as the internal representation, where as we propose a logic based notation as the internal representation. Logic based notation allows us to treat both mappings and rules uniformly, enabling us to process them together. The abstract operator model proposed by Orchid is similar to the model we use for representing data-flow graphs.

[15, 16] provide surveys of schema matching approaches. As discussed in section 3, these approaches provide initial correspondences between models. These have to be refined into mappings in consultation with domain experts.

6   Conclusion and Future Work

A mapping document that specifies relationships between source and target data elements is the starting point for most data migration implementation efforts. We have shown that using our modeling framework we can specify these mappings formally, at a conceptual level, closer to the business domain, and use model driven techniques to automatically generate data migration programs. The automation helped us eliminate manual efforts in various stages of data migration, thereby increasing productivity and reducing the chances of errors. We have also shown how queries can be migrated. We plan to extend this approach to migrate stored procedures and embedded queries by integrating it with a program migration framework. We also plan to explore how industry standard reference conceptual models, such as ACORD for insurance [21], can be exploited to facilitate data exchange among applications. These standard models are growing in popularity and many applications are adopting them as their reference conceptual models. Lack of good conceptual models is one of the stumbling blocks in adopting model driven approaches such as the one discussed in this paper. Adopting industry reference models addresses this problem. We map application specific models to the industry reference model. From these mappings we can automatically derive mappings between any two applications, and use them to facilitate data exchange between the applications.

References

1. Abiteboul S., Hull R., Vianu V. Foundations of Databases. Addison Wesley, Reading, Mass., USA (1995)
2. Ullman, J.D.: Information integration using logical views. In: Afrati, F.N., Kolaitis, P.G. (eds.) ICDT 1997. LNCS, vol. 1186, pp. 19–40. Springer, Heidelberg (1996)

3. Ullman, J.D.: Principles of database and knowledge-base systems, vol. I, II. Computer Science, Rockville, Md., USA (1989)
4. Halevy, A.Y.: Answering queries using views: A survey. The VLDB Journal 10(4), 270–294 (2001)
5. Maurizio, L.: Data integration: a theoretical perspective. In: Proceedings of the Twenty-First ACM SIGMOD-SIGACT-SIGART Symposium on Principles of Database Systems. ACM (2002)
6. Skoutas, D., Simitsis, A.: Designing ETL processes using semantic web technologies. In: Proceedings of the 9th ACM International Workshop on Data Warehousing and OLAP. ACM (2006)
7. Muñoz, L., Mazón, J.-N., Trujillo, J.: Automatic generation of ETL processes from conceptual models. In: Proceedings of the ACM Twelfth International Workshop on Data Warehousing and OLAP. ACM (2009)
8. Vassiliadis, P., Simitsis, A.: Extraction, transformation, and loading. Encyclopedia of Database Systems. Springer US, pp. 1095-1101 (2009)
9. Kulkarni, V., Reddy, S.: A model-driven architectural framework for integration-capable enterprise application product lines. In: IEEE European Conference on Model Driven Architecture - Foundations and Applications, Bilbao, Spain, July 2006
10. Dayal, U., et al.: Data integration flows for business intelligence. In: Proceedings of the 12th International Conference on Extending Database Technology: Advances in Database Technology. ACM (2009)
11. Dessloch, S., et al.: Orchid: integrating schema mapping and etl. In: IEEE 24th International Conference on Data Engineering, ICDE 2008. IEEE (2008)
12. Abinitio, March 2014. http://www.abinitio.com/#prod-cs
13. Informatica, March 2014. http://www.informatica.com/in/solutions/enterprise-data-integration-and-management/data-migration/
14. Talend, March 2014. http://www.talend.com/solutions/data-migration
15. Rahm, E., Bernstein, P.A.: A survey of approaches to automatic schema matching. The VLDB Journal (2001)
16. Shvaiko, P., Euzenat, J.: A survey of schema-based matching approaches. In: Spaccapietra, S. (ed.) Journal on Data Semantics IV. LNCS, vol. 3730, pp. 146–171. Springer, Heidelberg (2005)
17. Unifed Modeling Language. www.omg.org/spec/UML
18. Semantic Web Rule Language. http://www.w3.org/Submission/SWRL/#2
19. Object Query Language. Wikipedia. en.wikipedia.org/wiki/Object_Query_Language
20. Cohen, S., Nutt, W., Serebrenik, A.: Algorithms for rewriting aggregate queries using views. In: Masunaga, Y., Thalheim, B., Štuller, J., Pokorný, J. (eds.) ADBIS 2000 and DASFAA 2000. LNCS, vol. 1884, pp. 65–78. Springer, Heidelberg (2000)
21. ACORD. https://www.acord.org/

Model Conceptualisation
and Evolution

Interactive Recovery of Requirements Traceability Links Using User Feedback and Configuration Management Logs

Ryosuke Tsuchiya[1](✉), Hironori Washizaki[1], Yoshiaki Fukazawa[1],
Keishi Oshima[2], and Ryota Mibe[2]

[1] Department of Computer Science, Waseda University, Tokyo, Japan
`ryousuke_t@asagi.waseda.jp`, {`washizaki,fukazawa`}`@waseda.jp`
[2] Yokohama Research Laboratory of Hitachi, Ltd., Kanagawa, Japan
{`keishi.oshima.rj,ryota.mibe.mu`}`@hitachi.com`

Abstract. Traceability links between requirements and source code can assist in software maintenance tasks. There are some automatic traceability recovery methods. Most of them are similarity-based methods recovering links by comparing representation similarity between requirements and code. They cannot work well if there are some links independent of the representation similarity. Herein to cover weakness of them and improve the accuracy of recovery, we propose a method that extends the similarity-based method using two techniques: a log-based traceability recovery method using the configuration management log and a link recommendation from user feedback. These techniques are independent of the representation similarity between requirements and code. As a result of applying our method to a large enterprise system, we successfully improved both recall and precision by more than a 20 percent point in comparison with singly applying the similarity-based method (recall: 60.2% to 80.4%, precision: 41.1% to 64.8%).

Keywords: Traceability · Configuration management log · Interactive method

1 Introduction

Traceability of software development is defined as the ability to trace the relationships between software artifacts. We call these relationships "traceability links." Here we focus on links between requirements and source code files, which are called "requirements traceability links." For example, if there are the requirement "Recover links automatically" and the source code file "LinkRecover.java" implementing the requirement, a requirements traceability link exists between them. Grasping requirements traceability links is effective in several software maintenance tasks, especially for improving the modification efficiency for change requests [1,2,12].

Because software must be analyzed to identify and extract traceability links, if the size of the target software is large, it is difficult to recover requirements traceability links manually due to the massive number of combinations between requirements and

© Springer International Publishing Switzerland 2015
J. Zdravkovic et al. (Eds.): CAiSE 2015, LNCS 9097, pp. 247–262, 2015.
DOI: 10.1007/978-3-319-19069-3_16

source code files. Consequently, some methods to automatically recover requirements traceability links have been developed [2,3,4,6,17,18,19,20]. Most of them are similarity-based methods recovering links by comparing representation similarity between requirements and source code. Therefore, they cannot work well if there are some links independent of the representation similarity. To confirm the effectiveness for actual software products, we applied a typical similarity-based method to a large enterprise system developed by a company, and the method recovered links with a recall of 60.2% and a precision of 41.1%. This accuracy is unsuitable for practical use.

To cover weakness of the similarity-based method and improve the application effect, herein we propose a method that extends the similarity-based method using two techniques. The first technique is a log-based traceability recovery method using the configuration management log to compensate for the lack of information about the relationships between the requirements and the source code. The second technique is the "link recommendation" using user feedback which is results of validation for recovered links. Validation of links is an inevitable and ordinary cost in the traceability recovering process because traceability recovery methods retrieve some incorrect links and overlook some correct links. Therefore, employment of user feedbacks is not an additional burden for the users. The performance of these two techniques is independent of the representation similarity between requirements and source code.

We applied our refined method to the abovementioned enterprise system to evaluate the improvement in recall and precision. This system has more than 80KLOC. We recovered traceability links between 192 requirements and 694 source code files. The system has known 726 correct links. In this study, we evaluate recall and precision by comparing the known correct links to the links recovered by our refined method. This study addresses the following Research Questions.

- RQ1: How accurately can we recover links by the similarity-based method?
- RQ2: How much does the addition of the log-based method improve the recovery accuracy?
- RQ3: How much does the addition of link recommendations improve the recovery accuracy?

We answered these questions by conducting evaluation experiments. We recovered links with a recall of 80.4% and a precision of 64.8%, which is more than a 20 percent point improvement in both recall and precision. If users apply our refined method, they can recover 80% of the correct links when they validate about 1.3 links for each source code file compared to validating over 4 links using only the similarity-based method. Although our method uses user feedback, it will eventually require less effort of the user. The contributions of this study are:

- We propose a traceability recovery method that extends the similarity-based method by incorporating two techniques.
- We develop a prototype interactive tool to implement our refined method.
- We validate our refined method by comparative experiments with the similarity-based method using sufficiently large software.

The remainder of the paper is organized as follows. Section 2 provides background information. Section 3 describes our method, while section 4 evaluates our method. Section 5 discusses related works. Finally, section 6 provides a conclusion.

2   Background

2.1   Similarity-Based Method

To recover links automatically, most of previous methods compare the representation similarity between requirements and source code because related documents often share a lot of same words. We call them "similarity-based method." The vector space model (VSM) proposed by Salton et al. is one of the most typical techniques to calculate the representation similarity between documents [13]. When the similarity-based method using the VSM (e.g., [2]) compares the representation between requirements and source code files, terms are extracted from each artifact. For the requirements, terms are extracted from the requirement names or the requirement specification documents. For source code files, terms are extracted from the identifiers (e.g., the name of file, class, method, and field) and source code comments. Consequently, the effectiveness of this method depends on the similarity between these extracted terms, and it performs poorly in some scenarios. For example, in non-English speaking countries, engineers often use their native language in documents and source code comments to facilitate communications. If requirements are written in a non-English language, only the source code comments can be used to compare the representations. Moreover, if there are too few comments, the similarity cannot be calculated. On the other hand, even if requirements are written in English, this method does not work well when the identifier lacks meaningful terms (e.g., using an extremely shortened form).

2.2   Log-Based Method

As mentioned above, the similarity-based method cannot accurately recover links for some software. To recover links in such cases, we previously proposed a log-based traceability recovery method using the configuration management log [11]. The configuration management log contains information about modifications of software artifacts. We mainly considered the log of version control system such as Apache®[1] Subversion [14] or Git [15], which is composed of revisions that include messages and file paths (Figure 1). Hypothesizing that revision messages contain information about requirements, we designed a traceability recovery method using the log as an intermediary. Because revision messages, requirements and source code comments are often written in an engineer's native language, we can recover the links of software using a non-English language. However, this method cannot recover links with source code files that have no revision histories in the log. To resolve such weakness, herein we combine the similarity-based method with the log-based method.

---

[1]   Apache is registered trademarks of Apache Software Foundation.

Revision: 1234
Author: Ryosuke
Date: 2014/11/15 17:35:13
Message: Modified the method recover() reflecting the change request for "Recover links"
———
Modified: /.../.../.../LinkRecover.java

Fig. 1. Example of a revision in the configuration management log

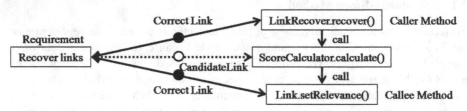

Fig. 2. Traceability links and call relationships

2.3   User's Validation and Call Relationships

Users must validate the recovered candidate links because they may contain incorrect links or overlook links. This cost is inevitable unless the method recovers links with perfect accuracy. Therefore, the results of user's validation can be used for accuracy improvement without an additional burden for the users.

A study by Ghabi et al. [10] confirmed that "Code elements sharing call relationships are often linked by the same requirement." The code element represents elements that comprise the source code (e.g., methods, classes and files). For example, in Figure 2, there is a high possibility that the method "ScoreCalculator.calulate()" is linked with the requirement "Recover links" because both the caller method "LinkRecover.recover()" and the callee method "Link.setRelevance()" are linked with the requirement. In our approach, we use this finding along with user feedback, as described above, in a technique called "Link Recommendation," which is described in detail in section 3.6.

2.4   Motivating Examples

We have applied the typical similarity-based method using the VSM to a large enterprise system, which was developed by a Japanese company. Hence, the requirement specification documents are written in Japanese. Although the source code comments are also written in Japanese, some source code files lack comments. Consequently, the method recovered links with a recall of 60.2% and a precision of 41.1%. This poor accuracy motivated us to extend the similarity-based method.

After improving some problems of the log-based method proposed, we applied it to the abovementioned enterprise system. As a result, we found that this method is superior to the similarity-based method under certain circumstances. When we limited the target source code files to those with sufficient revision histories in the configuration management log (the number of source code files decreases from 694 to 317), this method recovered links with a recall of 67.6% and a precision of 69.1%. Meanwhile, the similarity-based method only recovered links with a recall of 46.3% and a precision of 47.3% in the same situation. However, the log-based method cannot recover links of 377 source code files without revision histories. The superiority under certain circumstances and limited scope of application motivated us to combine the similarity-based method with the log-based method.

3   Approach

3.1   Overview

We propose a method to recover requirements traceability links. This method extends the similarity-based method using two techniques. In this study, we calculate the similarity between documents by using the VSM. Figure 3 shows the overview of our method. Our method requires three artifacts as inputs.

1. Requirements
   A list of requirement names is essential. In addition, we also use the requirement specification documents written in a natural language. In this study, we focus on requirements that are concrete and objective (i.e., software functional and non-functional requirements).
2. Source code files
   Because our method applies natural language processing and analyzes call relationships, our method can be applied to source code languages that the above two techniques are applicable for. The prototype tool for our method currently supports Java®[2] [16] (partly C and C++).
3. Revisions of the configuration management log
   We require the revision histories of the source code files. Our method mainly focuses on the log of the version control system. Our tool currently supports Subversion and Git. Prior to employing our method, unnecessary revisions, which indicate modification histories other than the source code files, are excluded. Moreover, revisions including simultaneous modification of too many source code files are excluded; that is, the tool excludes revisions involving over 10 source code files.

First, we create a document-term matrix (DTM) using the three input artifacts. The DTM is a matrix indicating the frequency of terms that occur in documents. Next, two kinds of relevance scores are calculated for each candidate link. The first score denotes the similarity score calculated by the similarity-based method. The second is the relevance score calculated by the log-based method. In this study, candidate links indicate all relationships between the target elements. For example, if the target system has 100 requirements, there are 100 candidate links for each source code file. However, the reliability as a score in the candidate links differs.

After calculating the score, users specify a target (requirement or source code file) that they want to recover links. Then our tool displays candidate links of the specified

---

[2]   Java is registered trademarks of Oracle and/or its affiliates.

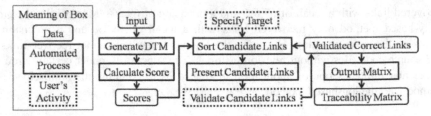

Fig. 3. Overview of our method

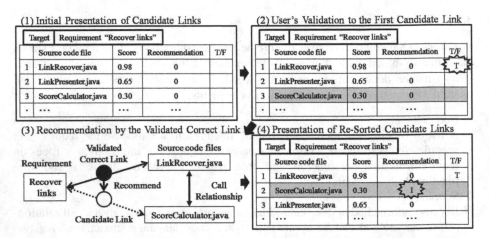

Fig. 4. Presentation and validation of sorted candidate links of a specified requirement

target after arranging the candidate links according to the sorting algorithm of our method. This algorithm sorts candidate links using two kinds of scores and user feedback. As shown in Figure 4, for example, if users specify the requirement "Recover links" as the target, the tool displays the sorted candidate links of the requirement.

Users then validate candidate links presented by our tool starting from the top. They judge the correctness of the candidate links, and each time, the result is provided as feedback to the tool. Then the tool re-sorts the order of the remaining candidate links according to the algorithm considering the user feedback. In Figure 4, by validating the correctness of the first presented link, the presentation order is re-sorted.

Finally, after users identify some correct links, users can determine the requirements traceability matrix at an arbitrary time. The matrix shows which source code files each requirement is related to. Below our method is described in detail.

3.2   Document-Term Matrix Generation

Requirements, source code files and revisions are treated as documents in this approach. In the VSM, each document is represented as a vector determined by valid terms (nouns, verbs, and adjectives) in the document. Terms of the requirement are extracted from the requirement name and the requirement specification document. Terms of the source code file are extracted from source code comments and

identifiers. Then, if the identifier is represented as the connected term (e.g., LinkRe-
cover, recover_Links()), the identifier is decomposed into individual terms. Terms of
revisions are extracted from revision messages.

Here, D represents a set of documents and T presents a set of terms. For a docu-
ment d_x ($\in D$) containing N valid terms [i.e., t_1, t_2,$\cdots$, t_N ($\in T$)], $w(t_p, d_x)$ ($1 \leq$
$p \leq N$) is the number of appearances of t_p in d_x. Consequently, d_x can be
represented by N-dimensional vector $\vec{v_x}$ as

$$\vec{v_x} = \big(w(t_1, d_x), w(t_2, d_x), \cdots, w(t_N, d_x)\big). \tag{1}$$

In the VSM, the vector of the document is represented as Formula (1). However, we
use the vector weighted by TF-IDF to more accurately represent the document characteristics. TF-IDF indicates the term frequency and inverse document frequency. Frequently used terms in a document have high importance for the document. On the
other hand, common terms used in many documents have low importance (e.g., general words). The term frequency value of t_p in d_x is defined as

$$tf(t_p, d_x) = \frac{w(t_p, d_x)}{\sum_N w(t_N, d_x)}. \tag{2}$$

If the number of documents is represented as M and the number of documents containing t_p is represented as $h(t_p)$, the inverse document frequency value of t_p is
defined as

$$idf(t_p) = \log_e \frac{M}{h(t_p)}. \tag{3}$$

Therefore, the vector weighted by TF-IDF is defined as

$$\vec{v'_x} = \big(tf(t_1, d_x) * idf(t_1), tf(t_2, d_x) * idf(t_2), \cdots, tf(t_N, d_x) * idf(t_N)\big). \tag{4}$$

The similarity between two documents d_i and d_j is obtained as the cosine of the
angle between the two document vectors $\vec{v'_i}$ and $\vec{v'_j}$, and is referred to as the cosine
similarity. $DSim(d_i, d_j)$ (Document Similarity, $0 \leq DSim \leq 1.0$) is defined using
the cosine similarity as

$$DSim(d_i, d_j) = \frac{\vec{v'_i} \vec{v'_j}}{|\vec{v'_i}||\vec{v'_j}|}. \tag{5}$$

To calculate the similarity between all documents (containing requirements, source
code files and revisions), a document-term matrix $DTM_{M \times N}$ with M rows and N
columns is generated. Here M represents the number of documents and N
represents the total number of terms in the documents. The matrix is defined as

$$DTM_{M \times N} = \begin{pmatrix} tf(t_1, d_1) * idf(t_1) & \cdots & tf(t_N, d_1) * idf(t_N) \\ \vdots & \ddots & \vdots \\ tf(t_1, d_M) * idf(t_1) & \cdots & tf(t_N, d_M) * idf(t_N) \end{pmatrix}. \tag{6}$$

The row of the matrix indicates the document vector mentioned in Formula (4). We calculate similarities between all documents using the DTM.

3.3 Calculating the Similarity-Based Score

In this approach, we calculate two kinds of relevance scores for each candidate link. First, we describe the first score in this section. In accordance with similarity-based methods, we directly calculate the similarity score between requirements and source code. We call this first score the "similarity-based score." Basically, $DSim$ is set to the similarity-based score. However, if the source code comments contain a requirement name, we set the maximized score (i.e., 1.0) to the similarity-based score. This exceptional process is designed on the basis of the hypothesis that engineers caring software traceability tend to record the name of relevant requirements in source code comments. The effectiveness of this process depends on the quality of comments.

Here, R represents a set of requirements and C is a set of source code files ($R, C \subset D$). The similarity-based score $SBScore$ between requirement r_i and source code file c_j ($r_i \in R$, $c_j \in C$) is defined as

$$SBScore(r_i, c_j) = \begin{cases} 1.0 \ (\text{if comments of } c_j \text{ contain the name of } r_i) \\ DSim(r_i, c_j) \ (\text{in other cases}) \end{cases} . \tag{7}$$

3.4 Calculating the Log-Based Score

Additionally, we calculate the second relevance score using the log-based method. We call the second score "log-based score." Because revisions contain file paths of the modified source code files, we can indirectly associate requirements with source code files by calculating the similarity between requirements and revisions. The log-based score is calculated by two elements: the similarity between requirements and revisions and the weight of the source code files for each revision.

Here L represents a set of revisions ($L \subset D$). The number of source code files modified in revision l_k ($l_k \in L$) is represented as $m(l_k)$. Then the weight of source code files c_j in revision l_k is defined as

$$Weight(c_j, l_k) = \begin{cases} \dfrac{1}{m(l_k)} \ (\text{if } c_j \text{ is modified in } l_k) \\ 0 \ (\text{in other cases}) \end{cases} . \tag{8}$$

Therefore, the log-based score $LBScore$ between requirement r_i and source code file c_j is defined as

$$LBScore(r_i, c_j) = \sum_{k=1}^{G} \left(DSim(r_i, l_k) * Weight(c_j, l_k) \right). \tag{9}$$

G represents the number of revisions. We calculate $DSim$ and $Weight$ for each revision and sum up their multiplied values ($DSim * Weight$).

3.5   Sorting Algorithms

After calculating scores, we present candidate links of the target specified by users. Here the target is either the requirement or source code file. Candidate links are sorted by our algorithm. The kind of target determines which algorithm is used.

As described in section 2.4, the log-based method is superior to the similarity-based method for recovering links of files with revision histories. Therefore, if the target is a source code file, we selectively use two kinds of score depending on the presence of the revision history. For a file without revision histories in the configuration management log (i.e., all log-based scores are 0), the candidate links are sorted in descending order of the similarity-based score. On the other hand, for a file with a revision history, the links are sorted in descending order of the log-based score.

If the target is a requirement, we basically use the similarity-based score. First, candidate links are sorted in descending order of the similarity-based score. However, on the other hand, candidate links get preferential rights if they have the highest log-based score in the group of candidate links when targeting any source code files. Candidate links with preferential rights are prior to links without the rights. (i.e., even if the similarity-based score is low, the link with the preferential right is preferentially presented to users.) Then candidate links with preferential rights are sorted in descending order of the log-based score.

3.6   Link Recommendations

Our tool presents sorted candidate links to users, and then the users validate the links starting from the top. Because their judgments are provided as feedbacks to the tool, our tool focuses on the call relationships of the source code file of the judged link. Here the call relationships of the source code file indicate the relationships of methods in the file. A validated correct link recommends other candidate links based on call relationships. We call this type of recommendation a "Link Recommendation."

In addition to the two types of relevance scores, candidate links have other two values: "RCR (Recommendation Count by calleR)" and "RCE (Recommendation Count by calleE)." These values increase when recommended by a correct link. For example, in Figure 2, if the link between the requirement "Recover links" and the source code file "LinkRecover.java" is judged as correct, the link recommends a candidate link between the requirement "Recover links" and the source code file "RelevanceCalculator.java" because the method "recover()" in the file "LinkRecover.java" is the caller of the method "calculate()" in the file "RelevanceCalculator.java." Then the value RCR of the candidate link increases by one. Likewise, if a link with the file "Link.java" is judged as correct, the value RCE of the candidate link increases by one.

3.7   Sorting Algorithm with User Feedback

Every time the candidate link is judged as correct, the remaining candidate links are sorted by the appropriate algorithm that extends the algorithms described in section 3.5 by two values RCR and RCE.

Rank	Link	RCR*RCE	RCR+RCE	SBScore	LBScore
1	A	2 (2*1)	3 (2+1)	0.55	0
2	B	0 (1*0)	1 (1+0)	0.60	0
3	C	0 (0*0)	0 (0+0)	0.95	0
4	D	0 (0*0)	0 (0+0)	0.42	0

Fig. 5. Example of link order

The algorithm is designed on the basis of the hypothesis that links recommended by both caller and callee are more reliable. First, the links are sorted in descending order of the value that multiplies *RCR* and *RCE*. Second, the links with the same multiplied value are arranged in descending order of the value obtained by adding *RCR* and *RCE*. Third, the links with the same added value are sorted by the algorithm mentioned in the section 3.5. In Figure 5 that shows an example of link order, the link A is the top of the order because it has the highest multiplied value (*RCR* * *RCE*). The link B is the second of the order because it has the highest added value (*RCR* + *RCE*) in the links with the same multiplied value (B, C, D). The links C and D are sorted in descending order of the similarity-based score.

4   Evaluation

4.1   Overview

To validate our method, we carried out experiments targeting an enterprise system developed by a Japanese company. Although this system has a very large scale, its subsystem has 726 known correct links. Hence, the following experiments target this subsystem, which has more than 80KLOC. We recovered traceability links between 192 requirements and 694 source code files where the requirements are extracted from the requirement specification documents. Source code files are implemented by Java®. We use 7090 revisions of the Subversion log. Requirements, source code comments and revision messages are written in Japanese.

To evaluate the improvement in recall and precision, we conducted three experiments. First, we recovered links by using only the similarity-based method. Second, we recovered links by using the method combining the similarity-based method and the log-based method. Third, we conducted an experiment evaluating the effectiveness of the link recommendation.

For each experiment, we recovered links by repeating the following cycle.

1. Specify a target (requirement or source code file).
2. Validate candidate links of the specified target starting from the top.
3. Validation of the target is complete when the validation count reaches the allowable validation count or all correct links of the target are recovered

Here the allowable validation count indicates how many candidate links users can validate in one cycle. For example, if the allowable validation count is one, users validate only the first presented link. The cycle is repeated as many times as the number of targets. Therefore, we repeated the cycle 192 times when targeting all requirements and also repeated 694 times when targeting all source code files. The recovery targeting requirements is independent of the recovery targeting source code files. Therefore, we can determine the recall and precision for both targeting requirements and targeting source code files. Recall, precision and F-measure (comprehensive measure of recall and precision) are defined as

$$recall = \frac{validated\ correct\ links}{all\ correct\ links}\ (0 \le recall \le 1.0), \tag{10}$$

$$precision = \frac{validated\ correct\ links}{all\ validated\ links}\ (0 \le precision \le 1.0), \tag{11}$$

$$F - measure = 2 * \frac{recall * precision}{recall + precision}\ (0 \le F - measure \le 1.0). \tag{12}$$

Because the correct links are known, all experiments were fully automated. When targeting requirements, we specified the requirement as the target in alphabetical order of the requirement name. However, the target order affects the accuracy when the targets are source code files and the link recommendation is used. Therefore, when targeting source code files in experiments, we tried using two kinds of orders: the best order (descending order of the highest relevance score of the candidate links) and the worst order (ascending order of the highest relevance score of the candidate links).

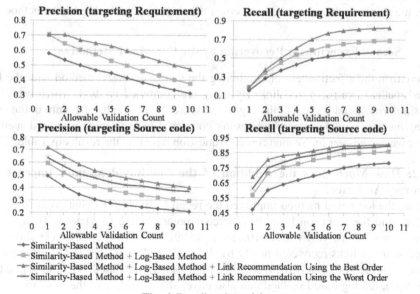

Fig. 6. Recall and precision

Figure 6 shows the experimental results for the recall and precision for each target where the horizontal axis indicates the allowable validation count and the vertical axis indicates the value of recall or precision. Table 1 lists the results with the highest F-measure for each method. In all methods, the highest F-measure occurs when the targets are source code files and the allowable validation count is two.

Table 1. Recall and precision when F-masure is highest

Method	Recall	Precision	F-measure
Similarity-Based Method	0.602	0.411	0.488
Similarity-Based Method + Log-Based Method	0.712	0.518	0.599
Similarity-Based Method + Log-Based Method + Link Recommendation Using the Best Order	0.804	0.648	0.718
Similarity-Based Method + Log-Based Method + Link Recommendation Using the Worst Order	0.751	0.571	0.648

4.2   First Experiment: Recovering by the Similarity-Based Method

First, we recovered links using only the similarity-based method, which used the similarity-based score to sort candidate links. Based on the results in Table 1, we can answer the first research question.

RQ1: How Accurately Can We Recover Links by the Similarity-Based Method?
The similarity-based method recovered links with a recall of 60.2% and a precision of 41.1%. This accuracy is not sufficiently high. However, 42.1% of the recovered correct links are the links with source code files that have no revision histories. Therefore, the similarity-based method can cover the weakness of the log-based method.

4.3   Second Experiment: Recovering by the Combined Method

To confirm the effectiveness of combining the similarity-based method with the log-based method, we recovered links by using the combined method, which used both the similarity-based score and the log-based score. In all graphs of Figure 6, the combined method provides improved results compared to the similarity-based method. Thus, we can answer the second research question based on the results in Table 1.

RQ2: How Much does the Addition of the Log-Based Method Improve the Recovery Accuracy?
Adding the log-based method improved the recall by an 11.0 percent point (60.2% to 71.2%) and the precision by a 10.7 percent point (41.1% to 51.8%). Then, the F-measure was improved by 0.111 (0.488 to 0.599). Moreover, the average similarity-based score of links recovered newly by the combined method is 0.227, whereas the average score of links recovered by the similarity-based method is 0.635. Therefore, the log-based method can also cover the weakness of the similarity-based method.

4.4   Third Experiment: Effectiveness of Link Recommendations

We recovered links by using the combined method with link recommendations to evaluate the effectiveness. Then we tried using two kinds of orders: the best order and the worst order. In Figure 6, the method with link recommendations is superior to that without link recommendations for all conditions except when the targets are requirements and the allowable validation count is one.

When targeting requirements, the link recommendation becomes effective from the second presented candidate link because the first presented link is not recommended by any other link. On the other hand, when targeting source code files, the link recommendation is effective from the first presented link excepting for the first targeted source code file, because the first presented link can be recommended by a link that has already been validated when targeting different source code files. Therefore, when targeting source code files, the targeting order affects the accuracy because the presentation order depends on the validation results of other source code files.

Thus, the experiments can answer the third research question.

RQ3: How Much Does the Addition of Link Recommendations Improve the Recovery Accuracy?

The link recommendation improved the recall by a 9.2 percent point (71.2% to 80.4%) and the precision by a 13.0 percent point (51.8% to 64.8%) when using the best order. Then, the F-measure was improved by 0.119 (0.599 to 0.718). On the other hand, when using the worst order, the effectiveness decreased in comparison with using the best order. Hence, the link recommendation is most effective when the validated correct link with the high relevance score recommends the unvalidated correct link with the low relevance score. Therefore, when we put on emphasis on the accuracy, we should preferentially target source code files that have candidate links with the high relevance score. In the experiment, we recovered many additional links that have low relevance scores by applying the link recommendation.

4.5   Threats to Validity

The fact that we validated our method by applying to only one software product is a threat to the external validity. The improvement in accuracy depends on the quality of the revision messages and software structure because our method employs the configuration management log and call relationships. Thus, we should evaluate the relationship between these factors for other software and the effectiveness of our method.

In our evaluation, we independently conducted the recovery targeting requirements and the recovery targeting source code files. However, in an actual application, users randomly specify targets based on their needs. The targeting consistency may affect the accuracy of the recovering links, which is a threat to the internal validity. Therefore, we should conduct an experiment with random targeting in the future.

Additionally, our method uses user feedback to improve the accuracy, which may result in human error. We should conduct experiments by subjects to evaluate the impact of the environment for real applications of our method.

5   Related Work

Arkley et al. conducted a survey of nine software projects using questionnaires and interviews [7], and identified issues of traceability including usability. As these findings suggest, we should improve usability of our tool because validation of the candidate links takes significant costs.

Mäder et al. conducted a controlled experiment with 52 subjects performing real maintenance tasks on two third-party development projects where half of the tasks were with and the other half were without traceability [1]. They showed that on average subjects with traceability perform 21% faster and create 60% more correct solutions. Their empirical study affirms the usefulness of requirements traceability links.

Blaauboer et al. have investigated how project managers make a decision on adopting requirements traceability [5]. They validated the factors relevant for the decision and found five dominant factors: development organization awareness, customer awareness, return on investment, stakeholder preferences, and process flow.

Some studies have compared the representation between requirements and source code to recover requirements traceability links [2,3,4,6,17,18,19,20] using different techniques, such as the VSM, the probabilistic model and the latent semantic index. Here we propose extended method based on the method using the VSM [2].

Chen et al. proposed an approach that combines three supporting techniques, Regular Expression, Key Phrases, and Clustering, with the VSM to improve the traceability recovery performance [8]. Except for Clustering, their supporting techniques depend on the representation similarity between the requirements and source code files. By contrast, our component techniques are independent of the representation similarity.

Wang et al. proposed a feature location approach that supports multi-faceted interactive program exploration [9]. Feature Location is a technique similar to recovering requirements traceability links for targeting requirements. Their approach automatically extracts multiple syntactic and semantic facets from candidate program elements. Then users can interactively group, sort, and filter feature location results by facets. Although our method is also an interactive method using user feedback, we require users only to validate correctness of candidate links.

Ghabi et al. proposed an approach to validate links through call relationships within the code [10]. They inputted set of candidate links with certain reliability and applied filtering by call relationships all at once, whereas we use only correct links validated by users and interactively apply the link recommendation by call relationships.

6   Conclusion and Future Work

We have proposed a traceability recovery method that extends the similarity-based method using two elemental techniques. The first technique is the log-based method using the configuration management log. The second is link recommendations using user feedback and the call relationships. We applied our method to an actual product and recovered links between 192 requirements and 694 source code files, confirming the effectiveness of applying two elemental techniques simultaneously. In the future, we plan conduct the additional experiments described in section 4.5, and investigate the applicability of other code relationships for link recommendations.

References

1. Mäder, P., Egyed, A.: Assessing the effect of requirements traceability for software maintenance. In: The 28th IEEE International Conference on Software Maintenance (ICSM 2012), pp. 171–180 (2012)
2. Antoniol, G., Canfora, G., Casazza, G., De Lucia, A., Merlo, E.: Recovering traceability links between code and documentation. IEEE Transactions on Software Engineering 28(10), 970–983 (2002)
3. Marcus, A., Maletic, J.I.: Recovering documentation to source code traceability links using latent semantic indexing. In: The 25th International Conference on Software Engineering (ICSE 2003), pp. 125–135 (2003)
4. Dagenais, B., Robillard, M.P.: Recovering traceability links between an API and its learning resources. In: The 34th International Conference on Software Engineering (ICSE 2012), pp. 47–57 (2012)
5. Blaauboer, F., Sikkel, K., Aydin, M.N.: Deciding to adopt requirements traceability in practice. In: Krogstie, J., Opdahl, A.L., Sindre, G. (eds.) CAiSE 2007 and WES 2007. LNCS, vol. 4495, pp. 294–308. Springer, Heidelberg (2007)
6. De Lucia, A., Oliveto, R., Tortora, G.: ADAMS re-trace: traceability link recovery via latent semantic indexing. In: The 30th International Conference on Software Engineering (ICSE 2008), pp. 839–842 (2008)
7. Arkley, P., Riddle, S.: Overcoming the traceability benefit problem. In: The 13th IEEE International Conference on Requirements Engineering (RE 2005), pp. 385–389 (2005)
8. Chen, X., Grundy, J.: Improving automated documentation to code traceability by combining retrieval techniques. In: The 26th IEEE/ACM International Conference on Automated Software Engineering, pp. 223–232 (2011)
9. Wang, J., Peng, X., Xing, Z., Zhao, W.: Improving feature location practice with multi-faceted interactive exploration. In: The 35th International Conference on Software Engineering (ICSE 2013), pp. 762–771 (2013)
10. Ghabi, A., Egyed, A.: Code patterns for automatically validating requirements-to-code traces. In: The 27th IEEE/ACM International Conference on Automated Software Engineering, pp. 200–209 (2012)
11. Tsuchiya, R., Washizaki, H., Fukazawa, Y., Kato, T., Kawakami, M., Yoshimura, K.: Recovering traceability links between requirements and source code in the same series of software products. In: The 17th International Software Product Line Conference (SPLC 2013), pp. 121–130 (2013)
12. Pooley, R., Warren, C.: Reuse through requirements traceability. In: The 3rd International Conference on Software Engineering Advances (ICSEA 2008), pp. 65–70 (2008)
13. Salton, G., McGill, M.J.: Introduction to modern information retrieval. McGraw-Hill, New York (1983)
14. Apache® Subversion. https://subversion.apache.org/
15. Git. http://git-scm.com/
16. Java®. https://www.java.net/
17. Jiang, H., Nguyen, T.N., Chen, I., Jaygarl, H., Chang, C.K.: Incremental latent semantic indexing for automatic traceability link evolution management. In: The 23rd IEEE/ACM International Conference on Automated Software Engineering, pp. 59–68 (2008)

18. De Lucia, A., Oliveto, R., Tortora, G.: IR-based traceability recovery processes: an empirical comparison of "one-shot" and incremental processes. In: The 23rd IEEE/ACM International Conference on Automated Software Engineering, pp. 39–48 (2008)
19. McMillan, C., Poshyvanyk, D., Revelle, M.: Combining textual and structural analysis of software artifacts for traceability link recovery. In: The 2009 ICSE Workshop on Traceability in Emerging Forms of Software Engineering, pp. 41–48 (2009)
20. Settimi, R., BenKhadra, O., Berezhanskaya, E., Christina, S.: Goal-centric traceability for managing non-functional requirements. In: The 27th International Conference on Software Engineering (ICSE 2005), pp. 362–371 (2005)

Detecting Complex Changes During Metamodel Evolution

Djamel Eddine Khelladi[1]([✉]), Regina Hebig[1], Reda Bendraou[1],
Jacques Robin[1], and Marie-Pierre Gervais[1,2]

[1] Sorbonne Universités, UPMC Univ Paris 06, UMR 7606, F-75005 Paris, France
djamel.khelladi@lip6.fr
[2] Université Paris Ouest Nanterre La Defense, F-92001 Nanterre, France

Abstract. Evolution of metamodels can be represented at the finest grain by the trace of atomic changes: add, delete, and update elements. For many applications, like automatic correction of models when the metamodel evolves, a higher grained trace must be inferred, composed of complex changes, each one aggregating several atomic changes. Complex change detection is a challenging task since multiple sequences of atomic changes may define a single user intention and complex changes may overlap over the atomic change trace. In this paper, we propose a detection engine of complex changes that simultaneously addresses these two challenges of variability and overlap. We introduce three ranking heuristics to help users to decide which overlapping complex changes are likely to be correct. We describe an evaluation of our approach that allow reaching full recall. The precision is improved by our heuristics from 63% and 71% up to 91% and 100% in some cases.

Keywords: Metamodel · Evolution · Complex change · Detection

1 Introduction

In the process of building a domain-specific modeling language (DSML) multiple versions are developed, tried out, and adapted until a stable version is reached. As by one of our industrial partners in the automotive domain, such intermediate versions of the DSML are used in product development, where often further needs are identified. A challenge hereby is that each time the metamodel of the DSML is changed to a next version, already developed models need to be co-evolved too. This is not only the case for DSMLs, but also for more generic metamodels, e.g. the UML officially evolved in the past every two to three years.

To cope with this evolution of metamodels, mechanisms are developed to co-evolve artifacts, such as models and transformations that may become invalid. A challenging task herein is to detect all the changes that lead a metamodel from a version n to a version $n+1$, called Evolution Trace (ET). Automatically detecting it, not only helps developers to automatically keep track of the metamodels' evolution, but also to trigger and/or to apply automatic actions based on these changes. For instance, models and transformations that are defined based on the metamodel are automatically co-evolved i.e. corrected based on the detected

© Springer International Publishing Switzerland 2015
J. Zdravkovic et al. (Eds.): CAiSE 2015, LNCS 9097, pp. 263–278, 2015.
DOI: 10.1007/978-3-319-19069-3_17

ET (e.g. [7,8]). Here the rate of automatically co-evolved metamodel changes depends significantly on the precision and accuracy of the ET.

In such a context, it becomes crucial to provide correct and *precise* detection of changes. Two types of changes are distinguished: a) *Atomic changes* that are additions, removals, and updates of a metamodel element. b) *Complex changes* that consist in a sequence of atomic changes combined together. In comparison to the atomic changes alone, complex changes include additional knowledge on the interrelation of these atomic changes. For example, move property[1] is a complex change, where a property is moved from one class to another via a reference. This is composed of two atomic changes: delete property and add property. During co-evolution of models, the move property provides the valuable information that instance values of the deleted property are not to be deleted, but moved to instances of the added property. Many further complex changes [10] are used in literature to improve co-evolution rate of models and transformations.

Therefore, the detection of complex changes is essential for automating co-evolution. One approach towards that are operator-based approaches. By directly applying complex changes in form of operators, the user traces complex changes himself. However, more than 60 different complex changes are known to occur in practice [10]. Modelers might not be willing to learn and remember such a high number of operators, increasing the likelihood of workarounds with atomic changes. Thus, operator based approaches cannot provide a guarantee that all complex changes are recorded.

Vision. Consequently, a detection of complex changes needs to work on the basis of atomic changes. This task has one inherent difficulty that one needs to be aware of: a guarantee that all identified complex changes are correct is hard to reach. Existing approaches [4,6,7,11,17] neither reach a 100% recall, nor 100% precision. This is due to the fact that recovering the user's intent during an evolution is never certain. For example, when a property *id* is removed in one class and another property *id* is added to another class. This might be detected as move property, although it is just a coincidence.

Thus, final decisions can only be made by the user. Two options exist after an initial list of complex changes has been detected: the user might correct the list by a) removing incorrectly detected changes (such as [17]) and/or b) manually forming further complex changes based on found atomic changes (such as [11]). The later step, however, implies much higher effort for the user than just picking correct and incorrect complex changes from a complete list.

Therefore, we think that a detection approach should aim at 100% recall, meaning that all potential complex changes should be detected. To further increase precision and support the user in making the selection, identified changes should be prioritized concerning their probability with the help of heuristics.

Problem Statement. Automatically detecting complex changes is a difficult task, mainly because of two reasons: *overlap* that is ignored so far and *indefinite length*.

i) *Overlap.* Different complex changes might be composed based on overlapping sets of atomic changes. Figure 1 shows an example, two complex changes

---

[1] For sake of readability we refer to metaclass and metaproperty as class and property.

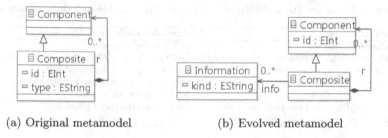

(a) Original metamodel   (b) Evolved metamodel

Fig. 1. An evolution example of a composite pattern

pull property (via the generalization) and *move property* (via the relation r) might be formed based on the same set of atomic changes: deleting property *id* from the Composite class and adding *id* to the Component class. Only one of the changes was intended by the user. However, since we cannot know which complex change is the correct one, both must be detected. This phenomenon is reinforced, when a lot of changes are performed on closely related or even the same metamodel elements.

ii) *Indefinite length.* Complex change types have variable numbers of involved atomic changes. For example, in Figure 1 property *id* is pulled from one subclass Composite, yet a pull might also be applied when multiple subclasses contain the same property. Thus, the number of property deletions varies with the number of involved subclasses. Both issues reduce the recall that can be reached with existing approaches.

iii) A further issue arises due to the fact that all existing approaches [4,6,7, 11,17] base the detection of complex changes on a set of atomic changes that has been computed as the difference between the old and the new version of the metamodel, the so-called difference model (DM). However, relying on the DM suffers from two main drawbacks:

(1) The first is that the DM cannot detect some changes that are *hidden* by other changes during evolution (called masked changes in [17]). Consequently, information might be lost, which impacts both recall and precision of the detection approaches. For example, in Figure 1 the move property *type* from class Composite to class Information is hidden by the change rename property *type* to *kind*. The DM cannot detect these last two changes, but sees only two independent operations: deletion of property *type* and addition of property *kind* as summarized in Table 1.

(2) The second drawback of the difference-based approach is that the DM returns an unordered sequence of all the detected changes. However, the chronological order of changes might be relevant during later co-evolution tasks, and can be used during complex change detection for improving precision.

Contributions. We address these challenges by four contributions:

– First, we propose to record at run-time the trace of atomic changes, by listening and logging modeler's editing actions within the modeling tool (editor). This way drawbacks of the difference-based approaches can be tackled.

Table 1. Recorded trace VS difference trace: An example of hidden changes

Applied Changes	Metamodel Difference Changes
1. *addClass(Information)*	1. *addClass(Information)*
2. *addProperty(info, Composite, Information)*	2. *addProperty(info, Composite, Information)*
3. *deleteProperty(id, Composite)*	3. *addProperty(id, Component, int)*
4. *deleteProperty(type, Composite)*	4. *addProperty(kind, Information, String)*
5. *addProperty(id, Component, int)*	5. *deleteProperty(id, Composite)*
6. *addProperty(type, Information, String)*	6. *deleteProperty(type, Composite)*
7. *renameProperty(type, kind, Information)*	

– Second, we propose a definition for complex changes that respects their variable character. Thus, all variants of a complex change can be detected.
– Third, we introduce a generic detection algorithm that consumes such variable complex change definitions as input together with the ET of atomic changes. In contrast to existing approaches [4,6,7,11,17], the algorithm systematically detects all possible candidates, even in case of *overlapping changes*, and thus reaching 100% recall. Furthermore, the approach can be easily extended to new complex changes, by just providing their definitions as input to the algorithm. We implemented the algorithm as a Complex Change Detection Engine (CCDE).
– Fourth, we propose to optimize precision by defining three heuristics that weight the detected overlapping complex changes. Especially, when many changes have been applied, these heuristics rank them in order of likelihood of correctness to the user, who can then pick and confirm the correct choice.

In this work, we apply our approach to detect seven complex changes: *move property, pull property, push property, extract super class, flatten hierarchy, extract class, and inline class* [10]. Our evaluation on two real case studies, including the evolution of GMF and UML Class Diagram metamodels, shows promising results by always reaching 100% recall of detection, and the precision is improved by our heuristics from 63% and 77% up to 95% and 100% in some cases.

In *Model-Driven Engineering* models are used in order to capture the different aspects of a system. This covers the system's architecture, its data structure or its design and GUI classses. While we focus in this paper on the evolution of metamodels, our approach for detecting complex changes theoretically applies on object-oriented models in general.

The rest of the paper is structured as follows. Section 2 illustrates our approach for detecting Complex changes. Sections 3 and 4 present the implementation and the evaluation of our approach. Sections 5 and 6 present the related work, discussion and conclude this paper.

2   An Approach for Complex Change Detection

This section presents an extensible approach to detect complex changes. We first describe how we obtain atomic changes, and then we introduce how a complex

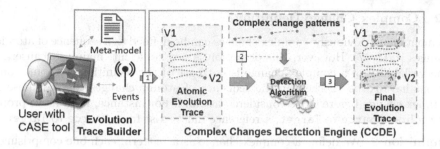

Fig. 2. Overall approach

change is defined, and what should be considered for its detection. After that, we present our detection algorithm, before applying it for seven complex changes.

Figure 2 depicts our overall approach. The atomic change trace is first recorded. Complex change patterns are then matched to it in order to generate a complex change trace. Based on the discussion of challenges in the introduction of this paper, we formulate four requirements for our approach:

– *R1. No changes must be hidden from the detection to not decrease the recall.*
– *R2. Detection must be able to cope with the variability to cover all possible variants of a complex change.*
– *R3. Detect all potential complex changes, i.e. high recall (100%). It means that no complex change is missed during the detection.*
– *R4. Prioritizing between overlapping complex changes to support the user in choosing those changes that conform to her intention.*

2.1 Atomic Change Detection

We propose a tracking approach that records at run-time all changes applied by users within a modeling tool without changing its interface. Thus, no changes are *hidden* or lost in the ET that serves for the detection of complex changes. This answers to the requirement R1, in contrast to the difference-based approaches. In order to implement the tracking mechanism we reuse an existing tool, Praxis [3] developed by our team. Praxis tool interfaces with a modeling editor to record all the changes that occur during an evolution. Existing works based on Praxis already provided good performances and scalability results [1–3,5].

Definition 1. We consider the following set of atomic changes that can be used during a metamodel evolution: *add, delete, and update* metametamodel elements. An *update*, changes the value of a property of an element, such as type, name, upper/lower bounds properties etc. The list of metametamodel elements that are considered in this work is: *package, class, attribute, reference, operation, parameter, and generalization.* Those elements represent the core feature of a metamodel, as in EMF/Ecore [15], MOF [13] metamodels.

2.2   Complex Change Definition

As mentioned previously, complex changes can be defined as a sequence of atomic changes [7,11,17]. However, this definition is not sufficient, mainly because: 1) The variability of a complex change is not part of the definition. 2) Some conditions have to be checked on the sequence of atomic changes that compose a complex change before to be considered as valid. For instance, for a move property p from `Source` to `Target`, a reference must exist from `Source` to `Target`.

Definition 2. We define a complex change as a pattern, each one comprising:

1. A set of atomic change types ($SOACT$) allowed to appear in the pattern, each with its multiplicity constraint. The multiplicity is a range between a minimum and a maximum [Min..Max]. For undefined Max value, a star is put instead, e.g. [1..*].
2. Conditions relating pairs of change type elements that additionally have to be satisfied for the pattern to match. Four types of conditions are used in our current approach:
   (a) Name equality between two named elements e_1 and e_2: $e_1.name == e_2.name$
   (b) Type equality between two typed elements e_1 and e_2: $e_1.type == e_2.type$
   (c) Equality between two typed elements e_1 and e_2: $e_1 == e_2 \Leftrightarrow e_1.name == e_2.name \wedge e_1.type == e_2.type$
   (d) Presence of a generalization relationship (Inheritance) between two classes c_1 and c_2: $c_1.inheritance.from == c_2$
   (e) Presence of a Reference relationship between two classes c_1 and c_2: $c_1.reference.type == c_2$

The above definition of a complex change answers to the requirement R2 of variability by explicitly specifying a multiplicity for each change.

2.3   Detection Algorithm of Complex Changes

The detection Algorithm 1 takes as input the pattern definitions of the complex changes that have to be detected and search for all their occurrences. In particular, our algorithm works in two passes. The first pass, (lines 1-11) generates all complex changes candidates, i.e. collects sets of atomic changes that might together form a complex change based on type and multiplicity of the pattern only. At each iteration, the algorithm browses through the evolution trace of n atomic changes, and if the current atomic change is part of a definition of a certain complex change, then a *candidate* is created with the current atomic change. After that, for all already existing candidates that might include this atomic change, we add a candidate instance that includes the current atomic change. The second pass (lines 12-13) scans the candidate set and only keeps those that satisfy the pattern, i.e. whether enough atomic changes could be identified and the conditions are fulfilled.

The main advantage of Algorithm 1 is its time complexity: it runs *one* time through the n atomic changes, and not k times for each complex change. The algorithm is designed to be extensible to detect other complex changes by defining additional definitions, the core detection remains unchanged. Its main drawback is the memory complexity, since it may create k candidates of complex

---

Algorithm 1. The Algorithm of Detection for Complex Changes.

Input: ET: The recorded evolution trace of atomic changes
          LDef: List of definitions of the complex changes
Output: L: List of detected complex changes
1: $CCC : CandidateComplexChanges \leftarrow \{\}$;   ▷ List of candidates of complex changes.
2: **while** *Not end of ET* **do**
          $current \leftarrow ET.current$;
3:      **for all** $c \in CCC$ **do**
4:          **if** $c.isItPossibleToAdd(current)$ **then** $c.add(current)$;
5:      **for all** $d \in LDef$ **do**
6:          **if** $current \in d$ **then** $x \leftarrow d.createCandiate()$;
          $x.add(current)$; $CCC.add(x)$;   ▷ add the atomic change to the created candidate and then to the list of candidates
7: **for all** $c \in CCC$ **do**
          $List < ComplexChanges >= c.validate()$; ▷ validate the candidate complex changes to confirm and return only the valid ones

---

changes at each iteration, in the worst case at the end, $n * k$ candidates need to be validates. We evaluate the practical occurrence of this worst case in section 4.

Algorithm 1 answers to the requirement R3 by systematically creating in pass 1 all complex changes candidates that match the type and multiplicity of the pattern. Thus, the algorithm achieves full recall by construction. It is guaranteed to always return all complex changes, However, it may return false positives by returning multiple overlapping complex changes reusing the same atomic changes occurrences. Thus, we propose heuristics to rank the overlapping complex changes to help users to decide which ones are correct. These heuristics are discussed in section 2.5.

2.4 Application to Concrete Complex Changes

In the literature, over sixty complex changes are proposed [10]. We apply the detection algorithm for a list of seven complex changes: *move property, pull property, push property, extract super class, flatten hierarchy, extract class, and inline class* [10]. A study of the evolution of GMF[2] in practice, showed that these seven changes constitute 72% of all the complex changes used during the evolution of GMF [9,11]. Table 2 lists the seven complex changes and their definitions as a set of atomic changes following the *Definition 2*.

2.5 Prioritizing Between Overlapping Complex Changes.

We define three optional heuristics to rank overlapping changes and help the user to quickly choose which ones to keep. The input of each heuristic is just the list of overlapping complex changes. The output is the same list of changes but prioritized from most probable correct complex change to the least probable.

---

[2] Graphical Modeling Framework http://www.eclipse.org/modeling/gmf.

Table 2. Definitions of seven complex changes

Complex Changes	Set of Atomic Changes
Move Property	$SOACT$ = {delete property p[1..1], add property p'[1..1]} Conditions: $(p == p')\wedge (\exists\ reference \in p.class : reference.type = p'.class)$
Pull Property	$SOACT$ = {delete property p [1..*], add property p' [1..1]} Conditions: $(\forall\ p : p == p')\wedge$ $(\forall\ p : \exists\ inheritance \in p.class : inheritance.from == p'.class)$
Push Property	$SOACT$ = {add property p [1..*], delete property p' [1..1]} Conditions: $(\forall\ p : p == p')\wedge$ $(\forall\ p : \exists\ inheritance \in p.class : inheritance.from == p'.class)$
Extract Class	$SOACT$ = {add class c [1..1], add property p [1..*], delete property p' [1..*]} Conditions: $(\exists!p, \exists!p' : p == p')\wedge (\forall p, p.class == c)\wedge$ $(\forall p', \exists\ reference \in p'.class : reference.type == c)$
Inline Class	$SOACT$ = {add property p [1..*], delete property p' [1..*], delete class c [1..1]} Conditions: $(\exists!p, \exists!p' : p == p')\wedge, (\forall p', p'.class == c)\wedge$ $(\forall p, \exists\ reference \in p.class, reference.type == c)$
Extract Superclass	$SOACT$ = {add class c [1..1], delete property p' [1..*], add property p' [1..*]} Conditions: $(\forall\ p : \exists!p' : p == p')\wedge (\forall\ p' : p'.class == c)\wedge$ $(\forall\ p : \exists\ inheritance \in p.class : inheritance.from == c)\wedge$ $(\forall\ p'_1, p'_2 \in p', \forall\ p_1 \in p : p'_1 == p_1, \exists\ p_2 \in p : p'_2 == p_2 \wedge p_1.class == p_2.class)$ $\wedge(\forall\ p'_1, p'_2 \in p', \forall\ p : (p == p'_1 \wedge p == p'_2) \Rightarrow p'_1 == p'_2)$
Flatten Hierarchy	$SOACT$ = {add property p [1..*], delete property p' [1..*], delete class c [1..1]} Conditions: $(\forall\ p : \exists!p' : p == p')\wedge (\forall\ p' : p'.class == c)\wedge$ $(\forall\ p : \exists\ inheritance \in p.class : inheritance.from == c)\wedge$ $(\forall\ p'_1, p'_2 \in p', \forall\ p_1 \in p : p'_1 == p_1, \exists\ p_2 \in p : p'_2 == p_2 \wedge p_1.class == p_2.class)$ $\wedge(\forall\ p'_1, p'_2 \in p', \forall\ p : (p == p'_1 \wedge p == p'_2) \Rightarrow p'_1 == p'_2)$

The first case of overlap between complex changes is when the first one is fully contained into the second one. The following heuristic handles this case.

Containment Level (h1). This heuristic assigns a containment level to each member of an overlapping complex change set. A complex change of higher containment level is ranked higher than one of lower containment level. For example, an extract class of one property p from class Source to class Target, contains the complex change move property p from Source to Target that is also detected. The former gets a higher priority than the latter. Figure 3a shows an example of containment between n complex changes.

The second case of overlap, is when several complex changes share only part of their atomic changes. The following two heuristics handle this case.

Distance of a complex change (h2). The atomic changes making up a complex change can be contiguous or not within the atomic change trace. A user who pulls a property p from half of the sub classes, then performs other actions, before coming back to pull p from the rest of the sub classes is an example of complex change composed of non-contiguous atomic changes. Heuristic 2: $Distance = \frac{S_{CC}-1}{E_P-SP}$, is the *Size of the Complex Change* divided by the *difference between the End Position and the Start Position* of the complex change in the ET. The distance is between 1 and 0. The higher is the distance value, the likelier the complex change to be the intended one among overlapping candidates.

Solving Overlapping Rate (h3). Our third heuristic ranks higher complex changes which removal from the candidate list minimizes the number of overlapping changes in this list. Users can rely on this heuristic to remove the least

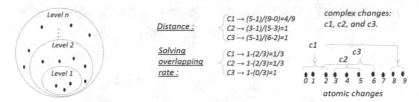

(a) Containment heuristic h1   (b) Distance and Solving rate heuristics h2 and h3

Fig. 3. Three prioritizing heuristics

possible complex changes. Heuristic 3: $SolvingOverlappingRate = 1 - \frac{N_{LOCC}}{N_{OCC}}$, where N_{LOCC} is the *Number of Left Overlapping Complex Changes* and N_{OCC} is the *Number of Overlapping Complex Changes*. The fraction represents the rate of the remaining overlapping complex changes when the current one is removed.

Examples of heuristics 2 and 3 are presented in Figure 3b. The three above heuristics answer the requirement R4.

3   Implementation

We extended the Praxis prototype [3] to support the detection of complex changes out of the recorded atomic changes. The algorithm and heuristics presented in Section 3 have been implemented as the Complex Change Detection Engine (CCDE) component and integrated within Praxis. It detects in the trace of atomic changes the seven most used complex changes we addressed in this paper based on their definitions in Table 2 (Other complex changes can easily be considered). The core functionalities of this component is implemented with Java (4946 LoC) and are packaged into an Eclipse plug-in that interfaces with the existing Praxis plug-ins.

Figure 4 displays a screenshot of this integration. Window (1) shows a metamodel drawn with EMF Ecore tool editor. Praxis builds the evolution trace of atomic changes while the user is evolving the metamodel as shown in Window (2). In Window (3) the CCDE detects complex changes over the atomic changes evolution trace and our heuristics can be used as a support for users. The final evolution trace contains both atomic and complex changes.

4   Evaluation

This section presents the evaluation of our approach. We first describe an experiment in which we use our tool to detect complex changes. After that we evaluate the quality of the approach based on the quality metrics in [14]: *precision, recall, and f-score*. Time performance and memory consumption are evaluated as well.

4.1   Experiment Set/Scenario

In our evaluation, we have chosen two real case studies. We first evaluate a real case study: UML Class Diagram (CD) evolution, in particular from version 1.5

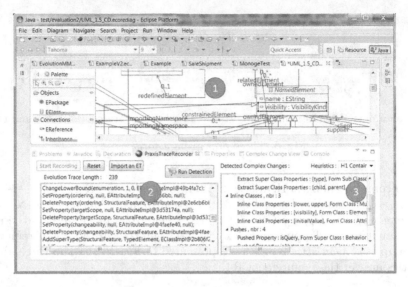

Fig. 4. Screenshot of the Tool

to 2.0, which contains significant changes. We manually analyzed beforehand the 238 atomic changes that leads UML CD 1.5 to 2.0 in order to know what are the expected complex changes. Without doing this analysis, we cannot assess the quality of detection of our tool, i.e. comparing what is expected against what is detected. In the UML CD case study, we expect 10 complex changes: 2 pulls properties, 4 pushes properties, 2 inlines class, and 2 extracts super class. The size of the UML CD metamodel 1.5 is of 143 elements.

For the second real case study we take the GMF graphical metamodel, GMF mapping metamodel, and GMF generator metamodels, all three making up the GMF metamodel. For the sake of simplicity, we will denote these three meta-models as "The GMF metamodel" in the rest of this paper. We thus consider the evolution of GMF metamodel from version 1.29 to version 1.74 that is inves-tigated in [9,11]. After we manually analyzed the 220 atomic changes that leads GMF 1.29 to 1.74, we expect in the GMF case study 10 complex changes: 1 move property, 2 pull properties, 3 push properties, 3 extracts super class, and 1 flatten hierarchy. The size of the GMF metamodel 1.29 is of 2339 elements.

To run the experiment, we take the UML CD 1.5 and the GMF 1.29 meta-models and we manually evolve them until versions UML CD 2.0 and GMF 1.74 are reached, while our tool records the modeling actions.

In this experiment, we measure the accuracy of our tool by using the three metrics [14] $precision = \frac{CorrectFoundChanges}{TotalFoundChanges}$, $recall = \frac{CorrectFoundChanges}{TotalCorrectChanges}$, $f-score = \frac{2*Recall*Precision}{Recall+Precision}$. The values of these metrics are between 0% and 100%. The higher the precision value, the smaller is the set of wrong detections (i.e. false positives). The higher the recall value, the smaller is the set of the complex changes that have not been detected (i.e. false negatives). f-score combines precision and recall into a single evaluation measure of the best trade-off between minimizing false positives and negatives. It is a useful metric since in most cases, methods manage to reach high precision with low recall and vice-versa. The higher the f-score the better the overall quality of our detection algorithm.

We measure the three quality metrics on the detected complex changes for the following cases: 1) without using the ranking heuristics defined in section 2.5, 2) using the heuristics separately. In our approach we do not remove complex changes from the overlapping list, but we only prioritize them with our heuristics, so that the user still has the chance to indicate that lower prioritized changes are correct instead of higher prioritized changes. While this prioritization supports the user, it does not impact the recall and precision. However, to nonetheless measure the quality of the heuristics, we simulate in this evaluation the situation that the user decides to keep only the highest prioritized changes. For the resulting list of complex changes we recalculate precision and recall. The whole process is performed once per heuristic.

Finally, we also measure the overall time of detection and memory consumption. We ran these experiments on a PC VAIO with i7 1.80 GHz Processor and 8GB of RAM with Windows 7 as OS.

4.2   Results

A. Without using heuristics. Figure 5 shows the results of the evaluation performed by our tool. Figure 5a shows the quality metrics on the raw detected complex changes without using heuristics. It shows 100% recall for both case studies UML CD and GMF metamodels evolutions without using any heuristics. This confirms the ability of our detection algorithm to reach our goal of a full recall that is essential in this paper.

In the UML CD case study, we detected 14 complex changes whereas we expected only 10. Three additional detected complex changes are due to the full overlapping issue when a change is contained in another one. In fact, each extract class, extract super class and flatten hierarchy respectively contain move, pull and push properties. Thus, in the UML CD case study, for each of the two applied extract super class, one of one reference and one of two references, we also detect three pulls of the same references that are incorrect.

One case of partly overlapping complex changes occurred in the UML CD case study, between one pull property *visibility* from sub classes `Feature` and `AssociationEnd` to super class `ModelElement`, and one unexpected inline class from `ElementOwnership` to `ModelElement` that contains the property *visibility*. They share only the add property *visibility* to the same class `ModelElement`. In this case, only the pull property *visibility* is correct and not the inline class. Thus, the precision is 10/14 that represents 71%.

In the GMF case study, we detected 16 complex changes whereas we expected only 10. All the six additional complex changes are due to the full overlapping issue. In the GMF evolution, we applied one extract super class of one reference that explains one additional pull reference. We also applied two extracts super class of two properties each that explain the four additional pull properties. For the one flatten hierarchy of one reference, we detect an additional push reference. Thus, the precision is 10/16, i.e. 63% as shown in Figure 5a. The overall f-score for the GMF and the UML CD case studies respectively reaches 78% and 87%.

B. Using only heuristic h1. Figure 5b shows the quality metrics after using the heuristic h1. For the GMF case study, h1 allows us to reach 100% of precision. This is possible since the case study contains only complex changes that overlap completely. The heuristic h1 ranks the additional push and pulls properties with a lower priority than the flatten hierarchy and the extracts super class, which are in our case study indeed the expected complex changes.

For the UML CD case study, h1 allows to reach 91% of precision (10/11), since the three additional pulls of a reference get a lower priority from h1 than the two expected extracts super class of the same references. Since the expected complex changes are ranked with the highest priority by h1, the recall thus stays 100% for both case studies. The f-score is improved to 95% and to 100% respectively for the UML CD and the GMF case studies.

C. Using only heuristic h2. Figure 5c shows the quality metrics after using the heuristic h2. For the GMF case study, h2 does not change the precision since there was no case of partly overlapping changes. However, for the UML CD case study, h2 allows to reach 77% of precision (10/13) by giving the highest priority to the pull property *visibility* that occurred at once in contrast to the unexpected inline class. Again, the recall stays unchanged for both case studies. The f-score reaches 87% for UML CD and stays unchanged for the GMF case study.

D. Using only heuristic h3. Figure 5d shows the results of the heuristic h3. It gives similar results as those when no heuristic is used, because h3 is useful when more than two complex changes partly overlap over different atomic changes, which is a situation that did not occur in our case studies. Note that for the UML CD case study, h3 fails to improve the precision by giving the same priority 1 that represents the rate of solving the overlap issue, to the two partly overlapping changes: the pull property *visibility* and the unexpected inline class.

E. Discussion. The results of the overall evaluation show that the recall is always 100% that denotes the completeness of our detection. The results also show that the heuristics h1 and h2 in some cases allow to improve the precision and thus the f-score. In the UML CD case study, we noticed five cases on *hidden* changes each by a rename action. Three properties in the two inlines class and two properties in the two extracts super class were all renamed afterward. One *hidden* change was noticed in the GMF case study regarding the one move property. Thus results of our detection engine would have been distorted if we have retrieved the atomic changes from the difference model.

In both case studies, the situation when a complex change partly overlap with other complex changes over different atomic changes, did not occur. Even though, it seems to be seldom in practice, we cannot exclude it. Heuristic h3 still could be useful in other case studies.

The evaluation experiments runs returned instantly and used insignificant memory. They detected all complex changes in less than 470 milliseconds over a trace of 220 atomic changes, while consuming less than 7.6 megabytes.

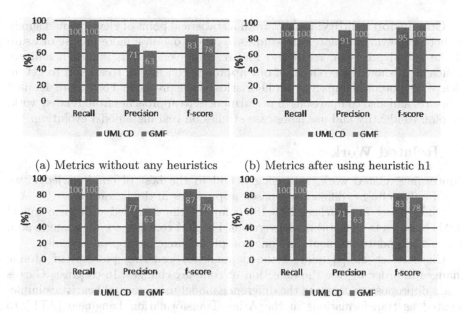

(a) Metrics without any heuristics   (b) Metrics after using heuristic h1

(c) Metrics after using heuristic h2   (d) Metrics after using heuristic h3

Fig. 5. Evaluation Results

4.3 Threats to Validity

Internal Validity: We had to apply the evolution of the metamodels ourselves to retrieve the ETs. We applied each complex change at once, i.e all its atomic changes were applied in sequence without being interrupted by other atomic changes. In consequence, the ET does not include cases where the actual expected change has a lower probability than 1 due to the distance between the involved atomic changes, which might lead to an over-estimation of the efficiency of the results for heuristic h2. However, we assume that only in seldom cases such a separate application at different timestamps happens. Therefore, this threat to validity is acceptable here. Yet, more experiments are needed to further evaluate the ranking heuristics. Furthermore, to be able to evaluate the benefit of the heuristics, we simulated the user choice by keeping only highest prioritized changes. Indeed a user might also decide differently. However, since we can assume that the user knows his intent, these deviating user decision can in practice only improve the precision compared to this evaluation.

External validity: The quality of the presented approach depends on the quality of the recorded trace, i.e. the logging mechanism of the underlying framework. This concerns correctness and granularity of the provided atomic changes. Thus, it is difficult to generalize the measured precisions, recalls, and f-scores for other modeling frameworks. However, since Ecore is one of the most used modeling frameworks, we think that this limitation is acceptable for now. In future work, we plan to evaluate on other modeling frameworks as well.

Conclusion validity: Finally, from a statistical point of view it would surely be better to evaluate more case studies in order to gain a more precise measure of the actual precision, recall and f-score. However, results gained herein are sufficient to show the strength of our approach concerning recall and to get an idea of the potential impact of our heuristics on the precision. For a more detailed measures and also comparisons of performances to approaches from related work, we plan to identify and use more case studies on real metamodel evolution.

5   Related Work

Concerning related work, surprisingly, and to the best of our knowledge, we found only delta i.e. differencing-based approaches in the literature.

Differencing approaches[12,16,18] compute the so-called difference model (DM) between two (meta) model versions.The DM contains atomic changes add, delete and updates element, and one complex change move property only.

Cicchetti et al. [4] address the dependency ordering problem of atomic changes in order to ease the detection of complex changes. In contrast, Garces et al. [6] propose to compute the difference model using several heuristics implemented as transformations in the Atlas Transformation Language (ATL) to detect atomic and also complex changes. Langer et al. [11] use graph-based transformation to define a complex change with the left-hand side (LHS) and the right-hand side (RHS). Garcia et al. [7] detect complex changes with predicates that check occurrences of atomic change class instances. The predicates are implemented as ATL transformation scripts for each complex change. However, neither [12] nor [17] address the complex changes of variable length. Vermolen et al. [17] propose to detect complex changes over a manually ordered sequence of atomic changes returned from a difference model. However, in contrast to [4,6,7,11], [17] consider the issue of variability inside a complex change.

All the previous approaches [4,6,7,11,17] are based on differencing approaches such as [12,16,18] or implement themselves a differencing approach as in [4,6]. Thus, they suffer from the drawbacks of non ordered, and potentially hidden changes. Only [4,17] considers the issue of atomic changes order in a difference model, by defining strategies to reorder the atomic changes. Only [17] considers the issue of hidden changes in a difference model by proposing to the user with some changes to add so that the effect of the evolution trace remains the same. In this paper, we overcome those two issues by relying on Praxis and recording the evolution trace at run-time.

No related work addresses the issue of overlapping changes. They thus cannot reach full recall in the general case. We tackle the overlap issue by proposing prioritization heuristics. To the best of our knowledge, we are the first to consider the overlap issue, to address it by proposing three ranking heuristics, and to cope simultaneously with the four above issues.

6   Conclusion and Future Works

In this paper, we addressed the topic of complex change detection when a metamodel evolves. We detect precisely complex changes by relying on the real evolution trace that is recorded by a user editing action observer. This approach has the advantage to preserve the evolution i.e. no changes are hidden from the detection. It thus supports full complex change recall, as shown in our evaluation. Relying on our tool, (meta) modelers are able to increase and to optimize the co-evolution percentage of artifact that relates to a metamodel, such as models. As mentioned previously, our approach can be applicable for object-oriented models in general, which can represent (1) the architecture of the system, (2) the design patterns on which it is based and (3) its data structures.

In a future work, we first aim to further improve the precision by optimizing the prioritizing heuristics and to propose new ones. In this paper, we applied the heuristics separately. Thus, we will assess how the precision is impacted by the different combinations of the heuristics.

Moreover, when recording the ET, there is a risk to record changes that cancel previous recorded changes. When there are ctrl-z events that undo the last changes, we can remove the last added changes from our ET. In case users perform a manual ctrl-z, we cannot deal with it. Yet, this does not impact the recall that remains 100%, but may lead to false positives. To cope with this issue, we will process the ET before the detection, searching for opposite changes that cancel each other and removing them from the ET.

Acknowledgments. The research leading to these results has received funding from the ANR French Project MoNoGe under grant FUI - AAP no. 15.

References

1. Bendraou, R., da Silva, M.A.A., Gervais, M.-P., Blanc, X.: Support for deviation detections in the context of multi-viewpoint-based development processes. In: CAiSE, pp. 23–31 (2012)
2. Blanc, X., Mougenot, A., Mounier, I., Mens, T.: Incremental detection of model inconsistencies based on model operations. In: van Eck, P., Gordijn, J., Wieringa, R. (eds.) CAiSE 2009. LNCS, vol. 5565, pp. 32–46. Springer, Heidelberg (2009)
3. Blanc, X., Mounier, I., Mougenot, A., Mens, T.: Detecting model inconsistency through operation-based model construction. In: ICSE 2008, pp. 511–520 (2008)
4. Cicchetti, A., Di Ruscio, D., Pierantonio, A.: Managing dependent changes in coupled evolution. In: Paige, R.F. (ed.) ICMT 2009. LNCS, vol. 5563, pp. 35–51. Springer, Heidelberg (2009)
5. da Silva, M.A.A., Blanc, X., Bendraou, R.: Deviation management during process execution. In: 26th IEEE/ACM ASE, pp. 528–531 (2011)
6. Garcés, K., Jouault, F., Cointe, P., Bézivin, J.: Managing model adaptation by precise detection of metamodel changes. In: Paige, R.F., Hartman, A., Rensink, A. (eds.) ECMDA-FA 2009. LNCS, vol. 5562, pp. 34–49. Springer, Heidelberg (2009)
7. García, J., Diaz, O., Azanza, M.: Model transformation co-evolution: a semi-automatic approach. In: Czarnecki, K., Hedin, G. (eds.) SLE 2012. LNCS, vol. 7745, pp. 144–163. Springer, Heidelberg (2013)
8. García, J., Dìaz, O., Cabot, J.: An adapter-based approach to co-evolve generated sql in model-to-text transformations. In: Jarke, M., Mylopoulos, J., Quix, C., Rolland, C., Manolopoulos, Y., Mouratidis, H., Horkoff, J. (eds.) CAiSE 2014. LNCS, vol. 8484, pp. 518–532. Springer, Heidelberg (2014)

9. Herrmannsdoerfer, M., Ratiu, D., Wachsmuth, G.: Language evolution in practice: the history of GMF. In: van den Brand, M., Gašević, D., Gray, J. (eds.) SLE 2009. LNCS, vol. 5969, pp. 3–22. Springer, Heidelberg (2010)
10. Herrmannsdoerfer, M., Vermolen, S.D., Wachsmuth, G.: An extensive catalog of operators for the coupled evolution of metamodels and models. In: Malloy, B., Staab, S., van den Brand, M. (eds.) SLE 2010. LNCS, vol. 6563, pp. 163–182. Springer, Heidelberg (2011)
11. Langer, P., Wimmer, M., Brosch, P., Herrmannsdorfer, M., Seidl, M., Wieland, K., Kappel, G.: A posteriori operation detection in evolving software models. Journal of Systems and Software **86**(2), 551–566 (2013)
12. Lin, Y., Gray, J., Jouault, F.: Dsmdiff: a differentiation tool for domain-specific models. European Journal of Information Systems **16**(4), 349–361 (2007)
13. OMG. Meta object facility (mof) (2011). http://www.omg.org/spec/MOF/
14. Rijsbergen, C.: Information retrieval. Butterworths (1979)
15. Steinberg, D., Budinsky, F., Merks, E., Paternostro, M.: EMF: eclipse modeling framework. Pearson Education (2008)
16. Toulmé, A.: Intalio Inc Presentation of emf compare utility. In: Eclipse Modeling Symposium, pp. 1–8 (2006)
17. Vermolen, S.D., Wachsmuth, G., Visser, E.: Reconstructing complex metamodel evolution. In: Sloane, A., Aßmann, U. (eds.) SLE 2011. LNCS, vol. 6940, pp. 201–221. Springer, Heidelberg (2012)
18. Xing, Z., Stroulia, E.: Umldiff: an algorithm for object-oriented design differencing. In: 20th IEEE/ACM ASE, pp. 54–65 (2005)

"We Need to Discuss the *Relationship*":
Revisiting Relationships as Modeling Constructs

Nicola Guarino[1] and Giancarlo Guizzardi[1,2(✉)]

[1] ISTC-CNR Laboratory for Applied Ontology (LOA), Trento, Italy
guarino@loa.istc.cnr.it, gguizzardi@inf.ufes.br
[2] Computer Science Department, Federal University of Espírito Santo (UFES), Vitória, Brazil

Abstract. In this paper we propose a novel ontological analysis of relations and relationships based on a re-visitation of a classic problem in the practice of conceptual modeling, namely *relationship reification*. Despite the two terms 'relation' and 'relationship' are often used interchangeably, we shall assume a radical difference between the two: a relation *holds*, while a relationship *exists*. Indeed, the relation holds *because* the relationship exists. We investigate the ontological the nature of relationships as *truthmakers*, proposing a view according to which they are *endurants*. Under this view, not only a relationship is responsible (with its existence) of the fact that a relation holds, but it also accounts (with its properties) of *the way a relation holds and develops in time*.

1   Introduction

"We need to discuss our relationship" is a statement that often occurs in our social every-day life. In such a context, a relationship is something that has its own life. Yet, in conceptual models relationships occur everywhere, but they tend to be considered as frozen entities. In this paper we argue for the need to (re)discuss the notion of relationship used in conceptual modeling, in order to better understand its ontological nature and to better capture the way it is used in describing application domains.

In his seminal paper [1], Chen describes relationships in E-R diagrams in the following manner: "*a relationship is an association among entities.* [However,] *it is possible that some people may view something (e.g., marriage) as an entity while other people may view it as a relationship. We think that this is a decision which should be made by the Enterprise Administrator*". In the same passage, Chen defines an Entity as a "thing" and claims that "*a specific person, a company, or an event is an example of an entity*". Further in the paper, he defines a *relationship type* as a "*mathematical relation*", that is, a set of tuples, and a relationship as one of such tuples. Chen also admits that relationships can bear properties. In one of his original examples, he illustrates how a *project-worker* relationship can have the attribute *percentage-of-time* representing an intrinsic property of the relationship itself.

We here subscribe to many of Chen's original intuitions. For example, as we argue in this paper, we agree with him on admitting that relationships can bear properties. However, in that paper, Chen does not take an explicit ontological stance on the very nature of relationships and, as a consequence, the real-world semantics of this

© Springer International Publishing Switzerland 2015
J. Zdravkovic et al. (Eds.): CAiSE 2015, LNCS 9097, pp. 279–294, 2015.
DOI: 10.1007/978-3-319-19069-3_18

construct (a fundamental one in his notation and in conceptual modeling, in general) is left underspecified. In a subsequent paper [2], he elaborates on some of these onto-logical aspects (albeit in an indirect form) via an analysis of the English sentence structure of textual descriptions. He states that entity types are the E-R counterpart of common nouns and that relationships are normally expressed by transitive verb phrases (e.g., *owns*, *belongs to*, *loves*). In addition, he recognizes that "nouns con-verted from a verb" (i.e., *verb nominalizations*) correspond to relationships (e.g., the *shipping* of the product to a customer or the *assigning* of an employee to a machine). Now, since verbs are typically the language proxy for events (including actions), it seems at first that Chen is committed to the view that relationships are events. Yet, in the very same paper he brings examples of relationship names such as *location of* or *part of*, which may not obviously correspond to events.

In any case, events are ontologically very different from tuples, so a question-begging issue that seems to be present since these early seminal papers on Conceptual Modeling is: what is a *relationship* after all? Is it just a tuple? Is it an event? Or is it something else? Moreover, is the difference between Entities and Relationships only a matter of a pragmatic modeling, as Chen seems to suggest, or there are aspects of the intrinsic nature of "real-world" entities that would justify such distinction?

In this paper we shall address the issues above by proposing a novel ontological analysis of relations and relationships based on a re-visitation of a classic problem in the practice of conceptual modeling, namely *relationship reification*. Despite the two terms 'relation' and 'relationship' are often used interchangeably, we shall assume a radical difference between the two: a relation *holds*, while a relationship *exists*. In-deed, our idea is that the relation holds *because* the relationship exists. A relationship is therefore a *truthmaker* [3] for the corresponding relation. However, as we shall see, such a truthmaker, in our view, not only is responsible (with its existence) of the fact that the relation holds, but it also accounts (with its properties) for *the way a relation holds and develops in time*. This means that a relationship includes aspects whose existence *entails* that the relation holds, as well as aspects whose existence is a *conse-quence* of the fact that the relation holds. So, when a worker works in a project as a result of job assignment, a new object emerges, in addition to the two *relata* (the worker and the project), whose properties and internal structure reflect, at each time, not only the *obligation* the worker has (which entails that the relation holds), but also the actual effort invested, the degree of satisfaction or stress, and so on. The latter aspects are indeed a *consequence* of the obligation, and together contribute to de-scribe the *way* the relation develops.

Our main claim is that relationships (at least those mostly interesting for us) are objects (*endurants*). The basic intuitions behind this claim were already present in Guizzardi's early works [4,5], later advanced in [6] and with an alternative version in [7]. In such works, reified relationships are conceptualized as *relators,* which are endurants of a special kind, with the power of connecting (*mediating*) other endurants. In this paper we shall revisit the foundations of this early work, investigating and clarifying the very nature of relators in the light of the notion of truthmaking, and ultimately identifying them with relationships. We shall also discuss the subtle connections between relationships, relations and events, and their implications on the practice of conceptual modeling.

The paper is structured as follows. In section 2, we revisit the notion of truthmaking and use it to briefly outline a typology of relations. We isolate a class of relations particularly relevant for conceptual modelling –*extrinsic relations*– and movivate the practical need to reify the corresponding relationships as truthmakers. In section 3, we explore more in detail the complex nature of such truthmakers. First, on ontological and linguistic grounds, we reject *facts* and tuples as alternatives. Then we also reject perdurants (event-like entities) as an alternative. In section 4 we investigate further the nature of relationships. We show that these are indeed *thing-like entities* and that they behave very much like all other thing-like entities. In particular, they can maintain their identity in time while possibly changing in a qualitative manner. In other words, we claim that relationships are *full-fledged endurants*, and as such they are the natural bearers of modal properties. In section 5, we explore some consequences of this view on the practice of conceptual modeling. We show that, by taking relationships as endurants, we have that their types can be organized in taxonomic structures exactly like object types, according to well-known and tested ontology-driven conceptual modeling design patterns. We also revisit a well-known approach towards relationship reification in conceptual modeling and show how our framework supports an ontological analysis and conceptual clarification of that approach. Finally, section 6 presents some final considerations for the paper.

2   Relationships as Truthmakers (of a Certain Kind)

2.1   Truthmakers and Kinds of Truthmaking

To start our analysis on the ontology of relations and relationships, we introduce the notion of *truthmaker*. We say that propositions, such as (*p1*) *"a is an apple"* or (*p2*) *"a is red"*, are *truthbearers,* in the sense that they can be either true or false, depending on what happens in the world. A *truthmaker* for one of such propositions is an entity in virtue of whose existence the proposition is true. There are several attempts to capture formally the notion of truthmaking [3], but for our purposes we shall take it as primitive, as a fundamental relation linking what is true to what exists. More in general, a truthmaker for a property or a relation is an entity in virtue of whose existence that property or relation holds. Suppose that in (*p1*) *a* denotes a particular apple. The very existence of *a* is enough for making the proposition true, so *a* is a truthmaker of *p1*. For *p2*, in contrast, the mere existence of *a* is only indirectly responsible of *p2*'s truth, since it is in virtue of the specific *way* the apple is (and not just in virtue of the apple's existence) that *p2* is true. In particular, there is something *inhering* to *a*, which we may call *a's redness*, which makes *a* red. Some philosophers term this redness an individualized property, or a *trope* (see also [8]). According to them, it is in virtue of such trope that the *red* property holds, so the trope (and not the apple) is the truthmaker. So, *being an apple* and *being red* are properties whose truthmakers are of a very different nature. We shall say that the former is a *formal property*, while the latter is a *qualitative property*. Formal properties account for *what* something is; qualitative properties account for *how* something is.

Let us shift now our focus from unary properties to (binary) relations. As we have anticipated, our first answer to the question discussed above, *"What are relationships, after all?"* is that *relationships are truthmakers of relations*. The nature and structure of such truthmakers determine different kinds of relations. A first kind is that of *formal relations*, whose arguments jointly constitute a truthmaker. For instance, the *successor-of* relation between integers is a formal relation, since it holds because of very nature of its arguments. In contrast, *qualitative relations* are those whose truthmaking depends on the existence of something in addition to the relata. Among qualitative relations, we include relations such as *being-taller-than*, whose truthmaking depend on particular intrinsic properties of the relata (i.e., their individual heights). In other words, the truthmaking of these relations depends solely on their intrinsic height tropes, i.e., no *relational trope* is involved. We term these *intrinsic relations*. In this paper, we are interested in a class of qualitative relations that are of far greater relevance to conceptual modeling, i.e., the so-called *extrinsic (or material) relations* [5].

Differently from intrinsic relations, the truthmakers of *extrinsic relations* are entities that are truly relational in nature, i.e., that cannot be reduced to intrinsic properties of the relata. These entities can only exist while connecting the relata, i.e., they exhibit mutual dependency patterns involving all the arguments, as well as dependencies on external entities besides the arguments. *Married-with* is a prototypical example of an extrinsic relation. For this relation to hold between John and Mary, we need more than the existence of John, Mary and their intrinsic properties. We need the occurrence of a wedding event (or the signing of a social contract), which, in turn, bestows John and Mary with individual qualities (e.g., commitments, claims, rights, obligations) that are truly relational in nature. For instance, a particular commitment of John towards Mary is a quality of John (inhering in John) but which is also existentially dependent on Mary.

Recognizing extrinsic relations is of fundamental importance for conceptual modeling. Firstly, because most of the relations represented in conceptual models are of this sort. For instance, *enrollments, employments, purchases, employee allocation to projects* and *presidential mandates* are of the very same ontological nature as the *marriage* in the previous paragraph, in strong contrast to relations such as *being-older-than* or *successor-of*. Secondly, as discussed in depth in [5,6], extrinsic relations must be represented in conceptual models differently from intrinsic relations. In particular, extrinsic relations cannot be suitably represented just as "mathematical relations", i.e., as sets of tuples. In the sequel, we elaborate on this issue.

2.2   The Need for Explicitly Representing Truthmakers of Extrinsic Relations

Take for instance the example discussed in [5] of a *treated-in* relation between *Patient* and *Medical Unit*. This is clearly neither a formal nor an intrinsic relation. For this relation to hold, it requires the existence of a third entity, such as an individual Treatment involving somehow a Patient and a Medical unit. So, independently of the nature of such third entity (which will be discussed in the rest of the paper), this is enough to classify this relation as an extrinsic relation. The presence of such third entity is at the origin of a specific practical problem, mentioned in [9] that affects the representation of extrinsic relations just as standard associations. In this particular example, let us assume we represent our relation as an association such that each patient can be treated in one-to-many medical units and that each unit can treat one-to-many patients. The problem is that these constraints are ambiguous, since many different interpretations can be given to it, including the following: (i) a patient is related to only one treatment in which possibly several medical units participate; (ii) a patient can be related to several treatments to which only one single medical unit participates; (iii) a patient can be related to several treatments to which possibly several medical units participate; (iv) several patients can be related to a treatment to which several medical units participate, and a single patient can be related to several treatments. To disambiguate among these different interpretations, we need a way to express constraints concerning how many patients and medical units can interact at each instance of the relation. In the literature, such constraints have been called *single tuple constraints* [9]. However, these constraints do not concern the single tuple, but the material conditions that justify the presence of that tuple in the relation, i.e., its truthmaker. So, to solve the problem, we must explicitly represent this truthmaker, i.e., the *treatment* itself.

This was indeed the solution adopted in [5], shown in Fig. 1, where the treatment is reified as a *relator*. As discussed in [4,5], the relation stereotyped as ‹‹*mediation*›› in fig.1 is a special type of existential dependence relation (a treatment only exists if both a patient and a medical unit exists). The figure also reports a dashed arc connectning the relator to the association between Patient and Medical Unit. This represents the *derivation* relation between a truthmaker and the tuples derived from it. In a nutshell, when a relation *R* is *derived* from a relator type *T*, then, for every *x*, *y*, *R(x,y)* holds if there is an instance *t* of *T* such that *mediates(t,x)* and *mediates (t,y)* hold. Both dependence and derivation are examples of formal relations.

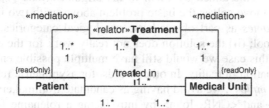

Fig. 1. Reifying Treatment as a relator solves the cardinality ambiguity problem (from [5])

In conclusion, we can see that by adopting the solution exemplified by Fig. 1 the cardinality ambiguity problem dissolves, since we can easily express the constraints on the number of patients and units involved in a single treatment. As demonstrated in [5], this problem manifests itself *for all extrinsic relations, and only for them.*

In summary, by recognizing extrinsic relations and reifying them as 'relators' we are able to address a number of classical problems related to the modeling of relations. These range from eliminating the ambiguity between *association specialization, subsetting and redefinition* [6] to solving the problem of transitivity of part-whole relations [4]. Independently of these modeling benefits, however, some fundamental questions still remain: what is the ontological nature of such relators? If they are truthmakers, what kind of truthmakers? How do they account for our idea of relationships as *ways* relations develop in time? This is the topic of next section.

3   What Kind of Truthmakers?

3.1   Are Relationships Facts?

One of the most common assumptions in conceptual modeling is that relationships are actually *facts*. Indeed, modeling approaches such as ORM [10] are normally called *fact-based approaches*. As we shall see, there are different ways of understanding relational facts, but none of them turns out to adequately account for the notion of relationship as truthmaker.

Suppose first that each instance of a relation (a tuple) directly represents a fact. So, for the relation *is-employed-by*, the tuple *<John, CNR>* represents the fact that John is employed by CNR. Take now the inverse relation *employs*. According to our assumption, the tuple *<CNR, John>* represents a different fact, since it is a different tuple. Indeed, the fact that John is employed at CNR is usually considered as different from the fact that CNR employs John, although, as argued in [11], in the world we have only one truthmaker, namely a state of affairs being described in two different ways. So, if we take that a relationship is just a syntactic instance of a relation, i.e., a tuple, then it cannot be a truthmaker.

A possibility to overcome the problem above is to associate specific roles to the arguments of the relation, so that the arguments' order is not crucial any more. This seems to be the position adopted by ORM and UML (with rolenames tied to association ends) and also entertained by Chen in his original article [1]. As discussed in depth in [11], this move solves the basic problem above, with two important caveats: (i) it makes *rolenames* as part of our basic ontological categories, instead of just a mere description tool; (ii) the solution does not really work for the case of symmetric relations, since in this case we would still have multiple possible entities standing for the same basic situation in reality. In other words, for asymmetric relations such as *is-employed-by* and *employs*, we avoid having as candidate truthmakers the distinct entities <John, CNR> and <CNR, John> by introducing a rolename for each argument position, say 'Employee' and 'Employer', and a unique entity that assigns the two relata to them {John→Employee, CNR→Employer}. However, for the case of symmetric relations such as *brother-of*, we would still have two distinct entities: {John→Brother1, Paul→Brother2} and {John→Brother2, Paul→Brother1} [11].

However, even ignoring (i) and (ii) above, there are more cogent reasons for ruling out the assumption that relationships are facts. In [3], Moltmann discusses a distinction between different types of *nominalizations*. Nominalization is the linguistic process of turning expressions of various categories into nouns. Examples include *John's wisdom*, *Mary's beauty*, *John and Mary's marriage*. In the case of relational expressions (such as the latter), these nominalizations are equivalent to relation reification as treated in the conceptual modeling literature. One of the issues addressed by Moltmann concerns the semantics of such nominalizations: they refer to particulars, but what kind of particulars? She contrasts three options for these referents: *(1) facts*, *(2) events*, and *(3) qualities*. On the basis of linguistic evidence, she then rejects option 1.

According to option 1, *Clara's enrollment at UNITN* would mean *the fact that Clara is enrolled at UNITN*. The problem, however, is that facts, by their very nature, are completely determined entities. In order to illustrate this point, let us consider the model of Fig. 2 below, which depicts an enrollment relationship with two optional attributes. If relationships are just facts, a possible instance of this model would be f_1: *the fact that Clara studies at UNITN*. However, suppose that at a later point we learn that Clara has a 9.5 GPA. Now, f_2: *the fact that Clara studies at UNITN with a 9.5 GPA* is clearly a different fact. Furthermore, if we learn later that Clara has accumulated 250 credits, we have f_3: *the fact that Clara studies at UNITN with 250 credits*, as well as f_4: *the fact that Clara studies at UNITN with a 9.5 GPA and 250 credits*. In other words, the creation of these multiple facts obscures the important issue that there is one single entity in reality, namely, Clara's enrollment at UNITN, underlining these facts. In contrast, when the referent of a nominalization is an event (option 1) or a quality (option 2), we have a concrete object of reference whose properties can be progressively uncovered and described. For instance, we linguistically accept *Peter described Clara's talk* and *Peter admired Clara's beauty*, but not *Peter described the fact that Clara gave a talk*, nor *Peter admired the fact that Clara was beautiful*.

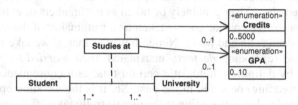

Fig. 2. Interpreting relationships as Facts

In conclusion, we think Moltmann brings enough evidence to discard facts as truthmakers of relations. The other two alternatives, events and qualities, deserve a bit of discussion. First of all, the use of the term 'quality' while referring to Moltmann's work is our choice, since she uses the term 'trope', admitting however that her tropes "are not tropes as most commonly understood". We believe that *individual qualities* in the sense of DOLCE [12] (or the so-called *moment persistents* in UFO [4]) are what she has in mind. Indeed, in her view qualities are understood as abstractions from tropes, which (differently from standard tropes) can change while maintaining their identity. For instance, in a sentence like *the color of the apple is changing*, we seem to make cognitive sense of an aspect of the apple that maintains its identity while changing in a qualitative way. After all, it is not 'red' that is changing; there is something there that changes while keeping existing as the referent for *the color of the apple*.

Now, coming to the difference between events and qualities from the point of view of their aptitude to act as truthmakers for relations, Moltmann highlights that qualities are capable of genuine changes while maintaining their numerical identity, while events are not. This latter point is further explored in next section.

3.2   Are Relationships Events?

At least since Chen's paper, the idea that relationships are events has been often implicitly present in the conceptual modeling literature. After all, entities like marriages, contracts, enrollments, from a linguistic point of view are verbal nominalizations, whose most obvious semantics, as discussed above, would be that of events (note that we use 'event' here in its most general sense, i.e., as a synonym of 'perdurant').

Before investigating the viability of this idea, let us first discuss a particular type of event that can be a candidate for our purposes, namely, what we call an *episode*. Suppose that *John runs* between 8:00 and 8:45 tonight. Any temporal subpart of this event (up to certain granularity) is an instance of a running event. Having such multitude of entities can cause many problems for conceptual modeling, in particular in the unambiguous specification of cardinality constraints, in a way similar to the problems of modeling quantities and collectives discussed in depth in [4]. For this reasons, we introduce the notion of *episode* as an event that is maximal given a certain unity criterion, i.e., given an episode *e* instantiating a property *P*, there is no event *e'* of which *e* is part such that *e'* also instantiates *P*. So, in our example, if John runs in a certain time interval there is at least one *running* episode that overlaps with that interval.

Consider now *relational* episodes, i.e., episodes involving multiple disjoint participants being in a certain relation. Clearly the existence of an *episode of being in relation R* entails that *R* holds for the time the episode lasts, so episodes (differently from *facts*, as discussed above) can genuinely be taken as truthmakers of extrinsic relations. For instance, a *marriage* episode can be taken as a truthmaker of the *married-to* relation holding between John and Mary. Notice however that, if we take marriage in the institutional sense (excluding *de facto* marriages), then *married-to* is an historical relation, which, by definition, holds at a certain time as a consequence of a specific episode (say, a wedding) occurred in the past. So, it is the wedding episode, and not the marriage episode, that is the ultimate (minimal) truthmaker of the *married-to* relation. Which of the two truthmakers shall we pick up as a candidate for the married-to relationship? To avoid the impasse we need to introduce a very plausible principle: a relationship is a truthmaker of a relational proposition *that lasts as long as the proposition holds*. In other words, a relationship is a *synchronous* truthmaker of a relation.

The principle above reconciles our general assumption that a relationship is a truthmaker of a relation with the hypothesis that a relationship is an episode. The question remains, however, whether this latter hypothesis suits our intuitions on relationships. Consider again the *marriage* episode. In our everyday talk (as the title of the present paper suggests), we say that a marriage relationship changes while it develops in time: it becomes more litigious or more passionate, new obligations arise because of children, and so on. Now, what is the subject of such changes? Clearly it cannot be the marriage episode, which, according to classical theories of events, is a 'frozen' extensional entity defined by the sum of its parts [13,14]. Indeed, in the traditional literature, a key difference between endurants and events is that the former can genuinely *change* in time while maintaining their identity [12], while the latter can just *vary* in time by exhibiting different properties for their temporal parts. So, if we model the marriage as an event (an episode), if it is peaceful at t_1 and litigious at t_2 it has two different temporal parts that bear otherwise incompatible properties. There is nothing that is entirely present throughout the duration of the marriage, and this is especially problematic while the episode is ongoing, since we have no way to say that the two parts at t_1 and at t_2 belong to *the same* marriage. A further problem concerns modal properties, which we often ascribe to relationships: could a marriage have been different from what it is, allowing us to consider counterfactual situations (e.g., *would their marriage have been different had they moved to Australia*)? Again, according to classical theories of events, we are forced to answer *no* to these questions. An event could not have been different from what it is.

In conclusion, conceiving relationships as episodes captures only partially our intuition that a relationship accounts for the way a relation holds and develops in time, because of the difficulties of properly modeling change. Yet, the explicit introduction of relational episodes in conceptual modeling can be extremely effective as a way to reify relationships in all those cases where we are only interested in keeping track of such episodes, without being interested in modeling change phenomena within them. For instance, the explicit introduction of a commitment episode for modeling services turned out to be very useful [15], although to describe complex service dynamics we adopted a different approach [16], based the notion of relator as described below.

4   Relationships as Full-Fledged Endurants

In the following, we shall elaborate on a different notion of relationships that conceives them as truthmakers of a special kind, namely endurants consisting of bundles of individual qualities, revising and extending Guizzardi's previous work.

Going back to one of Chen's original examples, consider the following proposition: a worker w *works-in* project p, as a result of an assignment event a. What are the truthmakers of such proposition? As we have seen, there is a minimal (asynchronous) truthmaker, the event a, and a synchronous truthmaker, a working episode e. Both are perdurants. There is however another synchronous truthmaker, which is an endurant: the *obligation* (o) the worker w has to work in p. This can be seen as a *relational quality* inhering in w. Its very existence at a certain time entails that the relation *works-in* holds at that time. Notice however that the permanence of the obligation to work in a certain project does not necessarily mean that the worker actually works there, so let's assume that 'works in' actually means 'is supposed to work in'. Indeed, we can consider another relational quality inhering in w, namely w's actual amount of *labour* currently (l) spent to fulfill o in the context of p. Clearly, l is dependent on the existence of o, besides being existentially dependent on p. Another relational quality depending on o may be w's degree of satisfaction while fulfilling o in the context of p. Other relational qualities existentially depending on o may emerge later, such as the collaboration attitude towards a new co-worker. Moreover, we have also qualities on the side of p depending on o, such as the amount of work assigned to w.

We see that, collectively, all these qualities (which are endurants, changing in time) describe in a very fine-grained way how the *works-in* relation develops in time, which is exactly our view of a relationship. Within these qualities, we can isolate a *nucleus*, in virtue of whose existence the relation holds, and a *shell* that is existentially dependent on the nucleus. We define a relationship as *an endurant that, at each time the relation holds, is constituted by the mereological sum of all these qualities* (the nucleus plus the shell). Thanks to this construction, we can see a relationship as a truthmaker of a certain kind, which accounts of the way a relation holds. In short, *a relationship is the particular way a relation holds* for a particular set of relata.

The summary of this discussion is illustrated in Fig. 3. Fig. 3a illustrates the inherence relation (i) between a worker, John, and those qualities of him that contribute to constitute the relationship with project *P#1*. We distinguish a nucleus of qualities that are directly existentially dependent (ed) on *P#*1, and a shell of qualities which, depending on the nucleus, are indirectly existentially dependent on *P#*1. Fig. 3b shows how the relationship, being a truthmaker of the *works-in* relation, mediates (m) between John and *P#1*.

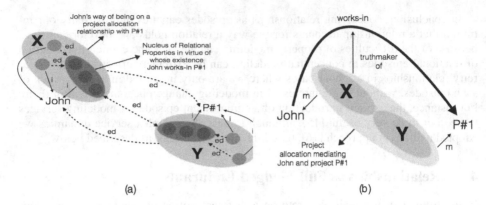

Fig. 3. (a) Relators (relationships) and their constituent relational qualities; (b) relators (relationships) as truthmakers of relations by mediating their relata

Let us now discuss the innovation with respect to the former work on relators. First, in the most recent formalization [7], relators where defined as sums of tropes. This played an important role in supporting reasoning in languages such as OWL. However, as we have seen (Section 3.1), classically speaking, tropes cannot change. In the present account (which makes justice of the original intuition [4]), since relationships are mereological sums of qualities and not tropes, they can change in all aspects in which their constituent qualities can change. For instance, an enrollment can change its accumulated credits or its GPA, and a medical treatment can change its cost. Note that, being an endurant, each relationship is an instance of a *kind*, which accounts for its identity conditions through time, determining the admissible extent of such changes. These kinds can be specialized and organized in various ways around distinctions such as those proposed by OntoClean and OntoUML (see discussion in section 5).

A further limitation of the original theory of relators was that it did not explicitly allow having relators that lose and gain qualities. Here we have defined a relationship as *constituted*, at each time it exists, by a mereological sum of qualities. Hence a relationship is a *variable embodiment* [17], which may have different constituent qualities at different times. So not only such qualities can have different values (qualia) at different times, but also that some of these qualities (those belonging to the shell) can cease to exist or come into being during the life of the relationship, exactly like the non-essential parts of a mechanical assembly. For instance, a service contract can contingently be insured, acquiring a 'level of insurance' quality.

Another innovation with respect to the previous approach concerns the role of *founding events* in determining the nature of relators. In Guizzardi's previous work, the focus was on relationships that hold as a consequence of an event (like the marriage as a consequence of a wedding), and the joint dependence on a single founding event was the unity criterion used to hold all the relator's qualities (or tropes) together. In our present view, since the identity of the nuclear qualities is given by the relator's kind and the non-nuclear qualities are just those dependent on the nucleus, the existence of a founding event is not required anymore, so the idea of relationships as endurants also applies to instantaneous relationships, such a ball hitting the floor.

Concerning the generality of this view, however, we have to observe that relators exist only for *genuine* relationships (as opposite to so-called *Cambridge relationships* [18]), which somehow impact on the properties of at least one of the relata. This means that the historical relationship existing between John and, say, a street he inadvertently crossed several years ago still has an (uninteresting) episode as a truthmaker, but none of John's qualities (and none of the street's qualities) keep memory of this, so to speak, so there is no relator. Indeed, the absence of a relator would mark the fact that the relationship is an uninteresting one.

On a final note, we should briefly comment on the connection between relationships and events (episodes). As we take (in general) events as manifestations of qualities, relational episodes are manifestations of relationships. The way the relation's arguments *participate* to the episode depends on the qualities constituting the relationship. For example, the *marriage episode* between John and Mary is the manifestation of the qualities constituting the marriage relationship [14]. Using a different terminology, we say that when an event is a manifestation of certain qualities, such qualities are the *focus* of that event. So *a relationship is the focus of a relational episode.*

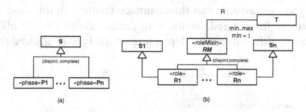

(a)   (b)

Fig. 4. Examples of OntoUML patterns for modeling taxonomic structures involving object types: (a) the phase pattern; (c) the role mixin pattern [20]

5   Practical Implications to Conceptual Modeling

5.1   Ontological Distinctions Applied to Relationship Types

Modal meta-properties play a fundamental role in conceptual modeling and ontology engineering. Indeed, in methodologies such as OntoUML [4] and OntoClean [19], there are a number of (meta)categories of types which are differentiated in terms of their modal meta-properties. For instance, while a *kind* such as *person* applies to its instances necessarily, a *phase* such as *teenager* or a *role* such as *student* apply to its instances only contingently. In other words, an instance of a person cannot cease to instantiate that type without ceasing to exist. In contrast, instances of a *phase* (teenager, living person) or *role* (student, employee) can move in an out of the extension of these classes without any impact of their identity. The ontology of types that underlies these approaches (containing these distinctions among many others) has proven to be one the most productive conceptual tools in ontology engineering [4, 19]. However, this ontology of types has been mainly used so far to structure *object* types (i.e., types of independent entities), and not *moment* types (i.e., types of dependent entities like qualities or relators). The choice of considering relationships as endurants, admitting genuine changes and modal properties, allows us to adopt for them the same general patterns that have proved very useful for modeling objects in these approaches.

For example, as discussed in [20], OntoUML has a pattern that is specific for modeling the connection between relator (relationship) types, relata types and derived material (extrinsic) relations (Fig. 1b). Now, if relators (relationships) are fully integrated in our ontology as genuine endurants, contingent types such as *phases*, *roles* and *role mixins* can also be used to model these types of individuals. As a consequence, for instance, a number of ontological patterns pertaining to the OntoUML language and related to the modeling of these types (e.g., those depicted in Fig. 4) can also be combined with the one in Fig. 1b [20]. Among these patterns, in particular, the *role mixin pattern* of Fig. 4b has proved effective for solving a classical recurrent problem regarding the modeling of roles [4, 20].

The model of Fig. 5 is an example of combination of these patterns. In this model, while *Enrollment* defines a certain *kind* of relationship (relator), *Active Enrollment* defines a phase for an enrollment. Supposing that some enrollments can be subject to insurance, thus entitling both relata to a certain rights, an *Insured Enrollment* is modeled as a role played by an Enrollment in a relation with an insurer. In fact, given that an insurer could insure a different kinds of relationships, we could apply here the role mixin pattern of Fig. 4b. In this model, both Enrollments and Employments can be insured. Here again, we assume that the insurance (policy) in this case entitles all the entities mediated by the insured relator with certain claims, while allowing for the possibility of having different claims depending on the type of insured relator.

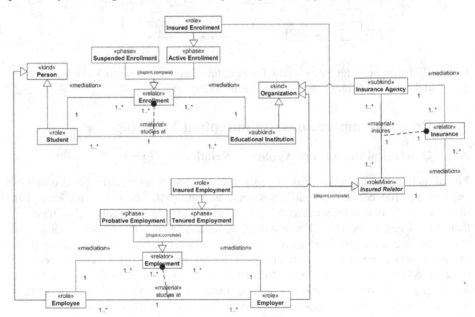

Fig. 5. An example of an extended OntoUML diagram with relator types

5.2   Olivé on Relationship Reification

In [21], Olivé discusses the issue of relationship reification and elaborates on the connection between reified relationships and their temporal properties. In that paper, he discusses the same example we have used above, namely the *works-in* relation. He assumes that, for each day a person works in a project, the number of hours worked is recorded (a day is conceptualized as a time point, i.e., as an atomic time interval). Moreover, for each convex time interval (i.e., continuous sequence of days) someone works in a project, he is assigned to a single task and has a single pre-fixed deadline. Finally, for the whole (non-convex) time interval the person works in a project, he has the same role and the same manager. Olivé then proposes three different types of temporal relationship reifications: *(1) per instant*: the relationship *r* is reified into a different entity *e* for each time point at which *r* holds. In this example, for each working day in a given project, we have a different entity *e* capturing the work in that day; *(2) per interval*: a relationship *r* is reified into a different entity *e'* for each (convex) temporal interval during which *r* holds. In this example, according to Olivé, *e'* can then capture properties such as the actual behavior with respect to deadlines and objectives; *(3) per life span:* a relationship *r* is reified into a single entity *e"*, which is the same during the whole life span of *r*. In this example, *e"* can then capture properties such as assigned role and manager.

In light of our discussion, an obvious question that comes to mind is: what kind of ontological entities these different types of reifications are intended to represent? If we take (1), in the solution presented by Olivé, the reified relationship (*workDay* by Olivé, although *work@Day* would be clearer) may have properties such as *hoursWorked* and (zero-to-many) *producedDeliverables*. Olivé highlights two meta-properties of this entity: it is instantaneous and can only exist in that instant. Given the chosen name (and these meta-properties), a salient interpretation is that the reified entity represents an *episode*. Since episodes cannot change in a qualitative way, then both the attributes *hoursWorked* and *producedDeliverables* are immutable. Now, if the instances of *workDay* are only recorded in *a posteriori* manner (which seems to be case since days are assumed to be instantaneous and mereologically atomic) then the only reason for representing them is to have a historical view on these relations. Thus, according to our framework, an instance of *WorkDay* is a fully determined entity and can be interpreted as an historical event or an historical fact derived from it (e.g., the fact that John worked 10 hours and produced deliverables d_1 and d_2 in March 20th, 2013). Also, in this case, of course the event only happens because of pre-existing endurants (e.g., capacities, rights, obligations) of the employee. In other words, also here, the *WorkDay* event is the manifestation of the *person-qua-employee's* qualities.

Let us take now case (2). In this case, Olivé's solution produces an entity termed *assignment* (which could perhaps be named *continuous assignment*), connecting an Employee and a Project for a continuous period of time. In this second case, representing an *assignment* as an episode may have some limitations, exactly because the *assignment* relationship may have modal and temporal properties: e.g., assignments can be fulfilled before the deadline or be delayed; can be realized in different ways (more or less accurately), can change in time in a qualitative way (for instance, the number of actual worked hours per day can change), can be suspended (because of an illness) or re-negotiated. In fact, an *Assignment* can even fail to manifest at all (for example, if the employee fails to actually work in the project).

Finally, let us analyze case (3). In that case, Olivé's solution reifies the relationship by something termed *participation*. Unlike cases (1) and (2), however, a participation is not correlated to a convex time interval. In other words, a participation can be active or inactive, being hence correlated with multiple disconnected time intervals. In this case, we believe that the most salient interpretation of this relationship is that of a complex bundle of commitments that can change qualitatively in many ways (e.g., in the number of working hours, or in the money paid per worked hour), can bear modal properties (e.g., being active or not because of medical leave) and can be manifested by a number of possible processes. In these different possible processes a person can have different task assignments, which can be fulfilled or not, with different performance evaluations, in different dates with different amounts of effort, etc.

The understanding of relationships proposed in this article allows us to analyze and clarify a number of interesting points regarding Olivé's proposal. In particular, reified relationships do clearly stand for episodes (events) only in the case of reification per instant. In the other cases, when the reified entity is possibly the subject of changes or modal properties, it is an endurant that is being represented. In any case, even when only a perdurant is represented, there are always some endurants (e.g., capacitites, dispositions, qualities, commitments) that are responsible for the happening of that perdurant [14].

6   Final Considerations

In this paper, we have contributed to the theory and practice of conceptual modeling by addressing one of its most fundamental constructs, namely, *relationships*. On the theoretical side, we have first used the notion of truthmaking to isolate a particular class of relations that are of fundamental relevance for conceptual modeling, namely, extrinsic relations. By pointing to the fact that these relations rely on external truthmakers (i.e., truthmakers that are neither the relata themselves nor are reduceable to their instrinsic properties), we have shown that these relations need a special representation treatment, i.e., the corresponding relationships need to be reified. Then, we have systematically investigated the nature of this reified entity. On ontological and linguistic grounds, we have eliminated facts as possible truthmakers of these relations, and argued for the limited practical utility of taking episodes as representatives of reified relationships, since they can't account for temporal and modal changes. So, we have defended a view according to which relationships are relational truth-makers *of a certain kind*: they are full-fledged endurants, i.e., thing-like entities that change in time while maintaining their identity, accounting for the *way* a relation holds and develops in time. Then we have explored the *internal structure* of such endurants, analysing them as bundles of qualities while revising and clarifying previous intuitions on relators. On the practical side, we have demonstrated how the interpretation of relationships as endurants enables the reuse of ontological patterns proven useful for the modeling of taxonomic structures involving other endurant types. Moreover, we have shown how this theoretical framework can support the ontological analysis and conceptual clarification of existing proposals for relation reification existing in the conceptual modeling literature.

As a next step in our research, we intend to re-engineer the OntoUML metamodel to accommodate the proposal put forth here. This shall have an impact not only in the language, but also in its supporting methodological and computational tools [20].

Moreover, in order to allow these distinctions to be formally reflected in the ontological semantics of the language, we need to extend its underlying foundational ontology (UFO). Thus, we intend to extend the formal theory of relations in UFO and characterize its connection to the formal theory of events presented in [14].

References

1. Chen. P.: The entity-relationship model: Towards a unified view of data. ACM Transactions on Database Systems **1**(1) (1976)
2. Chen, P.: English Sentence Structure and Entity-Relationship Diagrams. Information Sciences **29**(2–3), 127–149 (1983)
3. Moltmann, F.: Events, Tropes and Truthmaking, Philosophical Studies (2007)
4. Guizzardi, G., Ontological Foundations for Structural Conceptual Models, Telematics Instituut Fundamental Research Series, No. 015, ISSN 1388-1795, The Netherlands (2005)
5. Guizzardi, G., Wagner, G.: What's in a relationship: an ontological analysis. In: Li, Q., Spaccapietra, S., Yu, E., Olivé, A. (eds.) ER 2008. LNCS, vol. 5231, pp. 83–97. Springer, Heidelberg (2008)
6. Costal, D., Goméz, C., Guizzardi, G.: Formal Semantics and Ontological Analysis for Understanding Subsetting, Specialization and Redefinition of Associations in UML, 30th Int. Conf. on Conceptual Modeling (ER 2011), Brussels, Belgium (2011)
7. Guizzardi, G., Zamborlini, V., Using a Trope-Based Foundational Ontology for Bridging different areas of concern in Ontology-Driven Conceptual Modeling. Science of Computer Programming (2014)
8. Guizzardi, G. et al.: In the Defense of a Trope-Based Ontology for Conceptual Modeling: An Example with the Foundations of Attributes, Weak Entities and Datatypes, 25th Int. Conf. on Conceptual Modeling (ER'2006), Tucson
9. Bock, C., Odell, J.: A More Complete Model of Relations and Their Implementation: Relations as Object Types. Journal of Object-Oriented Programming **10**(3), June 1997
10. Halpin, T., Morgan, T., Information Modeling and Relational Dababases, Morgan Kaufman (2008)
11. Fine, F.: Neutral relations. The Philosophical Review **109**, 1–33 (2000)
12. Masolo, C., Borgo, S.: Foundational choices in DOLCE. In: Staab, S., Studer, R. (eds.) Handbook on Ontologies, pp. 361–381. Springer-Verlag, Berlin (2009)
13. Simons, P.: Parts: A Study in Ontology. Oxford University Press (1997)
14. Guizzardi, G., Wagner, G., de Almeida Falbo, R., Guizzardi, R.S., Almeida, J.P.A.: Towards ontological foundations for the conceptual modeling of events. In: Ng, W., Storey, V.C., Trujillo, J.C. (eds.) ER 2013. LNCS, vol. 8217, pp. 327–341. Springer, Heidelberg (2013)
15. Ferrario, R., Guarino, N.: Commitment-based modeling of service systems. In: Snene, M. (ed.) IESS 2012. LNBIP, vol. 103, pp. 170–185. Springer, Heidelberg (2012)
16. Nardi, J.C., de Almeida Falbo, R., Almeida, J.P.A., Guizzardi, G., Pires, L.F., van Sinderen, M.J., Guarino, N., Fonseca, C.M.: A Commitment-based Reference Ontology for Services, Information Systems, Elsevier (2015). doi:10.1016/j.is.2015.01.012
17. Fine, K.: Things and their Parts. Midwest Studies in Philosophy **23**(1), 61–74 (1999)
18. Mulligan, K., Smith, B.: A Relational Theory of the Act. Topoi **5**(2), 115–130 (1986)

19. Guarino, N., Welty, C.: An Overview of OntoClean. In: Staab, S., Studer, R. (eds.) Handbook on Ontologies, 2nd Edition. Springer-Verlag, pp. 201–220 (2009)
20. Guizzardi, G.: Ontological patterns, anti-patterns and pattern languages for next-generation conceptual modeling. In: Yu, E., Dobbie, G., Jarke, M., Purao, S. (eds.) ER 2014. LNCS, vol. 8824, pp. 13–27. Springer, Heidelberg (2014)
21. Olivé, A.: Relationship Reification: A Temporal View. In: Jarke, M., Advanced Information Systems Engineering: Proceedings of 11th Int. Conf., CAiSE 1999, pp. 396–410 (2009)

Process Mining, Monitoring and Predicting

PM²: A Process Mining Project Methodology

Maikel L. van Eck(✉), Xixi Lu, Sander J.J. Leemans,
and Wil M.P. van der Aalst

Eindhoven University of Technology, Eindhoven, The Netherlands
{m.l.v.eck,x.lu,s.j.j.leemans,w.m.p.v.d.aalst}@tue.nl

Abstract. Process mining aims to transform event data recorded in information systems into knowledge of an organisation's business processes. The results of process mining analysis can be used to improve process performance or compliance to rules and regulations. However, applying process mining in practice is not trivial. In this paper we introduce PM², a methodology to guide the execution of process mining projects. We successfully applied PM² during a case study within IBM, a multinational technology corporation, where we identified potential process improvements for one of their purchasing processes.

Keywords: Process mining · Methodology · Case study · Business process management.

1 Introduction

Process mining techniques can be used to automatically discover process models, check the conformance of process models to reality, and extend or improve process models using data of actual process executions [1]. Process mining analysis results can be used to improve the performance of processes or an organisation's compliance to rules and regulations. Hence, process mining provides the bridge between data mining or machine learning techniques and the business process management discipline.

Within the field of data mining, efforts have been made to establish methodologies to support organisations with their data mining projects [9,12]. The aim of these methodologies is to guide the planning and execution of such projects in order to save time and costs, e.g. by helping to avoid the presentation of irrelevant insights. This also results in a better understanding and acceptance of data mining projects [9]. Two widely used methodologies are CRISP-DM [16], developed by a consortium led by SPSS, and SEMMA, developed by SAS [12].

Efforts have also been made to create project methodologies that are tailored toward supporting process mining projects, as methodologies like CRISP-DM and SEMMA are very high-level and provide little guidance for process mining specific activities [1]. To the best of our knowledge, there are two well-known process mining methodologies: *Process Diagnostics Method* (PDM) [6], which has also been adapted for healthcare environments [14], and the *L* life-cycle*

© Springer International Publishing Switzerland 2015
J. Zdravkovic et al. (Eds.): CAiSE 2015, LNCS 9097, pp. 297–313, 2015.
DOI: 10.1007/978-3-319-19069-3_19

model [1]. PDM is designed to quickly provide a broad overview of a process, while L* covers many different aspects of process mining and touches on broader topics like process improvement and operational support.

Unfortunately, these methodologies are not suitable for every project. The scope of PDM is limited, covering only a small number of process mining techniques and emphasises on avoiding the use of domain knowledge during the analysis [6], which makes it less applicable for larger, more complex projects [18]. L* covers more techniques, but was primarily designed for the analysis of structured processes and aims at discovering a single integrated process model. Neither L* nor PDM explicitly encourages iterative analysis, which proved vital for both our own case study as well as the case study performed in [18]. Moreover, both methodologies can benefit from additional practical guidelines to help inexperienced practitioners to overcome common challenges.

To address these issues, we present PM^2: a Process Mining Project Methodology. PM^2 is designed to support projects aiming to improve process performance or compliance to rules and regulations. It covers a wide range of process mining and other analysis techniques, and is suitable for the analysis of both structured and unstructured processes. For each *stage* of PM^2, we define its *inputs* and *outputs* and discuss the concrete steps to be executed, referred to as *activities*. PM^2 supports quick analysis iterations and evolving insights, taking existing best practices into account. We provide practical guidance on using the methodology by discussing a case study performed together with IBM. There we applied PM^2 and used various process mining techniques to answer research questions related to the performance of a purchasing process.

The structure of the paper is as follows. In Sect. 2 we discuss the PM^2 methodology and explain each of its stages. The case study is discussed in Sect. 3 and the paper is concluded in Sect. 4.

2   The PM^2 Methodology

In this section we present the PM^2 methodology. We first give an overview of PM^2 and then discuss each stage of the methodology in detail.

PM^2 guides organisations performing process mining projects aimed at improving process *performance* or *compliance* to rules and regulations. The goals of a process mining project can be very concrete, e.g. achieving a cost reduction of 10% for a given process, or more abstract, e.g. obtaining valuable insights regarding the performance of several processes. Through PM^2, these goals are translated into concrete *research questions* which are iteratively refined and answered, resulting in findings that are the basis of improvement ideas for the selected process.

An overview of the PM^2 methodology is shown in Fig. 1. The methodology consists of six stages that relate to several different input and output objects of the following types: goal-related objects, data objects, and models. The four goal-related objects are (1) *research questions* derived from project goals, which are answered by (2) *performance findings* and (3) *compliance findings*, leading

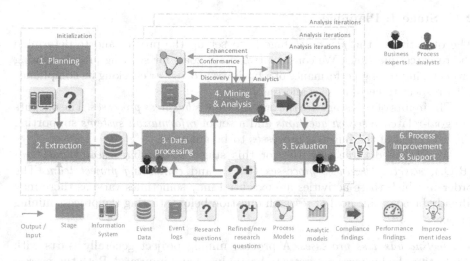

Fig. 1. An overview of the PM^2 methodology

to (4) *improvement ideas* to achieve the goals. The data objects denote the three different representations of process-related data: (1) *information systems* contain live process data in various forms, which can be extracted and linked to discrete events to form (2) *event data*. Event data can be transformed into (3) *event logs* by defining a case notion and event classes. We consider two types of models: (1) *process models* and (2) *analytic models*. Process models describe the ordering of activities in a process, possibly enhanced with additional information e.g. temporal constraints, resource usage or data usage. Moreover, we also consider business rules as (abstract) process models formally defining constraints with respect to the execution of business processes. Analytic models are any other type of models that give insight into the process, e.g. decision trees.

The first two stages of the methodology are (1) *planning* and (2) *extraction*, during which initial research questions are defined and event data are extracted. After the first two stages, one or more *analysis iterations* are performed, possibly in parallel. In general, each analysis iteration executes the following stages one or more times: (3) *data processing*, (4) *mining & analysis*, and (5) *evaluation*. An analysis iteration focusses on answering a specific research question by applying process mining related activities and evaluating the discovered process models and other findings. Such an iteration may take anywhere from minutes to days to complete, mainly depending on the complexity of the mining & analysis. If the findings are satisfactory then they can be used for (6) *process improvement & support*.

In the following we discuss each stage, its input and output, and the activities that are performed in it.

2.1 Stage 1: Planning

The objective of the *planning* stage is to set up the project and to determine the research questions. We consider two main goals for starting process mining projects: improving performance of a business process, or checking its compliance with respect to certain rules and regulations.

The inputs of this stage are the organisation's *business processes*. The outputs are goal-related *research questions* and a set of *information systems* supporting the execution of the business processes to be analysed.

We identified three activities for this stage: *identifying research questions* (R.Q.), *selecting business processes* (B.P.), and *composing project team*. The order in which these activities are executed may sometimes vary, as there may already be a specific goal or research question before starting the process mining project.

- *Selecting business processes.* A process mining project generally starts with selecting the business processes to be analysed and improved. Both the *process characteristics* as well as the *quality of event data* should be taken into account since they have large influence on the achievable results of the project [4]. Bose et al. [4] identified the four categories of problems related to the quality of event data: missing data, incorrect data, imprecise data and irrelevant data. For example, imprecise timing information for events affects the results of performance measurements, while the absence of unique identifiers to link all related events makes the event log creation harder [13]. In addition to these two factors, we also consider the *changeability* of the business processes, i.e. the organisation needs to be able to influence or adapt process executions based on the findings. This is important if process improvement is the main project goal. After selecting the business processes, the set of information systems that store the relevant process execution data is identified.
- *Identifying research questions.* During this activity, the goals are identified and translated into *research questions*, which we defined as *questions related to the selected process that can be answered using event data*. Research questions can be related to different aspects of business processes, e.g. quality, time, resource, cost. Various case studies [18] showed the importance of defining concrete research questions for a successful process mining project. However, we demonstrate in our case study that abstract research questions from the initialization phase can be refined through explorative analysis, resulting in concrete improvement ideas and valuable insights.
- *Composing project team.* The last activity involves selecting the people that work on the project. Earlier case studies and our own study show that project teams need experts with different backgrounds [18]. We define the following roles: business owners (who are in charge of the business processes), business experts (who know the business aspect and executions of the processes), system experts (who are familiar with the IT aspect of the processes and the systems supporting the processes), and process analysts (who are skilled in analysing processes and applying process mining techniques). The most important roles

are the business experts and the process analysts, between which collaboration is essential to evaluate the analysis findings and to ensure that the findings are relevant and usable.

2.2 Stage 2: Extraction

The *extraction* stage aims to extract *event data* and, optionally, *process models*. Inputs for this stage are the *research questions* and the *information systems* that support the execution of the selected business processes to be analysed. The outputs of this stage are *event data*, i.e. a collection of events without predefined case notion or event classes, and possibly *process models*.

We identified three activities for this stage: *determining scope*, *extracting event data*, and *transferring process knowledge*.

- *Determining scope*. This activity involves determining the scope of the data extraction, based on which the event data is to be created. We give four examples of questions to be considered: (1) with which *granularity* should be event data extracted (e.g. considering events related to purchase orders but neglecting events related to the items of purchase orders); (2) within which period; (3) which data attributes should be extracted; (4) which correlation between data should be used to collect them.
- *Extracting event data*. Once the extraction scope is determined, event data can be created by collecting the selected process related data from the relevant information systems and joining them into a single collection of events, for example, a table in which each entry represents an event.
- *Transferring process knowledge*. This activity can be executed simultaneously with the creation of event data. Tacit knowledge related to the selected business processes and the data attributes is exchanged between business experts and process analysts, through e.g. interviews or brainstorm sessions, which enables the analysts to be effective in the data processing and mining stages. Such process knowledge may include written process documentation or handmade process models. Process knowledge is shared throughout the project, but understanding of the process is essential for an effective data processing stage.

In contrast to existing process mining methodologies, we explicitly divided the event data extraction and the log creation and processing into two stages. One reason is that the event data extraction is time-consuming and less frequently repeated than data processing activities like filtering [13]. Another reason is that it is possible to create different views on the same event data that result in different event logs, as discussed in the next section.

2.3 Stage 3: Data Processing

The main objective of the *data processing* stage is to create event logs as different views of the obtained event data and to process event logs in such a way that it is optimal for the mining and analysis stage. In addition to the *event data* as our main input, one can also use *process models* as an input to filter the event data. The outputs are *event logs* that are used in the *mining and analysis* stage.

We identify four types of activities for this stage: *creating views, aggregating events, enriching logs* and *filtering logs*. Fig. 2 shows an overview of these activities and how they are applied.

- *Creating views.* Event logs are specific views on event data, created by defining case notions and event classes. Case notion relate events such that together they form a process instance, while event classes distinguish different activities within a process instance. Which view to create depends on the goal of the analysis, e.g. an order is a logical case notion to analyse throughput times, while the resource is a better case notion to analyse resource utilisation. A similar situation holds for defining the event classes: if every order is a process instance and the resource involved in an event is its event class, then process discovery algorithms produce handover of work graphs.

- *Aggregating events.* Aggregating events can help to reduce complexity and improve structure of mining results [5]. We distinguish two types of aggregation: *is-a* and *part-of*. The *is-a* aggregation considers different types of events belonging to an equivalent but more general event class while the number of events remains the same. For example, two events labeled with *Simple Manual Analysis* and *Complex Manual Analysis* are considered instances of event class *Manual Analysis* but remain as two events. In contrast, the *part-of* aggregation merges multiple events into larger events, as is the case with sub-processes. Both types of aggregation can also be applied in reverse, i.e. defining a specialisation. A more general technique is to define a hierarchy based on event attributes that can be used to aggregate events, as is discussed in [2], e.g. considering location at a city, country or continent level.

- *Enriching logs.* Event logs, as any other data, can be enriched with various additional attributes [11]. We discuss two ways of enriching an event log: (1) deriving or computing additional events and data attributes based on the log itself, or (2) adding external data. The throughput time of a case can be a computed data attribute, while adding information on the weather at the time an event occurred is an example of including external data.

- *Filtering logs.* Finally, filtering is a well-known and frequently used data processing step to reduce complexity or focus the analysis on a specific part of the dataset. This activity is often performed multiple times in an analysis iteration to obtain different perspectives on the event data. We distinguish three types of filtering techniques: *slice and dice* (also known as attribute filtering), *variance-based*, and *compliance-based*.

  - *Slice and dice* can be used to remove events or traces based on the values recorded for a specific attribute, e.g. activity name, resource identifier or timestamps of events, or based on simple statistics, e.g. number of events of a trace or case durations.

  - *Variance based filtering* groups similar traces, e.g. through clustering, which can be used to partition the event log in order to discover simpler process models for each of the partitions of a complex process [14].

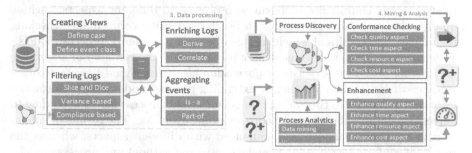

Fig. 2. An overview of different types of data processing activities

Fig. 3. An overview of the activities in *mining and analysis* stage

- *Compliance based filtering* can be used to remove traces or events that do not comply with a given rule or fit a given process model, which is a very flexible form of filtering.

2.4 Stage 4: Mining and Analysis

In the *mining & analysis* stage, we apply process mining techniques on event logs and aim to answer answer research questions and gain insight into processes *performance* and *compliance*. If the research questions are more abstract, explorative techniques combined with process discovery can be applied on event logs to get an overall view of the *business process*, e.g. its control-flow. Once more specific research questions have been defined, the analysis can focus on answering concrete research questions, e.g. the difference between the throughput times of the cases executed the activity *Manual analysis* and the cases that skipped this activity.

Inputs for this stage are *event logs*. In addition, if *process models* are available, they can also be used for conformance checking and enhancement activities. Output for this stage are findings that answer research questions related to *performance* and *compliance* goals.

We identify four types of activity for this stage: *process discovery, conformance checking, enhancement* and *process analytics*. The first three activities are well-known process mining techniques [1]. *Process analytics* are other complementary analysis techniques, e.g. data mining and visual analytics, which can be applied in the context of business processes [11]. Fig. 3 shows an overview the four activities.

- *Process Discovery.* Given an event log as input, we generally start with process discovery techniques, which return a fact-based process model as output. For discussions on different process discovery techniques, see e.g. [7].
- *Conformance Checking.* Given a process model, discovered or documented, describing intended behaviour, and an event log recorded real behaviour, conformance checking techniques *aim at the detection of inconsistencies between a process model and its corresponding execution log* [15]. Research questions

related to the compliance of business processes to different aspects, such as quality, time, resource and cost, can be checked using conformance checking techniques, the results of which can also be used to *enhance* process models.

- *Enhancement.* The enhancement activity is defined as *extending or improving an existing process model using information about the actual process recorded in an event log* [1], for example, by extending process model with performance information related to time or cost, or repairing the process model according to current executions shown by the corresponding event log. The results of enhancement are process models, e.g. enhanced with different aspects, whereas the results of conformance checking can be considered without any process model.

- *Process Analytics.* In addition to the three process mining activities, other analysis techniques can be applied in the context of event logs and process models, such as data mining techniques [11] or visual analytics (e.g. histograms of events per case), of which the results can be used to enhance process models with additional aspects.

2.5   Stage 5: Evaluation

The objective of the *evaluation* stage is to relate the analysis findings to improvement ideas that achieve the project's goals. The inputs are the *process models*, *performance* and *compliance* findings from the analysis stage. The outputs are *improvement ideas* or new *research questions*.

The activities for this stage are: *Diagnose*, and *Verify & Validate* (V&V).

- *Diagnose.* Diagnosing the findings obtained through mining and analysis includes the following: (1) correctly interpreting the results (e.g. understanding the process model discovered), (2) distinguishing interesting or unusual results from the expected ones (e.g. large set of abnormal executions), and (3) identifying or refining research questions for possible further iterations.

- *Verify & Validate.* The correctness of the (unexpected) findings is investigated. *Verification* compares the findings obtained to the original data and system implementations, while *validation* compares the findings to the claims of process stakeholders, e.g. interviewing the resources involved in processes. Both verification and validation may help identifying the underlying root causes and designing ideas for possible process improvements.

One of the challenges in process mining projects is often that the process analysts are not domain experts for the process they are analysing [6,18], which means that they may have difficulties determining the causes of unexpected analysis results. Therefore, it is essential that process experts are involved in the verification and validation of the results. Ideally, they would already be involved during the previous mining stage, guiding the analysis to make sure that the results are useful for the organisation.

2.6   Stage 6: Process Improvement and Support

The objective of the *process improvement & support* stage is to use the gained insights to modify the actual process execution. The inputs of this stage are the *improvement ideas* from the evaluation stage. The outputs of this stage are *process modifications*.

The activities are: *implementing improvements* and *supporting operations*.

- *Implementing improvements.* Achieving process improvements is often the main motivation for a process mining project. However, the actual implementation of process modifications is generally a separate project and a different area of expertise. The results of a process mining project then form the fact-based input of such process improvement efforts. Approaches that focus on this area include business process re-engineering and Six Sigma [8]. After changing the process, the improvements can be measured in another analysis project.
- *Supporting operations.* Process mining can provide operational support by detecting problematic running cases, predicting their future or suggesting recommended actions. To use process mining for operational support it is essential that the results are of high quality, and that there is an IT infrastructure in place that links these results to live event data. It is a challenging form of process mining, suitable only for very structured processes [1].

3   IBM Case Study

In this section we describe how PM² was applied in a concrete case study. The case study has been conducted at IBM, a leading multinational technology and consulting corporation. Among many other services, IBM provides hardware service plans. We have analysed a supporting process in this area: the purchasing process for spare parts. This process starts with the creation of a purchase requisition, after which an order is sent out to a supplier. The process ends when all ordered items are delivered, which occasionally requires multiple deliveries. There are three different types of orders: regular replenishment orders, emergency orders, and orders for the repair of parts. The process is performed independently at several different IBM facilities around the world.

For our case study, we mainly used the open-source process mining framework ProM toolkit [19] to support applying our methodology. The ProM is freely available[1] and contains some of the latest developments in process mining research, implemented as plug-ins.

In the following, we first discuss the activities executed in each stage of the methodology and the analysis results, listing only the tools and plugins used that were most important for our analysis. Following that we summarize the lessons learned from this case study.

---

[1] http://promtools.org/; November 2014

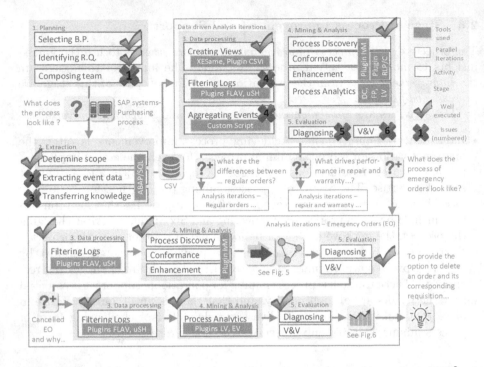

Fig. 4. An overview of the case study execution according to the stages of PM^2

3.1 Execution

An overview of the case study's activities is shown in Fig. 4. It gives the concrete inputs and outputs of each sage, which tools were used, and it shows where we deviated from PM^2 or encountered issues.

Planning. IBM's primary goal was to get detailed insights in the spare parts purchasing process' performance. This process was selected mainly due to the availability of good quality event data. Initially, there was only an abstract research question: *what does the process look like?* A project team was created consisting of a team leader, two business experts, two process analysts, and a system expert. Only the process analysts had previous experience with process mining.

Extraction. The scope of the extraction was limited to all purchase orders created in a single month. For each order, all events related to this order and its requisition were extracted from the SAP system, i.e. including events outside the specified month. Events related to the individual items of an order were not taken into account. This scope ensured that there was sufficient data to get a realistic overview of the workload of the entire process, while still being of a manageable size. The extracted event data contained hundreds of thousands of events related to thousands of orders.

Explorative Analysis Iteration. The first analysis iteration focussed on getting general insight into the process. In the *data processing* stage, multiple event logs were created. A view with the order as a case notion and the event types as the event classes was used for most analyses. Other views were created as well, e.g. the resource or supplier as a case notion for social network analysis. *Part-of* aggregation was used to divide the process into three sub-processes (related to requisitions, orders and deliveries) to obtain more structured models. Filtering was used for various purposes, e.g. simplifying the process by focussing on the events belonging to one sub-process.

The main activities performed during the *mining & analysis* stage were process analytics and discovery, with minor use of enhancement. Visual analytics and statistics provided basic insights related to e.g. the number of events per order or the case duration. The results showed clear weekly patterns and batch processing, such as orders being sent to the suppliers on a specific day. Process discovery on the aggregated log and the filtered logs of the sub-processes returned fact-based process models, which were enhanced with time information to show several bottlenecks.

We discuss some of the tools used during the data processing and mining stages. Event logs for different views are created using the XESame toolkit or by simply importing a CSV file *(CSVi)* in ProM [19]. Event log filtering is available through various plug-ins, e.g. *Filter Log by Attribute Values (FLAV)* or *using Simple Heuristics (uSH)*. The sub-process aggregation was performed using a custom script. For process analytics, the *Log Visualizer (LV)* provides basic statistics and can be used to inspect individual cases and events. Using the *Dotted Chart (DC)* plug-in [17], the events and cases of the log are visualised against time, revealing time patterns, concept drift and batch processing. There are many process discovery algorithms, but here the *Inductive visual Miner (IvM)* [10] was mainly used because it is fast and produces structured models that can be enhanced or analysed by other plug-ins. The *Replay a Log for Performance/Conformance Analysis (RLP/C)* [3] plug-in was used to enhance a model with time or model quality information. The *Feature Prediction (FP)* plug-in enriches the event log with additional attributes, e.g. case duration, and provides a general framework for deriving and correlating process characteristics [11].

The evaluation of the results by business experts, done without involving the process analysts, led to a clear definition of three separate processes (i.e. emergency orders, regular orders, and repair and warranty orders), and a list of very concrete research questions, which were mostly answered using process analytics techniques. In the following, we discuss how the three processes were investigated.

Analysis iteration - Emergency Orders. We started a new analysis iteration with the refined research question: *what is the process model of emergency orders according to the events recorded?* During the *data processing*, the event log was filtered on the order type and purchasing organisation to obtain the emergency orders. In addition, we only retained the event classes indicated as relevant by the

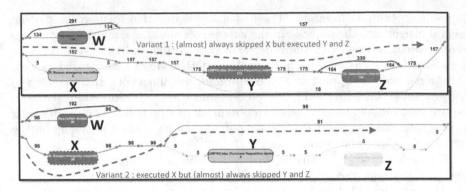

Fig. 5. Two variants of cancelling an emergency order, generally mutually exclusive

business experts. During the *mining and analysis* stage, we discovered a structured process model and enhanced the model with conformance results using *IvM* to show the frequencies of cases taking a certain path through the process model. During the *evaluation* stage, business experts identified an interesting combination of four event classes involved in two variants of cancelling an order that are usually mutually exclusive, shown in Fig. 5.

To further investigate the two variants, we started a second analysis iteration with the research question *what has exactly happened during these variants of executions and why did these executions happen?* The *data processing* activities were executed to focus on the two variants of cancelled emergency orders. We used analytic techniques in the *mining and analysis* stage to view variants of the remaining cases (using the ProM plug-in *Explore Variants (EV)*), while examining their corresponding complete executions in the original event log, shown by Fig. 6. We observed that the cancellation of some orders happened closely before the cancellation of the corresponding requisitions, which indicates users had to start two separate workflows to cancel the order and its related requisition, i.e. double work. Furthermore, we also observed that users sometimes sent a second order cancellation request even though the initial request was still pending in the workflow. During the *evaluation* stage, the business expert validated the observations by using the SAP system to see the workflows executed. The business expert concluded that an idea for improvement would be to provide the option to cancel an order and its corresponding requisition in one manual action and to inform users if an order is still pending to be cancelled, to prevent double work.

Analysis iteration - Regular Orders. We started another analysis iteration with the refined research question: *what are the differences between the business processes handling the regular orders of four different geographies?* We first used filtering to obtain one event log for each geography. Moreover, we only considered the 80% of cases with mainstream behaviour (known as the "happy flow") to make the differences more visible and filter out noise. We then used *IvM* to discover process models, and used the plug-in *Show deviations on process tree* to show the deviations between each process model and the other logs.

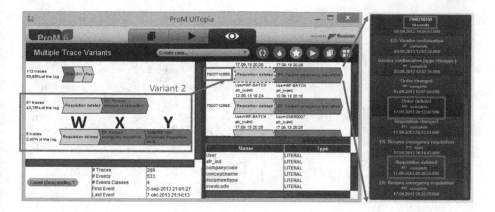

Fig. 6. Inspection of traces containing one variant of cancelling emergency orders

The obvious differences between the mainstream processes, shown in Fig. 7, triggered the refined research question: *what are then the differences between them with respect to the time aspect?* Again, we processed the logs and applied the plug-in *RLP/C*, indicating different bottlenecks as shown in Fig. 8.

Analysis iteration - Repair and Warranty Orders. This iteration's research question was: *what drives performance differences for the repair and warranty orders for different geographies?* In the data processing stage logs were created for each geography. Structured models were discovered with *IvM* and then manually compared, showing clear differences between geographies in the likelihood of orders being rejected by the suppliers. Detailed analysis revealed that one geography uses a pricing model where IBM pays a fee to the supplier even if a part is not successfully repaired, while other geographies use a pricing model where they only pay on successful repairs. Finally, the process models showed that in one geography an order confirmation from the supplier is not always recorded. This results in a risk that parts are not available when needed, so a concrete improvement idea is to implement order confirmations with all suppliers.

Process Improvement and Support. At the time of writing, this stage is still ongoing. The process owners are interested in further analysis and there are discussions on implementing the suggested process improvements based on the project findings.

3.2 Discussion

In this section we discuss the lessons learned and the open challenges encountered during the case study, as well as several good practices when using PM².

By applying PM² during the case study, the project team has successfully executed the process mining project. Detailed insights in the performance of IBM's

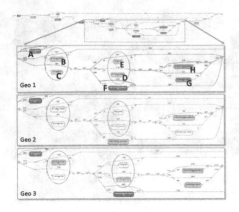

Fig. 7. The logs of three geographies, played-out on the model of the first. Lighter activities are less executed.

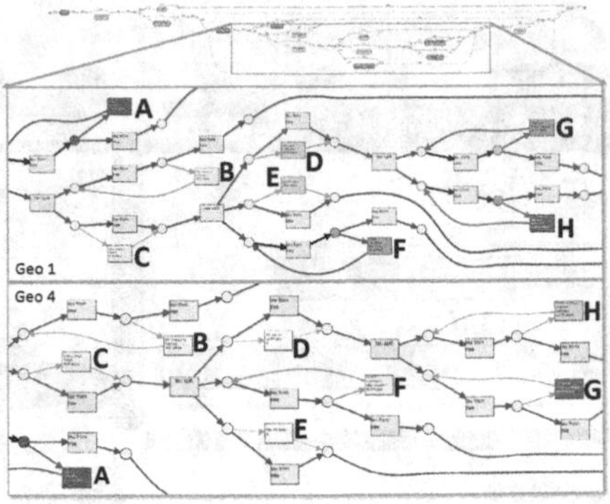

Fig. 8. A performance comparison for two geographies. Darker activities take longer.

spare part purchasing process have been delivered, achieving the project's goal. In addition, several concrete process improvement ideas have been generated.

A lesson learned is that process mining is most effective when process analysts work closely together with business experts in a highly iterative and interactive manner. This was observed when comparing the data-driven analysis iteration with the later analysis iterations. Initially, there were no business experts in the project team (Issue 1 in Fig. 4) and the transfer of knowledge was limited (Issue 3). The lack of domain knowledge in the data processing stage resulted in incorrect filtering and aggregation (Issue 4), leading to findings that were not representing the processes correctly (Issue 6). Business experts were added to the project team at the end of the data-driven iteration and the analysis that followed was executed in tandem by the business experts and process analysts. This tandem execution was considered to be "a golden combination" according to the stakeholders at IBM, as it led to faster analysis iterations and concrete process improvement ideas.

Another learning point is that a basic understanding of process mining is beneficial for all those involved in the evaluation stage. However, the business experts that joined the team had no previous experience with process mining. Hence, interpretation of the findings was difficult and time-consuming (Issue 5). A full-day process mining workshop was organised to improve process mining understanding for the business experts and business understanding for the process analysts. The evaluation stage became faster and more effective as a result.

We also learned that abstract research questions can be refined during the analysis to obtain valuable insights. It is known that concrete research questions guide a process mining project [18], however sometimes coming up with good research questions at the start of a project is difficult. Data-driven exploration can generate unexpected findings, leading to concrete research questions to explain the findings during further analysis.

A challenge we encountered during the project is that comparing process models is difficult. Some research questions were related to the process execution for different geographies. To answer these questions, process models were discovered and compared for each geography. However, manual comparison of these models is labour-intensive and existing tool support is limited.

Tool support for interactive analysis is important as well. In ProM, it is currently time-consuming to switch between different views or filter applications on the same data and to compare results. One possible solution would be to use process cubes [2].

A good practice that we identified during the project is to check the event data for errors using statistical techniques and manual inspection. In our project the event timestamps were not always created correctly (Issue 2), which led to incorrect results later in the analysis. Once this was discovered, the event data extraction and the analysis had to be redone. Checking the event data for errors would have prevented this.

Finally, a good practice for the data processing stage is to discuss ideas to simplify future analysis. Identifying sub-processes and process variants helped to reduce the complexity of the models and stimulated specific research questions in our project. Similarly, discussing the importance of events or the expected relations between events helped with the identification of unexpected patterns during the analysis evaluation.

4 Conclusion

In this paper, we have presented the PM² process mining project methodology. PM² is highly iterative and emphasises the need for close collaboration between process analysts and business experts. We have discussed and explained the inputs and outputs of each stage of the methodology, as well as the concrete activities that can be executed.

To illustrate the feasibility of PM² in practise and to provide practical guidance for its application, we performed a process mining project together with IBM. Their spare parts purchasing process was analysed in the case study using PM². We described a range of tools and techniques that were used, the results obtained, the challenges encountered and the lessons learned in the case study. We showed that we ran into issues when we deviated from our methodology, while applying PM² led to valuable insights and concrete process improvement ideas. IBM is currently discussing the implementation of the process improvement ideas generated in the project and considering the use of process mining in a wider and more structural manner.

We plan on continuing to work with IBM to further refine PM², and to provide even more discussion on its use. We also believe that there is still a need for more detailed practical guidance to help process mining practitioners tackle various challenges, e.g. determining how to choose a case notion, or when to use which mining algorithms. Such guidance could be given in the form of some kind of process mining "cookbook". Additionally, we plan to apply PM^2 in process mining projects within other organisations. Finally, we encountered challenges for which tool support is missing, e.g. model comparison, and we suggest further research into this.

Acknowledgments. We would like to thank the employees of IBM and in particular: Bart Pastoor, Jorn Kerkhof, Hans Nijssen, and Michiel Kuipers, who have worked closely with us during the case study described in this paper.

References

1. van der Aalst, W.M.P.: Process Mining: Discovery, Conformance and Enhancement of Business Processes. Springer (2011)
2. van der Aalst, W.M.P.: Process cubes: slicing, dicing, rolling up and drilling down event data for process mining. In: Song, M., Wynn, M.T., Liu, J. (eds.) AP-BPM 2013. LNBIP, vol. 159, pp. 1–22. Springer, Heidelberg (2013)
3. van der Aalst, W.M.P., Adriansyah, A., van Dongen, B.F.: Replaying history on process models for conformance checking and performance analysis. Wiley Interdisciplinary Reviews: Data Mining and Knowledge Discovery **2**(2), 182–192 (2012)
4. Bose, R.P.J.C., Mans, R.S., van der Aalst, W.M.P.: Wanna improve process mining results? In: 2013 IEEE Symposium on Computational Intelligence and Data Mining (CIDM), pp. 127–134. IEEE (2013)
5. Jagadeesh Chandra Bose, R.P., van der Aalst, W.M.P.: Abstractions in process mining: a taxonomy of patterns. In: Dayal, U., Eder, J., Koehler, J., Reijers, H.A. (eds.) BPM 2009. LNCS, vol. 5701, pp. 159–175. Springer, Heidelberg (2009)
6. Bozkaya, M., Gabriels, J., Werf, J.: Process diagnostics: a method based on process mining. In: International Conference on Information, Process, and Knowledge Management, eKNOW 2009, pp. 22–27. IEEE (2009)
7. De Weerdt, J., De Backer, M., Vanthienen, J., Baesens, B.: A multi-dimensional quality assessment of state-of-the-art process discovery algorithms using real-life event logs. Information Systems **37**(7), 654–676 (2012)
8. Harmon, P.: Business process change: A guide for business managers and BPM and Six Sigma professionals. Morgan Kaufmann (2010)
9. Kurgan, L.A., Musilek, P.: A Survey of Knowledge Discovery and Data Mining Process Models. The Knowledge Engineering Review **21**(01), 1–24 (2006)
10. Leemans, S.J.J., Fahland, D., van der Aalst, W.M.P.: Exploring processes and deviations. In: Fournier, F., Mendling, J. (eds.) BPM 2014 Workshops. LNBIP, vol. 202, pp. 304–316. Springer, Heidelberg (2015)
11. de Leoni, M., van der Aalst, W.M.P., Dees, M.: A general framework for correlating business process characteristics. In: Sadiq, S., Soffer, P., Völzer, H. (eds.) BPM 2014. LNCS, vol. 8659, pp. 250–266. Springer, Heidelberg (2014)
12. Mariscal, G., Marbán, Ó., Fernández, C.: A Survey of Data Mining and Knowledge Discovery Process Models and Methodologies. The Knowledge Engineering Review **25**(02), 137–166 (2010)
13. Nooijen, E.H.J., van Dongen, B.F., Fahland, D.: Automatic discovery of data-centric and artifact-centric processes. In: La Rosa, M., Soffer, P. (eds.) BPM Workshops 2012. LNBIP, vol. 132, pp. 316–327. Springer, Heidelberg (2013)

14. Rebuge, Á., Ferreira, D.R.: Business Process Analysis in Healthcare Environments: a Methodology based on Process Mining. Information Systems **37**(2), 99–116 (2012)
15. Rozinat, A., van der Aalst, W.M.P.: Conformance checking of processes based on monitoring real behavior. Inf. Syst. **33**(1), 64–95 (2008)
16. Shearer, C.: The crisp-dm model: the new blueprint for data mining. Journal of data warehousing **5**(4), 13–22 (2000)
17. Song, M., van der Aalst, W.M.P.: Supporting process mining by showing events at a glance. In: Workshop on Information Technologies and Systems, pp. 139–145 (2007)
18. Suriadi, S., Wynn, M.T., Ouyang, C., ter Hofstede, A.H.M., van Dijk, N.J.: Understanding process behaviours in a large insurance company in australia: a case study. In: Salinesi, C., Norrie, M.C., Pastor, Ó. (eds.) CAiSE 2013. LNCS, vol. 7908, pp. 449–464. Springer, Heidelberg (2013)
19. Verbeek, H.M.W., Buijs, J.C.A.M., van Dongen, B.F., van der Aalst, W.M.P.: Xes, xesame, and prom 6. In: Soffer, P., Proper, E. (eds.) CAiSE Forum 2010. LNBIP, vol. 72, pp. 60–75. Springer, Heidelberg (2011)

Completing Workflow Traces Using Action Languages

Chiara Di Francescomarino[1]([⊠]), Chiara Ghidini[1]([⊠]),
Sergio Tessaris[2], and Itzel Vázquez Sandoval[2]

[1] FBK-IRST, Via Sommarive 18, 38050 Trento, Italy
{dfmchiara,ghidini}@fbk.eu
[2] Free University of Bozen–Bolzano, piazza Università,
1, 39100 Bozen-Bolzano, Italy
tessaris@inf.unibz.it,
itzel.vazquezsandoval@stud-inf.unibz.it

Abstract. The capability to monitor process and service executions, which has gone to notably increase in the last decades due to the growing adoption of IT-systems, has brought to the diffusion of several reasoning-based tools for the analysis of process executions. Nevertheless, in many real cases, the different degrees of abstraction of models and IT-data, the lack of IT-support on all the steps of the model, as well as information hiding, result in process execution data conveying only incomplete information concerning the process-level activities. This may hamper the capability to analyse and reason about process executions. This paper presents a novel approach to recover missing information about process executions, relying on a reformulation in terms of a planning problem.

Keywords: Business processes · Planning · Execution logs

1 Introduction

In the last decades, the use of IT systems for supporting business activities has notably increased, thus opening to the possibility of monitoring business processes and performing on top of them a number of useful analysis. This has brought to a large diffusion of tools that offer business analysts the possibility to observe the current process execution, identify deviations from the model, perform individual and aggregated analysis on current and past executions, thus supporting process model re-design and improvement.

Unfortunately, a number of difficulties may arise when exploiting information system data for monitoring and analysis purposes. Among these, data may bring only partial information in terms of which process activities have been executed and what data or artefacts they produced, due to e.g., manual activities that are scarcely monitorable and hence not present in within the information system data (*non-observable activities*).

© Springer International Publishing Switzerland 2015
J. Zdravkovic et al. (Eds.): CAiSE 2015, LNCS 9097, pp. 314–330, 2015.
DOI: 10.1007/978-3-319-19069-3_20

To the best of our knowledge, none of the current approaches has tackled the latter problem. Only recently, the problem of dealing with incomplete information about process executions has been faced by few works [1,2]. However, either the proposed approach relies on statistical models, as in [1] or it relies on a specific encoding of a particular business process language, with limited expressiveness (e.g., it cannot deal with cycles), as in [2].

In this paper we tackle the problem of reconstructing information about incomplete business process execution traces, proposing an approach that, leveraging on the model, aims at recovering missing information about process executions using action languages. In order to address the problem we exploit the similarity between processes and automated planning [3], where activities in a process correspond to actions in planning. A (complete) process execution corresponds to a sequence of activities which, starting from the initial condition, leads to the output condition satisfying the constraints imposed by the workflow. Analogously, a total plan is a sequence of actions which, starting from the initial state, leads to the specified goal.

Given a workflow and an observed, incomplete, trace, we provide an algorithm to construct a planning problem s.t. each solution corresponds to a complete process execution and vice versa. In this way, by analysing all the possible plans we can infer properties of the original workflow specification (e.g. the number of valid cases, unused branches, etc.), including all the possible completions of the trace. The advantage of using automated planning techniques is that we can exploit the underlying logic language to ensure that generated plans conform to the observed traces without resorting to an ad hoc algorithm for the specific completion problem. In the literature different languages have been proposed to represent planning problems and in our work we use the language $\mathcal{K}$ based on the Answer Set Programming engine DLV$^{\mathcal{K}}$ (see [4]). This language, in the spirit of the well known $\mathcal{C}$ (see [5]), is expressive enough for our purposes and the integration within an ASP system enables a flexible and concise representation of the problem. On the other hand, the main ideas behind the encoding are general enough to be adapted to most of the expressive planning languages.

We focus on *block structured* workflows which, broadly speaking, means that they are composed of blocks, where every split has a corresponding join, matching its type, and of loops with a single entry and exit points [6]. This assumption rules out pathological patterns that are notoriously hard to characterise (e.g. involving nested OR joins); but they provide coverage for a wide range of interesting use cases [7].

2 A Motivating Example

We aim at understanding how to reconstruct information of incomplete process execution traces, given the knowledge about the process model (which we assume to be correct and complete). The input to our problem consists of: (i) an instance-independent component, the process model, which in this paper is described using the YAWL language[1] [6]; and (ii) an instance-specific component, that is, the input trace.

Hereafter we assume familiarity with YAWL, a workflow language inspired by Petri Nets, whose main constructs are reported in Figure 1.

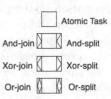

Fig. 1. YAWL

As a simple explanatory example of the problem we want to solve, consider the YAWL process in Figure 2. The process takes inspiration from the procedure for the generation of the Italian fiscal code: the registration module is created (CRM), the personal details of the subject are added (APD) and, before assigning the fiscal code, either the passport/stay permit information $(APPD)$ or the parents' data $(APARD)$ are added to the module. In the latter case, according to whether the child is foreigner $(foreigner)$ or not $(!foreigner)$, either the nationality code or the birth APSS code (AAC) is added to the module. Once data have been added $(APDC)$, the fiscal code is generated (GFC) and checked (CFC). If the fiscal code is correct $(FCOk)$, administrative offices (NA) and users (NU) can be notified (in parallel), otherwise $(!FCOk)$, the error reported (RE) and the fiscal code generation procedure iterated until successful. Specifically, for the user notification, according to whether the request is marked as a request for a child or not, either the parents (NP) or the requester (NR) are notified. After the notification the request module is finally registered (RRM).

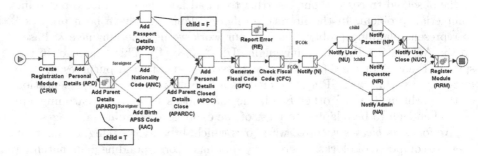

Fig. 2. A process for the generation of the Italian fiscal code

We assume that a run-time monitoring system is able to trace the execution of this process, by logging only the *observable activities APARD, RE* and *RRM*, marked in Fig. 2 with a small gears icon and the data observed by the system. An example of such a logged information (partial trace) is reported in (1). It lists 4 executions of observable activities and the corresponding observed data (enclosed in curly brackets):

$$APARD \; \{foreigner : T\}, \quad RE, \quad RE, \quad RRM \qquad (1)$$

---

[1] We use the YAWL modeling language but the approach can be extended to any other block-structured language.

Exploiting the available knowledge about the process model and the observed trace, we would like to know whether it is possible (and how) to reconstruct the complete trace. For instance, by knowing the process control flow in Fig. 2 and the fact that RRM was executed, we can infer that the workflow has been executed from the start until RRM. Thus, taking into account the YAWL semantics, this means that: (i) all the sequential and "parallel" activities CRM, APD, $APDC$, GFC, CFC, N, NU, NUC and NA have been executed; and (ii) exactly one among the mutually exclusive activities (a) $APPD$ or $APARD$ and $APARDC$, (b) ANC or AAC, and (c) NP or NR, have been executed. Moreover, by knowing from (1) that RE has been executed twice, it is possible to understand that the cycle has been iterated two times (and hence GFC and CFC have been executed three times). Similarly, by observing that $APARD$ has been executed, it is possible to understand that the execution also passed through $APARDC$ and not through $APPD$. As a result a possible extension of the trace in (1) is:

$$
\boxed{
\begin{array}{l}
CRM, \quad APD, \quad APARD \ \{foreigner : T\}, \quad APARDC, \quad APDC, \\
GFC, \quad CFC, RE, \quad GFC, \quad CFC, \quad RE, \quad GFC, \quad CFC, \quad N, \quad NU, \\
NUC, \quad NA \quad RRM
\end{array}
} \quad (2)
$$

However, at this point we are not able to completely reconstruct the trace as we cannot understand which of the alternatives among ANC or AAD, and NP or NR, have been executed. Data, both used for enriching the model and observed in the trace, provides a further source of useful knowledge which can help to discriminate about the missing activities. For example, by observing in the trace the value of the variable $foreigner$ just after the branching activity $APARD$, it is possible to understand that the branch executed by the considered execution trace is the one passing through ANC. Finally, it could happen that some further knowledge is available about data in a workflow, e.g., what are the activities in charge of manipulating those data. For instance, in this example, we could have further knowledge about the variable $child$: we could be aware that $child$ is a field of the registration module that is only set by the activity $APARD$ (to $true$) and $APPD$ (to $false$)[2]. This knowledge makes it possible to understand that the "child" branch, i.e., the branch passing through the parent notification (NP) should have been executed, thus reconstructing a complete trace, e.g.,

$$
\boxed{
\begin{array}{l}
CRM, \quad APD, \quad APARD \ \{foreigner : T\}, \quad ANC, APARDC, \quad APDC, \\
GFC, \quad CFC, RE, \quad GFC, \quad CFC, \quad RE, \quad GFC, \quad CFC, \quad N, \quad NU, \quad NP \\
NUC, \quad NA \quad RRM
\end{array}
} \quad (3)
$$

Although in this simple example understanding how to fill "gaps" in the incomplete trace is relatively easy, this is not the case for real world examples. In the next sections we show how to encode general problems in order to be able to automatically reconstruct a partial trace (if the incomplete information

---

[2] Note that the YAWL model in Figure 2 has been annotated with this additional information.

of the partial trace is compliant) or alternatively, to assess the non-compliance of the incomplete information of the partial trace). The output that we expect is hence either (a) the notification that the partial trace is inconsistent with the process model, or (b) a set of traces that complete the input partial trace (partially or in full).

3 The General Approach

IA (complete) process execution can be seen as a sequence of activities which, starting from the initial condition, leads to the output condition satisfying the constraints imposed by the workflow. Similarly, a total plan is a sequence of actions which, starting from the initial state, leads to the achievement of a specified goal.

By exploiting this similarity, given a workflow (that we assume to be correct and complete, as its actions) and an observed trace, we provide an algorithm to construct a planning problem such that each solution of the planning problem corresponds to a complete process execution and vice versa. In this way, we can (i) either assess the non-compliance of the incomplete information of the partial trace w.r.t. the workflow specification (if no compliant plan is found) or (ii) by analysing all the possible plans we can infer properties of the original workflow specification.

Our encoding includes two stages: firstly the given workflow is encoded into an equivalent planning problem; then further constraints are added to the gen-erated problem to ensure that the only admissible plans are those conforming to the observed traces.

The key of the bisimulation of the workflow processes using an action lan-guage lays in the fact that the semantics of YAWL is provided in terms of petri nets transition systems, where states are defined in terms of conditions connected to activities. Conditions may contain one or more tokens and the execution of activities causes transition between states by moving tokens from incoming to outgoing conditions according to their type (AND/OR/XOR join or split); e.g. in Figure 3a the execution of activity N, with an AND split, moves tokens from the input condition to both the output conditions. In a nutshell, the general idea of the bisimulation is to represent the position of tokens by means of states and execution of activities by (possibly non-deterministic) transitions between states (see Figure 3b).

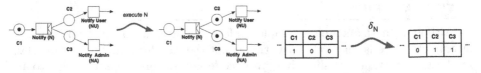

(a) Transition in a Petri Net   (b) Transition between states

Fig. 3. Encoding YAWL into a plan: an intuitive representation

Block structured workflows are *safe* in the sense that no more than one token accumulates in a single condition; therefore we do not need to keep track of the number of tokens in each condition but we just need to track the presence of a token by means of an appropriate mechanism (that of propositional fluents introduced below).

The execution of a workflow is encoded by using the main elements of an action language, that is *fluents* and *actions*. The formers represent the state of the system which may change by means of actions. Causality statements describe the possible evolution of the states and preconditions associated to actions describe which action can be executed according to the present state. The conditions in the workflow are represented by means of fluents and appropriate causality statements describe the transition by "simulating" the semantics of activities. The possibility of representing partial knowledge and non-determinism in $\mathcal{K}$, introduced in the next section, enables the precise modelling of complex workflow structures like OR-splits and loops.

The conformance to observed traces is enforced by means of additional fluents which, together with causality and pre-condition statements involving observable activities, rule out unwanted plans.

4   Encoding the Problem Using $\mathcal{K}$

We introduce our encoding in two different steps; firstly we provide a general algorithm that, given a block structured workflow, generates a planning problem that *bisimulates* the valid cases. Secondly, we show that given an observed trace we can modify the planning problem in order to exclude plans that are not conforming to the observations. Later we show that additional information about data used by the process can be easily incorporated into the framework, providing additional insight into the observed processes.

For lack of space, in this paper we introduce the main idea behind our technique. For the complete encoding and formal proofs the reader is referred to [8].

4.1   Overview of Action Language $\mathcal{K}$

A planning problem in $\mathcal{K}$ is specified using a Datalog-like language where fluents and actions are represented by literals (not necessarily ground). A problem specification includes the list of fluents, actions, initial state and goal conditions; moreover a set of statements specifies the dynamics of the planning domain using causation rules and executability conditions. The semantics of $\mathcal{K}$ borrows heavily from ASP paradigm. In fact, the system enables the reasoning with partial knowledge and provides both weak and strong negation.

A *causation rule* is a statement of the form

      caused f **if** $b_1, \ldots, b_k$, **not** $b_{k+1}, \ldots,$ **not** b_ℓ **after** $a_1, \ldots, a_m$, **not**
        $a_{m+1}, \ldots,$ **not** a_n.

where f is either a classical literal over a fluent or **false** (representing absurdity), the b_i's are classical literals (atoms or strongly negated atoms, indicated using -)

over fluents and background predicates and the a_j's are positive action atoms or classical literals over fluent and background predicates. Informally, the rule states that f is true in the new state reached by executing (simultaneously) some actions, provided that $a_1, \ldots, a_m$ are known to hold while $a_{m+1}, \ldots, a_n$ are not known to hold in the previous state (some of the a_j might be actions executed on it), and $b_1, \ldots, b_k$ are known to hold while $b_{k+1}, \ldots, b_\ell$ are not known to hold in the new state.

An *executability condition* is a statement of the form

executable a **if** $b_1, \ldots, b_k$, **not** b_{k+1}, ..., **not** b_ℓ.

where a is an action atom and $b_1, \ldots, b_\ell$ are classical literals (known as preconditions in the statement). Informally, such a condition says that the action is eligible for execution in a state, if $b_1, \ldots, b_k$ are known to hold while $b_{k+1}, \ldots, b_\ell$ are not known to hold in that state.

Terms in both kind of statements could include variables (starting with capital letter) and the statements must be safe in the usual Datalog meaning w.r.t. the first fluent or action of the statements. Additionally, $\mathcal{K}$ provides some macros to express commonly used patterns. These are internally expanded using the above two statements together with strong and weak negation. For example a fluent can be declared **inertial**, expressing the fact that its truth value does not change unless explicitly modified by an action, or it could be stated that after an action there should be total knowledge concerning a given fluent. For more details the reader should refer to [4].

4.2   Encoding of the Workflow

The main elements of a YAWL workflow are activities and conditions: the latter represent the current status by means of those where tokens are present, while the former "activate" according to the state of input conditions and move tokens in output conditions. To each activity X in the workflow is associated an action with the identifier x in the plan, moreover each condition is associated to a unique identifier. In our example this unique identifier is represented by the concatenation of the connected actions. For example, nu_np represents the condition connecting the activities NU and NP in the workflow in Fig. 2. States are represented by the inertial fluent enabled($\cdot$) ranging over the set of conditions in the workflow. The fact of the fluent being true corresponds to the presence of a token in the corresponding condition. In this way we can establish a one to one correspondence between planning and workflow states. In the examples below implicit conditions are named using the starting and ending activities. Workflow contains two special conditions called start and end respectively. These are encoded as the initial state and goal specification:

> **initially**: enabled(start).
> **goal**: enabled(end)?

The encoding is based on the activities of the workflow: each activity with input and output conditions translates to a set of $\mathcal{K}$ statements in a modular fashion. The kind of join determines the executability of the corresponding action according to the input conditions over the enabled($\cdot$) fluents. Values of the enabled($\cdot$) fluents associated to the output conditions are manipulated according to the kind of split by means of a set of causation rules.

Fig. 2 introduces two kinds of patterns: AND and XOR split/join representing parallelism and decision respectively. Parallelism makes sure that all the alternative branches are processed by activating all the output conditions and waiting for all the input conditions before enabling the closing activity:

> **caused** enabled(n_nu) **after** n.
> **caused** enabled(n_na) **after** n.
> **executable** rrm **if** enabled(nuc_rrm), enabled(na_rrm).

All tokens in input conditions are "consumed" by the activities and this is captured by using strong negation; e.g. for RRM:

> **caused** −enabled(nuc_rrm) **after** rrm.
> **caused** −enabled(na_rrm) **after** rrm.

Decision patterns (XOR) select *only one* condition, and the corresponding join expects just one of the input conditions to be activated:[3]

> **caused** enabled(apd_appd) **if not** enabled(apd_apard) **after** apd.
> **caused** enabled(apd_apard) **if not** enabled(apd_appd) **after** apd.
> **executable** apdc **if** enabled(appd_apdc).
> **executable** apdc **if** enabled(apardc_apdc).

All but the OR join can be characterised by *local* properties of the workflow; i.e. it is sufficient to consider input and output conditions associated to the activity. On the other hand, YAWL semantics for the OR join sanctions that the corresponding activity is executable iff there is a token in at least one of the input conditions and *no* tokens can reach empty input conditions later on. This specification is clearly non-local and requires the inspection of the status of conditions not directly connected with the action. However, the restriction to block structured workflows enables us to restrict the actual dependency only to conditions enclosed between the "opening" OR split corresponding to the join. By looking at the network we could determine which conditions might inject tokens into each one of the input conditions; therefore we can prevent the executability of the action unless there are no "active" conditions that might bring a token into any of the empty inputs. To this end we introduce the fluent delayed($\cdot$) which identifies such "waiting" conditions:

> **caused** delayed(Y) **if not** enabled(Y), reachable(Y,W), enabled(W).

The information concerning reachability is encoded into the predicate reachable($\cdot,\cdot$) which can be pre-computed during the encoding. Given these predicates, the encoding of the OR join for an action S with input conditions $c_1, \ldots, c_n$ correspond to an executability condition of the form:

> **executable** S **if** enabled(c_i), **not** delayed(c_1),..., **not** delayed(c_n).

for each of the input conditions.

---

[3] Split predicates associated to the edges will be discussed in a later section.

4.3   Encoding of Traces

Activities are divided in observable and non-observable. Traces are sequences of observed activities and generated plans should conform to these sequences in the sense that observable activities should appear in the plan only if they are in the traces and in the exact order.

In order to generate plans in which observable activities appear in the correct order, we introduce a set of fluents (indicated as *trace* fluents) to "inhibit" observable action activation unless it is in the right sequence. The action can be executed only if its corresponding trace fluent is satisfied; moreover trace fluents are set to true in the same order as the observed trace. An additional fluent indicating the end of the trace and included among the goal guarantees that all observed activities are included in the plan.

Trace fluents are in the form observed($\cdot,\cdot$) where the first argument is the name of the activity and the second one an integer representing the order in the sequence (observed(end,$k+1$) is the fluent indicating the end of a trace of length k). E.g. a trace $APARD, RRM$ for the example corresponds to the sequence of fluents

observed(apard,1), observed(rrm,2), observed(end,3)

The additional integer argument is necessary to account for multiple activations of the same activity in the trace; e.g. if RE has been observed twice there would be a fragment observed(re,n),observed(re,$n+1$) in the sequence of trace fluents.

To ensure that observable activities are included in plans only if required, all the pre-conditions of the executability conditions for observable actions are augmented with the corresponding trace fluents:

executable rrm **if** observed(rrm,N), enabled(nuc_rrm), enabled(na,rrm).

Once an action from the trace is included in the candidate plan, the action must not be repeated and the following activity could be considered; i.e. the corresponding trace fluents should be toggled:

caused observed(rrm,2) **after** observed(apard,1), apard.

caused −observed(apard,1) **if** observed(rrm,2).

Finally the initial status and goal should be modified in order to enable the first observable action and ensure the completion of the whole trace:

initially: enabled(start), observed(apard,1).

goal: enabled(end), observed(end,N)?

With the additional constraints related to the observed trace, the planner will select only plans that conform to the observation among all the possible ones induced by the workflow specification.

4.4   Encoding Information About Data

Although data within YAWL plays a crucial role in analysing process executions, to the best of our knowledge there is no formalisation suitable for automatising reasoning with workflows (see [9]).

As specified in YAWL, the conditions in which tokens are moved after the execution of (X)OR splits depend on the evaluation of the so called *branching tests* associated to the edges.[4] In order to provide an effective automated reasoning support for workflows manipulating data we considered common usage in use cases [10] and introduced a restricted form of data which enables the analysis of a wide range of workflows. The first restriction is that we focus on boolean variables, that is, with true or false value; and the second is that we restrict branching tests to literals; i.e. a variable or its negation.[5]

Data interacting with processes may arise in different contexts and from disparate sources; we distinguish two kind of variables according to how their value is established: *endogenous* and *exogenous*. The latter ones indicate variables whose value is determined by the environment in which the process actors interact (e.g. a query to a web service) or by events not directly represented within the workflow (e.g. an user action). For example, in Fig. 2, the variable *foreigner* is not "controlled" within the workflow but depends on the context in which the process is executed. Endogenous variables, on the contrary, are those which are completely characterised by the workflow description; i.e. for these variables we know which activities manipulate their value. For example, *CFC* in Fig. 2 sets the flag *FCOk* which signals whether code is not valid, and the value of this flag is used to control the loop in the workflow.

In our work we are not interested in capturing the whole data life cycle of processes but rather in being able to further restrict the set of execution traces to those conform to the observations about the data. E.g. the execution of a specific activity might be incompatible with a branch because of the value of a variable, and our system should be able to take this into account.

Endogenous variables. This kind of variables have a natural encoding within the action language by considering each variable a different inertial fluent which can be modified by actions. Branching tests involving these variables should be added to the causation rules defining the activation of the corresponding condition.

For example, activity *APARD* is known to set the variable *child* to true, therefore the encoding should include the causation rule "**caused** child **after** apard.". Similarly, branching depending on these variables affects the enabling of the corresponding conditions. For example, the condition connecting *NU* and *NP* depends on the truth value of *child* as well:

enabled(nu_nr) **after** nu.

Values of variables might be observed in traces, and in this case, before the advancing of the corresponding trace fluent, the value of the variable should be verified. This is encoded in the planning problem by adding the observed variable to the pre-conditions of the following trace fluent. For example, if in the trace *RRM* observes the value true for *child*, then the corresponding trace fluent should be "advanced" only if that value has been set by an action:

caused observed(end,$n + 1$) **if** child **after** observed(rrm,n), rrm.

---

[4] In the YAWL specification they are indicated as *branching conditions*, we use an alternative term to avoid confusion with the conditions themselves.

[5] This latter restriction can be lifted, although it simplifies the discussion in this paper.

Exogenous variables The behaviour of these variables is different because the process does not control but only accesses their value. In fact, in general, is not even possible to assume that their value would be constant through the complete run of the process. In terms of planning, this means that they cannot be characterised as inertial because their value might change without an explicit causation rule (e.g. external temperature below freezing). However, knowledge about their value might be exploited in specific context and this information could arise from two different sources: traces and branching tests.

In the trace shown in Equation (1), the value of exogenous variable foreigner is observed to be TRUE by the first activity (*APARD*); therefore we know its value right after the execution of the corresponding activity. This can be encoded into the following causation rules involving the fluent:

caused foreigner **after** observed(apard,1), apard.

The addition of the trace fluent is necessary to guarantee that the value is associated to the corresponding observation and not just each time the action is included in the plan (this is relevant for loops). Additional information about the nature of these variables can be used to further refine the encoding. E.g. knowing that the value of the variable would not change during the execution of the process would enable its declaration as inertial and this knowledge could be used in other parts of the workflow.

In general, exogenous variables which are part of a branching test cannot be used to select the right branch as shown in the case of endogenous variables. The reason being the fact that their value cannot be assumed. However, from the non-deterministic selection of a specific condition by means of the search for a valid plan the current value of a variable could be induced. Consider again the variable foreigner from the example in the case that its value would not have been observed in the trace, i.e., there is no information concerning which branch has been really taken). The planner would select non-deterministically between the two fluents apard_anc and apard_aac (see Fig. 2). From the selection of the first one we can assume that the value of variable foreigner must be TRUE. Indeed in any process execution in which that branching has been selected, the value of that variable had to be TRUE. This constraint can be imposed also for the encoding in the planning problem by adding the causation rule:

caused foreigner **if** enabled(apard_anc).

5   Evaluation

The problem of finding a (optimistic) plan for a $\mathcal{K}$ program is PSPACE-complete [11] and this result dominates the complexity of our algorithm. In fact, the proposed encoding generates a $\mathcal{K}$ program whose size is polynomially bound w.r.t. the size of the input problem (workflow and trace). Despite the upper-bound complexity, we are interested in investigating whether the approach is able to reconstruct incomplete traces in real scenarios and what kind of information is worth exploiting for the encoding.

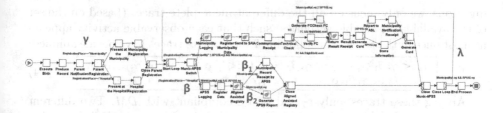

Fig. 4. Birth registration workflow

Specifically, we are interested in answering the following research questions:

RQ1 Is the ASP-based solver able to cope with the planning problems obtained encoding real scenarios?

RQ2 Is encoding information about data worth to be used by the solver to cope with the problem of reconstructing incomplete traces?

Experimental Setting. The process investigated in the experiment is the Italian procedure for the registration of births. The process, which involves several actors such as the public health service (APSS), the municipality, and the central national registry (SAIA), is reported (in the YAWL notation) in Figure 4[6]. It contains 38 activities (6 of which observable), 5 XOR blocks and 1 OR block, and it is enriched with data (specifically, 5 endogenous and 2 exogenous variables). Specifically, after that the activities devoted to prepare the procedure (γ) have been executed, the execution flow can take two alternative paths: the municipality path (path α) or the hospital one (path β), according to whether the parents decide to register the newborn first at the municipality and then the registration is passed to the hospital ($< \gamma, \alpha, \beta >$) or, first at the hospital and then the registration is passed to the municipality ($< \gamma, \beta, \alpha >$). A feedback loop ($\lambda$) allows the flow, once executed one of the two paths, to go back and execute the other one. Moreover, the β path also exhibits a mutually exclusive branch, such that, the subpath β_1 is executed if β is executed as first path, while the subpath β_2 is taken if the path β is executed as second path.

The control that both path α and β are executed exactly once, as well as the choice between the execution of β_1 or β_2 are realized through conditions imposed on data. Hence, based on the observable activities, the model enriched with data and conditions on data (DM) allows for only two possible compliant cases: $< \gamma, \alpha, \beta_2 >$ and $< \gamma, \beta_1, \alpha >$. Note that, when conditions imposed on data are not taken into account (i.e., the only control flow model M is considered), either β_1 or β_2 can be executed without any particular constraint and the feedback loop λ allows for the repetition of α and β. Although a potentially infinite number of different executions can be generated from M, in order to answer the research

---

[6] The figure is meant to provide an overview of the structure and size of the workflow; details are not essential in this context.

questions, we only focus on all the different incomplete traces (based on the set of the available observable activities) such that each observable activity appears at most once in the trace. The following 7 incomplete traces have been examined:

$$t_1 :< \gamma, \beta_1 >, \quad t_2 :< \gamma, \beta_2 >, \quad t_3 :< \gamma, \alpha >, \quad t_4 :< \gamma, \beta_2, \alpha >, \\ t_5 :< \gamma, \beta_1, \alpha >, \quad t_6 :< \gamma, \alpha, \beta_1 >, \quad t_7 :< \gamma, \alpha, \beta_2 > \tag{4}$$

Among these traces, only t_5 and t_7 are compliant with DM. Two different encodings have been investigated: (i) the one that considers only the information about the control flow (the M-based encoding) and the one relying on both control flow and data (the DM-based encoding). They contain about 35 actions and 142 (causation and executable) rules. For each incomplete trace we evaluated (both for the M and DM-encoding) the number of possible solutions (if any), as well as the time required for returning at least one solution of minimum size.

The experimentation has been performed on a pc running Windows 8 with 8GB RAM and a 2.4 GHZ Intel-core i7.

Experiment Results Table 1 reports for each incomplete trace, its size (i.e., the number of observable activities that it contains), the length of the plan (i.e., the size of the complete traces reconstructed by the planner), two metrics related to the planner exploration of the search space (i.e., the number of choice points and the recursion level), the number of alternative solutions (i.e., of the possible complete traces of minimum length) and the time required for reconstructing the missing information with and without using the information about data. Results in the table show that the planner with the DM encoding has correctly returned a complete trace only for t_5 and t_7, while it has classified the other traces as non-compliant. Indeed, the information about data, has a twofold advantage (**RQ2**):

- By constraining the execution flow through the information in the model and in the partial trace, it filters out non-compliant solutions. This also comes out by looking at the number of solutions of minimum length returned with the M and DM-encoding for t_5 and t_7: it is lowered down from 2 (c_9 and c_{13}) to 1 (c_{10} and c_{14}).
- By reducing the search space, it reduces the time required for the exploration. The time required for reconstructing the complete trace with the DM-encoding is almost a quarter of the one needed with the M-encoding.

By inspecting the time required by the planner to find a compliant plan, i.e., to find at least a possible complete trace of minimum size, results show that it depends on both the process model and the incomplete trace. For instance, the time required with the M-encoding seems to vary according to the plan length and, for plans of the same length, on the base of the type of path followed by the trace. Although the time required with the M-encoding can be high (e.g., see c_{10}), overall, the time required with the DM-encoding to find at least one possible complete trace, is of the order of a couple of minutes, which is still acceptable for a real case study (**RQ1**). Moreover, by inspecting the data, we found that for more complex (and hence time-consuming) cases, like c_{10} (which can even take

Table 1. Birth Management Procedure: statistics and time for trace completion

Check	Trace	With Data	Observable Activities	Plan Length	Choice Points	Recursion Level	Number of Plans	Completion Time
c_1	t_1	NO	1	17	1	1	2	696.0 ms
c_2	t_1	YES	1	non-compl.	-	-	-	-
c_3	t_2	NO	2	17	1	1	2	693.0 ms
c_4	t_2	YES	2	non-compl.	-	-	-	-
c_5	t_3	NO	4	22	1	1	2	1105.0 ms
c_6	t_3	YES	4	non-compl.	-	-	-	-
c_7	t_4	NO	6	31	707831	19	2	326224.0 ms
c_8	t_4	YES	6	non-compl.	-	-	-	-
c_9	t_5	NO	5	31	1050344	20	2	497429.0 ms
c_{10}	t_5	YES	5	31	385711	20	1	154157.0 ms
c_{11}	t_6	NO	5	31	189239	24	2	105574.0 ms
c_{12}	t_6	YES	5	non-compl.	-	-	-	-
c_{13}	t_7	NO	6	31	119850	22	2	84830.0 ms
c_{14}	t_7	YES	6	32	26348	22	1	18600.0 ms

10 minutes for getting a solution), the observability of a single extra activity drastically reduces the time required for the planning. For instance, observing 6 activities rather than only 5 in trace t_5 would allow us to halve the time needed for providing a solution (from 497429 ms to 244603 ms). This seems to suggest that a critical factor in terms of approach scalability is the ratio (and the type) of observable activities.

6   Related Work

The problem of incomplete traces has been faced in a number of works in the field of process mining, where it still represents one of the challenges [12]. Several works [13–15] have addressed the problem of aligning event logs and procedural models, without [13] and with [14] data, or declarative models [15]. All these works explore the search space of the set of possible moves to find the best one for aligning the log to the model. In our case, however, both goal and preconditions are different since we assume that the model is correct. Moreover, differently from [14], data are not used for weighting a cost function, by looking at their values, but rather their existence is exploited to drive the reconstruction of the complete trace.

The key role of data in the context of workflows and their interaction with the control flow has been deeply investigated by the artefact-centric approaches, in which processes are guided by the evolution of business data objects, i.e., artefacts [16]. The Guard-Stage-Milestone (GSM) approach [17] is an example of these approaches. It relies on a declarative description of the artefact life cycles, through a hierarchical structure of stages (sets of clusters of activities equipped with guards, controlling the stage activation, and milestones, determining when the stage goal is achieved). Although, similarly to these approaches, we also focus on the interaction between data and workflows, we are not interested to the data lifecycle, but rather we aim at exploiting data in order to further restrict the set of plans compliant with the available partial observations.

The reconstruction of flows of activities of a model given a partial set of information on it can be related to several fields of research in which the dynamics of a system are perceived only to a limited extent and hence it is needed to reconstruct missing information. Most of those approaches share the common conceptual view that a model is taken as a reference to construct a set of possible model-compliant "worlds" out of a set of observations that convey limited data. We can divide the existing proposals in two groups: quantitative and qualitative approaches. The former rely on the availability of a probabilistic model of execution and knowledge. For example, in a very recent work about the reconstruction of partial execution traces [1], the authors exploit stochastic Petri nets and Bayesian Networks to recover missing information (activities and their durations). The latter stand on the idea of describing "possible outcomes" regardless of likelihood; hence, knowledge about the world will consist of equally likely "alternative worlds" given the available observations in time. Among these approaches, the same issue of reconstructing missing information has been tackled in [2] by reformulating it in terms of a Satisfiability Modulo Theory (SAT) problem. In this work, the problem is reformulated as a planning problem (specifically in the form of an action language).

Other works focused on the use of planning techniques in the context of workflows [18,19], though with a different purpose (e.g. for verifying workflow constraints, for accomplishing business process reengineering). Planning techniques have also been applied for the construction and adaptation of autonomous process models [20–22]. For example in [21] YAWL is customized with *Planlets*, YAWL nets where tasks are annotated with pre-conditions, desired effects and post-conditions, to enable automatic adaptivity of dynamic processes at runtime. The same problem is addressed using continuous planning, in [22], where workflow tasks are translated into plan actions and task states into causes and effects, constraining the action execution similarly to the approach presented here. However, to the best of our knowledge, planning approaches have not yet been applied to specifically face the problem of incomplete execution traces.

7   Conclusions

The paper aims at supporting business analysis activities by tackling the limitations due to the partiality of information often characterising the business activity monitoring. To this purpose, a novel reasoning method for reconstructing incomplete execution traces, that relies on the formulation of the issue in terms of a planning problem, is presented.

Although preliminary experiments with significantly more complex workflows than the one used in the paper show that the approach can cope with real workflows, we plan to perform an exhaustive empirical evaluation to understand whether the planner can scale up to workflows deployed in practice. Another aspect to investigate is the different kind of data used in workflows and their interaction with the observed traces in order to discriminate relevant plans by augmenting the workflow with annotations. To this end we plan to consider the recent work on data-centric approaches to business processes (e.g. [16]) to characterise the data involved in process specification. Another line of research we have not yet considered is the analysis of the compatible completed traces. Since there could be several possible completions for an observed trace, it would be interesting to investigate how these can be aggregated and probabilistically ranked.

Acknowledgments. This work is partly funded by the European Union Seventh Framework Programme FP7-2013-NMP-ICT-FOF (RTD) under grant agreement 609190 - "Subject-Orientation for People-Centred Production".

References

1. Rogge-Solti, A., Mans, R.S., van der Aalst, W.M.P., Weske, M.: Improving documentation by repairing event logs. In: Grabis, J., Kirikova, M., Zdravkovic, J., Stirna, J. (eds.) PoEM 2013. LNBIP, vol. 165, pp. 129–144. Springer, Heidelberg (2013)
2. Bertoli, P., Di Francescomarino, C., Dragoni, M., Ghidini, C.: Reasoning-based techniques for dealing with incomplete business process execution traces. In: Baldoni, M., Baroglio, C., Boella, G., Micalizio, R. (eds.) AI*IA 2013. LNCS, vol. 8249, pp. 469–480. Springer, Heidelberg (2013)
3. Nau, D., Ghallab, M., Traverso, P.: Automated Planning: Theory & Practice. Morgan Kaufmann Publishers Inc., San Francisco (2004)
4. Eiter, T., Faber, W., Leone, N., Pfeifer, G., Polleres, A.: A logic programming approach to knowledge-state planning, ii: The dlvk system. Artificial Intelligence **144**, 157–211 (2003)
5. Lifschitz, V.: Action languages, answer sets and planning. In: The Logic Programming Paradigm: A 25-Year Perspective, pp. 357–373. Springer Verlag (1999)
6. van der Aalst, W.M.P., ter Hofstede, A.H.M.: Yawl: Yet another workflow language. Inf. Syst. **30**, 245–275 (2005)
7. Kiepuszewski, B., ter Hofstede, A.H.M., Bussler, C.J.: On structured workflow modelling. In: Seminal Contributions to Information Systems Engineering, pp. 241–255. Springer (2013)
8. Vázquez Sandoval, I.: Automated Reasoning Support for Process Models using Action Language. Master's thesis, Computer Science Faculty, Free University of Bozen-Bolzano (2014)
9. Russell, N.C.: Foundations of process-aware information systems. Thesis, Queensland University of Technology (2007)
10. Russell, N., ter Hofstede, A.H.M., Edmond, D., van der Aalst, W.M.P.: Workflow data patterns: identification, representation and tool support. In: Delcambre, L.M.L., Kop, C., Mayr, H.C., Mylopoulos, J., Pastor, Ó. (eds.) ER 2005. LNCS, vol. 3716, pp. 353–368. Springer, Heidelberg (2005)
11. Eiter, T., Faber, W., Leone, N., Pfeifer, G., Polleres, A.: A logic programming approach to knowledge-state planning: Semantics and complexity. INFSYS Research Report INFSYS RR-1843-01-11. TU Wien (2001)

12. van der Aalst, W., et al.: Process mining manifesto. In: Daniel, F., Barkaoui, K., Dustdar, S. (eds.) BPM Workshops 2011, Part I. LNBIP, vol. 99, pp. 169–194. Springer, Heidelberg (2012)
13. Adriansyah, A., van Dongen, B.F., van der Aalst, W.M.P.: Conformance checking using cost-based fitness analysis. In: Proc. of EDOC 2011, pp. 55–64 (2011)
14. de Leoni, M., van der Aalst, W.M.P., van Dongen, B.F.: Data- and resource-aware conformance checking of business processes. In: Abramowicz, W., Kriksciuniene, D., Sakalauskas, V. (eds.) BIS 2012. LNBIP, vol. 117, pp. 48–59. Springer, Heidelberg (2012)
15. de Leoni, M., Maggi, F.M., van der Aalst, W.M.P.: Aligning event logs and declarative process models for conformance checking. In: Barros, A., Gal, A., Kindler, E. (eds.) BPM 2012. LNCS, vol. 7481, pp. 82–97. Springer, Heidelberg (2012)
16. Cohn, D., Hull, R.: Business artifacts: A data-centric approach to modeling business operations and processes. Bulletin of the IEEE Computer Society Technical Committee on Data Engineering 32, 3–9 (2009)
17. Hull, R., Damaggio, E., Fournier, F., Gupta, M., Heath III, F.T., Hobson, S., Linehan, M., Maradugu, S., Nigam, A., Sukaviriya, P., et al.: Introducing the guard-stage-milestone approach for specifying business entity lifecycles (invited talk). In: Bravetti, M. (ed.) WS-FM 2010. LNCS, vol. 6551, pp. 1–24. Springer, Heidelberg (2011)
18. Regis, G., Ricci, N., Aguirre, N.M., Maibaum, T.: Specifying and verifying declarative fluent temporal logic properties of workflows. In: Gheyi, R., Naumann, D. (eds.) SBMF 2012. LNCS, vol. 7498, pp. 147–162. Springer, Heidelberg (2012)
19. Rodríguez-Moreno, M.D., Borrajo, D., Cesta, A., Oddi, A.: Integrating planning and scheduling in workflow domains. Expert Systems with Applications 33, 389–406 (2007)
20. da Silva, C.E., de Lemos, R.: A framework for automatic generation of processes for self-adaptive software systems. Informatica (Slovenia) 35, 3–13 (2011)
21. Marrella, A., Russo, A., Mecella, M.: Planlets: automatically recovering dynamic processes in yawl. In: Meersman, R., et al. (eds.) OTM 2012, Part I. LNCS, vol. 7565, pp. 268–286. Springer, Heidelberg (2012)
22. Marrella, A., Mecella, M., Russo, A.: Featuring automatic adaptivity through workflow enactment and planning. In: CollaborateCom 2011 (2011)

A Novel Top-Down Approach
for Clustering Traces

Yaguang Sun[✉] and Bernhard Bauer

Programming Distributed Systems Lab, University of Augsburg,
Augsburg, Germany
{yaguang.sun,bernhard.bauer}@informatik.uni-augsburg.de

Abstract. In the last years workflow discovery has become an important research topic in the business process mining area. However, existing workflow discovery techniques encounter challenges while dealing with event logs stemming from highly flexible environments because such logs contain many different behaviors. As a result, inaccurate and complex process models might be obtained. In this paper we propose a new technique which searches for the optimal way for clustering traces among all of the possible solutions. By applying the existing workflow discovery techniques on the traces for each discovered cluster by our method, more accurate and simpler sub-models can be obtained.

Keywords: Business process mining · Trace clustering · Greedy algorithm · Business process extension

1 Introduction

Business process mining techniques aim at discovering, monitoring and improving real processes by extracting knowledge from event logs recorded by enterprise information systems [1]. In general, current process mining techniques mainly consider three perspectives: workflow discovery, conformance checking and process extension [2]. The starting point of these analyses is usually an event log which is a set of cases, where each case is an instance of a business process. Every case in an event log has an attribute *trace* which is a set of ordered events. Cases and events are uniquely identified in the event log by *case id* and *event id* respectively. Additionally, typical event logs may contain much more process information, e.g., the performer and cost of each event.

However, in the real world many business processes are often executed in highly flexible environments, e.g., healthcare, customer relationship management (CRM) and product development [3]. As a result, the existing business process mining techniques might generate inaccurate and impalpable analysis results while dealing with event logs (real-life logs) stemming from such flexible environments. The problem is largely due to the dense distribution of cases with a high variety of behaviors in the real-life event log.

As one of the most crucial learning task in the business process mining area, the current workflow discovery techniques also encounter great challenges in the

© Springer International Publishing Switzerland 2015
J. Zdravkovic et al. (Eds.): CAiSE 2015, LNCS 9097, pp. 331–345, 2015.
DOI: 10.1007/978-3-319-19069-3_21

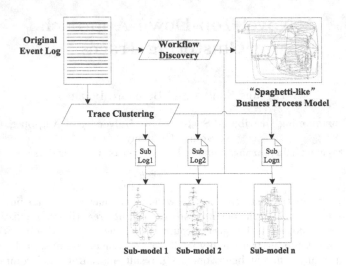

Fig. 1. Illustration of the basic trace clustering procedure in process mining

scenario of real-life event logs. For instance, "spaghetti-like" business process models might be generated by existing process discovery algorithms with an input of real-life event log [2]. Such models are often inaccurate and too complex to be well interpreted. Accordingly, some pioneering approaches have been developed to solve this problem. One efficient technique is *trace clustering* [3–7] which mines the structural behaviors[1] of traces (trace behaviors) in an event log and then groups the traces with similar behaviors into the same sub-log. Afterwards, by applying workflow discovery algorithms on each simpler sub-log, more accurate and comprehensible process models can be obtained. Figure 1 shows the basic procedure for *trace clustering*.

Nevertheless, most currently available *trace clustering* techniques treat all of the trace behaviors captured in the event log equally. As a result, the impacts of some important trace behaviors are reduced. Moreover, these techniques focus mainly on the discovery of various kinds of trace behaviors while the quality of the underlying process model for each cluster learned is not taken into account [3]. Hence, high-quality sub-process models from these trace clustering techniques can not be guaranteed. A promising method called *Active Trace Clustering* (ATC) was put forward in [3] which directly optimises the accuracy of each cluster's underlying process model. However, ATC only considers model accuracy metrics while the complexity of process models is neglected during trace clustering. The complexity of process models is also a very important metric and should not be ignored for *trace clustering*. Because a highly accurate process model can still be very complicated.

---

[1] Most trace clustering techniques only consider the structural behaviors of traces, while some consider the behaviors from both traces and other case attributes.

In this paper, the trace clustering problem is surveyed from a new perspective and redefined as an issue of searching for a global optimal solution in a solution space. The proposed technique employs a greedy strategy for searching for the optimal way to cluster the traces in an event log based on a specific model evaluation schema that considers both the accuracy and complexity of the potential sub-process models during the run time:

- The problem addressed by this paper is discussed in Section 2.
- Section 3.2 formalises definitions related to trace behaviors firstly. Afterwards, four different kinds of trace behaviors are defined for helping cluster the traces.
- In Section 3.3, a top-down approach is put forward which identifies the optimal solution for the trace clustering problem.
- To test the efficiency of our method, we carry out a case study in Section 4 by applying our approach to a real-life event log of the loan and overdraft approvals process from Business Process Intelligence Challenge 2012 (BPIC 2012).

2   Problem Description

Under certain conditions, an inaccurate and complex business process can be divided into several simpler and more accurate sub-processes where each sub-process performs some unique functions reflected by certain specific sub-process constructional behaviors. These behaviors can be recorded in the event log after the execution of the sub-process and expressed through the structural behaviors of traces (trace behaviors). In this paper, the trace behaviors that adhere to a more accurate and simpler sub-process model compared with the original model (generated by using the original event log) are called significant behaviors (defined in Section 3.2). Discovering these significant trace behaviors from the event log will assist in mining better sub-process models by clustering the traces based on these behaviors. However, due to the lack of domain knowledge about the significant trace behaviors, capturing them directly from the event log seems to be a difficult task.

In this paper, we transform the traditional trace clustering problem into the problem of finding the optimal way for clustering the traces among all possible solutions. As shown in Figure 2, each element in the solution space represents one strategy for clustering the traces from an event log into several subsets of traces. A best solution is defined as a solution which is able to divide the traces in the original event log into several subsets where the overall quality of the underlying sub-models for these subsets is optimal. Given a process model evaluation schema, how to find the optimal solution for clustering the traces from an event log is the main problem that this paper is going to solve.

In this paper, we propose a new technique which inherits the basic ideas of traditional trace clustering techniques and ATC for discovering the optimal way of clustering the traces. This technique considers both the behaviors of traces and the accuracy and complexity of each potential sub-process model during the mining procedure for the optimal solution.

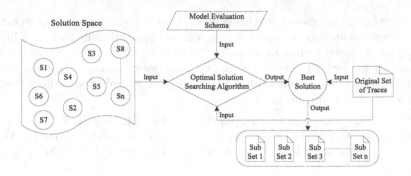

Fig. 2. The process for searching for the optimal solution for clustering traces

3   Approach Design

In this section we propose a new trace clustering technique which differs from existing correlative techniques because it searches for an optimal way for clustering the traces among all of the possible solutions. Four kinds of trace behaviors defined in Section 3.2 provide a basis for this technique to carry out the searching process.

3.1   Notation

Before introducing our method, we discuss some of the important basic concepts and notations. Let I be the set of all items, S be the set of all finite sequences over I. A sequence $S_j \in S$ of length n is denoted $<i_{j1}, i_{j2}, \ldots, i_{jn}>$, where each item i_{jk} represents an item from I. For any two sequences $\alpha = <a_1, a_2, \ldots, a_l>$ and $\beta = <b_1, b_2, \ldots, b_q>$ from S, α is a subsequence of β, denoted as $\alpha \sqsubseteq \beta$, if $1 \leq p_1 < p_2 < \cdots < p_l \leq q$ such that $a_1 = b_{p_1}, a_2 = b_{p_2}, \ldots, a_l = b_{p_l}$.

Let SC be the set of event logs, ST be the set of all sets of traces from SC, $\Omega : ST \to SY$ be a workflow discovery algorithm, where SY is the set of process models. $\Sigma : (SY, ST) \to SV$ represents a process model evaluation schema with an input of process model and a set of traces and an output of assessed value from SV (the set of all possible values output by Σ).

Let D be a database of sequences, for a given minimum support min_sup ($0 < min\_sup < 1$), a sequence λ is called a *sequential pattern* if $support(\lambda) \geq min\_sup \cdot |D|$, where $support(\lambda)$ is the number of sequences in D which contain λ and $|D|$ represents the total number of sequences in D. The set of *sequential patterns*, SP, contains all of the subsequences from D whose support values are no less than min_sup. The set of *closed sequential patterns* is defined as $CSP = \{\alpha | \alpha \in SP \text{ and } \nexists \beta \in SP \text{ such that } \alpha \sqsubseteq \beta \text{ and } support(\alpha) = support(\beta)\}$. $\Gamma : SD \xrightarrow{smin\_sup} SCSP$ represents a closed sequential pattern mining algorithm, where SD is the set of all databases of sequences, $SCSP$ is the set of all sets of closed sequential patterns and $smin\_sup$ is the set of all possible minimum supports. *CSP* effectively decreases the total number of sequential patterns generated but in the meantime preserves the complete information about all the sequential patterns. Additional information related to *sequential pattern mining* techniques can be found in [8,9].

In [10], the authors make some pioneering researches on identifying the factors that influence the comprehensibility of a business process model expressed as Petri net [11]. These factors primarily include the number of control-flows and the number of components (such as *and-joins, and-splits, xor-joins, xor-splits,* arcs, places and transitions, etc.) in the process model. Based on this previous research the authors of [3] develop an effective metric called *Place/Transition Connection Degree* (PT-CD) for quantifying the complexity of a Petri net. Let $|a|$ be the total number of arcs in the process model, $|P|$ be the number of places and $|T|$ be the number of transitions, the PT-CD is defined as [3]:

$$PT-CD = \frac{1}{2}\frac{|a|}{|P|} + \frac{1}{2}\frac{|a|}{|T|} \tag{1}$$

The greater the PT-CD is, the more complicated the model will be. In this paper we employ the *Heuristics Miner* (HM) [12] for generating the process models because HM is well designed to deal with real-life event logs and also has a good computational performance. Then the *Heuristic Net to Petri Net* plugin in ProM[2] is used for transforming the heuristic net output by the HM into a Petri Net. Afterwards, the PT-CD is used for evaluating the complexity of the Petri Net obtained.

3.2 Concepts Related to Trace Behaviors

Traces are generated performing a specific category of functions determined by business process-based domain criterion. Such criteria can be very diverse, e.g., presence or absence of activities, presence or absence of combinations of activities [3]. These underlying criteria are recorded in the event log and reflected by certain compositional behaviors of traces (trace behaviors). In the first step our technique searches for the structural behaviors of traces in an event log, then according to the identified trace behaviors the optimal solution searching process is carried out.

Trace Behaviors and Significant Trace Behaviors. Given a closed sequential pattern mining algorithm Γ and a minimum support *min_sup*, the set of trace behaviors *TB* from an event log C is defined as:

Definition 1. $TB = \{tb | tb \in \Gamma(T_C, min\_sup)\}$, where T_C is the set of traces from C.

According to Definition 1, a trace behavior *tb* is equivalent to a frequent pattern mined from T_C. In our opinion, certain frequently appeared subsequences

---

[2] http://www.promtools.org.

among traces in an event log are able to reveal some particularly important criteria of business processes and can help distinguish sub-process models with different functions hidden in the event log. Another benefit of utilising sequential patterns is that they can not only represent consecutive structural behaviors of traces, but inconsecutive trace behaviors as well. For instance, given an event log C_e that contains a set of traces $T_{C_e} = \{<A, C, D, E>, <A, C>, <A, E>\}$ and a minimum support $min\_sup = 0.4$, the set of trace behaviors $TB = \{<A>, <A, C>, <A, E>\}$ can be discovered, the sequential pattern $<A, C>$ is a consecutive trace behavior because activity C always appears right next to A in a trace, and $<A, E>$ is an inconsecutive trace behavior because activity A and E may appear in a trace discretely. However, most existing pattern-based trace clustering techniques are only able to capture consecutive trace behaviors in an event log. Moreover, employing frequent patterns is also in accordance with the main idea of most advanced process discovery techniques: only the frequent structures should be considered in the process mining procedure [2].

Additionally, we classify the behaviors of traces from a real-life event log into *significant behaviors* and *nonsignificant behaviors*. Let T_C be a set of traces from the event log C, tb is a trace behavior discovered from C, $C_1 \subseteq C$ is the sub-log of C, where T_{C_1} consists of all of the traces with a subsequence tb, $C_2 \subseteq C$ is the sub-log of C where T_{C_2} contains all of the traces without a subsequence tb, $V_C = \Sigma(\Omega(T_C))$, $V_{C_1} = \Sigma(\Omega(T_{C_1}))$ and $V_{C_2} = \Sigma(\Omega(T_{C_2}))$ are the assessed values obtained by performing the process model evaluation schema Σ on the process models for T_C, T_{C_1} and T_{C_2}. The significant behavior is conveyed by the following definition:

Definition 2. For a given minimum threshold μ, the trace behavior $tb \in TB$ is called a *significant trace behavior* (STB) if $((V_{C_1} + V_{C_2})/2 - V_C)/V_C \geqslant \mu$, otherwise tb is called an insignificant behavior.

As stated in Definition 2, a STB is able to divide the original set of traces into two subsets that lead to two process models of which the average quality should be increased by at least μ (a minimum threshold) compared with the quality of the model generated by utilising the original set of traces.

Sub-Model Improvement for STB. According to Definition 2, the starting point for identifying a STB is a process model evaluation schema Σ. As mentioned in Section 2, while evaluating a process model both the accuracy and complexity should be taken into account. Accordingly, the model evaluation schema Σ should contain two parts: the fitness[3] [2] computing schema Σ_f and the complexity evaluation schema Σ_c. Let Ω be a process model mining algorithm, T_C be a set of traces from the event log C, a trace behavior tb discovered from C separates T_C into T_{C_1} and T_{C_2}, where C_1 and C_2 stand for the sub-logs of C, the sub-model improvement SMI is defined as:

---

[3] Fitness is an important metric for calculating the accuracy of a process model which quantifies how good the behaviors in the event log can be expressed by the model.

$$SMI(T_{C_1}, T_{C_2}, T_C) = \alpha \times SMI_F(T_{C_1}, T_{C_2}, T_C) + \beta \times SMI_C(T_{C_1}, T_{C_2}, T_C) \quad (2)$$

$$SMI_F(T_{C_1}, T_{C_2}, T_C) = \frac{\frac{1}{2}(\Sigma_f(\Omega(T_{C_1})) + \Sigma_f(\Omega(T_{C_2}))) - \Sigma_f(\Omega(T_C))}{\Sigma_f(\Omega(T_C))} \quad (3)$$

$$SMI_C(T_{C_1}, T_{C_2}, T_C) = \frac{\Sigma_c(\Omega(T_C)) - \frac{1}{2}(\Sigma_c(\Omega(T_{C_1})) + \Sigma_c(\Omega(T_{C_2})))}{\Sigma_c(\Omega(T_C))} \quad (4)$$

According to Equation 2, the SMI is composed by two parts. The first part is related to the model accuracy and the second part is related to the model complexity. Our technique utilises the ICS fitness [13] and PT-CD for the evaluation of process models. The main reason for using the ICS fitness is that it has a computationally efficient calculative process and also includes a punishment schema for an underfitting process model (such models allow for many additional behaviors that are not registered in the event logs). In Equation 2, α and β represent the weights for the two parts and meet the condition of $\alpha + \beta = 1$. The values of α and β should be set upon the conditions of accuracy and complexity of the original model. For instance, if the original model has a good accuracy but suffers from a bad complexity then the value of β should be set higher than α and vice versa. According to Definition 2, given a minimum threshold μ, the trace behavior tb is a STB if $SMI(T_{C_1}, T_{C_2}, T_C) \geq \mu$.

Strict STB and Conditional Strict STB. The sub-model improvement criterion SMI considers both the fitness and complexity of the process models at the same time. However, in reality the fitness and complexity of a model are not associated with each other. The increment of fitness is not always accompanied by a decrement of the model complexity and vice versa. For example, let tb be a trace behavior from the event log C which divides the original set of traces T_C into T_{C_1} and T_{C_2}, pretend that $\mu = 0.15$, $\alpha = 0.5$, $\beta = 0.5$, $SMI_F(T_{C_1}, T_{C_2}, T_C) = -0.1$, $SMI_C(T_{C_1}, T_{C_2}, T_C) = 0.4$, according to Equation 2 and Definition 2, the $SMI(T_{C_1}, T_{C_2}, T_C) = 0.15$ is equal to the value of μ so tb is judged to be a STB. Even though the average fitness of the sub-models for T_{C_1} and T_{C_2} is decreased, the value of $SMI(T_{C_1}, T_{C_2}, T_C)$ augments because the average complexity of the sub-models is greatly reduced.

To avoid this situation, a stricter definition for STB needs to be developed. Let stb be a STB mined from a log C which divides the set of traces T_C into T_{C_1} and T_{C_2}, the *strict significant trace behavior* is defined as follows:

Definition 3. The stb is called a *strict significant trace behavior* (SSTB) if $SMI_F(T_{C_1}, T_{C_2}, T_C) \geq \mu_f$ and $SMI_C(T_{C_1}, T_{C_2}, T_C) \geq \mu_c$, where μ_f is a minimum threshold for the average fitness increment of the models for T_{C_1} and T_{C_2} compared with the original model and μ_c is a minimum threshold for the average complexity decrement of the models for T_{C_1} and T_{C_2}.

Based on Definition 3, a SSTB satisfies all the conditions for STB, in the meantime some additional conditions should be fulfilled: both the average fitness and average complexity of the related sub-models need to be improved to a certain extent.

Let Σ_f be a fitness computing schema, Σ_c be a complexity computing schema, Ω be a process model mining algorithm, given a minimum threshold φ_f and a maximum threshold φ_c:

Definition 4. The trace behavior tb is called a fitness-based conditional strict STB (FCSTB) if $(\Sigma_f(\Omega(T_{C_1})) + \Sigma_f(\Omega(T_{C_2})))/2 \geq \varphi_f$, $(SMI_C(T_{C_1}, T_{C_2}, T_C) \geq \mu_c \vee (\Sigma_c(\Omega(T_{C_1})) + \Sigma_c(\Omega(T_{C_2})))/2 \leq \varphi_c)$ and $SMI(T_{C_1}, T_{C_2}, T_C) \geq \mu$.

Definition 5. The trace behavior tb is called a complexity-based conditional strict STB (CCSTB) if $(\Sigma_c(\Omega(T_{C_1})) + \Sigma_c(\Omega(T_{C_2})))/2 \leq \varphi_c$, $(SMI_f(T_{C_1}, T_{C_2}, T_C) \geq \mu_f \vee (\Sigma_f(\Omega(T_{C_1})) + \Sigma_f(\Omega(T_{C_2})))/2 \geq \varphi_f)$ and $SMI(T_{C_1}, T_{C_2}, T_C) \geq \mu$.

The FCSTB is defined to deal with an event log of which the potential model has a high fitness but an inferior complexity. For instance, let tb be a trace behavior from the event log C which divides the original set of traces T_C into T_{C_1} and T_{C_2}, pretend that $\mu = 0.15$, $\alpha = 0.5$, $\beta = 0.5$, $SMI_F(T_{C_1}, T_{C_2}, T_C) = -0.1$, $SMI_C(T_{C_1}, T_C) = 0.4$, $\varphi_f = 0.9$, $(\Sigma_f(\Omega(T_{C_1})) + \Sigma_f(\Omega(T_{C_2})))/2 = 0.93$, according to Definition 2 and Definition 3, tb is a STB but not a SSTB. However, even though the average fitness of the sub-models decreases compared to the original model, it still remains a large value and greater than φ_f. In such a situation, the effect of tb should not be neglected. A corresponding definition to FCSTB is complexity-based conditional strict STB (CCSTB) which is defined in Definition 5. It should also be noticed that a tb can be both the FCSTB and the CCSTB at the same time.

3.3   A Top-Down Algorithm for Clustering Traces

In this section an algorithm is put forward for finding the optimal way to cluster the traces in an event log based on the definitions elaborated in Section 3.2. This algorithm applies a greedy strategy which discovers the best trace behavior (that is either a SSTB or a FCSTB or a CCSTB) for splitting the original set of traces for each stage according to the value of SMI. Let $\Pi(TB, T, \theta)$ be a trace behavior removing method, TB represents a set of trace behaviors mined from the set of traces T, a trace behavior $tb \in TB$ is able to divide T into two subsets: T_1 (contains the traces with a subsequence tb) and T_2 (contains the traces without a subsequence tb), if $|T_1| \leq \theta$ or $|T_2| \leq \theta$ then tb is removed from TB. In our technique θ stands for a minimum number of traces for each cluster. A trace behavior that leads to a cluster with a number of traces less than θ will not be considered. Given a workflow discovery algorithm Ω, a closed sequential pattern mining algorithm Γ, a process model fitness evaluation schema Σ_f and a process model complexity evaluation schema Σ_c, the details of our method is described in Algorithm 1.

To prevent the tendency of our technique to generate the clusters containing too few traces (too few traces means a very simple model), a minimum size θ of each potential cluster is requested to be set before starting the algorithm. Steps $4 - 9$ in Algorithm 1 check the number of traces in the original trace set and if there is no way to divide the trace set so that the sizes of both the subsets

---

Algorithm 1. Discovering the best solution for clustering traces (DBSCT)

Input: a set of traces T_C from event log C, the set of closed sequential patterns $CSP \leftarrow \Gamma(T_C, min\_sup)$ mined from T_C with a minimum threshold min_sup, the fitness weight α and complexity weight β for SMI, the minimum threshold μ for STB, the minimum thresholds μ_f and μ_c for SSTB, the minimum threshold φ_f for FCSTB, the maximum threshold φ_c for CCSTB, the minimum size θ for each cluster.

Let N, N_{left} and N_{right} be the nodes for a binary tree.
Let TB be a set of trace behaviors.
Let l be an array and $length(l) = 4$.
Let Φ be an algorithm which searches for the best *trace behavior* for splitting the original set of traces, the details about Φ is shown in Algorithm 2.

1: $N \leftarrow Null$ # create a node N
2: $N_{left} \leftarrow Null$ # N_{left} is the left child node of N
3: $N_{right} \leftarrow Null$ # N_{right} is the right child node of N
4: $l \leftarrow Null$
5: **if** $|T_C| \geq 2\theta$ **then**
6:    $TB = TB \cup \Pi(CSP, T_C, \theta)$
7: **else**
8:    return $N \leftarrow (T_C, \Omega(T_C), \Sigma_f(\Omega(T_C)), \Sigma_c(\Omega(T_C))$
         # label node N with a set of traces T, a process model $\Omega(T)$ and
         the quality information $\Sigma_f(\Omega(T))$ and $\Sigma_c(\Omega(T))$
9: **end if**
10: $l \leftarrow \Phi(TB, T_C, \alpha, \beta, \mu, \mu_f, \mu_c, \varphi_f, \varphi_c)$
11: **if** $l[trace\_behavior] = Null$ **then**
12:    return $N \leftarrow (T_C, \Omega(T_C), \Sigma_f(\Omega(T_C)), \Sigma_c(\Omega(T_C)))$
13: **else**
14:    $N_{left} \leftarrow DBSCT(l[trace\_set_1], CSP, \alpha, \beta, \mu, \mu_f, \mu_c, \varphi_f, \varphi_c, \theta)$
15:    $N_{right} \leftarrow DBSCT(l[trace\_set_2], CSP, \alpha, \beta, \mu, \mu_f, \mu_c, \varphi_f, \varphi_c, \theta)$
16: **end if**
17: return $N \leftarrow (T_C, \Omega(T_C), \Sigma_f(\Omega(T_C)), \Sigma_c(\Omega(T_C)))$
Output: a binary tree bt with a root node N

---

generated are larger than or equal to θ then the algorithm stops. Afterwards, the trace behaviors discovered in step 6 are filtered and all the trace behaviors that can't lead to a valid division of the original trace set according to the minimum size rule are removed. Step 10 searches for the best trace behavior among all of the behaviors found in step 6 through the algorithm Φ depicted in Algorithm 2. A best trace behavior is defined as a behavior (either a SSTB or a FCSTB or a CCSTB) which can help generate a maximum sub-model improvement *SMI* as shown in the steps 12–13 in Algorithm 2. The main reason to set the parameter *SMI* is: if the average quality of the sub-models can't be improved to a certain extent based on the division procedure compared with the quality of the original model, then it is not worth making the division (this requirement stems from the consideration for the balance between the integrity and the quality of the process model). Algorithm 1 takes a greedy strategy for clustering the traces step by step, the same procedure continues on the subsets of traces generated by

Algorithm 2. Searching for the best trace behavior (Φ)

Input: a set of trace behaviors TB, a set of traces T, the fitness weight α and complexity weight β for SMI, the minimum threshold μ for STB, the minimum thresholds μ_f and μ_c for SSTB, the minimum threshold φ_f for FCSTB, the maximum threshold φ_c for CCSTB.

Let T_1, T_2 be two sets of traces.
Let p be an array and $length(p) = 4$.
Let $SSTB\_FCSTB\_CCSTB$ be an algorithm which judges if a trace behavior tb is either a SSTB or a FCSTB or a CCSTB.

```
 1: T₁, T₂ ← ∅
 2: p[trace_behavior] ← Null; p[smi] ← −∞; p[trace_set₁], p[trace_set₂] ← ∅
 3: for each trace behavior tb ∈ TB do
 4:     for each trace t ∈ T do
 5:         if tb ⊑ t then
 6:             T₁ = T₁ ∪ {t}       # tb is a subsequence of t
 7:         else
 8:             T₂ = T₂ ∪ {t}       # tb is not a subsequence of t
 9:         end if
10:     end for
11:     if SSTB_FCSTB_CCSTB(T₁,T₂,T,α,β,μ,μ_f,μ_c,φ_f,φ_c) then
12:         if p[smi] ≤ SMI(T₁,T₂,T,α,β) then
13:             p[smi] ← SMI(T₁,T₂,T,α,β)
14:             p[trace_set₁] ← T₁
15:             p[trace_set₂] ← T₂
16:             p[trace_behavior] ← tb
17:         end if
18:     end if
19: end for
20: return p
```

Output: an array p which contains the information about the found trace behavior tb

the present stage as shown in the steps $11-15$ in Algorithm 1. Finally, a binary tree bt is output by Algorithm 1 where each leaf node in bt represents a found cluster of traces.

3.4 Assumptions

In this paper we assume that the inaccurate and complex business process subjected to our method is able to be divided into several simpler and more accurate sub-processes where each sub-process carries out some specific functions. These functions are identified by certain behaviors of traces recorded in the event log.

4 Case Study

We tested the effectiveness of our technique on a real-life event log of the loan and overdraft approvals process from Business Process Intelligence Challenge 2012

(BPIC 2012). This log contains 13087 traces and 36 event classes. A process model (as shown in Figure 3) which has an ICS fitness equal to 0.9268 and a *Place/Transition Connection Degree* (PT-CD) equal to 3.939 is generated by using the *Heuristics Miner* on this log.

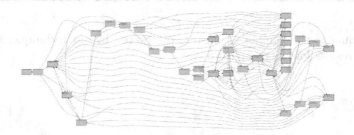

Fig. 3. Business process model of the loan and overdraft approvals process

Though this mined model has a good fitness, the whole model looks very complicated because it has a high complexity. So we set the fitness weight $\alpha = 0.4$ and the complexity weight $\beta = 0.6$ for calculating the *SMI*. The minimum support *min_sup* for the closed sequential pattern mining algorithm is set to 0.3, the minimum threshold μ for *SMI* is set to 0.04, both the minimum thresholds μ_f and μ_c for *SSTB* are set to 0.02, the minimum threshold φ_f for *FCSTB* is set to 0.84, the maximum threshold φ_c is set to 2.5 and the minimum size θ for each cluster is set to 655 (5% of the total number of traces in the event log). With these parameters set above, five clusters are generated by our technique. The weighted average ICS fitness[4], the weighted average control flows, the weighted average PT-CD and the weighted average number of and/xor join/splits for the process models mined from the traces clustered are calculated and shown in Table 1. The value on the right of the backslash in Table 1 is for the model mined by employing the original event log. Through the evaluation results exhibited in Table 1, we can see that the weighted average fitness of the sub-models from our technique is higher than the fitness of the original model, in the meantime the average complexity of these models has been greatly reduced. Such a result benefits from the thought of a trade-off between the accuracy and complexity in our technique.

We also compared our technique (OT) to other six trace clustering techniques which are 3-gram [6], MR and MRA [5], ATC [3], GED [4] and sequence clustering (SCT) [7]. Except for the original event log, four random sub-logs that contain 60%, 70%, 80% and 90% of the instances from the original log have been chosen for analysis. The number of clusters for the six trace clustering techniques

---

[4] Let j be the number of clusters, m_i denotes the number of traces in cluster i, where $1 \leq i \leq j$. Let $ICS-F_i$ represents the ICS fitness of the process model for cluster i, the weighted average ICS fitness is defined as: $WAICS-F = \frac{\sum_{i=1}^{j} m_i \times ICS-F_i}{\sum_{i=1}^{j} m_i}$.

Table 1. Evaluation results for the sub-models from the traces clustered by using our technique

Weighted average ICS fitness	Weighted average control flows	Weighted average PT-CD	Weighted Average and/xor join/splits	Time (Min)
0.9371/0.9268(raw model)	279/1635	2.87/3.94	55/147	6.8

is set to equal to the number of clusters discovered by our technique. Figure 4 shows the results for the comparison.

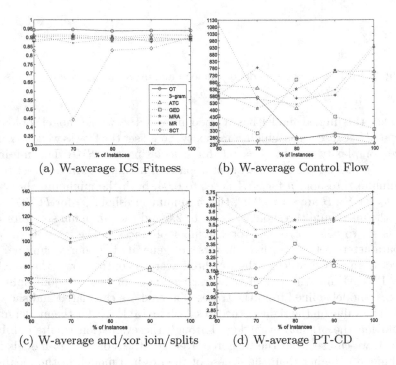

(a) W-average ICS Fitness   (b) W-average Control Flow

(c) W-average and/xor join/splits   (d) W-average PT-CD

Fig. 4. Comparison among different trace clustering techniques

For the entire accuracy of the sub-process models discovered, our technique and the ATC perform better than other trace clustering techniques. The main reason is that both our technique and the ATC try to optimise the accuracy of the potential model for each cluster during the run time. However the ATC doesn't consider the complexity of process models during the clustering procedure. As a result, the entire complexity of the sub-process models discovered by ATC is much higher. The models discovered by utilising our technique are less complicated than the models mined by other techniques. The sequence clustering technique performs better than our technique on the evaluation related to weighted average control flow. Nevertheless, the accuracy of the models mined by the sequence clustering technique is not as good as the accuracy of models discovered by our technique.

5   Related Work

In the literature, different trace clustering approaches have been put forward to overcome the negative impacts from high variety of behaviors stored in event logs. The basic idea is to transform the traces into vectors, then a distance metric can be defined among traces.

In [6] the authors propose an approach for expressing the traces by profiles so that a suitable environment can be built for clustering the traces. Each profile is a set of items that describe the trace from a specific perspective. Five profiles are recommended in [6] which are *activity profile*, *transition profile*, *case attributes profile*, *event attributes profile* and *performance profile*. By converting the profiles defined into an aggregate vector the distance between any two traces can be measured. One advantage of this technique is that it provides a full range of metrics for clustering traces.

In [14] the authors point out that a fully complete model (with high fitness) discovered may support a high variety of behaviors that are not registered in event log, as a result some significant structural features may be concealed in the mined model. Such a problem can be dealt with by considering the metric *soundness* [2] which measures the percentage of behaviors of the mined model that are recorded in the log among all of the behaviors supported by the model. An efficient technique is proposed in [14] which divides the whole process into a set of distinct sub-processes based on a greedy strategy which makes sure the further division of a process will lead to another increasingly sound sub-process. This method can also help solve the problem of high complexity of the initial model.

Context-aware trace clustering techniques are proposed in [5] and [4]. In [5] the authors indicate that the feature sets based on sub-sequences of different lengths are context-aware for the vector space model and can reveal some set of common functions. Two traces that have a lot of conserved features in common should be gathered in the same cluster. In [4] the authors present an edit distance-based approach for distributing traces into clusters such that each cluster consists of traces with similar structural behaviors. The cost of edit operations is associated with the contexts of activities so that the calculated edit distance between traces is more accurate.

The sequence clustering technique based on first-order Markov chains is presented in [7]. This technique learns a potential first-order Markov model for each cluster through an expectation-maximization algorithm. A sequence is assigned to a cluster which is able to generate it with higher probability. The technique proposed in this paper also inherits the idea from sequence clustering, the difference is our technique represents each cluster with a set of separate sequences (significant trace behaviors).

In [3] a novel technique for trace clustering is presented which directly optimises the fitness of each cluster's underlying process model during the run time.

This method doesn't consider the vector space model for trace clustering, it simply discovers the suitable traces for each cluster so that the combined accuracy of the related models for these clusters is maximised. This method sufficiently resolves the gap between the clustering bias and the evaluation bias.

6 Conclusion

In this paper we proposed a new trace clustering technique which is able to search for an optimal solution for clustering the traces from an event log among all of the possible solutions. This technique considers both the accuracy and complexity of the potential model for each cluster during the clustering procedure. Through the results from the experiment we demonstrated the effectiveness of our technique by comparing it with other six classical trace clustering techniques.

However, the technique presented in this paper encounters challenges on performance while dealing with event logs generated by totally unstructured business processes because such processes contain a tremendous number of behaviors. Our next main research task will be to focus on filtering the trival trace behaviors in the event logs so that the performance of our technique can be improved. In the meantime, we will also validate our methods on some other real-life cases.

References

1. van der Aalst, W.M.P., van Dongen, B.F., Herbst, J., Maruster, L., Schimm, G., Weijters, A.J.M.M.: Workflow Mining: A Survey of Issues and Approaches. Data and Knowledge Engineering 47(2), 237–267 (2003)
2. van der Aalst, W.M.P.: Process Mining: Discovery, Conformance and Enhancement of Business Processes. Springer, Heidelberg (2011)
3. Weerdt, J.D., vanden Broucke, S., Vanthienen, J., Baesens, B.: Active Trace Clustering for Improved Process Discovery. IEEE Transactions on Knowledge and Data Engineering 25(12), 2708–2720 (2013)
4. Bose, R.P.J.C., van der Aalst, W.M.P.: Context aware trace clustering: towards improving process mining results. In: SIAM International Conference on Data Mining, pp. 401–402 (2009)
5. Bose, R.P.J.C., van der Aalst, W.M.P.: Trace clustering based on conserved patterns: towards achieving better process models. In: Rinderle-Ma, S., Sadiq, S., Leymann, F. (eds.) BPM 2009. LNBIP, vol. 43, pp. 170–181. Springer, Heidelberg (2010)
6. Song, M., Günther, C.W., van der Aalst, W.M.P.: Trace clustering in process mining. In: Ardagna, D., Mecella, M., Yang, J. (eds.) Business Process Management Workshops. LNBIP, vol. 17, pp. 109–120. Springer, Heidelberg (2009)
7. Ferreira, D., Zacarias, M., Malheiros, M., Ferreira, P.: Approaching process mining with sequence clustering: experiments and findings. In: Alonso, G., Dadam, P., Rosemann, M. (eds.) BPM 2007. LNCS, vol. 4714, pp. 360–374. Springer, Heidelberg (2007)
8. Han, J., Kamber, M.: Data Mining: Concepts and Techniques. Morgan Kaufmann (August 2000)

9. Shengnan, C., Han, J., David, P.: Parallel mining of closed sequential patterns. In: KDD 2005 Proceedings of the Eleventh ACM SIGKDD International Conference on Knowledge Discovery in Data Mining, pp. 562–567. ACM, New York

10. Mendling, J., Strembeck, M.: Influence factors of understanding business process models. In: BIS, pp. 142–153 (2008)

11. van der Aalst, W.M.P.: The Application of Petri Nets to Workflow Management. The J. Circuits, Systems and Computers 8(1), 21–66 (1998)

12. Weijters, A.J.M.M., van der Aalst, W.M.P., Alves de Medeiros, A.K.: Process Mining with the Heuristics Algorithm. TU Eindhoven, BETA Working Paper Series 166 (2006)

13. de Medeiros, A.A.: Genetic Process Mining. Ph.D. thesis, Eindhoven University of Technology (2006)

14. Greco, G., Guzzo, A., Pontieri, L.: Discovering Expressive Process Models by Clustering Log Traces. IEEE Transactions on Knowledge and Data Engineering 18(8), 1010–1027 (2006)

Intra- and Inter-Organizational
Process Engineering

Extracting Decision Logic from Process Models

Kimon Batoulis[1]([⊠]), Andreas Meyer[1], Ekaterina Bazhenova[1], Gero Decker[2], and Mathias Weske[1]

[1] Hasso Plattner Institute, University of Potsdam, Potsdam, Germany
{kimon.batoulis,andreas.meyer,ekaterina.bazhenova,mathias.weske}@hpi.de
[2] Signavio GmbH, Berlin, Germany
gero.decker@signavio.com

Abstract. Although it is not considered good practice, many process models from practice contain detailed decision logic, encoded through control flow structures. This often results in spaghetti-like and complex process models and reduces maintainability of the models. In this context, the OMG proposes to use the Decision Model and Notation (DMN) in combination with BPMN in order to reach a separation of concerns. This paper introduces a semi-automatic approach to (i) identify decision logic in process models, (ii) to derive a corresponding DMN model and to adapt the original process model by replacing the decision logic accordingly, and (iii) to allow final configurations of this result during post-processing. This approach enables business organizations to migrate already existing BPMN models. We evaluate this approach by implementation, semantic comparison of the decision taking process before and after approach application, and an empirical analysis of industry process models.

Keywords: Process modeling · Decision modeling · BPMN · DMN

1 Introduction

Business process models are important artifacts in today's business organizations, since they provide expressive means to represent business logic. The corner stones of business process models are work activities, their logical ordering, data, and organizational responsibilities. With these models, organizations can improve, control, automatize, and measure their processes effectively [15]. In our studies of business process models from our project partners, we have also found situations, in which business process models were misused for modeling decision logic. The respective process models expose a complex routing structure, consisting of many exclusive gateways that represent different aspects of a decision. As a result, these process models are hard to comprehend, to implement, and to maintain.

In this paper, we argue that decision logic should be modeled separately from the process logic. Following the "separation of concerns" paradigm, this allows to keep the decision logic in a dedicated decision model and the process logic in a dedicated process model. To take advantage from existing information,

© Springer International Publishing Switzerland 2015
J. Zdravkovic et al. (Eds.): CAiSE 2015, LNCS 9097, pp. 349–366, 2015.
DOI: 10.1007/978-3-319-19069-3_22

we introduce an approach to semi-automatically detect decision logic in business process models and to generate decision models and corresponding decision tables from process models' decision logic. These decision models conform to the recently published Decision Model and Notation (DMN) [9] standard for decision modeling. Process models are represented with the industry standard: the Business Process Model and Notation (BPMN) [8]. The conceptual results are evaluated by sets of sample business processes from industry.

The paper contains two main contributions shaping its structure. First, we discuss the need to separate process and decision modeling (Section 2). Second, we introduce a semi-automatic approach to identify decision logic in business processes pattern-based (Section 3), to map these patterns into DMN models and to adapt the process model structure accordingly (Section 4) before we allow configuration of the results in post-processing (Section 5). Afterwards, Section 6 evaluates our approach and introduces our implementation. Section 7 is devoted to related work and Section 8 concludes the paper.

2   Process and Decision Modeling

Business process modeling is well established in business organizations and is highly supported by modern tools. Modeling languages as BPMN [8] are well suited for process experts as well as – thanks to tool support – end users. Process models allow documentation of business operations, enactment of business processes following the given execution semantics, and (automatic) process analysis regarding correctness, improvement, compliance, etc. In the course of process execution, multiple decisions are taken that influence the mentioned areas [2]. Analysis of industry processes reveals that such decisions include the assignment of actual resources to activities answering the question who shall execute a specific activity or evaluating a given set of data to calculate a decision indicating which path shall be followed at decision points (branching behavior). Furthermore, exceptional behavior is handled by pre-specified procedures for each case. Especially, in the insurance and banking domains, regulatory compliance highly influences process execution by specifying which guidelines must be followed.

Based on the analysis of 956 real world process models from, amongst others, insurance, banking, and health care, we recognized that part of the logic leading to decisions is often encoded in process models resulting in models that are hard to read and to maintain. BPMN allows to represent decisions and their impact or consequence respectively. However, BPMN is not meant to represent the detailed decision logic since modeling the decision logic often results in spaghetti like models (see Fig. 1 for an abstract example) or extensive natural language descriptions explaining the decision

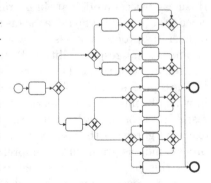

Fig. 1. Misuse of BPMN for decision logic modeling

taking process that are not analyzable automatically. Thus, decision logic modeling is out of scope for BPMN. Instead, decision tables [14] and further decision modeling concepts [7,16] are a reasonable and compact method to describe decision logic in scenarios with many input parameters. There exists the upcoming OMG standard for modeling decision diagrams: the Decision Model and Notation (DMN) [9]. DMN is meant to supplement BPMN and allows the "separation of concerns" [10] between process and decision logic modeling based on the actual scope of both modeling techniques. BPMN's scope comprises the business logic containing information on what activities need to be executed in which order by which resource utilizing which data objects while DMN covers the decision logic modeling by specifying which decision is taken based on which information, where to find it, and how to process this information to derive the decision result. Since both worlds existed long without proper integration, organizations misused BPMN by including decision logic into process models.

Thereby, data-based decisions are most common. A data-based decision is represented by a decision structure consisting of single and compound decision nodes we refer to as split gateways representing exclusive or inclusive alternatives based on external information. These decisions can be classified into three types: (i) An explicit decision task with succeeding branching behavior, e.g., in a task, the decision about a customer's loyalty is taken and based on the result, different actions (e.g., give or deny discount) are taken. (ii) Branching behavior is encoded in decision points, e.g., split gateways with decision logic (about the customer's loyalty) encoded in annotations to the gateways or to edges originating from such gateway. (iii) There exists a decision task without succeeding branching behavior, e.g., set discount for a customer based on her loyalty.

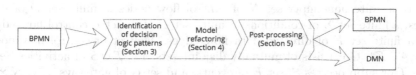

Fig. 2. Semi-automatic three step approach for process and decision logic separation

Fig. 2 visualizes the three main steps of our approach and the corresponding input and output. Given a BPMN model, we first identify decision logic patterns based on the specifications of Section 3. From the industry process model collections, we identified the three most often occurring patterns. We consider control-flow based decision structures only. Based on our insights into the industry process models, we defined three decision structures based on the occurrence of activities and gateways. However, we allow utilization of such information in the refactoring or the post-processing steps which follow in this order upon identification completion. The identification step is completed if a stakeholder approved the found patterns to be decision structures. Thereby, multiple patterns may match for parts of the process model such that the stakeholder also must decide which is the appropriate pattern. The refactoring is presented in Section 4 and comprises the translation of the identified patterns into a DMN model and the adaptation of the process model. The post-processing step, see Section 5, enables configuration of the resulting BPMN and DMN model. Two configuration options and their automatic application are discussed in the corresponding section. Finally, both models, the BPMN process model and DMN decision model are the outputs of our semi-automatic approach.

3   Patterns for Control-Flow-Based Decision Identification

We analyzed seven industry process model collections from the domains of insurance, banking, healthcare, energy, and information technology with each collection containing between 14 and 334 process models summing up to 956 process models in total. From these process models, the majority, 63%, contain data-based decisions. Note, that some process models contain multiple types of decisions. So, in total we observed 1,074 decision occurrences. Following the empirical results, in this paper, we focus on process models with data-based decisions that are taken within tasks directly preceding a split gateway where this gateway only routes the process flow based on the taken decision: branching behavior with explicit decision task. Fig. 3 presents such decision structure consisting of a single gateway in an insurance environment.

Each decision structure is a fragment of the process model the decision is taken in. We formally define the concepts of process model and process fragment as follows.

Definition 1 (Process model). *Process model* $m = (N, D, \Sigma, C, F, \alpha, \xi)$ consists of a finite non-empty set N of control flow nodes, a finite set D of data nodes, a finite set Σ of conditions, a finite set C of directed control flow edges, and a finite set F of directed data flow edges. The set of control flow nodes $N = A \cup E \cup G$ consists of mutually disjoint sets $A \subseteq T \cup S$ of activities being tasks T or subprocesses S, set E of events, and set G of gateways. $C \subseteq N \times N$ is the control flow relation such that each edge connects two control flow nodes. $F \subseteq (D \times A) \cup (A \times D)$ is the data flow relation indicating read respectively write operations of an activity with respect to a data node. Let Z be a set of control flow constructs. Function $\alpha : G \to Z$ assigns to each gateway a type in terms of a control flow construct. Function $\xi : (G \times N) \cap C \nrightarrow \Sigma$ assigns conditions to control flow edges originating from gateways with multiple outgoing edges.   ◇

Definition 2 (Process fragment). Let $m = (N, D, \Sigma, C, F, \alpha, \xi)$ be a process model. A *process fragment* $pf = (N', D', \Sigma', C', F', \gamma, \sigma)$ is a connected subgraph of process model m such that $N' \subseteq N$, $D' \subseteq D$, $\Sigma' \subseteq \Sigma$, $C' \subseteq C$, and $F' \subseteq F$. Functions γ and σ are restrictions of functions α and ξ respectively with corresponding new domains.   ◇

We use subscripts, e.g., A_m, α_m, and N_{pf}, to denote the relation of sets and functions to process model m or process fragment pf and omit the subscripts where the context is clear. The set of process fragments of process model m is denoted as PF_m. In this paper, we consider XOR and IOR as possible control flow constructs referring to an exclusive choice and an inclusive choice respectively. An XOR or IOR gateway with two or more outgoing edges is called split and an XOR or IOR gateway with two or more incoming edges is called join, whereby we assume that such gateway is either a split or a join. A gateway with multiple incoming and outgoing edges is transformed in two succeeding gateways with one representing the join and the other the split in this order.

As usual, we assume the process model to be structurally sound, i.e., m contains exactly one start and one end event and every node of m is on a path from the start to the end event. Further, we require each process fragment pf to consist of a single start node being an activity, multiple end nodes being activities (one for each alternative), each node is on a path from the start to some end node, and all nodes must not be a join gateway. We assume that decisions are taken in distinct tasks such that a split gateway only routes the process flow based on pre-calculated decision values, since it is good modeling practice to do so. "Omission of this decision task is a common mistake made by inexperienced BPMN users" [14].

We chose the top-three patterns in terms of occurrences in the industry process models as most prominent examples to show feasibility of combining BPMN and DMN automatically. A generalization of these patterns is out of scope for this paper due to the diverse nature of decision modeling. Next, we introduce these three identified patterns. Each pattern is represented as process fragment. Thereby, we utilize a fragment of a process model from the insurance domain dealing with assigning the correct discount for a customer. In the examples, for clarity reasons, we sometimes visualize two outgoing edges only for a split gateway. However, in practice, there can be any number of edges as covered by the corresponding formalisms.

3.1   P1 – Single Split Gateway

A fragment matching pattern P1 contains a decision structure of a task preceding a single split gateway with at least two outgoing control flow edges. On each path, an activity directly succeeds the split gateway. Thereby, pattern P1 subsumes optionality decisions as special case; paths directly connecting split and join gateways get automatically extended by τ-transitions. We assume, the decision is taken in the task preceding the gateway. Fig. 3 presents a corresponding process fragment

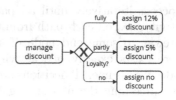

Fig. 3. Process fragment representing a split gateway with more than 2 outgoing edges

with three alternative paths at the split gateway; depending on the modeling style, the bottom activity *assign no discount* might not have been modeled such that it would have been added as τ-transition instead. Since, the gateway is of type XOR, only one alternative can be chosen. Based on the result of task *manage discount*, i.e., the taken decision about the customer's loyalty, the discount assigned to the customer is set to 12%, 5%, or 0% respectively. Possible results of the decision are fixed by the annotations on the edges originating from the split gateway.

Formally, we specify pattern P1 as follows.

Definition 3 (Pattern P1). Let pf be a process fragment of process model m and let Σ_{pf} denote the conditions assigned to control flow edges. Then, pf represents *P1* if

- $|G_{pf}| = 1 \wedge |g \bullet| \geq 2 \wedge (\gamma(g) = XOR \vee \gamma(g) = IOR), g \in G_{pf}$ (the fragment contains exactly one split gateway),
- $|A_{pf}| = |g\bullet|+1$ (the number of activities of pf equals the number of outgoing edges[1] of the split gateway g plus 1),
- $\bullet g = t \wedge |\bullet g| = 1, t \in T_{pf}$ (task t is the only predecessor of the split gateway),
- $|\bullet t| = 0$ (task t is the start node of pf),
- $\forall a \in A_{pf} \backslash t : \bullet a = g$ (all activities other than the one preceding the split gateway g directly succeed g),
- $\forall a \in A_{pf} \backslash t : |a \bullet| = 0$ (all activities other than the one preceding the split gateway g are end nodes of pf), and
- $\forall a \in A_{pf} \backslash t, c \in C_{pf}$ such that $(g, a) = c : \sigma(c) \in \Sigma_{pf}$ (all outgoing edges of the split gateway are annotated with a condition).   ◇

3.2   P2 – Sequence of Split Gateways (Decision Tree)

A fragment matching pattern P2 contains a decision structure of a task preceding a split gateway with at least two outgoing control flow edges. On each path, an activity or another split gateway with at least two outgoing control flow edges directly succeeds the split gateway. In case of a gateway, this proceeds iteratively until all paths reach an activity; i.e., on each path from the first split gateway to some end node of the fragment, there exists exactly one activity – the end node. We assume, all decisions are taken in the task preceding the first split gateway. Fig. 4

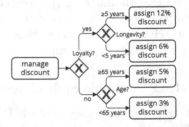

Fig. 4. Process fragment representing a sequence of split gateways that represents a decision tree

presents a corresponding process fragment with altogether four alternative paths after the first split gateway. Since, all gateways are of type XOR, only one alternative can be chosen. The actual routing based on the taken decisions is distributed over two split gateways. Based on the result for the customer loyalty, the second routing decision is either taken based on the longevity of the customer relationship (loyal customer) or the age of the customer (non-loyal customer). Due

---

[1] The number of outgoing (incoming) edges directly translates to the number of direct successors (predecessors) and vice versa.

to the dependency of a routing decision on the ones taken before, this pattern represents a decision tree. Analogous to pattern P1, the possible results of the decision are fixed by the annotations on the edges originating from some split gateway.

Formally, we specify pattern P2 as follows.

Definition 4 (Pattern P2). Let pf be a process fragment of process model m and let Σ_{pf} denote the conditions assigned to control flow edges. Then, pf represents $P2$ if

○ $\forall g \in G_{pf} : |g \bullet| \geq 2 \wedge (\gamma(g) = XOR \vee \gamma(g) = IOR)$ (all gateways of the fragment are split gateways),

○ $\exists t \in A_{pf} : |\bullet t| = 0 \wedge \forall a \in A_{pf}\backslash t : \bullet a = 1$ (t is the start node of pf),

○ $\forall a \in A_{pf}\backslash t : |a \bullet| = 0$ (activities other than the start node t are end nodes of pf),

○ $\forall g \in G_{pf} : \forall n \in g\bullet : n \in A_{pf} \cup G_{pf}$ (all successors of a gateway are an activity or a gateway), and

○ $\forall a \in A_{pf}\backslash t, g \in G_{pf}, c \in C_{pf}$ such that $(g,a) = c \vee (g,g) = c : \sigma(c) \in \Sigma_{pf}$ (all outgoing edges of a split gateway are annotated with a condition).

$\diamond$

3.3   P3 – Sequence of Split Gateways Separated by an Activity

A fragment matching pattern P3 contains a decision structure of a task preceding a split gateway with at least two outgoing control flow edges. On each path, an activity or another split gateway with at least two outgoing control flow edges directly succeeds the split gateway. A task – a specific type of activity – that succeeds a split gateway may be succeeded by another split gateway. Otherwise, it is an end node of the process fragment. Activities of type subprocess are also end nodes of the fragment. Iteratively, this proceeds until all paths reach an activity that is not succeeded by some split gateway. Fig. 5 presents a corresponding

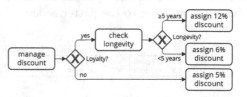

Fig. 5. Process fragment representing a sequence of split gateways separated by an activity

process fragment with altogether three alternative paths after the first split gateway. Since, all gateways are of type XOR, only one alternative can be chosen. Each task of this process fragment that is succeeded by a split gateway (tasks *manage discount* and *check longevity* in Fig. 5) takes the actual decisions for the subsequent routing decisions. In case there exist multiple split gateways (see decision tree in pattern P2), the task takes the decisions for the whole decision tree. This means, this pattern can be composed of multiple decision trees as well as single split gateways. Since multiple decisions are arranged in sequence, we consider this structure as additional pattern to preserve the decision dependencies instead of handling each decision separately. In Fig. 5, the choice between 12%

and 6% discount is taken based on two decisions (loyalty and longevity) while granting 5% discount is clear after the first decision for non-loyal customers.

Formally, we specify pattern P3 as follows.

Definition 5 (Pattern P3). Let pf be a process fragment of process model m and let Σ_{pf} denote the conditions assigned to control flow edges. Then, pf represents *P3* if

o $\forall g \in G_{pf} : |g \bullet| \geq 2 \wedge (\gamma(g) = XOR \vee \gamma(g) = IOR)$ (all gateways of the fragment are split gateways),

o $\exists t \in A_{pf} : | \bullet t| = 0 \wedge \forall a \in A_{pf} \backslash t : \bullet a = 1$ (t is the start node of pf),

o $\forall a \in A_{pf}$ such that $|a \bullet| = 1 : a \in T_{pf}$ (all activities being no end node are a task),

o $\forall g \in G_{pf} : \forall n \in g\bullet : n \in A_{pf} \cup G_{pf}$ (all successors of a gateway are an activity or a gateway),

o $\forall n \in N_{pf}$ such that $|n \bullet| = 0 : n \in A_{pf}$ (all end nodes are activities),

o $\forall a \in A_{pf} \backslash t, g \in G_{pf}, c \in C_{pf}$ such that $(g, a) = c \vee (g, g) = c : \sigma(c) \in \Sigma_{pf}$ (all outgoing edges of a split gateway are annotated with a condition).

◇

3.4   Pattern Identification Procedure

Given a process model, we check for the existence of decision logic by following the steps as shown in Fig. 6. For pattern identification, we first determine for all pairs of directly succeeding control flow nodes where the first one is a task, the decision task, and the second one is a split gateway. For each such pair of nodes, we traverse forward the process model and check for existence of a control flow structure aligning to the patterns defined above.

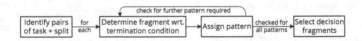

Fig. 6. Visualization of pattern identification process

For pattern P1, we check whether each path originating from the split gateway proceeds with an activity; such fragment is referred to pattern P1. Otherwise, P1-identification is stopped. For pattern P2, we traverse forward on each path until we identify a non-split-gateway control flow node, e.g., an activity or a join gateway, directly succeeding some split gateway. The initial split gateway must be followed by at least one other split gateway. Otherwise, P2-identification is stopped. For pattern P3, we traverse forward on each path until we identify a task that is directly succeeded by some control flow node that is no split gateway or until we identify a subprocess directly succeeding a split gateway. In case a split gateway is not succeeded by an activity or another split gateway or if a task is not succeeded by a split gateway, P3-identification is stopped.

After fragment determination, the fragment is referred to the pattern it was checked for if it was not stopped. Otherwise, the assignment is skipped. After checking each determined pair, the stakeholder gets presented all fragments that refer to some pattern and is required to decide which actually represent a decision. Thereby, process fragments indicating some decision may overlap. This needs to be resolved by the stakeholder resulting in non-overlapping fragments. For instance, consider the fragment f represented in Fig. 5. It refers to pattern P3. But there also exist two other fragments f_1, f_2 referring to pattern P1 and both are part of f – tasks *manage discount* and *check longevity* represent start nodes of fragments f_1 and f_2. The specification of non-overlapping fragments that actually represent a decision structure concludes the first step as visualized in Fig. 2.

4   Translation of BPMN Decision Logic to DMN

This section discusses the translation of a given process fragment referring to one of the introduced patterns to a DMN model. Before detailing the algorithm, we briefly introduce the Decision Model and Notation (DMN) and provide an example.

4.1   Decision Model and Notation

DMN defines two levels for modeling decision logic, the *decision requirements level* and the *decision logic level*. The first one represents how *decisions* depend on each other and what *input data* is available for the decisions. Therefore, these nodes are connected with each other through *information requirement edges*. A decision may additionally reference the decision logic level where its output is determined through an undirected association. The decision logic level describes the actual decision logic applied to take the decision. Decision logic can be represented in many ways, e.g., by an analytic model or a decision table. In this paper, we utilize decision tables.

Fig. 7 shows an example decision model; *decisions* are rectangles, *input data* are ellipsis, information requirement edges are solid, and the decision table association is dashed. The example is based on the fragment in Fig. 5 from the insurance domain. The decision to be taken refers to

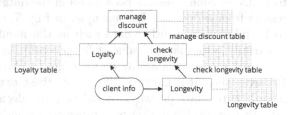

Fig. 7. Example decision model referring to Fig. 5

the *discount* given to a customer. The corresponding logic is defined in the associated decision table *manage discount table*. The decision cannot be taken directly, since it depends on second level decisions. Information about *Loyalty* and *Longevity* needs to be considered and the results of these decisions are referenced in the *manage discount table*. *Loyalty* can directly be derived from the input data *client info* while *check longevity* requires the result of *Longevity*.

4.2   Decision Model Extraction Algorithm

Next, we discuss the derivation of decision models from a process fragment satisfying one of the patterns described above. This means that the decision encoded in the fragment is partitioned into a top-level decision connected to sub-decisions with optional input data in DMN. If the decision logic is visible in the process model, we also provide associated decision tables. For this purpose, we devised Table 1 of corresponding model elements that dictates how both the decision requirements level and the decision logic level are constructed.

Table 1. Mapping of BPMN constructs to DMN constructs and the corresponding formalism representations. The black-lined constructs are affected by some mapping while the gray-lined constructs set the context where required.

BPMN	DMN	BPMN	DMN
◇ A	A	A → ◇	A ┄ (table)
A → ◇ B	A ↑ B	D ↘ A → ◇ C	C ↑ D
A →⋯→ B	A ↑ B	E → ◇ → C, A, B, D	A, B, E output / x, g, o1 / x, h, o2 / y, ⋮, ⋮ / z, ⋮

The left part of row one shows that data-based split gateways are mapped to DMN decision elements because often the data on which the routing is based results from a decision. For example, in Fig. 5, the value of *Loyalty* may need to be inferred from other data such as the number of purchases made so far. Contrarily, note that the value of *Longevity* in Fig. 5 can be observed directly so that in this case the gateway does not need to be mapped to any DMN element. However, since it is hard to differentiate these two situations automatically, the default is to map gateways to independent decision elements. The stakeholders can then decide during post-processing whether or not this is necessary, as described in Section 5.

The right part of row one shows that each BPMN decision task (tasks preceding a gateway) is mapped to a DMN decision element, which is additionally associated with a decision table. Notice that we are able to specify decision tables for decision tasks (right part of row one) but not for gateways (left part). This is because the concrete value of the variable on which the gateway routing is based usually is set by the task preceding it, and we cannot derive how this is done by only looking at the process model. In case of decision tasks, the situation is different since we can follow each path starting from task A and ending at another task and thereby construct a decision table, as will be explained below for the right part of row three. Because the decision table associated with a decision task will contain the value of the gateway variable, we map the connection of a decision task A and a succeeding gateway B in BPMN to a decision dependency between A and B in DMN. This is shown in the left part of row two.

The right part illustrates how BPMN data nodes are represented in DMN models, if they are available. As just mentioned, we assume that the decision task sets the following gateway's variable. If a data node is connected to this decision task, we assume that the data node is used to arrive at this value. Consequently, in the decision model, the data node is mapped to a DMN input data element providing input to the decision element corresponding to the gateway. The mapping shown in the left part of row three is similar to the one directly above. Decision task B succeeds A without further decision tasks in-between them. Then, in the decision model, decision A uses the output of B as input.

Finally, the right part of row three indicates how decision tables are derived. In general, decision tables consist of rules (represented as rows) having one or more conditions and one conclusion, the columns. Each decision table is associated with one decision element (as can be seen in the right part of the first row). The decision table belonging to decision task E will be made up of all gateways that either follow E or another gateway. The gateway labels are mapped to column headers, and the edge annotations to corresponding column values. There will be as many rows as there are individual paths starting from task E and ending at another task. If any of the gateways on the paths is of type IOR, the decision table's hit policy is set to *multi* since several paths (or rows) can be chosen; otherwise, *single* hit is chosen. The header of the conclusion column is derived from the decision task's label and placeholders are used for its cell values. They are used directly in the refactored process model and can be concretized by the process stakeholders during post-processing.

4.3 Exemplary Decision Model Extraction

This section gives an example for the decision model extraction step described in the previous section using the process fragment satisfying pattern P3 introduced in Section 3. The extraction procedure is best explained with the help of a figure that illustrates the correspondences shown in Table 1 using concrete process and decision models. On the left side of Fig. 8, one can see the process fragment, whereas on the right side the decision model is shown. The latter can be divided into the decision requirements level (top) and the decision logic level (bottom) consisting of decision tables. Also, we inserted arrows to point out the correspondences of the two models' elements. For the sake of clarity, we omitted arrows when the correspondence was already shown by another arrow. For example, arrow 1 shows that the process model's decision task *manage discount* corresponds to the decision element *manage discount* in the decision model

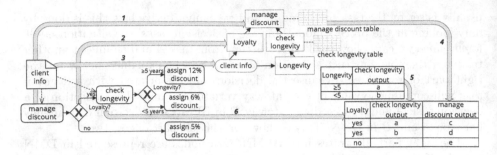

Fig. 8. Exemplary mapping for pattern P3: 1 – from BPMN activity to DMN decision; 2 – from BPMN gateway to DMN decision; 3 – from BPMN data node to DMN input data; 4 – from DMN decision table reference to actual DMN decision table; 5 – from DMN rule conclusions of sub-decision to DMN rule conditions; 6 – from BPMN gateway to DMN rule conditions

(right part of row one in Table 1). Consequently, we did not draw an arrow for the decision task *check longevity*.

Arrow 2 illustrates the left part of row one of Table 1 by mapping the gateway labeled *Loyalty?* to an equivalent decision element. The correspondence between BPMN data nodes and DMN input data elements (right part of row two in Table 1) is demonstrated by arrow 3. Note that the connections between the data node and the tasks in the process model result in connections between the gateway decision elements and the input data in the decision model. Furthermore, the mapping of the left part of row two in Table 1 is demonstrated by the fact that the *manage discount* decision has the *Loyalty* decision as an input requirement. Similarly, corresponding to the left part of row three of that table, since the task *check longevity* succeeds *manage discount*, the DMN decision *manage discount* also requires *check longevity* as an input.

Arrow 4 shows that decisions are connected to decision tables if the decision logic is visible in the process model and arrow 5 shows that the output column of the sub-decision is used as input column of the dependent decision. Arrow 6 visualizes that the headers of the condition columns correspond to the labels of the gateways following the decision task and the cell values equal the edge conditions (cf. right part of row three in Table 1).

4.4   Adaptation of BPMN Models

After extracting the decision logic from a process model to a decision model, the process model needs to be adapted in order to be usable together with the decision model. Basically, the entire decision logic is hidden inside of the first decision task of the pattern. For that purpose, BPMN offers *business rule tasks* that can be linked to decision models and that will output the value of the top-level decision of the decision model. Thus, for the adaptation we transform the task corresponding to this top-level decision to a business rule task. Since this decision potentially subsumes the decisions corresponding to following decision tasks, these tasks will not be required anymore in the adapted process model. Consequently, we delete each decision task other than the first from the process fragment. Basically, this means that also the gateways succeeding the deleted decision tasks can be removed, such that only the first decision task, the gateway succeeding it and the end nodes of the process fragment are kept. For each end node the gateway has an outgoing edge connected to it and the conditions with which the edges are annotated equal the row conclusions of the top-level decision table.

This situation is illustrated in Fig. 9. It is important to assign the correct conditions to the different edges originating from the split gateway. For example, the end node *assign 12% discount* in Fig. 9 is connected to an edge annotated with *c*. This is because in the original process fragment in Fig. 8 the conjunction of the conditions leading from the start node to this end node equals $yes \wedge (\geq 5 \ years)$ and the table row representing this conjunction has *c* as its output value.

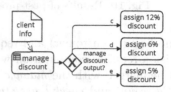

Fig. 9. Refactored process fragment for pattern P3

5   Post-Processing

The outcome of the model refactoring step is an adapted process model and corresponding DMN models, one for each decision. On a case basis, these resulting models are not finalized, because, for instance, decisions have been separated which are indeed taken collectively. Thus, we allow to configure the results in two directions: (i) activities taken based on a decision can be combined into single actions such that the branching behavior is replaced and (ii) two connected decisions in the DMN model can be combined. Considering the adapted process fragment shown in Fig. 9, the activities following on each path represent the same action *assign discount* based on some data input representing the actual discount value. In this paper, we require the stakeholder to explicitly specify that such decision shall be reduced with respect to configuration option (i). In future work, we plan to provide this configuration based on, for instance, label analysis. Choice of this option adapts a process fragment as follows: First, the initial split gateway and all succeeding control flow nodes are replaced by a single activity whose label the stakeholder has to specify. Secondly, we add a data node that is written by the decision task and read by the newly added activity. This data node represents the information transferred from the decision to the action taken based on the decision. For the fragment in Fig. 9, the corresponding adapted process fragment is shown in Fig. 10a. The added activity is labeled *assign discount* and the data node is labeled *discount*.

Referring to option (ii) and the DMN model presented in Fig. 8, decisions can be merged. For instance, decisions *Longevity* and *check longevity* can be merged since the first bases on information directly given in the customer information

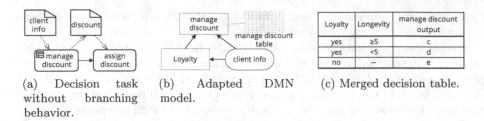

(a) Decision task without branching behavior.

(b) Adapted DMN model.

(c) Merged decision table.

Fig. 10. Results of post-processing for the example given in Section 4.3

(time being a customer) and requires no computation. In contrast, the *Loyalty* decision requires computation whether a customer is considered loyal and may not be merged with the *manage discount* decision. Furthermore, decisions *manage discount* and *check longevity* could be merged since both contribute to the decision which actual discount shall be awarded to a customer. Fig. 10b shows the adapted DMN model based on the discussed decision mergers for the outcome of the pattern P3 fragment given in Fig. 9. Merging decisions requires a merge of the corresponding decision tables, i.e., the dependent decision's table is inserted into the higher level decision's table. The resulting table of merging decisions *manage discount* and *check longevity* is shown in Fig. 10c.

After configuring the output models, the stakeholder may adapt the decision tables and the process model a final time. The annotations on the edges originating from a split gateway are intentionally abstract in our approach. The stakeholder may manually add more descriptive annotations by changing the corresponding edge labels or the corresponding rows in the decision task output column.

6 Evaluation

The evaluation is separated into two parts. First, we argue about the benefits of separating process logic and decision logic before we discuss the feasibility of our approach supported by some proof-of-concept implementation. With respect to Parnas [10], system and software design shall follow the concept of "separation of concerns" to utilize specialized concepts and especially one concept per problem resulting in easier maintenance, less complex systems, reusability, flexibility, shortened development time, comprehensibility, and reduced inter-dependencies. Transferring this concept to the process and decision modeling domains, both shall be separated resulting in the same advantages. In detail, a separation provides the following advantages. The complexity of the process model is reduced while, at the same time, precision, readability, and maintainability (of both the decision and the process model) get improved. Additionally, business logic and decision logic can be changed individually resulting in reduced changing costs and changing times, e.g., compliance experts can tune specific decision points without changing the process structure. Process models are considered stable and only to be adapted if the business changes while decision models are considered dynamic to react fast and flexible on temporary situations. Furthermore, separating the decision logic from process model logic allows reusability of the decision model in multiple decisions occurring in the same as well as different process models.

While separation of both worlds is easy for newly modeled processes, the existing ones need to be kept usable as well. Otherwise, the migration over- head is too large and organizations retain their BPMN misuse. For utilizing the advancements of simplicity, easy maintainability, high precision, and automatic analyzability, the original process model gets adapted to replace the decision logic fragment with a reference to the DMN model after its creation. Based on the assumption that the concept of separation of concerns can be transferred to the process and decision domains, the usefulness of the presented approach for stakeholders is directly given.

The ultimate goal with respect to separation of concerns of process and deci- sion logic is to remove the decision logic entirely from the process model. This results in a transformation of a decision – simple ones as represented by pattern P1 as well as most complex decision structures – into a single activity as shown in Fig. 10a.

To reason about applicability of our approach introduced in this paper, we generically compare the decision logic of both the original and the adapted pro- cess model fragments. As mentioned in Section 4, decision tables consist of rules made up of conjunctions of conditions and one conclusion. The conjuncts of a rule are equal to the conditions annotated to the edges originating from the split gate- ways that are on an individual path from start to end node of a fragment, while the conclusion is a placeholder to be used as an edge condition in the adapted frag- ment. Consequently, both the original and the adapted fragment together with the extracted decision tables represent the same decision logic. This directly shows that the same end node is reached in both process fragments.

We also implemented the introduced approach. We utilized an open source platform for research on process model repositories [4] that is based on the pipe and filter technique principle. Our implementation extending the platform with further modules, their documentation, and some example process models are available at *http://bpt.hpi.uni-potsdam.de/Public/BpmnDmn*. We used this implementation to validate the impact of our approach to the process model repositories of our project partners from the domains of insurance, banking, healthcare, energy, and information technology.

In total, we received 956 process models from them with 566 being syntactically cor- rect. Applying our implementation on these syntactically correct industry process models reveals that pattern P1 occurs in 59%, pat- tern P2 in 16%, and pattern P3 in 32% of all process models as visualized in Fig. 11. In total, we observed 680 occurrences of pattern P1 fragments, 113 occurrences of pattern P2 fragments, and 362 occurrences of pattern P3

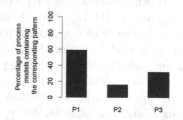

Fig. 11. Pattern occurrence in real world process models

fragments our set of 566 models. These numbers show that the identified patterns are frequently used in practice and thus, we already provide high impact by handling them.

7   Related Work

It is not considered good practice to model the detailed decision paths in the business process model. Thus, there is a demand for finding a good integration between decision and process modeling both in industry and academia. In order to deal with the changes which can arise from run-time contextual changes or the change of user requirements and preferences, different approaches on decision services modeling are used and proposed.

Similarly to our point of view, separation of decision from process logic is discussed in [3,6,14]. [6] presents a tool chain for creation of both models relying on concrete infrastructure and business rules. In contrast, we introduce generic means based on two standards of the OMG – BPMN and DMN. [14] and [3] also utilize these standards but do not provide the next step – as [6] also does not – that is important for practical usage: migration of existing process models into the new separated structure.

Apart from the DMN approach, there are other outlooks dedicated to model the separation of decision-making from application process logic. For instance, in [16], the authors come up with an approach which supports an asynchronous interaction such that the decision service can notify the process about new changes at any time and not only at predefined decision points. [7] presents a decision ontology for supporting decision-making in information systems. Another decision ontology is proposed in [1] as a "domain-specific modeling method that is integrated with an existing enterprise modeling method for describing and communicating decision processes". There are some industrial solutions for separation of decision from process logic, e.g., SAP Decision Service Management [13]. In contrast to our approach, these do not use standards; especially not those that have been designed to solve the advancement of logic separation. Here, BPMN provides rule-tasks that reference a DMN model allowing proper integration of both worlds. Thus, we decided to consider the DMN standard for exploiting the decision logic alongside BPMN for exploiting the process logic.

Another direction of extracting decision logic from process models is "decision mining" [11,12]. Though decision mining helps with the analysis of the dependencies within a process model, the advantage of our approach is that it is purely model-based and does not require additional information such as execution logs. Further, the existing approaches do not cover automatic refactoring of process models.

In [5], the authors state that declarative modeling approaches lead to more design- and run-time flexibility, better compliance guarantees, and higher expressibility. Since decision models are declarative in nature [14], combining them with business process models will provide these benefits as well and additionally preserves the benefits from the concept of separation of concerns.

8   Conclusion

In this paper, we elaborated on the advantages to separate process and decision logic resulting in simpler models with easy maintainability, high precision, and automatic analyzability. The separation especially fosters the differentiation of stable process models to be changed if the business model changes and dynamic decision models allowing flexible configuration of the currently applied business models. Since organizations long misused BPMN as decision modeling languages although it is not meant to capture these aspects, organizations require migration capabilities from misused, spaghetti like process models to a separation that we build of an adapted BPMN model and a DMN model. We provide a semi-automatic approach that allows identification of decision logic in process models, derivation of corresponding DMN models, adaptation of the original process model by replacing the decision logic accordingly, and final configuration of the result during post-processing. The identification is pattern-based derived from an intensive analysis of 956 real world process models provided by our project partners. We implemented this semi-automatic approach and provided statistical insights about pattern utilization in the industry process models. Since AND gateways do not influence decisions (neither AND forks nor merges) and since explicitly considering them would significantly increase the complexity of our approach and its formalization, we disregard AND gateways in this paper. Although not stated explicitly in the patterns, we also support loops like *WHILE x DO y*, since in these cases, the same decision is taken multiple times with varying input data values until the looping condition evaluates to false.

In future work, we will analyze further process model collections and reduce the assumption of control flow decision structures to identify more patterns and to provide a complete overview about decision logic modeling in process models. We also aim on pattern generalization. The mapping will be adjusted accordingly. Furthermore, we extend the configuration capabilities by, e.g., including label analysis. Finally, we plan to publish best practice guidelines on how to model processes and decisions separately.

Acknowledgments. The research leading to these results has been partly funded by DFG under grant agreement WE 1930/8-1. We thank Kristina Kirsten, Tobias Rohloff, and Thomas Zwerg for the support in analyzing the industry process repositories.

References

1. Bock, A., Kattenstroth, H., Overbeek, S.: Towards a modeling method for supporting the management of organizational decision processes. In: Modellierung, vol. 225, pp. 49–64. Gesellschaft für Informatik (2014)
2. Catalkaya, S., Knuplesch, D., Chiao, C., Reichert, M.: Enriching business process models with decision rules. In: Lohmann, N., Song, M., Wohed, P. (eds.) BPM 2013 Workshops. LNBIP, vol. 171, pp. 198–211. Springer, Heidelberg (2014)
3. Debevoise, T., Taylor, J.: The MicroGuide to Process Modeling and Decision in BPMN/DMN. CreateSpace Independent Publishing Platform (2014)

4. Eid-Sabbagh, R.-H., Kunze, M., Meyer, A., Weske, M.: A platform for research on process model collections. In: Mendling, J., Weidlich, M. (eds.) BPMN 2012. LNBIP, vol. 125, pp. 8–22. Springer, Heidelberg (2012)
5. Goedertier, S., Vanthienen, J., Caron, F.: Declarative business process modelling: principles and modelling languages. Enterprise Information Systems 9(2), 161–185 (2015)
6. Kluza, K., Kaczor, K., Nalepa, G.J.: Integration of business processes with visual decision modeling. Presentation of the HaDEs toolchain. In: Fournier, F., Mendling, J. (eds.) BPM 2014 Workshops. LNBIP, vol. 202, pp. 504–515. Springer, Heidelberg (2015)
7. Kornyshova, E., Deneckère, R.: Decision-making ontology for information system engineering. In: Parsons, J., Saeki, M., Shoval, P., Woo, C., Wand, Y. (eds.) ER 2010. LNCS, vol. 6412, pp. 104–117. Springer, Heidelberg (2010)
8. OMG: Business Process Model and Notation (BPMN), Version 2.0 (January 2011)
9. OMG: Decision Model and Notation (February 2014)
10. Parnas, D.L.: On the criteria to be used in decomposing systems into modules. Communications of the ACM 15(12), 1053–1058 (1972)
11. Petrusel, R.: Using markov decision process for recommendations based on aggregated decision data models. In: Abramowicz, W. (ed.) BIS 2013. LNBIP, vol. 157, pp. 125–137. Springer, Heidelberg (2013)
12. Rozinat, A., van der Aalst, W.M.P.: Decision mining in ProM. In: Dustdar, S., Fiadeiro, J.L., Sheth, A.P. (eds.) BPM 2006. LNCS, vol. 4102, pp. 420–425. Springer, Heidelberg (2006)
13. SAP: SAP Decision Service Management. http://scn.sap.com/docs/DOC-29158 (accessed: November 13, 2014)
14. Von Halle, B., Goldberg, L.: The Decision Model: A Business Logic Framework Linking Business and Technology. Taylor and Francis Group (2010)
15. Weske, M.: Business Process Management: Concepts, Languages, Architectures, 2nd edn. Springer, Heidelberg (2012)
16. Zarghami, A., Sapkota, B., Eslami, M.Z., van Sinderen, M.: Decision as a service: separating decision-making from application process logic. In: EDOC, pp. 103–112. IEEE (2012)

Equivalence Transformations for the Design of Interorganizational Data-Flow

Julius Köpke and Johann Eder[(✉)]

Department of Informatics-Systems, Alpen-Adria Universität, Klagenfurt, Austria
{julius.koepke,johann.eder}@aau.at

Abstract. Distributed interorganizational processes can be designed by first creating a global process, which is then split into processes or views for each participant. Existing methods for automating this transformation concentrate on the control flow and neglect either the data flow or address it only partially. Even for small interorganizational processes, there is a considerably large number of potential realizations of the data flow. We analyze the problem of generating message exchanges to realize the dataflow in depth and present a solution for constructing data flows which are optimal with respect to some design objectives. The approach is based on a definition of the correctness of data flow and a complete set of transformations which preserve correctness and allow to search for an optimal solution from a generated correct solution.

1 Introduction

Interorganizational business processes, a key technology to facilitate interorganizational cooperation and e-business, face the challenge to retain the advantages of *intra*organizational business process management for the design of enterprise information systems - which extensively takes advantage of a central coordination - while expanding the technology to fully distributed collaborations of autonomous entities. One of the major differences between centralized and distributed process management is the access to data: uniform access to a joint central data store versus distributed management of data with explicit exchange of data via messages.

We focus on a phase in the development of an interorganizational workflow where the explicit dataflow between participants is established. Starting point of our considerations is a process definition which assumes a global data store. This model is then augmented with messages for passing data between participants such that the process model can be executed in a fully distributed way, respectively projected onto the participants to define the interface of their internal process (e.g. by process views [3,4]). An initial process definition consists of a set of activities, the control flow between them, assignment of the activities to participants, and input and output parameters of activities. Many approaches such as [7,10,14,15,26,28] start with a global process definition and follow a top down or mixed strategy. A global process definition including input and output data already implicitly defines the data flow between participants. For the

© Springer International Publishing Switzerland 2015
J. Zdravkovic et al. (Eds.): CAiSE 2015, LNCS 9097, pp. 367–381, 2015.
DOI: 10.1007/978-3-319-19069-3_23

explicit realization of the data flow, however, there are numerous possibilities [17,21]. Nevertheless, there are no approaches which take this multitude of solutions explicitly into account and, therefore, cannot reason about the quality of the solution. While [25,26,28] do not consider data flow at all, [14,15] restrict the data flow to the distribution of decision variables. [7,10] address data flow, however, only a single solution based on one fixed strategy is generated.

Take for example the following trivial process chunk: lets an activity A produce the parameters x and y, the succeeding activity B updates x, and the third activity C needs x and y. There are basically two solutions: (a) *transitive transfer:* the interface of B is widened to also include y (assuming that B is also admitted to see y) such that B can pass y to C, or (b) *explicit data channel* [21]: A sends y directly to C which requires additional messaging activities which are not yet included in the process definition. Now consider that B is executed conditionally. A simple solution, as proposed by [7] is that A always sends x and y to C. On the one hand, this results in additional message overhead and on the other hand C may not even be allowed to get access to the (intermediate) value of x, if B is executed. If this is the case a better solution would be to only transfer x from A to C, if B is not executed later.

One can easily see that for a given process definition as above there are numerous solutions for establishing a correct explicit data flow. We can reason about properties of a solution and define criteria, such as the number of (additional) data transfers via messages, the number of transitively passed data, etc., for choosing among the possible solutions.

The major contribution of this paper is a set of equivalence transformations on processes with explicit data flow that allow us to define the complete solution space in which we can (heuristically) search for the best solution with respect to constraints and an objective function.

The results presented here can be used for several purposes: to automatically generate the explicit data flow in interorganizational workflows, to check whether a participant with a given unchangeable process interface can be accommodated to join the interorganizational workflow, or to verify and evaluate procedures and guidelines for establishing the data flow for interorganizational processes.

2   Process Model

2.1   Basic Process Model

We follow here the approach that an interorganizational business process is defined as a process rather than as a set of protocols between two participants. For defining the process we use block-structured workflow nets [9] supporting the usual basic control flow patterns sequence, par split / join, and xor split/join [24,27]. We focus on block structured workflow-nets as they prevent typical flaws of unstructured business processes dealing with data [1] and are also in line with the WS-BPEL [19] standard. The process definition is extended with data definition, i.e. global variables may be defined and for each activity we denote which variables are its input and its output. Furthermore, we assign to each activity and each control step one of the participants as actor.

In our notation, $A_a(R, W)$ is an activity step where A is the label of the task to be executed by participant a. R defines the set of input variables, W defines the set of output variables. Abstract blocks are placeholders for any sub-process (including empty ones) and are represented by their label. $SEQ(A, B)$ defines a sequence of the blocks A and B. Sequences can also be defined by nesting: $SEQ(A, SEQ(B, C)) \equiv SEQ(A, B, C)$. $XOR_{px,pj}(cb, A, B)$ defines a xor-block, where the xor-split is executed by participant px, the xor-join is executed by participant pj. Block A is executed, if the condition cb holds, otherwise B. $PAR_{ps,pj}(A, B)$ defines a par-split, where the split is executed by participant ps and the join is executed by participant pj. We also use a graphical representation which in analogy to the usual BPMN notation. The major difference is that we show which the participant executing a step as subscript, the set of input and output variables of activity-steps, and the condition of xor-splits. See Fig. 1, 2, 3, 4 for examples. A communication step (also called send-receive step) is denoted by $SR_s(X, pn, b)$. It defines that participant s sends the content of the set of variables X to participant pn, if the condition b holds. In the graphical notation we represent send-receive steps in analogy to BPMN choreography tasks. See the first step of $TS1a$ in Fig. 2 as an example for $SR_{p1}(X, pn, b)$. A communication step is implemented as a sending task in the local process of the sender and as a receiving task in the local process of the receiver.

2.2   Decision Model and Coordination

The xor-split requires special attention in interorganizational processes. There are the following possibilities: (1) The condition is not defined in the global process, or (2) the condition is defined using some global variables. In case (1) the actor of the XOR-split makes the decision and informs the other participants, if necessary. In case (2) each participant could make the decision. However, this requires that all participants receive all variables appearing in the condition to make the decision (i.e. evaluate the condition). This may result in additional communication overhead. Therefore and for providing a uniform treatment for both cases we treat case (2) like case (1): the actor of the xor-split evaluates the condition.

There are several possibilities for the coordination of different participants:

(1) deferred constructs, where the participants are implicitly informed by the message they receive or do not receive. For an example, step B_b in Fig. 1 does not need to know about the decision of the xor-split. Only when B_b is called participant b joins the process. In contrast participant a who executes the steps A_a and E_A must also be informed if E_a is not called. Otherwise, a would wait forever to be called. (See also death paths elimination in BPEL [10].)

(2) the actor sends the result of the decisions to the other participants. This allows each participant to execute each (required) xor-block locally.

We follow the second approach and require that for any $XOR_{ps,pj}(b, A, B)$ the condition b refers only to one single boolean variable called decision variable,

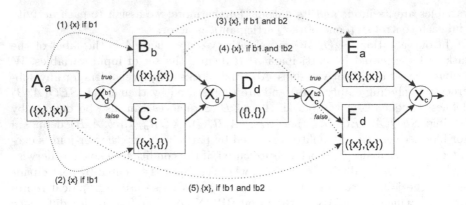

Fig. 1. Implicit data flow in an interorganizational process

which is output of a preceding activity called decision step $DESC_{xs}(\{...\}, \{b\})$ with the same actor as the xor-split. This is not a restriction of the generality as this pattern can be generated automatically. For the coordination it is important that all participants take the same decisions. Since variables can in general be updated, dependent xor-gateways or send-receive steps rely on the value a decision variable had when it was written by the deciding participant. To make our life (and that of workflow designers) easier, we require that decision variables must only be written once.

Data access within parallel blocks may lead to race conditions. In an intraorganizational setting this can be resolved by a transactional data store. For distributed processes we do not assume a distributed transactional data store and, therefore, do not allow parallel read-write or write-write dependencies between variables, i.e. if a variable is output of some activity it must not appear as input or output in branches parallel to this activity.

2.3   Realizing Interorganizational Data Flow

The process definition discussed above uses global variables as if there would be a global data store like in intraorganizational processes. This means it is assumed that each activity can access the most recent value of each variable. Implicitly this defines a data flow between the participants. For the fully distributed enactment of interorganizational processes we have to realize this implicit data flow by augmenting the process definition with explicit message exchanges which pass the content of variables between participants.

Fig. 1 presents an example process using the graphical representation. The first step is represented as $A_a(\{x\}\{x\})$ in the textual representation. Therefore, step A of participant a has variable x as input and as output.

In the example there are 5 data flow dependencies between tasks of different participants shown with dotted lines. Data flow dependencies can be conditional.

For example step E_a only needs x from B_b, if B_b and E_a are executed (if the conditions $b1$ and $b2$ hold). In order to support an interorganizational operation of the process, each data flow between different participants needs to be implemented by messages. Now there exist multiple solutions to support the data needs of E_a. We may add a message exchange right after the execution of B_b. In this case the message is only sent if B_b is executed. However, it will always be sent, even if E_a is not executed. The decision whether E_a is executed is made later. Therefore, it is impossible to predict whether the message needs to be sent or not. However, sending the message does not lead to an error in the data flow. A message is sent but its contents are not consumed as they are overwritten by a succeeding message. So this solution contains redundant message exchanges but it is correct. Another option is to add the message exchange sending x from b to a directly before E_a. However, in this case it must only be executed if B_b was executed. Otherwise a will get a wrong value for x. While b knows whether B_b was executed participant a does not and therefore needs to know whether a message will arrive.

To cope with this problem our process model supports the notion of conditional message exchanges (see Sect. 2.3) where the condition is a boolean expression consisting of decision variables. In our example, we can now add the send-receive step $SR_b(\{x\}, a, b1)$ directly before E_a to solve the previously discussed problem.

2.4 Process Model Definitions

A process model consists of sets of participants P, variables V (including boolean decision variables D), task labels T, and a block defined recursively as follows: Let S be a task label, R,W sets of variables, c a decision variable, b a boolean expression consisting of the decision variables $d_1, \ldots d_n$ then $S_{p1}(R, W)$ is a block (activity step), $SR_s(X, r, b)$ is a block (communication step), the empty block is a block, and if A and B are blocks, then $SEQ(A, \ldots, B)$, $XOR_{p1,p2}(c, A, B)$, $PAR_{p1,p2}(A, B)$ are blocks. All $p1, p2$ are called *actors* of their respective blocks, s is the sender and r is the recipient of a communication step, R, X, c, and $d_1, \ldots d_n$ are (sets of) input variables, W and X are output variables. In addition, a block inherits all input variables of its superordinate block.

Predecessor and successor relationships are defined as usual.

An *initial process* does not contain communication steps. An *augmentation* of an initial process P contains all the steps of P in the same topological order and some communication steps in addition. Each instantiation I of the set of decision variables of a process P constitutes an *instance type* P^I which is defined as a sub-model of P where each xor retains exactly one sub-block (depending on the value of the decision variable) and only those communication steps where the condition is *true* while the other sub-block is empty.

We now define that such an augmented process correctly realizes the implicit data flow of an interorganizational process if for centralized and distributed executions the value of each input variable of a step originates from the output of the same activity.

The *origin* of an input parameter x in block a of an instance type I, $o(P^I, a, x)$, is defined as follows: If b is the closest predecessor activity step of a with x as output parameter then $o(P^I, a, x) = b$.

An initial process is correct, if all input parameters of all steps have a unique origin. This correctness requirements covers the usual data flow faults like uninitialized variables and race conditions [23]. We emphasize that due to the hierarchical definition of process models it is not possible to define an incorrect workflow net.

For the distributed execution of an augmented process we have to consider that a participant only can access the content of a variable if it was produced locally or if it was received through a communication steps.

The *distributed origin* of the input parameter x in block a of an instance type P^I, $o^d(P^I, a, x)$ is defined as follows: Let p be the actor or sender of a and let b be the closest predecessor step of a with x as output parameter and p as actor (for activity steps) or recipient (for communication steps). If b is an activity step then $o^d(P^I, a, x) = b$, if b is a communication step $SR_s(X, p, b)$ then $o^d(P^I, a, x) = o^d(P^I, b, x)$.

Definition 1. Correct Augmentation. The augmentation P of a process is correct, iff for each instantiation I of decision variables, for each input variable x of each block a: $o(P^I, a, x)$ exists and is unique and $o^d(P^I, a, x) = o(P^I, a, x)$.

3   Equivalence Transformations on Augmented Processes

There exists numerous correct augmentations of the data flow of a process. For example all updated variables may be sent as soon as possible to all participants, they may be sent as late as possible or every data-exchange may follow the control-flow including transitive transfers. We present a set of transformations on augmented processes that allow to derive all other correct augmentations.

3.1   Equivalence Transformations on Sequences

We provide a graphical description of equivalence transformations on sequences in Fig. 2 and discuss each transformation shortly in the remainder of this section. The function $ref(b)$ returns the set of all variables, referenced by the boolean expression b.

TS1a - Swap (Send-Receive / Activity): A send-receive step c can be swapped with an activity a, unless a is the destination of c or a writes to some variable transmitted or referenced by c: $SEQ(SR_{p1}(X, pn, b), a_{p2}(R, W)) \equiv SEQ(a_{p2}(R, W), SR_{p1}(X, pn, b))$, unless $(W \cap X \neq \{\}) \vee (R \cap X \neq \{\} \wedge pn = p2) \vee ref(b) \subseteq W)$

TS1b - Swap (Send-Receive - Send-Receive): Two send-receive steps in a sequence can be swapped, unless one is the destination of the other.

$SEQ(SR_{p1}(X, pn, b1), SR_{p2}(Y, pm, b2)) \equiv SEQ(SR_{p2}(Y, pm, b2), SR_{p1}(X, pn,$
$b1))$, unless: $(pn = p2 \vee pm = p1) \wedge (X \cap Y \neq \{\} \vee ref(b1) \subseteq Y \vee ref(b2) \subseteq X)$.

TS2 - Change Sender: Directly sending variables to multiple participants is equivalent to transitive sending of the variables to these participants.
$SEQ(SR_{p1}(X, pn, b), SR_{pn}(X, pm, b)) \equiv SEQ(SR_{p1}(X, pn, b), SR_{p1}(X, pm, b))$

TS3 - Remove/Add at End: A send receive step at the end of a process
is equivalent to no send-receive step at the end of the process. $SEQ(A, SR_p(X,$
$p', b)) \equiv A$, when the sequence is located at the upper most level of the process.

TS4 - Absorb/Add: A send-receive step that sends only variables written by some succeeding activity step is equivalent to only the execution of
the activity-step: $SEQ(SR_{p1}(X, pn, b), a_{p2}(R, W)) \equiv a_{p2}(R, W)$ where $X \subseteq W$,
unless $R \cap X \neq \{\} \wedge pn = p2$.

TS5 - Split/Merge of Variables It is equivalent to transmit a set of
variables by one single send-receive step or by two send-receive steps:
$SEQ(SR_{p1}(X, pn, b), SR_{p1}(Y, pn, b)) \equiv SR_{p1}(X \cup Y, pn, b)$

TS6 - Split/Merge Conditions: Two send-receive steps in a sequence that
transfer the same set of variables from the same source participant to the same
target participant are equivalent to one single send-receive, which is executed if
at least one of the conditions holds:
$SEQ(SR_{p1}(X, pn, b_1), SR_{p1}(X, pn, b_2)) \equiv SR_{p1}(X, pn, \{b1 \vee b2\})$

3.2 Equivalence Transformations on XOR

We first introduce two predicates: *hasValue* and *takesPart*. *hasValue(p1,var,
pos)* returns *true*, if participant $p1$ certainly has the value of the variable *var*
before the execution of the block *pos*. *takesPart(xorBlock,participant)* returns
true, if the participant *participant* participates in any step of the xor-block
xorBlock (recursively). Fig. 3 shows all equivalence transformations on xor-
blocks.

TX1 - Passing XOR-splits One send-receive step s located directly before
a xor-split is equivalent to two send-receive steps with the same parameters
as s, where one is in each branch of the xor-split directly following the xor-
split, if the sender and the receiver of s have the current value of the decision
variable: $SEQ(SR_{p1}(X, pn, b), XOR_{p2,pj}(xb, A, B)) \equiv XOR_{p2,pj}(xb, SEQ(SR_{p1}$
(X, pn, b) , $A), SEQ(SR_{p1}(X, pn, b), B))$, if $hasValue(p1, xb, XS_{p2,pj} \wedge has$
$Value(pn, xb, XS_{p2,pj})$.

TX2 - Passing XOR-Join *TX2a Passing XOR-Join on true:* One send-
receive step s located directly before a xor-join in the *true* branch of a xor-split is
equivalent to one send-receive step s' directly after the xor-join, if all parameters
of s' and s are equivalent but the condition in s' is a conjunction of the one of s
and the decision variable of the xor-split. $XOR_{p2,pj}(xb, SEQ(A, SR_{p1}(X, pn, b)),$
$B) \equiv SEQ(XOR_{p2,pj}(xb, A, B), SR_{p1}(X, pn, \{b \wedge xb\})$

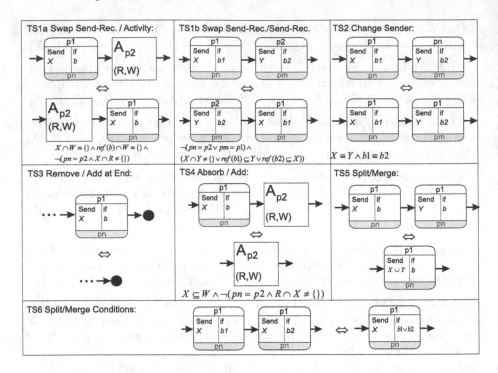

Fig. 2. Equivalence transformations on sequences

TX2b Passing Join on false: $XOR_{p2,pj}(xb, A, SEQ(B, SR_{p1}(X, pn, b))) \equiv$
$SEQ(XOR_{p2,pj}(xb, A, B), SR_{p1}(X, pn, \{b \wedge \neg xb\})$

TX3 - Jump over XOR-Block A send-receive step s, which is located directly before a xor-split is equivalent to a send-receive step directly after the corresponding xor-join, if s transmits only the decision variable of the xor-split and the target participant of s does not take part in the xor-block or any sub-block of it: $SEQ(SR_{p1}(X, pn, b), XOR_{p2,pj}(xb, A, B)) \equiv SEQ(XOR_{p2,pj}(xb, A, B), SR_{p1}(X, pn, b))$, if $\neg takesPart(XS_{p2}, pn) \wedge X \equiv \{xb\}$

TX4 - Inherit Conditions Given a send-receive step s with a condition b, which is nested into some xor-block x referencing the decision variable bx: $b \equiv b \wedge bx$, if s is in Block A of x and $b \equiv b \wedge \neg bx$ if s is in Block B of x.

TX1b - Add Send/Receive after XOR-Split Given a send-receive step s as a direct successor of a xor-split, we can add another send-receive step s' with the same parameter as s as a direct successor of the xor-split in the other branch. This is a one-way transformation. $XOR_{p2,pj}(xb, SEQ(SR_{p1}(Xpn, b), A), B) \vee XOR_{p2,pj}(xb, A, SEQ(SR_{p1}(Xpn, b), B)$
$\implies XOR_{p2,pj}(xb, SEQ(SR_{p1}(X, pn, b), A), SEQ(SR_{p1}(X, pn, b), B))$.

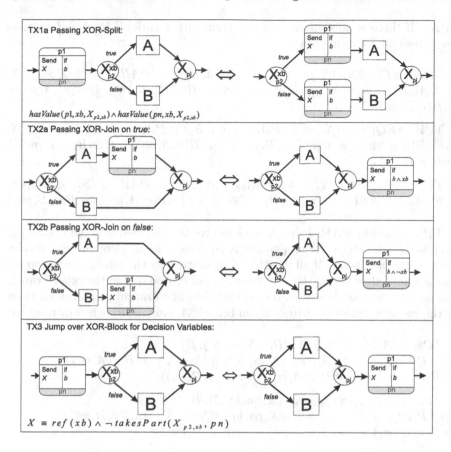

Fig. 3. Equivalence transformations for XOR

3.3   Equivalence Transformations on Parallel Blocks

Equivalence transformations on par-blocks need to consider in which branch reading or writing activities of the transmitted variables are located. We first define the predicates $hasWriter$, $hasReader$ and inB:
$hasWriter(var, Block)$ returns $true$ if the variable var is written anywhere in the block (recursively). $hasReader(var, block, participant)$ returns $true$, if the variable var is read by participant $participant$ in the block (recursively). $inB(var, Block, participant)$ is $true$, if $hasWriter(var, Block)$ or $hasReader$ $(var, block, participant)$. Fig. 4 illustrates $TP1a$, $TP1c$, $TP2a$ as examples.

TP1: Passing PAR-Split: A send-receive-step, which is located directly before a par-split is equivalent to a send-receive step in the first position of the branch with a consumer or a writer to every transferred variable. There are the following cases: A consumer or writer for every transmitted variable is in block A (TP1a), a consumer or writer for every transmitted variable is in block B (TP1b), a consumer for every transmitted variable is in Block A and in B

(TP1c). If there is no consumer of any transmitted variable in A and B, then also TP1a and TP1b applies.

TP1a: $SEQ(SR_{p1}(X, pn, b), PAR_{ps,pj}(A, B)) \equiv PAR_{ps,pj}(SEQ(SR_{p1}(X, pn, b), A), B)$, if $\forall v \in X : (inB(v, A, pn) \land \neg inB(v, B, pn)) \lor (\neg inB(v, A, pn) \land \neg inB(v, B, pn))$

TP1b: $SEQ(SR_{p1}(X, pn, b), PAR_{ps,pj}(A, B)) \equiv PAR_{ps,pj}(A, SEQ(SR_{p1}(X, pn, b), B))$, if $\forall v \in X : (inB(v, B, pn) \land \neg inB(v, A, pn)) \lor (\neg inB(v, A, pn) \land \neg inB(v, B, pn))$

TP1c: $SEQ(SR_{p1}(X, pn, b), PAR_{ps,pj}(A, B)) \equiv PAR_{ps,pj}(SEQ(SR_{p1}(X, pn, b), A), SEQ(SR_{p1}(X, pn, b), B))$, if $\forall v \in X : (inB(v, A, pn) \land inB(v, B, pn))$

TP2: Passing PAR-Join: A send-receive step located in some branch $B1$ of a par-split directly before a par-join is equivalent to an identical send-receive directly after a par-join, if all variables transmitted by the send-receive step are read or updated in branch $B1$ and none is read or updated in the other branch, or if none of the variables is read or updated in any branch. In particular there are the cases: A reader or writer only in branch A, only in Branch B or nowhere:

TP2a: $PAR_{ps,pj}(SEQ(A, SR_{p1}(X, pn, b)), B) \equiv SEQ(PAR_{ps,pj}(A, B), A, SR_{p1}(X, pn, b))$, if $\forall v \in X : (inB(v, A, pn) \land \neg inB(v, B, pn)) \lor (\neg inB(v, A, pn) \land \neg inB(v, B, pn))$

TP2b: $PAR_{ps,pj}(SEQ(SR_{p1}(X, pn, b), A), B) \equiv SEQ(PAR_{ps,pj}(A, B), A, SR_{p1}(X, pn, b))$, if $\forall v \in X : (inB(v, B, pn) \land \neg inB(v, A, pn)) \lor (\neg inB(v, A, pn) \land \neg inB(v, B, pn))$

3.4   Correctness and Completeness

Theorem 1 (Correctness of the Equivalence Transformations). Any application of any of the transformations on a correct augmentation of a process P (see Definition 1) P leads to another correct augmentation of the process P.

We prove the correctness of each transformation by showing that the transformation does not change origin and d-origin of all input variables of each block (details in [13]).

Theorem 2 (Completeness of the set of equivalence transformations). Every correct augmentation of a process P can be created by the application of the transformations starting from any correct augmentation of the process P.

We define a normal form for augmentations of a process and show that, if an augmentation cannot be transformed to this normal form it is incorrect. The theorem then follows from the fact that each transformation has an inverse (details in [13]).

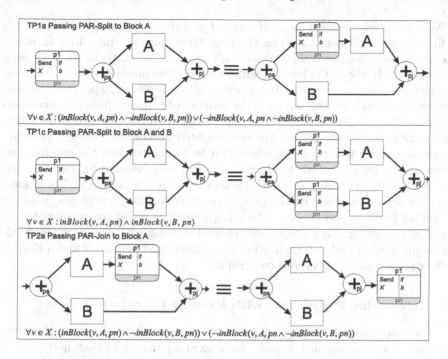

Fig. 4. Example equivalence transformations on PAR-split

4 Applications

The presented equivalence transformations provide a formal grounding for various applications dealing with data flow of interorganizational processes. We will present three applications scenarios as examples here.

4.1 Optimizing Message Exchanges Under Constraints

Given an interorganizational process without communication steps we can generate the complete solution space of correct implementations of the data flow. This allows to select the solution that best fits the needs of the participants based on objective functions and constraints. The best solutions heavily depends on user requirements. For example a major goal could be to achieve simple processes with minimal number of send-receive steps and favor message exchanges that can be integrated into the control-flow, while accepting some potentially redundant transfers. In another scenario minimizing the transferred data at runtime could be the major goal, when communications costs are high. For any of the previous examples additional constraints may exist. For example a participant may not be allowed to receive the value of a certain variable at all or after some specific step or a participant should not receive messages from a predefined set of other participants.

We have implemented a proof-of-concept prototype that uses best first search to find optimal solutions based on the transformations starting from an initial augmentation where all values are broadcasted to all participants after each modification. It allows the user to define an objective function based on various parameters including the weighted number of send-receive steps, the weighted number of transmitted variables and the number of transfers from unknown participants. The weight of send-receive steps is based on their nesting level within xor-blocks and their conditions. For the weighted number of send-receive we do not count communication steps, which can be integrated into the control-flow. When a solution is derived, local processes can be generated for each participant by simple projection of the steps onto each participant [15]. These local processes act as interfaces for the private processes of the participants. We have conducted initial experiments with our implementation and the generated solutions are promising. Future work will address starting with a more efficient initial augmentation and the application of sophisticated heuristics and a flexible framework for modeling various constraints.

4.2   Integrating Participants with Existing Processes

The previous scenario assumed a top-down development paradigm. However, in many cases participants already have existing processes that may not be changeable leading to a mixed approach. When participants with existing processes want to join an interorganizational process only solutions that match their (data) interfaces are applicable. Therefore, the rules can be applied both to test whether their (data) interfaces are compatible with the interorganizational process and to select the best solution based on an objective function.

This can be realized in analogy to the previous application scenario. The only difference is that we start with an interorganizational process with fixed (data) interfaces of one or more participants. In a next step an initial augmentation is created. Then solutions can be generated. However, only those are acceptable, where the participants with existing interfaces have only send-receive steps that are equivalent to their existing interfaces. In other words solutions are generated, where the non fixed participants act as mediators for the fixed ones. An example is the following: One participant needs to receive the variables a, b, c via one single message from participant e. However, a, b and c are all last updated by different other participants. Then the equivalence transformations can be used to generate solutions where participant e collects the results of the other participants and then sends the variables with one single message.

4.3   Validation of Guidelines and Methods

Using the equivalence definition we can also validate guidelines for designing the dataflow or procedures generating the dataflow by analyzing whether the resulting augmented processes can be transformed to a process known to be correct (e.g. the initial processes described in Section 4.1 above).

5 Related Work

We propose a set of equivalence transformations on the realization of the data flow of inter-organizational processes to derive (interfaces to) local processes from a global process definition. Approaches like the public to private approach and multi-party contracts [25, 26, 28] - address the projection of the control-flow onto different participants and the correct implementation of control-flow in the private process. Our approach complements these approaches for the correct implementation of the data flow specification using message exchanges.

Typical choreography approaches [2] either in form of interconnection modeling or in form of interaction-centric modeling are both supported by BPMN (2) [20]. Interconnection modeling wires multiple (collaboration) models together using message exchanges. Interaction-centric modeling is supported by choreography diagrams. An advantage of the interaction-centric style is that a global view of the choreography exists, preventing typical flaws of not properly aligned models. However, they still require that the message exchanges are modeled explicitly. We follow a different strategy. We begin with a global process describing the goals of the choreography in terms of control-and data flow requirements - message exchanges are not part of the global process. Instead our approach allows to automatically generate and optimize the required message exchanges (choreography) between the participants. We address the data flow perspective here, while the correct projection of the control flow is described in [14, 15].

A recent approach addressing data in choreographies is [16]. It proposes modeling guidelines that allow to derive message contents of a given choreography automatically. It is based on a global data model which is mapped to the local ones of each participant. Since our rules allow to automatically generate optimized message exchanges (choreographies) our output can be used as an input for [16] in order to resolve heterogeneities between the data representations of the participants. [17] proposes a set of design patterns for the implementation of data flows satisfying data dependencies. Instead of proposing a fixed set of common patterns we allow to automatically select the best solution according to the users requirements.

Numerous approaches deal with the automatic partitioning of BPEL processes with the aim to find assignments of participants that result in optimal data flow [5, 8, 18, 30]. This setting is very different from our goal, where the assignment of participants is fixed. Directly related to our approach are role based partitioning methods for executable processes such as [6, 7, 10–12]. These approaches also allow to derive processes for each participant. However, the implementation of the data flow is based on a fixed strategy and consequently provide only one solution is provided. An approach focusing on privacy aspects [29] allows to define which participants may exchange messages and to automatically find alternative paths if certain exchanges are forbidden. In contrast, we have provided a general approach for optimizing the implementation of data-transfers based on various criteria where privacy issues and constraints - among those also privacy constraints.

The correctness of the (implicit) data flow of *intra*organizational processes is addressed in works such as [22, 23]. In contrast, our approach spans the solution space for the correct realization of *inter*organizational data flow via message exchanges, taking a (correct) global process with implicit data flow as input.

6 Conclusion

Interorganizational business process management - a promising techniques to foster collaboration and e-business - still requires research and development, in particular in architecture, design and implementation techniques. There exists various implementations for the data flow of an interorganizational process. In this paper we have provided a comprehensive set of equivalence transformations that can act as a solid foundation for several applications such as: Top-down development of interorganizational processes including the automatic optimization of the data flow between different participants and the enforcement of various constraints (e.g. security / access rights), or the validation of methods and procedures for designing interorganizational processes with data flow. It allows to systematically test the compatibility of an existing process with some interorganizational process not only regarding the control-flow but also regarding the (optimized) data flow.

References

1. Combi, C., Gambini, M.: Flaws in the flow: the weakness of unstructured business process modeling languages dealing with data. In: Meersman, R., Dillon, T., Herrero, P. (eds.) OTM 2009, Part I. LNCS, vol. 5870, pp. 42–59. Springer, Heidelberg (2009)
2. Decker, G., Weske, M.: Interaction-centric modeling of process choreographies. Inform. Syst. **36**(2), 292–312 (2011)
3. Eder, J., Kerschbaumer, N., Köpke, J., Pichler, H., Tahamtan, A.: View-based interorganizational workflows. CompSysTech 2011, pp 1–10. ACM (2011)
4. Eder, J., Tahamtan, A.: Temporal consistency of view based interorganizational workflows. In: Kaschek, R., Kop, C., Steinberger, C., Fliedl, G. (eds.) Information Systems and E-business Technologies. LNBIP, vol. 5, pp. 96–107. Springer, Heidelberg (2008)
5. Fdhila, W., Dumas, M., Godart, C.: Optimized decentralization of composite web services. In: CollaborateCom 2010, pp. 1–10. IEEE (2010)
6. Fdhila, W., Godart, C.: Toward synchronization between decentralized orchestrations of composite web services. In: CollaborateCom 2009, pp. 1–10. IEEE (2009)
7. Fdhila, W., Yildiz, U., Godart, C.: A flexible approach for automatic process decentralization using dependency tables. In: ICWS 2009, pp. 847–855 (2009)
8. Goettelmann, E., Fdhila, W., Godart, C.: Partitioning and cloud deployment of composite web services under security constraints. In: IC2E 2013, pp. 193–200. IEEE (2013)
9. Hollingsworth, D.: The workflow reference model (1995)
10. Khalaf, R., Leymann, F.: Role-based decomposition of business processes using bpel. In: ICWS 2006, pp. 770–780 (2006)
11. Khalaf, R., Kopp, O., Leymann, F.: Maintaining data dependencies across BPEL process fragments. In: Krämer, B.J., Lin, K.-J., Narasimhan, P. (eds.) ICSOC 2007. LNCS, vol. 4749, pp. 207–219. Springer, Heidelberg (2007)

12. Khalaf, R., Leymann, F.: Coordination for fragmented loops and scopes in a distributed business process. Inform. Syst. **37**(6), 593–610 (2012)
13. Köpke, J., Eder, J.: Equivalence Transformations on Interorganizational Processes to Shift Communication Steps Technical report, AAU Klagenfurt (2014). http://isys.uni-klu.ac.at/PDF/2014-EQTrans.pdf
14. Köpke, J., Eder, J., Künstner, M.: Projections of abstract interorganizational business processes. In: Decker, H., Lhotská, L., Link, S., Spies, M., Wagner, R.R. (eds.) DEXA 2014, Part II. LNCS, vol. 8645, pp. 472–479. Springer, Heidelberg (2014)
15. Köpke, J., Eder, J., Künstner, M.: Top-down design of collaborating processes. In: iiWAS 2014. ACM (2014)
16. Meyer, A., Pufahl, L., Batoulis, K., Kruse, S., Lindhauer, T., Stoff, T., Fahland, D., Weske, M.: Automating data exchange in process choreographies. In: Jarke, M., Mylopoulos, J., Quix, C., Rolland, C., Manolopoulos, Y., Mouratidis, H., Horkoff, J. (eds.) CAiSE 2014. LNCS, vol. 8484, pp. 316–331. Springer, Heidelberg (2014)
17. Monsieur, G., Snoeck, M., Lemahieu, W.: Managing data dependencies in service compositions. J. Syst. Software **85**(11), 2604–2628 (2012)
18. Nanda, M.G., Chandra, S., Sarkar, V.: Decentralizing execution of composite web services. In: Proc. 19th Annual ACM SIGPLAN Conference on Object-oriented Programming, Systems, Languages, and Applications, OOPSLA 2004, pp. 170–187. ACM press (2004)
19. OASIS. OASIS Web Services Business Process Execution Language (WSBPEL) TC. Technical report, "OASIS" (2007)
20. Object Management Group (OMG). Business process model and notation (bpmn) version 2.0. Technical report (2011)
21. Russell, N., ter Hofstede, A.H.M., Edmond, D., van der Aalst, W.M.P.: Workflow data patterns: identification, representation and tool support. In: Delcambre, L.M.L., Kop, C., Mayr, H.C., Mylopoulos, J., Pastor, Ó. (eds.) ER 2005. LNCS, vol. 3716, pp. 353–368. Springer, Heidelberg (2005)
22. Sun, S.X., Zhao, J.L., Nunamaker, J.F., Sheng, O.R.L.: Formulating the data-flow perspective for business process management. Information Systems Research **17**(4), 374–391 (2006)
23. Trčka, N., van der Aalst, W.M.P., Sidorova, N.: Data-flow anti-patterns: discovering data-flow errors in workflows. In: van Eck, P., Gordijn, J., Wieringa, R. (eds.) CAiSE 2009. LNCS, vol. 5565, pp. 425–439. Springer, Heidelberg (2009)
24. van der Aalst, W.M.P.: Verification of workflow nets. In: Azéma, Pierre, Balbo, Gianfranco (eds.) ICATPN 1997. LNCS, vol. 1248. Springer, Heidelberg (1997)
25. van der Aalst, W.M.P.: Inheritance of interorganizational workflows: How to agree to disagree without loosing control? IT and Management **4**(4), 345–389 (2003)
26. van der Aalst, W.M.P., Lohmann, N., Massuthe, P., Stahl, C., Wolf, K.: Multiparty contracts: Agreeing and implementing interorganizational processes. Comput. J. **53**(1), 90–106 (2010)
27. van der Aalst, W.M.P., ter Hofstede, A.H.M., Kiepuszewski, B., Barros, A.P.: Workflow patterns. Distrib. Parallel Databases **14**(1), 5–51 (2003)
28. van der Aalst, W.M.P., Weske, M.: The P2P approach to interorganizational workflows. In: Dittrich, K.R., Geppert, A., Norrie, M. (eds.) CAiSE 2001. LNCS, vol. 2068, pp. 140–156. Springer, Heidelberg (2001)
29. Yildiz, U., Godart, C.: Information flow control with decentralized service compositions. ICWS **2007**, 9–17 (2007)
30. Zhai, Y., Hongyi, S., Zhan, S.: A data flow optimization based approach for BPEL processes partition. In: ICEBE 2007, pp. 410–413 (2007)

Automatic Generation of Optimized Process Models from Declarative Specifications

Richard Mrasek[✉], Jutta Mülle, and Klemens Böhm

Institute for Program Structures and Data Organization,
Karlsruhe Institute of Technology (KIT), Karlsruhe 76131, Germany
{richard.mrasek,jutta.muelle,klemens.boehm}@kit.edu

Abstract. Process models often are generic, i. e., describe similar cases or contexts. For instance, a process model for commissioning can cover both vehicles with an automatic and with a manual transmission, by executing alternative tasks. A generic process model is not optimal compared to one tailored to a specific context. Given a declarative specification of the constraints and a specific context, we study how to automatically generate a good process model and propose a novel approach. We focus on the restricted case that there are not any repetitions of a task, as is the case in commissioning and elsewhere, e. g., manufacturing. Our approach uses a probabilistic search to find a good process model according to quality criteria. It can handle complex real-world specifications containing several hundred constraints and more than one hundred tasks. The process models generated with our scheme are superior (nearly twice as fast) to ones designed by professional modelers by hand.

Keywords: Process synthesis · Automatic process generation · Commissioning processes · Business process modeling

1 Introduction

Scheduling tasks so that the overall execution is efficient and at the same time no constraints are violated continues to be a fundamentally important problem. Process models describe the possible arrangements of the tasks.

Example 1. Our application scenario is commissioning. Commissioning means configuring and testing the electronic components of a vehicle during its production. Process models describe the arrangement of the configuration and testing tasks. For instance, a factory worker has to configure the transmission and to activate the anti-theft system. The transmission can either be manual, i. e., Task M does the configuration, or automatic (Task A). Task T activates the anti-theft system. Before the activation, a central computer needs to generate a master key (Task G), and it opens the connection to the specific control unit (Task O). The connection has to be closed before the process finishes (Task C). The configuration of the transmission and the activation of the anti-theft system require a running engine; Task E turns it on. Figure 1(a) shows the tasks that may be

© Springer International Publishing Switzerland 2015
J. Zdravkovic et al. (Eds.): CAiSE 2015, LNCS 9097, pp. 382–397, 2015.
DOI: 10.1007/978-3-319-19069-3_24

a)

Task	proc. time
E : Start **E**ngine	1s
M : Conf. **M**anual transmission	5s
A : Conf. **A**utomatic transmission	2s
T : Activate anti-**T**heft system	1s
C : **C**lose Connection	1s
O : **O**pen Connection	1s
G : **G**enerate Master Key	5s

b)

Fig. 1. The Tasks for Commissioning (a) and the Ordering Relationship Graph (b)

part of the commissioning. The second column is the expected processing time. Commissioning always has a context, i.e., the variation of the vehicle, its components, their relationships and the constraints the vehicle currently tested must fulfill. The variation determines which tasks have to be executed, e. g., a car with a manual transmission requires different tasks than a car with an automatic one.

A context c determines the tasks $\mathcal{T}_c$ required for a process. It is infeasible to model all processes for each possible set of required tasks by hand. This calls for generic process models for several contexts. With such generic models however, one optimal arrangement of tasks for any context does not exist.

Example 2. The context characteristic transmission determines the required tasks as follows: If the vehicle has an automatic transmission, the commissioning requires execution of the tasks $\mathcal{T}_c =\{E, A, T, C, O, G\}$; for a manual transmission in turn the tasks are $\mathcal{T}_c =\{E, M, T, C, O, G\}$. Figure 1(b) shows the dependencies between the tasks as a graph. Directed edges represent ordering dependencies, while dashed lines represent exclusive dependencies. The graph is the declarative specification we generate the process model from. The extended version of this paper [17] shows how one can generate such a specification from input in other languages. Section 2 will introduce the notation behind that graph structure.

Figure 2 shows two generic process models that comply with the dependency graph of Figure 1(b). Figure 2(a) has a shorter processing time if the transmission is automatic (7s to 10s). For a manual transmission in turn, the process model in Figure 2(b) has a shorter processing time (8s to 10s).

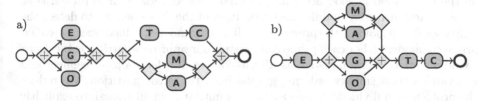

Fig. 2. Two Distinct Process Models for the Graph in Figure 1(b)

With at least one process model for each possible context, the number of such models increases exponentially with the number of context characteristics. For instance, 10 context characteristics that are Boolean in nature result in 1024 process models. Next, several models typically are possible for a given context. The problem studied here is how to generate a good process model for a given context from a declarative specification. The model should be good according to predefined quality criteria, e. g., throughput time. Process models that comply with the dependencies can be very different with respect to quality and performance criteria. Section 4 will show that models generated with our approach are about 50% faster than ones designed by professionals with years of experience. We focus on the restricted case that there are no repetitions, i. e., on process trees with inner nodes SEQ, AND, XOR, but not LOOP. There is a number of settings with this characteristic, for instance in manufacturing. In particular, loops are unnatural in commissioning processes, since a feature is tested only once. On the other hand, if a problem occurs and is fixed, a new commissioning process is started. Another assumption, which also holds for commissioning and elsewhere, is that context information together with experience from the past allows to reliably estimate the processing time of individual tasks.

The generation of a process model from a declarative specification bears several challenges. There often is a great variety of models that fulfill the specification, as mentioned before. To illustrate, the sequential arrangement of n nodes, in the absence of any constraint, give way to $n!$ different process models. For the largest process in our evaluation, 4.12×10^{340} models are possible. Generating all possible models is not possible. It is challenging to detect a good process model that does not violate any constraint.

Example 3. *There are four tasks A, B, C, and D. Suppose that the following constraints exist: B must always occur before A and C ($B \to A$, $B \to C$), and D always occurs before C ($D \to C$). It seems to be a good idea to put A and C in parallel, because this might reduce the throughput time. But putting A and C in parallel rules out having A and D in parallel.*

Related work in process synthesis is fully automatic only for processes that are fully specified by their dependencies [6][25]. In case of an under-specification, [6] requires a process modeler to manually make decisions, and [25] requires a manual clustering of the constraints. This is not practical, because of the daunting number of possible models. To this end, we propose a novel process synthesis algorithm whose output on the one hand complies with the dependencies and on the other hand is good according to predefined criteria. Our approach is as follows: First, it uses a modular decomposition of the dependencies to detect the fully specified regions of the process as well as the under-specified ones, so-called prime components. For each prime component, our approach partitions the corresponding ordering graph systematically, as follows. It selects a pivot element and generates several smaller ordering graphs from the pivot partition. We reduce the problem in a divide and conquer fashion until it is small enough to explicitly generate all possible models. We repeat this for different pivot elements to have a better coverage according to our quality criterion the throughput time of the process. Other criteria such as overall energy consumption are possible as well. As we show in the evaluation with thousands of non-trivial process models, our approach is efficient, i. e., is able to test thousands of models in under a second, checking for complex constraints. On average, our approach nearly halves the processing time compared to the reference processes, which already are the output of a careful intellectual design. Our approach can handle complex real-world specifications containing several hundred dependencies as well as more than one hundred tasks. In our evaluation, the process models generated contain between 98 and 185 tasks, and their arrangement typically is nontrivial.

Section 2 introduces some fundamentals. Section 3 describes our algorithm for the process generation. Section 4 features our evaluation. Section 5 discusses related work, and Section 6 concludes.

2   Fundamentals

A meaningful input for process synthesis is the declarative specification in the form of an ordering relation graph (ORG) [21]. The modular decomposition of a graph yields its components and implies a hierarchical structure of components called the Modular Decomposition Tree (MDT)[15], see Subsection 2.3. The MDT separates the under-specified regions from the fully specified ones.

2.1   Ordering Relation Graph

In an ordering relation graph, each node represents a task. Each edge represents a dependency between tasks. The dependencies consist of ordering dependencies, i. e., in which order do the tasks occur, and exclusive dependencies, i. e., when do two tasks exclude each other.

Definition 1. *The ordering relation graph is a directed attributed graph $G = (V, E)$, with V being nodes and $E \subseteq V \times V$ the edges. Each node corresponds to a task. E consists of two subsets $E_\rightarrow$ and $E_\#$ such that $E = E_\rightarrow \cup E_\#$ and $E_\rightarrow \cap E_\# = \emptyset$. $E_\rightarrow$ defines the ordering relation, i. e., two tasks that should be in a specific order have an edge in $E_\rightarrow$. $E_\rightarrow$ is transitive and anti-symmetric:*

$$(transitive) \quad \forall (x, y), (y, z) \in E_\rightarrow : (x, z) \in E_\rightarrow$$
$$(antisymmetric) \quad \forall (x, y) \in E_\rightarrow : (y, x) \notin E_\rightarrow$$

$E_\#$ defines the exclusiveness relation, i. e., if two tasks exclude each other they share an edge in $E_\#$. $E_\#$ is symmetric, i. e., $\forall (x, y) \in E_\# : (y, x) \in E_\#$. We do not allow self-edges, i. e., $\forall v \in V : (v, v) \notin E$.

Note that $E_\rightarrow$ does not contain any cycle. For each task we determine the processing time. The average error of the estimated execution times of our tasks from our application scenario is less than 17%. We had calculated these times by analyzing the logs of existing traces.

Definition 2. *The neighborhoods $N^{out}(v)$, $N^{in}(v)$ of a node v are defined as:*

$$N^{out}(v) := \{w \mid w \in V \wedge (v,w) \in E_{\rightarrow}\} \quad N^{in}(v) := \{w \mid w \in V \wedge (w,v) \in E_{\rightarrow}\}$$

$N^{out}(v)$ *is the set of nodes with an incoming ordering edge from v. $N^{in}(v)$ is the set of nodes that have an outgoing ordering edge to v. For a set of nodes V the incoming and outgoing set are defined as $N^{out}(V) := \bigcup_{v \in V} N^{out}(v)$ and $N^{in}(V) := \bigcup_{v \in V} N^{in}(v)$ respectively.*

In contrast to an imperative process language like BPMN, ORG is a declarative description and not necessarily fully specified.

2.2   Process Tree

We want to generate the process model in the form of a process tree (PT). In contrast to a graph-based process model, the process tree has two important characteristics. First, it can be easily transformed into an executable process language, see [17]. Second, a process tree is sound by default [10]. This means the following: First, the process will terminate properly. Second, for each task there is at least one process instance containing it. Each *process tree $PT = (\mathcal{V}, \mathcal{E})$* is an ordered tree, thus a rooted tree for which an ordering is specified for the children of each vertex. $\mathcal{V}$ consists of leaf nodes $\mathcal{V}_t$ and inner nodes $\mathcal{V}_c$, $\mathcal{V}_t \cup \mathcal{V}_c = \mathcal{V}$, $\mathcal{V}_t \cap \mathcal{V}_c = \emptyset$. Each leaf node corresponds to a task, and each inner node corresponds to a control structure. In this paper we consider three control structures, namely sequence SEQ, parallel AND and exclusive XOR. These control structures correspond to the basic control workflow patterns [2]. This study focuses on the synthesis of process models without cycles. Hence, we do not define a loop operator. It is possible to model the commissioning processes using those control structures. Each control structure can be translated to another block-oriented language, e. g., WS-BPEL, OTX, or to a graph-oriented process language, e. g., Petri nets, BPMN.

2.3   Modular Decomposition

We want to generate a process tree from the declarative specification, i. e., from the ORG. Let $G = (V, E)$ be such a graph. For any $W \subseteq V$ we say that $G_W(V^W, E^W)$ is the sub-graph induced by W, i. e., $V^W = W$ and $E^W = E \cap (W \times W)$. We call W a component iff $\forall v, v' \in W$, $N^{out}(v) \backslash W = N^{out}(v') \backslash W$ and $N^{in}(v) \backslash W = N^{in}(v') \backslash W$. Thus v and v' have identical neighborhoods outside of W. In other words, a component consists of tasks with the same dependencies regarding tasks outside of the component.

Example 4. *The set $\{T,C\}$ is a component of the graph in Figure 3(a). T has incoming edges from E, G, and O and no outgoing edge except the one to C, C shares the same edges, not considering the inner edge between T and C. The set $\{T,G\}$ is not a component because T has an incoming edge from E and G has not.*

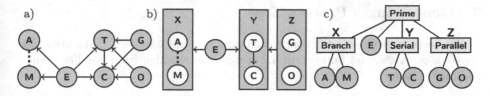

Fig. 3. An Ordering Relation Graph (a), its Modular Decomposition (b) and the Corresponding Modular Decomposition Tree (c)

In our use case, a component often consists of tasks operating on the same electronic control unit of the vehicle. W is a strong component if, for each component $W' \subseteq V$, one of the following holds: $W \cap W' = \emptyset$, $W \subseteq W'$, or $W' \subseteq W$.

Example 5. *Consider a graph G_2 with tree nodes A, B, C and no edges. $W = \{A, B\}$ and $W' = \{B, C\}$ are components. They are not strong because $W \cap W' \neq \emptyset$, $W \not\subseteq W'$, or $W' \not\subseteq W$. The strong components are $\{A, B, C\}$, $\{A\}$, $\{B\}$, $\{C\}$.*

The decomposition of a graph into strong components is called Modular Decomposition, and the resulting hierarchical structure is called Modular Decomposition Tree (MDT). Figure 3(a) shows the simple ordering relation graph of Figure 1, its decomposition in four components Figure 3(b) and the corresponding modular decomposition tree Figure 3(c). [15] shows that a node W in a MDT with children $S_1, S_2, \ldots, S_k$ is of one of the following:

Complete : $\forall I \subset \{1, \ldots, k\}$, with $1 < |I| < k : \bigcup_{i \in I} S_i$ is a component
Prime   : $\forall I \subset \{1, \ldots, k\}$, with $1 < |I| < k : \bigcup_{i \in I} S_i$ is not a component

Example 6. *The root node in Figure 3 (c) is a prime node. None of the subsets of the children with size 2 or 3, e.g., $\{X, E\}$ or $\{E, Y, Z\}$, do form a component.*

A complete component W with the induced graph $G_W(V^W, E^W)$ either does not contain any edges or is a clique in $E_\#^W$ or $E_\rightarrow^W$, see the proof of Lemma 1. A complete component can easily be transformed to a process tree deterministically, see [21]. For a prime component our approach will use a heuristic optimization.

Lemma 1. *A strong complete component W is of exactly one of four types:*

trivial : $|V^W| = 1$
serial   : *For every $v, v' \in V^W : (v, v') \in E_\rightarrow^W \lor (v', v) \in E_\rightarrow^W$. Recall that the edges in $E_\rightarrow^W$ are cycle-free.*
branch : *For every $v, v' \in V^W : (v, v') \in E_\#^W$*
parallel : *For every $v, v' \in V^W : (v, v') \notin E^W$*

Proof. The proofs of all lemmas are in [17]. □

[15] proves that the decomposition of a directed graph (V, E) can be done in $O(|V| + |E|)$, thus in time linear with the size of the graph – We use the MDT to transform the ORG into a process tree.

3   Generating a Process Tree

In this section we explain the conceptual design of our approach. Subsection 3.1 gives an overview, and Subsection 3.2 states how the algorithm handles under-specified regions.

Algorithm 1. Synthesize(ORG G, context c): ProcessTree PT

1: Determine $\mathcal{T}_c$ from c
2: $G \leftarrow$ subgraph G_W of G with the nodes $W = \mathcal{T}_c$
3: $PT \leftarrow$ Modular Decomposition of G
4: **for all** prime nodes $\mathcal{P} \in PT$ **do**
5:      Process tree PT$_\mathcal{P} \leftarrow synPrime(\mathcal{P})$
6:      Replace $\mathcal{P}$ with $PT_\mathcal{P}$
7: **end for**
8: **for all** leaf nodes $l \in PT$ **do**
9:      **if** l is a partition leaf node **then**
10:         $G_l \leftarrow$ ORG of l
11:         Process tree PT$_l \leftarrow synthesize(G_l, c)$
12:         Replace l with PT_l
13:     **end if**
14: **end for**
15: **return** PT

3.1   Overview of the Automatic Generation

Our goal is to automatically generate a process model from a declarative description. Algorithm 1 synthesizes a process tree from an ORG and a context c. The context c determines the required tasks $\mathcal{T}_c$ (Line 1). We then reduce the ORG G to the subgraph G_W with the nodes $W = \mathcal{T}_c$ (Line 2). The algorithm then computes a modular decomposition of the ORG (Line 3 in Algorithm 1). The resulting modular decomposition tree (MDT) may contain both complete and prime components. For complete components, a transformation to process fragments exists, cf. [21]. For a prime component in turn, several fragments are possible, see Figure 4. In other words, each prime component stands for an under-specified region. For each prime component $\mathcal{P}$, we use a probabilistic optimization to find a solution (Line 5). We replace $\mathcal{P}$ with the solution found (Line 6). $synPrime()$ splits the ORG of the prime components into partitions. It generates a graph with one node for each of these partitions. The algorithm recursively calls itself, in order to replace each node with a subtree. Finally, our approach transforms the PT into a process language, e. g., BPMN, WS-BPEL.

3.2   Under-Specified Regions

Each prime component $\mathcal{P}$ induces a graph $G_\mathcal{P} = (V_\mathcal{P}, E_\mathcal{P})$. $V_\mathcal{P}$ denotes the set of strong components that belong to $\mathcal{P}$. Figure 3 shows that the graph $G_\mathcal{P}$ for the

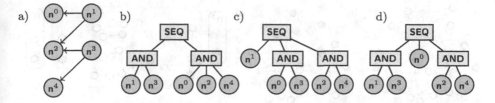

Fig. 4. The Neighborhood Graph to Directly Generate a Process Tree (a), three Possible Process Trees (b)(c)(d) for the Graph (a)

prime component $\mathcal{P}$ consists of $V_{\mathcal{P}} = \{X, R, Y, Z\}$ with $E_{\mathcal{P}} = \{(R \rightarrow X), (R \rightarrow Y), (Z \rightarrow Y)\}$. $\mathcal{P}$ is not fully specified and thus there does not exist a unique corresponding process tree. Due to the large number of possible process models for a prime graph $G_{\mathcal{P}}$ it is not feasible to construct every possible one.

The modular decomposition detects the fully specified and the under-specified regions of the process. Our overall idea is to reduce the size of the graph induced by a prime component iteratively until the number of remaining solutions is low (< 100) so that we can solve the problem. See Figure 4. Our intuition for the reduction is to select a pivot node v and detect which nodes (V_1) must occur before v, and which nodes (V_2) can be scheduled in parallel to v. V_1 as well as V_2 imply two smaller ordering graphs. We repeat this with several different pivot nodes. Our approach randomly selects a node $v \in V_{\mathcal{P}}$ with $N^{out}(v) = \emptyset$ as pivot node. Lemma 3 will show why we need this characteristic. The ORG $G_{\mathcal{P}}$ is cycle-free, and thus a node v with $N^{out}(v) = \emptyset$ always exists.

Definition 3. *The zero neighborhood of a pivot node v is $N^{(0)}(v) := \{v\}$, $N^{(1)}(v) := N^{in}(v)$. For $i \in \mathbb{N}$, $i > 1$ we define the i-neighborhood as:*

$$N^{(i)}(v) := \begin{cases} \left(\bigcup_{v' \in N^{(i-1)}(v)} N^{out}(v')\right) \setminus N^{(i-2)}(v) & \text{if } i \in \{2, 4, 6, \dots\} \\ \left(\bigcup_{v' \in N^{(i-1)}(v)} N^{in}(v')\right) \setminus N^{(i-2)}(v) & \text{if } i \in \{3, 5, 7, \dots\} \end{cases}$$

We use the neighborhood information to partition the graph. Each partition $n^{(i)}$ is a subgraph of the ORG $G_{\mathcal{P}}$ with the nodes $N^{(i)}(v)$. In other words, the partitioning implies a graph G_v where each $n^{(i)}$ is a node. We refer to this graph as the neighborhood graph. Formally, given a pivot node v, the neighborhood graph $G_v = (V_v, E_v)$ is as follows

$$V_v = \{n^i \mid N^{(i)}(v) \neq \emptyset\}$$
$$E_v = \{(n^i, n^{i+1}) \mid i \in \{1, 3, \dots\} \wedge n^i, n^{i+1} \in V_v\} \cup$$
$$\{(n^{i+1}, n^i) \mid i \in \{0, 2, \dots\} \wedge n^i, n^{i+1} \in V_v\}$$

The graph contains each non-empty neighborhood as a node.

Example 7. *For the graph in Figure 3(b) and the pivot Y the neighborhoods are: $N^{(0)}(Y) = \{Y\}$, $N^{(1)}(Y) = \{R, Z\}$, $N^{(2)}(Y) = \{X\}$, and for $i > 2$ $N^{(i)}(Y) = \emptyset$.*

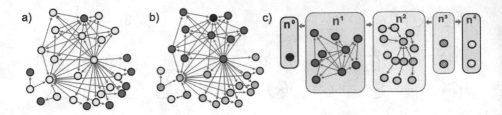

Fig. 5. A Prime Component (a), its Partitioning (b), and the Neighborhood Graph (c)

The neighborhood graph $G_Y(V_Y, E_Y)$ for the pivot Y is:

$$G_Y = (\{n^0, n^1, n^2\} , \{ (n^1, n^0) , (n^1, n^2) \})$$

Example 8. *Figure 5(a) shows a more complex graph which is a prime component, i.e., there is no unique corresponding tree. The possible pivot nodes are in violet. The pivot node at the top of Figure 5(a) leads to the partitioning in Figure 5(b). Figure 5(c) shows the respective neighborhood graph.*

Lemma 2. *The partitioning into the neighborhood graph for a pivot v preserves all order dependencies. In other words, for each edge $(v_1, v_2) \in E_P$, one of the following holds:*

(a) $\exists i \in \mathbb{N}_0 : v_1, v_2 \in N^{(i)}(v)$
(b) $v_1 \in N^{(i)}(v), v_2 \in N^{(j)}(v), i \neq j \Rightarrow (n^i, n^j) \in E_v$

Lemma 2 states that our approach does not loose any dependencies. A symmetric solution would be to select pivots with $N^{in}(v) = \emptyset$ and change the definition of the neighborhood accordingly. However, a pivot v with $N^{out}(v) \neq \emptyset \wedge N^{in}(v) \neq \emptyset$ would loose a dependency, see Lemma 3.

Lemma 3. *The neighborhood graph G_v for a pivot node v with $N^{out}(v) \neq \emptyset \wedge N^{in}(v) \neq \emptyset$ does not preserve the order dependencies.*

Algorithm 2. synPrime (Neighborhood Graph $G(V, E)$) : ProcessTree PT

1: Pivot v ← randomly select a node $v \in G$ with $N^{out}(v) = \emptyset$
2: $G_v(V_v, E_v)$ ← calculate neighborhood of v
3: **if** $N^{(\lambda)} = \emptyset$ **then**
4:     **return** (select tree pattern randomly)
5: **else**
6:     **return** $synPrime(G_v)$
7: **end if**

Algorithm 2 generates a process tree for an under-specified region, i.e., a prime component. First, the algorithm randomly selects a pivot node v (Line 1)

and calculates its neighborhood graph G_v (Line 2). The parameter $\lambda \in \mathbb{N}^+$ defines when the neighborhood graph is small enough to generate a process tree. If the neighborhood graph is too large, the algorithm calls *synPrime* again, and everything is repeated until the graph is processable. Figure 6 shows the reduction of a neighborhood graph. If our approach selects n^2 as the pivot element, it then builds the smaller graph on the right hand side.

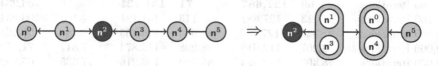

Fig. 6. Reduction of a Neighborhood Graph with the Pivot n^2

If the neighborhood graph is small enough ($N^{(\lambda)} = \emptyset$), Algorithm 2 randomly selects a tree pattern for it (Step 4). A tree pattern is a process tree for the neighborhood graph. The neighborhood graph in Figure 4(a) contains 5 nodes and 4 edges. For a graph with five nodes thousands of process trees are possible. For the graph in Figure 4(a) 53 trees are possible, given the constraints. For most of these 53 process trees, there is another tree with a lower overall processing time, for any processing times of the tasks. If we exclude these dominated trees, three trees remain. Figures 4(b) and (c) show two of them, randomly selected. The tree patterns define which additional dependencies have to be added to generate a block based process model for the specification. [17] shows and explains all tree patterns for $\lambda \in [1, 5]$. Figure 4(d) shows a process tree fulfilling the constraints in Figure 4(a), but the processing time of the tree in Figure 4(b) always is shorter.

For each ORG we have started out with, we calculate κ different process trees. The resulting trees differ depending on the probabilistic choices in Algorithm 2 (Line 1) and (Line 4). We select the best process tree found according to quality criteria, e. g., the processing time. We calculate a quality value of each tree as follows. The average processing time for each node in a process tree $PT(\mathcal{V}, \mathcal{E})$ is calculated recursively with function $fit \colon \mathcal{V} \to \mathbb{R}$.

$$fit(n) := \begin{cases} runtime(n) & \text{if } type(n) = task \\ \max_{c \in child_n} fit(c) & \text{if } type(n) = \text{AND} \\ \sum_{c \in child_n} fit(c) & \text{if } type(n) = \text{SEQ} \\ \max_{c \in child_n} fit(c) & \text{if } type(n) = \text{XOR} \end{cases}$$

$type \colon \mathcal{V} \to \{task, \text{AND}, \text{SEQ}, \text{XOR}\}$ is a function to determine the type of the tree node. $child_n := \{c \mid (n, c) \in \mathcal{E}\}$ is the set of nodes in the process tree with parent node n. The estimation for the XOR-Split is a worst case analysis, i.e., the processing time is smaller than the estimated one. If the probabilities of the splits are known a priori a more precise average case assumption is possible,

Table 1. Computation Time (CT) and Processing Time (PT) of our Approach

	PROCESS A		PROCESS B		PROCESS C	
NO. OF TASKS	171		185		116	
REF. PROCESS TIME	171 780ms		169 606ms		148 014ms	
	CT in ms	PT in ms	CT in ms	PT in ms	CT in ms	PT in ms
10 Iterations	35	188,420	34	227,260	**32**	**132,998**
50 Iterations	**69**	**127,687**	**71**	**131,121**	66	103,234
100 Iterations	113	127,687	113	131,121	104	103,234
1 000 Iterations	823	127 687	964	116,155	788	97,264
10,000 Iterations	8,207	112,918	8,298	113,874	7,817	71,513
100,000 Iterations	78,409	112,624	86,594	106,216	77,335	65,892
PT REDUCTION	34.437 %		37.375 %		50.456 %	

see [24]. The fitness of a process tree $fit(PT)$ is the fitness of its root node. The algorithm returns the process tree with the highest fitness value. The resulting process tree can easily be transformed to the notation required.

We have implemented the algorithms in C#. The program receives the ORG as input, see [17] on how to generate an ORG from a declarative specification. The output of the program is a process tree that is then transformed to the commissioning process notation OTX by a proprietary XSLT script written by us. The implementation can handle specifications with several hundreds of tasks and thousands of dependencies in a few minutes, see Section 4.

4   Evaluation

Our evaluation uses 21 process models from a car manufacturer that specify the testing and commissioning of middle-class vehicles. Each process model reflects several context characteristics which are attached for the generation. The context characteristics consist of properties of the vehicle project, of the factory and of the components to put in commission. Professional process developers have designed the process models. The tasks to be executed depend on the components built into the vehicle to be tested. In cooperation with those domain experts we have built the specification for the 21 process models, i. e., the ordering relationship graphs, automatically using a knowledge base. See [19]. The process models contain up to 185 tasks and over 3000 dependencies, including transitive ones. The parameter λ defines the maximum size of the process trees. The possible number of trees grows exponentially with the maximum size. Therefore, the correct and optimal tree patterns are harder to find for larger values of λ. Otherwise, a higher value could allow to find a process model with a better processing time. We choose $\lambda = 5$ for our evaluation.

Table 1 shows the results for commissioning process models A, B, and C. We have chosen A, B, and C because they are representative for the whole set, ranging from a relatively small one (C) to one of the largest (B). For a summary

Table 2. The Minimum, Maximum, and the Quartile for the Evaluation of 21 Commissioning Process Models

	Minimum		Median		Maximum
	$Q_{0.00}$	$Q_{0.25}$	$Q_{0.5}$	$Q_{0.75}$	$Q_{1.00}$
Nr. of Tasks	98	123	133	146	185
Ref. Process Time	144.232s	151.623s	157.513s	166.138s	178.606s
best found pt	64.643s	72.637s	84.529s	93.487s	108.496s
iterations (it)	5 090	15 523	37 733	76 035	94 271
calculation time (ct)	4.641s	12.356s	30.284s	63.392s	77.480s
pt reduction	33.39%	40.62%	47.54%	53.62%	58.03%

of all models see Table 2. The second row in Table 1 shows the processing time measured for the process model created by hand. Table 1 then lists the expected processing time of the process (PT) and the time our approach needs to generate the respective model (computation time CT) for 10 to 100,000 iterations. In all cases, the algorithm has been able to generate a process model in less than 100 ms that outperforms the reference process model. After 100,000 iterations (in less than 1.5 minutes) it could find process models with processing times 34%, 37%, and 50% lower than their manually generated counterparts.

For all 21 process models, Table 2 shows the minimum, maximum, and the quartile for 7 values of the evaluation. The process models contain between 98 and 185 tasks, and need up to 178s to perform. Our approach requires $\approx 30s$ and $\approx 37\,000$ iterations on average to generate the best result found. For all instances our approach has identified a solution that is better than the manually generated one in less than 100 ms. Our approach needs less than 3 iterations to do so in most cases. On average, it nearly halves the processing time of the commissioning process models (47.47%) compared to the reference points.

5 Related Work

[25] synthesizes a process model directly from its specification. The specifications are in PROPOLS [25], a temporal constraint specification language. The specifications are transformed into finite state machines and then integrated into one machine. Next, each accepting path is generated from the state machine. An algorithm similar to the α-algorithm [3] is applied to synthesize a process model from its set of paths. [25] can only be applied if the specification, i. e., the number of state machines, is small (≈ 6). To this end, [25] divides the specification into small groups, synthesizes a process fragment for each group and manually combines the fragments. For our use case, this approach would require over a hundred state machines for each commissioning process model, and the manual combination would not be feasible. [6] has specifications with LTL as starting point. It generates a pseudo model from the specification. This model lists all paths that fulfill the LTL formula. [6] generates an ordering relation graph from

the set of paths and uses it to synthesize a process tree. For our use case the generation of all paths would not be feasible. This is because the number of paths grows exponentially with the size of the specification. Even for the smallest process model we have evaluated calculating all paths has not been possible.

Process discovery means finding a process model that can reproduce the behavior given in a log [1]. [12] rediscovers a process model in the process-tree notation. It generates a graph (directly-follows graph) from the log and tries to find different kinds of cuts in the graph. Each kind of cut refers to a control structure in the process tree (SEQ, AND, XOR, LOOP). The cuts partition the graph and allow to hierarchically find a process tree for the log. In contrast to an ORG, a directly-follows graph is not transitive, and if two nodes are in parallel they share a two-way edge (no edge in the ORG). It is not possible to find a cut for a prime component, thus the approach of [12] does not help in case the specification is under-specified. Put differently, the problem statement in [12] is different from ours; the neighborhood graph of the complete log of a process tree never contains a prime component. For an incomplete log, a prime component can occur. [13] proposes to use probabilistic activity relations in the case of an incomplete log. The cut with the highest probability is chosen. This means that their algorithm generalizes from the incomplete log and assumes relationships that are not present. An ORG is an upper bound of the possible behavior. Assuming an additional relation would result in a violation of a constraint.

An approach different from generating the process model from scratch is to extract information from process models already specified and to create a similar process. [7] uses a CBR-based method to this end. The search is based on keywords that are annotations of the workflows. [9] guides the process designer with suggestions on how to complete data-oriented visualization models. The suggestions are generated from paths of existing visualization process models stored in a repository. [9] does not allow building a process model with an AND-Split and therefore is not sufficient in our case. [11] predicts which activity pattern (generic process fragment) will follow the partly modeled process. The paths of existing process models are extracted and analyzed with association rule mining. [9][11] extend an existing process model, while our approach generates one from a declarative specification. [7] requires annotations of the existing process models. None of the approaches mentioned optimize the runtime or consider constraints.

[21] transforms an unstructured model without cycles into a behaviorally equivalent structured process model. 'structured' means that for each Split-Gateway there is a corresponding Join-Gateway. Structured processes allow an effective verification [18] and are easy to understand [22]. [21] determines relationships between the tasks of a process model and generates an ORG using these relationships. Next, [21] decomposes the ORG into a Modular Decomposition Tree. In contrast to our approach, [21] generates the ORG from the behavior of an existing process model and not from a set of compliance rules. The behavior is definite, the result therefore is a unique process model. In our approach in turn, the behavior is under-specified, and several process models are possible.

AI planning is the task of defining a set of actions that achieve a specified aim [8]. In a nutshell, it is the search for an applicable plan in the solution space.

[23] uses a genetic algorithm to find a manufacturing plan. Some approaches that synthesize business processes are discussed next: [14] uses an AI planning approach to synthesize service compositions. Without calling it AI planning, [4] uses a similar approach for configuration-based workflow composition. [5] introduces a planning algorithm to compose data workflows. None of these studies focuses on optimizing the runtime of the process or considers requirements similar to ours. These approaches are not applicable to our problem statement.

In contrast to imperative process models, declarative workflows allow for any behavior fulfilling the declarative specification [16]. Thus, declarative workflows provide maximum flexibility not limited by a process model. In comparison, [25], [6] and our approach generate an imperative process model from the declarative specification. The enactment of declarative workflows is not trivial [20], and tool support by major vendors is missing. To our knowledge, there is no tool that executes declarative process models comparable to the commissioning of vehicles.

6 Conclusions

We have proposed a novel approach to generate a process model for a specific context automatically, given a set of constraints. We study the restricted case that there are not any repetitions of a task, as is the case in commissioning and elsewhere, e.g., manufacturing. We use a probabilistic search to find a good process model according to quality criteria that fulfills the constraints. Our approach can handle complex real-world specifications consisting of several hundred constraints and more than one hundred tasks. The process models generated with our scheme are superior (nearly twice as fast) to ones designed by professional process designers.

In future work we want to omit the cycle free limitation of process models. One approach could be to detect SESE (Single Entry Single Exit) loops in the graph, similarly to [21] Chapter 6.4. One could also extend the approach to resource dependencies limiting the possible number of parallel executions of certain tasks. One could detect such situations analyzing the graph structure and then add additional dependencies for the generation.

Acknowledgments. This research is supported by AUDI AG.

References

1. van der Aalst, W.M.P.: Process Mining: Discovery, Conformance and Enhancement of Business Processes. Springer Publishing Company, Incorporated, 1st edn. (2011)
2. van der Aalst, W.M.P., ter Hofstede, A.H.M., Kiepuszewski, B., Barros, A.P.: Workflow Patterns. Distributed and Parallel Databases **14**(1), 5–51 (2003)
3. van der Aalst, W.M.P., Weijters, T., Maruster, L.: Workflow mining: discovering process models from event logs. IEEE Transactions on Knowledge and Data Engineering **16**(9), 1128–1142 (2004)
4. Albert, P., Henocque, L., Kleiner, M.: Configuration based workflow composition. In: IEEE International Conference on Web Services, vol. 1, pp. 285–292, July 2005

5. Ambite, J.L., Kapoor, D.: Automatically composing data workflows with relational descriptions and shim services. In: Aberer, K., Choi, K.-S., Noy, N., Allemang, D., Lee, K.-I., Nixon, L.J.B., Golbeck, J., Mika, P., Maynard, D., Mizoguchi, R., Schreiber, G., Cudré-Mauroux, P. (eds.) ASWC 2007 and ISWC 2007. LNCS, vol. 4825, pp. 15–29. Springer, Heidelberg (2007)

6. Awad, A., Goré, R., Thomson, J., Weidlich, M.: An iterative approach for business process template synthesis from compliance rules. In: Mouratidis, H., Rolland, C. (eds.) CAiSE 2011. LNCS, vol. 6741, pp. 406–421. Springer, Heidelberg (2011)

7. Chinthaka, E., Ekanayake, J., Leake, D., Plale, B.: CBR based workflow composition assistant. In: IEEE World Conference on Services, pp. 352–355, July 2009

8. Hendler, J., Tate, A., Drummond, M.: AI Planning: Systems and Techniques. Tech. rep., University of Maryland at College Park, College Park, MD, USA (1990)

9. Koop, D., Scheidegger, C., Callahan, S., Freire, J., Silva, C.: VisComplete: Automating Suggestions for Visualization Pipelines. IEEE Transactions on Visualization and Computer Graphics 14(6), 1691–1698 (2008)

10. Kopp, O., Martin, D., Wutke, D., Leymann, F.: The Difference Between Graph-Based and Block-Structured Business Process Modelling Languages. Enterprise Modelling and Information Systems Architecture 4(1), 3–13 (2009)

11. Lau, J.M., Iochpe, C., Thom, L., Reichert, M.: Discovery and analysis of activity pattern cooccurrences in business process models. In: Int'l Conf. on Enterprise Information Systems, Milan, Italy, pp. 83–88, May 2009

12. Leemans, S.J.J., Fahland, D., van der Aalst, W.M.P.: Discovering block-structured process models from event logs - a constructive approach. In: Colom, J.-M., Desel, J. (eds.) PETRI NETS 2013. LNCS, vol. 7927, pp. 311–329. Springer, Heidelberg (2013)

13. Leemans, S.J.J., Fahland, D., van der Aalst, W.M.P.: Discovering block-structured process models from incomplete event logs. In: Ciardo, G., Kindler, E. (eds.) PETRI NETS 2014. LNCS, vol. 8489, pp. 91–110. Springer, Heidelberg (2014)

14. Matskin, M., Rao, J.: Value-added web services composition using automatic program synthesis. In: Bussler, C.J., McIlraith, S.A., Orlowska, M.E., Pernici, B., Yang, J. (eds.) CAiSE 2002 and WES 2002. LNCS, vol. 2512, pp. 213–224. Springer, Heidelberg (2002)

15. McConnell, R.M., de Montgolfier, F.: Linear-time modular decomposition of directed graphs. Discrete Applied Mathematics 145(2), 198–209 (2005)

16. Montali, M., Pešić, M., van der Aalst, W.M.P., Chesani, F., Mello, P., Storari, S.: Declarative Specification and Verification of Service Choreographies. ACM Trans. Web 4(1), 3:1–3:62 (2010)

17. Mrasek, R., Mülle, J., Böhm, K.: Automatic Generation of Optimized Process Models from Declarative Specifications. Technical Report 2014–15, KIT, Karlsruhe, November 2014. http://digbib.ubka.uni-karlsruhe.de/volltexte/1000044586

18. Mrasek, R., Mülle, J., Böhm, K.: A new verification technique for large processes based on identification of relevant tasks. Information Systems (2014)

19. Mrasek, R., Mülle, J., Böhm, K., Becker, M., Allmann, C.: User-friendly property specification and process verification – a case study with vehicle-commissioning processes. In: Sadiq, S., Soffer, P., Völzer, H. (eds.) BPM 2014. LNCS, vol. 8659, pp. 301–316. Springer, Heidelberg (2014)

20. Pešić, M., Bošnački, D., van der Aalst, W.M.P.: Enacting declarative languages using LTL: avoiding errors and improving performance. In: van de Pol, J., Weber, M. (eds.) Model Checking Software. LNCS, vol. 6349, pp. 146–161. Springer, Heidelberg (2010)

21. Polyvyanyy, A.: Structuring Process Models. University of Potsdam, Potsdam (2012)
22. Reijers, H., Mendling, J.: A Study Into the Factors That Influence the Understandability of Business Process Models. IEEE Transactions on Systems, Man and Cybernetics, Part A: Systems and Humans **41**(3), 449–462 (2011)
23. Váncza, J., Márkus, A.: Genetic algorithms in process planning. Computers in Industry **17**(2–3), 181–194 (1991)
24. Yang, Y., Dumas, M., García-Bañuelos, L., Polyvyanyy, A., Zhang, L.: Generalized aggregate Quality of Service computation for composite services. Journal of Systems and Software **85**(8), 1818–1830 (2012)
25. Yu, J., Han, Y.B., Han, J., Jin, Y., Falcarin, P., Morisio, M.: Synthesizing Service Composition Models on the Basis of Temporal Business Rules. Journal of Computer Science and Technology **23**(6), 885–894 (2008)

Process Compliance and Alignment

Towards the Automated Annotation
of Process Models

Henrik Leopold[1]([⊠]), Christian Meilicke[2], Michael Fellmann[3], Fabian Pittke[4],
Heiner Stuckenschmidt[2], and Jan Mendling[4]

[1] VU University Amsterdam, De Boelelaan 1081,
1081 HV Amsterdam, The Netherlands
h.leopold@vu.nl
[2] Universität Mannheim, 68159 Mannheim, Germany
{christian,heiner}@informatik.uni-mannheim.de
[3] Universität Osnabrück, Katharinenstr. 3, 49074 Osnabrück, Germany
michael.fellmann@uni-osnabrueck.de
[4] WU Vienna, Welthandelsplatz 1, 1020 Vienna, Austria
{fabian.pittke,jan.mendling}@wu.ac.at

Abstract. Many techniques for the advanced analysis of process models build on the annotation of process models with elements from predefined vocabularies such as taxonomies. However, the manual annotation of process models is cumbersome and sometimes even hardly manageable taking the size of taxonomies into account. In this paper, we present the first approach for automatically annotating process models with the concepts of a taxonomy. Our approach builds on the corpus-based method of second-order similarity, different similarity functions, and a Markov Logic formalization. An evaluation with a set of 12 process models consisting of 148 activities and the PCF taxonomy consisting of 1,131 concepts demonstrates that our approach produces satisfying results.

Keywords: Process model · Taxonomy · Automatic annotation

1 Introduction

Nowadays, many organizations use business process models for documenting and improving their operations. However, only a few have recognized the full potential their process models offer. In particular semantic technologies facilitate a wide range of possibilities that go beyond the documentation of business operations [27]. For example, there are techniques available that use process models for checking business process compliance [9,22], for checking the interoperability of business processes [10], and for discovering semantic weaknesses in business processes [2]. However, the limitation of all these approaches is that they build on an existing annotation of the process model activities, for instance, with concepts from a taxonomy. Recognizing this drawback, user-friendly approaches for semantic annotation have been proposed [4]. Still, the manual effort that is required for annotating process models is considerable and, in many cases, even

© Springer International Publishing Switzerland 2015
J. Zdravkovic et al. (Eds.): CAiSE 2015, LNCS 9097, pp. 401–416, 2015.
DOI: 10.1007/978-3-319-19069-3_25

hardly manageable taking into account that taxonomies often contain hundreds or even thousands of concepts.

In this paper, we present the first approach for automatically annotating process models with the concepts of a taxonomy. At this stage, we focus on activity-based taxonomies such as the Supply-Chain Operations Reference-model (SCOR) [24], the MIT process handbook [17], and the Process Classification Framework (PCF) [1]. To this end, we define an approach that combines semantic similarity measurement with probabilistic optimization. In particular, we use different types of similarity between the process model and the taxonomy as well as the distance between the taxonomy concepts to guide the matching with a Markov Logic formalization. In contrast to prior approaches in the domain of process modeling, we do not measure the similarity using WordNet, but build on the more powerful corpus-based approach of second-order similarity. An evaluation of our approach with a set of 12 process models consisting of 148 activities and the PCF taxonomy with 1,131 concepts shows that our technique performs significantly better than a naive baseline and indeed produces satisfying results.

The rest of the paper is structured as follows. Section 2 illustrates the problem of automatically annotating process models with taxonomy concepts. Section 3 introduces the similarity functions we use for computing the input for our probabilistic optimization. Section 4 introduces Markov Logic Networks and defines the probabilistic optimization problem using a Markov Logic formalization. Section 5 presents the evaluation of our approach. Section 6 discusses related work before Section 7 concludes the paper.

2   Problem Illustration

The goal of this paper is to present an approach for the automated annotation of process models with the concepts of an activity-based taxonomy. It builds on two types of input: a process model P consisting of a set of activities A_p and an activity taxonomy T, which is specified as follows:

Definition 1 (Activity Taxonomy). An activity taxonomy is a tuple $T = (A_t, r, H)$ such that

- A_t is a finite and non-empty set of activities. We refer to them as *concepts*.
- $r \in A$ represents the taxonomy root.
- $H \subseteq A \times (A \setminus \{r\})$ is the set of parent-child relationships such that $(a_1, a_2) \in H$ if a_1 is a parent of a_2.
- H is an acyclic and coherent relation such that each concept $a \in A \setminus \{r\}$ has exactly one direct parent.

We further use $C = \{a \mid (r, a) \in H\}$ to refer to the direct children of the taxonomy root r. They represent the roots of what we refer to as taxonomy categories. The function $c(a) = \{c_a \mid c_a \in C \wedge (c_a, a) \in H^+\}$ returns the category a concept $a \in A_t$ belongs to. Note that the taxonomy categories are disjoint and, hence, $|c(a)| = 1$.

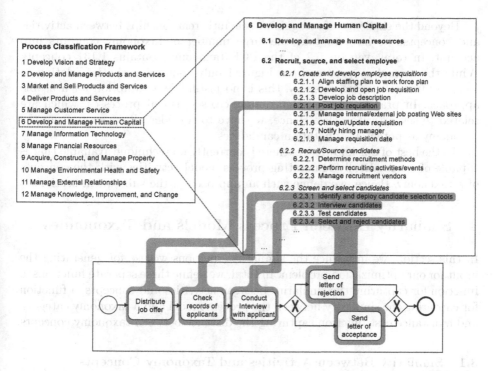

Process Classification Framework

1 Develop Vision and Strategy
2 Develop and Manage Products and Services
3 Market and Sell Products and Services
4 Deliver Products and Services
5 Manage Customer Service
6 Develop and Manage Human Capital
7 Manage Information Technology
8 Manage Financial Resources
9 Acquire, Construct, and Manage Property
10 Manage Environmental Health and Safety
11 Manage External Relationships
12 Manage Knowledge, Improvement, and Change

6 Develop and Manage Human Capital

6.1 Develop and manage human resources
...

6.2 Recruit, source, and select employee

  6.2.1 *Create and develop employee requisitions*
    6.2.1.1 Align staffing plan to work force plan
    6.2.1.2 Develop and open job requisition
    6.2.1.3 Develop job description
    6.2.1.4 Post job requisition
    6.2.1.5 Manage internal/external job posting Web sites
    6.2.1.6 Change//Update requisition
    6.2.1.7 Notify hiring manager
    6.2.1.8 Manage requisition date

  6.2.2 *Recruit/Source candidates*
    6.2.2.1 Determine recruitment methods
    6.2.2.2 Perform recruiting activities/events
    6.2.2.3 Manage recruitment vendors

  6.2.3 *Screen and select candidates*
    6.2.3.1 Identify and deploy candidate selection tools
    6.2.3.2 Interview candidates
    6.2.3.3 Test candidates
    6.2.3.4 Select and reject candidates
    ...

Distribute job offer — Check records of applicants — Conduct Interview with applicant — Send letter of rejection / Send letter of acceptance

Fig. 1. Correspondences between an exemplary process model and the PCF taxonomy

The annotation of a process model P with the concepts of an activity taxonomy T are captured by the relation $\mathcal{A} : A_p \times A_t$. An element $(a_p, a_t) \in \mathcal{A}$ defines that the activity a_p is annotated with the concept a_t, i.e., they both represent similar semantics. Note that each activity is annotated with at most one concept. However, one concept can be used as annotation for several activities.

Figure 1 illustrates the challenges associated with the automated annotation by showing a simple hiring process and its annotations with the concepts from the PCF taxonomy. In total, the process consists of five activities. First, the job offer is distributed. Afterwards, the records of the applicant are checked and an interview is conducted. Based on the result of the interview, the applicant is either rejected or accepted. Once the corresponding letter was sent, the process is finished. The grey shades visualize the annotations of the activities of the process model with the taxonomy concepts. We observe that all activities belong to the category *Develop and Manage Human Capital*. Considering the annotations in more detail, it becomes clear that the automatic identification of these annotations is by no means trivial. While the activity *Distribute job offer* and the corresponding concept *Post job requisition* at least share the common word *job*, the connection between *Check records of applicants* and *Identify and deploy candidate selection tools* is purely semantic. A similar situation can be observed for the activities *Send letter of rejection* and *Send letter of acceptance*, which are both annotated with the concept *Select and reject candidates*.

Beyond the challenge of recognizing semantic relationships between activities and concepts, we have to take the large number of taxonomy concepts into account. In total, version 5.2 of the PCF taxonomy contains 1,131 concepts. While the exemplary process from Figure 1 only contains activities relating to concepts from the same category, this is no justifiable assumption for a usable approach. In practice, we may encounter cross-sectional processes, which are related to several categories. Hence, we have to consider all concepts from the taxonomy as potential annotation candidates.

To the best of our knowledge, there is currently no technique available that is capable of automatically annotating process model activities with the concepts of a taxonomy. Hence, we define such an approach in the subsequent sections.

3   Similarity Between Process Models and Taxonomies

In this section, we introduce the similarity functions we use for generating the input for our optimization problem. In total, we define three separate functions: a function for capturing the similarity between activities and concepts, a function for capturing the similarity between the process model and a taxonomy category, and a distance cost function capturing the distance between taxonomy concepts.

3.1   Similarity Between Activities and Taxonomy Concepts

To measure the similarity between a process model activity and a taxonomy concept, we automatically decompose them into their semantic components. As pointed out in [18], activities can be characterized by three components: an action, a business object on which the action is performed, and an optional additional information fragment that is providing further details. As an example, consider the process model activity *Perform interview with employee*. It consists of the action *perform*, the business object *interview*, and the additional information fragment *with employee*. The same procedure can be applied to the concepts of an activity taxonomy. In order to accomplish this decomposition in an automated way, we employ the technique defined in [15].

Building on the decomposition, we compute the semantic similarity between the actions, business objects, and additional information fragments of the considered activity-concept pair. A challenge in this context is the usage of specific terminology from business settings, which is often not fully captured by standard natural language tools such as WordNet [19]. Hence, we determine the similarity between two components using a corpus-based method called second-order similarity [11]. The approach of second-order similarity is based on the statistical analysis of co-occurrences in large text collections and has been implemented in several tools such as NLS [5] or DISCO [13]. In comparison to WordNet, second-order similarity has the advantage that it is not restricted to a set of manually predefined term relations and, hence, is more powerful for our purposes. In order to calculate the semantic similarity between a process model activity a_p and an taxonomy concept a_t, we introduce three functions: a component similarity function $cpsim$, a coverage function cov, and a activity-concept similarity function sim, combining the latter two into a final result.

The function $cpsim$ calculates the semantic similarity between two components cp_1 and cp_2 derived from an activity-concept pair. In general, the second-order similarity sim_{SO} is returned. In case one or both of the concepts represent an empty string, $cpsim$ returns zero.

$$cpsim(cp_1, cp_2) = \begin{cases} 0 & \text{if } cp_1 = \epsilon \lor cp_2 = \epsilon \\ sim_{SO}(cp_1, cp_2) & \text{if } cp_1 \neq \epsilon \land cp_2 \neq \epsilon \end{cases} \quad (1)$$

The coverage function cov is used to determine the number of components of an activity or a concept $a \in A_p \cup A_t$. Note that the index act in the definition denotes an action, bo a business object and add an additional information fragment.

$$cov(a) = |\{cp \mid cp \neq \epsilon \land cp \in a_{act}, a_{bo}, a_{add}\}| \quad (2)$$

To combine the similarity results from the previously defined functions, we introduce the function sim. It calculates the arithmetic mean of the similarity values for action, business object, and the additional information fragment. This is accomplished by dividing the sum of $cpsim_{act}$, $cpsim_{bo}$ and $cpsim_{add}$ by the maximum coverage among the input activity-concept pair $a_p \in A_p$ and $a_t \in A_t$. As a result, we obtain the overall semantic similarity for an activity-concept pair.

$$sim(a_p, a_t) = \frac{cpsim_{act}(a_p, a_t) + cpsim_{bo}(a_p, a_t) + cpsim_{add}(a_p, a_t)}{\underset{a \in \{a_p, a_t\}}{\arg \max} \, cov(a)} \quad (3)$$

By calculating sim for every activity-concept pair, we obtain a set of similarity values. These values form the basis for our automatic annotation approach.

3.2 Similarity Between Process Models and Taxonomy Categories

For activities containing frequently occurring words the sole consideration of the similarity function sim may not be sufficient for identifying the best fitting concept. As an example, consider the activity *Develop strategy*, whose business object *strategy* occurs in six categories of the PCF taxonomy. In such a situation, it would be helpful to quantify the similarity between the entire process model and the different taxonomy categories. The resulting values could complement the individual similarity scores derived from sim in order to truly identify the best fitting candidate.

To quantify the similarity between a process model and a taxonomy category, we adopt the general idea of term frequency-inverse document frequency (tf-idf) and the vector space model from the domain of information retrieval [23] and modify them to meet the characteristics of our problem. Using the tf-idf it is possible to determine the discriminative power of a word. In the context of a taxonomy, the tf-idf assigns high weights to words that frequently occur in a particular category but rarely in the entire taxonomy. Contrarily, words that occur in many or even all categories have hardly any discriminative power and hence receive a low weight. Let A_c denote the concepts from a category $c \in C$ and $f(w, c)$ the frequency of a word w among the concepts of c. Then, the tf-idf is defined as follows:

$$tf\text{-}idf(w, c) = f(w, c) \times log\frac{|C|}{|c \in C : w \in A_c|} \tag{4}$$

Based on the tf-idf values, we can create a vector representation for the entire process model as well as for taxonomy categories. Therefore, we calculate the tf-idf values for each word from A_p and A_c and store them in the vectors v_p and v_c. As a result, we obtain a vector representation of the process model and the category in a vector space. Using the cosine similarity, it is now possible to measure the distance between these vectors and to quantify the similarity between a process model and a category. Accordingly, we introduce the similarity function rel, which we define as follows:

$$rel(c) = cos(v_p, v_c) = \frac{v_p \cdot v_c}{||v_p||\,||v_c||} = \frac{\sum\limits_{i=1}^{n} v_{pi} \times v_{ci}}{\sqrt{\sum\limits_{i=1}^{n}(v_{pi})^2} \times \sqrt{\sum\limits_{i=1}^{n}(v_{ci})^2}} \tag{5}$$

By calculating rel for each category $c \in C$, we receive a set of similarity values which complement the similarity values from sim.

3.3   Distance Costs Between Taxonomy Concepts

Besides the semantic perspective, we also need to take the structure of the process model and the taxonomy into account. Assuming that process models describe the underlying process in a rather coherent fashion, we would not expect large "leaps" between the annotations of two neighboring activities. For instance, we would assume that two subsequent activities are rather annotated with concepts *6.2.1* and *6.2.6* than with *7.1* and *3.2.1.5*. To penalize such leaps, we introduce a distance cost function dc based on concept similarity introduced by Wu and Palmer [28]. It quantifies the distance between two concepts based on the graph structure of the taxonomy and their least common superconcept a_s. Given two concepts $a_1, a_2 \in A_t$, we define dc as follows:

$$dc(a_1, a_2) = \left(-0.5 + \frac{2 \times N3}{N1 + N2 + 2 \times N3} \right) \times 2 \tag{6}$$

where N1 is the number of concepts on the path from a_1 to a_s, N2 is the number of concepts on the path from a_2 to a_s, and N3 is the number of concepts on the path from a_s to the taxonomy root r.

By calculating dc for each concept pair, we obtain a set of distance cost values in the interval [-1,1], i.e., only big leaps are penalized. Together with the previously introduced similarity values they form the input for our probabilistic annotation model.

4 Using Markov Logic for Automatic Annotation

Markov Logic (ML) is a formalism that combines first order logic with undirected probabilistic models, i.e., Markov Networks [21]. A Markov Logic formalization of a given problem consists of a set of weighted and unweighted logical formulae. These formulae describe observations relevant to the concrete problem instance and general constraints that have to hold for each instance of the problem class. By replacing variables with concrete values, which is called grounding, it is possible to transform the Markov Logic formalization into a Markov Logic Network. For technical details we refer to [21].

Two types of inference can be applied to a Markov Logic Network, known as marginal inference and maximum a-posteriori (MAP) inference. In the context of our work, we are interested in MAP inference. MAP inference computes the most probable assignment of truth values to the ground atoms of the given formalization. The MAP state, which is the result of applying MAP inference, corresponds in our setting to the most probable annotation of activities with concepts. Since the underlying probabilistic model is log linear, the MAP state is the solution which is maximal with respect to the sum of weights attached to the formulae.

In the previous section, we introduced functions for measuring similarity, relatedness, and distance costs. To incorporate these functions into our Markov Logic formalization, we introduce a predicate for two of these functions and weigh each grounded atom with the value that results from applying the corresponding similarity function. For the sake of simplicity, we use the same names for these predicates as introduced for the corresponding similarity measures, i.e., we use

- $sim(a_p, a_t)$ to express that activity a_p and concept a_t are similar.
- $dc(a_t, a_t')$ to express that a_t and a_t' are located close to each other.

These predicates are used to generate a comprehensive set of weighted atoms by computing all possible groundings. Additionally, we add unweighted formulae that describe the sequence flow in the given process model and the structure of the taxonomy. In particular, we use the predicates

- $suc(a_p, a_p')$ to express that activity a_p directly succeeds activity a_p',
- $cat(c, a_t)$ to express that a_t belongs to the category c, i.e., $c(a_t) = c$.

Now we define the constraints that relate the given evidence to the *annotate* predicate. The groundings of the *annotate* predicate correspond to the solution of the annotation problem. First of all, we add a constraint that enforces to annotate each activity with only one concept, i.e., we define the predicate *annotate* to be functional.

$$\langle annotate(a_p, a_t) \wedge annotate(a_p, a_t') \rightarrow a_t = a_t', \; \infty \rangle \tag{7}$$

Note that we represent a weighted formula as a pair, where the first element is the formula itself and the second element is the associated weight. Using ∞ as weight we refer to a hard (unweighted) formula that has to be true in every possible world. Now we link the activity-concept similarity to the *annotate* predicate.

$$\langle sim(a_p, a_t) \rightarrow annotate(a_p, a_t), \ \infty \rangle \qquad (8)$$

This formula means that the weight attached to $sim(a_p, a_t)$ is added only to the objective of our optimization problem if $annotate(a_p, a_t)$ is part of the solution. The model we defined so far will create a functional mapping as MAP state that is optimal with respect to the similarity weights given in our evidence with the guarantee that the mapping is functional. We extend this model by taking the relatedness score into account. For each category c we add one weighted formula using the following schema.

$$\langle cat(c, a_t) \wedge annotate(a_p, a_t), \ rel(c) \rangle \qquad (9)$$

If c is the category to which a_t belongs to and if a_p is annotated with a_t, the relevance score $rel(c)$ of category c is added to the objective. By adding these weighted rules, we ensure that concepts from a category that are more relevant with respect to the given process model are preferred over concepts from less relevant categories.

Finally, we want to penalize pairs of annotations where two consecutive activities a_p and a'_p are annotated with two concepts a_t and a'_t that are located at different places in the taxonomy. Since a_p and are a'_p are directly connected by a sequence flow, we would expect that their counterparts are located closely to each other in the taxonomy. The following constraint enforces that we have to add the distance cost, which is the weight associated to $dc(a_t, a'_t)$, whenever two consecutive activities a_p and a'_p are annotated with a_t and a'_t.

$$\langle annotate(a_p, a_t) \wedge annotate(a'_p, a'_t) \wedge suc(a_p, a'_p) \rightarrow dc(a_t, a'_t), \infty \rangle \qquad (10)$$

The positive impact of this constraint can be best explained with the help of Figure 1. Suppose that the concepts *6.2.3.2* and *6.1.2.3* have similarly high similarity values for the activity *Conduct Interview with Applicant*. Further suppose that our approach detected a high similarity between *Send letter of rejection* and concept *6.2.3.4*. Due to Formula 10, *6.2.3.2* will now be preferred over *6.1.2.3* as annotation for *Conduct Interview with Applicant*, because there is a large distance between *6.1.2.3* and *6.2.3.4*, while *6.2.3.2* and *6.2.3.4* are located close to each other. This illustrates nicely that our approach solves the annotation problem as a whole taking interdependencies between potential annotations into account.

5   Evaluation

To demonstrate the applicability of our approach, we conduct an evaluation with a set of manually annotated process models and the PCF taxonomy. The goal of the evaluation is to learn how well our approach can approximate the manual annotation. Section 5.1 introduces the data set we use for the evaluation. Section 5.2 introduces the details of the evaluation setup. Finally, Section 5.3 presents the evaluation results.

5.1 Test Collection

As we are the first to present an automated approach for annotating process models with taxonomy concepts, there is currently no commonly accepted test sample available. Hence, we use a set of BPMN process models that was created during a PCF case study by students from the University of Osnabrück, Germany. In the context of this case study, groups of students were asked to model a set of three fictitious business processes from the area of change management, product development, and human resources using BPMN. In addition, they had to annotate the activities of the models with the corresponding PCF concepts. We use the original annotations created by the students without any modifications. The resulting model set comprises twelve manually annotated BPMN process models consisting of a total of 148 activities.

Table 1. Overview of the test collection

Model	#Activities	Topic	PCF Categories
1	9	Change Management	12
2	8	Change Management	12
3	9	Change Management	12
4	9	Change Management	12
5	12	Product Development	2, 3
6	15	Product Development	1, 2, 3, 4
7	14	Product Development	2, 3
8	16	Product Development	2
9	10	Human Resources	6
10	11	Human Resources	6
11	19	Human Resources	6
12	15	Human Resources	6

Table 1 gives an overview of the model characteristics including the number of activities, the main topic of the model, and the PCF categories the activities of the process model were assigned to. It shows that the models vary in size as well as their coverage of the different PCF categories. Moreover, some models are cross sectional (i.e., models 5, 6, and 7) while others only belong to a single PCF category. Thus, we believe that the test set is well-suited to demonstrate the applicability of our annotation approach.

5.2 Setup

For evaluating the approach presented in this paper, we implemented it in the context of a prototype. The prototype is based on the activity analysis technique from [15], the second-order similarity implementation DISCO [13], and the Markov Logic Network implementation RockIt [20]. We used our prototype to automatically generate the annotations for the models from our test set and the text-based PCF taxonomy version 5.2. We then compared the automatically generated annotations $\mathcal{A}$ with the manual annotation from the students $\mathcal{R}$. Based on this comparison, we can assess the quality of the annotation by computing the metrics precision and recall:

$$pre(\mathcal{A}, \mathcal{R}) = \frac{|\mathcal{A} \cap \mathcal{R}|}{|\mathcal{A}|} \qquad rec(\mathcal{A}, \mathcal{R}) = \frac{|\mathcal{A} \cap \mathcal{R}|}{|\mathcal{R}|}$$

In our context, precision is the number of correct annotations computed by our approach divided by the number of annotations our approach proposed. Recall is the number of correct annotations computed by our approach divided by the total number of annotations according to the manually created gold standard.

However, the drawback of the standard precision and recall metrics for our context is that they only consider annotations that are correct up to the last sub category. As an example, consider an activity a_p that was manually annotated with the concept $6.2.1.4$. If our approach proposes to annotate a_p with the concept $6.1.2.2$, this would be simply considered as incorrect although the first three levels of the manually annotated concept were actually identified correctly. To provide for a more fine granular perspective on our results, we introduce a level-based form of precision and, recall which is in line with the approach presented in [8].

To this end, we introduce a function $parent_i(a_t)$, which returns the ith parent of a concept $a_t \in A_t$. We define $parent_i(a_t) = parent(parent_{i-1})$ for all $i > 0$ and $parent_i(a_t) = a_t$ for all $i \leq 0$. Thus, for instance, $parent_2(a_t)$ returns the concept 6.2 for the input concept $6.2.1.4$. We further introduce a function $level(a_t)$, which returns the level of a concept a_t in the taxonomy. It, for example, returns 4 for the concept $6.2.1.4$ and 2 for the concept 6.2. Based on these definitions, we introduce a function l_n, which maps a set of annotations $\mathcal{A}$ to a set of less fine-grained annotations from level n:

$$l_n(\mathcal{A}) = \bigcup_{(a_p, a_t) \in \mathcal{A}} (a_p, parent_{level(a_t)-n}(a_t))$$

As an example, consider the set of annotations $\{(Distribute\ job\ offer, 6.2.1.4), (Recruit\ employees, 6.2.2)\}$. For these annotations, l_2 would return $\{(Distribute\ job\ offer, 6.2), (Recruit\ employees, 6.2)\}$ and l_1 would return $\{(Distribute\ job\ offer, 6), (Recruit\ employees, 6)\}$. Based on l_n, we are now able to define the level-based form of precision and recall.

$$pre_n(\mathcal{A}, \mathcal{R}) = \frac{|l_n(\mathcal{A}) \cap l_n(\mathcal{R})|}{|\mathcal{A}|} \qquad rec_n(\mathcal{A}, \mathcal{R}) = \frac{|l_n(\mathcal{A}) \cap l_n(\mathcal{R})|}{|\mathcal{R}|}$$

As the PCF taxonomy that is used in the context of this evaluation has four levels, we accordingly use four levels of precision and recall to evaluate our results. In addition, we report the f-measure fm_n for each level, which is the harmonic mean of pre_n and rec_n. Respectively, the metrics pre_4, rec_4, fm_4 provide information about annotations that are correct up to the forth level and pre_1, rec_1, fm_1 provide information about annotations that are at least correct with respect to the main category.

5.3   Results

To demonstrate the applicability of the approach presented in this paper, we tested different configurations:

- **Baseline**: As baseline configuration, we annotated each activity $a_p \in A_p$ with the concept $a_t \in A_t$ with the highest value for $sim(a_p, a_t)$. We did not include any aspects from the above introduced ML formalization.
- **ML with Wu & Palmer**: For this configuration we used our ML formalization to compute the best annotations based on the activity-concept similarity sim and the distance dc between taxonomy concepts.
- **ML with Category Weighting**: For this configuration we used our ML formalization to compute the best annotations based on the activity-concept similarity sim and the category weights rel.
- **Full ML Configuration**: For the full configuration we included all previously discussed aspects into the ML formalization: the activity-concept similarity sim, the distance dc between taxonomy concepts, and the category weights rel.

Table 2 summarizes the results of our experiments. It shows that the baseline configuration without Markov logic yields quite low results. The value of 0.20 for the metric pre_1 indicates that only one out of five activities is annotated with a concept from the correct main category. The consideration of the additional similarity measures in the context of our Markov implementation improves the results significantly. While the sole use of the Wu & Palmer distance improves the results only slightly, the sole use of the category weighting already has a big effect. The f-measure fm_1 of the category weighting configuration rises from 0.20 to 0.76 and fm_2 rises from 0.18 to 0.38. Apparently, the additional category weight helps to rule out candidates that have high values for sim, but generally cannot be related to the process model. The positive effect of the Wu & Palmer distance can be observed for the full configuration. The combination of the category weighting and the Wu & Palmer distance causes an additional increase of fm_2 from 0.38 to 0.45. The value of fm_1, however, remains identical. This effect can be explained by the fact that the Wu & Palmer distance does not cause the approach to consider additional (and potentially correct) concepts. It rather improves the coherence of the annotations among the already considered candidates. Hence, it improves fm_2 without affecting fm_1. In addition, it does not compromise fm_3 and fm_4 too much. The small losses can be explained by a dominance of

Table 2. Evaluation Results

Configuration	n	pre$_n$	rec$_n$	fm$_n$
Basline	1	0.20	0.21	0.20
	2	0.11	0.11	0.11
	3	0.07	0.08	0.07
	4	0.03	0.03	0.03
ML with Wu & Palmer	1	0.29	0.23	0.25
	2	0.21	0.17	0.18
	3	0.10	0.08	0.08
	4	0.04	0.03	0.04
ML with Category Weighting	1	0.76	0.77	0.76
	2	0.37	0.38	0.38
	3	0.16	0.17	0.16
	4	0.07	0.08	0.08
Full ML Configuration	1	0.76	0.77	0.76
	2	0.44	0.45	0.45
	3	0.14	0.14	0.14
	4	0.05	0.06	0.06

the Wu & Palmer distance on the third and fourth level where the *sim* value would have actually indicated the correct annotation.

Altogether, the results suggest that both the category weights as well as the Wu & Palmer distance are helpful for finding correct and ruling out incorrect annotations. Taking the huge complexity of the annotation problem into account - each activity has more than thousand potential annotations - the results have to be considered as good. About 76% of all activities were annotated with a concept from the correct main category and 44% of all activities were annotated with the correct subcategory. Figure 2 gives an indication of where our approach could be improved by showing the values of fm_n for each model separately.

From the numbers from Figure 2 we can learn that particularly the zero values for models 3 and 8 negatively affect the overall result. The reason for these numbers can be found in the use of highly specific words for which we were not able to obtain a similarity value. As a result, the weight *rel* dominates the small values from *sim* and causes an erroneous annotation of the entire process model. In fact, the use of specific words also causes a major share of the incorrect annotations among the other models. As an example, consider the activity *Sales contact OEM for details* from model 8. Due to the domain specific abbreviation *OEM*, the values *sim* do not help us to identify the correct concepts from the taxonomy.

Besides the problem with specific words, the reason for the sub optimal results on the levels three and four is given by the fact that some concepts are semantically quite close. As an example, consider the activity *Recommend candidate*

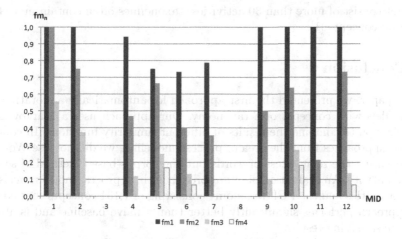

Fig. 2. Detailed results of fm_n for each model from the test set

from model 9. Our approach annotated this activity with the concept *6.2.4.3 Recommend/not recommend candidate* whereas the manual annotation assigned it to *6.2.3.4 Select and reject candidates*. Although the manual annotation is an arguably better choice than the computed one, both concepts represent semantically similar choices.

6 Related Work

The work presented in this paper relates to two major streams of research: process model annotation and process model matching.

Research addressing process model annotation typically aims at describing general guidelines and strategies [16] or the benefits and potentials associated with the annotation [25]. Some approaches also automatically filter relevant concepts from the considered ontology [3,4,7]. The final decision about the annotation is, however, still taken by the user. Hence, we are, to the best of our knowledge, the first who present an automatic approach for annotating process models.

Process model matching aims at the automatic identification of correspondences between two process models. In prior work, a plethora of process model matching approaches has been proposed [6]. Typically, they build on a combination of structural or behavioral properties with different types of textual similarity. Some rely on rather simplistic techniques such as the Levenshtein distance [26], others use WordNet for computing textual similarity [12,14]. However, so far, no approach has considered the use of second-order similarity. Besides these conceptual differences, it is worth noting that the overall complexity of automated annotation is considerably higher. While a process model typically does not consist of more than 30 activities, taxonomies often contain more than thousand concepts [1].

7 Conclusion

In this paper, we presented the first approach for automatically annotating process models with concepts of a taxonomy. Our approach uses a Markov Logic formalization to combine the results of different similarity functions. In contrast to prior approaches from the area of process modeling, we did not use WordNet for measuring the relatedness of words but the corpus-based method of second-order similarity. An evaluation of our approach with 12 process models consisting of 148 activities and the PCF taxonomy consisting of 1,131 concepts showed that our approach performs significantly better than a naive baseline and is able to compute satisfying results.

As for future work, we consider two main directions. First, we aim at improving the performance of our approach. Promising directions for accomplishing this goal include the consideration of additional information of the process model such as the control flow and the improvement of the similarity measurement by training DISCO with domain-specific corpora. Second, we plan to study to what extent our approach can be transferred to other types of ontologies as, for instance, the MIT Process Handbook, which uses both part-of as well as is-a relations to structure business activities.

References

1. APQC. Apqc process classification framework (pcf) - cross industry - pdf version 5.2.0. Technical report (2012)
2. Becker, J., Bergener, P., Räckers, M., Weiß, B., Winkelmann, A.: Pattern-based semi-automatic analysis of weaknesses in semantic business process models in the banking sector (2010)
3. Bögl, A., Schrefl, M., Pomberger, G., Weber, N.: Semantic annotation of EPC models in engineering domains to facilitate an automated identification of common modelling practices. In: Filipe, J., Cordeiro, J. (eds.) Enterprise Information Systems. LNBIP, vol. 19, pp. 155–171. Springer, Heidelberg (2009)
4. Born, M., Dörr, F., Weber, I.: User-friendly semantic annotation in business process modeling. In: Weske, M., Hacid, M.-S., Godart, C. (eds.) WISE Workshops 2007. LNCS, vol. 4832, pp. 260–271. Springer, Heidelberg (2007)
5. Cai, Z., McNamara, D.S., Louwerse, M., Hu, X., Rowe, M., Graesser, A.C.: Nls: A non-latent similarity algorithm. In: Proc. 26th Ann. Meeting of the Cognitive Science Soc. (CogSci 2004), pp. 180–185 (2004)
6. Cayoglu, U., Dijkman, R., Dumas, M., Fettke, P., Garcıa-Banuelos, L., Hake, P., Klinkmüller, C., Leopold, H., Ludwig, A., Loos, P., et al.: The process model matching contest 2013. In: 4th International Workshop on Process Model Collections: Management and Reuse (PMC-MR 2013) (2013)

7. Di Francescomarino, C., Tonella, P.: Supporting ontology-based semantic annotation of business processes with automated suggestions. In: Halpin, T., Krogstie, J., Nurcan, S., Proper, E., Schmidt, R., Soffer, P., Ukor, R. (eds.) Enterprise, Business-Process and Information Systems Modeling. LNBIP, vol. 29, pp. 211–223. Springer, Heidelberg (2009)
8. Ehrig, M., Euzenat, J., et al.: Relaxed precision and recall for ontology matching. In: Proc. K-Cap 2005 workshop on Integrating ontology, pp. 25–32 (2005)
9. Governatori, G., Hoffmann, J., Sadiq, S., Weber, I.: Detecting regulatory compliance for business process models through semantic annotations. In: Ardagna, D., Mecella, M., Yang, J. (eds.) Business Process Management Workshops. LNBIP, vol. 17, pp. 5–17. Springer, Heidelberg (2009)
10. Hofferer, P.: Achieving business process model interoperability using metamodels and ontologies (2007)
11. Islam, A., Inkpen, D.: Second order co-occurrence pmi for determining the semantic similarity of words. In: LREC, pp. 1033–1038 (2006)
12. Klinkmüller, C., Weber, I., Mendling, J., Leopold, H., Ludwig, A.: Increasing recall of process model matching by improved activity label matching. In: Daniel, F., Wang, J., Weber, B. (eds.) BPM 2013. LNCS, vol. 8094, pp. 211–218. Springer, Heidelberg (2013)
13. Kolb, P.: Disco: a multilingual database of distributionally similar words. In: Proceedings of KONVENS-2008, Berlin (2008)
14. Leopold, H., Niepert, M., Weidlich, M., Mendling, J., Dijkman, R., Stuckenschmidt, H.: Probabilistic optimization of semantic process model matching. In: Barros, A., Gal, A., Kindler, E. (eds.) BPM 2012. LNCS, vol. 7481, pp. 319–334. Springer, Heidelberg (2012)
15. Leopold, H., Smirnov, S., Mendling, J.: On the refactoring of activity labels in business process models. Information Systems 37(5), 443–459 (2012)
16. Lin, Y., Strasunskas, D., Hakkarainen, S.E., Krogstie, J., Solvberg, A.: Semantic annotation framework to manage semantic heterogeneity of process models. In: Martinez, F.H., Pohl, K. (eds.) CAiSE 2006. LNCS, vol. 4001, pp. 433–446. Springer, Heidelberg (2006)
17. Malone, T.W., Crowston, K., Herman, G.A.: Organizing business knowledge: the MIT process handbook. MIT press (2003)
18. Mendling, J., Reijers, H.A., Recker, J.: Activity Labeling in Process Modeling: Empirical Insights and Recommendations. Information Systems 35(4), 467–482 (2010)
19. Miller, G., Fellbaum, C.: WordNet: An Electronic Lexical Database. MIT Press, Cambridge (1998)
20. Noessner, J., Niepert, M., Stuckenschmidt, H.: Rockit: exploiting parallelism and symmetry for map inference in statistical relational models. Statistical Relational Artificial Intelligence. In: AAAI Workshop (2013)
21. Richardson, M., Domingos, P.: Markov logic networks. Machine learning 62(1–2), 107–136 (2006)
22. Sadiq, W., Governatori, G., Namiri, K.: Modeling control objectives for business process compliance. In: Alonso, G., Dadam, P., Rosemann, M. (eds.) BPM 2007. LNCS, vol. 4714, pp. 149–164. Springer, Heidelberg (2007)
23. Salton, G., McGill, M.J.: Introduction to modern information retrieval (1983)
24. Stephens, S.: Supply chain operations reference model version 5.0: A new tool to improve supply chain efficiency and achieve best practice. Information Systems Frontiers 3(4), 471–476 (2001)

25. Thomas, O., Fellmann, M.: Semantic Process Modeling - Design and Implementation of an Ontology-Based Representation of Business Processes. Business & Information Systems Engineering **1**(6), 438–451 (2009)
26. Weidlich, M., Dijkman, R., Mendling, J.: The ICoP framework: identification of correspondences between process models. In: Pernici, B. (ed.) CAiSE 2010. LNCS, vol. 6051, pp. 483–498. Springer, Heidelberg (2010)
27. Wetzstein, B., Ma, Z., Filipowska, A., Kaczmarek, M., Bhiri, S., Losada, S., Lopez-Cob, J.-M., Cicurel, L.: Semantic business process management: a lifecycle based requirements analysis. In: SBPM (2007)
28. Wu, Z., Palmer, M.: Verbs semantics and lexical selection. In: Proceedings of the 32nd Annual Meeting on Association for Computational Linguistics, pp. 133–138. Association for Computational Linguistics (1994)

Discovery and Validation of Queueing Networks in Scheduled Processes

Arik Senderovich[1], Matthias Weidlich[2(✉)], Avigdor Gal[1],
Avishai Mandelbaum[1], Sarah Kadish[3], and Craig A. Bunnell[3]

[1] Technion – Israel Institute of Technology, Haifa, Israel
sariks@tx.technion.ac.il, {avigal,avim}@ie.technion.ac.il
[2] Imperial College London, London, UK
m.weidlich@imperial.ac.uk
[3] Dana-Farber Cancer Institute, Boston, MA, USA
{sarah_kadish,craig_bunnell}@dfci.harvard.edu

Abstract. Service processes, for example in transportation, telecommunications or the health sector, are the backbone of today's economies. Conceptual models of such service processes enable operational analysis that supports, e.g., resource provisioning or delay prediction. Automatic mining of such operational models becomes feasible in the presence of event-data traces. In this work, we target the mining of models that assume a resource-driven perspective and focus on queueing effects. We propose a solution for the discovery and validation problem of scheduled service processes - processes with a predefined schedule for the execution of activities. Our prime example for such processes are complex outpatient treatments that follow prior appointments. Given a process schedule and data recorded during process execution, we show how to discover Fork/Join networks, a specific class of queueing networks, and how to assess their operational validity. We evaluate our approach with a real-world dataset comprising clinical pathways of outpatient clinics, recorded by a real-time location system (RTLS). We demonstrate the value of the approach by identifying and explaining operational bottlenecks.

1 Introduction

Service systems play a central role in today's economies, e.g., in transportation, finance, and the health sector. Service provisioning is often realized by a *service process* [1,2]. It can be broadly captured by a set of activities that are executed by a service provider and designated to both attain a set of organizational goals and add value to customers.

Independently of the domain, service processes can be classified by the amount of interactions between service providers and customers and the level of demand predictability and capacity flexibility. A service can be *multi-stage*, in the sense that service provisioning involves a series of interactions of a customer with a provider, or specific resources at a provider's end. Further, a process can be *scheduled*, meaning that the number of customers to arrive is known in advance, up

© Springer International Publishing Switzerland 2015
J. Zdravkovic et al. (Eds.): CAiSE 2015, LNCS 9097, pp. 417–433, 2015.
DOI: 10.1007/978-3-319-19069-3_26

to last moment cancellations and no-shows. Then, customers follow a pre-defined series of activities, with every activity having a planned starting time for its execution, a duration, and a set of involved resources. Multi-stage scheduled processes are encountered, for instance, in outpatient clinics, where various types of treatments are provided as a service to patients [3]. Here, a schedule determines when a patient undergoes a specific examination or treatment. Another example of multi-stage scheduled processes is public transportation, where schedules determine which vehicle serves a certain route at a specific time [4].

In this work, we focus on the following operational question for multi-stage scheduled service processes: *how to assess the conformance of the schedule of a service process to its actual execution?* To address this question, we develop an approach that is based on discovery and validation of resource-centered models. First, we discover a deterministic model that represents a planned execution of a service process (schedule). Second, we check the conformance of a schedule against a log of recorded process executions.

Our choice of formalism to capture a resource-centered view of service processes is driven by two challenges that arise from multi-stage scheduled service processes, namely dependencies and synchronization. Specifically, in multi-stage processes, customers go through a complex network of resources prior to service completion. Hence, resource demand does not arrive at random, and dependencies between arrivals at different resources must be taken into account. Second, in scheduled processes, customers are delayed not only due to scarce capacity of providers (*resource queues*), but also in *synchronization queues* where customers, for whom activities are executed concurrently, experience delays before they can proceed towards subsequent service phases. The formalism that we select captures the resource perspective in service processes is *queueing networks* and more specifically, *Fork/Join networks* [5]. The Fork/Join networks allow for performance analysis and optimization of parallel queueing systems [35]. Adopting this formalism, the contribution of this paper is summarized as follows:

(1) We propose a technique to discover a deterministic Fork/Join network from a *schedule* of a service process.
(2) We present a conformance checking technique that assesses the validity of a deterministic Fork/Join network based on recorded process executions.

We demonstrate the value of the proposed discovery and validation methods by applying them to RTLS-based data from a real-world use-case of scheduling in a large outpatient oncology clinic. Our experiments demonstrate the usefulness of the proposed methods in detecting operational bottlenecks in the schedule, specifically longer-than-planned synchronization delays, and diagnosing the root-cause to those problems.

The remainder of the paper is structured as follows. Section 2 presents a detailed use-case of a process in an outpatient clinic. The models for schedules and log data of service processes is outlined in Section 3. Fork/Join networks and their discovery from a schedule are discussed in Section 4. The technique to check conformance of schedule-driven models against recorded process executions is presented in Section 5. An empirical evaluation of our approach is given in

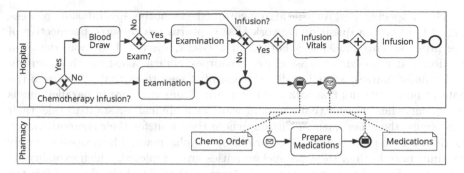

Fig. 1. The control-flow perspective of patient flow in the day hospital

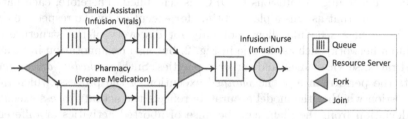

Fig. 2. A Fork/Join network that depicts the scheduled process from the resource perspective

Section 6. Section 7 discusses related work, followed by concluding remarks and future work (Section 8).

2   A Service Process in an Outpatient Clinic

We illustrate the challenges that arise from operational analysis of multi-stage scheduled service processes through a process in the Dana-Farber Cancer Institute (DFCI), a large outpatient cancer center in the US. In this hospital, approximately 900 patients per day are served by 300 health care *providers*, e.g. physicians, nurse practitioners, and registered nurses, supported by approximately 70 administrative staff. The hospital is equipped with a Real-Time Location System (RTLS). We use the movements of patients, personnel, and equipment recorded by this system to evaluate our approach.

We focus on the service process for a particular class of patients, the on-treatment patients (OTP). This process applies to 35% of the patients, yet it generates a large fraction of the workload due to the long service times. Hence, operational analysis to balance quality-of-service and efficiency is particularly important for this process. Figure 1 depicts the control-flow perspective of the process as a BPMN diagram: Arriving patients may directly receive examination by a physician, or shall undergo a chemotherapy infusion. For these patients, a blood draw is the initial appointment. Then, they either move to the infusion stage directly, or first see a provider for examination.

For a specific part of the aforementioned chemotherapy infusion process, Fig. 2 illustrates a queueing network that captures the resource perspective of the process. This model is a Fork/Join network, discussed in more detail in Section 4. It represents the associated resources: clinical assistants, a pharmacy, and infusion nurses, as well as dependencies between them that follow from the patient flow. Patients first fork and enter two *resource queues* in parallel: one is the queue where they actually sit and wait for a clinical assistant to take their vital signs; the other queue is virtual, where they wait for their chemotherapeutic drugs to be prepared by the central hospital pharmacy. The process can only continue once both of these parallel activities are completed, which explains the existence of *synchronization queues* in front of the join of the flows. After the join, patients are enqueued to wait for a nurse and chair to receive infusion.

The provisioning of infusions in DFCI is scheduled. Therefore, each patient has a schedule that assigns a planned time for execution by the respective activities. As such, a schedule allows not only for discovery of the structure of a Fork/Join network, such as the one in Fig. 2, but also its annotation in terms of arrival rates, service times, and server capacities. Such a *schedule-driven model* reflects the performance of the *planned* execution of the process, which raises the question whether the model accurately reflects the actual process execution. Any deviation from the plan, e.g., because of aborted activities or differences in resource scheduling policies, negatively impacts the validity of the schedule-driven model. In the presence of recorded process executions, however, conformance checking as presented in this work can be used to assess the behavioral, conceptual, and operational validity of the schedule-driven model.

3   Schedules and Event Logs of Service Processes

In this work, we provide a multi-level analysis approach that exploits two types of input data, namely a *schedule* and a *log* of recorded actual executions of activities. Such multi-level representation enables analysis that is richer than the state-of-the-art. Below, we formalize the models for schedules and event logs.

Schedule. A schedule represents the plan of a multi-staged service process for *individual customers*. It comprises *tasks* that are partially ordered. We define a task to be a relation between customers, activities, resources at a time, for a duration, e.g., customer *Smith* is to perform a *blood draw* with nurse *Greenberg* on Monday, 03/02/2016 8:00, for 5 minutes. We denote the universe of tasks by T.

Definition 1 (Schedule). *A schedule is a set of planned tasks, $T_P \subseteq T$, having a schema (set of functions) $\sigma_P = \{\xi_p, \alpha_p, \rho_p, \tau_p, \delta_p\}$, where*

- $\xi_p : T \to C$ *assigns a customer to a task.*
- $\alpha_p : T \to A$ *assigns an activity to a task.*
- $\rho_p : T \to R$ *assigns a resource to a task.*
- $\tau_p : T \to \mathbb{N}^+$ *assigns a timestamp representing the planned start time to a task.*

– $\delta_p : T \to \mathbb{N}^+$ *assigns a duration to a task.*
The timestamps assigned by τ_p *induce a partial order of tasks, denoted by* $\prec_P \subseteq T_P \times T_P$.

Log. A log contains the data recorded during the execution of the service process, e.g., by a Real-Time Location System (RTLS) as in our use-case scenario (Section 2). Task events in the log relate to a customer, resource, activity, and the timestamps of execution, thereby representing a unique instantiation of an activity executed by a resource for a customer at a certain time.

Definition 2 (Log). *A log is a set of sequences of executed tasks,* $T_A \subseteq T^*$, *having a schema* $\sigma_A = \{\xi_a, \alpha_a, \rho_a, \tau_{start}, \tau_{end}\}$, *where*

– $\xi_a : T \to C$ *assigns a customer to a task.*
– $\alpha_a : T \to A$ *assigns an activity to a task.*
– $\rho_a : T \to R$ *assigns a resource to a task.*
– $\tau_{start} : T \to \mathbb{N}^+$ *assigns a timestamp representing the observed start time to a task.*
– $\tau_{end} : T \to \mathbb{N}^+$ *assigns a timestamp representing the observed end time to a task.*

4 Discovering Queueing Networks for Scheduled Processes

The approach taken in this paper is outlined in Figure 3. We first discover a deterministic F/J network from a schedule (see Definition 1). Then, data-driven techniques create an enriched F/J network that is used for validation. This section focuses on the discovery stage, by first defining Fork/Join networks (Section 4.1), before elaborating on the actual discovery (Section 4.2). Enrichment and validation are detailed in Section 5.

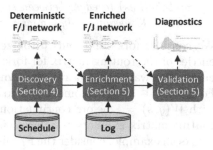

Fig. 3. An outline of our approach

4.1 F/J Queueing Networks: Structure and Dynamics

Queueing networks are directed graphs, with each node corresponding to either a server (a resource) or a queue, see Fig. 2. We consider single-class (customers are of one type), open (customers arrive from outside the system and depart eventually), Fork/Join (F/J) queueing networks [5]. F/J networks extend 'classical' queueing networks with support for splitting and joining of customer instances, which makes them particularly suited to model concurrent actions in service processes.

To define F/J networks, we first need to specify server dynamics. To capture these dynamics, we adopt a version of Kendall's notation [8], so that every server is characterized by, $\mathcal{A}/\mathcal{B}/\mathcal{C}+\mathcal{P}$ where $\mathcal{A}$ is the arrival rate for queues with *external* arrivals, given as the joint distribution of inter-arrival times; $\mathcal{B}$ is the service time of processing a single customer, given as the distribution of this time; and $\mathcal{C}$ is the capacity, given as the number of resources. Note that arrivals, service times, and resource capacity may be defined in a time-varying manner. Further, component $\mathcal{P}$ is the service policy that sets both the order of entry-to-service, among the enqueued customers, and selects the resource, among available resources, to serve a customer. For example, the most well-known service policy for queues is the First-Come First-Served Policy (FCFS), which is often combined with a server selection strategy that choses the first server that becomes available.

F/J networks support two types of queues: *resource queues* are formed because of limited resource capacity; *synchronization queues* result from simultaneous processing by several resources. Servers can be of three types: regular (services with capacity), fork, and join. A routing matrix defines the flow between servers and queues. With $\mathcal{K}$ being the universe of possible dynamics models for a server, we define F/J network as follows.

Definition 3 (F/J Network). *An F/J network is a quadruple $\langle S, Q, W, b \rangle$, where*
- $S = S_R \cup S_F \cup S_J$ *is a set of servers, with S_R being a set of resources and S_F, S_J being sets of forks and joins, respectively;*
- $Q = Q_R \cup Q_S$ *is a set of queues, with Q_R being a set of resource queues and Q_S being a set of synchronization queues;*
- $W : (Q \times S) \cup (S \times Q) \rightarrow [0, 1]$ *is a routing matrix that assigns weights (or probabilities) to edges between servers and queues;*
- $b : S \rightarrow \mathcal{K}$ *assigns a dynamics model to servers.*

We consider forks and joins to be zero-delay, single-server nodes. Further, the entries of the routing matrix for forks and joins are binary. For a fork $s \in S_F$, a customer always continues in *all* downstream queues $q \in Q$ for which $W(s, q) = 1$. For a join $s \in S_J$, a customer needs to be selected from *all* upstream queues $q \in Q$ with $W(q, s) = 1$ before continuation. An F/J network for which the complete routing matrix is binary is *deterministic*, otherwise the network is *probabilistic*.

As an example, consider the F/J network in Fig. 2. It contains three resources, a fork, a join, three resource queues (preceding resources), and two synchronization queues (succeeding resources). Note that the structure given in Fig. 2 can only be a deterministic F/J network as all queues and servers, which are not forks, have a single outgoing edge.

4.2   Discovering a Scheduled Queueing Network

Under the assumption that the process follows the schedule in terms of the execution of activities for customers by resources, i.e., there may only be temporal deviations, the network structure is directly derived from the schedule. The timestamps of the schedule tasks in T_P induce a partial order $\prec_P$, which gives raise to a dependency graph between activities and, thus, resource nodes. The structure of the F/J network is then created by inserting the required forks and joins, at resource nodes with more than one predecessor or successor, respectively. Further, resource queues are inserted for all incoming edges of resource nodes, which are no forks or joins. Finally, synchronization queues are added for all incoming edges of joins.

To extract the dynamics models, for each resource node $s \in S_R$, we shall assume that the number of resources as function of time, $K_s(t)$, can easily be extracted from the schedule log (see also [9] for a respective method). To extract the arrivals $(\mathcal{A})$, service times $(\mathcal{B})$, and service policy $(\mathcal{P})$ from a schedule of tasks T_P with schema $\sigma_P = \{\xi_p, \alpha_p, \rho_p, \tau_p, \delta_p\}$, partially ordered by $\prec_P$, we proceed as follows.

Arrival Times. For each of the most upstream resource nodes $s \in S_R$, arrival times

$$A(s, T_P, \sigma_P, \prec_P) = \{\tau_p(t) \mid t \in T_P \land \rho_p(t) = s \land \forall\, t' \in T_P : \xi_p(t) = \xi_p(t') \Rightarrow t' \nprec_P t\},$$
(1)

are defined by the first event in the schedule for the planned process execution for each customer. Arrivals into downstream resource nodes are assumed to correspond to end-of-processing times of previous nodes.

Service Times. For a resource node $s \in S_R$, services times

$$B(s, T_P, \sigma_P, \prec_P) = \{\delta_p(t) \mid t \in T_P \land \rho_p(t) = s\},$$
(2)

are defined by the planned duration of the respective activity.

Service Policy. A service policy is a, potentially time-dependent, function that selects a task to be served from a set of waiting tasks. A typical schedule assumes that tasks are served according to an *earliest-due-date* (EDD) policy with the additional constraint that tasks arriving ahead of their due time do not get served. Formally, given a set of waiting tasks, $\{t_1, \ldots, t_n\}$ at time t, the EDD policy is given by:

$$P(\{t_1, \ldots, t_n\}, t) = \operatorname{argmin}_{t' \in \{t_1, \ldots, t_n\}, \tau_p(t') < t} \{\tau_p(t')\}.$$
(3)

5 Validating Schedule-Driven Networks with Logs

A F/J network discovered from a schedule enables operational analysis of the planned process behavior under the assumption that there are no deviations from the plan. In most cases, however, such deviations are likely to be observed, which calls for validation of the schedule-driven model. In the presence of a log of recorded process executions, such validation can be achieved by conformance checking.

Below, we first review dimensions of validity for operational models, i.e., behavioral, operational, and conceptual validity (Section 5.1). Given the rich body of literature on methods to ensure behavioral validity, we focus on the other dimensions and present a methodology to ensure operational validity (Section 5.2) and conceptual validity (Section 5.3). For both dimensions, we also instantiate the methodology and outline methods to validate specific model aspects, i.e., processing delays and service policies. Finally, we elaborate on the link between conceptual and operational validity (Section 5.4).

5.1   Dimensions of Validity

Validity relates to *behavioral, operational,* and *conceptual* model aspects [10].

Behavioral Validity. Given a process model, its behavioral relevance with respect to the real process is of crucial importance. Four complementary notions of behavioral validity are given in the literature, namely *fitness, simplicity, precision* and *generalization* [11]. Various techniques to assess behavioral validity have been proposed, among some *trace replay* [12], also known as trace-based simulation [7], *trace alignment* [13], the comparison of behavioral relations [14], and the injection of negative events [15].

Deterministic F/J networks are equivalent to decision-free Petri-Nets [16]. Therefore, the aforementioned techniques to assess behavioral validity can directly be lifted to the resource perspective of a process that is given as a deterministic F/J network.

Operational Validity. Operational validity concerns model performance measures and the accuracy of conclusions drawn from it. Operational models and recorded executions of a process may be consistent in terms of ordering, i.e., the model is behaviorally valid. However, the same model may show low operational validity and be inaccurate in the operational sense. An example would be too coarse-grained abstractions, e.g., a schedule consisting of a single activity per customer and logs that record only the execution of this activity. The discovered model, while behaviorally valid, may be useless for operational analysis. Specifically, execution times for the single activity that would result from the model may not match their corresponding times from the log, because of their large variability that stems from the aggregation of customers that are served differently.

Conceptual Validity. Conceptual validity is defined as the checking of the assumptions and theories that underlie a model [10]. For the context of F/J networks, conceptual validity relates to its structure and the dynamics models of server nodes. Operational models are typically built with assumptions related to the distribution of execution times, customer arrival rates, and routing probabilities. Moreover, some operational models rely on approximations and therefore, should be tested for their applicability against data. To determine conceptual validity, various techniques can be used, for example, statistical tests can be applied to verify model assumptions and quantify the deviation between assumed values (e.g., first-moments) and actual measurements (data) [10].

5.2   Operational Validity: Detecting and Quantifying Performance Deviations

Methodology for Operational Validity. To assess operational validity of a model, model-based performance measures are compared to their counterparts in the recorded log data. The specific measures to consider may vary among scenarios. However, the comparison between the model and the recorded data typically exploits a discrepancy metric between the two, based on a specific performance measure (or output).

Formally, let $D : O \times O \rightarrow X$ be the deviation between an output of a model and the corresponding actual measurements (or the output of another model), where O is the output domain (e.g., processing delays) and X is the domain of the measure for deviation (e.g. the distance between processing delays is also a delay).

Once the performance measures and distance function are set, one can apply a replay technique, see [12], to collect sample values of D for every planned task $t \in T_P$ that also exists in the log, i.e., $t \in T_A$. The replay will result in sample of the deviations between two outputs, $\{D(t) \mid t \in (T_P \cap T_A)\}$. This sample can, in turn, be analyzed via statistical techniques for measuring goodness-of-fit between two models.

Validation of Processing Delays. We now turn to an instantiation of the methodology to assess operational validity for a specific model aspect. We take up the aforementioned case of Dana-Farber, where quality improvement teams focus on *delays* of individual patients per activity with respect to the maximum between the scheduled time and the time of arrival at the respective resource. To investigate this aspect, a distribution is constructed from the individual delays. Then, the difference between the measure from the log and its equivalent from the deterministic F/J network is quantified.

Using a continuous time model, the specific deviation function for processing delays is defined as $D_D : \mathbb{R} \times \mathbb{R} \rightarrow \mathbb{R}$. For convenience, we assume $T_A \subseteq T_P$, i.e., no unplanned tasks arrived to the system. While this assumption is not necessary for the demonstrated approach, it simplifies the definitions in the remainder.

Delays in processing may be caused by resource capacity (customers wait in a resource queue) or synchronization (customers wait in a synchronization queue). Hence, for a task $t \in T_A$, there is a resource delay $\widehat{W_R(t)}$ and a synchronization delay $\widehat{W_S(t)}$, and the total delay is their sum, $\widehat{W(t)} = \widehat{W_R(t)} + \widehat{W_S(t)}$. The resource delay is the difference between the current time and the maximum between synchronization time between previous tasks and the scheduled time for the task. The synchronization delay is the difference of the earliest and latest entry in one of the synchronization queues.

From the schedule, for resource $s \in S_R$, we extract the planned delay $W(t, s)$ as the timestamp difference between the task and its direct successors. Then, we define $D_D(t) = D(\widehat{W(t)}, W(t))$ as one of the well-established metrics for deviations between two outputs, e.g. the squared deviation. This way, deviations in processing delays between the schedule and the observed process execution are detected and quantified.

5.3   Conceptual Validity: Checking Model Assumptions

Methodology for Conceptual Validity. We approach the conceptual validity of a deterministic F/J network discovered from the schedule by means of *enhancement* and *comparison*. That is, the deterministic F/J network is enhanced based on the log data, which yields a stochastic F/J network. Conceptually, this step is similar to enhancement operations known for process models that focus on the control-flow perspective, see [17]. As a by-product of applying the enhancement algorithm, however, our approach directly compares the two models, specifically, the server dynamics of the deterministic, schedule-driven model to the dynamics of the stochastic, data-driven model.

An *enhancement function* creates a stochastic F/J network from a deterministic F/J network and a log. In practice, enhancement boils down to fitting all model elements of the stochastic F/J network with the log data, namely identifying the model structure and, for every server, discovering its dynamics. Generally speaking, enhancement combines several process mining and statistical techniques:

- To extract the model structure, process discovery algorithms that exploit direct successorship of activities and detect concurrency can be used, e.g., the family of α-algorithms [18, Ch.5].
- The routing matrix can be inferred by its empirical equivalent, i.e. counts over sums of historical transitions between nodes.
- Service policies for routing customers can be discovered using the policy-mining techniques presented in [19].
- The distribution of inter-arrival and service times can be fitted via techniques that were developed and applied in [20,21].

Differences in the structure and server dynamics of the schedule-driven model and the data-driven model are assessed by statistical comparison techniques, e.g., hypothesis testing [22]. This allows for quantifying deviations and concluding on their significance.

Validation of Service Policies. Next, we instantiate the methodology and demonstrate a statistical comparison method for service policies that determine the routing of customers to resources. We focus on a single resource node $s \in S_R$ and assume that it has been previously diagnosed (via the techniques to assess operational validity) to cause delays downstream. Hence, we aim at comparing that server's service policy and verify whether the schedule-driven policy indeed holds.

Formally, let P be the assumed policy that has to be checked against all historical decisions on the next customer to enter service, which are represented in the log. Policy P supposedly follows Equation 3, i.e., for a set of tasks $\{t_1, \ldots, t_n\}$ waiting in the respective resource queue at time t, the task that has the earliest scheduled timestamp is selected. To assess to which extent this policy holds true, we define a respective indicator $\mathbb{1}_{P(i)}$, which is equal to one if indeed the i-th past decision corresponds to Equation 3. Then, we define a statistic that quantifies the level of compliance to policy P:

$$\chi_P = \frac{1}{|n|} \sum_{i=1}^{n} \mathbb{1}_{P(i)}, \tag{4}$$

This is an estimate of the probability that P holds, i.e., $\mathbb{E}[\mathbb{1}_P] = \mathbb{P}(P)$ with P being the compliance-to-policy-P event. We use this estimate to test several plausible policies, e.g., First-Come First-Serve, and decide on the best-fitting policy.

5.4 Continuous Validity

We tighten the relations between conceptual and operational validity by adopting the paradigm of *continuous validity*. This paradigm means that two models that are equivalent in the conceptual domain, will also be equivalent in the operational domain. The notion of conceptual equivalence between two models can be derived from model comparison as described above, while operational equivalence can be defined with respect to our measure for deviations, D (see Section 5.2). The result of continuous validation can be interpreted in two ways. First, assuming that the schedule is the normative process, one should fix the causes for deviation in process executions. Alternatively, if the actual execution is the reference point, the schedule is to be repaired accordingly.

6 Evaluation

This section presents an empirical evaluation of our approach based on the case study of the Dana-Farber Cancer Institute, see Section 2. Specifically, we use the appointment schedule, RTLS data, and pharmacy data to discover a schedule-based queueing network. Then, we demonstrate an operational validation of the model that searches for deviations from the scheduled process in the temporal sense. Last, we check the conceptual validity to locate the root-cause of these deviations.

Below, Section 6.1 describes the datasets and experimental setup. Section 6.2 discuss the obtained discovery and validation results.

6.1 Datasets and Experimental Setup

Our experiments combine three data sources from the Dana-Farber Cancer Institute: an *appointment schedule*, an *RTLS log* recording movements of badges (patients and service providers), and a *pharmacy log* that records checkpoints in the medication-production process. The resolution of the RTLS can be as accurate as 3 seconds, depending on the amount of movement of a badge. From the pharmacy log, we only extracted the start and end events for the production process, since we consider the pharmacy as a separate server. The experiments involve three weekdays, April 14-16, 2014, which are days of 'regular' operation (approximately 600 OTP patients) as was verified with local contacts.

Our experiments involved the following steps. First, we discovered a deterministic F/J network from the schedule. Second, we performed an operational validation of the model against log data, with a focus on deviations in processing delay. Third, we assessed conceptual validity. We enhanced the model to obtain a stochastic, data-driven F/J network and then focus on one of the server nodes, for which operational deviations had been detected in the second step, and analyzed its dynamics.

We implemented our experiments in two software frameworks, SEEStat and SEEGraph. Both tools have been developed in the Service Enterprise Engineering lab,[1] and enable, respectively, statistical and graphical analysis of large operational datasets. In particular, they enable the creation of new procedures for server dynamics (SEEStat), and for the discovery of structure and routing in queueing networks (SEEGraph).

6.2 Results

Model Discovery. As a first step, we discovered a deterministic schedule-driven F/J network. An excerpt of the result is presented in Fig. 4. Note that the excerpt shows only the activities that are conducted by staff of the outpatient clinic, i.e., the preparation of medications by the pharmacy is not shown[2]. Note that the SEEGraph notation for the queueing network dis-

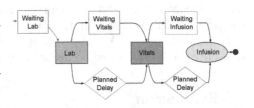

Fig. 4. Schedule-driven process (appointments) extracted from the RTLS data

tinguishes two types of customer delays, i.e., time spent before the scheduled time (*Planned Delay*) and the processing delay after the time the customer was scheduled (*Waiting Lab/Vitals/Infusion*).

Operational Validity: Delay Deviations. Next, we enacted the operational validation and tracked down deviating performance measures. Here, we provide the results for the example that is outlined in Fig. 2: a patient that is scheduled to enter infusion waits for two concurrent activities, namely pre-infusion vital signs (vitals) and medication production. The scheduled time between the end of vitals and the beginning of infusion is actually zero and most of the delay is planned for the beginning of vitals.

Figure 5 presents the actual distribution of time between vitals and the beginning of infusion, based on the RTLS data. We observe that, indeed, a large portion of patients go into infusion within a minute from vitals. However, the distribution presents a long tail of patients, who wait for the next step (average delay of 23 minutes). For most patients, this is due to synchronization delays since they wait for their medications. In many occasions, one can observe in the RTLS data that patients wait, while infusion nurses are available for service. This again points toward synchronization delays between the vitals activity and the pharmacy. According to schedule, the central pharmacy is planned to deliver the medication in synchronization with vitals (within 30 minutes). The operational insight of long synchronization delays, however, hints at a conceptual issue regarding the just-in-time arrival of the medication.

---

[1] http://ie.technion.ac.il/labs/serveng/
[2] An animation can be found at http://youtube.com/watch?v=ovXu3DB9RuQ

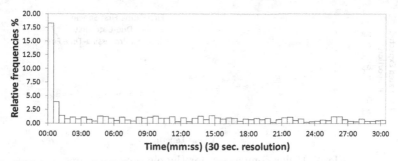

Fig. 5. Waiting time for Infusion (after vitals); Sample size = 996, Mean = 25min, Stdev = 29min

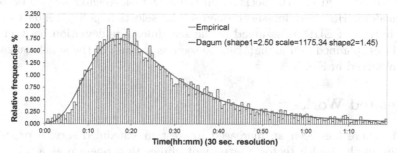

Fig. 6. Medication production time; Sample size = 7187, Mean = 30min, Stdev = 24min

Conceptual Validity: Production Times and Policy. To check for a conceptual issue related to the 'Pharmacy' resource, we investigated its dynamics. We assume that the fork in Fig. 2 is zero-delay and that pharmacy is notified once the patient is ready for infusion. Therefore, we assume that the arrival times do not deviate, and diagnose the two remaining dynamics: production time and service policy. Figure 6 shows the distribution of production times (for April 2014), and the fitted 'Dagum' distribution. Here, we observe that the stochastic model shares a first moment with the planned duration: both are 30 minutes on average. Therefore, in alignment to our continuous-validity paradigm, the root-cause for operational deviations is not the length of drug production.

We now turn to the second dynamic component, the service policy for the drug production. Here, we focus on the time until the first drug has been prepared. Although patients often require more than one drug, the first medication is the one that is needed for the process to flow. Using the method proposed in Section 5.3, we estimated the expected indicators for three policies: (1) Earliest-Due-Date (EDD) First, which corresponds to the plan, (2) First-Come First-Served (FCFS), which produces according to the order of prescription arrivals and (3) Shortest Processing Time (SPT) first, which implies that priority will be given to patients with shorter infusion durations.

Figure 7 presents the estimated proportion of compliance to policy, as a function of the number of medication orders in queue. To see an effect of selection

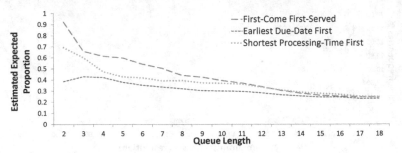

Fig. 7. Policy comparison for the pharmacy resource

based on a policy, the comparison starts with a queue of size two. We observe that as the queue grows, the decision on the next task to enter service becomes more random. However, for short queues, the selection policy tends towards FCFS, instead of EDD as assumed in the schedule. The deviation between the two policies, planned and actual, can be seen as a cause of the synchronization delays observed in Fig. 5.

7 Related Work

Recently, there has been an increased interest in scheduled service processes, especially in the health sector. Outpatient clinics that operate as a scheduled multi-stage process, are of particular interest, due to their pervasiveness and growth over the past years [3]. Performance questions for scheduled multi-stage processes relate to bottleneck identification, dynamic resource allocation, and optimal control (decision making).

Traditionally, such performance analysis is based on techniques from Operations Research disciplines, such as Scheduling [23] and Queueing Theory [24]. These methods use hand-made (highly abstract) models of the reality, and apply the relevant (model-specific) analysis. Validation of the results is typically performed by simulating the 'reality' (again a hand-made model), and comparing the outputs of the modeled reality and the simulated reality, neglecting the benefits of data-driven validation, c.f. [25].

The rapidly evolving field of *process mining*, in turn, is driven by the available data [18]. Models are discovered from and validated against event data that stems from recorded process executions, see [26]. Mined models are used as the basis for prediction [27,28], simulation [17], and resource-behavior analysis [29,30]. However, much work in this field focuses on the *control-flow perspective*, i.e. the order of activities and their corresponding resources, times and decisions [18, Ch.8], so that the created models cannot benefit from the analysis techniques developed in Operations Research. In earlier work, therefore, we argued for an explicit representation of the *queueing perspective* and demonstrated its value for several real-world processes [9,19]. However, the existing techniques all considered the simplistic setting of a single-station system, whereas, this paper addressed the more complex scenario of service processes that are scheduled and have a multi-stage structure that involves resource synchronization.

Our approach of discovering a model from a schedule is similar to the transformation of schedules to Petri-Nets presented in [31]. However, our target formalism is Fork/Join networks to leverage existing analysis techniques for queueing networks. Also, we employ log data to answer structural and operational questions regarding the schedule.

One of the main questions in scheduled processes is that of conformance of the actual process execution to the plan. Techniques for model validation in process mining primarily focus on behavioral validity, see [12–15]. However, a few works also addressed time and resource validity of discovered models [32,33], where the replay method, as in [34], is used to quantify deviations in performance measures. However, in these approaches, conceptual validity (model assumptions) is confounded with operational validity (resulting performance measures). This paper argues for a clear separation between behavioral, operational and conceptual validity, and introduces a methodology for assessing the operational and conceptual validity of Fork/Join networks.

8 Conclusion

In this work, we provided a framework for the operational analysis of scheduled multi-stage service processes, as they are observed in such domains as healthcare and transportation. To assess the conformance of the schedule of a process and its actual execution, we presented an approach based on discovery and validation of queueing networks. First, we showed how a deterministic Fork/Join network is discovered from a schedule. Second, we presented a method that exploits log data to assess the operational and conceptual validity of the discovered model. We evaluated the approach with real-world data from an outpatient clinic and showed how our approach leads to the identification of operational bottlenecks and supports the analysis of the root-causes of these bottlenecks.

In future work, we would like to test the value of the stochastic Fork/Join network in the context of queue mining, e.g. for delay prediction in a network. Also, we hope to extend our validation techniques to incorporate features of stochastic analysis, when comparing two models, e.g., by developing similarity measures for Fork/Join networks.

Acknowledgments. This work was supported by the EU INSIGHT project (FP7-ICT 318225). We are grateful to the SEELab members, Dr. Valery Trofimov, Igor Gavako and especially Ella Nadjharov, for their help with the statistical analysis. We also thank Kristen Camuso, from Dana-Faber Cancer Institute for the insightful data discussions.

References

1. Dumas, M., Rosa, M.L., Mendling, J., Reijers, H.A.: Fundamentals of Business Process Management. Springer, Heidelberg (2013)
2. Daskin, M.S.: Service Science. Wiley. com (2011)

3. Froehle, C.M., Magazine, M.J.: Improving scheduling and flow in complex outpatient clinics. In: Handbook of Healthcare Operations Management, pp. 229–250. Springer (2013)
4. Gal, A., Mandelbaum, A., Schnitzler, F., Senderovich, A., Weidlich, M.: Traveling Time Prediction in Scheduled Transportation with Journey Segments. Tech. Rep., Technion (2014)
5. Ammar, M.H., Gershwin, S.B.: Equivalence relations in queueing models of fork/join networks with blocking. Performance Evaluation 10(3), 233–245 (1989)
6. Mandelbaum, A.: Service engineering (science, management): A subjective view. Technical report, Technion-Israel Institute of Technology (2007)
7. Bolch, G., Greiner, S., de Meer, H., Trivedi, K.S.: Queueing Networks and Markov Chains - Modeling and Performance Evaluation with Computer Science Applications. Wiley (2006)
8. Kendall, D.G.: Stochastic Processes Occurring in the Theory of Queues and their Analysis by the Method of the Imbedded Markov Chain. The Annals of Mathematical Statistics 24(3), 338–354 (1953)
9. Senderovich, A., Weidlich, M., Gal, A., Mandelbaum, A.: Queue mining – predicting delays in service processes. In: Jarke, M., Mylopoulos, J., Quix, C., Rolland, C., Manolopoulos, Y., Mouratidis, H., Horkoff, J. (eds.) CAiSE 2014. LNCS, vol. 8484, pp. 42–57. Springer, Heidelberg (2014)
10. Sargent, R.G.: Verification and validation of simulation models. In: WSC, pp. 183–198 (2011)
11. Buijs, J.C.A.M., van Dongen, B.F., van der Aalst, W.M.P.: Quality dimensions in process discovery: The importance of fitness, precision, generalization and simplicity. Int. J. Cooperative Inf. Syst. 23(1) (2014)
12. Rozinat, A., van der Aalst, W.M.P.: Conformance checking of processes based on monitoring real behavior. Inf. Syst. 33(1), 64–95 (2008)
13. Bose, R.P.J.C., van der Aalst, W.M.P.: Process diagnostics using trace alignment: Opportunities, issues, and challenges. Inf. Syst. 37(2), 117–141 (2012)
14. Weidlich, M., Polyvyanyy, A., Desai, N., Mendling, J., Weske, M.: Process compliance analysis based on behavioural profiles. Inf. Syst. 36(7), 1009–1025 (2011)
15. vanden Broucke, S.K.L.M., Weerdt, J.D., Vanthienen, J., Baesens, B.: Determining process model precision and generalization with weighted artificial negative events. IEEE Trans. Knowl. Data Eng. 26(8), 1877–1889 (2014)
16. Dallery, Y., Liu, Z., Towsley, D.: Equivalence, reversibility, symmetry and concavity properties in fork-join queuing networks with blocking. J. ACM 41(5), 903–942 (1994)
17. Rozinat, A., Mans, R., Song, M., van der Aalst, W.M.P.: Discovering simulation models. Information Systems 34(3), 305–327 (2009)
18. van der Aalst, W.: Process Mining: Discovery, Conformance and Enhancement of Business Processes. Springer, Heidelberg (2011)
19. Senderovich, A., Weidlich, M., Gal, A., Mandelbaum, A.: Mining resource scheduling protocols. In: Sadiq, S., Soffer, P., Völzer, H. (eds.) BPM 2014. LNCS, vol. 8659, pp. 200–216. Springer, Heidelberg (2014)
20. Brown, L., Gans, N., Mandelbaum, A., Sakov, A., Shen, H., Zeltyn, S., Zhao, L.: Statistical Analysis of a Telephone Call Center. Journal of the American Statistical Association 100(469), 36–50 (2005)
21. Zhang, P., Serban, N.: Discovery, visualization and performance analysis of enterprise workflow. Computational statistics & data analysis 51(5), 2670–2687 (2007)
22. Bickel, P., Doksum, K.: Mathematical Statistics: Basic Ideas and Selected Topics. Holden-Day series in probability and statistics, vol. 1. Prentice Hall (2001)

23. Pinedo, M.: Planning and scheduling in manufacturing and services. Springer (2005)
24. Buzacott, J.A., Shanthikumar, J.G.: Stochastic Models of Manufacturing Systems. Prentice Hall, Englewood Cliffs, NJ (1993)
25. Mans, R.S., Russell, N.C., van der Aalst, W.M.P., Moleman, A.J., Bakker, P.J.M.: Schedule-aware workflow management systems. In: Jensen, K., Donatelli, S., Koutny, M. (eds.) Transactions on Petri Nets and Other Models of Concurrency IV. LNCS, vol. 6550, pp. 121–143. Springer, Heidelberg (2010)
26. Rogge-Solti, A., van der Aalst, W.M.P., Weske, M.: Discovering stochastic petri nets with arbitrary delay distributions from event logs. In: Lohmann, N., Song, M., Wohed, P. (eds.) BPM 2013 Workshops. LNBIP, vol. 171, pp. 15–27. Springer, Heidelberg (2014)
27. van der Aalst, W.M.P., Schonenberg, M., Song, M.: Time prediction based on process mining. Information Systems 36(2), 450–475 (2011)
28. Rogge-Solti, A., Weske, M.: Prediction of remaining service execution time using stochastic petri nets with arbitrary firing delays. In: Basu, S., Pautasso, C., Zhang, L., Fu, X. (eds.) ICSOC 2013. LNCS, vol. 8274, pp. 389–403. Springer, Heidelberg (2013)
29. Pika, A., Wynn, M.T., Fidge, C.J., ter Hofstede, A.H.M., Leyer, M., van der Aalst, W.M.P.: An extensible framework for analysing resource behaviour using event logs. In: Jarke, M., Mylopoulos, J., Quix, C., Rolland, C., Manolopoulos, Y., Mouratidis, H., Horkoff, J. (eds.) CAiSE 2014. LNCS, vol. 8484, pp. 564–579. Springer, Heidelberg (2014)
30. Nakatumba, J., van der Aalst, W.M.P.: Analyzing resource behavior using process mining. In: Rinderle-Ma, S., Sadiq, S., Leymann, F. (eds.) BPM 2009. LNBIP, vol. 43, pp. 69–80. Springer, Heidelberg (2010)
31. Van der Aalst, W.: Petri net based scheduling. Operations-Res.-Spektr. 18(4), 219–229 (1996)
32. Taghiabadi, E.R., Gromov, V., Fahland, D., van der Aalst, W.M.P.: Compliance checking of data-aware and resource-aware compliance requirements. In: Meersman, R., Panetto, H., Dillon, T., Missikoff, M., Liu, L., Pastor, O., Cuzzocrea, A., Sellis, T. (eds.) OTM 2014. LNCS, vol. 8841, pp. 237–257. Springer, Heidelberg (2014)
33. de Leoni, M., van der Aalst, W.M.P., van Dongen, B.F.: Data- and resource-aware conformance checking of business processes. In: Abramowicz, W., Kriksciuniene, D., Sakalauskas, V. (eds.) BIS 2012. LNBIP, vol. 117, pp. 48–59. Springer, Heidelberg (2012)
34. Adriansyah, A., van Dongen, B.F., van der Aalst, W.M.P.: Conformance checking using cost-based fitness analysis. In: EDOC, IEEE Computer Society, pp. 55–64 (2011)
35. Atar, R., Mandelbaum, A., Zviran, A.: Control of fork-join networks in heavy traffic. In: 50th Annual Allerton Conference on Communication, Control, and Computing, pp. 823–830 (2012)

Verification and Validation of UML Artifact-Centric Business Process Models

Montserrat Estañol[1(✉)], Maria-Ribera Sancho[1,2], and Ernest Teniente[1]

[1] Universitat Politècnica de Catalunya, Barcelona, Spain
{estanyol,ribera,teniente}@essi.upc.edu
[2] Barcelona Supercomputing Center, Barcelona, Spain

Abstract. This paper presents a way of checking the correctness of artifact-centric business process models defined using the BAUML framework. To ensure that these models are free of errors, we propose an approach to verify (i.e. there are no internal mistakes) and to validate them (i.e. the model complies with the business requirements). This approach is based on translating these models into logic and then encoding the desirable properties as satisfiability problems of derived predicates. In this way, we can then use a tool to check if these properties are fulfilled.

Keywords: Artifact-Centric BPM · UML · Verification · Validation

1 Introduction

Business process modeling (BPM) is a critical task in the business's definition, as these processes are directly involved in the achievement of an organization's goals. Business processes may be modeled following an artifact-centric approach which represents both the dynamic (i.e. the activities or tasks) and the structural (i.e. the data) dimensions of the process. Including the data in the model makes it possible to define precisely what each of the tasks does. This is why this approach has grown in importance in recent years.

It is essential to evaluate the correctness of these models as early as possible, to avoid the propagation of errors through the development of the business. Several research has been done on this topic [2,6,9,17]. However, most of these specify the processes in different variants of logic, resulting in specifications that are complex and difficult to understand by the domain experts. They have also been proposed at a theoretical level: there is no tool that can perform the tests.

The correctness of an artifact-centric BPM can be assessed from two different perspectives. *Verification* ensures that the model is right, i.e. that it does not include contradictions or redundancies. *Validation* guarantees that we are building the right BPM, i.e., that the model fulfills the business requirements.

The main contribution of our work is to propose an approach to verify and validate an artifact-centric BPM specified in *BAUML* [4], which uses a combination of UML and OCL models. To do this, we provide a method to translate

© Springer International Publishing Switzerland 2015
J. Zdravkovic et al. (Eds.): CAiSE 2015, LNCS 9097, pp. 434–449, 2015.
DOI: 10.1007/978-3-319-19069-3_27

all *BAUML* components into a set of logic formulas. The result of this translation ensures that the only changes allowed are those specified in the model, and that those changes are taking place according the order established by the model. Having obtained this logic representation, these models can be validated by any existing reasoning method able to deal with negation of derived predicates. We also show the feasibility of our approach by using an implementation of an existing method that is able to carry out verification and validation tests.

To our knowledge, ours is the first approach able to check the correctness of artifact-centric BPMs in practice with reliable results since previous proposals always dealt with this problem at a theoretical level or bounded the number of objects considered. It is also the first one to handle together reasoning on class diagrams, state transition diagrams, activity diagrams and operation contracts.

This paper extends our previous work in several ways. In [8] we dealt with this problem at a theoretical level. In [14] we did not consider the notion of business artifact, nor state transition diagrams and activity diagrams during reasoning. In [4] we identified sufficient conditions over *BAUML* models which guarantee decidability of verification, and which can be applied to this work.

2   Motivation and Running Example

We base our work on the BALSA framework [12], which establishes four different dimensions that should be present in any artifact-centric business process model. They are the following. **Business Artifacts** represent the information required by the business, whose evolution we wish to track. **Lifecycles** are used to represent the evolution of an artifact during its life, from the moment it is created until it is destroyed. **Associations** establish the execution flow for services. **Services** (also known as tasks) are atomic units of work in the business process. As such, they make changes to artifacts by creating, updating and deleting them. Apart from artifacts, businesses keep data which may change but whose potential states are not relevant from the business's point of view. We will refer to it as *objects*.

In this paper we adopt the *BAUML* modeling approach [4], which represents the BALSA dimensions using UML and OCL: UML class diagrams for business artifacts; UML state transition diagrams for lifecycles; UML activity diagrams for associations, and OCL operation contracts for services.

As an example, consider the artifact-centric BPM of a city bicycle rental system. Figure 1 shows its UML class diagram. *Bicycle* is the only business artifact since we wish to track in the system the bicycle's evolution. A *Bicycle* may be in state *Available*, *InUse* or *Unusable* (we shortened the names for convenience; they should be called *AvailableBicycle*, etc.). The rest of the classes correspond to objects and specify the data required to rent a bicycle.

The textual constraints for Figure 1 are shown below.

1. *Bicycles* and *Users* are identified by their *id*. *AnchorPoints* by their *number*.
2. *inServiceSince* must be earlier or equal to *lastReturn*, *startTime*, and *date* in Unusable.
3. *expectedReturn* must be later or equal to *startTime*.

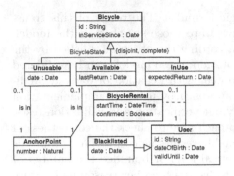

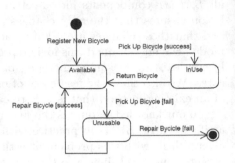

Fig. 1. Class diagram of our example   **Fig. 2.** State diagram of *Bicycle*

Figure 2 shows the lifecycle of the artifact *Bicycle*. When a *Bicycle* is registered it is *Available*. When a *User* picks it up to rent it, he may return it to its anchor point if it is not in good shape and the bicycle is *Unusable*. Otherwise, it is *InUse*. When the user returns the bicycle, it is *Available* again. An *Unusuable* bicycle may be repaired, so that it is again *Available*. Otherwise, it is destroyed.

Figure 3 shows the activity diagram for transition *Register New Bicycle*. To do this, the bicycle has to be created first and then assigned to an anchor point.

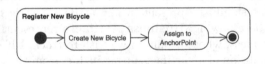

Fig. 3. Activity diagram of *Register New Bicycle*

The operation contracts for the tasks in Figure 3 are shown below. For the sake of simplicity, and without loss of generality, we leave out class attributes.

```
operation createNewBicycle(): Bicycle
post: Available.allInstances()->exists (b | b.oclIsNew() and
      result=b.oclAsType(Bicycle))
```

```
operation assignToAnchorPoint(b: Bicycle, ap: AnchorPoint)
pre: AnchorPoint.allInstances()->includes(ap) and ap.available->isEmpty()
     and ap.unusable->isEmpty()
post: ap.available = b.oclAsType(Available)
```

BAUML provides a high-level of abstraction that allows specifying artifact-centric BPMs from a technology-independent perspective, making these models understandable to model experts. However, it is very difficult to manually assess that the model is correct. For instance, is it possible to create an *unusable* bicycle? Will external event *Pick Up Bicycle* ever be executed? Are *Blacklisted* users forbidden from renting a bicycle? Automated reasoning techniques can aid the designer in this important task. This is the main goal of this paper.

3   Basic Concepts

This section formally presents the BALSA UML models that we use and the logic formalization in which they are translated in order to check their correctness.

The BAUML Model. A BAUML model $\mathcal{B}$ is a tuple $\langle \mathcal{M}, \mathcal{S}, \mathcal{P}, \mathcal{T} \rangle$, describing the four dimensions of the BALSA framework:

Class Diagram: $\mathcal{M}$ is a UML class diagram, in which some classes represent (business) artifacts. We denote the set of artifacts in $\mathcal{M}$ as ARTIFACTS($\mathcal{M}$) and, when convenient, we use ARTIFACTS($\mathcal{B}$) interchangeably. Each artifact is the top class of a hierarchy whose leaves are subclasses with a dynamic behavior (their instances change from one subclass to another). Each subclass represents a specific state in which an artifact instance can be at a certain moment in time. These subclasses must fulfill the covering and disjointness constraints (i.e. the artifact must exactly have one of the subclasses type at a certain point in time.) We denote the classes in $\mathcal{M}$ as CLASSES($\mathcal{M}$), and the associations in $\mathcal{M}$ as ASSOCIATIONS($\mathcal{M}$). When convenient, we may refer to them as CLASSES($\mathcal{B}$) and ASSOCIATIONS($\mathcal{B}$). A class diagram will also have a set of graphical and textual (defined in OCL) integrity constraints, which we denote as $\mathcal{O}$.

State Transition Diagrams: $\mathcal{S}$ is a set of UML state transition diagrams, one per artifact in ARTIFACTS($\mathcal{M}$). More formally, for each artifact $\mathtt{A} \in$ ARTIFACTS($\mathcal{M}$), $\mathcal{S}$ contains a state transition diagram $S_{\mathtt{A}} = \langle V, V_0, E, T \rangle$, where V is a set of states, $V_0 \subseteq V$ is the set of initial states, E is a set of events, and $T \subseteq V \times OCL_{\mathcal{M}} \times E \times C \times V$ is a set of transitions between pairs of states, where $OCL_{\mathcal{M}}$ is an OCL condition over $\mathcal{M}$ and C is a tag on the result of the execution of the event in E. The states V of $S_{\mathtt{A}}$ exactly mirror the subclasses of $\mathtt{A}$.

Transitions have the following form (elements inside parenthesis are optional): ([$OCL_{\mathcal{M}}$]) ExternalEvent($a_1, ..., a_n$) ([C]), where $a_1, ..., a_n$ are the artifacts manipulated by ExternalEvent. The transition will take place if $OCL_{\mathcal{M}}$ is true when the external event is received. The execution of the event results in tag C (as we shall see, its possible values are success and fail).

$OCL_{\mathcal{M}}$ is an OCL boolean expression over $\mathcal{M}$. ExternalEvent($a_1, ..., a_n$) must appear at least in a transition of the state transition diagram of each artifact a_i. The execution of external events and the tags C resulting from this execution are driven by activity diagrams.

Activity Diagrams: $\mathcal{P}$ is a set of UML activity diagrams, such that for every state transition diagram $S = \langle V, V_0, E, T \rangle \in \mathcal{S}$, and for every event $\varepsilon \in$ EXTEVENTS(S) there exists exactly one activity diagram $P_\varepsilon \in \mathcal{P}$.

P_ε is a tuple $\langle N, n_o, n_f, F \rangle$, where N is a set of nodes, $n_o \in N$ is the initial node, $n_f \subset N$ is the set of final nodes and $F \subseteq N \times G \times C \times N$ is a set of transitions between pairs of nodes where C is a tag (success or fail) denoting the correct or incorrect execution of the transition, and G a guard condition.

There are four different types of nodes $n \in N$ in an activity diagram P_ε: initial nodes (denoted as INI(P_ε)), final nodes (FINAL(P_ε)), gateways (GATEWAYS(P_ε)

and tasks (TASKS(P_ε)). *Initial* and *final* nodes indicate the points where the activity diagram flow begins and ends, respectively. *Gateways* are used to control the sequence flow, they include *decision nodes* and *merge nodes*. Finally, each task is associated to an *operation contract*, which expresses a precondition on the executability of the task, and a postcondition describing its effect, both formalized in terms of OCL queries over $\mathcal{M}$.

We only allow guard conditions over a transition $f = \langle n_s, g, c, n_t \rangle \in F$ if n_s is a decision node, and g corresponds to an OCL condition over $\mathcal{M}$. Similarly, we only allow c over $f \in F$ such that $f = \langle n_s, g, c, n_t \rangle$ and $n_t \in$ FINAL(P_ε).

We make the following assumptions: decision nodes have one incoming flow and more than one outgoing flow; merge nodes have more than one incoming flow and exactly one outgoing flow; tasks have exactly one incoming and one outgoing flow; initial nodes have no incoming flow and exactly one outgoing flow; and final nodes have one or several incoming flows but no outgoing flow. In addition, the external event must, at the end of its execution, bring the artifact to the target state of the transition in the state machine diagram.

During the execution of an activity diagram the constraints may be violated, but they must be met at the end of the execution, otherwise the transition in the state transition diagram does not take place and the changes are rolled back.

Tasks: $\mathcal{T}$ is a set of atomic tasks, each of which has an OCL operation contract. A task can only be executed when the current information base satisfies its precondition and, once executed, it brings the information base to a new state that satisfies its postcondition. If, during the execution of an activity diagram the precondition of one of the tasks is not met, then we assume that the corresponding transition does not take place and that no changes are made.

Given an artifact $A \in \mathcal{M}$, we denote by TASKS(A) the set of tasks appearing in the state transition diagram S_A, also considering all activity diagrams related to S_A. Moreover, we assume that every task in TASKS(A) that does not belong to the activity diagram of an initial transition has as input an instance of the artifact in S_A.

Logic Formalization. For the formalization of our models, we use formulas in first-order logic. A term T is a variable or a constant. If p is a n-ary predicate and $T_1, ..., T_n$ are terms, then $p(T_1, ..., T_n)$ or $p(\overline{T})$ is an atom. An ordinary literal is either an atom or a negated atom. A built-in literal has the form of $A_1 \theta A_2$, where A_1 and A_2 are terms. θ is either $<, \leq, >, \geq, =$ or $\neq$.

A normal clause has the form: $A \leftarrow L_1 \wedge ... \wedge L_m$ with $m \geq 0$, where A is an atom and each L_i is an ordinary or built-in literal. All the variables in A, and in each L_i, are assumed to be universally quantified over the whole formula. A is the head and $L_1 \wedge ... \wedge L_m$ is the body of the clause. A normal clause is either a *fact*, $p(\overline{a})$, where $p(\overline{a})$ is a ground atom, or a *deductive rule*, $p(\overline{T}) \leftarrow L_1 \wedge ... \wedge L_m$ with $m \geq 1$, where p is the derived predicate defined by rule.

A condition is a formula of the (denial) form: $\leftarrow L_1 \wedge ... \wedge L_m$ with $m \geq 1$. Finally, a schema S is a tuple (DR, IC) where DR is a finite set of deductive rules and IC is a finite set of conditions. All formulas are required to be *safe*, i.e.

every variable occurring in their head or in negative or built-in literals must also occur in an ordinary positive literal of the same body. An instance of a schema S is a tuple (E, S) where E is a set of facts about base predicates. $DR(E)$ denotes the whole set of ground facts about base and derived predicates that are inferred from an instance (E, S), and corresponds to the fixpoint model of $DR \cup E$.

4   Verification and Validation of BAUML Models

Given a BAUML model, our goal is to ensure that it is correct (verification) and that it satisfies the user requirements (validation). To do so, we need to transform the model into the logic described in section 3. After this, we will obtain a set of derivation rules and conditions (a schema) representing the BAUML model. A desirable property of the model will be then tested by checking the satisfiability of a derived predicate.

The work we present here clearly differs from [14], where only class diagrams and operation contracts were considered. Note that in this case no restrictions were imposed on the execution of the tasks nor on the checking of the constraints.

4.1   Translation Algorithms

Our translation process is divided into four steps, shown in Algorithm 1. To begin with, we focus on the generic steps: obtaining derivation rules for classes and associations, translating the integrity constraints, generating the derivation rules from the tasks, and adding the required conditions to ensure that tasks execute properly, in the context given by state transition and activity diagrams.

The first step creates the derivation rules for the read-write set of classes and associations. To determine if a class or association is read-only or read-write, it is only necessary to examine the postcondition of all the tasks as described in [14]. The predicate corresponding to each read-write class and association will have a time component t indicating that the element exists at time t, whereas read-only elements will not include the time t and will be treated as base predicates.

The algorithm also takes into consideration if a class is *created* or *created and deleted* in the model. The general form of these rules is:

$$C(oid, \overline{p}, t) \leftarrow addC(\overline{p}, t_1) \wedge \neg deletedC(\overline{p}_j, t_1, t) \wedge t \geq t_1 \wedge time(t),$$

where $\overline{p}$ corresponds to the attributes in the class (including its OID [unique object identifier]) or the participants in the association, $\overline{p}_j$ represents the identifier of the class (its OID) or association (OID of the classes that participate and identify it) C, and thus $\overline{p}_j \subseteq \overline{p}$, and t and t_1 represent the time. We will see how $addC(...)$ and $deletedC(...)$ are obtained later on.

The rule basically states that a class or an association will exist at time t if it has been created previously, at t_1 ($t_1 \leq t$), and it has not been deleted in the meantime. For instance, Bicycle is encoded as:

$$Bicycle(b, t) \leftarrow addBicycle(b, t_1) \wedge time(t) \wedge \neg deletedBicycle(b, t_1, t) \wedge t_1 \leq t,$$

Algorithm 1. TranslateToLogic($\mathcal{B} = \langle \mathcal{M}, \mathcal{S}, \mathcal{P}, \mathcal{T} \rangle$)

// Step 1: Creating rules for read/write classes and associations
$r := \emptyset$
for all $c \in$ CLASSES($\mathcal{M}$) **do**
    if c is created in $\mathcal{P} \wedge c$ is <u>not</u> deleted in $\mathcal{P}$ **then**
        $r := r \cup \{C(\overline{p}, t) \leftarrow addC(\overline{p}, t_1) \wedge time(t) \wedge t \geq t_1\}$
    else if c is created in $\mathcal{P} \wedge c$ is deleted in $\mathcal{P}$ **then**
        $r := r \cup \{C(\overline{p}, t) \leftarrow addC(\overline{p}, t_1) \wedge \neg deletedC(\overline{p}_j, t_1, t) \wedge t \geq t_1 \wedge time(t)\}$
        $r := r \cup \{deletedC(\overline{p}_j, t_1, t_2) \leftarrow delC(\overline{p}_j, t) \wedge time(t_1) \wedge time(t_2) \wedge t \leq t_2 \wedge t > t_1\}$
    end if
end for
for all $a \in$ ASSOCIATIONS($\mathcal{M}$) **do**
    if a is created in $\mathcal{P} \wedge a$ is <u>not</u> deleted in $\mathcal{P}$ **then**
        $r := r \cup \{A(\overline{p}, t) \leftarrow addA(\overline{p}, t_1) \wedge time(t) \wedge t \geq t_1\}$
    else if a is created in $\mathcal{P} \wedge a$ is deleted in $\mathcal{P}$ **then**
        $r := r \cup \{A(\overline{p}, t) \leftarrow addA(\overline{p}, t_1) \wedge \neg deletedA(\overline{p}_j, t_1, t) \wedge t \geq t_1 \wedge time(t)\}$
        $r := r \cup \{deletedA(\overline{p}_j, t_1, t_2) \leftarrow delA(\overline{p}_j, t) \wedge time(t_1) \wedge time(t_2) \wedge t \leq t_2 \wedge t > t_1\}$
    end if
end for
// Step 2: Translate integrity constraints
$icSet := translateIC(\mathcal{O})$
for all condition $cond \in icSet$ **do**
    $cond := cond + \{\wedge validState(t)\}$
end for
$taskRules := \emptyset$
// Step 3: Generate rules for class and association creation and deletion for every task
for all $t \in \mathcal{T}$ **do**
    $resRules := translateTask(t)$
    $taskRules := taskRules \cup resRules$
end for
// Step 4: Generate necessary rules and conditions to ensure correct execution order
$taskRules := taskRules \cup generateConstraintsTaskExecution(\mathcal{B})$
return $\langle r, icSet, taskRules \rangle$

---

whereas User is encoded as $User(u)$. Bicycle is a derived predicate created and deleted by some of the tasks. On the other hand, User is a base predicate as it is not created nor deleted by any task.

Step 2 of the algorithm translates the constraints $\mathcal{O}$ into a set of formulas in denial form, following [15], but we need to add an atom $\wedge validState(t)$ to each of them to ensure that they are only checked at the end of the execution of a state transition diagram transition, following the semantics of the framework.

For instance, the covering constraint in the hierarchy of Bicycle indicates that a Bicycle must have one of its subclasses' type. Then the condition: $\leftarrow Bicycle(b, t) \wedge \neg IsKindOfBicycle(b, t) \wedge validState(t)$ states that there cannot be a bicycle which has not any of its subtypes (predicate $IsKindOfBicycle$), where $IsKindOfBicycle$ is a derived predicate from $InUse$, $Available$ and $Unusuable$. This condition only applies when there are no transitions taking place, indicated by predicate $validState$.

Step 3 is the most complex and it is decomposed into various algorithms. It generates the derivation rules that link the creation and deletion of the classes and associations with the tasks that perform these changes, and ensures that all tasks execute at the right time. This is done by calling Algorithms 2 and 3.

Finally, step 4 generates the remaining necessary constraints to ensure the correct execution of the tasks by calling Algorithm 4. For instance, if there is

---

Algorithm 2. translateTask(*task*)

$rules := \emptyset$
$prevRules := getContextPreviousTasks(task, t)$ // t represents a time term
$createList$ contains the classes and associations created by $task$
$delList$ contains the classes and associations deleted by $task$
for all $ruleFragment \in prevRules$ **do**
    for all $el \in createList$ **do**
        $r := addEl(\overline{p}, t) \leftarrow task(\overline{p}, \overline{x}, t) \wedge pre_{task}(t-1) \wedge time(t) \wedge ruleFragment$
        $rules := rules \cup r$
    end for
    for all $el \in delList$ **do**
        $r := delEl(\overline{p}_j, t) \leftarrow task(\overline{p}_j, \overline{y}, t) \wedge pre_{task}(t-1) \wedge time(t) \wedge ruleFragment$
        $rules := rules \cup r$
    end for
    $rules := rules \cup \{task'(p_a, t) \leftarrow task(p_a, \overline{z}, t) \wedge pre_{task}(t-1) \wedge time(t) \wedge ruleFragment\}$
end for
return $rules$

---

a sequence of tasks that execute in the activity diagram, it ensures that all of them execute and creates the derivation rules to generate predicate *validState* at the end of the execution of the activity diagram.

We will now analyze the details of the remaining algorithms. Algorithm 2 is aimed at translating the atomic tasks. As they make changes to the instances of the class diagram, this translation will result in the derivation rules that generate predicates *addEl* and *delEl*, where *el* is a class or an association. In [14], these rules are generated by analyzing the postcondition of each task and determining if the task creates or deletes some instance. If the task has a precondition, then its translation (following [15]) is also added to the body of the derivation rule to ensure that it is true at time $t-1$, where t represents the time the task executes.

However, this translation does not impose any restrictions over the order for task execution. In BAUML tasks execute following the restrictions and the order established by the state transition and activity diagrams. In particular, $task_k$ can only execute if pre_{task_k} is true and the previous task $task_{k-1}$ has executed at $t-1$.

Algorithm 2 generates the creation and deletion rules as described, invoking Algorithm 3 to obtain the part of the rule that refers to the successful execution of the previous tasks. At the end, Algorithm 2 generates a rule of the form:

$$task'(p_a, t) \leftarrow task(p_a, \overline{z}, t) \wedge pre_{task}(t-1) \wedge time(t) \wedge ruleFragment,$$

where p_a corresponds to the OID of the business artifact, which we use to ensure the proper evolution of the system, and $\overline{z}$ corresponds to the remaining parameters or terms of *task*. The derived predicate of this rule, $task'(...)$, will be used as an indicator that *task* has executed properly by the next task.

Algorithm 3 is in charge of generating the part of the derivation rules that depends on the previous node(s) of a certain node. Its complexity lies in the fact that we consider not only linear activity diagrams, but that we also allow decision and merge nodes. We assume that control nodes do not add execution time to our diagrams and that they are traversed immediately. So, given a node n that belongs to an activity diagram P_ε and time t, the algorithm:

Algorithm 3. getContextPreviousTasks(n,t)

$result := \emptyset$
$prevSet$ contains the previous nodes of n
for all $n_p \in prevSet$ **do**
  if n_p is task **then**
    $result := result \cup n'_p(p_a, t - 1)$
  else if n_p is decision node **then**
    $guard := getGuard(n_p, n)$
    $res := getContextPreviousTasks(n_p, t)$
    for all $el \in res$ **do**
      $result := result \cup \{el \wedge guard(t - 1)\}$
    end for
  else if n_p is merge node **then**
    $res := getContextPreviousTasks(n_p, t)$
    $result := result \cup res$
  else if n_p is initial node **then**
    $transitions$ contains the transitions in which the activity diagram appears
    for all $t \in transitions$ **do**
      s_s is the source state of t
      $cond$ is the translation of condition of t
      if s_s is not initial pseudostate $\wedge$ $cond$ is not empty **then**
        $result := result \cup \{s_s(\overline{p}, t - 1) \wedge cond(t - 1)\}$
      else if s_s is not initial pseudostate **then**
        $result := result \cup \{s_s(\overline{p}, t - 1)$
      else if $cond$ is not empty **then**
        $result := result \cup \{cond(t - 1)\}$
      end if
    end for
  end if
  return $result$
end for

---

1. Obtains the previous nodes of n, stores them in $prevSet$ and initializes $result$ to the empty set.
2. For each $n_p \in prevSet$, it checks its type.
   (a) If n_p is a task, it then adds the $n'_p(...)$ predicate to the existing $result$, indicating that the task n_p will have executed successfully.
   (b) If n_p is a decision node, the algorithm needs to obtain the predicates corresponding to the tasks that may execute before n_p; therefore it invokes itself, but this time with n_p and t as input. As n_p is a decision node, there will be a guard condition in the edge between n_p and n. This guard will be translated as if it was a precondition and it will have to be true at $t - 1$ in order for the task to execute. Then, it will add the guard condition to each rule-part obtained by the self-invocation,
   (c) If n_p is a merge node, it invokes itself with parameters n_p and t, and it adds the result of this invocation to variable $result$.
   (d) If, on the other hand, n_p is an initial node, it adds the source state of the state transition diagram of the transitions in which the activity diagram appears. If there is an OCL condition, it also adds the translation of the condition.
3. The algorithm returns variable $result$, containing a set of rule fragments.

For instance, for task *Assign to Anchor Point*, we have the following rules:

$$addAvailableIsIn(b, a, t) \leftarrow assignToAnchPoint(a, b, t) \land AnchorPoint(a)$$
$$\land precondAssToAP(a, t-1) \land Bicycle(b, t) \land createNewBicycle'(b, t-1)$$
$$assignToAnchPoint'(b, t) \leftarrow assignToAnchPoint(a, b, t) \land AnchorPoint(a)$$
$$\land precondAssToAP(a, t-1) \land Bicycle(b, t) \land createNewBicycle'(b, t-1)$$

The task creates an instance of the *available is in* association. It has a precondition which must be true at $t-1$, and its translation appears in the derivation rule of *addAvailableIsIn*. In addition to this, the body of the rule includes the predicate *createNewBicycle'*, that guarantees that the previous operation (*Create New Bicycle*) has executed successfully.

Algorithm 4. generateConstraintsTaskExecution($\mathcal{B}$)

$constr := \emptyset$
for all $task \in$ TASKS($\mathcal{B}$) **do**
   n_n is next node of $task$
   if n_n is task **then**
      $constr := constr \cup \{\leftarrow task(p_a, \overline{z}, t) \land \neg n'_n(p_a, t+1)\}$
   else if n_n is decision node $\lor$ n_n is merge node **then**
      $r := \leftarrow task(p_a, \overline{z}, t) \land \neg nextTask(p_a, t+1)$
      $res := generateConstraintsNextTasks(n, task)$
      $constr := constr \cup r \cup res$
   else if n_n is final node **then**
      $constr := \{validState(t) \leftarrow task'(p_a, t)\}$
   end if
end for
return $constr$

With the algorithms that we have seen so far we have restricted the order for the tasks execution in one direction, ensuring that task $task_k$ can only execute if $task_{k-1}$ has taken place. We also need to ensure that, once an activity diagram begins execution, it finishes. Algorithm 4 generates the necessary constraints to do so. For each task, it obtains its next node and, if the next node n_n is a task, it creates a rule of the form: $\leftarrow task(p_a, \overline{z}, t) \land \neg n'_n(p_a, t+1)$, where predicate n'_n corresponds to the derived predicate generated by Algorithm 2 to ensure that task n_n has executed properly. For instance, for the tasks *Create New Bicycle* and *Assign to Anchor Point* we have the following condition and derivation rule: $\leftarrow createNewBicycle(b, t) \land \neg assignToAnchorPoint'(b, t+1)$.

On the other hand, if n_n is a decision node or a merge node, there is the possibility that there will be more than one task that can be executed. For this reason, the algorithm generates this rule: $\leftarrow task(p_a, \overline{z}, t) \land \neg nextTask(p_a, t+1)$, meaning that if $task$ has executed at t one of its next tasks must have executed at $t+1$. $nextTask$ is a derived predicate resulting from the execution of any of the next tasks. These derivation rules are created in Algorithm 5 and have the following form: $nextTask(p_a, t) \leftarrow task'_n(p_a, t)$. The algorithm iterates over the nodes until the next task(s) are found. Guard conditions are not considered because they have already been translated by the other algorithms.

Finally, if a task is followed by a final node, we need to generate rule: $validState(t) \leftarrow task'(p_a, t)$. This rule will ensure that the restrictions of the model are checked at the end of the execution. For instance, in our example the successful execution of task *Assign To AnchorPoint* generates predicate *validState* as it is the last task in the activity diagram: $validState(t) \leftarrow assignToAnchorPoint'(b, t)$.

Algorithm 5. generateConstraintsNextTasks(n,task)

$result := \emptyset$
$nextSet$ contains the set of next nodes of n
for all $n_n \in nextSet$ **do**
   if n_n is task **then**
      $nextTask(p_a, t) \leftarrow n'_n(p_a, t)$
   else if n_n is decision node $\vee$ n_n is merge node **then**
      $res := generateConstraintsNextTasks(n_n, task)$
      $result := result \cup res$
   else if n_n is final node $\wedge$ n is decision node **then**
      $guard$ contains the guard condition from n to n_n
      $nextTask(p_a, t) \leftarrow task'(p_a, \overline{z}, t) \wedge guard(\overline{y}, t)$
      $validState(t) \leftarrow task'(p_a, \overline{z}, t) \wedge guard(\overline{y}, t)$
   end if
end for
return $result$

There is a special case, however. If there is a decision node n and one of the next nodes $n_n \in \text{FINAL}(P_\varepsilon)$ is a final node, then these rules are needed:

$$nextTask(p_a, t) \leftarrow task'(p_a, \overline{z}, t) \wedge guard(\overline{y}, t)$$
$$validState(t) \leftarrow task'(p_a, \overline{z}, t) \wedge guard(\overline{y}, t),$$

which will ensure that after the execution of *task*, the diagram terminates if the corresponding guard condition is met.

4.2   Verification and Validation Tests

After applying the translation described in the previous section, we are now interested in checking certain properties to guarantee the model's correctness. All tests are represented as checking the satisfiability of a derived predicate. Any satisfiability checking method that is able to deal with negation of derived predicates can be used to validate the schema. Note that we use the translation of our whole running example to perform the tests.

Verification Tests. The goal of verification tests is to ensure that there are no inherent contradictions or mistakes in the model. They can be generated and performed automatically without requiring intervention from the modeler.

The **liveliness test** of a class or an association will ensure that an instance of it can be successfully created and that it persists in the system until the transition that has created it ends. Logically, it only makes sense to apply the tests to read-write classes and associations. The general form of the test is the following, where el is the name of the class or association: $livelinessTestEl() \leftarrow el(\overline{p}, t) \wedge validState(t)$. Remember that $validState$ is a derived predicate generated by the last task that executes in a transition. For instance, to test the liveliness of $Bicycle$, we would define the following derivation rule: $livelinessTestBicycle() \leftarrow Bicycle(b, t) \wedge validstate(t)$.

The **applicability test** will check whether a certain task can be executed, that is, if the necessary requirements for its execution are met. The test will have the following form, for task $task_i$: $applicabilityTask() \leftarrow pre_{task}(\overline{y}, t) \wedge task'_{i-1}(p_a, t)$.

The **executability test** will check if a certain task can be executed. It is particularly useful for those activity diagrams with decision nodes to ensure that all paths can be taken. The test will have the following form: $executabilityTask() \leftarrow task'(p_a, t)$. Notice that it is equivalent to checking if the predicate $task'$ can be generated, as $task'$ represents precisely the successful execution of $task$. For instance, to check the executability of task *Confirm Return*, we would run the following test: $execConfirmReturn() \leftarrow confirmReturn'(b, t)$.

Validation Tests. On the other hand, validation tests ensure that the model is aligned to the user requirements. In the general case, validation tests require the intervention from the user and thus cannot be generated automatically from the model. An interesting validation test in our example would be to check if a blacklisted user can rent a bicycle: $blacklistUserRent() \leftarrow Blacklisted(u) \wedge BicycleRental(b, u, i, t) \wedge validState(t)$. The $validState$ predicate is needed to ensure that the BicycleRental is not deleted before the end of a transition.

5   Implementing our Approach Within SVTe

We have studied the feasibility of our approach by using an existing tool, SVTe, that is able to perform the tests described previously. This tool uses the CQC_E method [16] which is aimed at building a consistent state of a database schema that satisfies a given goal, represented as a set of one or more literals. The method starts with an empty solution, and given the goal, the database schema, the constraints and the derivation rules, tries to obtain a set of base facts that satisfy the goal without violating any of the constraints. The CQC_E method is a semidecision procedure for finite satisfiability. This means that it does not terminate in the presence of solutions with infinite elements. However, termination is assured if the model satisfies the conditions identified in [4].

To instantiate the variables during the inference process, the method uses Variable Instantiation Patterns (VIPs), which generate only the relevant facts that need to be added to the schema to satisfy the goal. If no instance that satisfies the database schema and the constraints is found, then the VIPs guarantee that the goal cannot be achieved with the given schema and constraints.

Figure 4 shows the result of some of the previous tests: i.e. the outcomes of the bicycle liveliness test (top), the executability test for task *Confirm Return* (middle) and the validation test (bottom). Notice that all the tests execute successfully, that is, there exists an instantiation of the database schema (i.e. the translation of our model) that fulfills the given goals. The tool shows the set of base predicates (corresponding to tasks and read-only classes and associations) that prove the satisfiability of the test. However, notice that although the last test also gives a positive result, it is not what should be: blacklisted users should *not* be allowed to rent bicycles. The reason for this is that an integrity constraint is missing in the class diagram, forbidding blacklisted users to have bicycle rentals.

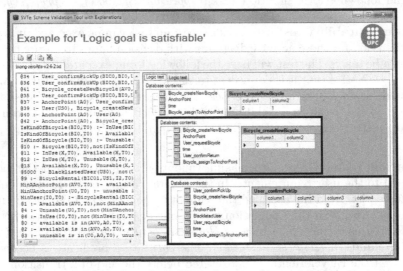

Fig. 4. Screenshots from SVTe showing the results of the test

6   Related Work

We examine validation and verification in two different areas related to our work: artifact-centric business process models and UML diagrams.

Several approaches to reasoning on artifact-centric BPM use data-centric dynamic systems (DCDSs), grounded on logic, as the basis for reasoning [1–3]. [2] uses a relational database to represent the data, together with a set of condition-action rules and actions defined in logic. In contrast, [1] uses a Knowledge and Action Base defined in a variant of Description Logics to represent this data. Similarly, [3] maps an ontology to a DCDS in order to verify certain temporal properties expressed in a variant of μ-calculus.

Similarly, [6] represents artifacts using a set of variables, which are updated by services defined by pre and postconditions in first-order logic. They check whether the resulting model fulfills a set of properties defined in LTL-FO, which is not as powerful as μ-calculus.

All these works represent artifact-centric business process models in languages derived from logic. Consequently, the models under consideration are formal, but they are not practical for business people. Moreover, they have been proposed at a theoretical level and do not have a tool that implements them.

In contrast, the Guard-Stage-Milestone (GSM) approach provides a business-friendly representation of artifact-centric business processes. [17] studies the decidability of verification over GSM models by translating them into a DCDSs. However, the presented results are theoretical, as there is no tool that can actually perform the reasoning. [11] presents a system to model and execute artifact systems. However, to our knowledge, the system is limited to simulating the behavior of the model given certain data and this is different to our work in this paper. [10] performs model checking over GSM models from a multi-agent perspective; however the bound placed on the number of objects may sometimes lead to unreliable results when this bound is exceeded.

Similarly to our work, [18] performs verification over process models considering the meaning of the tasks. These are annotated with preconditions and effects defined in logic, and use an ontology to define the underlying data. Time is not considered explicitly, which only allows for analysis of the current state of the system, whereas in our case we can analyze the system's evolution.

On the other hand, most of the proposals for reasoning on UML models deal with only one diagram. For instance, [15] focuses on the class diagram, [5] handles state-machine diagrams, and [7] focuses on activity diagrams. As far as approaches examining various UML diagrams, [13] offers a systematic literature review but only four of the analyzed papers perform reasoning on more than one of the diagrams in our approach: they can handle class and state machine diagrams. [14] handles both the class diagram and the operation contracts, but it does not consider state transition nor activity diagrams.

7   Conclusions

We have presented a way of validating and verifying artifact-centric business process models defined using the *BAUML* framework. This framework provides us with a set of models which can be defined and are understandable by the modelers. Checking the correctness of these models as early as possible is important to avoid the propagation of errors to the execution stage of the process. These errors can result from mistakes in the models themselves (e.g. contradictions) or errors in the sense that the models do not fulfill the business requirements.

To ensure that they are free of errors, we translate the BAUML models into logic and encode the desirable properties as derived predicates. We can then use an existing tool to check if the properties are fulfilled. To the best of our knowledge, there is no other proposal that is able to check the correctness of artifact-centric BPMs with reliable results.

We are aware that, in some instances, the tool may not perform efficiently, and even not terminate for some tests, due to the temporal cost of the search for a solution and its potential infinity. Improving the efficiency of the tool and the translation of parallelism is left as further work.

Acknowledgments. This work has been partially supported by the Ministerio de Ciencia e Innovación under project TIN2011-24747 and by UPC.

References

1. Bagheri Hariri, B., et al.: Verification of description logic knowledge and action bases. In: Raedt, L.D., et al. (eds.) ECAI. Frontiers in Artificial Intelligence and Applications, vol. 242, pp. 103–108. IOS Press (2012)
2. Bagheri Hariri, B., et al.: Verification of relational data-centric dynamic systems with external services. In: PODS, pp. 163–174. ACM (2013)
3. Calvanese, D., De Giacomo, G., Lembo, D., Montali, M., Santoso, A.: Ontology-based governance of data-aware processes. In: Krötzsch, M., Straccia, U. (eds.) RR 2012. LNCS, vol. 7497, pp. 25–41. Springer, Heidelberg (2012)
4. Calvanese, D., Montali, M., Estañol, M., Teniente, E.: Verifiable UML artifact-centric business process models. In: Li, J., Wang, X.S., Garofalakis, M.N., Soboroff, I., Suel, T., Wang, M. (eds.) CIKM 2014, pp. 1289–1298. ACM (2014)
5. Choppy, C., Klai, K., Zidani, H.: Formal verification of UML state diagrams: a Petri net based approach. ACM SIGSOFT Soft. Eng. Notes **36**(1), 1–8 (2011)
6. Damaggio, E., Deutsch, A., Vianu, V.: Artifact systems with data dependencies and arithmetic. ACM Transactions on Database Systems **37**(3), 1–36 (2012)
7. Eshuis, R.: Symbolic model checking of UML activity diagrams. ACM Trans. Softw. Eng. Methodol. **15**(1), 1–38 (2006)
8. Estañol, M., Sancho, M.-R., Teniente, E.: Reasoning on UML data-centric business process models. In: Basu, S., Pautasso, C., Zhang, L., Fu, X. (eds.) ICSOC 2013. LNCS, vol. 8274, pp. 437–445. Springer, Heidelberg (2013)
9. Gerede, C.E., Su, J.: Specification and verification of artifact behaviors in business process models. In: Krämer, B.J., Lin, K.-J., Narasimhan, P. (eds.) ICSOC 2007. LNCS, vol. 4749, pp. 181–192. Springer, Heidelberg (2007)
10. Gonzalez, P., Griesmayer, A., Lomuscio, A.: Model checking GSM-based multi-agent systems. In: Lomuscio, A.R., Nepal, S., Patrizi, F., Benatallah, B., Brandić, I. (eds.) ICSOC 2013. LNCS, vol. 8377, pp. 54–68. Springer, Heidelberg (2014)
11. Heath III, F.T., Boaz, D., Gupta, M., Vaculín, R., Sun, Y., Hull, R., Limonad, L.: Barcelona: a design and runtime environment for declarative artifact-centric BPM. In: Basu, S., Pautasso, C., Zhang, L., Fu, X. (eds.) ICSOC 2013. LNCS, vol. 8274, pp. 705–709. Springer, Heidelberg (2013)
12. Hull, R.: Artifact-centric business process models: brief survey of research results and challenges. In: Meersman, R., Tari, Z. (eds.) OTM 2008, Part II. LNCS, vol. 5332, pp. 1152–1163. Springer, Heidelberg (2008)
13. Lucas, F.J., Molina, F., Álvarez, J.A.T.: A systematic review of UML model consistency management. Information & Software Technology **51**(12), 1631–1645 (2009)
14. Queralt, A., Teniente, E.: Reasoning on UML conceptual schemas with operations. In: van Eck, P., Gordijn, J., Wieringa, R. (eds.) CAiSE 2009. LNCS, vol. 5565, pp. 47–62. Springer, Heidelberg (2009)
15. Queralt, A., Teniente, E.: Verification and validation of UML conceptual schemas with OCL constraints. ACM Trans. Softw. Eng. Methodol. **21**(2), 13 (2012)

16. Rull, G., Farré, C., Teniente, E., Urpí, T.: Providing explanations for database schema validation. In: Bhowmick, S.S., Küng, J., Wagner, R. (eds.) DEXA 2008. LNCS, vol. 5181, pp. 660–667. Springer, Heidelberg (2008)
17. Solomakhin, D., Montali, M., Tessaris, S., De Masellis, R.: Verification of artifact-centric systems: decidability and modeling issues. In: Basu, S., Pautasso, C., Zhang, L., Fu, X. (eds.) ICSOC 2013. LNCS, vol. 8274, pp. 252–266. Springer, Heidelberg (2013)
18. Weber, I., Hoffmann, J., Mendling, J.: Beyond soundness: on the verification of semantic business process models. Distributed and Parallel Databases **27**(3), 271–343 (2010)

Enterprise IT Integration and Management

Empirical Challenges in the Implementation of IT Portfolio Management: A Survey in Three Companies

Lucy Ellen Lwakatare[✉], Pasi Kuvaja, Harri Haapasalo, and Arto Tolonen

Department of Information Processing Science, University of Oulu, Oulu, Finland
{lucy.lwakatare,pasi.kuvaja,
harri.haapasalo,arto.tolonen}@oulu.fi

Abstract. The study explores the implementation challenges of Information Technology (IT) portfolio management in three companies. The portfolio approach to IT assets is significant for enabling organisations to make effective use of limited resources by prioritising IT initiatives and also for monitoring and evaluating their performance. In practice, the process facilitates the provision of necessary information for decision makers, allowing them to make rational decisions about IT investments. We found that there is a significant gap between IT portfolio management as discussed in the literature and its actual practice. The analysis showed that there was high flexibility when specifying IT projects, which caused companies to implement IT portfolios that were too broad. As a consequence, resources were not effectively utilised, and IT portfolio evaluations post implementation were rarely conducted. Our research contribution identifies important gaps to be filled in the literature and presents case studies related to IT portfolio management.

Keywords: IT portfolio management · IT governance · IT project portfolio

1 Introduction

Information Technology (IT) has, in many cases, proven to be a useful enabler in achieving the strategic mission of an organisation, though it is often constrained by various factors such as high costs. For companies, yearly increases in expenditure on IT shows a relationship between the strategic implementation of IT and the ability to achieve corporate objectives and goals [1]. Conversely, some studies have argued that the causal relationship between IT investments and business value has remained partially unexplained [2, 3]. The notion here is that large investments in IT do not guarantee long-term success, but rather appropriate governance of IT investments is crucial if an organisation is creating value through IT investments [4]. Applying appropriate governance to IT investments includes adopting suitable methods and practices for selecting and evaluating IT initiatives. Generally, IT constitutes a company's total investments in computing and communication technologies that facilitate information sharing and help to support a variety of business processes, such as R&D, in achieving its goals. Typically, companies have a dedicated or separate IT function that is responsible for acquiring IT products and services.

© Springer International Publishing Switzerland 2015
J. Zdravkovic et al. (Eds.): CAiSE 2015, LNCS 9097, pp. 453–467, 2015.
DOI: 10.1007/978-3-319-19069-3_28

The decision to invest in any aspect of IT is often complex and multi-phased [5]. It consists of a series of actions, starting from the identification of a need (problem) and continuing until the investment is approved as an IT project [6]. The literature on IT investments emphasises basing investment decisions on correct, suitable and up-to-date information rather than on feelings and intuition [6, 7]. Given that there are few widely accepted methodologies directing IT investments in organisations, this raises the question of how to invest in IT wisely for optimum benefit. This study explores portfolio theory as a widely accepted methodology that has been adopted in the field of information systems [8].

IT Portfolio Management (ITPM), which has its roots in the modern portfolio theory of Markowitz, enables senior managers to make informed decisions about their investment alternatives [8]. We identified that a growing number of studies on IT portfolios have focused on theoretical issues related to portfolios, such as portfolio diversification, strategic alignment, portfolio synergies and models for portfolio selection. Thus, there is a need for studies that provide insight into ITPM implementation and adaptation in companies, which to date have been scarce [9]. The aim of this study is to fill this gap by investigating how ITPM practices have been implemented in three selected medium-sized companies. In addition, we present ITPM challenges as perceived by these companies, revealing a significant gap between the literature and empirical findings. The findings of our work were guided by the following research questions:

1. To what extent is IT portfolio management practised in the selected companies?
2. What are the perceived challenges of IT portfolio management in the selected companies?

This paper is organised as follows. Section 2 presents related work and an analysis framework for ITPM. The research approach of the study is presented in Section 3. In Section 4, the findings from the companies are presented followed by a discussion and conclusion in sections 5 and 6, respectively.

2   Related Work and Analysis Framework for ITPM

The literature on ITPM, and especially on IT project portfolios, is mostly studied in Information Systems (IS), project management and operational research [10]. ITPM has been described by Jeffery and Leliveld [11] as managing "a portfolio of assets similar to a financial portfolio and striving to improve the performance of the portfolio by balancing risk and return". Although there is a significant difference between financial portfolios and IT portfolios, their purpose is to maximise the expected return of an investment at a minimum risk [10]. IT initiatives represent IT investment opportunities and assets composed of IT projects, IT infrastructure, IT application and IT services [12]. IT initiatives can be further categorised as strategic, transactional, informational and infrastructural depending on their contribution in fulfilling organisation's objective [9], [13]. ITPM is an instance of IT governance because it supports and implements the internal controls and procedures needed to ensure accountability, transparency and the efficient use of IT investments [13, 14]. It also provides central oversight of IT budgets, IT risk management and strategic alignment of IT investments. As such, IT governance frameworks such as IT infrastructure library (ITIL) and Control Objectives for Information and Related Technology (COBIT) have addressed the ITPM concepts of ensuring the recognition of value and risks associated with IT initiatives [14].

The ITPM process establishes an investment framework for IT project selection for the construction of IT portfolios that is based on maximised expected returns and minimised risk. The IT project selection literature has predominantly focused on developing quantitative models derived from financial and operational research disciplines [10]. The main reason for the quantitative models is to make the decision making process rational with the use of rigorous and evidence-based comparisons [5], [15]. This is particularly important because other issues such as conflict, disagreements, coalitions and power of decision makers can obstruct the decision making process [16]. The quantitative models also aim at complementing decision makers' beliefs—acquired through observation and experience—about the future performance of proposed IT initiatives. Despite their benefits, empirical research has shown that quantitative models lack adoption in companies mainly due to their complexity and practitioners' lack of understanding regarding the models [11].

On the other hand, the literature has focused least on the activities and methods required after IT project selection, especially regarding the termination or de-escalation of commitment to misaligned or failing IT initiatives [9]. The termination of existing IT initiatives in IT portfolios is critical for discontinuing or removing initiatives that are either misaligned with the company's objectives or that do not realise the expected benefits [5]. Such actions allow resources to be freed up to create room for other opportunities. According to Kester et al. [5], termination decisions are often difficult to make because the individuals' responsible for certain projects have their emotions involved in the project, making them reluctant to terminate it. Also, even when other persons are involved, there is a risk that they may influence decisions through "overly positive evaluation of the project" [5]. In the IS literature, the evaluations methods of IT initiatives and assets both before (ex ante) and after (ex post) their implementation have been greatly studied [3]. The main challenge has been to explain the link between IT investment and value attained as well as how and from whose perspective that is value measured [3].

Although in literature ITPM is considered to constitute to a well-defined and structured process, few ITPM methodological frameworks exist [15]. This not only suggests the fact that contextual factors have a huge impact but also suggests the complexity and diversity in ITPM implementation. However, there is a consensus that the process involves continuous identification, prioritisation, balancing, allocation and review of IT initiatives making up IT portfolios [18]. Some studies have applied ITPM practices to an IT investment framework with three phases—namely, selection, control and evaluation [18-20]. In this study, we consider these phases to create an ITPM analysis framework. In the framework, an IT initiative can concurrently be active in more than one phase. For instance, an IT initiative is subjected to reselection throughout the control phase. Also, if an IT initiative has not met the goals originally specified or if the goals have been modified to reflect changes in the strategy, a decision must be made on whether to continue to invest in the IT initiative. Generally, "deselection" is one of the most difficult steps to implement, but it is necessary if resources are to be better utilised elsewhere. We further describe the activities in each of the named phases.

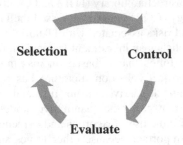

Selection   **Control**

Evaluate

Fig. 1. A framework for IT portfolio management

2.1   IT Portfolio Selection

The portfolio selection phase describes how different proposals for IT initiatives will be defined, prioritised and selected for investment. From the literature [5] [10-22], summary of the aspects emphasised in the IT portfolio selection phase include:

— The availability of data for use in quantitative models
— The use of quantitative models in the information provided for decision making
— The nature of the decision making process (e.g. evidence-based, opinion-based)
— The criteria used for making the decision
— A consideration of individual IT projects at the portfolio level (e.g. IT project synergies)

Generally, the selection phase involves identifying, analysing and evaluating the risks and returns of IT initiatives both individually and collectively with other initiatives. Then, using certain criteria in the evaluation of risk and returns, IT initiatives are selected for inclusion in a portfolio.

There are various models proposed in the literature for the IT portfolio selection phase. For instance, return on investment (ROI) and net present value (NVP) for evaluating the returns and Analytical Hierarchical for evaluating the strategic fit [5]. A multi-criteria approach is favoured in IT project selection because the value of IT initiatives cannot only be captured in financial metrics due to the nature of IT projects e.g. exhibit   high interdependencies [21, 22].

2.2   IT Portfolio Control

In the IT portfolio control phase, selected IT initiatives are monitored and tracked during implementation to ensure that the objectives and benefits are met at an expected or minimised level of risk and cost [18-20]. Periodic reviews, such as project review meetings, ensure that monitored information is provided to help assess the performance of IT initiatives against the specified targets [23]. In the control phase, companies should be able to make adjustments or address problems when the company's objectives have changed or problems arise during implementation.

The measures (both qualitative and quantitative models) need to be able to capture the progress against the targets.

2.3   IT Portfolio Evaluation

The evaluation phase involves post-implementation reviews (ex post evaluation) to compare the expected returns and objectives of IT initiatives against their actual performance [18-20]. It also involves examining and verifying the associated risks and impacts of selected IT initiatives regarding the achievement of the company's goals and objectives. Some of the important issues identified from the literature [3],[5],[10-22] regarding IT evaluation include:

— The approaches used for evaluation models need to include a consideration of contextual factors and organisational transformation when being interpreted
— Assessment of the contribution of IT initiatives to other types of performances
— Clarity in the definition of benefits and risks

This phase serves the purpose of identifying the needed changes or modifications to the existing IT initiatives and also of revising the ITPM process based on the lessons learned from the existing ITPM process.

3   Research Process and Method

An explorative qualitative study was used to investigate ITPM in three companies. The aim was to understand ITPM practices in a real-world context where contextual information is important [24]. The focus was on identifying ITPM practices in each phase of the ITPM framework. Figure 1 shows the research process of our study.

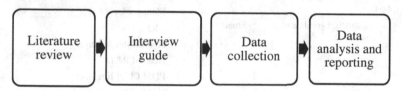

Fig. 2. Research process of the study

Literature Review. Relevant literature on ITPM was retrieved from the IS, project management and operational research disciplines that have influenced research on ITPM [10]. The studies were retrieved using the Google Scholar and Science Direct databases. In addition, we looked at the references of the retrieved studies to identify other relevant studies. The literature review served two main purposes: first, to provide a synthesis of previous research on ITPM, and second, to form an analysis framework for empirical investigation in the selected companies.

Interview Guide. The interview guide was developed using the findings from the literature review. The interview guide consisted of semi-structured questions divided into four sections: (1) ITPM understanding and IT governance; (2) current practices of ITPM in selection, control and evaluation; and (3) ITPM challenges, benefits and drivers. The semi-structured interview questions allowed for the collection of rich data and the necessary flexibility in an explorative study [24].

Data Collection. The data collection process was designed to carefully consider threats to validity. Empirical data was primarily collected through semi-structured interviews with practitioners from three companies. Based on the network of the research team, three companies were selected, and interview invitations were sent to key contact persons. The key contact persons agreed to take part in the study and also nominated other potential interview participants. The companies are reported anonymously in this study, owing to a confidentiality agreement. All interviews took place on the premises of the companies with a total of 10 interviewees who had varying roles in the companies, as presented in Table 1. Each of the three separate, in-depth, face-to-face interview sessions that lasted about three hours. All interview sessions were recorded and transcribed. The interview transcripts were sent back to interviewees for review so as to strengthen interpretive validity [24]. Additionally, an interview guide used in the interviews helped to reduce researchers' reactivity bias [24]. The companies represent small and medium-sized companies in Finland with IT expenditures of 2 percent (B), 4 percent (A) and 10 percent (C) of the companies' revenue. Henceforth, the interviewees are referred to as practitioners in the study.

Table 1. Companies and roles of interviewees

Company	Industry	Size	Interviewees
A	Telecommunications (equipment manufacturer)	Medium	IT Stakeholder Manager for R&D
			IT Portfolio and Enterprise Release Manager for R&D
B	Industrial goods and services	Small	CIO
			IT Portfolio Manager
			Head of R&D
			PDM Chief Engineer
			Head of Factory and Logistics
C	Telecommunications (service provider)	Medium	IT Service Director
			Solutions Manager
			Development Director

Data Analysis and Reporting. For data analysis, the transcribed and reviewed interview transcripts were analysed using NVivo[1]. From the transcripts, we coded responses to the following themes: IT governance, ITPM understanding, ITPM practices (in the three phases of the ITPM framework), ITPM challenges, ITPM benefits and ITPM drivers. The structure of the interview guide helped in the analysis as different themes were identified beforehand as well as in setting the direction of what to

---

[1] Qualitative data analysing software (http://www.qsrinternational.com/)

look for in the data. The analysis of one company enabled its comparison with the other companies so as to further determine similar and/or differing patterns of ITPM practices in the ITPM framework.

4   Findings of ITPM in the Companies

This section presents the findings of ITPM in the surveyed companies using the ITPM process framework. In summary, practitioners described ITPM as including the types of IT services (or IT projects) that the companies currently had or that were planned for as well as how they were being prioritised, valued and managed across their entire lifecycle. Table 2 gives an overview of the findings using the analysis framework presented in Section 2.

Table 2. ITPM practices in the surveyed companies

ITPM		Company A	Company B	Company C
Selection	Information provided for selection	Business Case (ROI, NPV, break-even), Project Plan	Business Case (ROI, increases in margin, risk, payback time), Project Plan	Business Case (NPV, ROI, risks, delivery time and costs), Project Plan, Strategic Initiatives
	Selection and prioritisation criteria	1. Strategy 2. Company-specific 5 level criteria 3. Business case	1. Strategy 2. Business case	1. Strategy 2. Business case
Control	Tracked and monitored information	Status of projects, cost, schedules, scope, risk and quality	Costs, schedules, risks and quality	Schedule deviations
	Corrective actions	Corrective actions agreed upon for underperforming Cancellation only when there are changes to strategy	Action taken for risks that can be contained or minimised	Corrective actions for key risks
Evaluation	Information provided for evaluation	SLA, KPI of services and actual costs, risks and benefits	IT operational performance, Process KPI	Actual benefits, Operational performance of IT using KPIs

4.1   IT Governance

IT governance—in terms of how activities are organised (centralised or decentralised) and management teams responsible for making IT investment decisions—was crucial to the understanding of the ITPM processes in the companies.

In two companies, B and C, IT was centralised, whereas in Company A IT was both centralised and decentralised. The decentralised IT in Company A took the form of individual business units such as R&D being responsible for overseeing their own specific IT needs. In centralised IT, one division is responsible for overseeing common IT needs across different business units. For Company B, IT was centralised to enable business by providing IT tools and services to the main business units of the company such as customer services, logistics etc., with the exception of R&D. The IT tools for R&D, such as those for software development and simulation, were not supported by centralised IT and were thus the responsibility of the R&D division. Similarly, in Company C, IT was centralised. However, unlike company B, the IT tools for R&D were also supported by centralised IT.

All companies had clearly defined the roles and responsibilities for the management teams responsible for making IT investment decisions. In addition, flexibility in the structure enabled decision escalations to take place whenever necessary. It was also noticed that the size and nature of the IT initiatives influenced the hierarchical level at which the decision took place. The highest level of IT governance was the board of directors, which was responsible for providing leadership on the company's strategy and oversight. The next level was the executive board, which was responsible for allocating the budget as well as making investment decisions. Company B had its big IT projects approved at this level, whereas Company A and Company C had IT projects approved at the next lower level. The corporate development steering team responsible for selecting and reviewing the bigger IT initiatives that impact more than one business unit (process) was at the third level. It consisted of heads of business units (process), the Chief Financial Officer (CFO) and the Chief Information Officer (CIO). Typically, the team was also responsible for process development, cooperation and management between the different organisational processes and IT. According to the practitioners of companies A and C, this was also the IT review group, which had the authority to delay, cancel or approve projects. The next level was made up of a solution area or business unit steering team, which mainly consisted of a process owner and CIO, who together selected and prioritised initiatives specific to a particular business unit. The last level was occupied by other management teams such as the project steering team, who oversaw the execution of one specific project. As such, in all companies, IT investment decisions were not made solely by IT or business experts but rather through a common understanding between business and IT.

4.2   IT Portfolio Selection

In all companies, the determination of the IT annual budget preceded the selection process of IT initiatives as it was allocated as part of the annual corporate budgeting. The top-down approach of setting the cost framework for IT activities upfront also considered the bottom-up approach. In the bottom-up approach, business units annually developed and proposed IT investment plans in advance of the upcoming financial year.

In Company A, IT portfolio selection for R&D involved allocating a part of the assigned IT budget to the different IT projects, services and applications that enabled

R&D to rapidly develop and deliver products to markets. Business cases which included quantitative financial models (ROI, NPV, break-even) were used for proposing new IT initiatives. Often, the selection and prioritisation decisions were made based on the specified company's strategy and goals and were formalised according to five levels of criteria. Following the approval of IT initiatives, project plans were presented and used for making decisions to start and end new projects. The project steering team of the approved project oversaw project implementation at different milestones and set targets to be tracked. Unlike Company A, Company B did not have harmonised selection and prioritisation criteria for selecting IT initiatives. IT initiatives were selected through discussion and common understanding between the main business units and IT in a forum consisting of business process owners, the CIO and the portfolio manager. During the discussions, the forum analysed and evaluated business effect, ROI, increases in margin, risk and payback time for the proposed IT initiatives. It was stated by the practitioners that there is no harmonized criteria because they tend to be subjective: "we have a huge Excel containing all of our projects for evaluation in the common forum. There are many criteria inside the Excel like company's top priority said by the management team this year, a critical project but I would agree it's subjective. And in our case even if we would have specified selection criteria it would not be the guiding factor for starting the projects because resource bottleneck is the guiding principle for how many can be started at once and are then prioritized accordingly". Although the practitioners had different opinions regarding the importance of explicitly specifying the selection and prioritisation criteria, they commonly agreed that it helped in the development of IT project plans: "with that list, we were actually able to create a prioritised list of initiatives; and even though all the resourcing does not agreeing with it, there is still some understanding that we are now providing proper project plans for each by defining more clearly what is needed and when,". In Company C, a business case including information about NPV, expected benefits and returns (e.g. ROI, risks, delivery time and costs) was used as a source of information for selecting new IT projects, particularly capability building IT projects: "IT projects get prioritised if they have a business case. There is a list that contains initiatives in priority order, and these have cumulative expenditures and there is a point where the expenditure hits available budget. As there is a fixed budget, decisions go through prioritizations of available resources or through the priorities set by business owners (IT also gives inputs)."

In companies A and C, Microsoft Excel was used to make quantitative financial calculations that were then presented in the business case. The program was also used for storing a list of IT project inventory. As the quantitative models were included as templates in Microsoft Excel, there was a tendency for individuals to not fully understand them. Due to the limitations of Microsoft Excel, the companies were in the process of acquiring portfolio management tools.

4.3   IT Portfolio Control

After the selection of IT initiatives and during their implementation, different ITPM control activities were incorporated.

In Company A, IT portfolio control involved the frequent monitoring of status, cost, schedules, scope, risk and quality for the selected IT initiatives against the annual cost plan etc. This was reported and reviewed monthly at the business unit level by the specific steering teams, by the IT performance and assurance teams and occasionally by the corporate steering team. For IT services, the company frequently measured its service level agreement (SLA) and projects' key performance indicators (KPIs). When there was risk, schedule and cost deviations, and decisions on corrective actions were made on a case by case basis: "corrective actions are taken on a case by case basis because there is something unexpected. Sometimes, when there is some issue already known, there can be different options for how to correct it, and the project manager can say we have a problem and state some corrective actions, and the project steering team decides". Also, if there are changes in strategy, then existing IT initiatives are reviewed and changed accordingly: "during the prioritisation of projects, we noticed that some projects were categorised according to old criteria (the criteria were changed in December of last year) and thus were reviewed according to the new criteria, and all projects are now updated". In Company B, the forum responsible for initiating IT projects did not participate in IT portfolio control. The IT portfolio control is conducted by the project steering teams, where they review and track costs, schedules, risks and quality. Corrective actions are taken to minimise and contain risks when necessary. For Company C, portfolio control was conducted for IT projects through reviews of project schedule deviations: "we measure how development projects go through the process and projects schedules deviations. Currently many projects are overrun though not considered a problem in our organization".

4.4   IT Portfolio Evaluation

In the three companies, portfolio management reviews were either conducted informally or not at all. If they were not conducted, it was because they were considered to be officially conducted at the project level by the project steering groups.

For Company A, IT portfolio evaluations involved assessing SLAs, KPI of services and the actual costs, risks and benefits of IT initiatives. In Company B, ITPM evaluations involved evaluating the KPIs of the process to see whether there had been any progress that had been anticipated, the actual implementation costs and IT operational performance. The company mostly followed spending to see if it matched with the business cases' calculations, but it did not follow feedback from users: "spending is followed but not user feedback. We follow whether were able to match business case calculations in reality as these are defined in the process but not really controlled. We try to improve in that by not allowing the closure of the project without having approval from the executive management team; as a part of that process, you need to present the return". The practitioners identified this to be important and an area needing to be improved. For Company C, portfolio evaluations post implementation of IT initiatives varied depending on the projects. For large IT projects, the company conducts interviews and reviews to evaluate the benefits that have been achieved. However, the IT is normally evaluated for operational performance using KPIs: "They are measured depending on projects; for larger ones, we have interviews and reviews to evaluate whether the benefits have been achieved, but this is not done comprehensively for all projects. At centralized IT, what is measured is KPI at the operational level: number of critical failures (and how successfully new systems are taken into production), user satisfaction, staying on budget. Critical ones are reported monthly, and targets of the measures are set on a half-year basis"

4.5   ITPM Challenges

ITPM is highly relevant and practised to an extent in the surveyed companies. The main key driver for ITPM implementation in the companies was that it provided a framework to control IT investment and ongoing IT initiatives. ITPM was also viewed as beneficial in providing visibility and transparency of IT activities throughout the company. Additionally, according to practitioners, ITPM provided useful information to senior management to aid in making decisions. However, the companies faced several challenges when implementing ITPM. The identified challenges are listed in Table 3 and further described below.

Table 3. IT portfolio management challenges in the companies

Challenge	Company		
	A	**B**	**C**
Lack of clear focus, resulting in too broad a portfolio		√	√
Inadequate categorisation of IT initiatives to help achieve comparable measures		√	√
In some cases, decisions were based on intuitions, opinions and power		√	√
Lack of focused post-implementation evaluations		√	√
Lack of a portfolio mind-set in identifying synergies and limiting redundant IT applications	√	√	√
Decisions to end IT initiatives rarely occur	√	√	√

One of the challenges related to the ITPM process was that companies often implemented too broad a portfolio. IT projects which had high flexibility in terms of what could be done at times posed a disadvantage, especially when the company focus was not clearly defined or communicated. This also gave the impression that there was no limit to the number of IT initiatives a company could implement at given a time, and as a consequence resources were not effectively utilised or termination decisions were hard to make: "when there are too many new things, there is a risk of not utilizing resources effectively…Currently, priorities change during the year, and in some cases it is justified, but in other cases it is easier to change than make hard decisions. As a result, momentum is lost. There is a need to have more clear focus areas and ensure these go through rather than implementing too broad a portfolio".

All IT projects, regardless of the differences in their contributions (e.g. strategic or informational) were competing on equal grounds. Inadequacy in the categorisation of IT initiatives to reflect their contribution made it challenging for companies to achieve comparable results and also difficult to find appropriate measures: "It is challenging to really have projects with comparable weighted KPIs which would help to make a good portfolio so we are able to highlights that these are important, these are strategic ones, etc."

Despite the business cases, the selection of IT initiatives is based on beliefs, opinions and intuition: "Although we have business cases and clearly defined the structure in decision making process to be able to make better fact based decision,   there are still places where the loudest person gets projects implemented over the silent person". It was also observed that at times, individuals' level of power can also be the deciding factor for IT investment: "factors and intuitions are used and the person allocating the money is calling the shots".

Another challenge that was identified in the companies was related to the IT portfolio evaluation phase of the ITPM process framework. After the implementation of IT initiatives, the companies did not conduct IT evaluations systematically: "It should ne systematic that once an IT system has been implemented, IT together with the process owners should ensure the development activities create/improve value and efficiencies through some specified set of targets, like having better turnaround of inventory or better time to market". Additionally, when IT portfolio evaluations were done, they had limited focus or that the companies had no good measures (e.g. focused on error tickets with no user satisfaction surveys): "we currently don't have any SLAs that oversee how different requests are being fulfilled. We have from agile project methods that are targeting efficiency and visibility etc.   Otherwise there are no good measures of how IT is meeting demand."

The companies also lacked a "portfolio mind-set" to help determine synergies amongst IT initiatives, which would help to limit redundant IT applications: "we have enterprise architecture look for redundant IT applications, and also each of us working in business units should see that there aren't applications doing the same things. For some reason there still are". All companies had consolidation plans that had been developed but that are yet to be implemented. Additionally, most redundant IT applications that were either no longer serving the business but that were used by a few individuals or resulted from mergers still remained and were not removed from the IT portfolio. The reasons for this lack of removal relate to the unwillingness of the few users to "let go" and also the failure of consolidations plans to be realised.

5   Discussion

The findings of the study revealed that companies experienced various challenges when implementing ITPM. Additionally, companies had no an explicitly defined ITPM framework. This lack of an explicitly defined ITPM process framework illustrates the dynamic nature of the ITPM process [5] and a gap in the literature [13]. IT initiatives are constantly subjected to technological and environmental changes. This necessitates the need for agility in the decision making process as well as in ITPM practices [5]. Recent advances in the way IT applications are developed and acquired in companies (e.g. Agile/lean methods, virtualisation, Software as Service (SaaS) in the cloud and increased use of Open Source Software) further emphasise the need for flexibility in ITPM. This relates to the organisational transformation dimension that is often ignored in IT evaluation approaches [3]. For instance, as a result of the advances mentioned, ITPM requires less detailed plans and also measures of how IT fulfilling the organisational needs.

As all companies in this study rarely conducted IT portfolio evaluations, these findings are consistent with other studies of IT (ex ante and ex post) evaluations reported in the IS literature [3], [25-27]. The latter studies observed that IT evaluation processes occur too infrequently in many organisations mainly due to imprecise and vague definitions of benefits and risks in the business cases and a lack of contextual considerations in the evaluation techniques. Inadequate IT portfolio evaluations prevent (or prolong) the taking of corrective actions where there are misaligned objectives or wrong intuitions. As a result of this observation, we included a "Termination" phase in the ITPM process framework. The termination phase would allow companies to evaluate whether an existing IT initiative (or the sub-components of that initiative) in their IT portfolio should be removed or reselected based on the results of the ITPM evaluation phase. As a result, companies will free up resources and also be able to identify specific areas in the current IT portfolio that need improvement as well as areas that are underserved, over served or misaligned with the company's strategy and objectives.

It was evident in this study that IT governance plays an important role in ITPM. It has been identified in previous studies that a certain degree of IT centralisation has an impact on the management of IT application redundancies, the exploitation of IT synergies and the level at which IT initiatives are selected [6]. Our findings support this previous research but also reveal that redundant IT applications can exist despite the centralisation of IT. This suggests that a "portfolio mind-set" amongst decision makers is also necessary in identifying IT project synergies and redundant IT applications. IT governance also has an important role in developing and communicating the strategy and areas of focus of the company. From our findings, we identified that effective communication of the strategy and focus areas enabled the effective implementation of ITPM practices. This is because the strategy was used to develop the selection and prioritisation criteria, and changes in the strategy greatly impacted the IT portfolio evaluation and control phases. If it is not well communicated, companies lack focussed efforts—both long term and short term—and effective ITPM. From our findings, a missing IT portfolio selection criterion that is explicitly defined demonstrated poor communication plan of the strategy or continuous changes in project priorities.

The following proposition and research implications can be drawn from our study findings. First, the ITPM process framework needs to be further improved given the different contextual conditions, agility in IT and organisational transformations. We have proposed the inclusion of a "Termination" phase in the presented ITPM process framework. Second, there needs to be more research on the subsequent phases of ITPM after the selection phase so as to identify the needed improvements and also to take into consideration the removal or retirement misaligned IT initiatives.

To practitioners our findings recommend that companies first acquire knowledge about the different ITPM evaluation techniques (both ex ante and ex post) and the circumstances in which they can be used. Also practitioners' need to incorporate 'portfolio mind-set' in the selection of IT project so as to identify synergies in IT projects and redundant IT applications. Moreover, to avoid multiple interpretations, companies still need to have a clear set of criteria for use in the selection and evaluation processes.

6   Conclusion

ITPM practices exist in almost every organisation. Our study investigated ITPM practices and challenges in three selected companies.

The findings revealed a gap between the literature and the empirical implementation of IT portfolio management. The major misalignment between theory and practice was that portfolio reviews representing portfolio control and post-implementation IT evaluations as described in the literature were rarely conducted in practice or were conducted with limited scope. Moreover, in the literature, a variety of portfolio selection models have been proposed, but the companies mostly used business cases with few models to select IT initiatives for inclusion in their IT portfolio. Some of the challenges related to ITPM in the companies included: lack of clear focus resulting to too broad a portfolio, and that decisions to remove IT initiatives are rarely made.

The research implication of our study is that it provides background for future research and case studies evaluating ITPM in a larger number of companies. Specifically, the use of the chosen framework provided a sound basis for analysing the state of the practice in the companies studied. Additionally, based on our findings, there is still a need for more empirical research which investigates ITPM activities after the selection phase in order to obtain a more general understanding of such an undertaking.

References

1. Laudon, K., Laudon, J.: Management Information Systems: Managing the Digital Firm. Prentice Hall, New Jersey (2012)
2. Lin, W., Shao, B.: The Business Value of Information Technology and Inputs Substitution: the Productivity Paradox Revisited. Decision Support Systems 42, 493–507 (2006)
3. Schryen, G.: Revisiting IS business value research: What We Already Know, What We Still Need to Know, and How We Can Get There. European Journal of Information Systems 22, 139–169 (2012)
4. Stratopoulos, T., Dehning, B.: Does Successful Investment in Information Technology Solve the Productivity Paradox? Information & Management 38, 103–117 (2000)
5. Kester, L., Griffin, A., Hultink, E.J., Lauche, K.: Exploring Portfolio Decision-Making Processes*. Journal of Product Innovation Management 28, 641–661 (2011)
6. Cho, W., Shaw, M.: Portfolio Selection Model for Enhancing Information Technology Synergy. IEEE Transactions on Engineering Management 60, 739–749 (2013)
7. Xue, Y., Liang, H., Boulton, W.: Information Technology Governance in Information Technology Investment Decision Processes: The Impact of Investment Characteristics, External Environment, and Internal Context. MIS Quarterly 32, 67–96 (2008)
8. Dolci, P., Maçada, A.: Portfolio theory: the contribution of markowitz's theory to information system area. In: Dwivedi, Y.K., Wade, M.R., Schneberger, S.L. (eds) Information Systems Theory. LNCS, vol. 28, pp. 199–211. Springer, New York (2012)

9. Kumar, R., Ajjan, H., Niu, Y.: Information Technology Portfolio Management: Literature Review, Framework, and Research Issues. Information Resources Management Journal **21**, 64–87 (2008)
10. Frey, T., Buxmann, P.: IT project portfolio management - a structured literature review. In: Proceedings of the 20th European Conference on Information Systems. AIS Electronic Library, Paper No. 167 (2012)
11. Jeffery, M., Leliveld, I.: Best Practices in IT portfolio Management. MIT Sloan Management Review **45**, 41–49 (2004)
12. Roebuck, K.: IT Portfolio Management: High-Impact Strategies - What You Need to Know: Definitions, Adoptions, Impact, Benefits, Maturity, Vendors. Emereo Pty Limited (2011)
13. Kaplan, J.: Strategic IT Portfolio Management: Governing Enterprise Transformation. Pittiglio Rabin Todd & McGrath (PRTM) Inc, California (2005)
14. Moller, R.: Executive's Guide to IT Governance: Improving Systems Processes with Servive Management, COBIT and ITIL. John Wiley & Sons (2013)
15. Marchewka, J., Keil, M.: Portfolio Theory Approach for Selecting and Managing IT projects. Information Resources Management Journal **8**, 5–16 (1995)
16. Hansen, L., Kræmmergaard, P.: There is more to IT portfolio management than top-management making the right decisions: a review of the literature. In: The 34th Information Systems Research Seminar in Scandinavia, pp. 144–186 (2011)
17. Stettina, C.J., Hörz, J.: Agile Portfolio Management: An Empirical Perspective on the Practice in Use. International Journal of Project Management **33**, 140–152 (2015)
18. Cunha Dolci, P., Carlos Gastaud Maçada, A., Grant, G.: IT Investment Management and Information Technology Portfolio Management. Journal of Enterprise Information Management **27**, 802–816 (2014)
19. United States General Accounting Office, (US-GAO): Information Technology Investment Management – A Framework for Assessing and Improving Process Maturity. http://www.gao.gov/assets/80/76790.pdf
20. Van Over, D.: Use of Information Technology Investment Management to Manage State Government Information Technology Investments. Strategic Information Technology and Portfolio management. Idea Group Inc, New York (2009)
21. Rahmani, N., Talebpour, A., Ahmadi, T.: Developing a Multi Criteria Model for Stochastic IT Portfolio Selection by AHP Method. Procedia - Social and Behavioral Sciences, pp. 1041–1045 (2012)
22. Chou, T., Chou, S., Tzeng, G.: Evaluating IT/IS Investments: A Fuzzy Multi-Criteria Decision Model Approach. European Journal of Operational Research **173**, 1026–1046 (2006)
23. Phillips, B.: Information Systems Portfolio Management: The impact of portfolio management practices (2008)
24. Yin, R.K.: Qualitative Research from Start to Finish. Guilford Press (2010)
25. Seddon, P., Graeser, V., Willcocks, L.: Measuring Organizational IS Effectiveness: an Overview and Update of Senior Management Perspectives. ACM SIGMIS Database **33**, 11–28 (2002)
26. Kasi, V., Keil, M.: The post mortem paradox: a Delphi study of IT specialist perceptions. European Journal of Information Systems **17**, 62–78 (2008)
27. Gwillim, D., Dovey, K., Wieder, B.: The politics of post-implementation reviews. Information Systems Journal **15**, 307–319 (2005)

Integration Adapter Modeling

Daniel Ritter[✉] and Manuel Holzleitner

Technology Development, SAP SE, Dietmar-Hopp-Allee 16,
Walldorf 69190, Germany
{daniel.ritter,manuel.holzeitner}@sap.com

Abstract. *Integration Adapters* are a fundamental part of an integration system, since they provide (business) applications access to its messaging channel. However, their modeling and configuration remain under-represented. In previous work, the integration control and data flow syntax and semantics have been expressed in the Business Process Model and Notation (BPMN) as a semantic model for message-based integration, while adapter and the related quality of service modeling were left for further studies.

In this work we specify common adapter capabilities and derive general modeling patterns, for which we define a compliant representation in BPMN. The patterns extend previous work by the adapter flow, evaluated syntactically and semantically for common adapter characteristics.

Keywords: Business Process Model and Notation (BPMN) · Conceptual modeling · Language design · Message endpoints · Quality of service

1 Introduction

Enterprise Application Integration (EAI) continues to receive widespread focus by organizations offering them as means of integrating their conventional business applications with each other, with the growing amount of cloud applications and with their partners' systems. In many cases, the integration middleware systems serve as the enabling technology for distributed, mission-critical business processes. For that, these systems offer well-defined modeling capabilities to describe integration semantics (e. g., message creation, transformation, routing) as well as runtime systems that interpret the definitions for efficient message processing. Figure 1 shows a typical conceptual overview of application-to-application (A2A) and business-to-business (B2B) integration, which can be found in many organizations (cf. Reese [12]). The dominating aspects are the many connections or integration adapters, which are currently under-represented in the (integration) modeling domain. Integration semantics are generally described based on a comprehensive (often graphically depicted) syntax and execution semantics (process model). In their best practices book Enterprise Integration Patterns (EIP), Hohpe and Woolf [7] have collected a widely used and accepted collection of integration patterns that are typical concepts used when implementing a messaging system and have proven to be useful in practice. However, they do not specify a semantic

© Springer International Publishing Switzerland 2015
J. Zdravkovic et al. (Eds.): CAiSE 2015, LNCS 9097, pp. 468–482, 2015.
DOI: 10.1007/978-3-319-19069-3_29

model for the formalization of the integration syntax and semantics. Most noticeable, the integration adapter modeling with its manifold characteristics is reduced to a *Channel Adapter* icon.

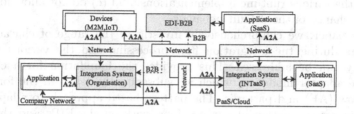

Fig. 1. Conceptual View on integration architecture of organizations

In previous work, we studied and provided a Domain-specific Language (DSL) with well-defined building blocks for modeling EIPs in the Business Process Model and Notation (BPMN) [11], which is a "de-facto" standard for modeling business process semantics and their runtime behavior [14]. We mapped EIPs to BPMN compatible syntax and defined execution semantics adapted to message processing. We extended that notion to end-to-end flows of messages, called *Integration Flow* (IFlow) [13]. In a nutshell, an IFlow can be seen as message-based integration from a sending application (Sender, *BPMN Participant*) to one or many receiving applications (Receiver(s), *BPMN Participant*) via *BPMN Message Flow* configurations (denoting the inbound and outbound adapters) and dedicated participant(s) that specify an integration process (composition of EIPs). We decided on BPMN for defining a "message-based integration" DSL due to its sufficient coverage of control flow, data and exception flow, process modeling capabilities and execution semantics [13,16]. The work on "Data in Business Processes" [8] shows that besides *Configuration-based Release Processes* (COREPRO) [10], which mainly deals with data-driven process modeling, (business) object status management, and UML activity diagrams, BPMN achieves the highest coverage in the categories relevant for our approach. Compared to BPMN and apart from the topic of "object state" representation, neither *Workflow Nets* [20] nor petri nets support data modeling at all [8]. For instance, Figure 2 shows an excerpt of an asynchronous integration scenario from the *Internet of Things* (IoT) domain, syntactically expressed in BPMN according to [13]. The encrypted incoming message is of type "TD" (short for *Telemetry Data*), which has to be normalized with respect to its timestamps using a *Message Transformation* pattern [7]. The *Message Queue Telemetry Transport* (MQTT)[1] is used as transport protocol, which is a common, lightweight queuing protocol frequently used in the IoT domain. The approach to specifying integration semantics and its runtime works well for common integration scenarios [13]. More complex scenarios have to deal with non-trivial combinations

---

[1] Message Queue Telemetry Transport: http://mqtt.org/

of message exchange pattern (MEP) and quality of service (QoS) levels. These notions are mostly induced during the adapter processing and continued into the integration process. Currently, integration modeling approaches (a) do not classify adapter characteristics, (b) leave the default adapter processing (mostly) hidden in the various runtime implementations, and (c) do not allow for configuration or change of the default behavior.

In this paper, we comprehensively investigate the range of characteristics of adapters during the integration flow processing and the various ways, in which they can be addressed. This provides the foundation for a classification of the adapter modeling, which we subsequently define in the form of an adapter flow (AF) and patterns. The pattern-based approach to adapter classification is a continuation of our previous work on the EIPs and the IFlow.

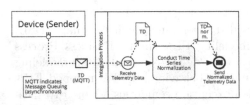

Fig. 2. IoT: Devices enqueue messages (asynch.) for time series normalization

The adapter processing patterns have proven to be intuitive to both practitioners and researchers alike and have been widely utilized for a variety of purposes including customer and partner content development. They provide the conceptual foundations for the SAP HANA Cloud Integration (HCI)[2] system, which is an Integration as a Service (INTaaS) implementation based on Apache Camel [3], an open-source integration system. The motivation for this paper is to provide a conceptual framework for classifying the adapter processing capabilities of middleware systems more generally based on the IFlow modeling approach, while being independent of the specific runtime platforms. The major contributions of this work are (1) a comprehensive classification of common adapter characteristics in integration systems and beyond, (2) an extension of the BPMN-based IFlow model for adapter flows (AFs) that make default processing visible to the user for all identified categories from (1) and allows for change of the default behavior, (3) the derivation of common adapter processing patterns and their representation in BPMN, as well as (4) the application to an existing open source middleware system, the technical analysis and discussion of the proposed approach as experimental validation in two examples. In a nutshell, we propose an answer to the underlying questions of the observations (a-c), e. g., "which QoS does the IFlow in Figure 2 have?" and "how can the default handling be adapted to custom requirements?".

Section 2 discusses adapter modeling characteristics, before we derive adapter processing patterns as an extension to the IFlow in Section 3, which we prototypically applied in two examples in Section 4. Section 5 summarizes our experiences, Section 6 discusses related work, and Section 7 concludes.

---

[2] SAP HANA Cloud Integration: http://help.sap.com/cloudintegration

2   Adapter Modeling Characteristics

In this section, we introduce a generalized integration system architecture, classify adapter characteristics and formulate them as modeling requirements. The adapter type classification is based on [7], supported by an analysis of 151 message endpoints, contributed to Apache Camel [3], and an integration expert workshop with 20 experienced integration experts from 7 different companies (cf. Suppl. Material [15]). As illustrated in Figure 3 conventional integration systems consist of a set of event-based or polling consumer adapters, an integration process engine, which executes sets of routing and message transformation tasks, and a set of producer adapters. The adapters represent the *Message Endpoint* pattern [7] and have to deal with security concerns and (possibly) format conversions from the sender format $F_s(msg)$ to an internal format $F_{cdm}(msg)$ (i. e., Canonical Data Model (CDM) [7]) that is used for the integration processing, and eventually conversions from the CDM to the target format $F_r(msg)$ understood by the receiver.

The internal messages are either distributed to Message Queues (asynchronously) or directly sent to the integration system process engine (synchronously). This engine uses a set of outbound adapters to actively interact with external systems. During the whole integration process, the recoverability should be ensured; thus, the internal message representations have to be stored locally using an operational data store or are queued for cross-process or cross-system message exchange. The execution environment of the consumer and producer adapters is an adapter runtime, which is part of the application server for conventional integration systems, however, can be an arbitrary software stack. The connections to related parts of the system (e. g., Messaging System, Data Store) are discussed subsequently as part of the classification. We consider five main categories, which allow to comprehensively describe adapters. Hence we discuss common capabilities from these categories and derive requirements $(R\text{-}X)$ for a general adapter modeling approach.

Adapter Type. Adapters can be canonically differentiated by their type: consumer or producer (as seen before). A consumer adapter allows the message

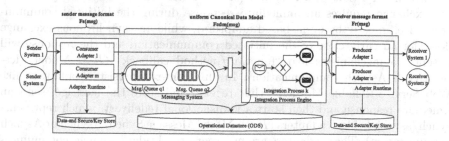

Fig. 3. Conceptual view on a conventional integration system with a slight emphasis on the consumer and producer adapters

sender applications to connect to the integration system. Message consumers are further sub-devided by their behavior into polling and event-based adapters. The polling adapter (e. g., File, (S)FTP) is configured to actively check for messages to read and process them (*R-1*: Model Polling Consumer). Hereby, settings like the polling interval, location, (initial) delay and format, can be specified. In contrast, an event-based consumer specifies an endpoint configuration (e. g., Servlet URI), on which it registers a "passive" listener that waits for events or callbacks from the sender (*R-2*: Model Event-based Consumer). A producer adapter forwards the messages to their receivers (*R-3*: Model Producer). The analysis of the 119 Apache Camel component bundles supports this differentiation (cf. [15]), by showing ten "consumer only" (6.6%), 33 "producer only" (22%) and 108 "consumer+producer" adapters. Despite the difficult task of determining "active" adapters, at least 34% of the sender adapters are "polling".

Configuration Complexity. The analysis of 119 component bundles resulted to 151 single components, or adapters. In other words, components like mail encapsulate multiple endpoints represented by protocols like smtp, pop3, imap (*R-4*: Model Multi-Component Adapter). Another outcome of the analysis showed that 30/151 components require more complex configurations, e. g., for the parameterization of connection and credential details like Java bean, key/trust store references as shown in Figure 3 (*R-5*: Allow for complex model references). Complementarily the user study resulted into a strong vote for scenario specific adaptations of the adapter's behavior. That means, an adapter shall provide extension points to hook in one or more custom processors, which can be modeled similar to an IFlow [13]. Evidence for such a requirement can be found in concepts like "channel modules" in SAP's *Process Integration*[3] middleware system. This is an extension to adapters, which can be combined to the notion of "message channel" modeling, similar to the integration process (*R-6*: Model Message Channels). Hence a message channel consists of consumer/producer adapters and arbitrarily many ordered processors.

Integration Styles. The *Message Exchange Pattern* (MEP) defines whether a message is sent inOnly (i. e., one-way) or inOut (i. e., two-way). A "two-way" message requires an (a)synchronously sent response, while a "one-way" message will never result to a response (*R-7*: Model MEP). A synchronous message exchange requires an immediate response during the initiated communication (i. e., mostly by event-based adapters), while an asynchronous exchange allows for an early close of the initiated communication and the response will be sent via mechanisms like "function/method callback" (*R-8*: Model Message Synch/Asynch communication). In this context, persistent adapters like "Web Service-Reliable Message" that receive and store the message, send an immediate response and then start a transactional redelivery, which represents "synch/asynch bridge" adapters (*R-9*): Model Message Synch/Asynch or Asynch/Synch communication). These adapters are necessary to "bridge" asynch. communication to synch. endpoints and vice versa.

---

[3] SAP Process Integration: http://help.sap.com/nwpi

Quality of Service. The most common service qualities of an integration system, which can be induced or supported by adapters are abbreviated as *BE, ALO, EO, EOIO* (sorted by the increasing quality level). The *Best Effort* (BE) messaging can be summarized as "fire-and-forget", which means that no guarantee for the delivery of a message is given. If a message shall be delivered *At Least Once* (ALO), it has to be persistently stored and redelivered from an adapter or the integration process (*R-10*: Model Message Redelivery (from a Message Store)).

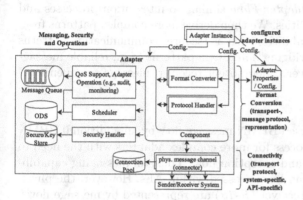

Fig. 4. Adapter Micro-Architecture

In case the message shall be delivered *Exactly Once* (EO), ALO has to be enhanced by the *Idempotent Receiver* [7], which stores the primary identifier of a message and filters out known messages (*R-11*: Model an Idempotent Receiver). Although the receiver itself should behave idempotent, producer adapters or the integration process can try to act in its place. For some integration cases, the strict adherence to a message sequence is important (e. g., create business object, before update). That means, messages shall be send *Exactly Once In Order* (EOIO). Therefore, EO is extended by a *Resequencer* pattern [7], which collects messages to emit them in the correct order (*R-12*: Model Resequencer).

Adapter Architecture and Tasks. Figure 4 draws a conceptional view on the internal architecture of a common adapter. Each adapter specifies a *Connector* or connection handler. The connector establishes a physical connection to the message endpoints (*R-13*: Model Physical Connection). For secure connections (e. g., user/password, certificates), a *Security Handler* is used (*R-14*: Model Security Relevant Configurations). Polling consumers might require a *Scheduler* for the configuration of the polling interval (cf. similar to *R-1*). For the QoS and monitoring support (e. g., message and channel monitoring), an operational data store or a message queue has to be used (*R-15*: Model (Queued-) Persistence, similar to R-10). The counterpart to the transport protocol handling connector (e. g., HTTP, FTP, JMS) is the *Format Conversion* (e. g., XML, JSON, CSV). An adapter shall be able to transform the sender format $F_s(msg)$ to the internal representation $F_{cdm}(msg)$ and eventually to the receiver format $F_r(msg)$ (*R-16*: Model Control and Data Flow). The modeled adapter shall be re-used in different adapter instances/configurations (*R-17*: Approach shall allow for re-use).

3   Adapter Modeling Approach

Following the IFlow modeling approach of Ritter [13,14] adapters are represented as message flows in BPMN (cf. Figure 2). To model integration processes
with "simple" adapter configuration this approach is sufficient, although it over-
defines BPMN message flows, makes the characteristics of an adapter implicit
and does not allow for modeling of complex logic other than on second-level
property sheets. For more complex adapter processing (cf. *R-6*), we subsequently
define an explicitly modeled *Adapter Flow* similar to integration processes and
discuss basic processing capabilities. We then derive more complex patterns from
the requirements to model capabilities such as (secure) communication patterns
(e. g., request/response and "bridging") and QoS patterns (e. g., reliable messaging with (transactional) redelivery, idempotent receiver, message resequencer).

3.1   Adapter Flow

An AF replaces the currently used BPMN message flow by an additional BPMN
pool outside the integration process for more complex adapters with the need to
specify an own control-, data- and exception flow. Thus, all messaging capabilities as described in the EIPs can be expressed within AFs. However, the physical connections to the sender/receiver (*R-13*) are represented by message flows.

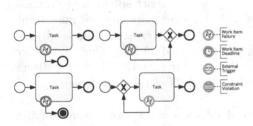

The AF of adapters with several
selectable transport protocols (*R-4*),
represented by connector and protocol handler (cf. Figure 4), remain stable, while the entering message flow
of consumer and the leaving message
flow of producer adapters changes
based on selections. Basic "processing capabilities / patterns", as modeled in Figure 5, can be used within
AFs, including skipping of processing
steps based on conditions or errors
(top-right) and message redelivery

Fig. 5. AF message processing patterns

(bottom-right; *R-10*). These mechanisms are explicitly modeled using BPMN
Exclusive Gateway elements. An adapter can decide to terminate the processing of one message (top-left) or the whole process (bottom-left) in exceptional
situations or through other events. In case of synch. communication, a response
is returned to the sender. When the basic processing capabilities are combined,
more complex "adapter processing" can be expressed. To avoid re-occurring,
complex adapter modeling patterns for communication and QoS support are
required (cf. *R-17*).

3.2   Communication Patterns

The (adapter) communication patterns specify several more complex interactions
of adapters and integration processes within and outside an organization.

Communication Styles and Bridge Patterns. Common (business) applications support interfaces for synchronous (synch) and/or asynchronous (asych) communication styles. Synch. communication means applications respond to requests (e. g., with error codes or resulting data), while the requesting application is blocking in order to get the response (RPC-style). In asynch. communication, the sending application sends requests without waiting for responses from other applications and immediately continues with its processing after sending a message (non-blocking). However, the sending application may offer callback interfaces for getting responses back for it's previously and asynchronously sent requests. Integrating applications that do not share the same communication style requires an adapter that bridges/translates between both communication styles. Such a bridging adapter is modelled in Figure 6(a), which shows the

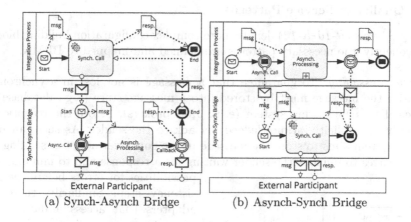

(a) Synch-Asynch Bridge   (b) Asynch-Synch Bridge

Fig. 6. Adapter Bridge Patterns

modeled data and control flow for a synch to asynch bridge (cf. *R-16*, *R-8*), in which the synchronous call follows the inOut message exchange pattern (*R-7*). The *Synch. Call* in the integration process is modelled as BPMN *Service Task* which connects with a message flow to the Synch-Asynch Bridge BPMN *Pool*. The message is forwarded to an *Async. Call* represented as a BPMN *Intermediate Message End Event* that connects via a message flow to the *External Participant*. It continues with asynch. processing that reacts to *Callback* messages in an BPMN *Intermediate Message Start Event* and forwards the response to the *Synch. Call* service task. Following the same pattern, Figure 6(b) shows a model for a asynch to synch bridge (cf. *R-9*) and includes the handling of responses and forwarding them to callback interfaces. Both bridge adapter modeling patterns can be reused, applied and adjusted in other IFlows (cf. *R-17*) or "inlined" to the integration process of an IFlow.

Processing Patterns. The AFs can be modeled to adapt between two integration processes across tenant or network boundaries (A2A and B2B), for which an integration process is associated to one tenant or network. In the case of cross-tenant integration, the IFlow of tenant T_a can adapt to an IFlow in another tenant T_b by representing the IFlow T_b as an delegate in IFlow T_a and vice versa. As such, IFlows are either "local" to one tenant, which means that they are locally visible and modifiable or they are "remote" which means that they can only be connected from "local" IFlows but not made visible or modified. Hereby, for synch. communication the "remote" IFlow could be represented as a collapsed BPMN *Pool* (which cannot be expanded) and connected to the "local" integration process with request/response BPMN message flows. For (reliable) asynchronous communication a shared data store is used to make the necessary queuing step explicit. As a representative pattern, this "remote" IFlow delegate can be used to model across networks or IFlows, by changing its type.

3.3   Quality of Service Patterns

The QoS levels (R-10–R-12) denote more complex configuration building blocks. Subsequently, the necessary patterns are defined and mapped to BPMN.

Reliable Messaging. To guarantee that a message is not lost in asynchronous scenarios the message must be stored into a message store (e. g., database) or enqueued to a messaging system (e. g., JMS brokers), before the reception is explicitly or implicitly acknowledged via `ack` to the sender. As such, an integration system aims to store the message in the consumer adapter, sending the `ack` messages to unblock the sender waiting for a response and to minimize the possibilities for errors before the persistency step. Similarly, there are adapters that access a data store/queue for cross-applications and software systems (e. g., JDBC, JMS). AFs could connect to BPMN data store to model key and trust stores (cf. R-5). For instance, Figure 7 uses AFs to model JMS adapters and the access to queues in a message broker, which is represented as a BPMN *Data Store* (cf. R-15). This allows to attach configurations to the data store (such as connection details) and to the BPMN *Data Association* (cf. R-16), and the enqueue/dequeue tasks in the pro-

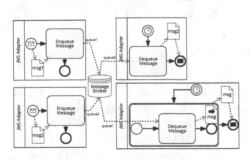

Fig. 7. Adapter modeling with message queuing via data-stores and transactional subprocess in consumer adapter

ducer adapter (cf. R-3) to the data store (such as queue/topic names). Through BPMN *Timer Event*, the polling behavior of a consumer adapter can be modeled (R-1). For instance, Figure 7 (bottom, right) shows the periodical, transactional dequeue of messages using a BPMN *Task* within a transactional subprocess, which specifies the transactional boundaries. In case of exceptions during the task processing within these boundaries, the message is not dequeued from the queue. A message redelivery would be attempted in the next polling interval (cf. *R-10*). Although *Topics* for publish/subscribe scenarios could be modeled similarly, they could be represented by BPMN signal end/start events (cf. Section 3.5 in [15]). The transferred message would be determined by the associated BPMN *Data Object* and the corresponding events would be identifiable by their matching names. Clearly this would make the inner mechanics implicit, but would allow for the modeling of an event-based consumer adapter (cf. *R-2*). For (reliable) asynchronous, inOut messaging (cf. Figure 8), we assume a "reply-to" header field attached to the `req-msg` indicating that the AF (right JMS Adapter) should reply to the specified queue. The (queued) response is correlated to the waiting integration process instance by using the identifier of the `req-msg`.

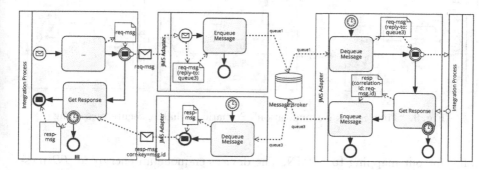

Fig. 8. Adapter modeling with message queuing via data-stores and explicit modeling of request/reply via response queues

Idempotency Repository. To support AMO and EO (in combination with *Reliable Messaging*), the integration system needs to take care that messages are not sent twice to the receiver (cf. *R-11*). This is modeled by a flow step the integration process (or AF) that filters already sent messages, which is preferably executed just before the message is sent to the receiving application in a producer AF. Figure 10 shows the filter processing as part of a producer AF (bottom) by accessing an *Idempotency Repository* [7], which is represented as a BPMN data store, storing the identifiers of already processed messages against it checks the current message identifier.

Message Resequencing. The resequencer (cf. [14]) can be used for *In-Order* (IO) scenarios, for which the messages have to be ordered according to a sequence number. Alternatively, order preserving queues (e. g., specified in JMS) are used to keep messages in sequence. The EOIO processing additionally requires the combination of *Reliable Messaging* with redelivery semantics and a filter step using the *Idempotency Repository* to guarantee that the messages are sent exactly once and in order (cf. *R-12*).

4   Examples

Let us apply the rather abstract BPMN AF definitions and integration patterns to two intriguing integration scenarios, which cover secure, reliable messaging as well as most difficult QoS configurations. Coming back to the motivating example and questions around the visualization (2) and re-configuration (3) of the expected default exception handling and compensation in the "Reliable Time Series Normalization" scenario (Section 1) Figure 9 shows the syntax proposal

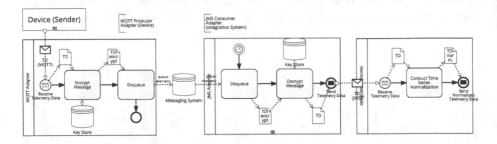

Fig. 9. "Time Series Normalization" Scenario: Reliable, secure messaging

following our mapping to BPMN. The devices enqueue an encrypted *TD* message to the `telemetry` queue in the messaging system using an *MQTT* adapter (cf. *R-6*). The integration process listens to the queue using a *JMS* adapter, which decrypts the received messages (cf. *R-14*) and passes them to the integration process, where the message content is normalized.

The QoS support is crucial for integration systems. When sending a message synchronously to a receiver, BE is applied (i. e., delivery will be attempted otherwise the sender will receive an exception message). In case of asynchronous, reliable, in-order messaging this is not sufficient. The message has to be persistently stored and a retry has to be started to guarantee its delivery (cf. *R-10*), e. g., in a message queue, since the sender cannot be notified. In addition, the order of the messages according to a *Message Sequence* [7] has to be guaranteed using a *Resequencer* pattern (cf. *R-12*). If in addition, duplicate messages are filtered out during the processing (cf. *R-11*), the QoS is called EOIO, syntactically in Figure 10. The consumer AF starts with a synchronous part by storing the message and sending a response. Hereby, the "Redelivery on Exception" sub-process acts as a combined ALO, synch/asynch bridge pattern, which then starts the asynchronous delivery of the message to the integration process, which collects messages and orders them along defined sequences using a "Resequencer" sub-process pattern and synchronously emits the messages to the producer adapter. The producer adapter checks whether a message has already been processed and synchronously sends it to the receiver. The receiver's response (i. e., acknowledgement or exception) is passed to the integration process, which triggers a message redelivery on exception.

5 Qualitative Analysis and Experiences

This section discusses "ex-post", practical experiences with the defined adapter modeling based on an evaluation with integration experts from different enterprises as interviews, workshops and surveys (cf. Suppl. Material [15]). The evaluation of the approach can be summarized to the topics subsequently discussed. In general, the integration models with an explicit AF are experienced as more complex (i. e., contradicting the aimed usage of BPMN by business experts [11]), however, the visibility of the default adapter characteristics allow for better insights into the integration flow modeling, ease of use, a more intuitive and faster modeling through the identified patterns.

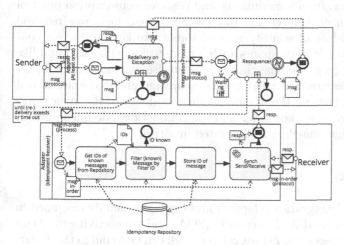

Fig. 10. "EOIO": message redelivery in the consumer adapter, resequencer in the integration process, and idempotent message handling in the producer adapter

Modeling Complexity. Some BPMN syntax elements are not applicable to the integration environment in an useful way. For example, the lane element has no semantic meaning and could only be used to structure certain aspects of the integration systems, such as distinguishing normal logic from AF logic. Though this would increase the size of the diagram leading to a confusing model. Additionaly, in Figure 7, for queuing with a message broker the data association to the message broker is denoted with the queue name to/from messages should be enqueued/dequeued. Although this was rated as complex (e. g., the adapter on top-left communicates with the adapter on bottom-right, while the adapter on top-right seems more related to the adapter on top-left), it was favored over the BPMN *Signal* approach proposed for topics. In case of many connections to the message broker, a partitioning of the IFlow into several smaller diagrams would help to make the single parts more understandable (cf. "in-context" editing), while tool support would be needed to show the complete IFlow on demand. The alternative of modeling several instances of one broker in one IFlow, which are then connected to related adapters only, was not seen as desirable solution.

Modeling Preferences. The modeling of AFs was very well received, while the participants differentiated between producer and consumer adapter modeling. The producer adapter modeling allows for adding scenario-specific "pre-processing" capabilities to the system, before entering the integration process (e. g., especially for bridges). The consumer AFs were seen limited to the QoS support, while potential "post-processing" logic could be executed in the integration process. However, from a modularity and resource consumption point of view, a clear separation of adapter and integration process logic was received well. The explicit modeling of security related topics like key stores was controversially discussed. While participants with a more technical background like the proposed approach (e. g., helping them to be precise in the security aspect modeling), more business related participants complaint about the additional complexity. Both parties agreed that a more explicit modeling of the inner workings of a message broker is not necessary and the transactional de-queuing with the BPMN *Transactional Sub-Process* was rated intuitive.

6   Related Work

Recently, the topics of "integration adapter" and QoS were mainly discussed in the areas of "Service-oriented Architectures" (SOA) and connectivity to "Data Warehouses" (DW). However, the closest related work can be found in the *Enterprise Integration Pattern* (EIP) icon notation collected by Hophe et al. [7]. The EIP notation defines modeling building blocks for core integration aspects (e. g., resequencer, publish/subscribe, durable (topic) subscriber and channel adapter). In addition, to these pattern, our approach has a representation of an idempotent receiver, a messaging system for "store-and-forward" processing (guaranteed message delivery) and different levels of service quality can be modeled.

Quality of Service. Most of the QoS definitions, from this work, can be found in standard industry middleware systems, too. For instance, the *WebLogic* system [9] knows EO, ALO as "duplicates only mode", and "At-Most Once" (AMO), which can be modeled by our approach through an idempotent receiver pattern. From a modeling point of view, adapters are reduced to one icon and a property sheet, similar to the EIP icon notation. Closer to our approach, Gönczy et al [5] define a proprietary meta-model for reliable messaging with acknowledgements for some QoS (i. e., ALO, EO) and target to apply verification approaches using graph transformations [6]. However, other service qualities, e. g., IO, AMO, EOIO, are currently undefined.

Model-driven Adapter Development and Re-configuration. There are some approaches for automatic adapter generation and re-configuration from the SOA domain, to which we aligned our terminology, however, they do not define a (conceptual) modeling approach for integration adapters. Nezhad [4] summarizes work on model-driven development of web services, while highlighting the importance of a QoS support. Other approaches target the self-adapting adapters in terms of signature-/protocol-level and quality related re-configurations and planning (e. g., [19]). We consider these approaches complementary to our work.

Data-Intensive Adapter Modeling. Through data warehouse connectivity scenarios, the *Extract-Transform-Load* (ETL) domain gained interest in the conceptual modeling of more "data-intensive" adapters (e. g., [17]). Although characteristics like QoS are not relevant for data warehouse connectivity, these modeling approaches can be seen as domain-specific, complementary work. For instance, Akkaoui et al. mapped ETL processes to BPMN [1] and provided a maintenance framework for [2], which can be seen as subset of our approach. There are several UML-based approaches, e. g., for modeling data mining with time-series data [21] or ETL data flows [18], which mostly define new icon notations, similar to the EIP notation. Their focus on the data flow limits the modeling to data transformation.

7   Concluding Remarks

In this paper, we (a) define common adapter types within integration systems (starting from literature and small empirical studies), (b) extend our BPMN-based definition of IFlows [13,14] by AF constructs and patterns to make the default adapter behavior visible, and thus (c) provide a basis for a scenario-specific adapter configuration. We started with a systematical analysis of common adapter characteristics (cf. R-1–9, R-13–17), spanning to edge cases like QoS modeling (cf. R-10-12).

The mapping of these adapter characteristics to BPMN allowed us to link them to the integration flows and define common integration adapter processing capabilities and patterns. We applied our approach to the real-world "internet of things" integration scenario and the "exactly-once-in-order" QoS case. The evaluation exclusively targets the syntactical feasibility and applicability of the approach. The presented examples show some minor shortcomings due to BPMN's focus on control over data flow and advice to change the proposed, which we solved by explicit modeling of AFs as separate BPMN pools.

The brief discussion of the experiences from the presented and many more real-world case studies as well as integration expert and partner interviews show the value of the modular, pattern-based and explicit modeling approach, however, highlights topics for further (quantitative) analysis. A solution for some of the mentioned issues with BPMN can be found in further investigations of the possibilities to use BPMN extensions. However, as pre-existing elements may not be modified and the syntax of BPMN models (such as conditional data flows) may not be changed, the mitigations might go beyond the current BPMN syntax.

References

1. El Akkaoui, Z., Mazón, J.-N., Vaisman, A., Zimányi, E.: BPMN-Based Conceptual Modeling of ETL Processes. In: Cuzzocrea, A., Dayal, U. (eds.) DaWaK 2012. LNCS, vol. 7448, pp. 1–14. Springer, Heidelberg (2012)

2. Akkaoui, Z.E., Zimányi, E., Mazón, J., Trujillo, J.: A bpmn-based design and maintenance framework for ETL processes. IJDWM **9**(3), 46–72 (2013)
3. Anstey, J., Zbarcea, H.: Camel in Action. Manning (2011)
4. Benatallah, B., Casati, F., Toumani, F., Ponge, J., Nezhad, H.R.M.: Service mosaic: A model-driven framework for web services life-cycle management. IEEE Internet Computing **10**(4), 55–63 (2006)
5. Gnczy, L., Varr, D.: Modeling of reliable messaging in service oriented architectures. In: International Workshop on Web Services Modeling and Testing (2006)
6. Gönczy, L., Kovács, M., Varró, D.: Modeling and verification of reliable messaging by graph transformation systems. Electr. Notes Theor. Comput. Sci. **175**(4), 37–50 (2007)
7. Hohpe, G., Woolf, B.: Enterprise Integration Patterns: Designing, Building, and Deploying Messaging Solutions. Addison-Wesley, Boston (2003)
8. Meyer, A., Smirnov, S., Weske, M.: Data in business processes. EMISA Forum **31**(3), 5–31 (2011)
9. Mountjoy, J., Chugh, A.: WebLogic - the definitive guide. O'Reilly (2004)
10. Müller, D.: Management datengetriebener Prozessstrukturen. PhD thesis (2009)
11. O. M. G. (OMG). Business process model and notation (bpmn) version 2.0. Technical report (January 2011)
12. Reese, G.: Cloud Application Architectures: Building Applications and Infrastructure in the Cloud. O'Reilly Media Inc. (2009)
13. Ritter, D.: Experiences with Business Process Model and Notation for Modeling Integration Patterns. In: Cabot, J., Rubin, J. (eds.) ECMFA 2014. LNCS, vol. 8569, pp. 254–266. Springer, Heidelberg (2014)
14. Ritter, D.: Using the business process model and notation for modeling enterprise integration patterns. CoRR, abs/1403.4053 (2014)
15. Ritter, D., Holzleitner, M.: Qualitative Analysis of Integration Adapter Modeling. CoRR, abs/1503.02007 (2015)
16. Ritter, D., Sosulski, J.: Modeling exception flows in integration systems. In: 18th IEEE International Enterprise Distributed Object Computing Conference, EDOC 2014, Ulm, BW, Germany, September 3–5 (2014)
17. Simitsis, A., Vassiliadis, P.: A methodology for the conceptual modeling of ETL processes. In: The 15th Conference on Advanced Information Systems Engineering (CAiSE 2003), Klagenfurt/Velden, Austria, 16–20 June, Workshops Proceedings, Information Systems for a Connected Society (2003)
18. Trujillo, J., Luján-Mora, S.: A UML Based Approach for Modeling ETL Processes in Data Warehouses. In: Song, I.-Y., Liddle, S.W., Ling, T.-W., Scheuermann, P. (eds.) ER 2003. LNCS, vol. 2813, pp. 307–320. Springer, Heidelberg (2003)
19. van den Heuvel, W., Weigand, H., Hiel, M.: Configurable adapters: the substrate of self-adaptive web services. In: 9th International Conference on Electronic Commerce: The Wireless World of Electronic Commerce, Minneapolis, USA (2007)
20. van der Aalst, W.M.P.: The application of petri nets to workflow management. Journal of Circuits, Systems, and Computers **8**(1), 21–66 (1998)
21. Zubcoff, J.J., Pardillo, J., Trujillo, J.: A UML profile for the conceptual modelling of data-mining with time-series in data warehouses. Information & Software Technology **51**(6), 977–992 (2009)

Service Science and Computing

Modelling Service Level Agreements
for Business Process Outsourcing Services

Adela del–Río–Ortega[✉], Antonio Manuel Gutiérrez, Amador Durán,
Manuel Resinas, and Antonio Ruiz–Cortés

Universidad de Sevilla, Sevilla, Spain
{adeladelrio,amgutierrez,amador,resinas,aruiz}@us.es

Abstract. Many proposals to model service level agreements (SLAs)
have been elaborated in order to automate different stages of the service
lifecycle such as monitoring, implementation or deployment. All of them
have been designed for computational services and are not well–suited
for other types of services such as business process outsourcing (BPO)
services. However, BPO services supported by process–aware information systems could also benefit from modelling SLAs in tasks such as
performance monitoring, human resource assignment or process configuration. In this paper, we identify the requirements for modelling such
SLAs and detail how they can be faced by combining techniques used to
model computational SLAs, business processes, and process performance
indicators. Furthermore, our approach has been validated through the
modelling of several real BPO SLAs.

Keywords: Service level agreement · Business process outsourcing service · Process performance measure · Process aware information System ·
Process performance indicator

1 Introduction

Service level agreements (SLAs) have been used by many proposals in the last
decade to automate different stages of the service lifecycle, using a formal definition of the different parts of an SLA such as *service level objectives* (SLOs),
penalties, or metrics, to automate their negotiation [1], the provisioning and
enforcement of SLA–based services [2], the monitoring and explanation of SLA
runtime violations [3], or the prediction of such violations [4]. What all of these
proposals have in common is that most of them have been designed for computational services. Therefore, they are aimed at enhancing software that supports
the execution of computational services such as network monitors, virtualisation

This work has received funding from the European Commission (FEDER), the
European Union's Horizon 2020 research and innovation programme under the
Marie Sklodowska-Curie grant agreement No 64575, the Spanish and the Andalusian R&D7&I programmes (grants TIN2012-32273 (TAPAS), TIC-5906 (THEOS)
and COPAS (P12-TIC-1867)).

© Springer International Publishing Switzerland 2015
J. Zdravkovic et al. (Eds.): CAiSE 2015, LNCS 9097, pp. 485–500, 2015.
DOI: 10.1007/978-3-319-19069-3_30

software, or application servers with SLA–aware capabilities, where there are no human or non-automatic tasks involved in service comsumption.

On the other hand, *business process outsourcing* (BPO) services are non–computational services such as logistics, supply–chain, or IT delivery services, that are based on the provisioning of business processes as services, providing partial or full business process outsourcing. Like computational services, their execution is regulated by SLAs and supported by specific software [5,6]. In this case, since BPO services are process–oriented, the software that supports them is usually a *process–aware information systems* (PAIS) such as ERPs, CRMs, or *business process management systems* (BPMSs). However, unlike computational services, there is little work related to the extension of PAIS with SLA–aware capabilities to support BPO services.

A PAIS with SLA–aware capabilities, i.e. an SLA–aware PAIS, is a PAIS that uses explicit definitions of SLAs to enable or improve the automation of certain tasks related to both the SLAs and their fulfilment such as performance monitoring, human resource assignment or process configuration [7]. For instance, an SLA–aware PAIS could be automatically instrumented according to the metrics defined in the SLA so that when there is a risk of not meeting an SLO, an alert is raised allowing the human actors involved in the process to take measures to mitigate the risk. Another example could be the automated configuration of the process, *e.g.* removing or adding activities, executed by the SLA–aware PAIS depending on the conditions of the SLA agreed with the client.

Apart from the benefits derived from the automation of these tasks, the need for a SLA–aware PAIS becomes more critical in a *business–process–as–a–service* scenario. A business–process–as–a–service is a new category of cloud–delivered service, which, according to Gartner [8], can be defined as "the delivery of BPO services that are sourced from the cloud and constructed for multitenancy. Services are often automated, and where human process actors are required, there is no overtly dedicated labour pool per client. The pricing models are consumption–based or subscription–based commercial terms. As a cloud service, the business–process–as–a–service model is accessed via Internet–based technologies." In this setting, the conditions of the SLA agreed with each client may vary. Therefore, it is crucial for the PAIS that supports the business–process–as–a–service to behave according to the SLA agreed with the client. An example could be the prioritisation of the execution of tasks for those clients whose SLAs have bigger penalties if they are not met.

In this paper, we focus on the formalization of BPO SLAs as a first step to enable such SLA–aware PAIS. To this end, after analysing the modelling requirements of such SLAs, four main aspects involved in their formalization have been identified, namely: 1) the description of the business process provided by the service; 2) the SLOs guaranteed by the SLA; 3) the penalties and rewards that apply if guarantees are not fulfilled; and 4) the definition of the metrics used in these guarantees. Then, we detail how these aspects can be formalized by means of generic models for the definition of computational SLAs and techniques used to model process performance indicators. Furthermore, we have validated our approach through the modelling of several real BPO SLAs.

The remainder of the paper is structured as follows. In Section 2, a running example is introduced. Section 3 details the four elements that must be formalized in SLAs for BPO services and Section 4 shows how they can be modelled using WS–Agreement, a specification from Global Grid Forums to describe Service Level Agreements[1]. Next, Section 5 reports on how the running example can be formalized using our proposal and discusses some limitations identified during the definition of the SLA metrics. Section 6 reports on work related to the definition of SLAs for BPO services. Finally, conclusions are detailed in Section 7.

2 Running Example

Let us take one of the BPO SLAs to which our approach has been applied as running example throughout this paper. The SLA takes place in the context of the definition of statements of technical requirements of a public company of the Andalusian Autonoumous Government, from now on *Andalusian Public Company*, APC for short. Statements of technical requirements are described in natural language and include information about the services required as well as their SLA. Although the running example includes one service only, further information on this or the rest of services, as well as on other application scenarios, is available at http://www.isa.us.es/ppinot/caise2015.

The statement of technical requirements document of this example is defined for the Technical Field Support for the Deployment of the Corporative Telecommunication Network of the Andalusian Autonomous Government. It is presented in a 72–page document written in natural language including the SLAs defined for five of the required services, namely: 1) field interventions; 2) incidents; 3) network maintenance; 4) installations and wiring; and 5) logistics. In particular, we focus on the *field interventions* (FI) service. The term *field intervention* makes reference to the fact of requiring the presence of a technician at any headquarter of the APC for different reasons: troubleshooting technical assistance, installations supervision or restructure, for instance.

From a high–level perspective, the FI service can be defined as follows: the APC requires an FI, which can have different levels of severity, from the contractor staff. Then, the contractor plans the FI and performs it at headquarters. In some cases, it is necessary for the contractor to provide some required documentation and, if such documentation is considered incomplete or inadequate by the APC, it needs to be resubmitted by the contractor until it fulfils the APC's quality requirements.

For this service, the statement of technical requirements document presents the following information: 1) the committed times by the contractor (see Table 1); 2) the general objective defined for FIs —the SLO of the SLA— represented as AFIP > 95%, where the AFIP (*accomplished FIs percentage*) metric is defined as:

$$AFIP = \frac{\text{\# accomplished FIs}}{\text{\# FIs}} \times 100$$

---

[1] https://www.ogf.org/documents/GFD.107.pdf

and 3), the penalties applied in case the SLO is not accomplished (see Table 2). These penalties are defined over the monthly billing by the contractor for the FI service. In addition, the statement of technical requirements document presents the following definitions for the referred times in Table 1:

Response Time Elapsed time between the notification of the FI request to the contractor and its planning, including resources assignment, *i.e.* technicians.

Presence Time Elapsed time between resource (technician) assignment and the beginning of the FI, *i.e.* technician arrival.

Resolution Time Elapsed time between the technician arrival and the end and closure of the FI.

Documentation Time If documentation, *i.e.* reports, is required, it is defined as the elapsed time between the end and closure of the FI and documentation submission. If the APC considers such documentation as incomplete or inadequate, it will be returned to the contractor and documentation time is again activated and computed.

3 Requirements for Modelling SLAs of BPO Services

The requirements for modelling BP SLAs in the context of SLA–aware PAIS have been identified after a study of the state of the art in SLAs for both computational and non–computational services, and the analysis of more than 20 different BPO SLAs developed by 4 different organisations in 2 different countries. The conclusion is that four elements must be formalized in SLAs for BPO services, namely: 1) the business process; 2) the metrics used in the SLA; 3) the SLOs guaranteed by the SLA; and 4) the penalties and rewards that apply if guarantees are not fulfilled. Next we describe each of them.

3.1 Business Process

An SLA is always related to one or more specific services. The way such services must be provided is usually defined by describing the underpinning business process, and this is often done in natural language. Consequently, the formalization of SLAs for BPO services requires the formalization of the business process itself.

Table 1. Committed times by the contractor (in hours) for the FI Service SLA

Criticality Level	Response Time	Presence Time	Resolution Time	Document. Time	Timetable	Calendar
Critical	0.5	4	2	4	8:00 – 20:00	Local
High	2	8	4	12	8:00 – 20:00	Local
Mild	5	30	6	24	8:00 – 20:00	Local
Low	5	60	8	48	8:00 – 20:00	Local

Table 2. Penalties definition (in monthly billing percentage) for the FI Service SLA

AFIP	Penalty
94% ≤ AFIP < 95%	-1%
93% ≤ AFIP < 94%	-2%
92% ≤ AFIP < 93%	-3%
91% ≤ AFIP < 92%	-4%
90% ≤ AFIP < 91%	-5%
AFIP < 90%	-10%

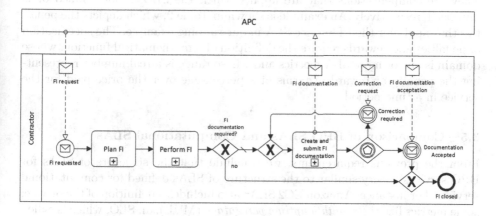

Fig. 1. BPMN model of Field Intervention (FI) service

Note that it is not required for the SLA to detail the low level business process that will be enacted by the provider's PAIS since most SLAs do not delve into that level of detail and just focus on main activities and the consumer–provider interaction (cf. Fig 1 for the high–level business process of the running example). However, it should be possible to link this higher level business process to the lower level business process enacted by the PAIS.

3.2 SLA Metrics

These are the metrics that need to be computed so that the fulfilment of the SLA can be evaluated. For instance, in the running example, *response time*, *presence time*, or AFIP are examples of such metrics. The mechanism used to define these metrics must have two main features. On the one hand, it must be *expressive*, i.e. it must allow the definition of a wide variety of metrics. On the other hand, it must be traceable with the business process so that it enables their automated computation. In addition, it is convenient that the metrics are defined in a declarative way because it reduces the gap between the SLA defined in natural language and the formalised SLA and decouples the definition of the metric from its computation.

3.3   Service Level Objectives (SLOs)

These are the assertions over the aforementioned metrics that are guaranteed by the SLA and, hence, must be fulfilled during the execution of the service. For instance, the running example defines AFIP > 95% as an SLO for AFIP metric of the FI service. In general, SLOs can be defined as mathematical constraints over one or more SLA metrics.

3.4   Penalties and Rewards

They are compensations that are applied when the SLO is not fulfilled or is improved, respectively. An example is shown in Table 2, which depicts the penalties that apply for the FI Service SLA in our running example. The specification of penalties and rewards require the definition of a mathematical function, whose domain is one or more SLA metrics and whose range is a real number representing the penalty or reward in terms of a percentage over the price paid for the service in a time period.

3.5   Comparison of BPO SLAs and Computational SLAs

From the previous requirements, we conclude that the structure of SLAs for BPO services is very similar to the structure of SLAs defined for computational services. For instance, Amazon EC2 SLA[2] also includes a definition of the service; some metrics like the *monthly uptime percentage* (MUP); an SLO, which is called *service commitment*, defined as $MUP \geq 99.95\%$; and a penalty based on the MUP and defined in terms of a percentage over the price paid in the last month.

In contrast, the description of the service and the definition of the SLA metrics of BPO SLAs and computational SLAs present significant differences. The main reason is that, unlike computational services, BPO services are process–aware and, hence, their description and their SLA metrics are based on that process.

4   Modelling SLAs for BPO Services

Based on the requirements described in the previous section, and on the similarities and differences between BPO SLAs and computational SLAs, we propose modelling BPO SLAs by combining the agreement structure and mechanisms for the definition of SLOs, penalties, and rewards that have been already proposed for computational SLAs, with notations used to model processes and *Process Performance Indicators* (PPIs), such as [9–13]. PPIs are quantifiable metrics that allow the efficiency and effectiveness of business processes to be evaluated; they can be measured directly by data that is generated within the process flow and are aimed at the process controlling and continuous optimization [14].

---

[2] http://aws.amazon.com/ec2/sla/

Specifically, in this paper we propose using WS–Agreement [15] as the agreement structure; BPMN as the language to model business processes; PPINOT [13] as the mechanism to model PPIs; the predicate language defined in iAgree [16] to specify SLOs, and the compensation functions introduced in [17] to model penalties and rewards. These proposals have been chosen because of two reasons. Firstly, they are amongst the most expressive proposals of their kind, which is necessary to model the different scenarios that appear in BPO SLAs. Secondly, they have a formal foundation that enables the development of advanced tooling support that can be reused in a SLA–aware PAIS environments. For instance, it is possible to automatically analyse a WS–Agreement document with iAgree predicates to detect conflicts such as inconsistencies between agreement terms or dead terms (i.e., conditional terms that can never be applied) [16].

In the following, we introduce the basic structure of an SLA in WS–Agreement and then, we detail how it can be used together with other languages and models to define a BPO SLA. Furthermore, we also provide more details about the aforementioned models and the tooling support that has been developed for them.

4.1 WS–Agreement in a Nutshell

WS–Agreement is a specification that describes computational service agreements between different parties. It defines both a protocol and an agreement document metamodel in the form of XML schema [15]. According to this metamodel, an agreement is composed of an optional name, a context and a set of terms. The *context* section provides information about participants in the agreement (*i.e.* service provider and consumer) and agreement's lifetime. The *terms* section describes the agreement itself, including *service* terms and *guarantee* terms.

Figure 2 shows the overall structure of a WS–Agreement document using iAgree syntax [16], which is designed for making WS–Agreement documents more human–readable and compact than with the original XML syntax. All examples included in this paper are defined using iAgree.

Service terms describe the provided service, and are classified in *service description terms*, *service properties* and *service references*. Service description terms (lines 9–10) describe the features of the service that will be provided under the agreement. They identify the service itself, so there is no reason to monitor them along service lifecycle. Service properties (lines 11–12) are the set of monitorable variables relevant to the agreement, for which a name and a metric are defined. Finally, service references (line 8) point to an electronic service using endpoints references.

Guarantee terms (lines 13–18) define SLOs that the obligated party must fulfil together with the corresponding penalties and rewards. An SLO in WS–Agreement is an assertion over monitorable properties that must be fulfilled during the execution of the service. SLOs can be guarded by a *qualifying condition*, which indicates a precondition to apply the constraint in the SLO. Both SLOs and qualifying conditions are expressed using any suitable user–defined assertion language. penalties and rewards.

```
 1  Agreement Example version 1
 2  Provider as Responder
 3    Metrics
 4      ServiceCreditMeasure: Percentage
 5      AvailabilityMeasure: Percentage
 6      CostMeasure: Integer
 7    AgreementTerms
 8      Service Example @ http://mycloud.com/service.wsdl
 9      DescriptionTerms
10        Cost : CostMeasure = 10
11      MonitorableProperties
12        Availability : AvailabilityMeasure
13      GuaranteeTerms
14        G1: Provider guarantees
15          Availability > 99
16          with monthly penalty of
17          ServiceCredit : ServiceCreditMeasure = 25
18            if Availability ≤ 99
19  EndAgreement
```

Fig. 2. Computational SLA in WS–Agreement using iAgree syntax

4.2   Materialising BPO SLAs with WS–Agreement

WS–Agreement leaves consciously undefined the languages for the specification of service description terms, SLOs, or qualifying conditions. This flexibility makes WS–Agreement a good choice for modelling BPO SLAs since it allows embedding any kind of model in its terms. In this paper, we propose the following *WS–Agreement Configuration* [16] for defining BPO SLAs.

Service Description Terms. In BPO services, this description can be provided in terms of the underpinning business process. In this paper we use the BPMN (*Business Process Model and Notation*) standard since it is a well–known standard widely used in both industry and academy.

Service Properties. In BPO services, these metrics can be specified using a PPI–oriented approach. Specifically, we propose defining metrics using PPINOT [13] measure definitions. This choice has been made based on the analysis performed in [13] of the different available PPI–oriented approaches. In particular, PPINOT has been chosen because of its expressiveness, since it allows the definition of certain PPIs not possible with other existing approaches, and its traceability with BPMN models, since it provides explicit connections to their elements. Furthermore, PPINOT has been used at the core of a software tool called the *PPINOT Tool Suite* [18], which includes the definition of PPIs using either a graphical or a template–based textual notation [19], their automated analysis at design–time, and their automated computation based on the instrumentation of open source BPMSs.

PPINOT measure definitions can be classified into three main categories depending on the number of process instances involved and the nature of the measure: base measures, aggregated measures, and derived measures[13].

Base measures They are obtained directly from a single process instance and do not require any other measure to be computed. Aspects that can be measured include: 1) the duration between two time instants (*time measures*); 2) the number of times something happens (*count measures*); 3) the fulfilment of certain condition in both running or finished process instances (*condition measures*); and 4) the value of a certain part of a data object (*data measures*). The definition of this kind of measures also includes certain conditions that are applied to the corresponding business process elements. For instance, the events (e.g. an activity starts or an event is triggered) associated to the time instants used to compute a time measure or the attribute of a data object that is measured in a data measure.

Aggregated measures Sometimes, it is interesting knowing not only the value of a measure for a single process instance (*base measures*) but an aggregation of the values for multiple instances of a process. For these cases, *aggregated measures* are used, together with an aggregation function such as *average*, *maximum*, etc.

Derived measures They are defined as functions of other measures. Depending on whether the derivation function is defined over single or multi–instance measures, derived measures are classified accordingly as *derived single–instance measures* or *derived multi–instance measures* (see [13] for details).

Guarantee Terms. To define SLOs, we use the predicate language defined in iAgree [16], which is a domain-indpendent language that includes relational, logical and common arithmetic operators. Apart from a concrete syntax, iAgree also provides semantics to define SLOs expressions as a constraint satisfaction problem, which enables the automation of analysis operations on SLAs such as detecting conflicts within an agreement document [16] or explaining SLA violations at run–time [3].

Concerning penalties and rewards, they are defined using the notion of *compensation functions* defined in [17]. Let SP be the set of all possible values to the service properties of the agreement, a compensation function is a function from SP to $\mathbb{R}$ that associates a compensation, expressed as a real number, to each of the values of the service properties. As a normalised convention, a positive compensation is associated to penalties and a negative compensation is associated to rewards. The compensation can be defined in absolute terms (e.g. in euros) or in relative terms (e.g. as a percentage of the service monthly bill).

5   Applicability of our Approach

In order to validate the applicability of our approach, we have used it to model a subset of the SLAs analysed in Section 3. In particular, 9 different services designed by 3 different organisations were modelled. In the following, we show how WS–Agreement and PPINOT can be used to model the running example and then, discuss the limitations we have found and how they can be solved. The remaining SLAs that have been modelled are available at http://www.isa. us.es/ppinot/caise2015.

5.1 SLA for the Running Example

Figure 3 shows an excerpt of the SLA for the running example, in which the three elements of the BPO SLA are specified as follows.

Service Description Terms. Service description terms (lines 34–36) specify the high level BPMN model associated to the FI service derived from the corresponding SoTR, as described in Section 2.

Service Properties. Once the high level business process has been modelled, service properties relevant to the SLA are defined, namely AFIP (lines 37–38). This service property is computed according to the AFIP_Measure metric (lines 15–28), that measures the percentage of *accomplished* FIs (AFI_Measure) with respect to the total number of FIs (FI_Measure), as described informally in Section 2. The definition of these metrics is done by means of the measure definitions that PPINOT provides to detail how PPIs are measured (see [13] for details).

Guarantee Terms. Finally, the guarantee terms of the SLA including its SLOs and penalties are specified. In this case, according to Tables 1 and 2, the percentage of accomplished interventions must be greater than 95%. This can be defined in terms of the previously defined service properties as AFIP $> 95\%$ (line 40). Additionally, penalties are defined as a percentage discount of the monthly billing if the SLO is not achieved. This is 1% of discount per each 1% of accomplished percentage under the objective, or 10% if the percentage is under 90%, as depicted in Table 2.

5.2 Limitations of our Approach

The application of the proposed approach for defining the SLAs of nine BPO services and the analysis of another number of them, all from real scenarios, showed up some limitations concerning the definition of SLA metrics, whereas WS–Agreement and the models used to define business processes, SLOs, penalties, and rewards proved to be capable to model all possible situations.

Concerning SLA metrics, although most of them could be successfully modelled using PPINOT, there were a few types that could not be represented properly. As far as we know, this limitation is not specific to PPINOT, since there is not any other PPI modelling approach that can model all of the metrics that appear in the analysed SLAs. We believe that the main reason why we have found this limitation is that, although related, the purpose of PPIs and SLA metrics are slightly different. PPIs are used internally by the organisation that performs the process as a mechanism to improve its performance. In contrast, SLA metrics are aimed at providing service–level guarantees to the service consumer or defining penalties when guarantees are not met. As a consequence, SLA metrics are much more focused on the customer and its expectations than the former.

```
1    Agreement FI_Service_SLA version 1
2    Provider Corporate as Responder;
3      Metrics for FI_Service:
4        ResponseTime: LinearTimeMeasure
5          from event FI requested is triggered
6          to activity Plan FI becomes completed
7          considering only working hours and local calendar
8        PresenceTime: LinearTimeMeasure ...
9        ResolutionTime: LinearTimeMeasure ...
10       DocumentationTime: CyclicTimeMeasure aggregation Sum
11         from activity Create and submit doc becomes active
12         to activity Create and submit FI documentation becomes completed
13         considering only working hours and local calendar
14       CLevel: DataMeasure criticalityLevel of Intervention
15       AFI_Measure: AggregatedMeasure with function sum
16         aggregates DerivedMeasure with function A & B & C & D where
17           A: DerivedMeasure with function
18             CLevel = critical => ResponseTime    < 0.5 & PresenceTime    < 4 &
19                                  ResolutionTime < 2   & DocumentationTime < 4
20           B: DerivedMeasure with function
21             CLevel = high    => ResponseTime    < 2 & PresenceTime    < 8 &
22                                  ResolutionTime < 4 & DocumentationTime < 12
23           C: DerivedMeasure with function
24             CLevel = mild    => ResponseTime    < 5 & PresenceTime    < 30 &
25                                  ResolutionTime < 6 & DocumentationTime < 24
26           D: DerivedMeasure with function
27             CLevel = low     => ResponseTime    < 5 & PresenceTime    < 60 &
28                                  ResolutionTime < 8 & DocumentationTime < 48
29       FI_Measure: AggregatedMeasure with function sum
30         aggregates CountMeasure when event FI closed is triggered
31       AFIP_Measure: DerivedMeasure with function ( AFI_Measure / FI_Measure ) * 100
32
33   AgreementTerms
34     Service FI_Service
35       process:
```

```
36
37   MonitorableProperties
38     AFIP: AFIP_Measure
39   Guarantee Terms
40     G1: Provider guarantees AFIP > 95%
41       with monthly penalty
42       of Penalty = 95 - AFIP if 90% ≤ AFIP < 95%
43       of Penalty = 10       if AFIP < 90%
44     ...
```

Fig. 3. Excerpt of the FI service SLA in *iAgree* syntax

Specifically, we found four types of metrics that cannot be modelled neither with PPINOT nor with most of the other PPI modelling approaches:

Metrics that involve exclusion of idle time, suspend time, calendars or timetables In the running example, when defining times like *resolution* time, *documentation* time, *etc*, the SoTR document usually specified that idle time should be ignored for those measures, and that the local calendar and working hours were considered to compute time for them. This ability to exclude time according to some criteria is not usually present in PPI modelling approaches.

Metrics that involve delays with respect to a date given in a data object These metrics require comparing the time instant when an activity had started or finished, or when an event was triggered, with respect to a due date contained in a document like a project plan, a replacement requirement or any other in order to compute possible delays. This is a rather frequent metric in SLAs since it is directly related with customer expectations. However, it is much less frequent as a PPI metric and, hence, it is not supported by PPI modelling approaches.

Metrics that involve human resources These metrics are used in SLAs in which the task performer profile must be taken into account when applying penalties, so that a different coefficient is applied, according to the different profiles, to calculate the penalty. For instance, in one of the studied scenarios, the general penalty of each metric had to be multiplied by the monthly profile rate of the person involved in the non-fulfilment. This metric is again closely related with the customer. In this case, with the fact that the customer expects a fair compensation depending on the task performer profile that failed to fulfilled the guarantees. However, current PPI modelling approaches do not support any metric that involve information related with the human resources that performed the task.

Metrics that involve different processes Some SLA metrics have to be defined over two or more process instances. This happens when a metric require execution information from two different processes to be computed. An example was found in one of the analysed BPO SLAs, where the number of incidents post production had to be obtained, and this metric required information from the incidents and the software delivery processes. Again, this metric cannot be modelled using current PPI modelling approaches, since a PPI focus on just one process by definition.

Some of these limitations could be easily addressed in PPINOT just by doing minor changes in its metamodel. However, others are left as future work since they require more significant changes. In particular, the first two type of metrics can be supported just by defining filters over *time measures*, so that idle time, suspend time, calendars or timetables can be taken into account when computing the time for the measure; and by adding a new type of measure, *time instant measure*, that measures the date and time in which an event takes place instead of the duration between two events. The metrics that involve human resources can be partially addressed using an extension to PPINOT to define resource–aware PPIs [20]. Finally, the metrics that involve different processes can be defined as a *derived measure* that relates measures in each process instance, but it is necessary to include information on how to correlate process instances when defining them, which is something that will be addressed in future work.

6 Related Work

A number of research efforts have focused on proposing models for SLA definition in computational and non–computational domains. *WSLA Framework* [21] provides an *agreement document model* (WSLA), which is the origin of the WS–Agreement specification, and provides foundations to monitor SLA fulfillment. Sauvé *et al.* [22] propose a methodology to calculate SLO thresholds to sign IT services SLAs according to service function cost from a business perspective. In all these cases, guarantees are proposed upon computational metrics (e.g. response time or availability). Therefore, it is useful only for SLAs that apply to the software infrastructure that support business processes and not for the business processes offered as a service. Kieninger *et al.* [23] describe a categorization of IT services and outline a mechanism to obtain efficient SLOs for them. However, they do that in a conceptual level and do not detail how they can be formalised to enable their automated management. Daly et al. [24] propose an SLA model based on the different elements in the service provision, *i.e.* application, servers, network, etc, related to service provision system. Cardoso et al. [25] propose a description language for services that include business characteristics together with technical or operational parameters. Unlike our proposal of managing a business process as a service, this work is focused on managing services including business perspective. Finally, Wieder et al. [26] define a *Service Oriented Architecture* with their own SLA model. The model has to be refined on each specific domain and there is an independent proposal to define measurements. The problem with all these approaches is that their SLA model offers no mechanism to model a business process nor to define metrics in terms of this business process. This seriously limits their applicability for building SLA–aware PAIS, in which processes play a key role.

Perhaps, the proposal closer to ours is Chau *et al.* [27]. It relates SLAs and business process artifacts where guarantees over the process are defined through process events. However, although similar to our work, this approach has a couple of limitations. First, the language to define metrics is imperative. Instead, PPINOT expressions are declarative, which eases the adaptation to different PAIS and makes it possible to define them in an user-friendly way by means of linguistic patterns as detailed in [19]. Second, the authors use their own model for SLA definitions, which limits the interoperability of their proposal and the reusability of existing proposals to analyse SLAs such as [3, 16].

7   Conclusions and Future Work

In this paper, we have shown how BPO SLAs can be modelled by combining mechanisms for modelling computational SLAs with mechanisms to model business processes and PPIs. Specifically, we first analysed the requirements for modelling BPO SLAs after a study of the state of the art in SLAs for both computational and non–computational services and the analysis of more than 20 different BPO SLAs developed by 4 different organisations. The conclusion of this analysis was that the structure of SLAs for BPO services and the definition of SLOs, penalties, and rewards are very similar to those of SLAs defined for computational services. However, the service description and the definition of the SLA metrics of BPO SLAs and computational SLAs present significant differences. The reason is that, unlike computational services, BPO services are process–aware and this has a strong influence on how they are described.

On the light of these requirements, our proposal to model BPO SLAs combines well founded approaches and standards for modelling computational SLAs and PPIs. Specifically, we rely on WS–Agreement [15], which provides the general SLA structure, BPMN [28], which is used to model the business process related to the service, PPINOT [13], which allows the definition of metrics, and iAgree [16], which provides a language to define SLOs and penalties.

The application of the proposed approach to a number of real scenarios allowed us to conclude that our approach is able to model all possible situations in these scenarios except for some limitations concerning the definition of SLA metrics as detailed in Section 5.2. Some of them could be solved by applying minor changes to the PPINOT metamodel. However, other limitations require more significant changes that shall be carried out in future work.

Apart from addressing these limitations, there are two lines of future work. On the one hand, we want to build a SLA–aware PAIS that uses these models to improve the automation of certain tasks related to both the SLAs and their fulfilment. To this end, we plan to take advantage of the existing tool support for iAgree and PPINOT to automate the definition, monitoring and analysis of the aforementioned SLAs for BPO services. On the other hand, we want to include additional information in SLAs to cover not only performance guarantees, but other aspects that are relevant for the customer such as compliance or audit–related issues [29].

References

1. Resinas, M., Fernández, P., Corchuelo, R.: A bargaining-specific architecture for supporting automated service agreement negotiation systems. Science of Computer Programming **77**(1), 4–28 (2012)
2. Emeakaroha, V.C., Brandic, I., Maurer, M., Dustdar, S.: Cloud resource provisioning and SLA enforcement via LoM2HiS framework. Concurrency and Computation: Practice and Experience **25**(10), 1462–1481 (2013)
3. Müller, C., Oriol, M., Franch, X., Marco, J., Resinas, M., Ruiz-Cortés, A., Rodriguez, M.: Comprehensive Explanation of SLA Violations at Runtime. IEEE Transactions on Services Computing **7**(2), 163–183 (2014)

4. Leitner, P., Ferner, J., Hummer, W., Dustdar, S.: Data-driven and automated prediction of service level agreement violations in service compositions. Distributed and Parallel Databases **31**(3), 447–470 (2013)
5. Gutiérrez, A.M., Cassales Marquezan, C., Resinas, M., Metzger, A., Ruiz-Cortés, A., Pohl, K.: Extending WS-Agreement to Support Automated Conformity Check on Transport and Logistics Service Agreements. In: Basu, S., Pautasso, C., Zhang, L., Fu, X. (eds.) ICSOC 2013. LNCS, vol. 8274, pp. 567–574. Springer, Heidelberg (2013)
6. Marquezan, C.C., Metzger, A., Franklin, R., Pohl, K.: Runtime Management of Multi-level SLAs for Transport and Logistics Services. In: Franch, X., Ghose, A.K., Lewis, G.A., Bhiri, S. (eds.) ICSOC 2014. LNCS, vol. 8831, pp. 560–574. Springer, Heidelberg (2014)
7. van der Aalst, W.M.P.: Business process configuration in the cloud: How to support and analyze multi-tenant processes? In: 9th IEEE European Conference on Web Services, ECOWS 2011, Lugano, Switzerland, September 14–16, pp. 3–10 (2011)
8. Gartner Inc: Business Process as a Service (BPaaS). Gartner IT Glossary (2013) Available from http://www.gartner.com/it-glossary/business-process-as-a-service-bpaas
9. Popova, V., Sharpanskykh, A.: Modeling organizational performance indicators. Information Systems **35**(4), 505–527 (2010)
10. Wetzstein, B., Ma, Z., Leymann, F.: Towards measuring key performance indicators of semantic business processes. Business Information Systems **7**, 227–238 (2008)
11. Pedrinaci, C., Lambert, D., Wetzstein, B., van Lessen, T., Cekov, L., Dimitrov, M.: Sentinel: a semantic business process monitoring tool. In: International Workshop on Ontology-Supported Business Intelligence (OBI), pp. 26–30 (2008)
12. Delgado, A., Weber, B., Ruiz, F., de Guzmán, I.G.R., Piattini, M.: An integrated approach based on execution measures for the continuous improvement of business processes realized by services. Information & Software Technology **56**(2), 134–162 (2014)
13. del-Río-Ortega, A., Resinas, M., Cabanillas, C., Ruiz-Cortés, A.: On the Definition and Design-time Analysis of Process Performance Indicators. Information Systems **38**(4), 470–490 (2012)
14. Chase, G., Rosenberg, A., Omar, R., Taylor, J., Rosing, M.: Applying Real-World BPM in an SAP Environment. SAP Press, Galileo Press (2011)
15. Andrieux, A., Czajkowski, K., Dan, A., Keahey, K., Ludwig, H., Nakata, T., Pruyne, J., Rofrano, J., Tuecke, S., Xu, M.: Web services agreement specification (ws-agreement). Specification from the Open Grid, Forum (OGF) (2007)
16. Müller, C., Resinas, M., Ruiz-Cortés, A.: Automated Analysis of Conflicts in WS-Agreement. IEEE Transactions on Services Computing, 1 (2013)
17. Müller, C., Gutiérrez, A.M., Martín-Díaz, O., Resinas, M., Fernández, P., Ruiz-Cortés, A.: Towards a formal specification of SLAs with compensations. In: Meersman, R., Panetto, H., Dillon, T., Missikoff, M., Liu, L., Pastor, O., Cuzzocrea, A., Sellis, T. (eds.) OTM 2014. LNCS, vol. 8841, pp. 295–312. Springer, Heidelberg (2014)
18. del-Río-Ortega, A., Cabanillas, C., Resinas, M., Ruiz-Cortés, A.: PPINOT Tool suite: a performance management solution for process-oriented organisations. In: Basu, S., Pautasso, C., Zhang, L., Fu, X. (eds.) ICSOC 2013. LNCS, vol. 8274, pp. 675–678. Springer, Heidelberg (2013)
19. del-Río-Ortega, A., Resinas, M., Durán, A., Ruiz-Cortés, A.: Using templates and linguistic patterns to define process performance indicators. Enterprise Information Systems (2014) (in press)

20. del-Río-Ortega, A., Resinas, M., Cabanillas, C., Ruiz-Cortés, A.: Defining and analysing resource-aware process performance indicators. In: Proc. of the CAiSE 2013 Forum at the 25th International Conference on Advanced Information Systems Engineering (CAiSE), pp. 57–64 (2013)
21. Keller, A., Ludwig, H.: The wsla framework: Specifying and monitoring service level agreements for web services. Journal of Network and Systems Management 11(1), 57–81 (2003)
22. Sauvé, J.P., Marques, F., Moura, A., Sampaio, M.C., Jornada, J., Radziuk, E.: SLA Design from a business perspective. In: Schönwälder, J., Serrat, J. (eds.) DSOM 2005. LNCS, vol. 3775, pp. 72–83. Springer, Heidelberg (2005)
23. Kieninger, A., Baltadzhiev, D., Schmitz, B., Satzger, G.: Towards service level engineering for IT services: defining IT services from a line of business perspective. In: 2011 Annual SRII Global Conference, pp. 759–766 (2011)
24. Daly, D., Kar, G., Sanders, W.: Modeling of service-level agreements for composed services. In: Feridun, M., Kropf, P., Babin, G. (eds.) Management Technologies for E-Commerce and E-Business Applications. Lecture Notes in Computer Science, vol. 2506, pp. 4–15. Springer, Berlin Heidelberg (2002)
25. Cardoso, J., Barros, A., May, N., Kylau, U.: Towards a unified service description language for the internet of services: Requirements and first developments. In: 2010 IEEE International Conference on Services Computing (SCC), pp. 602–609 (2010)
26. Wieder, P., Butler, J., Theilmann, W., Yahyapour, R., eds.: Service Level Agreements for Cloud Computing, vol. 2506. Springer (2011)
27. Chau, T., Muthusamy, V., Jacobsen, H.a., Litani, E., Chan, A., Coulthard, P.: Automating SLA modeling. In: Proceedings of the 2008 Conference of the Center for Advanced Studies on Collaborative Research: Meeting of Minds, pp. 10:126–10:143 (2008)
28. Object Management Group (OMG): Business process model and notation (BPMN) version 2.0 (2011) Available from: http://www.omg.org/spec/BPMN/2.0/PDF
29. Accorsi, R., Lowis, L., Sato, Y.: Automated Certification for Compliant Cloud-based Business Processes. Business & Information Systems Engineering 3(3), 145–154 (2011)

Deriving Artefact-Centric Interfaces for Overloaded Web Services

Fuguo Wei(✉), Alistair Barros, and Chun Ouyang

Queensland University of Technology, Brisbane, Australia
{f.wei,alistair.barros,c.ouyang}@qut.edu.au

Abstract. We present a novel framework and algorithms for the analysis of Web service interfaces to improve the efficiency of application integration in wide-spanning business networks. Our approach addresses the notorious issue of large and overloaded operational signatures, which are becoming increasingly prevalent on the Internet and being opened up for third-party service aggregation. Extending upon existing techniques used to refactor service interfaces based on derived artefacts of applications, namely business entities, we propose heuristics for deriving relations between business entities, and in turn, deriving permissible orders in which operations are invoked. As a result, service operations are refactored on business entity CRUD which then leads to behavioural models generated, thus supportive of fine-grained and flexible service discovery, composition and interaction. A prototypical implementation and analysis of web services, including those of commercial logistic systems (FedEx), are used to validate the algorithms and open up further insights into service interface synthesis.

Keywords: Web service · Business entity · Service interface synthesis · Service interface analysis

1 Introduction

Services have become the standard way of exposing applications, beyond technology and organisational boundaries, to allow functional capabilities to be accessed and composed, based on loosely coupled collaborations. Web Services Description Language (WSDL), REST and proprietary application programming interfaces (API) are rapidly growing, especially with the rise of Internet-based applications, software-as-a-service and cloud computing, in turn leading to larger vendors providing openly available interfaces for large and otherwise "in-house" software installations, notably in the enterprise systems segment (e.g. ERP and CRM systems). Consequently, the number, range of types, size, and overall complexity of services are progressively increasing, compounding the challenges of

This work is sponsored by Smart Service CRC Australia and in part by ARC Discovery Grant DP140103788.

© Springer International Publishing Switzerland 2015
J. Zdravkovic et al. (Eds.): CAiSE 2015, LNCS 9097, pp. 501–516, 2015.
DOI: 10.1007/978-3-319-19069-3_31

integrating services and vastly outpacing the conventional means to adapt services to support application interoperability in diffuse network settings.

Consider, for example, SAP's Enterprise (Web) services, as analysed in [1], where the input message of the goods movement service operation has 104 parameters, out of which only 12 are mandatory for the correct invocation of the service, with the other 92 data types and properties factoring in different usages of the service across different industries. As another example, FedEx provides 12 Web services[1] with the open shipping service demonstrating the highest complexity. It has 22 operations with the average number of input parameters of 307; 111 of them are nested types on average; an average number of hierarchical levels is 6. The operation which has the largest number of input parameters is createOpenShipment, with 1335 parameters, 442 of which are complex and the total levels of hierarchy are 9. More contemporary services from Internet players, too, have non-trivial operations as seen in the e-commerce services provided by Amazon, requiring comprehension of large and technically intricate documentation[2]. From a service consumer's perspective, several problems arise from this level of service complexity: (1) It is difficult to comprehend what each parameter means as the number is very large (2) It is challenging to know which parameter should go along with which for a particular purpose, as a large number of these parameters are optional and there are certain dependencies between them which consumers often do not have sufficient comprehension. For example, parameter B may become compulsory because parameter A is used in a specific invocation (3) How are operations related to each other? In other words, are there any sequence constraints to invoke these operations? (4) How are operations in one service related to ones in other services?

In general, integration of heterogeneous applications requires adapters to mediate across data types of operations (structural aspects) and the permissible orders in which operations are invoked (behavioural aspects). Despite advances in automated support for service adaptation, complex interfaces such as those from SAP, FedEx, Amazon and many others require manual effort and reliance on providers or specialist integrators, to design and implement the required service adapters [2]. In fact, most service providers, especially enterprise systems vendors, do not disclose structural and behavioural interfaces needed for service adaptation, but instead publish interface signatures such as WSDL specifications [3]. Thus, service adaptation incurs significant lead times and costly maintenance to yield service adapters, and their productivity in the context of dynamic service growth on the scale of the Internet is restricted.

This paper extends upon a recent and complementary strategy to conventional service adaptation, whereby the details of service interfaces and knowledge required to interact with them can be unilaterally synthesised by service consumers. Existing interface synthesis techniques build on type elicitation and data dependencies by automatically analysing service interfaces [4,5]. These are useful for identifying the focal artefacts of applications, namely the *business entities*,

---

[1] http://www.fedex.com/us/web-services/

[2] http://aws.amazon.com/ecommerce-applications/

which forms the basis for the creation of a simplified and fine-grained interface layer, allowing access (create, read, update and delete) operations against individual business entities. We extend upon these techniques to derive key *relationships* between business entities, which then provides a refined understanding of derived business entities and their dependencies, allowing invocation dependencies across their operations to be derived. For example, if one business entity such as a purchase order strictly contains another business entities such as line items, the container business entity should be created before the contained entities. In all, we develop heuristics for three relationship categories: strong containment, weak containment, and association. These, in turn, result in different business entity operation invocation dependencies, providing indispensable knowledge for generating behavioural aspects of service interfaces.

The remainder of this paper is structured as follows. Section 2 reviews state of the art and this is followed by the elaboration on the key components of our interface synthesis framework and the development of detailed insights into its most novel features in Section 3. Section 4 evaluates the framework by experimenting the implemented prototype with a variety of services and reveals some open issues. Finally, Section 5 concludes the paper and outlines the future work.

2   Related Work

Service analysis techniques have been proposed over many years to address challenges of service integration concerning structural and behavioural aspects of interfaces. Different approaches have been proposed including the utilisation of semantic ontologies to annotate interfaces to facilitate discovery, use, and composition of services. As an example, Falk et al. [6] adapted automata learning to the problem of service interaction analysis. This proposal usefully combines automated analysis with semantic ontologies in that it needs semantically annotated interface descriptions showing preconditions and effects as the prerequisite to learn interaction protocols. These semantically annotated descriptions are usually not provided by service providers in practice, and the development and maintenance of semantic ontologies requires significant lead times and adoption. Complementary to semantic techniques, log mining algorithms [7] have been proposed for matching data type of target services for service requests, which can also be used at design-time to develop adapters. These incur overheads for aggregating logs and can suffer from missing information for derivation of association dependencies. As we discussed above, our approach concerns static analysis of service interfaces in order to derive the structure and behaviour of services, complementary to semantic and mining approaches.

The first challenge of static service interface analysis is to identify business entities in operations, noting that operations of especially larger systems can have more than one entity, with potential overloading arising from bad service interface design. Identification of business entities is a complex problem requiring an insight into the clustering of different attributes which imply structural type cohesion of an entity. Proposals for static interface analysis proceed from assumptions of attribute to entity type associations based on the use of prior matching techniques (ontology or mining based). The approach of Kumaran et al. [5] proposes heuristics for understanding basic business entity relationships based on the domination theory of business entities, however the derived relationship type is strict containment, which leads to a limited understanding of operation invocation dependencies across services. A more advanced proposal for behavioural interface synthesis has been proposed by [4] based on data dependencies between service operations' input and output parameters, but the study has not been exposed to overloaded service interfaces such as the aforementioned examples from enterprise and Internet players.

Service composition approaches have also been used in the context of service adaptation, the common problem being addressed is "how to automatically generate a new target service protocol by reusing some existing ones" [8]. However, this technique assumes that the interfaces of individual services involved in a composition are available.

3   Service Interface Synthesis

To address the aforementioned problems, this section presents the details of a service interface synthesis framework. It consists of two main modules: Service interface analysis and Service interface refining.

The service interface analysis module is comprised of two components (Fig. 1): *BE data model derivation* and *Service operation refactoring*. They analyse service structural interfaces and determine the order of invoking operations provided by a service. Services essentially focus on addressing and transferring states of resources and business entities are the primary resource manipulated by services in the context of global business networks. Therefore, our service analysis is carried out based on the notion of business entity (i.e., entity types) - a concept widely adopted in Object Role Modelling [9]. The *BE data model derivation* component analyses the input and output parameters of operations on a service and map them to a business entity-based service data model (BE data model). The *Service operation refactoring* component categorises operations provided by a service according to what each operation does to a business entity (i.e, to CREATE, READ, UPDATE or DELETE (CRUD) a business entity). This component also generates behavioural interfaces for each CRUD operation of a business entity.

As a result of structural and behavioural interface analysis, a complex service interface is mapped onto a BE data model and a behavioural interface model. The former presents business entities and the relations among them inherent in the service, and the later depicts the behavioural constraints that service consumers are required to follow. These models form the refactored service interfaces, which encapsulate and simplify complex and overloaded service interfaces. Having these structured service interfaces, valid combinations of input parameter sets can be easily derived. The *Service interface refining* component then utilises a Monte Carlo statistic approach [10] to search for possible valid combinations and then invoke services using these combinations with sample data values in order to determine and test their validity. An Interface Layer is formed in the end, and it exhibits much simpler service interface with possible valid combinations and behavioural specifications so that service consumers can easily consume services. Due to space limit, this paper only addresses the first module: service interface analysis, which simplifies service structural interfaces and generates service behavioural interfaces.

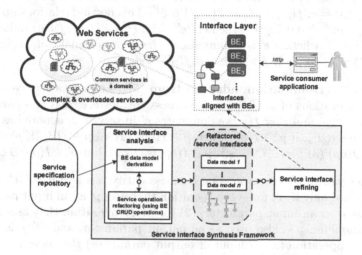

Fig. 1. An overview of the service interface synthesis framework

3.1 BE Data Model Derivation

Definition 1 (Operation and Parameter). Let s be a service, OP_s is a set of operations of s. For each operation $op \in OP_s$, $\mathcal{N}(op)$ is the name of op, $\mathcal{I}(op)$ is the set of input parameters and $\mathcal{O}(op)$ is the set of output parameters of op.

Let P be a set of parameters. For each $p \in P$, $\mathcal{N}(p)$ is the name of p, $\gamma(p) \in \{primitive, complex\}$ indicates whether p is of a primitive or a complex type (i.e., an user-defined type), and $type(p)$ specifies the type of data (e.g. string, LineItem) carried by p.

$P_C = \{p \in P | \gamma(p) = complex\}$ denotes the set of complex parameters in P. $\xi^P \subseteq P_C \times P$ specifies the (direct) nesting relation between two parameters. ξ^P is transitive and irreflexive. $\lambda^P : \xi^P \rightarrow \{true, false\}$ indicates for each $(p, p') \in \xi^P$ whether p' is a compulsory ($true$) or optional ($false$) element of p. □

Definition 2 (Business Entity). E is a set of business entities. For each $e \in E$, $\mathcal{N}(e)$ is the name of e, $key(e)$ is the unique identifier of e, and $\mathcal{A}(e)$ is the set of attributes associated with e. For each attribute $a \in \mathcal{A}(e)$, $\mathcal{N}(a)$ is the name of a and $type(a)$ is the type of data carried by a. □

Definition 3 (Parameter and Business Entity Mapping). Let P_C be a set of complex parameters, ξ^P the nesting relation between parameters, and E a set of business entities. There exists a surjective mapping $f : P_C \to E$ where $\forall p, p' \in P_C, (p, p') \in \xi^P \Rightarrow f(p) \neq f(p')$, i.e. two nesting parameters cannot be mapped to the same business entity. □

Definition 4 (Business Entity Nesting Relation). Let P_C be a set of complex parameters, ξ^P the nesting relation between parameters, E a set of business entities, and f the mapping from P_C to E. The nesting relation between two business entities can be defined as $\xi^E \subseteq E \times E$ where $\forall (e, e') \in \xi^E, \exists \ p, p' \in P_c$ such that $f(p) = e$, $f(p') = e'$, and $(p, p') \in \xi^P$. This nesting relationship is transitive, i.e., if $e\xi^E e'$ and $e'\xi^E e''$, then $e\xi^E e''$. $\lambda^E : \xi^E \to \{true, false\}$ indicates for each $(e, e') \in \xi^E$ whether e' is a compulsory (*true*) or optional (*false*) element of e. $\lambda^E(e, e') = \lambda^P(p, p')$ if $f(p) = e$ and $f(p') = e'$. □

Definition 5 (Domination, adapted from [5]). Let s be a service and OP_s the set of operations of s. Given two business entities e, e' and two parameters p, p' s.t. $e = f(p)$ and $e' = f(p')$, e dominates e' in service s, denoted as $e \mapsto e'$, iff: (1) $\forall \ op \in OP_s$, if $p' \in I(op)$, then $p \in I(op)$ (2) $\forall \ op \in OP_s$, if $p' \in O(op)$, then $p \in O(op)$ (3)$\exists \ op \in OP_s$, s.t. $p \in I(op) \cup O(op)$, but $p' \notin I(op) \cup O(op)$. □

In other words, p's corresponding business entity is e and p''s is e', e dominates e', if and only if (1) for every operation that uses p' as an input parameter, p is also used as an input parameter, (2) for every operation that uses p' as an output parameter, p is also used as an output parameter, and (3) p is used by at least one operation (as its input or output parameter) that does not use p'.

Definition 6 (Strong Containment). Given two business entities e and e', e' is strongly contained in e iff $e\xi^E e'$, $e \mapsto e'$, and $\nexists e'' \in E \setminus \{e\}$ s.t. $e'' \mapsto e'$. τ captures the set of strong containment relations between business entities. □

Definition 7 (Weak Containment). Given two business entities e and e', e' is weakly contained in e iff $e\xi^E e'$ and $e' \mapsto e$. φ captures the set of weak containment relations between business entities. □

Definition 8 (Association). Given two business entities e and e' where $(e, e') \in \varphi$, e and e' are associated with each other if there exist two parameters p, p' such that $e = f(p)$ and $e' = f(p')$, and there exist an operation op such that $p' \in I(op)$ and $p \in O(op)$. ω captures the set of association relations between business entities. □

Definition 9 (Business Entity Data Model). A business entity data model M is a tuple $(E, \xi^E, \varphi, \tau, \omega)$ which consists of a set business entities E and their nesting relations ξ^E, strong containment relations τ, weak containment relations φ, and association relations ω.

Given a service specification such as a WSDL file, the BE model derivation derives the BE data model for each operation provided by the service. This can

---

Algorithm 1. IDENTIFYBEANDRELATION

---

input: (complex) parameter p, parameters nesting relation ξ^P, business entity e, business entity set E, business entity nesting relation ξ^E, business entity repository $\mathcal{E}$

    /* *Find a matching business entity from the repository via ontology check* */
    $e' := $ ONTOLOGYCHECK$(\mathcal{N}(p), type(p), \mathcal{E})$
    /* *Record the business entity and derive the relation with its parent entity* */
    if $e' \neq \perp$ **then**
        for each $(p, p') \in \xi^P$ **do**
            $\mathcal{A}(e) := \mathcal{A}(e) \cup \{$CONVETTOENTITYATTR$(p')\}$
        end for
        $E := E \cup \{e'\}$
        if $e \neq \perp$ **then**
            $\xi^E := \xi^E \cup \{(e, e')\}$
        end if
        /* *Recursively call this algorithm for each complex parameter nested in p* */
        for each $(p, p') \in \xi^P \wedge \gamma(p') = complex$ **do**
            IDENTIFYBEANDRELATION$(p', \xi^P, e', E, \xi^E, \mathcal{E})$
        end for
    end if
    return (E, ξ^E)

---

be achieved through algorithm 1 and 2. The first algorithm generates E and ξ^E and the second refines the relation ξ^E to derive φ, τ, and ω for the operation. For each service, we iterate its operations and then loop through each complex input and output parameter of each operation to identify the BE data model. There is an overview algorithm which calls algorithm 1 to do so and the details of the algorithm can be found in our report [11].

Algorithm 1 contains three main steps. The first mainly involves the function ONTOLOGYCHECK which takes name $(\mathcal{N}(p))$ and type $(type(p))$ of a complex parameter $p \in P_C$, and the business entity repository $(\mathcal{E})$ as the inputs, and returns an entity e' s.t. $e' = f(p)$. It will return nothing if there is no match found. For each complex parameter p, we check if there is a business entity that maps onto p. To do this, the service synthesis framework allows users to designate business entities for a particular context at design time. These business entities are stored in a repository $\mathcal{E}$, and p is checked against it to determine if there is a matching business entity in it. To semantically match a parameter with a business object, we assure the existence of an ontology that allows users to designate business objects for a particular context at design time. Semantic matching techniques have been well studied and this research adopts S-Match [12], a widely used semantic matching algorithm. The second step keeps the business entity and its nesting relation. If there is a mapping business entity e', parameters that are nested in p are converted and added to e''s attribute list $\mathcal{A}(e')$. The conversion involves interpreting these nested parameters as attributes of e' and skipping parameters that should not be attributes. Then e is added to op's entity set E_{op}, which stores all business entities discovered in op. If there is

---

Algorithm 2. REFINEBERELATION

---

input: service operation set OP, service operation op ($op \in OP$), set of business entity
sets $\bigcup_{z \in OP} E_z$, business entity nesting relation ξ_{op}^E, set of mappings from parameters
to business entities f

/* Set flags for indication of whether a specific relation holds */
$r^\tau := \perp$ /* flag for strong containment relation */
$r^\omega := \perp$ /* flag for association relation */
for each $e \in E_{op}$ **do**
    /* Iterate for all the business entities nested in e */
    for each $(e, e') \in \xi_{op}^E$ **do**
        /* Iterate for all the operations manipulating e' until a strong containment
        relation fails to hold */
        $X := OP$
        while $X \neq \varnothing \wedge r^\tau \neq false$ **do**
            Select $x \in X$ s.t. $e' \in E_x$
            $Y := E_x$
            while $Y \neq \varnothing \wedge r^\tau \neq false$ **do**
                Select $e'' \in Y$ s.t. $e'' \mapsto e'$
                $r^\tau := (e'' = e)$
                $Y := Y \setminus \{e''\}$
            end while
            $X := X \setminus \{x\}$
        end while
        /* Collect strong containment, weak containment, and association relations */
        if $r^\tau = true$ **then**
            $\tau_{op} := \tau_{op} \cup \{(e, e')\}$ /* collect strong containment relation */
        else if $e' \mapsto e$ **then**
            for each $z \in OP$ **do**
                Search for p, p' s.t. $p' \in I(op) \wedge f(p') = e' \wedge p \in O(op) \wedge f(p) = e$
                if there exist such p and p' **then**
                    $r^\omega := true$
                    $\omega_{op} := \tau_{op} \cup \{(e, e')\}$ /* collect association relation */
                end if
            end for
            if $r^\omega := false$ **then**
                $\varphi_{op} := \varphi_{op} \cup \{(e, e')\}$ /* collect weak containment relation */
            end if
        end if
    end for
    /* Reset flags for relation indication */
    $r^\tau := \perp$
    $r^\omega := \perp$
end for
return $(\tau_{op}, \varphi_{op}, \omega_{op})$

---

a business entity e containing e', this relation is recorded as nesting, which is a
part of op's BE data model ξ_{op}^E. e is an input parameter of algorithm 1 and it

refers to the parent entity of current entity e'. The final step takes every complex parameter p' that is nested in p and recursively calls the algorithm itself to process each p'. The current e' is passed on to next invocation to form the nesting relation because it is the parent of each $f(p')$. Essentially, algorithm 1 incrementally updates op's BE data model until all entities and nesting relationships are processed.

Once E_{op} and ξ_{op}^{E} are identified, we can call algorithm 2 to refine the relations and derive the other three types of relations for op: strong containment (τ_{op}), weak containment (φ_{op}), and association (ω_{op}) to complete the BE data model for op. Algorithm 2 iterates each business entity e in op's BE data model and then assesses the relationship between e and every business entity e' that is nested in e. This assessment is carried out according to the definitions of strong containment (Definition 6), weak containment (Definition 7), and association (Definition 8).

3.2 Service Operation Refactoring

The above algorithms show how a BE model for an operation (i.e., M_{op}) is generated. A BE data model for a service M_s is an aggregation of BE data models of all operations provided by s. Based on the service BE data model M_s, the service operation refactoring component derives the behavioural interface for s. For any business entity e derived, there are a number of operations that manipulate e and these operations can be categorised into four groups: C_e, R_e, U_e, and D_e, which denote the set of operations for creating, reading, updating, and deleting an instance of e respectively. To categorise operations provided by a service into the four modular operations of a business entity, we identified the following mapping rules.

CREATE If the invocation of an operation requires some input parameters which are actually attributes of e and returns a reference to a business entity (i.e., $key(e)$), the operation is for creating an instance of e. In other words, an operation that is designed to create a business entity e usually requires its users to pass in values for some parameters which are attributes of e. For instance, to create a shipment order, a create operation often needs to know details of shipment order such as what goods are to be shipped, where these goods are shipped from and to. As a result, the create operation should return a reference (i.e., id) of the shipment order created. There may be multiple operations designed for creating a business entity, and the set C_e is used to keep these operations.

READ If the invocation of an operation requires information of $key(e)$ and it returns the values of parameters that are attributes of the business entity e, the operation is for reading an instance of e. The set (i.e., R_e) that stores READ operations is singleton because there is usually only one operation to read an instance of e.

UPDATE If the invocation of an operation requires information of $key(e)$ and some input parameters which are actually attributes of e, the operation is for updating an instance of e.

DELETE If the invocation of an operation requires information of $key(e)$ and returns nothing related to e but just a status, the operation is for deleting an instance of e.

We propose an algorithm that invokes each operation op that manipulates a business entity e and then analyses the input and output parameters according to the aforementioned mapping rules to determine the category of op, i.e. whether op is to create, read, update or delete e. As a result, the algorithm groups each op and adds it into one of the following sets: C_e, R_e, U_e, and D_e. The details of this algorithm can be found in our report [11]. At this stage, there could be many operations in C_e, U_e, and D_e. For example, to create a shipping order, there are a number of operations and a service consumer needs to follow certain sequence constraints, so the next step is to generate these sequences for each modular operation.

Service behavioural interfaces (i.e., protocols) depict a set of sequencing constraints and they define legal order of messages. In this paper, a behavioural interface is formalised as business entity-based behavioural model (BE model). A BE behavioural model is a Petri net (Q, T, F). T is a set of transitions that specify service operations, Q a set of places that specify the pre- and post-conditions of service operations, and $F \subseteq (Q \times T \cup T \times Q)$ a set of flow relations that connect a (pre-)condition to an operation or an operation to a (post-)condition.

For each $e \in E_s$, we generate BE models for its CRUD operations. For example, the model for CREATE operation defines the operations and their invocation order for creating an instance of a business entity. To derive such a model for e, we firstly retrieve entities that are strongly contained in, weakly contained in, and associated with e. When a business entity e' is weakly contained in or associated with business entity e, an instance of e' and an instance of e can be created in any order if $\lambda(e, e') = false$, otherwise if (i.e. $\lambda(e, e') = true$), an instance of e' must be created before the creation of an instance of e. If a business entity e' is strongly contained in another business entity e, an instance of e' cannot be created unless an e is instantiated. The second step is to retrieve all operations in C_e and identify their sequence through trial/error invocation. Each op is called and the response is analysed. If it is positive, the invocation is in sequence. Otherwise, other operations in C_e are called. This process proceeds until either all operations are in order or all operations have been checked.

Fig. 2 (b_1) and Fig. 2 (b_2) present the BE behavioural model derived based on the e_1 focused data model shown in Fig. 2 (a). Specifically, Fig. 2 (b_1) presents the model for the situation when the compulsory factor $\lambda(e, e')$ between all the entities that are related is true. As e_3 is associated with e_1, it has to be created before e_1's creation, the same can be said for e_4 and e_2. In this case, $C_{e_1} = \{op_1, op_2, op_3\}$ and we assume the sequence of creating e_1 is $op_1 - op_1 - op_2$, so the invocations of these three operations can create an instance of e_1. As e_2 is strongly contained in e_1, it can only be created after e_1's creation. Similarly, e_5 is created after e_2's creation. Fig. 2 (b_2), on the other hand, depicts the sequence derived for the situation when the compulsory factor is false. e_3 can be created concurrently with e_1's creation and e_4 can be created in parallel with

e_2's creation. The detailed algorithm for BE Behavioural model derivation can be found in our report [11].

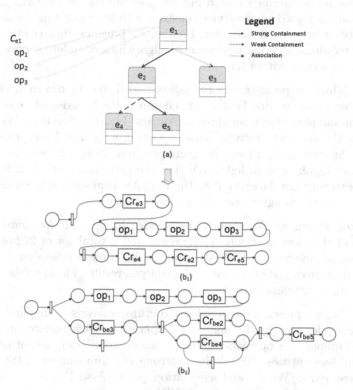

Fig. 2. An abstract demonstration for BE Behavioural model derivation

4   Implementation and Validation

To validate the service interface synthesis framework, we have developed a prototype that analyses service interfaces and generates BE data models for CRUD of a business entity. This prototype is called Service Integration Accelerator and it implements the algorithms presented in the previous section. This section presents the details of the experiments we conducted on *service interface analysis* and evaluates the framework using their results.

Hypotheses. We define three hypotheses to assess the effectiveness of the service interface synthesis framework. The first one is simplification - the service interface analysis mechanism simplifies overloaded and complicated service interfaces, so service consumers are able to utilise the structural analysis results as a guidance to facilitate their comprehension of service interfaces. As a result, this reduces the amount of time that they need in order to comprehend and then invoke services correctly. Another criteria to be examined is accuracy - the service interface analysis mechanism derives all possible business entities, however a rate of 25% of false positives is allowed as some entities may not be business entities in one specific context, but are possibly business entities in another context. Therefore, we allow service consumers to filter out those which should not be entities in a specific context. Finally, we presume that the performance fulfils our requirement - the implemented algorithms complete service interface analysis on a service within ten seconds.

Objects. Thirteen popular services (shown in Table 1) drawn from xmethods.net[3], Amazon.com, and FedEx were chosen as the experiment objects. These experiment samples were from three categories: Internet Services (IS), i.e., services from the Internet, Software-as-a-Service (SaaS), and Enterprise Services (ES) and the complexity of services increases from IS to ES. Services in the IS category are highlighted in light grey (i.e, the first three services); Services in the SaaS category are darkgray (i.e., the four Amazon services); Services in the ES category are in dimgray (i.e., the six FedEx services).

Validation Process. We applied the Service Integration Accelerator to the interfaces of the aforementioned 13 services, and a total set of 272 operations, 12962 input parameters, and 29700 output parameters were analysed. Then, we asked the domain experts to examine the analysis results, identify false positives, and do some adjustments if necessary.

Results. Table 1 presents the detailed structural analysis results and it reports the following details: (1) the number of operations each service provides, (2) the mean number (per operation) of input parameters (IPs), output parameters (OPs), business entities (BE) derived, strong containment pairs (SCP), weak containment pairs (WCP), and association pairs (Asso Pairs), (3) The mean (per operation) of false positive rate (FPR).

According to the results, Internet services usually do not involve business entities, because they often only have a few operations with a handful of parameters. For example, the Weather Forecast service only has two operations 'GetCitiesByCountry(Country)' and 'GetForecastByCity(City, Country)'. Therefore, although the Service Integration Accelerator can pick up and present the Internet services' parameters, which provides guidance on the structural interface of these services, Internet service consumers will not benefit significantly from the analysis results because the interface is not complex.

As for services in the SaaS category, their interfaces present intermediate complexity. The number of operations provided in the four Amazon web services ranges from 9 to 157 and the average number of input parameters is between 4 and 24. There are around 3 business entities derived per operation. It may seem that service consumers can cope with this type of services as the number of input parameters for some operations is not very large, but the number of operations is quite significant and service users may find it difficult to know

---

[3] http://www.xmethods.net:5868/ve2/index.po

the sequential constraints among these operations. Having a proper structural analysis is essential to derive such constraints.

Services in the ES category are the most complex ones and they usually have a large of number of input and output parameters. Therefore, it is worthwhile to reduce complexity so that service consumers can understand the interfaces. The result shows that the Service Integration Accelerator works effectively for enterprise services. The six FedEx services in Table 1 show how these complex services are simplified. For example, the Open Shipping service has 22 operations and the average number of input parameters is 309 and the output parameter is 575. After the structural analysis, on average, we derived 11 entities per operation, which dramatically reduce the complexity as users can more easily understand the interface by looking at these business entities and their relationships. Taking the FedEx Open Shipping service as an example, the operation - 'createOpenShipment' has 1336 input parameters and 596 output parameters, by analysing these parameters, we derived 14 key business entities and their relationships as shown in Fig. 3 (b).

Regarding false positive rate, as the Service Integration Accelerator treats all complex parameters as business entities, it sometimes generates entities that should not be. For example, in the generated Amazon S3 service structural analysis result in Fig. 3 (a), 'CopyObject' and 'PutObject' should be combined as one entity, which is 'Object', and 'SetBucketLoggingStatus' should not be an entity. These false positives are 12% of total entities (32) derived. Overall, the results for majority of services experimented fulfil the hypothesis, which is 25% false positive rate, plus we allow domain experts to manually revise the business entity model and to correct these false positives. These false positives can cause the Service Integration Accelerator to derive incorrect behavioural models, but they are assessed by domain experts prior to the derivation of behavioural interfaces, so invalid ones will be prevented.

The time taken to analyse each service is not listed in Table 1 as it was fairly quick to complete the analysis, even the most complicated service - FedEx Open Shipping - took only 7 seconds, indicating the hypothesis about performance has been met.

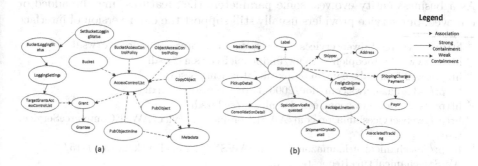

Fig. 3. Interface analysis results of Amazon S3 and Fedex createOpenshipment services

Table 1. Structural Analysis Results of the 13 services (Mean)

Services	Operations	IPs	OPs	BE derived	SCP	WCP	Asso Pairs	FPR (%)
Weather Forecast[4]	2	2	5	0	0	0	0	0
Find People[5]	3	2	1	0	0	0	0	0
MailBox Validator[6]	1	2	6	0	0	0	0	0
Amazon S3[7]	16	9	4	2	1	1	0	12
Amazon EC2[8]	157	4	8	2	1	1	1	20
Amazon Advertising[9]	9	24	243	4	3	1	0	2
Amazon Mechanical[10]	44	11	271	3	2	1	0	10
FedEx Ship[11]	5	709	239	34	40	8	1	28
FedEx Pick up[11]	3	137	41	25	23	8	1	5
FedEx Return[11]	1	20	15	3	1	0	0	0
FedEx Close[11]	6	47	18	4	3	1	1	12
Open Shipping[11]	22	309	575	11	9	3	5	24
Address Validation[11]	1	31	51	5	3	0	0	0

Open issues. Having examined the experiment results, we find that another two types of relationships between entities: inclusive and exclusive specialization. The former refers to subtypes of business entities, i.e., a set of attributes of a business entity *be* may form a new business entity be_{sub}, which is a subtype of *be*. For example, in Fig. 3 (a), 'BucketAccessControlPolicy' should be an inclusive specialization of 'AccessControlPolicy'. However, this relationship is currently considered weak containment. Inclusive specialization can also be derived using our Monte Carlo statistic based Service operation refining mechanism. That is to say, if a valid combination is a sub set of a business entity (*be*)'s attributes, this combination may become a new business entity, which is a specialization of *be*. Exclusive specialization denotes different versions of a business entity. As a business entity evolves, some parameters (i.e., features) may be added or removed, but service providers usually still support the older version of interface

---

[4] http://www.restfulwebservices.net/wcf/WeatherForecastService.svc?wsdl

[5] http://www.findpeoplefree.co.uk/findpeoplefree.asmx?wsdl

[6] http://ws2.fraudlabs.com/mailboxvalidator.asmx?wsdl

[7] http://s3.amazonaws.com/doc/2006-03-01/AmazonS3.wsdl

[8] http://s3.amazonaws.com/ec2-downloads/ec2.wsdl

[9] http://webservices.amazon.com/AWSECommerceService/AWSECommerceService.wsdl

[10] http://mechanicalturk.amazonaws.com/AWSMechanicalTurk/2013-11-15/AWSMechanicalTurkRequester.wsdl

[11] http://www.fedex.com/us/web-services/

because of compatibility. Therefore, our interface analysis should be able to cope with the analysis of different version of business entities. We will examine these two types of specializations in our future work.

5 Conclusion

This paper presented a service interface synthesis framework for addressing the service interoperability challenges in the context of open and diffuse setting of global business networks. Specifically, it described a few key components of the framework, detailing service interface analysis. We also validated the framework using a variety of services. The study has demonstrated that the business entity based service interface analysis technique is an effective solution to simplify services with large, overloaded operations in interfaces. Future work will complete the framework by composing different service invocations and then validate them using a Monte Carlo statistic approach. We will also extend the prototype to support service operation refactoring to derive service behavioural interfaces and validate them.

References

1. Stollberg, M., Muth, M.: Efficient business service consumption by customization with variability modelling. Journal of Systems Integration 1(3), 17–32 (2010)
2. Motahari Nezhad, H.R., Benatallah, B., Martens, A., Curbera, F., Casati, F.: Semi-automated adaptation of service interactions. In: Proceedings of the 16th International Conference on World Wide Web (WWW 2007), pp. 993–1002. ACM, New York (2007)
3. Issarny, V., Bennaceur, A., Bromberg, Y.-D.: Middleware-Layer Connector Synthesis: Beyond State of the Art in Middleware Interoperability. In: Bernardo, M., Issarny, V. (eds.) SFM 2011. LNCS, vol. 6659, pp. 217–255. Springer, Heidelberg (2011)
4. Bertolino, A., Inverardi, P., Pelliccione, P., Tivoli, M.: Automatic synthesis of behavior protocols for composable web-services. In: Proceedings of the the 7th Joint Meeting of the European Software Engineering Conference, ESEC/FSE 2009, pp. 141–150. ACM, New York (2009)
5. Kumaran, S., Liu, R., Wu, F.Y.: On the Duality of Information-Centric and Activity-Centric Models of Business Processes. In: Bellahsène, Z., Léonard, M. (eds.) CAiSE 2008. LNCS, vol. 5074, pp. 32–47. Springer, Heidelberg (2008)
6. Howar, F., Jonsson, B., Merten, M., Steffen, B., Cassel, S.: On Handling Data in Automata Learning. In: Margaria, T., Steffen, B. (eds.) ISoLA 2010, Part II. LNCS, vol. 6416, pp. 221–235. Springer, Heidelberg (2010)
7. Motahari-Nezhad, H., Saint-Paul, R., Benatallah, B., Casati, F.: Protocol discovery from imperfect service interaction logs. In: IEEE 23rd International Conference on Data Engineering, pp. 1405–1409 (2007)
8. Ragab Hassen, R., Nourine, L., Toumani, F.: Protocol-Based Web Service Composition. In: Bouguettaya, A., Krueger, I., Margaria, T. (eds.) ICSOC 2008. LNCS, vol. 5364, pp. 38–53. Springer, Heidelberg (2008)

9. Halpin, T., Morgan, A., Morgan, T.: Information modeling and relational databases, Morgan Kaufmann series in data management systems. Elsevier/Morgan Kaufmann Publishers (2008)
10. Robert, C.P., Casella, G.: Monte Carlo Statistical Methods (Springer Texts in Statistics). Springer-Verlag New York Inc., Secaucus (2005)
11. Wei, F., Barros, A., Ouyang, C.: Deriving artefact-centric interfaces for overloaded web services (February 2015)
12. Giunchiglia, F., Shvaiko, P., Yatskevich, M.: S-Match: an Algorithm and an Implementation of Semantic Matching. In: Bussler, C.J., Davies, J., Fensel, D., Studer, R. (eds.) ESWS 2004. LNCS, vol. 3053, pp. 61–75. Springer, Heidelberg (2004)

Tutorials

CAiSE 2015 Tutorials

This volume includes a collection of extended abstracts of the tutorials presented at the Conference on Advanced Information Systems Engineering (CAiSE 2015), in Stockholm, Sweden. A total of 17 proposals were considered, from researchers coming from Australia, Austria, Belgium, Canada, Israel, Romania, Spain, South Africa, Switzerland, UK, and the USA. These proposals were carefully reviewed by the tutorial chairs. After this process, 5 tutorials were accepted. We would like to thank the authors who considered CAiSE as a forum for the presentation of their highquality work. In the sequel, we elaborate on these selected tutorials.

In the tutorial titled *"Work Systems Theory: A Bridge between Business and IT views of Systems"*, Steven Alter presents the main concepts and ideas of the Work Systems Theory (WST) and its applications to various issues that are relevant for Information Systems engineering.

In *"Fundamental Systems Thinking Concepts for IS Engineering: Balancing between Change and Non-change"*, Gil Regev raises challenges that stem from resistance to change, which accompanies the introduction of new IT systems. He indicates that in anticipation of such resistance, IS researchers and practitioners need to alleviate it for the success of the system.

In the tutorial *"Know-how Mapping with ME Maps"*, Arnon Sturm and Eric Yu show how Means-Ends diagrams, well known in Requirements Engineering, can be used for mapping practical knowledge, referred to as "know-how". Such maps can be used for visualizing existing knowledge in a domain, identifying gaps, and setting grounds for new research and for evaluating the impact of research outcomes.

In *"Model Matching: Processes and Beyond"*, Matthias Weidlich and Avigdor Gal provide an overview of a body of research and the state of the art in the area of process model matching. They further indicate possible generalizations of these results to conceptual models in general, in support of model reuse, similarity assessment, and variability management.

Finally, in *"FEDS2: A Practical Tutorial on the Framework for Evaluation in Design Science Research (v. 2)"* John Venable describe a practical approach for conducting design science research, with an emphasis on the evaluation phase. As the paradigm of design science is central in IS engineering, this tutorial provides valuable guidance to researchers in this area.

April 2015

Ilia Bider
Pnina Soffer

© Springer International Publishing Switzerland 2015
J. Zdravkovic et al. (Eds.): CAiSE 2015, LNCS 9097, p. 519, 2015.
DOI: 10.1007/978-3-319-19069-3

Work System Theory: A Bridge Between Business and IT Views of Systems

Steven Alter

University of San Francisco
alter@usfca.edu

Abstract. This tutorial explains the most current version of work system theory and related ideas that were developed over several decades in an attempt to create a systems analysis and design method that could be used by business professionals. This tutorial covers: 1) work system theory (WST), 2) application of WST in various versions of the work system method (WSM), and 3) extensions of WST including work system principles, work system design spaces, a work system metamodel that reinterprets basic work system ideas in a detailed way that is more directly useful for IT-related analysis and design, linkages between WST and service systems, and application of work system ideas in a theory of workarounds and proposed theory of system interactions.

Keywords: Work system, work system framework, work system life cycle model, work system metamodel

Tutorial Details

A longstanding shortcoming of systems analysis and design, software engineering, business informatics, and enterprise architecture is the lack of readily usable and easily teachable concepts, frameworks, tools, and methods that bridge the gap between two worlds. Those worlds are the people- and business-oriented sociotechnical world of business professionals and the abstract, technology-centric world of IT professionals and IS/IT researchers. That gap contributes to widely recognized difficulties in communicating and collaborating around creating, implementing, and improving ITreliant systems in organizations. Some experienced consultants and consulting companies have proprietary methods, but those are not readily available for use by others.

This tutorial explains the most updated version of WST and related ideas that were developed over several decades. WST has three components [1,2]:

1. the definition of work system
2. the work system framework, a static view of the work system as it exists during a particular time interval when it retains its identity and integrity even though it may change slightly through small adaptations, workarounds, personnel changes, and even unintentional drift
3. the work system lifecycle model, a dynamic view of how work systems change over time through a combination of planned and unplanned change.

© Springer International Publishing Switzerland 2015
J. Zdravkovic et al. (Eds.): CAiSE 2015, LNCS 9097, pp. 520–521, 2015.
DOI: 10.1007/978-3-319-19069-3

WSM applies WST but is not part of WST. WSM is designed to help business professionals, IT professionals, students, and researchers think about current and proposed work systems. Various versions of WSM all involve identifying the main problems or opportunities that launched an analysis, identifying the smallest work system that exhibits those problems or opportunities. summarizing the "as is" work system using a formatted one page table, evaluating the work system's operation at an appropriate level of detail, summarizing changes that will appear a proposed "to be" work system, and describing the likely improvement in work system performance. WSM has been used by many hundreds of MBA or Executive MBA students in the United States, China, Vietnam, and India to produce preliminary management briefings about possible improvements in real world work systems in their own organizations [1, 3, 4].

Recent developments include extensions of WST into areas that were not anticipated in the earlier research, such as work system principles [1], work system design spaces [1], various versions of a work system metamodel [2, 5], linkages between WST and service systems [5, 6], possible uses of WST as a front end to object oriented analysis and design [7], possible links between WST and BPM [8], a theory of workarounds [9], and possible uses of the work system framework as part of a scaffolding for a body of knowledge related to information systems and other systems in organizations [10].

References

1. Alter, S., Work System Theory: Overview of Core Concepts, Extensions, and Challenges for the Future. Journal of the Association for Information Systems, 14(2), 72-121. 2013.
2. Alter, S., Work System Theory as a Platform: Response to a Research Perspective Article by Niederman and March, Journal of the Association for Information Systems, 2015. (in press).
3. Truex, D., Alter, S., Long, C., Systems Analysis for Everyone Else: Empowering Business Professionals through a Systems Analysis Method that Fits Their Needs, Proceedings of ECIS 2010, European Conference on Information Systems, 2010.
4. Alter, S., The Work System Method: Connecting People, Processes, and IT for Business Results. Larkspur, CA: Work System Press, 2006.
5. Alter, S., Metamodel for Service Analysis and Design Based on an Operational View of Service and Service Systems, Service Science, 4(3), 218-235, 2012.
6. Alter, S., Service System Fundamentals: Work System, Value Chain, and Life Cycle, IBM Systems Journal, 47(1), 71-85, 2008.
7. Alter, S., Bolloju, N., A Work System Front End for Object-Oriented Analysis and Design, 11th SIGSAND Symposium, Vancouver, Canada, 2012.
8. Alter, S., Using Work System Theory to Link Managerial and Technical Perspectives on BPM, IEEE International Conference on Business Informatics, Vienna, Austria, 2013.
9. Alter, S., Theory of Workarounds, Communications of the Association for Information Systems, 34(55), 1041-1066, 2014.
10. Alter, S., The Knowledge Cube: Scaffolding for a Body of Knowledge about Information Systems, Proceedings of ECIS 2012, European Conference on Information Systems, Barcelona, Spain, 2012.

Fundamental Systems Thinking Concepts for IS Engineering: Balancing Between Change and Non-change

Gil Regev

Ecole Polytechnique Fédérale de Lausanne (EPFL), School of Computer and
Communication Sciences, CH-1015 Lausanne, Switzerland
gil.regev@epfl.ch

Abstract. The introduction of a new IT system in an organization is always accompanied by changes to business processes, and sometimes to reporting structures and customer relationships. Resistance to change is a well-known response to these initiatives. By going to the roots of systems thinking it is possible to explain this resistance through homeostasis, the maintenance of the identity of a system in a changing environment. Understanding the necessity and inevitability of this resistance can help both researchers and practitioners. Researchers will better understand the nature of organizations enabling them to design better research initiatives. Practitioners will be able to design better change initiatives in their organization.

Tutorial Details

The concept of system is omnipresent in IS discourse, as evidenced by the very name of the field: Information Systems. A thorough understanding of systems concepts should therefore be a pre-requisite to every IS researcher and practitioner. Most systems discourse is based on the cybernetics paradigm, with its host of goal-oriented terms: goals, objectives, aims, targets, ends and means.

In this tutorial we will introduce more fundamental and more profound systems principles. These are: system as a worldview [4], survival [5], requisite variety [1], homeostasis [1,2,5] and balancing-optimizing of relationships [3].

References

1. Ashby, W.R.: An Introduction to Cybernetics. Chapman Hall. London (1956)
2. Cannon, W:B.: Organization for Physiological Homeostasis, Physiological Reviews IX(3) (1929) 399-431
3. Cannon, W.B.: The Wisdom of the Body, Norton & Company, New York (1939)
4. Vickers, Sir G.: Value Systems and Social Process. Tavistock, London (1968)
5. Weick, K. E.: The Social Psychology of Organizing, second edition. McGraw-Hill (1979)
6. Weinberg, G. M.: An Introduction to General Systems Thinking. Wiley & Sons (1975)

© Springer International Publishing Switzerland 2015
J. Zdravkovic et al. (Eds.): CAiSE 2015, LNCS 9097, p. 522, 2015.
DOI: 10.1007/978-3-319-19069-3

Know-how Mapping with ME-map

Eric Yu[1] and Arnon Sturm[2]

[1] University of Toronto
eric.yu@utoronto.ca
[2] Ben-Gurion University of the Negev
sturm@bgu.ac.il

Abstract. Know-how, which refers to the practical knowledge that connects desired objectives to actions that can achieve those objectives, is a crucial foundation for today's advanced technological society. As more new know-how is constantly being created, methods and techniques are needed for organizing, visualizing, understanding, and applying know-how. In this tutorial, we elaborate on the needs for mapping out such knowledge, provide an overview for approaches for addressing these needs, and elaborate on ME-map, a particular approach we developed for mapping know-how.

Keywords: Knowledge Mapping, Know-How, Requirement Engineering, Modeling

Tutorial Details

The term know-how is generally used to refer to knowledge about how to accomplish something effectively and efficiently. While it is widely acknowledged that a great deal of know-how is tacit, the body of literature in each technical domain reflects the cumulative store of the articulated know-how for that domain. Mapping out the conceptual structure of a body of know-how facilitates learning about the domain. Practitioners can use a map to seek out solutions to problems, and compare strengths and weaknesses of alternate solutions. Researchers can use a map to uncover gaps and guide research directions. In this part, we will introduce the notions and the benefits of know-how mapping.

As part of the landscape exploration of the of knowledge mapping domain we discuss the desired properties from a knowledge mapping approach and analyze potential approaches for mapping out know-how in light of the desired properties (such as Ease of Use, Expressiveness, Evolution, Reasoning, and Process Support). These approaches include literature review [4,5], classification [6], citation graphs [2], cause maps [3], concept maps [7], and claim-oriented argumentation [8].

This research is partially supported by the Israel Science Foundation (Grant No. 495/14) and by the Natural Sciences and Engineering Research Council of Canada.

J. Zdravkovic et al. (Eds.): CAiSE 2015, LNCS 9097, pp. 523–524, 2015.
DOI: 10.1007/978-3-319-19069-3

The ME-map approach centres around the means-ends relationship prominent in goal-oriented requirements engineering (hence the name ME-map) [10], for depicting alternative solutions to problems and the trade-offs among them [9]. By visualizing and analyzing the structure of the body of know-how in a domain, one can discover gaps in knowledge (open problems with missing or inadequate solutions), thereby guiding research directions and facilitating the evaluation of the impact of research results. Synergies across domains can potentially be discovered by making connections across know-how maps, creating new solutions. The progress of knowledge over time can be visualized as an animation, as newly-invented methods and techniques are incrementally overlaid on top of the map of the existing body of know-how. We illustrate the approach and our experiences with examples from a number of areas in information system engineering, such as: variability in modeling business processes, architecture description languages, architecture documentation, agent-oriented software engineering, and data mining. We also outline research challenges for know-how mapping.

References

1. Abrishamkar, S.: Goal-Oriented Know-How Mapping- Modelling Process Documentation, a Prototype, and Empirical Studies, M.I. Thesis, University of Toronto (2013)
2. Chen, C. M., Paul, R. J., O'Keefe, B.: Fitting the jigsaw of citation: Information visualization in domain analysis. Journal of the American Society for Information Science and Technology, 52(4), 315-330 (2001)
3. Eden, C., Ackermann, F., Cropper, S.: The analysis of cause maps. Journal of Management Studies, 29(3), 309-324 (1992)
4. Jesson, J., L. Matheson, and F.M. Lacey: Doing Your Literature Review: Traditional and Systematic Techniques, Sage Publication (2011)
5. Kitchenham, B., Brereton, P., Budgen, D., Turner,M., Bailey, J., Linkman, S.: Systematic literature reviews in software engineering - A systematic literature review. Inf. Softw. Technol. 51 (1), 7-15 (2009)
6. Kwasnik, B.: The role of classification in knowledge representation and discovery. Library Trends, 48, 22-47 (1999)
7. Novak, J. D., Cañas, Al. J.: The Theory Underlying Concept Maps and How To Construct and Use Them, Institute for Human and Machine Cognition (2006)
8. Shum, S. B., Motta, E., Domingue, J.: ScholOnto: An ontology-based digital library server for research documents and discourse. International Journal of Digital Libraries, 3(3), 237248 (2000)
9. Sturm, A., Gross, D., Wang, J., Yu, E.: Analyzing Engineering Contributions using a Specialized Concept Map. CAiSE (Forum/Doctoral Consortium), 89-96 (2014)
10. Yu, E., Giorgini, P., Maiden, N., Mylopoulos, J.: Social Modeling for Requirements Engineering, MIT Press (2011)

Model Matching - Processes and Beyond

Avigdor Gal[1] and Matthias Weidlich[2]

[1]Technion – Israel Institute of Technology
avigal@ie.technion.ac.il
[2]Imperial College London
m.weidlich@imperial.ac.uk

Abstract. Conceptual models in general, and process models in particular, have been established as a means to design, analyze, and improve information systems [1]. The creation, utilization, and evolution of such models is supported by manifold concepts and techniques that offer, for instance, re-use driven modelling support, harmonization of model variants, model-based system validation, and effective management of model repositories. Many of these techniques share reliance on the identification of correspondences between the entities of different models, also termed model matching. The accuracy and therefore usefulness of techniques supporting the creation, utilization, and evolution of models is highly dependent on the correctness and completeness of the result of model matching. This tutorial takes up recent advances in matching process models in particular and provides information systems engineers (both practitioners and researchers) with a comprehensive overview of concepts and matching techniques in this domain. We first clarify terminology and essential notions of process model matching and elaborate on use cases in which model matching proved to be useful tool. Then, we review similarity measures that span the textual, structural, and behavioral dimension of models and form the basis of matching techniques. Although we focus on the case of matching process models, the tutorial also outlines how other types of conceptual models can be matched with these techniques. The tutorial further includes a discussion of practical considerations for the application of process model matching, based on insights from the Process Model Matching Contest conducted in 2013 [2]. Finally, we elaborate on open research challenges related to the integration of user feedback, evaluation measures, and the use of model documentation in the matching process.

Keywords: Conceptual models · model matching · process model matching

Tutorial Details

This tutorial provides information systems engineers (both practitioners and researchers) with a comprehensive overview of concepts and techniques for model matching. It gives an introduction to the underlying concepts and algorithms, but also discusses practical considerations. On the one hand, it enables participants to apply process model matching methods as part of specific approaches for process model creation,

© Springer International Publishing Switzerland 2015
J. Zdravkovic et al. (Eds.): CAiSE 2015, LNCS 9097, pp. 525–526, 2015.
DOI: 10.1007/978-3-319-19069-3

utilization, and evolution. On the other hand, participants learn about the state- of-the-art in the field, thereby allow young researchers to identify new research horizons on model matching. At the end of the 90 minutes tutorial a participant will have a basic coverage of the state-of-the-art in model matching (and in particular process model matching) methods.

The intended audience of the tutorial consists of academics, graduate students and practitioners of information systems engineering, who are interested in research and applications of techniques for model matching. The tutorial will be on a basic level, yet familiarity with essential notions of process modelling is desirable.

The comparison of different process models is at the core of many approaches that aim at effective creation, utilization, and evolution of models, which themselves are a means for effective engineering of information systems. Specifically, virtually all approaches to manage process model collections (see the International Workshop on Process Model Collections series3 or a related special issue on managing large collection of process models in Computer in Industry [3]) rely on techniques for model matching.

In recent years, a large number of techniques for process model matching have been proposed – some of which have been evaluated in the Process Model Matching Contest in 2013.4 However, it is cumbersome to get a comprehensive overview of the state-of-the- art in this area since most techniques focus on a specific perspective of process model matching (e.g., structural matching or the semantics of activity labels). This tutorial aims at introducing the basic concepts and existing techniques of model matching in a comprehensive and pedagogical manner, enabling the participants to take up existing results for their own applications and research projects. Also, the coverage of practical considerations of model matching benefit participants with an industry background.

References

1. Dumas, M., La Rosa, M., Mendling, J., Reijers, H.: Fundamentals of Business ProcessManagement. Springer (2012)
2. Cayoglu, U., Dijkman, R.M., Dumas, M., Fettke, P., Garc´ıa-Ban˜ uelos, L., Hake, P., Klinkmu¨ ller, C., Leopold, H., Ludwig, A., Loos, P., Mendling, J., Oberweis, A., Schoknecht, A., Sheetrit, E., Thaler, T., Ullrich, M., Weber, I., Weidlich, M.: Report: The process model matching contest 2013. In Lohmann, N., Song, M., Wohed, P., eds.: Business Process Management Workshops - BPM 2013 International Workshops, Beijing, China, August 26, 2013, Revised Papers. Volume 171 of Lecture Notes in Business Information Processing., Springer (2013) 442–463
3. Dijkman, R.M., Rosa, M.L., Reijers, H.A.: Managing large collections of business process models - current techniques and challenges. Computers in Industry 63(2) (2012) 91–97

FEDS2: A Practical Tutorial on the Framework for Evaluation in Design Science Research (v. 2)

John R. Venable

School of Information Systems, Curtin University, Perth WA 6845, Australia
j.venable@curtin.edu.au

Abstract. The goals of this tutorial are to (1) describe the newest version of the FEDS (Framework for Evaluation in Design Science Research) frameworks and method (FEDS2), (2) provide a deeper understanding of the FEDS2 approach than that provided in available publications, (3) provide opportunities to practice applying the FEDS2 technique to the participants' own research, and (4) help the participants to progress and improve their DSR work.

Keywords: Design Science Research, DSR, Evaluation, Research Method, Research Design

Tutorial Details

Design Science Research is a research paradigm relevant to technology invention or development. Venable and Baskerville [1] define Design Science Research (DSR) as "Research that invents a new purposeful artefact to address a generalised type of problem and evaluates its utility for solving problems of that type." Evaluating new artefacts is essential to impart scientific rigor to the research. The Framework for Evaluation in Design Science Research version 2 (FEDS2) supports researchers with a comprehensive approach to planning and designing the evaluation strategies, approaches, and activities that are an essential component of high quality DSR. FEDS2 was co-developed by the presenter and colleagues and is based on, combines, and extends two earlier approaches [2,3]. FEDS2 includes several frameworks and a process for applying them to guide DSR researchers.

This mini-tutorial is intended for practicing and student Design Science Researchers who wish to learn and apply a practical approach for determining how to effectively and efficiently (within resource constraints) evaluate designed purposeful artefacts and design theories about them. It should be highly relevant and suitable for those novice and experienced researchers who wish to learn more about DSR, develop and progress their own DSR work, and/or supervise DSR projects. This tutorial is more relevant to researchers than to practitioners, although practitioners are often engaged de facto in DSR or collaborate with DSR researchers.

© Springer International Publishing Switzerland 2015
J. Zdravkovic et al. (Eds.): CAiSE 2015, LNCS 9097, pp. 527–528, 2015.
DOI: 10.1007/978-3-319-19069-3

The goals of this tutorial are to describe the newest version of the FEDS2 frameworks and method, provide a deeper understanding of the FEDS2 approach than that provided in available publications, to provide opportunities to practice applying the FEDS2 technique to the participants' own research, and to help the participants to progress and improve their DSR work.

The teaching method to be used will be a combination of:

- Introduction and presentation of FEDS2 by the presenter,
- Discussion of FEDS2 and an example with the participants,
- Application of FEDS2 by participants to their own research, and
- Individualised feedback and group discussion on the participants' applications of FEDS2.

The tutorial presumes a basic familiarity with the DSR research paradigm, its more common methods, and Design Theory, although questions and discussion about these and the DSR approach generally are welcome.

References

1. Venable, J. R., Baskerville, Eating Our Own Cooking: Toward a More Rigorous Design Science of Research Methods, Electronic Journal of Business Research Methods. 10, 141153, online open access at http://www.ejbrm.com/volume9/issue2 (2012)
2. Venable, J. R., Pries-Heje, J., Baskerville, R., A Comprehensive Framework for Evaluation in Design Science Research, In: Peffers, K., Rothenberger, M. (eds.) 7th International Conference on Design Science Research in Information Systems and Technology (DESRIST 2012), Springer, Berlin, Germany (2012)
3. Venable, J. R., Pries-Heje, J., Baskerville, R., FEDS: A Framework for Evaluation in Design Science Research, European Journal of Information Systems, advance online open access publication at http://www.palgrave-journals.com/doifinder/10.1057/ejis.2014.36 (2014)

Author Index

Abubahia, Ahmed 133
Alter, Steven 520
Amyot, Daniel 181
Arellano, Cristóbal 20
Arruda, Narciso 214
Azanza, Maider 20

Barros, Alistair 501
Batoulis, Kimon 349
Bauer, Bernhard 331
Bazhenova, Ekaterina 349
Bellatreche, Ladjel 199
Bendraou, Reda 263
Böhm, Klemens 382
Brown, Pieta 118
Brown, Ross 166
Bunnell, Craig A. 417

Cabanillas, Cristina 53
Casanova, Marco A. 214
Cocea, Mihaela 133
Collet, Philippe 181

Das, Prasenjit 230
De Giacomo, Giuseppe 84
Decker, Gero 349
Delmas, Rémi 151
del–Río–Ortega, Adela 485
Di Francescomarino, Chiara 314
Díaz, Oscar 20
Dumas, Marlon 84
Durán, Amador 485

Eder, Johann 367
Estañol, Montserrat 434

Fellmann, Michael 401
Fukazawa, Yoshiaki 247
Fukusumi, Shun 3

Gal, Avigdor 417, 525
Gervais, Marie-Pierre 263
Ghidini, Chiara 314

Grossniklaus, Michael 35
Guarino, Nicola 279
Guizzardi, Giancarlo 279
Gutiérrez, Antonio Manuel 485

Haapasalo, Harri 453
Harman, Joel 166
Hebig, Regina 263
Heine, Antje 69
Holzleitner, Manuel 468

Johnson, Daniel 166
Jokela, Mikko 103

Kadish, Sarah 417
Kannengiesser, Udo 166
Khelladi, Djamel Eddine 263
Khouri, Selma 199
Kitagawa, Hiroyuki 3
Knuplesch, David 53
Köpke, Julius 367
Koschmider, Agnes 69
Kuvaja, Pasi 453

Leemans, Sander J.J. 297
Leme, Luiz Paes 214
Leopold, Henrik 401
Link, Sebastian 118
Lopes, Giseli Rabello 214
Lu, Xixi 297
Lwakatare, Lucy Ellen 453

Maggi, Fabrizio Maria 84
Mandelbaum, Avishai 417
Meilicke, Christian 401
Mendling, Jan 53, 401
Meyer, Andreas 349
Mibe, Ryota 247
Montali, Marco 84
Morishima, Atsuyuki 3
Mrasek, Richard 382
Mülle, Jutta 382

Oberweis, Andreas   69
Oshima, Keishi   247
Ouyang, Chun   501

Palmieri, Anthony   181
Pittke, Fabian   401
Polacsek, Thomas   151

Reddy, Sreedhar   230
Regev, Gil   522
Reichert, Manfred   53
Renso, Chiara   214
Resinas, Manuel   53, 485
Rinderle-Ma, Stefanie   166
Ritter, Daniel   468
Roberval, Mariano   214
Robin, Jacques   263
Ruiz–Cortés, Antonio   53, 485

Sancho, Maria-Ribera   434
Sandoval, Itzel Vázquez   314
Scholl, Marc H.   35
Semassel, Kamel   199
Senderovich, Arik   417
Siren, Anni   103
Smolander, Kari   103

Stuckenschmidt, Heiner   401
Sturm, Arnon   523
Sun, Yaguang   331

Teniente, Ernest   434
Tessaris, Sergio   314
Tolonen, Arto   453
Tsuchiya, Ryosuke   247

Ullrich, Meike   69

van der Aalst, Wil M.P.   297
van Eck, Maikel L.   297
Venable, John R.   527
Vidal, Vânia M.P.   214

Washizaki, Hironori   247
Wei, Fuguo   501
Weidlich, Matthias   417, 525
Weiler, Andreas   35
Weske, Mathias   349

Yeddula, Raghavendra Reddy   230
Yu, Eric   523

Printed in the United States
By Bookmasters